Fodor's 3rd Edition

New Mexico

The complete guide, thoroughly up-to-date

Packed with details that will make your trip

The must-see sights, off and on the beaten path

What to see, what to skip

Vacation itineraries, walking tours, day trips

Smart lodging and dining options

Essential local dos and taboos

Transportation tips

Key contacts, savvy travel advice

When to go, what to pack

Clear, accurate, easy-to-use maps

Books to read, videos to watch, background essay

Fodor's Travel Publications • New York, Toronto, London, Sydney, Auckland
www.fodors.com

Fodor's New Mexico

EDITOR: Christina Knight

Editorial Contributors: Andrew Collins, Jeanie Puleston Fleming, Marilyn Haddrill, Kathleen McCloud, Sharon Niederman
Editorial Production: Rebecca Zeiler Wintle
Maps: David Lindroth, *cartographer;* Rebecca Baer and Bob Blake, *map editors*
Design: Fabrizio La Rocca, *creative director;* Guido Caroti, *art director;* Jolie Novak, *photo editor*
Cover Design: Pentagram
Production/Manufacturing: Jessie Markland
Cover Photo (Santa Fe Museum of Fine Arts): Thomas Hoepker/Magnum Photos, Inc.

Copyright

Third Edition

ISBN 0–679–00584–6

ISSN 1526–4734

Special Sales

Fodor's Travel Publications are available at special discounts for sales promotions or premiums. Special editions, including personalized covers, excerpts of existing guides, and corporate imprints, can be created in large quantities for special needs. For more information, write to Special Marketing, Fodor's Travel Publications, 280 Park Avenue, New York, NY 10017. In the United Kingdom, write to Fodor's Travel Publications, 20 Vauxhall Bridge Road, London, England SW1V 2SA.

PRINTED IN THE UNITED STATES OF AMERICA

10 9 8 7 6 5 4 3 2 1

Important Tip

Although all prices, opening times, and other details in this book are based on information supplied to us at press time, changes occur all the time in the travel world, and Fodor's cannot accept responsibility for facts that become outdated or for inadvertent errors or omissions. So **always confirm information when it matters,** especially if you're making a detour to visit a specific place.

CONTENTS

Maps

ON THE ROAD WITH FODOR'S

EVERY VACATION IS IMPORTANT. So here at Fodor's, we've pulled out all stops in preparing *Fodor's New Mexico*. To guide you in putting together your New Mexico experience, we've created multiday itineraries and neighborhood walks. And to direct you to the places that are truly worth your time and money, we've rallied the team of endearingly picky know-it-alls we're pleased to call our writers. Having seen all corners of New Mexico, they're real experts. If you knew them, you'd poll them for tips yourself.

Former Fodor's editor **Andrew Collins,** who authored *Fodor's Gay Guide to the USA,* updated the Northwestern and Northeastern New Mexico chapters. He writes a weekly syndicated column on gay travel for numerous newspapers and Web sites, and he's the travel columnist for *Fairfield County Magazine,* in Westport, Connecticut. He lives in Santa Fe; Washington, New Hampshire; and Roxbury, Connecticut.

Jeanie Puleston Fleming is an avid hiker and skier in the mountains of northern New Mexico where she has lived for the past 20 years. She writes about the Southwest for national and regional publications.

Native New Mexican **Marilyn Haddrill** has explored many overlooked crannies of the southern part of the state. A veritable fountain of practical information about the entire state, she was the perfect updater for the Smart Travel Tips A to Z section and the Destination: New Mexico chapter. Marilyn has coauthored two suspense novels and writes for various publications, including *Final Frontier* and the *Dallas Morning News.* Her wildest experience while on assignment? Trying to drive through a herd of hungry, bleating sheep to investigate a remote ranch.

Kathleen McCloud, a visual artist and arts writer for local and national publications, has lived in the Santa Fe area for 12 years. Her expertise is in the traditional arts of the Southwest, particularly textile arts, as well as contemporary art. Her knowledge and appreciation of Southwestern architecture comes after many years of living with a house designer/builder, and hands-on experience building three houses in northern New Mexico.

Sharon Niederman, a New Mexico resident for two decades, is addicted to driving the state's open highways and back roads. Her ambition is to visit each of New Mexico's 100 cities, a goal she got closer to reaching as the updater of the Albuquerque chapter and author of the Northwestern New Mexico and Northeastern New Mexico chapters. Sharon has written five books about New Mexico's history, culture, and cuisine. Two have received the Border Regional Library Award for their contributions to the history and culture of the Southwest.

Don't Forget to Write
Keeping a travel guide fresh and up-to-date is a big job. So we love your feedback—positive and negative—and follow up on all suggestions. Contact the New Mexico editor at editors@fodors.com or c/o Fodor's, 280 Park Avenue, New York, New York 10017. And have a wonderful trip!

Karen Cure
Editorial Director

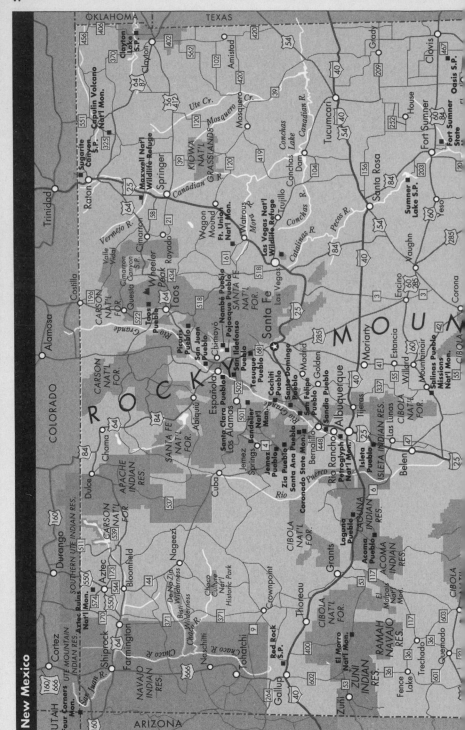

New Mexico

SMART TRAVEL TIPS A TO Z

Basic Information on Traveling in New Mexico, Savvy Tips to Make Your Trip a Breeze, and Companies and Organizations to Contact

AIR TRAVEL

BOOKING

When you book **look for nonstop flights** and **remember that "direct" flights stop at least once.** Try to avoid connecting flights, which require a change of plane.

CARRIERS

Once you've landed in one of New Mexico's two gateways, Albuquerque or El Paso, Texas, you can take advantage of some regional airlines. Mesa Airlines offers shuttle flights to larger communities in the state including Las Cruces and Roswell. Rio Grande Air operates daily flights between Albuquerque and Taos. Charter flights also are available. Costs are significantly higher per air mile when you venture off a major air carrier onto a shuttle or charter flight with fewer passengers, but you can weigh those costs against convenience. Since choices are few, you are unlikely to find airfare bargains once you leave a major airport.

➤ MAJOR AIRLINES: **American** (☎ 800/433–7300). **Continental** (☎ 800/525–0280). **Delta** (☎ 800/221–1212). **Northwest** (☎ 800/692–7000). **TWA** (☎ 800/221–2000). **United** (☎ 800/241–6522). **US Airways** (☎ 800/428–4322).

➤ SMALLER AIRLINES: **America West** (☎ 800/235–9292). **Frontier** (☎ 800/432–1359). **Mesa Airlines** (☎ 800/637–2247). **Rio Grande Air** (☎ 877/435–9742). **Southwest Airlines** (☎ 800/435–9792).

➤ FROM THE U.K.: **British Airways** (☎ 0345/222–111). **Delta** (☎ 0800/414–767). **United Airlines** (☎ 0800/888–555).

CHECK-IN & BOARDING

Assuming that not everyone with a ticket will show up, airlines routinely overbook planes. When everyone does, airlines ask for volunteers to give up their seats. In return, these volunteers usually get a certificate for a free flight and are rebooked on the next flight out. If there are not enough volunteers, the airline must choose who will be denied boarding. The first to get bumped are passengers who checked in late and those flying on discounted tickets, so **get to the gate and check in as early as possible,** especially during peak periods.

Always **bring a government-issued photo I.D. to the airport.** You may be asked to show it before you are allowed to check in.

CUTTING COSTS

The least expensive airfares to New Mexico must usually be purchased in advance and are nonrefundable. It's smart to **call a number of airlines, and when you are quoted a good price, book it on the spot**—the same fare may not be available the next day. Always **check different routings** and look into using different airports. Travel agents, especially low-fare specialists (☞ Discounts & Deals, *below*), are helpful.

Consolidators are another good source. They buy tickets for scheduled international flights at reduced rates from the airlines, then sell them at prices that beat the best fare available directly from the airlines, usually without restrictions. Sometimes you can even get your money back if you need to return the ticket. Carefully read the fine print detailing penalties for changes and cancellations, and **confirm your consolidator reservation with the airline.**

➤ CONSOLIDATORS: **Cheap Tickets** (☎ 800/377–1000). **Discount Airline Ticket Service** (☎ 800/576–1600). **Unitravel** (☎ 800/325–2222). **Up & Away Travel** (☎ 212/889–2345). **World Travel Network** (☎ 800/409–6753).

FLYING TIMES

Flying time between Albuquerque and Los Angeles is 1 hour and 45 minutes; Chicago, 3 hours and 35 minutes; New York, 5 hours and 15 minutes (there are no direct flights); Dallas, 1 hour and 40 minutes.

HOW TO COMPLAIN

If your baggage goes astray or your flight goes awry, complain right away. Most carriers require that you **file a claim immediately.**

➤ AIRLINE COMPLAINTS: U.S. Department of Transportation **Aviation Consumer Protection Division** (⊠ C-75, Room 4107, Washington, DC 20590, ☎ 202/366–2220, airconsumer@ost.dot.gov, www.dot.gov/airconsumer). **Federal Aviation Administration Consumer Hotline** (☎ 800/322–7873).

AIRPORTS

The major gateway to New Mexico is Albuquerque International Sunport, which grants quick access to Albuquerque but is still 65 mi southwest of Santa Fe and 130 mi south of Taos. There is no regular air service between Albuquerque and Santa Fe, but air shuttle service is offered to Carlsbad and Las Cruces on Mesa Air and to Taos on Rio Grande Air (☞ Smaller Airlines, *above*).

The gateway to southern New Mexico is El Paso International Airport, several miles from El Paso, Texas, off I–10. The flight between El Paso and Albuquerque takes 50 minutes. The state's easternmost side can also be accessed via major airports in Texas including Midland, Lubbock, and Amarillo.

➤ AIRPORT INFORMATION: **Albuquerque International Sunport** (⊠ Sunport Blvd. off I–25, 5 mi south of downtown, ☎ 505/842–4366). **El Paso International Airport** (⊠ 6701 Convair Dr., off I–10's Exit 25, ☎ 915/772–4271).

➤ MUNICIPAL AIRPORTS: **Cavern City Air Terminal (McCausland Aviation), Carlsbad** (⊠ 1505 Terminal Dr., off U.S. 62/180 in south Carlsbad, ☎ 505/885–5236). **Four Corners Regional Airport, Farmington** (⊠ 1300 W. Navajo St., ☎ 505/599–1395).

Grant County Airport (Silver City area) (⊠ 188 Airport Rd., Hurley, NM, 20 mi southeast of Silver City, ☎ 505/388–4554). **Las Cruces International Airport** (⊠ 9000 Zia Rd., off I–10 west of Las Cruces, ☎ 505/524–2762). **Roswell Municipal Airport** (⊠ 1 Jerry Smith Circle, 5 mi south of Roswell via Main St., ☎ 505/347–5703). **Santa Fe Municipal Airport** (⊠ Airport Rd./NM 284 west of NM 14, ☎ 505/473–7243). **Sierra Blanca Regional Airport (Ruidoso area)** (⊠ 1 Airport Rd., 16 mi northeast of Ruidoso, ☎ 505/336–8111). **Taos Municipal Airport** (⊠ U.S. 64, 12 mi west of Taos, ☎ 505/758–4995). **Truth or Consequences Municipal Airport (Enchantment Aviation)** (⊠ NM 181 N, 5 mi north of Truth or Consequences, take Exit 83 off I–25, ☎ 505/894–6199).

TRANSFERS

Shuttle buses between the Albuquerque International Sunport and Santa Fe take about 1 hour and 20 minutes and cost approximately $20 each way. Shuttle service between Albuquerque and Taos takes 2¾ hours and costs $30–$35. In southern New Mexico there are daily trips between El Paso International Airport and Las Cruces. The trip takes 60 minutes and costs $26 for the Las Cruces Shuttle and $18 for Silver Stage. Shuttle costs between El Paso and Carlsbad are about $45 for a three-hour journey; it's $33 for the three-hour trip to Silver City. Between El Paso and Deming, costs are about $28 for a two-hour trip. Reservations are advised on all shuttles. Ask about round-trip and group discounts.

➤ BETWEEN ALBUQUERQUE AND SANTA FE: **Express Shuttle USA** (☎ 800/256–8991). **Sandia Shuttle Express** (☎ 505/474–5696).

➤ BETWEEN ALBUQUERQUE AND TAOS: **Faust's Transportation** (☎ 505/758–7359). **Pride of Taos** (☎ 505/758–8340). **Twin Hearts Express** (☎ 505/751–1201).

➤ BETWEEN EL PASO AND SOUTHERN NEW MEXICO DESTINATIONS: **Las Cruces Shuttle Service** (☎ 505/525–1784). **Silver Stage** (☎ 800/522–0162).

BUS TRAVEL

Bus service on Texas, New Mexico & Oklahoma Coaches, affiliated with Greyhound Lines, is available between major cities and towns in New Mexico, except Silver City, which is served by Silver Stage. Silver Stage offers personalized service in addition to airport transportation, giving door-to-door service between cities including El Paso, Carlsbad, Las Cruces, Deming, and Silver City.

FARES & SCHEDULES

A one-way ticket from Albuquerque to Santa Fe costs about $12; to Taos, about $22. Make reservations several weeks in advance of major holidays or other special events such as the Kodak Albuquerque International Balloon Fiesta in October. Space might be limited at these times.

➤ BUS INFORMATION: **Greyhound Albuquerque** (✉ 300 2nd St. SW Albuquerque, ☎ 505/243–4435 or 800/231–2222). **Faust's Transportation** (☎ 505/758–7359). **Sandia Shuttle Express** (☎ 505/474–5696). **Silver Stage** (☎ 800/522–0162). **Texas, New Mexico & Oklahoma Coaches** (✉ 490 N. Valley Dr., Las Cruces, ☎ 800/231–2222).

BUSINESS HOURS

BANKS & OFFICES

Banks generally are open in Santa Fe on weekdays between 9 and 3 and on Saturday between 9 and noon. In Taos they are open on weekdays between 9 and 5, and in Albuquerque on weekdays between 9 and 4. Some branches are open between 10 and noon on Saturday. In the rest of the state, hours vary but most banks are open at least on weekdays from 9 to 3. In Santa Fe and Albuquerque the main post offices are open on weekdays from 8 to 5 (from 9 to 5 in Taos) and on Saturday between 9 and noon. The Las Cruces main post office and branches generally are open Saturday mornings from 9 to noon.

GAS STATIONS

A few gas stations in Albuquerque are open 24 hours, but it's best to purchase gasoline before 10 PM. Gas stations in rural areas often close in the early evening; it's wise to gas up before the sun sets.

MUSEUMS & SIGHTS

Museums in Santa Fe, Taos, Albuquerque, and around the state are generally open daily from 9 or 10 AM to 5 or 6 PM, although hours may vary from season to season. Even during the summer, a peak travel season, some facilities close at 4 PM. Many are closed on Monday. Some are open for extended hours on Friday evening. Some pueblos are closed to visitors for short periods throughout the year.

PHARMACIES

There aren't many all-night pharmacies in New Mexico, so plan ahead. Taos does not have a 24-hour pharmacy.

➤ 24-HOUR PHARMACIES: **Walgreens** (✉ 6201 Central Ave. NE, Albuquerque, ☎ 505/255–5511; 5001 Montgomery Blvd. NE, Albuquerque, ☎ 505/881–5050). **Walgreens** (✉ 1096 S. St. Francis Dr., Santa Fe, ☎ 505/982–9811).

SHOPS

Most shops and galleries are open between 10 and 5 or 6, with limited hours on weekends. Store and commercial hours also vary according to the flux of tourist seasons.

CAMERAS & PHOTOGRAPHY

New Mexico's wildlife and rugged landscape are extremely photogenic. The striking red sandstone cliffs and soil of northern New Mexico make a terrific backdrop. Photographers also flock to White Sands National Monument, where the stark white sand dunes offer unlimited opportunity for abstract shots such as sand ripples or contrast for brightly dressed models. New Mexico air generally is so clean and pure (except during dust storms) that you can't go wrong. It's best to take photographs in the early morning or late evening to take advantage of more subtle lighting and escape the glare of the bright sun. Before you take photographs on Indian reservations, **check the rules.** In many cases, you must purchase a permit. Restrictions can range from no built-in telephoto lenses to no photography altogether. Be sure you have permission to photograph any Native American you encounter, since beliefs regarding this practice vary. Additionally, your actions might be interpreted as downright rude.

➤ PHOTO HELP: **Kodak Information Center** (☎ 800/242–2424). *Kodak Guide to Shooting Great Travel Pictures,* available in bookstores or from Fodor's Travel Publications (☎ 800/ 533–6478; $18 plus $5.50 shipping).

EQUIPMENT PRECAUTIONS

Always **keep your film and tape out of the sun.** Carry an extra supply of batteries, and **be prepared to turn on your camera or camcorder** to prove to security personnel that the device is real. Always **ask for hand inspection of film,** which becomes clouded after repeated exposure to airport X-ray machines, and **keep videotapes away from metal detectors.** In New Mexico, dust can be a problem. Keep cameras and video equipment in cases while not in use. Also, keep in mind that extreme heat can ruin film. Don't leave your equipment in a hot car or under direct sunlight.

CAR RENTAL

A typical rate at the Albuquerque International Sunport is about $40 daily and $200 weekly for an economy car with air-conditioning, automatic transmission, and unlimited mileage. Prices are about the same in Santa Fe. If you want to explore the backcountry, consider renting a 4x4, which will cost you almost double the price of an economy car. Tax on car rentals is 10.75% with an additional $2 per day surcharge.

➤ MAJOR AGENCIES: **Alamo** (☎ 800/ 327–9633; 020/8759–6200 in the U.K.). **Avis** (☎ 800/331–1212; 800/ 879–2847 in Canada; 02/9353–9000 in Australia; 09/525–1982 in New Zealand). **Budget** (☎ 800/527–0700; 0144/227–6266 in the U.K.). **Dollar** (☎ 800/800–4000; 020/8897–0811 in the U.K., where it is known as Eurodollar; 02/9223–1444 in Australia). **Hertz** (☎ 800/654–3131; 800/263– 0600 in Canada; 020/8897–2072 in the U.K.; 02/9669–2444 in Australia; 03/358–6777 in New Zealand). **National Car Rental** (☎ 800/227–7368).

CUTTING COSTS

To get the best deal, **book through a travel agent, who will shop around.** Also **price local car-rental companies,** although the service and maintenance may not be as good as those of a major player. Remember to ask about required deposits, cancellation penalties, and drop-off charges if you're planning to pick up the car in one city and leave it in another. If you're traveling during a holiday period, also make sure that a confirmed reservation guarantees you a car. By renting your car elsewhere, you can duck a hefty 9% tax charged extra at the Albuquerque International Sunport and other municipal airports.

Do **look into wholesalers,** companies that do not own fleets but rent in bulk from those that do and often offer better rates than traditional car-rental operations.

➤ LOCAL AGENCIES: **Enterprise** (☎ 800/325–8007). **Sears** (☎ 800/527– 0770). **Thrifty** (☎ 800/367–2277).

➤ WHOLESALERS: **Kemwel Holiday Autos** (☎ 800/678–0678, FAX 914/ 825–3160, www.kemwel.com).

INSURANCE

When driving a rented car you are generally responsible for any damage to or loss of the vehicle as well as for any property damage or personal injury that you may cause. Before you rent see what coverage your personal auto-insurance policy and credit cards already provide.

For about $15 to $20 per day, rental companies sell protection, known as a collision- or loss-damage waiver (CDW or LDW), that eliminates your liability for damage to the car. In most states you don't need a CDW if you have personal auto insurance or other liability insurance. However, **make sure you have enough coverage to pay for the car.** If you do not have auto insurance or an umbrella policy that covers damage to third parties, purchasing liability insurance and a CDW or LDW is highly recommended.

REQUIREMENTS & RESTRICTIONS

In New Mexico you must be 21 to rent a car, and rates may be higher if you're under 25. You'll pay extra for child seats (about $3 per day), which are compulsory for children under five, and for additional drivers (about $2 per day). Non-U.S. residents will need a reservation voucher, a passport, a driver's license, and a travel policy that covers each driver, when picking up a car.

SURCHARGES

Before you pick up a car in one city and leave it in another, **ask about drop-off charges or one-way service fees,** which can be substantial. Note, too, that some rental agencies charge extra if you return the car before the time specified in your contract. To avoid a hefty refueling fee, **fill the tank just before you turn in the car,** but be aware that gas stations near the rental outlet may overcharge.

CAR TRAVEL

A car is a basic necessity in New Mexico, as even the larger cities have minimal public transportation. Distances may seem great, but you can make excellent time on long stretches of interstate and other four-lane highways with speed limits of up to 75 mph. If you wander off major thoroughfares, slow down. Speed limits here generally are only 55 mph, and for good reason. Many such roadways have no shoulders and if you're on a twisting, turning road in the mountains or foothills, you'll be creeping along sometimes at speeds as low as 25 mph. For the most part, the scenery you'll take in while driving makes the drive sightseeing in itself.

Interstate 40 runs east–west across the middle of the state. Interstate 10 cuts across the southern part of the state from the Texas border at El Paso to the Arizona line, through Las Cruces, Deming, and Lordsburg. Interstate 25 runs north from the state line at El Paso through Albuquerque and Santa Fe, then angles northeast to the Colorado line near Raton.

U.S. highways connect all major cities and towns with a good network of paved roads. State roads go to the smaller towns; most of the state roads are paved two-lane thoroughfares, but some are well-graded gravel. Roads on Native American lands are designated by wooden, arrow-shape signs and you'd best adhere to the speed limit; some roads on reservation or forest land aren't paved.

EMERGENCIES

Depending on the location, either the New Mexico State Police or the county sheriff's department responds to road emergencies. Call the city or village police departments if you encounter trouble within the limits of a municipality. Indian reservations have tribal police headquarters, and rangers assist travelers within U.S. Forest Service boundaries.

GASOLINE

There's a lot of high, dry, lonesome country in New Mexico. For a safe trip **keep your gas tank full.** Self-service gas stations are the norm in New Mexico, though in some of the less populated regions you'll find stations with one or two pumps and an attendant who provides full service (pumping your gas, checking your tires and oil, washing your windows). At press time, the cost of unleaded gas at self-service stations in New Mexico was about $1.50 per gallon, though typically higher in Santa Fe by at least a few pennies. Bargains can be found by distancing yourself from interstates, where stations typically hike their prices to take advantage of travelers in a hurry. Don't complain too much about higher prices in rural or isolated areas. These remote gas stations pay a premium to ship in their product and must pass along these costs to their customers.

ROAD CONDITIONS

Arroyos, dry washes or gullies, are bridged on major roads, but lesser roads often dip down through them. These can be a hazard during the rainy season of July, August, and September. Even if it looks shallow, **don't try to cross an arroyo filled with water**—it may have an axle-breaking hole in the middle. Wait a little while, and it will drain off almost as quickly as it filled. If you stall in a running arroyo, get out of the car and onto high ground if possible. If you are in backcountry, never drive (or walk) in a dry arroyo bed if the sky is dark anywhere upstream. A sudden thunderstorm 15 mi away could send a raging flash flood down a wash that was perfectly dry a few minutes earlier.

Unless they are well graded and graveled, **avoid unpaved roads in New Mexico when they are wet.** The soil has a lot of caliche, or clay, in it that gets very slick when mixed with water. During winter storms roads may be shut down entirely; call the State Highway Department to find out road conditions.

At certain times during the fall or spring, New Mexico winds can be vicious for large vehicles like RVs. Driving conditions can be particularly treacherous in passages through foothills or mountains where wind gusts are concentrated.

➤ ROAD CONDITIONS: **State Highway Department** (☎ 800/432–4269).

ROAD MAPS

The New Mexico Department of Tourism provides a detailed map of the state on request. GTR Mapping produces a topographical map of the state that depicts many backroads and recreational sites. The GTR maps are sold at convenience and grocery stores, bookstores, and department stores like Kmart and Wal-Mart.

➤ MAPS: **New Mexico Department of Tourism** (☎ 505/827–7400 or 800/545–2070). **GTR Mapping** (☎ 719/275–8948).

RULES OF THE ROAD

The speed limit along the interstates in much of New Mexico is 70 or 75 mph; it's 65 to 70 on U.S. highways (55 in more populated areas). In most areas you can turn right at a red light provided you come to a full stop and check to see that the intersection is clear first. Speed limits are more strictly enforced along interstates, but you can still encounter a patrol car lurking behind a billboard. Radar detectors are legal in New Mexico. U.S. Border Patrol checkpoints are set up on all major roadways from El Paso, Texas, into southern New Mexico. If stopped, you'll be asked what your citizenship is.

The use of seat belts in the front of the car is required by law in New Mexico.

Always **strap children under age five into approved child-safety seats.** The state has an unusually high incidence of drunken driving–related accidents, and you might encounter sobriety checkpoints. The legal adult blood alcohol content (BAC) limit is .08.

CHILDREN IN NEW MEXICO

FLYING

If your children are two or older, **ask about children's airfares.** As a general rule, infants under two not occupying a seat fly at greatly reduced fares or even for free.

Experts agree that it's a good idea to use safety seats aloft for children weighing less than 40 pounds. Airlines set their own policies: U.S. carriers usually require that the child be ticketed, even if he or she is young enough to ride free, since the seats must be strapped into regular seats. Do **check your airline's policy about using safety seats during takeoff and landing.** And since safety seats are not allowed just everywhere in the plane, get your seat assignments early.

When reserving, **request children's meals or a freestanding bassinet** if you need them. But note that bulkhead seats, where you must sit to use the bassinet, may lack an overhead bin or storage space on the floor.

LODGING

Most hotels in New Mexico allow children under a certain age to stay in their parents' room at no extra charge, but others charge for them as extra adults; be sure to **find out the cutoff age for children's discounts.** Another lodging option when traveling with kids is to consider resort accommodations. In many cases, especially for larger families, these work out to be much cheaper than hotels. Adventure holidays for children and families abound in the Southwest. Operators will organize wagon rides, safaris, and other activities for children and adults.

➤ BEST CHOICES: **Best Western Hotels** (☎ 800/528–1234). **Bishop's Lodge** in Santa Fe (☎ 505/983–6377 or 800/732–2240). **Holiday Inns** (☎ 800/465–4329).

THE GOLD GUIDE / SMART TRAVEL TIPS

THE GOLD GUIDE / SMART TRAVEL TIPS

➤ CONDOMINIUMS AND RESORTS: **Ft. Marcy Hotel Suites** (⊠ 320 Artist Rd., Santa Fe 87501, ☎ 505/982–6636).

SIGHTS & ATTRACTIONS

Carlsbad Caverns National Park and White Sands National Monument (☞ Chapter 7) are otherworldly settings that will impress even the most jaded 13-year-old. The many rural areas in this sparsely populated state offer many outdoor activities for energetic kids, ranging from hiking to fishing, and ample numbers of family restaurants can be found. If you're planning to travel into Mexico even for a few hours with children, *see* Southwestern New Mexico A to Z *in* Chapter 8 for document requirements. Places that are especially appealing to children are indicated by a rubber duckie icon in the margin.

➤ ADVENTURE HOLIDAYS: **Santa Fe Detours** (⊠ 54½ E. San Francisco St., Santa Fe 87501, ☎ 505/983–6565 or 800/338–6877).

CONSUMER PROTECTION

Whenever shopping or buying travel services in New Mexico, **pay with a major credit card** so you can cancel payment or get reimbursed if there's a problem. If you're doing business with a particular company for the first time, **contact your local Better Business Bureau and the attorney general's offices** in your own state and the company's home state, as well. Have any complaints been filed? Finally, if you're buying a package or tour, always **consider travel insurance** that includes default coverage (☞ Insurance, *below*).

➤ BBBs: **Better Business Bureau**(⊠ 2625 Pennsylvania NE, Suite 2050, Albuquerque, NM 87110, ☎ 505/ 884–0500 or 800/873–2224 in NM, FAX 505/346–0696, www.bbbnm. com). **Council of Better Business Bureaus** (⊠ 4200 Wilson Blvd., Suite 800, Arlington, VA 22203, ☎ 703/ 276–0100, FAX 703/525–8277, www.bbb.org).

DINING

New Mexico has some of the best Mexican food in the Southwest, and ingredients and style vary even within the state. Most longtime residents like their chiles with some fire. In the Santa Fe, Albuquerque, and Las Cruces areas, chile is sometimes celebrated for its ability to set off smoke alarms. Most restaurants offer a choice of red or green chile with one type typically being milder than the other (both colors can be hot or mild). Excellent barbecue and steaks also can be found throughout New Mexico. The restaurants we list are the cream of the crop in each price category.

CATEGORY	COST*
$$$$	over $30
$$$	$20–$30
$$	$10–$20
$	under $10

per person for a three-course meal, excluding drinks, service, and sales tax (5.6%–7%)

RESERVATIONS & DRESS

Reservations are always a good idea: we mention them only when they're essential or not accepted. Book as far ahead as you can, and reconfirm as soon as you arrive. State-wide, many kitchens stop serving around 8 PM, so **don't arrive too late** if you're looking forward to a leisurely dinner. We mention dress only when men are required to wear a jacket or a jacket and tie. Even at nicer restaurants in New Mexico, dress is usually casual.

SPECIALTIES

The glossary in Chapter 9 explains various Southwestern ingredients and dishes you'll find on menus.

WINE, BEER & SPIRITS

Like many other states, New Mexico has some fine microbreweries with the largest production facility found in the unlikely and highly remote location of Carrizozo, in south-central New Mexico. New Mexico also has a modest number of vineyards, along with wine production. Franciscan monks first planted their vines here before moving more successfully to northern California.

DISABILITIES & ACCESSIBILITY

Most of the region's national parks and recreational areas have accessible visitor centers, rest rooms, campsites, and trails.

➤ LOCAL RESOURCES: **National Park Service, Intermountain Support Office** (✉ Box 728, Santa Fe 87504, ☎ 505/988–6011).

LODGING

In Carlsbad, the Best Western Motel Stevens has two large, accessible guest rooms with parking directly outside the rooms. Accessible kitchenettes also are available. Four Kachinas Bed & Breakfast in Santa Fe has an accessible room among the four offered. This room includes a 5-ft turning circle, and grab bars at the toilet and tub. The sink has knee clearance and lever faucets. The Hyatt Regency in Albuquerque has eight accessible rooms in both smoking and non-smoking sections. The rooms have flashing alarm lights, with TTY and closed-captioned television available. Braille guidebooks can also be obtained here. Shadow Mountain Lodge in Ruidoso offers one accessible room on the ground floor, with a rest room equipped with a handheld showerhead and grab bars.

➤ ACCESSIBLE ROOMS: **Best Western Motel Stevens** (☎ 505/887–2851). **Four Kachinas Bed & Breakfast** (☎ 505/982–2550). **Hyatt Regency** (☎ 505/842–1234). **Shadow Mountain Lodge** (☎ 505/257–4886).

RESERVATIONS

When discussing accessibility with an operator or reservations agent, **ask hard questions.** Are there any stairs, inside *or* out? Are there grab bars next to the toilet *and* in the shower/tub? How wide is the doorway to the room? To the bathroom? For the most extensive facilities meeting the latest legal specifications, **opt for newer accommodations.**

SIGHTS & ATTRACTIONS

Santa Fe is an old city, so its narrow streets and walkways aren't always convenient for wheelchairs. The same is true of Old Mesilla near Las Cruces. Carlsbad Caverns National Park is accessible on the 1¼-mi Red Tour that goes directly into the Big Room via elevator; wheelchair users are advised never to try this alone. Reserved parking is available at the cavern's lower amphitheater, where the summer

bat flights take place. Parking and picnic areas at White Sands National Monument are wheelchair accessible, but only limited access is available to the sand dunes, where there are no developed trails. New Mexico has several free guidebooks for travelers with disabilities.

➤ NEW MEXICO GUIDEBOOKS: **Albuquerque Convention and Visitors Bureau** (☎ 800/284–2282). **Developmental Disabilities Planning Council** (☎ 800/552–8195). **Governor's Concerns on the Handicapped** (☎ 505/827–6465).

TRANSPORTATION

Specially equipped vehicles can be rented from **Wheelchair Getaways** (✉ Box 93501, Albuquerque 87199, ☎ 505/247–2626), a franchise organization based in Albuquerque. Automatic wheelchair lifts or ramps along with hand controls are included in vans, which will be delivered to the Albuquerque International Sunport upon request. Rentals also are available from this franchise for the El Paso, Texas, area.

➤ COMPLAINTS: **Disability Rights Section** (✉ U.S. Department of Justice, Civil Rights Division, Box 66738, Washington, DC 20035–6738, ☎ 202/514–0301 or 800/514–0301; TTY 202/514–0383 or 800/514–0383, FAX 202/307–1198, www.usdoj.gov/crt/ada/adahom1.htm) for general complaints. **Aviation Consumer Protection Division** (☞ Air Travel, *above*) for airline-related problems. **Civil Rights Office** (✉ U.S. Department of Transportation, Departmental Office of Civil Rights, S-30, 400 7th St. SW, Room 10215, Washington, DC 20590, ☎ 202/366–4648, FAX 202/366–9371) for problems with surface transportation.

TRAVEL AGENCIES

In the United States, the Americans with Disabilities Act requires that travel firms serve the needs of all travelers. Some agencies specialize in working with people with disabilities.

➤ TRAVELERS WITH MOBILITY PROBLEMS: **Access Adventures** (✉ 206 Chestnut Ridge Rd., Scottsville, NY 14624, ☎ 716/889–9096, dltravel@

prodigy.net), run by a former physical-rehabilitation counselor. **Flying Wheels Travel** (✉ 143 W. Bridge St., Box 382, Owatonna, MN 55060, ☎ 507/451–5005 or 800/535–6790, FAX 507/451–1685, thq@ll.net, www.flyingwheels.com). **Hinsdale Travel Service** (✉ 201 E. Ogden Ave., Suite 100, Hinsdale, IL 60521, ☎ 630/325–1335, FAX 630/325–1342, hinsdaletravel@hinsdaletravel.com).

DISCOUNTS & DEALS

Be a smart shopper and **compare all your options** before making decisions. A plane ticket bought with a promotional coupon from travel clubs, coupon books, and direct-mail offers may not be cheaper than the least expensive fare from a discount ticket agency. And always keep in mind that what you get is just as important as what you save.

DISCOUNT RESERVATIONS

To save money, **look into discount reservations services** with toll-free numbers, which use their buying power to get a better price on hotels, airline tickets, even car rentals. When booking a room, always **call the hotel's local toll-free number** (if one is available) rather than the central reservations number—you'll often get a better price. Always ask about special packages or corporate rates.

➤ AIRLINE TICKETS: ☎ **800/FLY–ASAP.**

➤ HOTEL ROOMS: **RMC Travel** (☎ 800/245–5738, www.rmcwebtravel.com). **Steigenberger Reservation Service** (☎ 800/223–5652, www.srs-worldhotels.com). **Turbotrip.com** (☎ 800/473–7829, www.turbotrip.com).

PACKAGE DEALS

Don't confuse packages and guided tours. When you buy a package, you travel on your own, just as though you had planned the trip yourself. Fly-drive packages, which combine airfare and car rental, are often a good deal.

ECOTOURISM

New Mexico has a wide variety of cactus species, which grow so abundantly that it might seem harmless to dig up a plant or two as a souvenir. Don't do it. New laws prohibit this practice, as certain species are becoming scarce. Avoid picking up lizards or related species, which also are becoming increasingly protected. It's also illegal to carry off Indian artifacts such as arrowheads or pottery from public land. On U.S. Bureau of Land Management land, it's okay to collect many types of rock samples, but you might want to clarify rules depending on the district you're visiting. Southern New Mexico has many caves open to visitors mostly by permit. If you visit a cave, don't leave any traces of yourself (pack it in, pack it out) and don't touch the delicate formations.

ETIQUETTE & BEHAVIOR

See Reservations and Pueblos *in* the Pleasures and Pastimes section of Chapter 1 for information about proper etiquette when visiting Native American lands.

GAY & LESBIAN TRAVEL

Although Santa Fe doesn't have a highly visible gay community or a swinging gay nightlife (at press time the city had but one gay bar), lesbians and gay men have long been a presence, and a short section of North Guadalupe Street is developing into a local hangout. A few gay businesses are clustered around in the Nob Hill Historic District in Albuquerque. The monthly *Out! Magazine* (no relation to the national magazine *Out*) provides coverage of New Mexico. A chapter in *Fodor's Gay Guide to the USA* covers Santa Fe, Taos, and Albuquerque.

➤ RESOURCES: *Fodor's Gay Guide to the USA,* available in bookstores or from Fodor's Travel Publications (☎ 800/533–6478; $20 plus $4 shipping). *Out! Magazine* (☎ 505/243–2540).

➤ GAY- & LESBIAN-FRIENDLY TRAVEL AGENCIES: **Different Roads Travel** (✉ 8383 Wilshire Blvd., Suite 902, Beverly Hills, CA 90211, ☎ 323/651–5557 or 800/429–8747, FAX 323/651–3678, leigh@west.tzell.com). **Kennedy Travel** (✉ 314 Jericho Tpk., Floral Park, NY 11001, ☎ 516/352–4888 or 800/237–7433, FAX 516/354–8849, main@kennedytravel.com, www.kennedytravel.com). **Now Voyager** (✉ 4406 18th St., San Francisco, CA 94114, ☎ 415/626–1169 or 800/255–6951, FAX 415/626–8626, www.nowvoyager.com). **Skylink Travel and Tour** (✉ 1006 Mendocino Ave., Santa Rosa, CA 95401, ☎ 707/546–9888 or 800/225–5759, FAX 707/546–9891, skylinktvl@aol.com, www.skylinktravel.com), serving lesbian travelers.

HOLIDAYS

New Mexico is an exceptional destination at Christmastime, particularly Santa Fe and Taos. There's an excellent chance for snow to put you in the holiday mood, but usually not too much of it and at tolerable temperatures. Farolitos (paper bag lanterns) line sidewalks and adobe buildings. Similar scenes are repeated throughout most of New Mexico, reflecting traditions dating back several centuries. In a nationally recognized Christmas tour at Carlsbad, home owners provide several miles of brightly lit backyard displays for the benefit of evening boat cruises along the Pecos River.

Major national holidays include New Year's Day (Jan. 1); Martin Luther King, Jr., Day (3rd Mon. in Jan.); Presidents' Day (3rd Mon. in Feb.); Memorial Day (last Mon. in May); Independence Day (July 4); Labor Day (1st Mon. in Sept.); Thanksgiving Day (4th Thurs. in Nov.); Christmas Eve and Christmas Day (Dec. 24 and 25); and New Year's Eve (Dec. 31).

INSURANCE

The most useful travel-insurance plan is a comprehensive policy that includes coverage for trip cancellation and interruption, default, trip delay, and medical expenses (with a waiver for preexisting conditions).

Without insurance you will lose all or most of your money if you cancel your trip, regardless of the reason. Default insurance covers you if your tour operator, airline, or cruise line goes out of business. Trip-delay covers expenses that arise because of bad weather or mechanical delays. Study the fine print when comparing policies.

Always **buy travel policies directly from the insurance company**; if you buy them from a cruise line, airline, or tour operator that goes out of business you probably will not be covered

for the agency or operator's default, a major risk. Before making any purchase, **review your existing health and home-owner's policies** to find what they cover away from home.

➤ TRAVEL INSURERS: In the U.S.: **Access America** (✉ 6600 W. Broad St., Richmond, VA 23230, ☎ 804/285–3300 or 800/284–8300, FAX 804/673–1583, www.previewtravel.com), **Travel Guard International** (✉ 1145 Clark St., Stevens Point, WI 54481, ☎ 715/345–0505 or 800/826–1300, FAX 800/955–8785, www.noelgroup.com).

FOR INTERNATIONAL TRAVELERS

CAR TRAVEL

Interstate highways—limited-access, multilane highways whose numbers are prefixed by "I–"—are the fastest routes. Interstates with three-digit numbers encircle urban areas, which may have other limited-access expressways, freeways, and parkways as well. Tolls may be levied on limited-access highways. So-called U.S. highways and state highways are not necessarily limited-access but may have several lanes.

Along larger highways, roadside stops with rest rooms, fast-food restaurants, and sundries stores are well spaced. State police and tow trucks patrol major highways and lend assistance. If your car breaks down on an interstate, pull onto the shoulder and wait for help, or have your passengers wait while you walk to an emergency phone. If you carry a cell phone, dial *55, noting your location on the small green roadside mileage markers.

Driving in the United States is on the right. Do **obey speed limits** posted along roads and highways. Watch for lower limits in small towns and on back roads. On weekdays between 6 and 10 AM and again between 4 and 7 PM **expect heavy traffic.** Parking violations are enforced more strictly in larger cities.

Book stores, gas stations, convenience stores, and rest stops sell maps (about $3) and multiregion road atlases (about $10). See Car Travel, *above*, for information on gasoline and more rules of the road and requirements.

CONSULATES & EMBASSIES

➤ AUSTRALIA: ✉ 2049 Century Park E, 19th floor, Los Angeles, ☎ 310/229–4840.

➤ CANADA: ✉ 300 S. Grand Ave., Los Angeles, ☎ 213/346–2700.

➤ NEW ZEALAND: ✉ 4365 Executive Dr., No. 1600, San Diego, ☎ 619/699–2993.

➤ UNITED KINGDOM: ✉ 11766 Wilshire Blvd., No. 400, Los Angeles, ☎ 310/477–3322.

CURRENCY

The dollar is the basic unit of U.S. currency. It has 100 cents. Coins include the copper penny (1¢); the silvery nickel (5¢), dime (10¢), quarter (25¢), and half-dollar (50¢); and the golden $1 coin, replacing a now-rare silver dollar. Bills are denominated $1, $5, $10, $20, $50, and $100, all green and identical in size; designs vary. The exchange rate at press time was $1.44 per British pound, 67¢ per Canadian dollar, 56¢ per Australian dollar, and 42¢ per New Zealand dollar.

CUSTOMS & DUTIES

When shopping, **keep receipts** for all purchases. Upon reentering the country, **be ready to show customs officials what you've bought.** If you feel a duty is incorrect or object to the way your clearance was handled, note the inspector's badge number and ask to see a supervisor. If the problem isn't resolved, write to the appropriate authorities, beginning with the port director at your point of entry.

Australian residents who are 18 or older may bring home $A400 worth of souvenirs and gifts (including jewelry), 250 cigarettes or 250 grams of tobacco, and 1,125 milliliters of alcohol (including wine, beer, and spirits). Residents under 18 may bring back $A200 worth of goods. Prohibited items include meat products. Seeds, plants, and fruits need to be declared upon arrival.

Canadian residents who have been out of Canada for at least 7 days may bring home C$500 worth of goods duty-free. If you've been away fewer than 7 days but more than 48 hours, the duty-free allowance drops to C$200; if your trip lasts 24–48 hours, the allowance is C$50. You may not pool allowances with family members. Goods claimed under the C$500 exemption may follow you by mail; those claimed under the lesser exemptions must accompany you. Alcohol and tobacco products may be included in the 7-day and 48-hour exemptions but not in the 24-hour exemption. If you meet the age requirements of the province or territory through which you reenter Canada, you may bring in, duty-free, 1.14 liters (40 imperial ounces) of wine or liquor *or* 24 12-ounce cans or bottles of beer or ale. If you are 16 or older you may bring in, duty-free, 200 cigarettes and 50 cigars. Check ahead of time with Revenue Canada or the Department of Agriculture for policies regarding meat products, seeds, plants, and fruits. You may send an unlimited number of gifts worth up to C$60 each duty-free to Canada. Label the package UNSOLICITED GIFT—VALUE UNDER $60. Alcohol and tobacco are excluded.

Homeward-bound New Zealand residents 17 or older may bring back NZ$700 worth of souvenirs and gifts. Your duty-free allowance also includes 4.5 liters of wine or beer; one 1,125-milliliter bottle of spirits; and either 200 cigarettes, 250 grams of tobacco, 50 cigars, or a combination of the three up to 250 grams. Prohibited items include meat products, seeds, plants, and fruits.

From countries outside the European Union, including the United States, residents of the United Kingdom may bring home, duty-free, 200 cigarettes or 50 cigars; 1 liter of spirits or 2 liters of fortified or sparkling wine or liqueurs; 2 liters of still table wine; 60 milliliters of perfume; 250 milliliters of toilet water; plus £136 worth of other goods, including gifts and souvenirs. If returning from outside the EU, prohibited items include meat products, seeds, plants, and fruits.

➤ IN AUSTRALIA: **Australian Customs Service** (Regional Director, ✉ Box 8, Sydney, NSW 2001, ☎ 02/9213–2000, 𝖥𝖠𝖷 02/9213–4000, www.customs.gov.au).

➤ IN CANADA: **Revenue Canada** (✉ 2265 St. Laurent Blvd. S, Ottawa, Ontario K1G 4K3, ☎ 613/993–0534; 800/461–9999 in Canada, FAX 613/991–4126, www.ccra-adrc.gc.ca).

➤ IN NEW ZEALAND: **New Zealand Customs** (Custom House, ✉ 50 Anzac Ave., Box 29, Auckland, New Zealand, ☎ 09/359–6655, FAX 09/359–6732).

➤ IN THE U.K.: **HM Customs and Excise** (✉ Dorset House, Stamford St., Bromley, Kent BR1 1XX, ☎ 020/7202–4227, www.hmce.gov.uk).

➤ IN THE U.S.: **U.S. Customs Service** (✉ 1300 Pennsylvania Ave. NW, Washington, DC 20229, www.customs.gov; inquiries ☎ 202/354–1000; complaints c/o ✉ 1300 Pennsylvania Ave. NW, Room 5.4D, Washington, DC 20229; registration of equipment c/o ✉ Resource Management, ☎ 202/354–1000).

ELECTRICITY

The U.S. standard is AC, 110 volts/60 cycles. Plugs have two flat pins set parallel to each other.

EMERGENCIES

For police, fire, or ambulance, **dial 911.**

INSURANCE

Britons and Australians need extra medical coverage when traveling overseas.

➤ INSURANCE INFORMATION: In the U.K.: **Association of British Insurers** (✉ 51–55 Gresham St., London EC2V 7HQ, ☎ 0207/600–3333, FAX 0207/696–8999, info@abi.org.uk, www.abi.org.uk). In Australia: **Insurance Council of Australia** (☎ 03/9614–1077, FAX 03/9614–7924). In Canada: **Voyager Insurance** (✉ 44 Peel Center Dr., Brampton, Ontario L6T 4M8, ☎ 905/791–8700; 800/668–4342 in Canada).

MAIL & SHIPPING

Other than at a post office, you can also deposit mail in the stout, dark blue, steel bins at strategic locations everywhere and in the mail chutes of large buildings; pickup schedules are posted.

For mail sent within the United States, you need a 33¢ stamp for first-class letters weighing up to 1 ounce (22¢ for each additional ounce) and 20¢ for domestic postcards. For overseas mail, you pay 60¢ for ½-ounce airmail letters, 50¢ for airmail postcards, and 35¢ for surface-rate postcards. For Canada you need a 52¢ stamp for a 1-ounce letter and 40¢ for a postcard. For 50¢ you can buy an aerogram—a single sheet of lightweight blue paper that folds into its own envelope, stamped for overseas airmail.

To receive mail on the road, have it sent c/o General Delivery at your destination's main post office (use the correct five-digit zip code). You must pick up mail in person within 30 days and show a driver's license or passport.

PASSPORTS & VISAS

The best time for Americans to apply for a passport or to renew is in fall and winter. Before any trip, check your passport's expiration date, and, if necessary, renew it as soon as possible. When traveling internationally, **carry your passport** even if you don't need one (it's always the best form of I.D.) and **make two photocopies of the data page** (one for someone at home and another for you, carried separately from your passport). If you lose your passport, promptly call the nearest embassy or consulate and the local police.

Visitor visas are not necessary for Canadian citizens or for citizens of Australia, New Zealand, and the United Kingdom staying fewer than 90 days.

➤ AUSTRALIAN CITIZENS: **Australian Passport Office** (☎ 131–232). The **U.S. Office of Australia Affairs** (✉ MLC Centre, 19-29 Martin Pl., 59th floor, Sydney, NSW 2000).

➤ CANADIAN CITIZENS: **Passport Office** (☎ 819/994–3500 or 800/567–6868).

➤ NEW ZEALAND CITIZENS: **New Zealand Passport Office** (☎ 04/494–0700 for application procedures; 0800/225–050 in New Zealand for application-status updates). **U.S. Office of New Zealand Affairs** (✉ 29 Fitzherbert Terr., Thorndon, Wellington).

➤ U.K. CITIZENS: **London Passport Office** (☎ 0990/210–410) for appli-

THE GOLD GUIDE / SMART TRAVEL TIPS

cation procedures and emergency passports. **U.S. Embassy Visa Information Line** (☎ 01891/200–290). **U.S. Embassy Visa Branch** (✉ 5 Upper Grosvenor Sq., London W1A 1AE); send a self-addressed, stamped envelope. **U.S. Consulate General** (✉ Queen's House, Queen St., Belfast BTI 6EO).

TELEPHONES

All U.S. telephone numbers consist of a three-digit area code and a seven-digit local number. Within most local calling areas, dial only the seven-digit number. Within the same area code, dial "1" first. To call between area-code regions, dial "1" then all 10 digits; the same goes for calls to numbers prefixed by "800," "888," and "877"—all toll-free. For calls to numbers preceded by "900" you must pay—usually dearly.

For international calls, dial "011" followed by the country code and the local number. For help, dial "0" and ask for an overseas operator. The country code is 61 for Australia, 52 for Mexico, 64 for New Zealand, 44 for the United Kingdom. Calling Canada is the same as calling within the United States. Most local phone books list country codes and U.S. area codes. The country code for the United States is 1.

For operator assistance, dial "0". To obtain someone's phone number, call directory assistance, 555–1212 or occasionally 411 (free at public phones). To have the person you're calling foot the bill, phone collect; dial "0" instead of "1" before the 10-digit number.

At pay phones, instructions are usually posted. Usually you insert coins in a slot (35¢ for local calls in New Mexico) and wait for a steady tone before dialing. When you call long distance, the operator will tell you how much to insert; prepaid phone cards, widely available in various denominations, are easier.

LODGING

The lodgings we list are the cream of the crop in each price category. We always list the facilities that are available—but we don't specify whether they cost extra: when pricing accom-

modations, always ask what's included and what costs extra. Accommodations in New Mexico include inexpensive chain hotels, many bed-and-breakfasts, small alpine lodges near the primary ski resorts, and low-budget motels. Rates are highest during the peak tourist months of July and August and during Christmas and winter ski season. Off-season rates, which fluctuate, tend to be 20% lower than peak rates, and reservations are easier to obtain at this time. You can book rooms (and rental cars and outdoor and other activities) by calling New Mexico Central Reservations.

Assume that hotels operate on the European Plan (EP, with no meals) unless we specify that they use the **Continental Plan** (CP, with a Continental breakfast) or **Breakfast Plan** (BP, with a full breakfast).

CATEGORY	COST*
$$$$	over $150
$$$	$100–$150
$$	$65–$100
$	under $65

All prices are for a standard double room, excluding tax (5.6%–7%), in peak season.

➤ RESERVATIONS: **New Mexico Central Reservations** (☎ 800/466–7829).

APARTMENT & VILLA RENTALS

If you want a home base that's roomy enough for a family and comes with cooking facilities, **consider a furnished rental.** These can save you money, especially if you're traveling with a group. Home-exchange directories sometimes list rentals as well as exchanges.

➤ INTERNATIONAL AGENTS: **Hideaways International** (✉ 767 Islington St., Portsmouth, NH 03801, ☎ 603/430–4433 or 800/843–4433, FAX 603/430–4444, info@hideaways.com www.hideaways.com; membership $99).

LOCAL AGENTS

Vacation home, condo, and cabin rentals are numerous, particularly in mountain resort areas of New Mexico. Management companies include Craig Management Co. in Taos and Green Mountain Real Estate in Cloudcroft.

► MANAGEMENT COMPANIES: **Craig Management Co.** (☎ 800/800–4754). **Green Mountain Real Estate** (☎ 800/748–2537).

B&BS

B&Bs in New Mexico run the gamut from rooms in locals' homes to grandly restored adobe or Victorian homes. Rates in Santa Fe and Taos tend to be high; they're a little lower in Albuquerque and rival those of chain motels in the outlying areas. Good deals can be found in southern New Mexico as well.

► RESERVATION SERVICES: **Bed and Breakfast of New Mexico** (☎ 505/982–3332). **New Mexico Bed and Breakfast Association** (☎ 505/766–5380 or 800/661–6649).

CAMPING

If you're into camping the way the pioneers did, New Mexico is the place for you. Primitive sites, where you'll likely not see a ranger (or even another camper) for miles, are plentiful. Many of the state and national parks have developed sites. The New Mexico Department of Tourism (☞ Visitor Information, *below*) has information about public and private campgrounds in the state. The state also has a surprising number of lakes, including the expansive Elephant Butte and Navajo Lake. Campers can load up their boats with gear and head for primitive backcountry away from roads and crowds.

HOME EXCHANGES

If you would like to exchange your home for someone else's, **join a home-exchange organization,** which will send you its updated listings of available exchanges for a year and will include your own listing in at least one of them. It's up to you to make specific arrangements.

► EXCHANGE CLUBS: **HomeLink International** (✉ Box 650, Key West, FL 33041, ☎ 305/294–7766 or 800/638–3841, FAX 305/294–1448, usa@homelink.org, www.homelink.org; $98 per year). **Intervac U.S.** (✉ Box 590504, San Francisco, CA 94159, ☎ 800/756–4663, FAX 415/435–7440, www.intervac.com; $89 per year includes two catalogs).

HOSTELS

No matter what your age, you can **save on lodging costs by staying at hostels.** New Mexico hostel accommodations range from the elegant surroundings of a bed-and-breakfast in Silver City (The Carter House) to the casual, camping out–style environment of a hot springs locale in Truth or Consequences (Riverbend Hot Springs) to the no-frills friendliness of the Abominable Snowmansion in Arroyo Seco (north of Taos).

In some 5,000 locations in more than 70 countries around the world, Hostelling International (HI), the umbrella group for a number of national youth-hostel associations, offers single-sex, dorm-style beds and, at many hostels, rooms for couples and family accommodations. Membership in any HI national hostel association, open to travelers of all ages, allows you to stay in HI-affiliated hostels at member rates; one-year membership is about $25 for adults (C$26.75 in Canada, £9.30 in the U.K., $30 in Australia, and $30 in New Zealand); hostels run about $10–$25 per night. Members have priority if the hostel is full; they're also eligible for discounts around the world, even on rail and bus travel in some countries.

► ORGANIZATIONS: **Hostelling International—American Youth Hostels** (✉ 733 15th St. NW, Suite 840, Washington, DC 20005, ☎ 202/783–6161, FAX 202/783–6171, hiayhserv@hiayh.org, www.hiayh.org). **Hostelling International—Canada** (✉ 400–205 Catherine St., Ottawa, Ontario K2P 1C3, ☎ 613/237–7884, FAX 613/237–7868, info@hostellingintl.ca, www.hostellingintl.ca). **Youth Hostel Association of England and Wales** (✉ Trevelyan House, 8 St. Stephen's Hill, St. Albans, Hertfordshire AL1 2DY, ☎ 01727/855215 or 01727/845047, FAX 01727/844126, customerservices@yha.org.uk, www.yha.org.uk). **Australian Youth Hostel Association** (✉ 10 Mallett St., Camperdown, NSW 2050, ☎ 02/9565–1699, FAX 02/9565–1325, www.yha.com.au). **Youth Hostels Association of New Zealand** (✉ Box 436, Christchurch, New Zealand, ☎ 03/379–9970, FAX 03/365–4476, book@yha.org.nz, www.yha.org.nz).

HOTELS

If you plan to visit Albuquerque in October, be sure and check dates for the Kodak Albuquerque International Balloon Fiesta or you might be stranded if you haven't booked at least four months in advance. Premium hotel rooms in the state capital of Santa Fe tend to fill up during sessions of the New Mexico Legislature, typically conducted during the first three months of the year. The Fourth of July weekend can pack hotel rooms in smaller tourist-oriented communities such as Ruidoso, Taos, and Carlsbad, so make sure you have reservations in advance. All hotels listed have a private bath unless otherwise noted.

➤ TOLL-FREE NUMBERS: Baymont Inns (☎ 800/428–3438, www.baymontinns.com). Best Western (☎ 800/528–1234, www.bestwestern.com). Choice (☎ 800/221–2222, www.hotelchoice.com). Clarion (☎ 800/252–7466, www.choicehotels.com). Colony (☎ 800/777–1700. www.colony.com). Comfort (☎ 800/228–5150, www.comfortinn.com). Days Inn (☎ 800/325–2525, www.daysinn.com). Doubletree and Red Lion Hotels (☎ 800/222–8733, www.doubletree.com). Embassy Suites (☎ 800/362–2779, www.embassysuites.com). Fairfield Inn (☎ 800/228–2800, www.marriott.com). Four Seasons (☎ 800/332–3442, www.fourseasons.com). Hilton (☎ 800/445–8667, www.hiltons.com). Holiday Inn (☎ 800/465–4329, www.basshotels.com). Howard Johnson (☎ 800/654–4656, www.hojo.com). Hyatt Hotels & Resorts (☎ 800/233–1234, www.hyatt.com). La Quinta (☎ 800/531–5900, www.laquinta.com). Marriott (☎ 800/228–9290, www.marriott.com). Quality Inn (☎ 800/228–5151, www.qualityinn.com). Radisson (☎ 800/333–3333, www.radisson.com). Ramada (☎ 800/228–2828. www.ramada.com), Sheraton (☎ 800/325–3535, www.sheraton.com).Sleep Inn (☎ 800/753–3746, www.sleepinn.com). Westin Hotels & Resorts (☎ 800/228–3000, www.westin.com). Wyndham Hotels & Resorts (☎ 800/822–4200, www.wyndham.com).

MOTELS

➤ TOLL-FREE NUMBERS: Econo Lodge (☎ 800/553–2666). Hampton Inn (☎ 800/426–7866). La Quinta (☎ 800/531–5900). Motel 6 (☎ 800/466–8356). Rodeway (☎ 800/228–2000). Super 8 (☎ 800/848–8888).

MEDIA

Because of its sparse and scattered communities, New Mexico has more demand for radio stations and newspapers than ordinarily found (per capita) in more urbanized areas. These islands of population generally have their own media outlets, except for network television stations that are concentrated in Albuquerque and El Paso, Texas. Albuquerque television station affiliates are set up in Roswell, while public television and radio stations operate on university campuses at Albuquerque, Las Cruces, and Portales.

NEWSPAPERS & MAGAZINES

New Mexico has about 50 daily and weekly newspapers. Only one newspaper, the *Albuquerque Journal,* circulates statewide. the *Santa Fe New Mexican* often takes a political tone, since it is based in the state's capital city. In more rural areas, agriculture reporting is predominant in newspapers such as the *Courier* in Hatch and *Quay County Sun* in Tucumcari. Two magazines with headquarters in Santa Fe, *New Mexico* (travel and cultural features), and *Outside* (outdoor recreation articles), are nationally recognized publications. Find out what's happening in the arts, culture, and nightlife by picking up the free weeklies that are available in Albuquerque, Santa Fe, and Taos: the *Alibi, Crosswinds Weekly,* and the *Santa Fe Reporter.*

RADIO & TELEVISION

National Public Radio affiliates are found on major university campuses in New Mexico, including KUNM (89.9 FM) at Albuquerque's University of New Mexico, KRWG (90.7 FM) at New Mexico State University in Las Cruces, and KENW (89.5 FM) at Eastern New Mexico State University in Portales. The state has about 40 radio stations, ranging from Christian broadcasts to rock to country-and-western. Major network affiliates in New Mexico are all based in Albuquerque, including **KOB** (NBC, Channel 4), **KASA** (Fox, Channel 2), **KRQE** (CBS, Channel 13) and **KOAT** (ABC, Channel 7). Major network affiliates in El Paso, Texas serve many southern New Mexico locations. Public television station outlets are found on university campuses, including **KNME** (Channel 5) in Albuquerque, **KRWG** (Channel 22) in Las Cruces, and **KENW** (Channel 3) in Portales.

MEXICO SIDE TRIPS

Visitors to El Paso, Texas, and other border towns often make an excursion into Mexico. If you're planning to cross the border to Mexico, **note the travel requirements** detailed in Southwestern New Mexico A to Z in Chapter 8 and passport and customs information under International Travelers, *above*.

SAFETY

The U.S. State Department has issued a warning regarding travel in Ciudad Juárez. Crime rates in Juárez are high, and gangland-style hits associated with internal drug wars have taken place in public places.

Since tourists are sometimes targeted for foul play, **don't take the family van with U.S. license plates into Mexico** and never drive in Mexico after dark. Desirable model vehicles from the United States are often stolen when left parked in unsupervised areas.

Be cautious about eating in smaller restaurants, since water and food quality controls are not as stringent here as they are in the United States. It's best to order bottled beverages and packaged food, if you're in doubt. **Never carry firearms across the border,** as there are severe penalties, including long-term incarceration.

The odds of encountering trouble are slim, as long as you obey laws and practice common-sense precautions that would apply in any large metropolitan area. You can peruse travel warnings for many international locations including Mexico at the U.S. State Department Web site.

➤ U.S. CONSULATE GENERAL'S OFFICE: ⊠ Avenida Lopez Mateos 924-N,

Ciudad Juárez Mexico, ☎ 011/52–16–113000.

➤ U.S. STATE DEPARTMENT: ⊠ U.S. Department of State, 2201 C St. NW, Washington, DC 20520, ☎ 202/647–4000, www.travel.state.gov.

MONEY MATTERS

In New Mexico, Santa Fe is by far the priciest city: meals, gasoline, and motel rates are all significantly higher in the state's capital. Lodging costs in Santa Fe typically run 30% higher than in any other New Mexico city. Taos, too, can be a little expensive because it's such a popular tourist destination, but you have more choices for economizing there than in Santa Fe. Lodging and meals throughout much of the rest of the state are a genuine bargain. Depending on the establishment, $7 can buy you a savory Mexican-food dinner in Farmington, Old Mesilla, or Silver City. As the state's largest metropolitan area, Albuquerque has a full range of price choices. Prices throughout this guide are given for adults. Substantially reduced fees are almost always available for children, students, and senior citizens. For information on taxes, *see* Taxes, *below.*

ATMS

Look for ATMs in larger communities, since isolated rural areas are not as widely served. ATMs are available in banks, bank branches, chain grocery stores, and shopping malls.

CREDIT CARDS

Throughout this guide, the following abbreviations are used: AE, American Express; D, Discover; DC, Diners Club; MC, MasterCard; and V, Visa.

➤ REPORTING LOST CARDS: **American Express** (☎ 800/300–8765). **Diners Club** (☎ 800/234–6377). **Discover-Card** (☎ 800/347–2683). **MasterCard** (☎ 800/826–2181). **Visa** (☎ 800/336–8472).

OUTDOORS & SPORTS

The New Mexico Department of Tourism (☞ Visitor Information, *below*) distributes a booklet, *Outdoors New Mexico,* with information about the many recreational activities that take place within the state.

BIKE TRAVEL

A detailed recreational map showing elevations and roadways throughout New Mexico can be ordered from *New Mexico* magazine. The New Mexico Public Lands Information Center also has a variety of maps and information for outdoor recreation. Cycling events in New Mexico include the Santa Fe Century (50- or 100-mi recreational rides), the Sanbusco Hill Climb (a race to the Santa Fe Ski Area), and the Tour de Los Alamos (road race and criterium).

Most airlines accommodate bikes as luggage, provided they are dismantled and boxed. For bike boxes, often free at bike shops, you'll pay about $5 (at least $100 for bike bags) from airlines. International travelers can sometimes substitute a bike for a piece of checked luggage at no charge; otherwise, the cost is about $100. Domestic and Canadian airlines charge $25–$50.

➤ BIKE MAPS: *New Mexico* magazine (☎ 800/898–6639). **New Mexico Public Lands Information Center** (✉ 1474 Rodeo Rd., Santa Fe 87505, ☎ 505/438–7542, FAX 505/438–7582 www.publiclands.org).

➤ CYCLING EVENTS: **New Mexico Touring Society** (☎ 505/298–0085).

BIRD-WATCHING

New Mexico is fortunate to be home to tens of thousands of migrating birds, and the refuges offer viewing platforms for observing the flocks of snow geese, sandhill cranes, and other migratory birds using this popular stopover.

➤ REFUGES: **Bitter Lake National Wildlife Refuge** (✉ 4065 Bitter Lakes, Box 7, Roswell 88202, ☎ 505/622–6755). **Bosque del Apache National Wildlife Refuge** (✉ Box 1246, Socorro 87801, ☎ 505/835–1828).

CANOEING, KAYAKING, AND RIVER RAFTING

Most of the hard-core river rafting is done in the Taos area; for statewide information concerning river recreational activities, contact the New Mexico Department of Tourism (☞ Visitor Information, *below*). For additional operators, *see* the A to Z

listings at the end of individual chapters or contact local tourism offices.

FISHING

Anyone over 12 who wishes to fish must **buy a New Mexico fishing license.** Including a trout-validation stamp, the license costs out-of-state visitors $8 per day or $16 for five days. Habitat stamps also must be purchased for an extra $5 for fishing on U.S. Forest Service or Bureau of Land Management lands. The year-round nonresident fee is $39 ($17.50 for state residents). About 225 sporting-goods and other stores (among them Kmart and many convenience stores), in addition to the offices of the New Mexico Game and Fish Department, sell fishing licenses. The New Mexico Guides Association has information about guided fishing trips.

Fishing on Native American reservations is not subject to state regulations but will require tribal permits; the Indian Pueblo Cultural Center (☞ Visitor Information, *below*) can provide further information.

➤ INFORMATION: **New Mexico Game and Fish Department** (✉ Villagra Building, 408 Galisteo St., Box 25112, Santa Fe 87503, ☎ 505/827–7911). **New Mexico Guides Association** (☎ 505/988–8022). **Sport Fishing Promotions Council toll-free hot line** (☎ 800/275–3474).

GOLF

➤ INFORMATION: **Sun Country Amateur Golf Association** (✉ 10035 Country Club La. NW, No. 5, Albuquerque 87114, ☎ 505/897–0864) has a list of courses and telephone numbers for each club regarding greens fees and hours.

HIKING

Hiking opportunities abound throughout the state—whether in the Gila National Forest, the Lincoln National Forest, Sandia Mountains, Taos Ski Valley, or Santa Fe area.

➤ INFORMATION AND MAPS: **New Mexico State Parks Division** (✉ Energy, Minerals, and Natural Resources Dept., 2040 S. Pacheco, Box 1147, Santa Fe 87504, ☎ 505/827–7173 or 888/667–2757).

HORSE RACING

➤ TRACKS: **Downs at Santa Fe** (⊠ 5 mi south of Santa Fe, ☎ 505/471–3311). **Downs at Albuquerque** (⊠ New Mexico State Fairgrounds, E. Central Ave., ☎ 505/266–5555). **Ruidoso Downs Racetrack** (⊠ 1461 Hwy. 70 W, ☎ 505/378–4431). **Sunland Park Racetrack** (⊠ 5 mi north of El Paso, TX, ☎ 505/589–1131).

SKIING

Winter in New Mexico mountains can be particularly pleasant for skiers, because bright sunshine often beams down on mounds of snow. However, compared with other notable ski areas, the state also is more susceptible to extended periods of dry weather that can create massive melt downs. Major ski resorts have snow machines, but you should **check conditions first** or you might be in for a disappointment.

➤ INFORMATION: **Ski New Mexico** (☎ 800/755–7669), for a free "Skier's Guide."

➤ DOWNHILL: **Angel Fire Resort** (⊠ Drawer B, Angel Fire 87710, ☎ 800/633–7463). **Enchanted Forest Cross-Country Ski Area** (⊠ Box 521, Red River 87558, ☎ 505/754–2374). **Pajarito Mountain Ski Area** (⊠ Box 155, Los Alamos 87544, ☎ 505/662–7669 or 505/662–5725). **Red River Ski Area** (⊠ Box 900, Red River 87558, ☎ 505/754–2223). **Sandia Peak Ski Area** (⊠ 10 Tramway Loop NE, Albuquerque 87122, ☎ 505/242–9133). **Ski Santa Fe** (⊠ 2209 Brothers Rd., Suite 220, Santa Fe 87505, ☎ 505/982–4429). **Sipapu Lodge and Ski Area** (⊠ Box 29, Vadito 87579, ☎ 505/587–2240). **Ski Apache** (⊠ Box 220, Ruidoso 88345, ☎ 505/336–4356). **Village of Taos Ski Valley** (⊠ Box 90, Taos Ski Valley 87525, ☎ 505/776–2291).

PACKING

Typical of the Southwest, temperatures can vary considerably from sunup to sundown. You should **pack for warm days and chilly nights.**

The areas of higher elevation are considerably cooler than the low-lying southern portions of the state. In winter pack warm clothes—coats, parkas, and whatever else your body's thermostat and your ultimate destination dictate. Sweaters and jackets are also needed in summer, because though days are warm, nights at the higher altitudes can be extremely chilly. And **bring comfortable shoes;** you're likely to be doing a lot of walking.

New Mexico is one of the most informal and laid-back areas of the country, which for many is much a part of its appeal. Probably no more than three or four restaurants in the entire state enforce a dress code, even for dinner, though men are likely to feel more comfortable wearing a jacket in the major hotel dining rooms, and anyone wearing tennis shoes may receive a look of stern disapproval from the maître d'.

The Western look has, of course, never lost its hold on the West, though Western-style clothes now get mixed with tweed jackets, for example, for a more conservative, sophisticated image. You can wear your boots and big belt buckles in even the best places in Santa Fe, Taos, or Albuquerque, but if you come strolling through the lobby of the Eldorado Hotel looking like Hopalong Cassidy, you'll get some funny looks.

Don't neglect to **bring skin moisturizers** if dry skin's a problem, and **bring sunglasses** to protect your eyes from the glare of lakes or ski slopes. High altitude can cause headaches and dizziness, so check with your doctor about medication to alleviate symptoms. Sunscreen is a necessity.

In your carry-on luggage, **pack an extra pair of eyeglasses or contact lenses** and **enough of any medication you take** to last the entire trip. You may also ask your doctor to write a spare prescription using the drug's generic name, since brand names may vary from country to country. In luggage to be checked, **never pack prescription drugs or valuables.** To avoid customs delays, carry medications in their original packaging. And don't forget to carry with you the addresses of offices that handle refunds of lost traveler's checks. If you are traveling with a wine opener, pocketknife, or any other kind of knife, or toy weapons **pack them in check-in luggage.** These are consid-

THE GOLD GUIDE / SMART TRAVEL TIPS

ered potential weapons and are not permitted as carry-on items.

CHECKING LUGGAGE

How many carry-on bags you can bring with you is up to the airline. Most allow two, but some allow only one (including United, a major carrier in New Mexico), so make sure that everything you carry aboard will fit under your seat or in the overhead bin, and get to the gate early. Note that if you have a seat at the back of the plane, you'll probably board first, while the overhead bins are still empty.

If you are flying internationally, note that baggage allowances may be determined not by piece but by weight— generally 88 pounds (40 kilograms) in first class, 66 pounds (30 kilograms) in business class, and 44 pounds (20 kilograms) in economy.

Airline liability for baggage is limited to $1,250 per person on flights within the United States. On international flights it amounts to $9.07 per pound or $20 per kilogram for checked baggage (roughly $640 per 70-pound bag) and $400 per passenger for unchecked baggage. You can buy additional coverage at check-in for about $10 per $1,000 of coverage, but it excludes a rather extensive list of items, shown on your airline ticket.

Before departure, **itemize your bags' contents** and their worth, and label the bags with your name, address, and phone number. (If you use your home address, cover it so potential thieves can't see it readily.) Inside each bag, **pack a copy of your itinerary.** At check-in, **make sure that each bag is correctly tagged** with the destination airport's three-letter code. If your bags arrive damaged or fail to arrive at all, file a written report with the airline before leaving the airport. Attendants at Albuquerque's and El Paso's airports match your luggage's baggage claim ticket to the number placed on your boarding pass envelope, **so have the envelope handy as you exit the baggage claim area.**

PARKS & FORESTS

There are 12 national monuments in New Mexico and a few state monuments and parks preserving natural or cultural treasures such as northern Indian cliff dwellings or the white sands in the south. Several monuments yield insight into the 19th-century Territorial period of New Mexico, including exploits of the infamous Billy the Kid.

Carlsbad Caverns National Park, in the southeastern part of the state, has one of the largest and most spectacular cave systems in the world. For information about New Mexico's five national forests and the Kiowa National Grasslands (part of the Cibola National Forest), contact the U.S.D.A. Forest Service (☞ Visitor Information, *below*).

See also Pleasures and Pastimes *in* Chapter 1, and individual park and monument listings *in* Chapters 2 through 8.

➤ GENERAL INFORMATION: **Monument Division, Museum of New Mexico** (⊠ Box 2087, Santa Fe 87504, ☎ 505/ 476–5085). **State Parks and Recreational Division** (⊠ Energy, Minerals, and Natural Resources Dept., 2040 S. Pacheco, Box 1147, Santa Fe 87505, ☎ 505/827–7183 or 888/667–2757). **National Park Service** (⊠ Box 728, Santa Fe 87504, ☎ 505/988–6011).

➤ NATIONAL MONUMENTS AND PARKS: **Aztec Ruins National Monument** (⊠ Box 640, Aztec 87410, ☎ 505/334– 6174). **Bandelier National Monument** (⊠ HCR 1, Box 1, Suite 15, Los Alamos 87544, ☎ 505/672–0343). **Capulin Volcano National Monument** (⊠ Box 94, Capulin 88414, ☎ 505/ 278–2201). **Carlsbad Caverns National Park** (⊠ 3225 National Parks Hwy., Carlsbad 88220, ☎ 505/785– 2251). **Chaco Culture National Historical Park** (⊠ Star Rte. 4, Box 6500, Bloomfield 87413, ☎ 505/ 786–7014). **El Malpais National Monument and Conservation Area** (⊠ Box 939, Grants 87020, ☎ 505/ 285–4641). **El Morro National Monument** (⊠ Rte. 2, Box 43, Ramah 87321-9603, ☎ 505/783–4226). **Fort Union National Monument** (⊠ Box 127, Watrous 87753, ☎ 505/425– 8025). **Gila Cliff Dwellings National Monument** (⊠ Rte. 11, Box 100, Silver City 88061, ☎ 505/536–9461 or 505/757–6032). **Guadalupe Moun-**

tains National Park (✉ HC 60, Box 400 Salt Flat, TX 79847 ☎ 915/828–3251). **Pecos National Historic Park** (✉ Drawer 418, Pecos 87552, ☎ 505/757–6032 or 505/757–6414). **Petroglyph National Monument** (✉ 6900 Unser Blvd. NW, Albuquerque 87120, ☎ 505/897–8814). **Salinas Pueblo Missions National Monument** (✉ Box 517, Mountainair 87036, ☎ 505/847–2585). **White Sands National Monument** (✉ Box 1086, Holloman AFB, NM 88330-1086, ☎ 505/479–6124).

➤ NATIONAL FORESTS: **Carson National Forest** (✉ 208 Cruz Alta Rd., Taos 87571, ☎ 505/758–6200). **Cibola National Forest** (✉ 2113 Osuna Rd. NE, Suite A, Albuquerque 87113, ☎ 505/346–2650). **Gila National Forest** (✉ 3005 E. Camino del Bosque, Silver City 88061, ☎ 505/388–8201). **Lincoln National Forest** (✉ Federal Building, 1101 New York Ave., Alamogordo 88310, ☎ 505/434–7200). **Santa Fe National Forest** (✉ 1474 Rodeo Rd., Box 1689, Santa Fe 87504, ☎ 505/438–7400).

➤ STATE MONUMENTS: **Coronado State Monument** (✉ NM 44, off I–25, Box 95, Bernalillo 87004, ☎ 505/867–5351). **Fort Selden** (✉ Radium Springs exit off I–25, 13 mi north of Las Cruces, Box 58, Radium Springs 88054, ☎ 505/526–8911). **Fort Sumner** (✉ 2 mi east of the town Fort Sumner, on Billy the Kid Rd., NM 1, Box 356, Fort Sumner 88119, ☎ 505/355–2573). **Jemez State Monument** (✉ NM 4, 1 mi north of Jemez Springs, Box 143, Jemez Springs 87025, ☎ 505/829–3530). **Lincoln State Monument** (✉ U.S. 380, 12 mi east of Capitan, Courthouse Museum, Box 36, Lincoln 88338, ☎ 505/653–4372).

DISCOUNT PASSES

Look into discount passes to save money on park entrance fees. The National Parks Pass ($50) gets you and your companions free admission to all parks for one year. (Camping and parking are extra.) Both the Golden Age Passport ($10), for those 62 and older, and the Golden Access Passport (free), for travelers with disabilities, entitle holders to free entry to all national parks, plus 50%

off fees for the use of many park facilities and services. You must show proof of age and of U.S. citizenship or permanent residency (such as a U.S. passport, driver's license, or birth certificate) and, if requesting Golden Access, proof of disability. The Golden Age and Golden Access passes are available at all national parks wherever entrance fees are charged. The National Parks and Golden Access passes are available by mail or through the Internet.

➤ PASSES BY MAIL: **National Park Service** (✉ National Park Service National Office, 1849 C St. NW, Washington, DC 20240-0001, ☎ 202/208–4747, www.nps.gov). **National Parks Pass** (✉ 27540 Ave. Mentry, Valencia, CA 91355, ☎ 888/GO–PARKS, www.nationalparks.org).

SENIOR-CITIZEN TRAVEL

Many stores, restaurants, and tourist attractions in New Mexico offer senior-citizen discounts, and certain RV parks throughout the state are designated for senior citizens.

To qualify for age-related discounts, **mention your senior-citizen status up front** when booking hotel reservations (not when checking out) and before you're seated in restaurants (not when paying the bill). When renting a car, ask about promotional car-rental discounts, which can be cheaper than senior-citizen rates.

➤ EDUCATIONAL PROGRAMS: **Elderhostel** (✉ 75 Federal St., 3rd floor, Boston, MA 02110, ☎ 877/426–8056, FAX 877/426–2166, www.elderhostel.org). **Interhostel** (✉ University of New Hampshire, 6 Garrison Ave., Durham, NH 03824, ☎ 603/862–1147 or 800/733–9753, FAX 603/862–1113, learn.dce@unh.edu, www.learn.unh.edu).

SHOPPING

New Mexico is a treasure trove of antiques originating from old ranch houses and attics of family homes. You can find some real bargains in out-of-the-way places. Authentic Indian jewelry and handcrafted items, along with goods imported from nearby Mexico, like leatherwork and ceramics, are unique to this region.

You can stock up on Western-style clothing and cowboy boots here too. The Wingspread Collectors Guide compiles useful listings of art galleries throughout the state.

➤ WINGSPREAD GUIDES OF NEW MEXICO, INC.: **Wingspread Guides of New Mexico, Inc.** (✉ Box 13566-T, Albuquerque, NM 87192, ☎ 505/292–7537 or 800/873–4278, www.collectorsguide.com).

KEY DESTINATIONS

Old Town in Albuquerque is full of wares reflecting the state's Spanish and Indian origins. Santa Fe once was a trading post, and its downtown area retains an atmosphere of barter with outdoor vendors, shops, and galleries scattered among historic adobe buildings. Old Mesilla near Las Cruces is an authentic Mexican-style adobe village where shops and galleries offer high-quality handcrafted jewelry and clothing at bargain prices. Taos is an artist's haven, and an array of styles appears in the galleries. Most pueblos or reservations sell Native American arts, crafts, and jewelry. Shops there are often also artisan's homes, and you should check for signage indicating open hours.

SMART SOUVENIRS

Authentic Navajo blankets are always a good buy, since they gain in value over time. In Taos and other New Mexico outlets, the Overland Sheepskin Co. markets sheepskin footwear, coats, hats, and mittens. In El Paso, Texas, you can find Old West items such as famous handcrafted Tony Lama boots and far-out souvenirs such as hand-painted cow skulls. New Mexicans love their roadrunners (the state bird) so you'll find plenty of depictions of this feathered denizen.

WATCH OUT

In New Mexico and other Southwestern states, shysters marketing fake Indian jewelry and blankets are a continuing problem. Your best guarantee of authenticity, particularly involving Navajo blankets, is to purchase directly from a reputable reservation outlet; the goods sold at the Palace of the Governors in Santa Fe are also all guaranteed handmade by Indian artisans and are high quality. At other shops, **ask for a certificate of authenticity, written verification of a piece's origin, or a receipt** which lists the materials that make up an item. The Indian Arts and Crafts Association offers free information on what to look for in Indian-made goods and sells buyers' guides as well.

➤ INDIAN ARTS AND CRAFTS ASSOCIATION: IACA ✉ Box 29870, Santa Fe 87592-9780 ☎ 505/265–9149, FAX 505/474–8924.

STUDENTS IN NEW MEXICO

Four-year universities can be found in cities such as Albuquerque, Silver City, Socorro, Las Cruces, and Portales. Many branch colleges are located in other communities. Discounts are commonly offered to university students.

➤ I.D.s & SERVICES: **Council Travel** (CIEE; ✉ 205 E. 42nd St., 14th floor, New York, NY 10017, ☎ 212/822–2700 or 888/268–6245, FAX 212/822–2699, info@councilexchanges.org, www.councilexchanges.org) for mail orders only, in the United States. **Travel Cuts** (✉ 187 College St., Toronto, Ontario M5T 1P7, ☎ 416/979–2406 or 800/667–2887 in Canada, www.travelcuts.com).

TAXES

Tax rates vary, depending on which community you're visiting. But some typical sales taxes in major communities are 5.8% in Albuquerque, 6.3% in Santa Fe, 6.9% in Taos, 6.2% in Carlsbad, and 6.4% in Las Cruces.

SALES TAX

The standard state gross receipts tax rate is 5%, but municipalities and counties enact additional charges at varying rates. Even with additional charges, you will encounter no sales tax higher than 7%.

TIME

New Mexico and a small portion of west Texas (including El Paso) observe Mountain Standard Time, switching over with most of the rest of the country to Daylight Saving Time in the spring through fall. In New Mexico, you'll be two hours behind New York and one hour ahead of Arizona and California.

TIPPING

In New Mexico as elsewhere in the country, a 15%–20% tip is standard for restaurant service.

TOURS & PACKAGES

Because everything is prearranged on a prepackaged tour or independent vacation, you'll spend less time planning—and often get it all at a good price.

BOOKING WITH AN AGENT

Travel agents are excellent resources. But it's a good idea to collect brochures from several agencies, as some agents' suggestions may be influenced by relationships with tour and package firms that reward them for volume sales. If you have a special interest, **find an agent with expertise in that area**; ASTA (☞ Travel Agencies, *below*) has a database of specialists worldwide.

Make sure your travel agent knows the accommodations and other services of the place being recommended. Ask about the hotel's location, room size, beds, and whether it has a pool, room service, or programs for children, if you care about these. Has your agent been there in person or sent others whom you can contact?

Do some homework on your own, too: local tourism boards can provide information about lesser-known and small-niche operators, some of which may sell only direct.

BUYER BEWARE

Each year consumers are stranded or lose their money when tour operators—even large ones with excellent reputations—go out of business. So **check out the operator.** Ask several travel agents about its reputation, and try to **book with a company that has a consumer-protection program.** (Look for information in the company's brochure.) In the United States, members of the National Tour Association and the United States Tour Operators Association are required to set aside funds to cover your payments and travel arrangements in the event that the company defaults. It's also a good idea to choose a company that partici-

pates in the American Society of Travel Agents' Tour Operator Program (TOP); ASTA will act as mediator in any disputes between you and your tour operator.

Remember that the more your package or tour includes the better you can predict the ultimate cost of your vacation. Make sure you know exactly what is covered, and **beware of hidden costs.** Are taxes, tips, and transfers included? Entertainment and excursions? These can add up.

➤ TOUR-OPERATOR RECOMMENDATIONS: **American Society of Travel Agents** (☞ Travel Agencies, *below*). **National Tour Association** (NTA; ✉ 546 E. Main St., Lexington, KY 40508, ☎ 606/226–4444 or 800/ 682–8886, www.ntaonline.com). **United States Tour Operators Association** (USTOA; ✉ 342 Madison Ave., Suite 1522, New York, NY 10173, ☎ 212/599–6599 or 800/468–7862, FAX 212/599–6744, ustoa@aol.com, www.ustoa.com).

➤ ARCHAEOLOGY: **Archaeological Conservancy** (✉ 5301 Central Ave. NE, No. 1218, Albuquerque 87108– 1517, ☎ 505/266–1540).

➤ ART/CULTURE: **Atwell Fine Art** (✉ 1430 Paseo Norteno St., Santa Fe 87505, ☎ 505/474–4263 or 800/ 235–8412, FAX 505/474–4602).

TRAIN TRAVEL

Amtrak trains stop in Albuquerque, Gallup, Lamy (near Santa Fe), Raton, Las Vegas, and Deming. Amtrak also services El Paso, Texas.

➤ TRAIN INFORMATION: **Amtrak** (☎ 800/872–7245).

TRANSPORTATION AROUND NEW MEXICO

A tour bus or car is the best way to take in the entire state. Public transportation options do exist in metropolitan areas, but they are not very convenient. City buses and taxi service are available only in a few larger communities such as Albuquerque, Santa Fe, and Las Cruces. Don't expect to find easy transportation for rural excursions. Bus or van service exists for virtually every community on the map, but be prepared for frequent stops for pickups along rural routes.

TRAVEL AGENCIES

A good travel agent puts your needs first. Look for an agency that has been in business at least five years, emphasizes customer service, and has someone on staff who specializes in your destination. In addition, **make sure the agency belongs to a professional trade organization.** The American Society of Travel Agents (ASTA), with 27,000 agents in some 170 countries, is the largest and most influential in the field. Operating under the motto "Integrity in Travel," it maintains and enforces a strict code of ethics and will step in to help mediate any agent-client disputes if necessary. ASTA also maintains a Web site that includes a directory of agents. If a travel agency is also acting as your tour operator, *see* Buyer Beware *in* Tours & Packages, *above*.

➤ LOCAL AGENT REFERRALS: **American Society of Travel Agents** (ASTA; ☎ 800/965–2782 24-hr hot line, ℻ 703/684–8319, www.astanet.com). **Association of British Travel Agents** (✉ 68–71 Newman St., London W1P 4AH, ☎ 020/7637–2444, ℻ 020/7637–0713, information£abta.co.uk, www.abtanet.com). **Association of Canadian Travel Agents** (✉ 1729 Bank St., Suite 201, Ottawa, Ontario K1V 7Z5, ☎ 613/237–3657, ℻ 613/521–0805, acta.ntl@sympatico.ca). **Australian Federation of Travel Agents** (✉ Level 3, 309 Pitt St., Sydney 2000, ☎ 02/9264–3299, ℻ 02/9264–1085, www.afta.com.au). **Travel Agents' Association of New Zealand** (✉ Box 1888, Wellington 10033, ☎ 04/499–0104, ℻ 04/499–0827, taanz@tiasnet.co.nz).

VISITOR INFORMATION

For general information before you go, contact the city and state tourism bureaus. If you're interested in learning more about the area's national forests, contact the U.S.D.A. For information about Native American attractions, call or visit the Indian Pueblo Cultural Center.

➤ CITY INFORMATION: **Albuquerque Convention and Visitors Bureau** (✉ 20 1st Plaza NW, Suite 601, Albuquerque 87102, ☎ 505/842–9918 or 800/733–9918. www.abqcvb.org). **Santa Fe Convention and Visitors Bureau** (✉ Box 909, Santa Fe 87504, ☎ 505/984–6760 or 800/777–2489, ℻ 505/984–6679. www.santafe.org). **Taos County Chamber of Commerce** (✉ Drawer I, Taos 87571, ☎ 505/758–3873 or 800/732–8267, ℻ 505/758–3872. www.taoschamber.com).

➤ STATEWIDE INFORMATION: **New Mexico Department of Tourism** (✉ 491 Old Santa Fe Trail, Santa Fe 87503, ☎ 505/827–7400 or 800/545–2070, ℻ 505/827–7402. www.newmexico.org).

➤ NATIONAL FORESTS: **U.S.D.A. Forest Service, Southwestern Region** (✉ Public Affairs Office, 517 Gold Ave. SW, Albuquerque 87102, ☎ 505/842–3292, ℻ 505/842–3800. www.fs.fed.us/r3).

➤ NATIVE ATTRACTIONS: **Indian Pueblo Cultural Center** (✉ 2401 12th St. NW, Albuquerque 87102, ☎ 505/843–7270; 800/766–4405 outside NM, ℻ 505/842–6959).

➤ FROM THE U.K.: **New Mexico Tourism** (✉ 302 Garden Studios, 11–15 Betterton St., Covent Garden, London WC2H 9BP, ☎ 020/7470–8803, ℻ 020/7470–8810).

WEB SITES

Do check out the World Wide Web when you're planning your trip. You'll find everything from current weather forecasts to virtual tours of famous cities. Fodor's Web site, www.fodors.com, is a great place to start your on-line travels. When you see a 🕮 in this book, go to www.fodors.com/urls for an up-to-date link to that destination's site.

Official Web sites of tourism offices are listed under Visitor Information (☞ *above*). Information about cultural events in north-central New Mexico is found on Albuquerque's alternative newsweekly *Alibi*, www.weeklywire.com/alibi/. A great guide to the Kodak Albuquerque International Balloon Fiesta in October is www.balloonfiesta.com. If you'll be visiting northwestern New Mexico, check out www.

farmingtonnm.org. Taos County Lodgers Association runs the site www.taoswebb.com/taos.

WHEN TO GO

Most ceremonial dances at the Native American pueblos occur in the summer, early fall, and at Christmas and Easter. The majority of other major events—including the Santa Fe Opera, Chamber Music Festival, and Indian and Spanish markets—are geared to the traditionally heavy tourist season of July and August. The Santa Fe Fiesta and New Mexico State Fair in Albuquerque are held in September, and the Kodak Albuquerque International Balloon Fiesta is in October.

The relatively cool climates of Santa Fe and Taos are a lure in summer, as is the skiing in Taos and Santa Fe in winter. Christmas is a wonderful time to be in New Mexico because of Native American ceremonies as well as the Hispanic religious folk plays, special foods, and musical events. Hotel rates are generally highest during the peak summer season but fluctuate less than those in most major resort areas. If you plan to come in summer, **be sure to make reservations in advance for July and August.** You can avoid most of the tourist crowds by coming during spring or fall.

CLIMATE

Depending on where you're headed in New Mexico, you may find the sun strong, the air dry, and the wind hot and relentless. Northern New Mexico is significantly cooler on the whole than destinations in the southern part of the state, although mountain regions are scattered throughout. Timing is everything in this land of seasonal temperature extremes. Desert regions can be delightful in late fall and winter months, but can surprise you with rare snowfall. Spring weather is unpredictable; it can be mild and cool, or hot and gusty. Certain desert regions in summer months can see temperatures climb above 100°F. During these times, you should head for the cool mountains. Higher elevations are usually within a reasonable drive just about anywhere in New Mexico. October is one of the best months to visit: the air is crisp, colors are brilliant, and whole mountainsides become fluttering cascades of red and gold.

➤ FORECASTS: **Weather Channel Connection** (☎ 900/932–8437), 95¢ per minute from a Touch-Tone phone.

The following are average daily maximum and minimum temperatures for areas of the state.

ALBUQUERQUE

Jan.	46F	8C	May	78F	26C	Sept.	84F	29C
	24	−4		51	11		57	14
Feb.	53F	12C	June	89F	32C	Oct.	71F	22C
	28	−2		60	16		44	7
Mar.	60F	16C	July	91F	33C	Nov.	57F	14C
	33	1		64	18		32	0
Apr.	69F	21C	Aug.	89F	32C	Dec.	48F	9C
	42	6		64	18		26	−3

LAS CRUCES

Jan.	56F	13C	May	87F	31C	Sept.	87F	31C
	29	−2		57	14		62	17
Feb.	62F	17C	June	97F	36C	Oct.	78F	26C
	34	1		64	18		50	10
Mar.	70F	21C	July	96F	36C	Nov.	66F	19C
	40	4		68	20		38	3
Apr.	79F	26C	Aug.	94F	34C	Dec.	57F	14C
	48	9		67	19		30	−1

THE GOLD GUIDE / SMART TRAVEL TIPS

RUIDOSO AREA

Jan.	45F	7C	May	71F	22C	Sept.	73F	23C
	19	−7		37	3		41	5
Feb.	49F	9C	June	82F	28C	Oct.	66F	19C
	19	−7		44	7		30	−1
Mar.	53F	12C	July	82F	28C	Nov.	52F	11C
	24	−4		47	8		23	−4
Apr.	62F	17C	Aug.	77F	25C	Dec.	53F	12C
	27	−3		46	8		19	−7

SANTA FE

Jan.	39F	4C	May	68F	20C	Sept.	73F	23C
	19	−7		42	6		48	9
Feb.	42F	6C	June	78F	26C	Oct.	62F	17C
	23	−5		51	11		37	3
Mar.	51F	11C	July	80F	27C	Nov.	50F	10C
	28	−2		57	14		28	−2
Apr.	59F	15C	Aug.	78F	26C	Dec.	39F	4C
	35	2		55	13		19	−7

1 DESTINATION: NEW MEXICO

A LAND APART

ALMOST EVERY New Mexican has a tale or two to tell about being perceived as a "foreigner" by the rest of the country. There is the well-documented case of the Santa Fe man who tried to purchase tickets to the 1996 Olympic Games in Atlanta, only to be shuffled over to the department handling international requests. Even the U.S. Postal Service occasionally returns New Mexico–bound mail to its senders for insufficient "international" postage.

Though annoying to residents, such cases of mistaken identity are oddly apt (keep an ear open to how often New Mexicans themselves refer to their state, one of the nation's poorest, as a Third World country). New Mexico is, in many ways, an anomaly: it has its own cuisine, architecture, fashion, and culture, all of these an amalgam of the designs and accidents of a long and intriguing history. In prehistoric times Native Americans hunted game in New Mexico's mountains and farmed along its riverbanks. Two thousand years ago Pueblo Indians began expressing their reverence for the land through flat-roofed earthen architecture, drawings carved onto rocks, and rhythmic chants and dances. The late-16th and early 17th centuries brought the Spanish explorers who, along with the Franciscan monks, founded Santa Fe as a northern capital of the empire of New Spain, a settlement that was contemporaneous with the Jamestown colony of Virginia.

Although the clash of the Native American and Spanish cultures was often violent, during the course of several hundred years tolerance has grown and traditions have commingled. Pueblo Indians passed on their uses for chile, beans, and corn, and the Spanish shared their skill at metalwork, influencing the Native American jewelry that has become symbolic of the region. The Spanish also shared their architecture, which itself had been influenced by 700 years of Arab domination of Spain, and the acequia method of irrigation still in use in the villages of northern New Mexico.

The last of the three main cultures to make their mark was that of the Anglo (any non–Native American, non-Hispanic person in New Mexico is considered an Anglo—even groups who don't normally identify with the Anglo-Saxon tradition). Arriving throughout the 19th century, Anglos mined the mountains for gold, other precious metals, and gemstones and uncovered vast deposits of coal, oil, and natural gas. Their contributions to New Mexican life include the railroad, the highway system, and—for better or worse—the atomic bomb.

The resulting mélange of cultures has produced a character that is uniquely New Mexican: Spanish words are sprinkled liberally through everyday English parlance; Spanish itself, still widely spoken in the smaller villages, contains numerous words from the Pueblo Indian dialects. Architectural references and culinary terms in particular tend to hew to the original Spanish: you'll admire the vigas and bancos that adorn the restaurant where you'll partake of posole or chiles rellenos. (These and other often-used words are defined in the glossary in Chapter 9.)

But beyond the linguistic quirks, gastronomic surprises, and cultural anomalies that give New Mexico its sense of uniqueness, there remains the most distinctive feature of all—the landscape. At once subtle and dramatic, the mountains and mesas seem almost surreal as they glow gold, terra-cotta, and pink in the clear, still air of the high desert. The shifting clouds overhead cast rippling shadows across the land, illuminating the delicate palette of greens, grays, and browns that contrast with a sky that can go purple or dead black or eye-searingly blue in a matter of seconds. It's a landscape that has inspired writers (such as D. H. Lawrence and Willa Cather), painters (Georgia O'Keeffe), and countless poets, dreamers, and assorted iconoclasts for centuries.

Indeed, watching the ever-changing sky is something of a spectator sport here, especially during the usual "monsoons" of summer. So regular that you could almost set your watch by them, the thunderheads start to gather in late afternoon, giving enough visual warning before the inevitable downpour. In the meantime, the sky dazzles with its interplay of creamy white clouds edged by charcoal, sizzling flashes of lightning, and dramatic shafts of light shooting earthward from some ethereal perch.

The mountains absorb and radiate this special illumination, transforming themselves daily according to the whims of light and shadow. The very names of the major ranges attest to the profound effect their light show had on the original Spanish settlers. The Franciscan monks named the mountains to the east of Santa Fe *Sangre de Cristo*, or "blood of Christ," because of their tendency to glow deep red at sunset. To the south, east of Albuquerque, the Sandia Mountains ("watermelon" in Spanish) also live up to their colorful name when the sun sets. Georgia O'Keeffe once joked about the Pedernal mesa in the Jemez range, "It's my private mountain, it belongs to me. God told me if I painted it enough, I could have it."

The awe-inspiring beauty of the landscape renders New Mexico's tag lines more than just marketing clichés. The state is truly a "Land of Enchantment," and Santa Fe is indisputably "the City Different." Surrounded by mind-expanding mountain views and filled with sinuous streets that promote foot over car traffic, Santa Fe welcomes with characteristic adobe warmth. Rapid growth and development have prompted many local residents to worry about becoming too much like "everywhere else," but the surfeit of trendy restaurants, galleries, and boutiques that tout regional fare and wares, both authentic and artificial, are still distinctly Santa Fean. Commercialism notwithstanding, Santa Fe's deeply spiritual aura affects even nonreligious types in surprising ways, inspiring a reverence probably not unlike that which inspired the Spanish monks to name it the "City of Holy Faith." (Its full name is La Villa Real de la Santa Fe de San Francisco de Asís, or the Royal City of the Holy Faith of St. Francis of Assisi.) A kind of mystical Catholicism blended with ancient Native American lore and beliefs flourishes throughout northern New Mexico in tiny mountain villages that have seen little change through the centuries. Tales of miracles, spontaneous healings, and spiritual visitations thrive in the old adobe churches that line the High Road that leads north of Santa Fe to Taos.

F SANTA FE IS SPIRITUAL, sophisticated, and occasionally superficial, Taos, 65 mi away, is very much an outpost despite its relative proximity to the capital. Compared with Santa Fe, Taos is smaller, feistier, quirkier, tougher, and very independent. Taoseños are a study in diverse convictions, and most anyone will share theirs with you if you lend them an ear. Rustic and comfortably unpretentious, the town contains a handful of upscale restaurants with cuisines and wine lists as innovative as what you might find in New York. It's a haven for aging hippies, creative geniuses, cranky misanthropes, and anyone else who wants a good quality of life in a place that accepts new arrivals without a lot of questions—as long as they don't offend longtime residents with their city attitudes.

Sixty miles south of Santa Fe, Albuquerque adds another distinctive perspective to the mix. New Mexico's only big city by most standards, it shares many traits with cities its size elsewhere: traffic, noise, crime, and congestion. But what sets it apart is its dogged determination to remain a friendly small town, a place where pedestrians still greet one another as they pass, and where downtown's main street is lined with angle parking (a modern-day version of the hitching post). Old Town, a congenial district whose authentic historical appeal is tempered by the unabashed pursuit of the tourist buck, is a typical example of how traditional small-town New Mexico flourishes amid a larger, more demanding economy, without sacrificing the heart and soul of the lifestyle. San Felipe de Neri Catholic Church, built in 1793, is still attended by local worshipers.

The unifying factor among these and other towns and the terrain around them is the appeal of the land and the people. From the stunning natural formations of Carlsbad Caverns to the oceanic sweep of the "badlands" north of Santa Fe, it's the character of the residents and respect for the land that imbue New Mexico with its enchanted spirit. First-time visitors discover the unexpected pleasures of a place where time is measured not only by linear calculations of hours, days, weeks, and years but also by the circular sweep of crop cycles, gestation periods, the rotation of generations, and the changing of seasons.

Summer is traditionally the high season, when the arts scene explodes with gallery openings, opera performances at Santa Fe's open-air opera house, and a variety of festivals and celebrations. In autumn, the towering cottonwoods that hug the riverbanks turn gold, days are warm and sunny, and the nights crisp. Those beehive-shape kiva fireplaces get a workout in winter, a time when life slows down to accommodate occasional snowstorms, and the scent of aromatic firewood like piñon and cedar fill the air like an earthy incense.

Even after you leave, New Mexico will sneak into your consciousness in unexpected ways. As much a state of mind as it is a geographic entity, a place where nature can be glimpsed simultaneously at its most fragile and most powerful, New Mexico truly is a land of enchantment.

— Nancy Zimmerman

WHAT'S WHERE

Albuquerque and Vicinity

With the state's only international airport, Albuquerque is the gateway to New Mexico and the state's business, finance, education, and industry capital. Like many other areas of New Mexico, this sprawling city more or less in the center of the state is filled with artists, writers, poets, filmmakers, and musicians. Its population, like its architecture, foods, art, and ambience, reflects the state's three primary cultures: the original Native Americans and its subsequent Hispanic and Anglo settlers.

Northeastern New Mexico

The brilliantly clear light of northeastern New Mexico—the area east of Taos that includes parts of the Carson National Forest, a large portion of the Santa Fe Trail, and Wild West towns like Cimarron and Raton—illuminates seemingly endless high-desert plains. Hawks soar overhead and antelope gallivant across the same open landscape traversed by the Native Americans and the pioneers, cowboys, ranchers, miners, and railroaders who settled the West.

Northwestern New Mexico

Roads branch out west and north from Albuquerque, to the ruins of Anasazi civilization and the dances and drumbeats of their descendants' ceremonies in pueblos that have survived time and change. Journey through red-rock canyons that shelter ancient hamlets or to high, fortresslike plateaus crowned by Native American villages, and you'll encounter cultures whose art, architecture, spirituality, and knowledge of nature have ensured their existence for millennia. Gallup and Farmington are the region's two largest cities; Chaco Canyon, Zuñi Pueblo, Aztec Ruins, and Salmon Ruins are among the major attractions.

Santa Fe

On a 7,000-ft-high plateau at the base of the Sangre de Cristo Mountains in north-central New Mexico, Santa Fe is one of the most popular cities in the United States, with an abundance of museums, one-of-a-kind cultural events, art galleries, first-rate restaurants, and shops selling Southwestern furnishings and cowboy gear. Among the smallest state capitals in the country, the city is characterized by its Pueblo Revival–style homes and buildings made of adobe. The remnants of a 2,000-year-old Pueblo civilization surround the city, and this also echoes its nearly 250 years of Spanish and Mexican rule. Other area highlights include Chimayó, a small Hispanic village famous for weaving, regional food, and the Santuario shrine.

Southeastern New Mexico

Carlsbad, just above the Texas border and along the Pecos River, is a popular destination with historic museums, 30 parks, beaches, the Living Desert Zoo and Gardens State Park, and, the main attraction, Carlsbad Caverns National Park, one of the largest and most spectacular cave systems in the world. Roswell's alien reputation draws those interested in *other*worldly things.

Northwest of Carlsbad are the historic towns of Lincoln County (Ruidoso, San Patricio, and Lincoln, where Billy the Kid was jailed). The highly elevated Lincoln National Forest creates a lush ecosystem above the desert brush, and in south-central New Mexico, White Sands National Monument is an otherworldly wonderland of shifting gypsum sand dunes.

Southwestern New Mexico

Southwestern New Mexico has its own mystique, where shimmering mirages born of desert heat hover above mesquite-covered sand dunes. But the area isn't all desert. Near Silver City, the ore-rich mountains are dotted with old mining ghost towns. Silver City itself is establishing a reputation as an artists' haven amid the grandeur of the Gila National Forest. The Mexican-style village of Old Mesilla near Las Cruces has appealing shops and galleries occupying historic adobe buildings in the downtown plaza. Outdoor enthusiasts fish, swim, and boat along the miles of lake water at Elephant Butte Reservoir, near Truth or Consequences.

Taos

On a rolling mesa at the base of the Sangre de Cristo Mountains, Taos is a world-famous artistic and literary center that attracts artists and collectors to its museums and galleries. Romantic courtyards, stately elms and cottonwood trees, narrow streets, and a profusion of adobe buildings are but a few of the charms of this city of 6,500 people. Three miles northwest of the commercial center lies Taos Pueblo, and south of town is Ranchos de Taos, a farming and ranching community first settled centuries ago by the Spanish. The fabulous slopes of the Taos Valley Ski Area and Rio Grande rafting trips are yet other draws.

NEW AND NOTEWORTHY

Will wolves in the wild attract tourists or drive them away? The debate raged during 2000 after Albuquerque mayor Jim Baca stated that the release of Mexican gray wolves in the **Gila National Forest** of southwestern New Mexico could boost the state's tourism trade. Plans remain firm to reintroduce wolves to the forest lands, primarily to preserve the species in natural habitats, but also in hope that they will pique travelers' interest in the great outdoors.

In a setback to New Mexico's environment, a controlled burn of the underbrush at Bandolier National Monument in May 2000 turned into a fierce wildfire. More than 200 homes were destroyed in **Los Alamos,** though Los Alamos National Laboratory did not suffer serious damage. At the same time, the state was suffering its worst drought in 30 years. Drenching rains later in the summer, however, helped much of the state's mountain and desert areas to begin recovering from dry conditions.

The controversial issue of casinos on Native American lands remained in the news in 2000 as more tribes announced plans to get in on the gaming action. More than half of New Mexico's 22 tribes are now involved. Plans were in the works or construction already begun on new or expanded casinos at **San Juan Pueblo,** the **Jicarilla Apache Reservation, Laguna Pueblo,** and **Acoma Pueblo.** New Mexico has the nation's second-largest per capita population of Native Americans, but not all tribal members think economic benefits of casinos outweigh intrusions upon lifestyle represented by glittering gaming establishments. Others argue that revenues are being put to good use to help preserve Native American traditions.

While the **Navajo** tribe has voted to reject gaming, officials are exploring a novel idea for attracting tourists. Navajo families have begun opening up their private hogans to guests willing to pay for the experience. These huts built of logs and mud are commonly seen throughout Navajo reservation land in the northwest's Four Corners area.

Albuquerque now has a professional basketball team known as the **New Mexico Slam.** Part of the newly formed International Basketball League, the team will play at the **Albuquerque Convention Center** with its 6,200 seating capacity.

Las Cruces in southern New Mexico continues efforts to establish its own mystique by exploiting the region's close ties to centuries of Hispanic culture, arts, and folklore. The city's **Museum of Fine Arts And Culture** opened in late 1999 as part of the Cultural Complex, which includes the **Log Cabin Museum** and **Branigan Cultural Center.** A **New Mexico Railroad & Transportation Museum** was scheduled to open at an old Santa Fe Railroad train depot during 2001.

PLEASURES AND PASTIMES

Dining

New Mexico's cuisine is a delicious and extraordinary mixture of Pueblo, Spanish colonial, and Mexican and American frontier cooking. Recipes that came from Spain via Mexico were adapted for local ingredients—chiles, corn, pork, wild game, pinto beans, honey, apples, and piñon nuts—and have remained much the same ever since.

In northern New Mexico, babies cut their teeth on **fresh flour tortillas** and quickly develop a taste for **sopaipillas,** deep-fried, puff-pastry pillows drizzled with honey. But it's the **chile pepper,** whether red or green, that is the heart and soul of northern New Mexican cuisine. The question most asked of diners in New Mexico—"red or green?"—is often responded to with the query "Which is hotter?" The answer might be either—or neither. Green is made from roasted fresh chile pods harvested beginning in late July, and red is concocted from pods of the same plant, ripened and dried. Can't decide? Order the "Christmas" combination. Like the altitude, chile may take getting used to, but once you develop a taste for it, it is addictive. For those not chile-inclined, most Mexican and New Mexican restaurants also prepare recognizable "gringo food."

You might be a bit surprised to learn that *ristras,* those strings of bright red chiles that seem to hang everywhere, are sold more for eating here than for decoration. More varieties of chiles—upward of 90—are grown in New Mexico than anywhere else in the world. Mighty wars have been waged over the spelling of chile and chili. Most New Mexicans prefer the spelling chile for the peppers and chili for the spicy dish with red chile, beans, and meat. ("If you want chili, go to Texas.") *See* the glossary *in* Chapter 9 for the names and terms of traditional New Mexican dishes.

Restaurants serving New Mexican cuisine are especially popular and are almost universally inexpensive. Some serve buffalo meat (stews, steaks, and burgers), particularly in southern New Mexico—"cowboy country." Of course, there are trendy restaurants serving nouvelle cuisine, particularly in Santa Fe and Taos, as well as a respectable offering of grill rooms and plenty of ethnic eateries.

Outdoor Activities and Sports

BIRD-WATCHING➤ Bird-watchers have wonderful opportunities to spot feathered friends migrating along the **Rio Grande flyway** from the jungles of South America to the tundra of the Arctic Circle. The **Bosque del Apache National Wildlife Refuge,** 90 mi south of Albuquerque, is the winter home of tens of thousands of migrating birds, including one of only two wild flocks of the rare whooping crane. The **Bitter Lake National Wildlife Refuge,** north of Roswell, also serves as a stopover for migrating flocks of snow geese, sandhill cranes, and other exotic birds. If you can't spot golden eagles in northeastern New Mexico at the **Maxwell Wildlife Refuge,** south of Raton off I–25, dust off your binoculars!

CANOEING AND RIVER RAFTING➤ You can either take it easy or challenge yourself on New Mexico's rivers. The **Taos Box,** a 17-mi run through the churning rapids of the Rio Grande, is one of America's most exciting rafting experiences. (Most of the hard-core river rafting is done in the Taos area.) More leisurely trips can be had aboard the sightseeing craft that ply the Rio Chama and other meandering rivers. Depending on the amount of spring runoff from snowmelts, river rafting also is popular in the **Silver City** area of the **Gila National Forest.**

FISHING➤ Good fishing spots include the **Rio Grande,** which traverses New Mexico north to south; **Abiquiu Lake,** 40 mi northwest of Santa Fe; the 6,000-acre **Heron Lake,** 20 mi southwest of Chama via U.S. 64 and NM 96, which has rainbow trout, lake trout, and kokanee salmon; and **Blue Water Lake,** 28 mi west of Grants via NM 371. In the northwest corner of the state, the **San Juan River**'s high-quality water regulations make for some of the best trout fishing in the country. In northeastern New Mexico at **Cimarron Canyon State Park** and **Lake Maloya** your chances are great at pulling in your limit of browns and rainbows. Trout fisherfolk will also find pleasure in the sparkling streams of the **Sangre de Cristo range,** north of Santa Fe. The **Pecos River** and its tributaries offer excellent backcountry fishing. Anglers also can try their luck in the rivers, lakes, and streams of the **Gila National Forest** and **Lincoln National Forest** of southern New Mexico. World-class bass tournaments take place at **Elephant Butte Reservoir** near **Truth or Consequences.** Fishing on Native American reservations is not subject to state regulations but requires tribal permits.

HIKING➣ New Mexico's air is clean and crisp, and its ever-changing terrain is aesthetically rewarding as well. **Carlsbad Caverns National Park** in the southeast has more than 50 mi of scenic hiking trails. You'll find superb hiking of all levels in northeastern New Mexico at **Sugarite State Park,** above Raton along quiet, wildflower-filled trails. Try the McKittrick Canyon trail in **Guadalupe Mountains National Park** of west Texas to view a gorgeous, tree-lined stream gurgling in the midst of desert terrain. In the **Gila National Forest and Wilderness,** you can explore miles of pristine country and soak sore muscles in delightful natural hot springs.

HORSE RACING➣ Horse racing with pari-mutuel betting is very popular in New Mexico. Two of the more favored of the state's tracks are **Downs at Santa Fe,** 5 mi south of town, and **Downs at Albuquerque,** a glass-enclosed facility in the center of the city at the New Mexico State Fairgrounds. Quarter-horse racing's Triple Crown events—Kansas Futurity, Rainbow Futurity, and All-American Futurity—take place in mid-June, mid-July, and on Labor Day, respectively, at the **Ruidoso Downs** tracks in Lincoln County. The **Sunland Park Racetrack** is 5 mi north of El Paso, Texas.

RODEOS➣ Rodeos are a big draw from early spring through autumn. Besides big events in **Santa Fe, Albuquerque,** and **Gallup,** every county in the state has a rodeo competition during its county fair. Major Native American rodeos take place at Stone Lake on the **Jicarilla Apache Reservation** in north-central New Mexico, on the **Mescalero Apache Reservation** in southeastern New Mexico, at the **Inter-Tribal Ceremonial** in Gallup, and at the **National Indian Rodeo Finals** in Albuquerque.

SKIING➣ New Mexico contains many world-class downhill ski areas. Snowmaking equipment is used in most areas to ensure a long season, usually from Thanksgiving through Easter. The **Santa Fe Ski Area** averages 250 inches of dry-powder snow a year; it accommodates all levels of skiers on more than 40 trails. Within a 90-mi radius of Taos are resorts with slopes for all levels of skiers, as well as snowmobile and cross-country ski trails. The **Taos Ski Valley** resort is recognized internationally for its challenging terrain and European-style ambience.

The **Enchanted Forest** near Red River, with miles of groomed trails, is the state's major Nordic ski area allowing ample cross-country access. Head to the **Sangre de Cristos,** the **Jemez,** the **Sandias,** or the **Manzanos** for other cross-country skiing terrain. There are also exciting trails north of Chama along the New Mexico–Colorado state line and in the south in the **Gila wilderness** and the **Sacramento Mountains. Ski Apache** near Ruidoso has 55 trails covering 750 acres.

Parks and Monuments

New Mexico's outstanding parks and monuments contain outdoor recreational facilities, campgrounds, and historic exhibits. New Mexico's state-park network includes nearly four dozen parks, ranging from high-mountain lakes and pine forests in the north to the Chihuahuan Desert lowlands of the south. There are also five national forests—**Carson, Cibola, Gila, Lincoln,** and **Santa Fe**—and the **Kiowa National Grasslands** (part of the Cibola National Forest), as well as several state monuments and historic parks with ruins of prehistoric Native American pueblos and 17th-century mission churches. The best place to see ancient pueblos—the communities (cities, really) built by the Anasazi ancestors of today's Pueblo people—is northwest New Mexico, where **Aztec Ruins, Salmon Ruins,** and **Chaco Canyon** stun the imagination.

There are plenty of parks and monuments close to Santa Fe and Albuquerque. In southern New Mexico the biggest draws are **Carlsbad Caverns National Park, White Sands National Monument,** and **Elephant Butte Lake State Park.**

Reservations and Pueblos

The Indian reservations of New Mexico are among the few places left in the United States where traditional Native American culture and skills are retained in largely undiluted form. There are two general classifications of Native Americans in New Mexico: Pueblo, who established an agricultural civilization here more than seven centuries ago; and the descendants of the nomadic tribes who later came into the area—the Navajos, Mescalero Apaches, and Jicarilla Apaches.

The **Jicarilla Apaches** live on a reservation of three-quarters of a million acres in north-central New Mexico, the capital of which is Dulce. The terrain varies from mountains, mesas, and lakes to high grazing land, suited to cattle and horse ranching. The tribe has a well-defined tourist program (☞ Visitor Information *in* Northwestern New Mexico A to Z *in* Chapter 6) that promotes fishing and camping on a 20,000-acre game preserve. Nearly all the tribe members gather at Stone Lake in mid-September for the fall festival—two days of dancing, races, and a rodeo.

A reservation of a half million acres of timbered mountains and green valleys is home to the **Mescalero Apaches** in southeastern New Mexico. The tribe owns and operates the fine Inn of the Mountain Gods resort, as well as Ski Apache, 16 mi from Ruidoso. For detailed information, *see* Ruidoso *in* Chapter 7.

The **Navajo Reservation,** home to the largest Native American group in the United States, covers 17.6 million acres in New Mexico, Arizona, and Utah. Many Navajos are still seminomadic, herding flocks of sheep from place to place and living in hogans (mud-and-pole houses). There are a few towns on the reservation, but for the most part it is a vast area of stark pinnacles, colorful rock formations, high desert, and mountains. The land encompasses several national and tribal parks, some of which include campgrounds. Navajos are master silversmiths and rug weavers, and their work is available at trading posts scattered throughout the reservation. The tribe encourages tourism; for more information, contact the **Navajo Nation Tourism Office** (☞ Visitor Information *in* Northwestern New Mexico A to Z *in* Chapter 6).

New Mexico's pueblo cultures, each with its own reservation and distinct but overlapping history, art, and customs, evolved out of the highly civilized Anasazi culture that built Chaco Canyon. Pueblos dating back centuries are located near Santa Fe, Taos, and Albuquerque; the best times to visit them are during their many year-round public dance ceremonies. Admission is free to pueblos unless otherwise indicated. Donations, however, are always welcome.

Before venturing off to visit any one of the pueblos, you might want to visit the **Indian Pueblo Cultural Center** in Albuquerque, which exhibits and sells the best of arts and crafts from all the New Mexico pueblos, or the **Museum of Indian Arts and Culture** in Santa Fe.

Fall, when the pueblos celebrate the harvest with special ceremonies, dances, and sacred rituals, is the best time to visit. The air is fragrant with curling piñon smoke. Drums throb with an insistent cadence. Dancers adorn themselves with some of the most beautiful turquoise jewelry seen anywhere. The atmosphere is lighthearted, evocative of a country fair.

The pueblos around Santa Fe—San Ildefonso, Nambé, Pojoaque, and Santa Clara—are more infused with Spanish culture than are those in other areas. Dwellers here also have the keenest business sense when dealing with the sale of handicrafts and art and with matters touristic. The famous **Taos Pueblo,** unchanged through the centuries, is the quintessence of classic pueblo Native American culture. Sports enthusiasts from Albuquerque regularly escape urban life to fish in the well-stocked lakes and reservoirs of the nearby pueblos—Acoma ("Sky City"), Isleta, Jemez, Laguna, and Santo Domingo. The legendary **Acoma Pueblo,** probably the most spectacular of the pueblo communities, is only a short drive from the city. For detailed information about the individual pueblos, *see* listings *in* Chapters 2, 3, 5, and 6.

ETIQUETTE AND RULES➣ When visiting pueblos and reservations, you're expected to follow a certain etiquette. Each pueblo has its own regulations for the use of still and video cameras and video and tape recorders, as well as for sketching and painting. Some pueblos, such as Santo Domingo, prohibit photography altogether. Others, such as Santa Clara, prohibit photography at certain times, such as during ritual dances. Still others allow photography but require a permit, which usually costs from $10 to $20, depending on whether you use a still or video camera. The privilege of setting up an easel and painting all day will cost you as little as $35 or as much as $150 (at Taos Pueblo). Associated fees for using images also can vary widely, depending on what kind of reproduction rights you might require. Be sure to ask permission before photographing anyone in the pueblos; it's also customary to give the subject a dollar or two for agreeing to be photographed. Native American law prevails on the pueblos, and violations of photography regulations could result in confiscation of cameras.

Specific restrictions for the various pueblos are noted in the individual descriptions. Other rules are described below.

- Possessing or using drugs and/or alcohol on Native American land is forbidden.

- Ritual dances often have serious religious significance and should be respected as such. Silence is mandatory—that means no questions about ceremonies or dances while they're being performed. Don't walk across the dance plaza during a performance, and don't applaud afterward.

- Kivas and ceremonial rooms are restricted to pueblo members only.

- Cemeteries are sacred. They're off-limits to all visitors and should never be photographed.

- Unless pueblo dwellings are clearly marked as shops, don't wander or peek inside. Remember, these are private homes.

- Many of the pueblo buildings are hundreds of years old. Don't try to scale adobe walls or climb on top of buildings, or you may come tumbling down.

- Don't litter. Nature is sacred on the pueblos, and defacing land can be a serious offense.

- Don't bring your pet, or feed stray dogs.

- Even off reservation sites, state and federal laws prohibit picking up artifacts such as arrowheads or pottery from public lands.

Shopping

Santa Fe, Old Mesilla near Las Cruces, Taos, and Old Town in Albuquerque are all filled with one-of-a-kind, locally owned specialty shops; national boutique chain stores have only recently arrived. There's plenty of opportunity to buy goods directly from their makers, be it from a pueblo jewelry maker to a chile farmer. Western wear, leather goods, handwoven shawls, Mexican imports, handcrafted items, fine arts—it's all here.

ANTIQUES➤ As New Mexico is the oldest inhabited region of the United States, it can be great fun to browse through its antiques shops and roadside museums. You'll find everything in these shops, from early Mexican typewriters to period saddles, ceramic pots, farm tools, pioneer aviation equipment, and yellowed newspaper clippings about Kit Carson and D. H. Lawrence.

ART➤ Native American art, Western art, Hispanic art, fine art, sculpture, photography, prints, ceramics, jewelry, folk art, junk art—it can all be found throughout the state. Santa Fe, with more than 150 galleries, is a leading fine arts center nationally as well as the arts capital of the Southwest. Taos, a town dense with artists, is not far behind. You'll find a small art colony in Silver City, and Old Mesilla near Las Cruces has an impressive array of galleries displaying regional talent. In autumn in northern New Mexico you can tour artists' studios.

CRAFTS➤ Hispanic handcrafted furniture and artwork command high prices from collectors. Images of elongated and dour-faced *santos* (saints) come in either the form of carved wooden *bultos* sculptures or *retablos*, paintings on wood or tin. Colorful handwoven Hispanic textiles, tinwork, ironwork, and straw appliqué are also in demand. Native American textiles, rugs, katsina dolls, baskets, silver jewelry, turquoise, pottery, beadwork, ornamental shields, drums, and ceramics can be found almost everywhere in New Mexico, from Santa Fe Plaza to the Native American pueblos throughout the state. Prices range from thousands of dollars for a rare 1930s katsina doll to a few cents for hand-wrapped bundles of sage, juniper, sweet grass, and lavender that are used by Native Americans in healing ceremonies, gatherings, and daily cleansing of the home. Ignited like incense, this herbal combination gives off a sacred smoke; passing it once around the room is enough to change and charge the air. If you love Indian jewelry, head to Gallup, which has many old trading posts that sell silver, turquoise, and beadwork.

SPICES➤ Roadside stands sell chile ristras, and shops carry chile powder and other spices. You'll catch the smell of chile peppers from the road; walk in a store and your eyes may water and your salivary glands begin to work. For many, especially natives of the Southwest, *picante* is the purest, finest word in the Spanish language. It means hot—spicy hot. All around you, in boxes, bags, packets, jars, and cans, there's everything picante—salsas, chile pastes, powders, herbs, spices, peppers, barbecue sauce, and fiery potions in bottles.

Studio Tours

Northwestern New Mexico is a region of artists' colonies, and from the last weekend of September through the first weekend of December the artists and artisans in the villages of **Galisteo, the Pecos Valley, El Rito, Abiquiu, Dixon,** and **Madrid** take turns hosting studio-tour weekends. Homes and studios are open for browsing, shopping, and conversing; maps are provided to guide you to the open houses, where you'll find reasonably priced arts and crafts. Wares include everything from pottery and paintings to wreaths, ristras, and dried-flower arrangements; homemade jellies, pestos, chile sauces, and other food items; fresh produce such as garlic, chiles, and shallots; and wood carvings, religious paintings, clothing, and handmade furniture.

The quality varies, but bargains are abundant. Of course for many the real fun is the opportunity to experience village life and to get inside those charming old adobes that you can only pass by at other times of the year. Many of the villagers provide refreshments, and you're encouraged to wander at a leisurely pace.

Because studio-tour planning passes from one chairperson to another each year, there is no central number to call for information. But if you're in the Santa Fe area during the fall season, check "Pasatiempo," the Friday supplement of the *Santa Fe New Mexican,* for a report about which village is open for touring and what items are for sale. The one constant is the Dixon tour, which takes place every year on the first weekend in November. About a half hour south of Taos, Dixon was the first village to host a studio tour, and its version has the largest number of participating artists and the greatest variety of merchandise.

GREAT ITINERARIES

If You Have 3 Days

If you've flown into ▦ **Albuquerque,** it's logical to begin your tour here. Poke through the shops of Old Town Plaza and spend some time at the New Mexico Museum of Natural History and Science. After lunch, head north to the Indian Pueblo Cultural Center and then west to Petroglyph National Monument. Return east for a sunset ride on the Sandia Aerial Tramway.

On day two, head to ▦ **Santa Fe** on I–25, or travel the Turquoise Road—the beauty of it is worth the extra time it takes. Explore the adobe charms of the downtown central Plaza. Stop first at the Palace of the Governors on the plaza's north side, then investigate the crafts and wares of Native American outdoor vendors, then visit the Museum of Fine Arts to view exhibits of works by Southwestern artists. East of the plaza, the Romanesque-style Saint Francis Cathedral is worth a look.

Orient yourself to Santa Fe's cultural roots with a visit to the Museum of Indian Arts and Culture, after which you can head north to the Hispanic pilgrimage town of **Chimayó** and either **San Ildefonso Pueblo** or **Santa Clara Pueblo.**

On the third day, drive to ▦ **Taos,** noted for its galleries and colony of independent artists. Reserve time for **Taos Pueblo,** which still retains the mud-and-straw adobe walls of its original construction almost 1,000 years ago. Stay overnight in Taos or return to Santa Fe. The two routes between Santa Fe and Taos are equally scenic. Take the High Road when you can allow for a longer drive, and the Rio Grande route (NM 68) when you have less time.

If You Have 5 Days

It's a long drive to ▦ **Carlsbad,** but after you've spent the first three days visiting **Albuquerque, Santa Fe,** and **Taos,** you should make southern New Mexico your next destination. Set aside the morning of the fourth day to drive the 265 mi from Santa Fe to Carlsbad (the distance will be 338 mi if you've spent your third night in Taos). Spend the rest of the day visiting **Living Desert Zoo and Garden State Park** (it's open until

8 PM from Memorial Day to Labor Day and until 5 the rest of the year) and strolling scenic pathways along the Pecos River at **Lake Carlsbad Recreation Area.**

On the fifth day, take the walking tour into the enormous caves of **Carlsbad Caverns National Park.** You can spend at least a half day here. If you need to head back to the northern part of the state, consider driving northwest through the mountain area of **Cloudcroft** and drop down to **White Sands National Monument.** If you have only a few hours of daylight left, make White Sands your priority. It's a dazzling vista of glistening white dunes.

If You Have 8 Days

Follow most of the above five-day itinerary, but plan to spend three extra days in southern New Mexico after you've reached ⛱ **Carlsbad.** Once you've made the long journey down, you might be surprised at what you'll find in out-of-the-way corners. You can be more leisurely about visiting **Carlsbad Caverns** on the fifth day. Round out your tour with a scenic drive through **Walnut Canyon;** then return at sunset (if you're there during summer months) for the evening bat flight. On day six, take U.S. 62/180 south from Carlsbad to **Guadalupe Mountains National Park.** Stop over at the visitor center, and consider a short hike along a nature trail. Eat lunch or a late breakfast at delightfully ornery, middle-of-nowhere Cornudas Café; then drive on to ⛱ **El Paso.** If your time is limited, drive through El Paso straight to ⛱ **Las Cruces,** where you can spend the night. In the afternoon, take in the galleries and sights of **Old Mesilla,** where you can dine at one of several excellent restaurants.

On the seventh day, take U.S. 70 northeast to **White Sands National Monument.** Proceed to **Alamogordo** and visit the Space Center if you have time. For a beautiful scenic drive take U.S. 82 east to **Cloudcroft;** then turn north onto NM 24, where you'll drive through the **Mescalero Apache Reservation** to ⛱ **Ruidoso.** Spend the night and your eighth day here. Nearby is the Old West historical town of **Lincoln.** If you're in the area in colder months, consider winter sports at **Ski Apache.** If it's summer, you might want to spend some time betting on the ponies at **Ruidoso Downs.**

FODOR'S CHOICE

Historic Buildings

Acoma Pueblo. Rising out of a mesa in the northwest quadrant of the state, Acoma Pueblo's Sky City humbled the first Spanish explorers. Parts of the multistory complex are thought to be more than 1,500 years old.

Palace of the Governors, Santa Fe. The oldest public building in the United States, this Pueblo-style structure has served as the residence for 100 Spanish, Native American, Mexican, and American governors; it is now the state history museum.

San Francisco de Asis Church, Ranchos de Taos. Built in the 18th century as a spiritual and physical refuge from raiding Apaches, Utes, and Comanches, this church outside Taos is a spectacular example of adobe Mission architecture. Its simple form has inspired generations of painters and photographers, including Georgia O'Keeffe, Paul Strand, and Ansel Adams.

San Miguel Mission, Santa Fe. This simple, earth-hue adobe structure built in about 1625 is the oldest church still in use in the continental United States. Priceless statues and paintings are within, as well as the San José Bell, said to have been cast in Spain in 1356.

Santuario de Chimayó, Chimayó. Tens of thousands make pilgrimages each year to this small frontier adobe church just north of Santa Fe. Built on the site where a mysterious light is said to have come out of the ground on Good Friday night in 1810, the chapel holds a sacred *pozito* (a small well). The dirt from the pozito is believed to have miraculous healing properties.

Taos Pueblo, Taos. For nearly 1,000 years the Taos-Tiwas have lived in or near this community, which has the largest existing multistory pueblo structure in the United States. The pueblo is a UNESCO World Heritage site.

Dining

Geronimo, Santa Fe. The menu changes daily at this chic restaurant in the historic Borrego House. Enjoy such dishes as mesquite-grilled Black Angus rib eye with a spicy smoked corn and tomato salsa or the superb Sunday brunch. *$$$$*

Trading Post Cafe, Taos. Imaginative variations on Continental and other dishes have made this restaurant a town favorite. $$$–$$$$

Cafe Pasqual's, Santa Fe. This festive, local favorite pleases with its zesty regional and Latin American dishes. Three meals a day are served and there's a communal table for those who want to beat the lines or make acquaintances. $$–$$$$

Artichoke Cafe, Albuquerque. Diners appreciate the excellent service and New American, Italian, and French dishes prepared at this outstanding café, whose chefs use organic produce. $$–$$$

Rancho de Chimayó, Chimayó. This favorite for northern New Mexico cuisine, more notable for its ambience than its food, has cozy dining rooms within a century-old adobe hacienda tucked into the mountains. $$–$$$

Cattleman's Steakhouse, El Paso. Savory steak will win over experienced and inexperienced red meat eaters alike at this ranchlike setting 20 mi east of El Paso, Texas. $–$$$

Plaza Café, Santa Fe. A fixture on the Plaza since 1918, this vintage restaurant serves excellent American, New Mexican, and Greek fare. $$

La Fonda, Artesia. For decades, residents of both Carlsbad and Roswell have driven to this Mexican-food establishment to dine on celebrated specialties such as the Guadalajara plate of seasoned beef, cheese, and guacamole. $–$$

La Posta, Old Mesilla. Dine on authentic Mexican dishes and Southwestern favorites at this old adobe structure, once a way station for the Butterfield Overland Mail and Wells Fargo stages. $–$$

The State Line, El Paso. Aside from its unique location directly atop the New Mexico–Texas state line near El Paso, this area favorite is noted for serving mounds of delicious barbecue with generous side dishes. $–$$

Lodging

The Bavarian, Taos. A luxurious hideaway, this re-creation of a Bavarian ski lodge has the only mid-mountain accommodations in the Taos Ski Valley. $$$$

Hotel Santa Fe. If you're looking for casual but polished comforts and more insight into Native American culture, this Picurís Pueblo-owned hotel offers attractive Southwestern decor and informal talks on Native American history. $$$$

Inn of the Anasazi, Santa Fe. In the heart of the historic Plaza district, this beautifully crafted hotel has individually designed rooms, each with a beamed ceiling, kiva fireplace, four-poster bed, and handcrafted desk, dresser, and tables. $$$$

Hyatt Regency Albuquerque. This gorgeous hotel's soaring desert-color tower climbs high above the city skyline. The Hyatt is totally modern and luxurious, from the on-site spa to the well-regarded restaurant and shopping promenade. $$$–$$$$

Hacienda del Sol, Taos. Once a house for guests of art patron Mabel Dodge Luhan, this bed-and-breakfast contains kiva-style fireplaces, Spanish antiques, Southwestern-style handcrafted furniture, and original artworks. $$–$$$$

Touchstone Inn, Taos. This peaceful bed-and-breakfast overlooking the Taos Pueblo is filled with a tasteful mix of antiques and modern artworks by the talented owner, Ben Price. $$–$$$$

Inn of the Mountain Gods, Mescalero. The Mescalero Apaches own and operate this spectacular year-round resort on the shore of Mescalero Lake, about 3 mi southwest of Ruidoso. $$$

The Cottages, Silver City. You can wander this 80-acre, forested estate in search of a lost silver mine if you're so inclined. The European-style inn also has detached cottages. $$–$$$

La Posada de Albuquerque. Zsa Zsa Gabor honeymooned at this historic downtown hotel, which overflows with Southwestern charm, from its tiled lobby fountain, massive vigas, encircling balcony, and fixtures of etched glass and tin to the Native American war-dance murals behind the reception desk. $$–$$$

Meson de Mesilla, Old Mesilla. A glass-enclosed atrium and a spectacular Mesilla Valley location with lofty views of the Organ Mountains set the atmosphere of this B&B, which offers rooms from affordable to pricey. $–$$$

Lundeen Inn of the Arts, Las Cruces. Architect Gerald Lundeen seamlessly joined two 1895 adobe houses, one Mexican colonial and the other Territorial. Guest rooms are decorated in honor of Western artists like Georgia O'Keeffe and Frederic Remington. *$$*

Best Western Stevens Inn, Carlsbad. Scenes of cavern formations and Carlsbad's historic courthouse are etched in mirrored glass and carved into wooden doors at this motel, which provides a touch of elegance at bargain prices. *$*

Outdoor Adventures

★ **Fishing.** New Mexico offers practically every range of experience except for saltwater oceans. You can launch your boat onto Navajo Lake in northern New Mexico or Elephant Butte to the south. Stream fishing abounds in the Farmington area, while catfishing reigns in the lazy currents of the Pecos or Rio Grande rivers.

★ **Hot-air ballooning.** More than 800 balloons lift off from Albuquerque during the Kodak International Balloon Fiesta, and there are year-round opportunities to soar above the city. In Taos, balloonists will thrill you with dips into the Rio Grande Gorge.

★ **Hot springs soaking, Ojo Caliente.** Get a massage or soak in one of five different hot springs at this cliff-backed spa, which is on the National Register of Historic Places. You can also take a horseback tour or guided hike to ancient ruins.

★ **Sand surfing, White Sands National Monument.** Wipe out on your surfboard and dive headlong into the powdery soft sand. Okay, so the New Mexico version of surfing makes landings a little hard. But you can slide plastic saucers down the dips and curves of the tall gypsum dunes and let your imagination run wild in this white landscape.

★ **White-water rafting, Taos.** As snows melts and water runs swift, there's no better spot for this sport than the northern Rio Grande. You can pick the degree of adventure you want, from mildly flowing water to the spectacular dips and thrills of roaring white water.

Scenic Drives

★ **Enchanted Circle.** This 84-mi loop from Taos winds through alpine country, with a few colorful mining towns along the way.

★ **High Road to Taos.** On the old road linking Santa Fe and Taos, the stunning drive—with a rugged alpine mountain backdrop—encompasses rolling hillsides studded with orchards and tiny picturesque villages noted for weavers and wood-carvers.

★ **Lake Valley National Back Country Byway.** The winding two-lane byway passes through 48 mi of forest and desert, with mountain ranges looming in the distance. The route is accessible 18 mi south of Truth or Consequences. Take the Hillsboro exit off I–25.

★ **Mountains to Desert.** For a dramatic ride that runs from high, cool, green mountains to hot, dry desert near White Sands National Monument, drive the stretch of U.S. 82 in south-central New Mexico that drops 6,000 ft in altitude between Cloudcroft and Alamogordo.

★ **Turquoise Trail.** Full of ghost towns, this old route between Albuquerque and Santa Fe ventures into backcountry, with views worth skipping the interstate for.

FESTIVALS AND SEASONAL EVENTS

WINTER

DEC.➤ **Christmas Native American Dances** (☎ 505/758–1028) take place at most pueblos. The Spanish-inspired dance-drama *Los Matachines* is performed at Picurís Pueblo. There are also pine-torch processions and katsina dances at Taos Pueblo, and Basket, Buffalo, Deer, Harvest, Rainbow, and Turtle dances at Acoma, Cochiti, San Ildefonso, Santa Clara, and Taos pueblos.

During the **Christmas season** Santa Fe is at its most festive, with incense and piñon smoke sweetening the air and the darkness of winter illuminated by thousands of farolitos. A custom believed to have derived from Chinese lanterns, the glowing farolitos are everywhere, lining walkways, doorways, rooftops, walls, and window sills. The songs of Christmas are sung around corner bonfires (luminarias, as the holiday bonfires are called in Santa Fe). With glowing lights reflected on the snow, Santa Fe is never lovelier.

During the 10 days of **Las Posadas** at San Miguel Mission (✉ 401 Old Santa Fe Trail, ☎ 505/983–3974) the story of Mary and Joseph's journey to Bethlehem is reenacted. The **Feast Day of Our Lady of Guadalupe,** December

12, is grandly celebrated at the Santuario de Guadalupe, and **Christmas at the Palace** resounds with hours of festive music emanating from the Palace of the Governors in mid-December.

At **Christmas on the Pecos** (☎ 505/887–6516) in Carlsbad, glittering backyard displays can be viewed from boats that cruise the Pecos River. Tickets usually sell out early and are available beginning in August.

JAN.➤ During **Native American New Year's Celebrations** (☎ 505/758–1028) at many pueblos, Comanche, Deer, Turtle, and other traditional dances are performed.

SPRING

MAR.➤ For a $7 admission, the one-weekend **Fiery Foods Show** (☎ 505/298–3835) in Albuquerque covers everything you ever wanted to know about the international scope of New Mexico's favorite spicy food. Chile in all its incarnations, from sizzling salsas and dips to unusual beer and chocolate concoctions, is the featured spice here. The festival started in 1988 with just 35 booths and has expanded to more than 240 exhibitors from throughout the world.

In Columbus, the events surrounding Mexican revolutionary Pancho Villa's 1917 invasion of Columbus, and the subsequent return of the U.S. soldiers who hunted for him, are commemorated during **Raid Day** (☎ 505/531–2663). It takes place the weekend closest to March 9.

MAR.–APR.➤ The **Chimayó Pilgrimage** (☎ 505/753–2831) takes place on Good Friday; thousands of New Mexicans and out-of-state pilgrims trek on foot to the Santuario de Chimayó, a small church north of Santa Fe that is believed to be the scene of miracles. People line U.S. 285 for miles en route to this sacred spot.

APR.➤ **Frontier Days** (☎ 505/526–8911) at Fort Selden State Monument features historic displays and events commemorating the 1865 founding of this remote adobe outpost near Las Cruces. The **Taos Talking Picture Festival** (☎ 505/751–0637) honors cinematographers and storytellers.

Gathering of Nations Powwow (☎ 505/758–1028), in Albuquerque, is the largest such gathering in the nation. This popular event attracts Native American dancers from across North America, who are dressed in incredible costumes and compete for large prizes. Arts-and-crafts exhibitions, traditional foods, and a beauty contest are other highlights.

The **Silver City Cowboy Jamboree** (☎ 505/538–5431) in Silver City attracts poets, storytellers, and balladeers in a weekend of entertaining sessions highlighted by a jamboree show.

During the last weekend of April, Truth or Consequences holds the **Ralph Edwards Truth or Consequences Fiesta** (☎ 505/894–2946). Residents parade and celebrate the 1950 decision to switch the town name from Hot Springs to that of a popular game show.

MAY➤ The **Taos Spring Arts Celebration** (☎ 800/732–TAOS) is a two-week festival of contemporary visual arts, music, poetry readings, and dance.

The weeklong **Mescal Roast & Mountain Spirit Dances** (☎ 505/887–5516) at Carlsbad's Living Desert Zoo and Garden State Park celebrates the mystic connection Mescalero Apaches have long had with the Guadalupe Mountains of this area, where mescal plants were traditionally gathered for food.

The **New Mexico Wine and Chile War Festival** (☎ 505/646–4543) pits some of the most accomplished regional chile chefs and wine makers against each other in competitions that also offer visitors a taste of the creations. The event is held at Doña Ana County Fairgrounds, west of Las Cruces.

Mariachi music and swirling Mexican dancers are among attractions at the **Cinco de Mayo Festival** (☎ 505/525–1965), May 5, in the Old Mesilla Plaza.

SUMMER

EARLY JUNE–AUG.➤ During **Shakespeare in Santa Fe** (☎ 505/982–2910), free performances of Shakespearean plays take place on Friday, Saturday, and Sunday. An outdoor theater on the campus of St. John's College provides a beautiful backdrop.

JUNE➤ On the last weekend of the month, Albuquerque's New Mexico State Fairgrounds hosts the **New Mexico Arts and Crafts Fair** (☎ 800/284–2282), at which more than 200 artists and craftspeople come together to display their talents. Spanish, Native American, and other North American cultures are represented, and there's plenty of food and entertainment.

El Paso's annual musical drama **Viva El Paso!** (☎ 915/565–6900 or 800/915–8482) lights up a canyon amphitheater from June through August. A diverse cast, from flamenco and ballet dancers to guitarists and actors, brings the multicultural history and legends of the region to life.

LATE JUNE OR EARLY JULY–AUG.➤ The world-famous indoor-outdoor **Santa Fe Opera** (☎ 505/986–5955) opens for the summer season in a beautiful facility tucked into a hillside. World premieres and classics are presented. Opening night is one of *the* social events of the year in New Mexico.

JULY➤ For a small-town Fourth of July with a balloon rally and glorious fireworks, head to **Raton** (☎ 505/445–3689 or 800/638–6161). Age comes before youthful beauty at the **Magdalena Old-Timers Reunion** (☎ 505/854–2201), where the queen must be at least 60 years old. The reunion, held on the first weekend after the Fourth of July, includes three days of rodeo (one day a kids' rodeo), a big chuck wagon cook-off, and outdoor dancing.

Out-of-this-world **Encounter Festival** (☎ 505/624–6860) festivities celebrate Roswell's notoriety as the home of the 1947 crash of a supposed UFO. Guest lecturers and events like alien costume competitions are part of the fun.

MID–LATE JULY➤ The arts and crafts of Native Americans from across the country are auctioned and for sale at the **Arts and Crafts Show** (☎ 505/852–4265) at San Juan Pueblo.

Rodeo de Santa Fe (☎ 505/471–4300) brings a taste of the Old West, with calf roping, bull riding, and a traditional rodeo parade. World-champion rodeo competitors come from all parts of the United States and Canada to this four-decades-old event.

You can smell the burritos, tamales, and chile for blocks around the festive **Spanish Market** (☎ 505/983–4038) held on the Santa Fe Plaza during the last full weekend of July. Along with the good food, Hispanic arts and crafts are for sale. Many exhibitors are from remote villages, where outstanding works are produced.

Aug.➤ Santo Domingo's **Corn Dance** (☎ 505/465–2214) takes place in early August when hundreds of dancers fill the plaza in thanks for the corn harvest.

The **Bat Flight Breakfast** (☎ 505/785–2232), on the second Thursday of the month, is when early risers gather at the entrance to Carlsbad Caverns to eat breakfast and watch tens of thousands of bats fly back into the cave after a night of feeding on insects.

Launched in 1922, Gallup's **Inter-Tribal Indian Ceremonial** (☎ 800/233–4528) is one of the oldest Native American gatherings in the nation; the Ceremonial is an informal and festive reunion of old friends and visitors. Native American dances, a huge arts-and-crafts fair, several parades, and an all-Native American rodeo are some of the attractions of this event, held outside town in Red Rocks State Park.

Santa Fe's **Indian Market** (☎ 505/983–5220) is the world's most prestigious gathering of Native American potters, jewelers, weavers, painters, basket makers, katsina carvers, and other artists and craftspeople. At least 800 artists and craftspeople show their work at this event, held on the Plaza on the third weekend in August.

During **Old Lincoln Days** (☎ 505/653–4025), this Old West town's early prominence in the violent Lincoln County Wars is depicted in numerous events lasting several days, including performances of the "Last Escape of Billy the Kid" Pageant.

AUTUMN

Sept.➤ **Las Fiestas de Santa Fe** (☎ 505/988–7575), the city's biggest celebration, begins the first Friday after Labor Day and commemorates the reconquest of Santa Fe from the Pueblos by Don Diego de Vargas in 1692. A pet parade, dancing, religious observances, ethnic foods, fireworks, and the burning of *Zozobra* (Old Man Gloom) are all part of the event.

The **New Mexico State Fair** (☎ 505/265–1791) takes place at the New Mexico State Fairgrounds in Albuquerque, with arts, crafts, livestock shows, entertainment, and a rodeo.

Wagon Mound, once the pinto-bean capital of New Mexico, celebrates its heritage on **Bean Day** (☎ 505/666–2011), held on Labor Day weekend. Pitch horseshoes, watch the rodeo, and line up for the noon barbecue.

If you love pie, head to Pie Town on the second weekend in September for the **Pie Festival** (☎ 505/772–2755). Some of the participants arrive a few days early to set up operations and start rolling the crusts of their specialties. The festival celebrated its 20th anniversary in 2000.

Oct.➤ The **Kodak Albuquerque International Balloon Fiesta** (☎ 505/821–1000) is the single most popular event in the state, with about 1 million spectators viewing the mass ascensions of more than 800 hot-air and gas balloons. This major event in the world of ballooning—you'll never see anything like it—takes place at Balloon Fiesta Park for two weekends beginning the first full weekend in October.

The **Whole Enchilada Fiesta** (☎ 505/541–2444), in Las Cruces, lasts several days and attracts thousands with food, arts and crafts, and the concoction of the world's largest enchilada—which is shared with the crowd.

At the **Lincoln County Cowboy Symposium** (☎ 505/378–4142), cowboy poets, musicians, chuck wagon cooks, and artisans congregate in Ruidoso's rugged mountain settings for festivities lasting several days.

Portales residents go nuts at harvest time over their specialty crop, Valencia peanuts, grown in the red sandy soil of New Mexico's eastern plains. Arts-and-crafts displays along with treats made with the peanuts are featured during the **Peanut Valley Festival** (☎ 505/562–2227).

Nov.➤ Costumed characters in the garb of the Middle Ages enliven the **Renaissance Craftfaire** (☎ 505/523–6403), singing songs and selling their wares in a Las Cruces park. The event is conducted during the first full weekend in November.

The **International Mariachi Conference** (☎ 505/523–1888) during the second weekend of November in Las Cruces is a celebration in song, music, and dance of the Hispanic culture and traditions.

2 SANTA FE

WITH SIDE TRIPS TO AREA
PUEBLOS AND HISTORIC SITES

Take a high-desert plateau with crystalline
air at the foot of snowcapped peaks; layer
in almost 400 years of Spanish, Mexican,
and Native American influences; and
sprinkle on an odd assortment of artists,
writers, health nuts, and urban refugees,
and you get Santa Fe, America's most
un-American city.

Updated by
Kathleen
McCloud

WITH ITS CRISP, CLEAR AIR and bright, sunny weather, Santa Fe couldn't be more welcoming. On a plateau at the base of the Sangre de Cristo Mountains—at an elevation of 7,000 ft—the city is surrounded by remnants of a 2,000-year-old Pueblo civilization and filled with reminders of almost four centuries of Spanish and Mexican rule. The town's placid central Plaza, which dates from the early 17th century, has been the site of bullfights, public floggings, gunfights, battles, political rallies, promenades, and public markets over the years. A uniquely appealing destination, Santa Fe is fabled for its rows of chic art galleries, superb restaurants, and shops selling Southwestern furnishings and cowboy gear.

La Villa Real de la Santa Fe de San Francisco de Asísi (the Royal City of the Holy Faith of St. Francis of Assisi) was founded in the early 1600s by Don Pedro de Peralta, who planted his banner in the name of Spain. In 1680 the region's Pueblo people rose in revolt, burning homes and churches and killing hundreds of Spaniards. After an extended siege in Santa Fe, the Spanish colonists were driven out of New Mexico. The tide turned 12 years later, when General Don Diego de Vargas returned with a new army from El Paso and recaptured Santa Fe.

To commemorate de Vargas's victory, Las Fiestas de Santa Fe have been held every year since 1712. The nation's oldest community celebration takes place on the weekend after Labor Day, with parades, mariachi bands, pageants, the burning of Zozóbra—also known as Old Man Gloom—and nonstop parties. "Fiesta" (as it's referred to locally) is but one of many annual opportunities for revelry—from the arrival of the rodeo and the opening week of the Santa Fe Opera in summer to traditional Pueblo dances at Christmastime.

Following de Vargas's defeat of the Pueblos, the then-grand Camino Real (Royal Road), stretching from Mexico City to Santa Fe, brought an army of conquistadors, clergymen, and settlers to the northernmost reaches of Spain's New World conquests. In 1820 the Santa Fe Trail—a prime artery of U.S. westward expansion—spilled a flood of covered wagons from Missouri onto the Plaza. A booming trade with the United States was born. After Mexico achieved independence from Spain in 1821, its subsequent rule of New Mexico further increased this commerce.

The Santa Fe Trail's heyday ended with the arrival of the Atchison, Topeka & Santa Fe Railway in 1880. The trains, and later the nation's first highways, brought a new type of settler to Santa Fe—artists who fell in love with its cultural diversity, history, and magical color and light. Their presence attracted tourists, who quickly became a primary source of income for the largely poor populace.

Santa Fe is renowned for its arts, tricultural (Native American, Hispanic, and Anglo) heritage, and adobe architecture. The Pueblo people introduced adobe to the Spanish, who in turn developed the adobe brick style of construction. In a relatively dry, treeless region, adobe was a suitable natural building material. Melding into the landscape with their earthen colors and rounded, flowing lines, the pueblos and villages were hard to see from afar and thus somewhat camouflaged from raiding nomadic tribes. The region's distinctive architecture no longer repels visitors, it attracts them.

Among the smallest state capitals in the country, Santa Fe has no major airport (Albuquerque's is the nearest). The city's population, an estimated 70,000, swells to nearly double that figure in summer. In winter the skiers arrive, lured by the challenging slopes of Ski Santa Fe and Taos Ski Valley (☞ Chapter 3). Geared for tourists, Santa Fe can put a serious dent in your travel budget. Prices are highest in June, July, and August. Between September and November and in April they're lower, and (except for the major holidays) from December to March they're the lowest.

EXPLORING SANTA FE

Humorist Will Rogers said on his first visit to Santa Fe, "Whoever designed this town did so while riding on a jackass, backwards, and drunk." The maze of narrow streets and alleyways confounds motorists, but with shops and restaurants, a flowered courtyard, or an eye-catching gallery at nearly every turn they're a delight for pedestrians. The trickle of water called the Santa Fe River runs east, parallel to Alameda Street, from the Sangre de Cristos Mountains to the open prairie southwest of town, where it disappears into a narrow canyon before joining the Rio Grande. But in New Mexico there is a *dicho,* or old saying, "*agua es vida*"—"water is life"—be it ever so humble.

There are four state museums in Santa Fe, and purchasing a Museum of New Mexico pass is this most economic way to to visit them all. The four-day pass costs $10 and is sold at all of the four museums, which include the Palace of the Governors, Museum of Fine Arts, Museum of Indian Arts and Culture, and Museum of International Folk Art.

Santa Fe Plaza

Much of the history of Santa Fe, New Mexico, the Southwest, and even the West has some association with Santa Fe's central Plaza, which New Mexico governor Don Pedro de Peralta laid out in 1607. The Plaza, already well established by the time of the Pueblo revolt in 1680, was the site of a bullring and of fiestas and fandangos. Freight wagons unloaded here after completing their arduous journey across the Santa Fe Trail. The American flag was raised over the Plaza in 1846, during the Mexican War, which resulted in Mexico's loss of all its territories in the present southwestern United States. For a time the Plaza was a tree-shaded park with a white picket fence. In the 1890s it was an expanse of lawn where uniformed bands played in an ornate gazebo. Particularly festive times on the Plaza are the weekend after Labor Day, during Las Fiestas de Santa Fe, and at Christmas, when all the trees are filled with lights and rooftops are outlined with *farolitos,* votive candles lit within paper-bag lanterns.

Numbers in the text correspond to numbers in the margin and on the Santa Fe map.

A Good Walk
To get started, drop by the information booth at the northwest corner of the plaza, across the street from the clock, where Palace Street meets Lincoln Street (in front of the bank) to pick up a free map. From there, begin your walk around the plaza. You can get an overview of the history of Santa Fe and New Mexico at the **Palace of the Governors** ①, which borders the northern side of the Plaza on Palace Avenue. Outside, under the Palace portal, dozens of Native American craftspeople sell their wares. From the Palace, cross Lincoln Street to the **Museum of Fine Arts** ②, where the works of regional masters are on display. The **Georgia O'Keeffe Museum** ③, on nearby Johnson Street, exhibits the works of its namesake, New Mexico's best-known painter.

From the O'Keeffe Museum, return to the Plaza and cut across to its southeast corner to Old Santa Fe Trail, where you can find the town's oldest hotel, **La Fonda** ④, a good place to soak up a little of bygone

Santa Fe

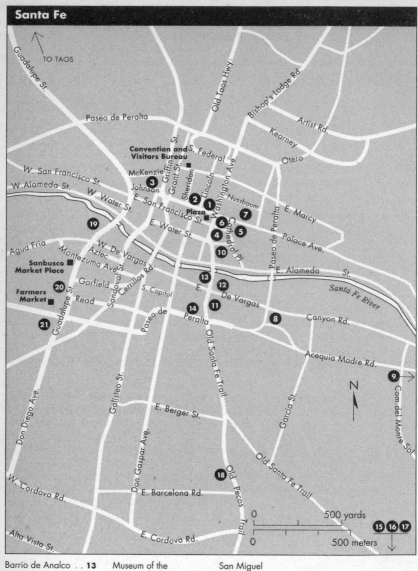

TO TAOS

Guadalupe St.

Paseo de Peralta

Old Taos Hwy.

Bishop's Lodge Rd.

Artist Rd.

Kearney

Otero

Convention and Visitors Bureau

S. Federal

McKenzie

Griffin St.

Grant St.

Sheridan

Lincoln

Washington Ave.

Nussbaum

E. Marcy

W. San Francisco St.

W. Alameda St.

Johnson

W. Water St.

E. San Francisco St.

Plaza

E. Water St.

Cathedral Pl.

Paseo de Peralta

Palace Ave.

Agua Fria

W. De Vargas

Aztec

Montezuma Ave.

E. Alameda

St.

Santa Fe River

Sanbusco Market Place

Garfield

Sandoval

Cerrillos Rd.

S. Capitol

E.

De Vargas

Farmers Market

Read

Guadalupe St.

Paseo de Peralta

Old Santa Fe Trail

Canyon Rd.

Acequia Madre Rd.

Com. del Monte Sol

Don Diego Ave.

Galisteo St.

E. Berger St.

Garcia St.

Old Santa Fe Trail

N

Don Gaspar Ave.

E. Barcelona Rd.

Old Pecos Trail

W. Cordova Rd.

E. Cordova Rd.

Alta Vista St.

0   500 yards

0   500 meters

Barrio de Analco . . **13**

Cristo Rey
Church **9**

Georgia O'Keeffe
Museum **3**

Gerald Peters
Gallery **8**

La Fonda **4**

Loretto Chapel **10**

Museum of
Fine Arts **2**

Museum of
Indian Arts and
Culture **15**

Museum of the
Institute of American
Indian Arts **6**

Museum of
International
Folk Art **16**

New Mexico State
Capitol **14**

The Oldest
House **12**

Palace of the
Governors **1**

St. Francis
Cathedral **5**

San Miguel
Mission **11**

Santa Fe
Children's
Museum **18**

Santa Fe Southern
Railway **20**

Santuario de
Guadalupe **19**

Sena Plaza **7**

SITE Santa Fe **21**

Wheelwright Museum
of the American
Indian **17**

Santa Fe. One block east on Cathedral Place looms the imposing facade of **St. Francis Cathedral** ⑤. Across from the cathedral is the **Museum of the Institute of American Indian Arts** ⑥. A stone's throw from the museum is cool, quiet **Sena Plaza** ⑦, accessible through two doorways on Palace Avenue.

TIMING

It's possible to zoom through this compact area in about five hours—two hours exploring the Plaza and the Palace of the Governors, two hours seeing the Museum of Fine Arts and the Museum of the Institute of American Indian Arts, and an hour visiting the other sites.

Sights to See

🖉 *following the text of a review is your signal that the property has a Web site, where you will find details and, usually, images; for a link, visit www.fodors.com/urls.*

❸ Georgia O'Keeffe Museum. One of many East Coast artists who visited New Mexico in the first half of the 20th century, O'Keeffe fell in love with the region and returned to live and paint here, eventually emerging as the demigoddess of Southwestern art. This private museum devoted to the works of this Modernist painter opened in 1997. O'Keeffe's innovative view of the landscape is captured in *From the Plains*, inspired by her memory of the Texas plains, and *Jimson Weed*, a quintessential O'Keeffe study of one of her favorite plants. Special exhibitions with O'Keeffe's modernist peers are on view throughout the year. ✉ *217 Johnson St.,* ☎ *505/995–0785.* 🖾 *$5, free Fri. 5–8 PM.* ☉ *July–Oct., Tues–Sun. 10–5, (extended hrs Wed. and Fri. 'til 8); Nov.–June, Tues., Thurs.–Sun. 10–5, (extended hrs Fri. 'til 8).* 🖉

❹ La Fonda. A Santa Fe landmark, La Fonda (☞ Lodging, *below*) faces the southeast corner of the Plaza. A *fonda* (inn) has stood on this site for centuries. Architect Isaac Hamilton Rapp, whose Rio Grande–Pueblo Revival structures put Santa Fe style on the map, built this hotel in 1922. The hotel was remodeled in 1926 by another luminary of Santa Fe architecture, John Gaw Meem. The hotel was sold to the Santa Fe Railway in 1926 and became one of Fred Harvey's Harvey House hotels until 1968. Because of its proximity to the Plaza and its history as a gathering place for cowboys, trappers, traders, soldiers, frontier politicians, movie stars (Errol Flynn stayed here), artists, and writers, it is referred to as "The Inn at the End of the Trail." Major social events still take place here. ✉ *E. San Francisco St. at Old Santa Fe Trail,* ☎ *505/982–5511.*

★ **❷ Museum of Fine Arts.** Designed by Isaac Hamilton Rapp in 1917, the museum contains one of America's finest regional collections. It's also one of Santa Fe's earliest Pueblo Revival structures, inspired by the adobe structures at Acoma Pueblo. Split cedar *latillas* (branches set in a crosshatch pattern) and hand-hewn vigas make up the ceilings. The 8,000-piece permanent collection emphasizes the work of regional and nationally renowned artists, including the early Modernist Georgia O'Keeffe; realist Robert Henri; the "Cinco Pintores" (five painters) of Santa Fe (including Fremont Elis and Will Shuster); and members of the Taos Society of Artists (Ernest L. Blumenschein, Bert Geer Philips, Joseph Henry Sharp, and Eanger Irving Couse, among others). Many excellent examples of Spanish colonial–style furniture are on display. An interior *placita* (small plaza) with fountains, murals, and sculpture, and the St. Francis Auditorium are other highlights. Concerts and lectures are often held in the auditorium. ✉ *W. Palace Ave.,* ☎ *505/476–5072, www.nmculture.org.* 🖾 *$5, 4-day pass $10, free Fri. 5–8 PM.* ☉ *Tues.–Thurs. and weekends 10–5, Fri. 10–8.*

⑥ **Museum of the Institute of American Indian Arts.** Inside the handsomely renovated former post office, this museum contains the largest collection of contemporary Native American art in the United States. The paintings, photography, sculptures, prints, and traditional crafts exhibited here were created by past and present students and teachers. The institute itself, which moved to the College of Santa Fe campus, was founded as a one-room studio classroom in the early 1930s by Dorothy Dunn, a beloved art teacher who played a critical role in launching the careers of many Native American artists. In the 1960s and 1970s it blossomed into the nation's premier center for Native American arts. Artist Fritz Scholder taught here for years, as did the sculptor Allan Houser. Among their disciples was the painter T. C. Cannon. ⊠ *108 Cathedral Pl.,* ☎ *505/988–6211 for events and parking information.* 🎟 *$4.* ⊙ *Daily 10–5.*

★ 🖐 ❶ **Palace of the Governors.** A humble-looking one-story adobe on the north side of the Plaza, the palace is the oldest public building in the United States. Built at the same time as the Plaza, circa 1607, it was the seat of four regional governments—those of Spain, Mexico, the Confederacy, and the U.S. territory that preceded New Mexico's statehood, which was achieved in 1912. The building was abandoned in 1680, following the Pueblo Revolt, but resumed its role as government headquarters when Don Diego de Vargas successfully returned in 1692. It served as the residence for 100 Spanish, Mexican, and American governors, including Governor Lew Wallace, who wrote his epic *Ben Hur* in its then drafty rooms, all the while complaining of the dust and mud that fell from its earthen ceiling.

The palace has been the central headquarters of the Museum of New Mexico since 1913 and houses the main section of the **State History Museum.** Permanent exhibits chronicle 450 years of New Mexico history, using maps, furniture, clothing, housewares, weaponry, and village models. With advance permission, students and researchers have access to the museum's extensive research library and its rare maps, manuscripts, and photographs (more than 120,000 prints and negatives). The palace is also home to the **Museum of New Mexico Press,** which prints books, pamphlets, and cards on antique presses and hosts bookbinding demonstrations, lectures, and slide shows. There is also an outstanding gift shop and bookstore. ⊠ *Palace Ave., north side of the Plaza,* ☎ *505/476–5100, www.nmculture.org.* 🎟 *$5, 4-day pass $10 (good at all 4 state museums in Santa Fe), free Fri. 5–8.* ⊙ *Tues.–Thurs. and weekends 10–5, Fri. 10–8.* 🖐

Dozens of Native American vendors gather daily under the portal of the Palace of the Governors to display and sell pottery, jewelry, bread, and other goods. With few exceptions, the more than 500 artists and craftspeople registered to sell here are Pueblo or Navajo Indians. The merchandise for sale is required to meet Museum of New Mexico standards: all items are handmade or hand-strung in Native American households; silver jewelry is either sterling (92.5% pure) or coin (90% pure) silver; all metal jewelry bears the maker's mark, which is registered with the museum. Prices tend to reflect the high quality of the merchandise. Don't take photographs without permission.

★ ❺ **St. Francis Cathedral.** This magnificent cathedral, a block east of the Plaza, is one of the rare significant departures from the city's ubiquitous pueblo architecture. Construction was begun in 1869 by Jean Baptiste Lamy, Santa Fe's first archbishop, working with French architects and Italian stonemasons. The Romanesque style was popular in Lamy's native home in the southwest of France. The circuit-riding cleric was sent by the Catholic Church to the Southwest to change the religious practices of its native population (to "civilize" them, as one period document puts it), and is buried in the crypt beneath the church's high altar. He was the inspiration behind Willa Cather's novel *Death Comes for the Archbishop* (1927).

A small adobe chapel on the northeast side of the cathedral, the remnant of an earlier church, embodies the Hispanic architectural influence so conspicuously absent from the cathedral itself. The chapel's *Nuestra Señora de la Paz* (Our Lady of Peace), popularly known as *La Conquistadora,* the oldest Madonna statue in the United States, accompanied Don Diego de Vargas on his reconquest of Santa Fe in 1692, a feat attributed to the statue's spiritual intervention. Every Friday the faithful adorn the statue with a new dress. Just south of the cathedral, where the parking lot meets Paseo de Peralta, is the **Archives of the Archdiocese Museum,** a small museum where many of the area's historic, liturgical artifacts are on view. ⊠ *231 Cathedral Pl.,* ☎ *505/982–5619.* ⊙ *Daily 8–5:45, except during mass. Mass celebrated Mon.–Sat. at 7 and 8:15 AM, 12:10 and 5:15 PM; Sun. at 6, 8, and 10 AM, noon, and 7 PM. Museum weekdays 9–4.*

❼ Sena Plaza. Two-story buildings enclose this courtyard, which can be entered only through two small doorways on Palace Avenue. Surrounding the oasis of flowering fruit trees, a fountain, and inviting benches are unique, low profile shops. The quiet courtyard is a good place for repose. The buildings, erected in the 1700s as a single-family residence, had quarters for blacksmiths, bakers, farmers, and all manner of help. ⊠ *125 E. Palace Ave.*

Canyon Road

Once a Native American trail and an early 20th-century route for woodcutters and their burros, Canyon Road is now lined with art galleries, shops, and restaurants, earning it the nickname "the Art and Soul of Santa Fe." The narrow road begins at the eastern curve of Paseo de Peralta and stretches for about 2 mi at a slight incline toward the base of the mountains.

Most establishments are in authentic, old adobe homes with undulating thick walls that appear to have been carved out of the earth. Within many are contemporary and traditional works by artists from internationally renowned names like Fernando Botero to anonymous weavers of ancient Peruvian textiles.

There are few places as festive as Canyon Road on Christmas Eve, when thousands of farolitos illuminate walkways, walls, roofs, and even trees. In May, the scent of lilacs wafts over the adobe walls, and in August red hollyhocks enhance the surreal color of the blue sky on a dry summer day.

A Good Walk

Begin on Paseo de Peralta at the **Gerald Peters Gallery** ⑧, which has an enormous collection as well as an ample parking lot. Continue a half block north to Canyon Road. Turn right (east) and follow the road, which unfolds in shadows of undulating adobe walls. Street parking is at a premium, but there is a city-owned pay lot at the corner of Camino del Monte Sol, four blocks up. Between visits to galleries and shops, take a break at one of the courtyards or fine restaurants. At the intersection of Upper Canyon and Cristo Rey you'll find the massive **Cristo Rey Church** ⑨. Wear good walking shoes and watch out for the irregular sidewalks, which are built of stone and can get icy in winter.

TIMING

A tour of Canyon Road could take a whole day or as little as a few hours. If art is more than a curiosity to you, you may want to view the Gerald Peters Gallery apart from your Canyon Road tour. There is so much to see there that visual overload could hit before you get halfway up the road. Even on a cold day the walk can be a pleasure, with massive, glistening icicles hanging off roofs and a silence shrouding the side streets.

Sights to See

❾ Cristo Rey Church. Built in 1940 to commemorate the 400th anniversary of Francisco Vásquez de Coronado's exploration of the Southwest, this church is the largest Spanish adobe structure in the United States and is considered by many the finest example of Pueblo-style architecture anywhere. The church was constructed in the old-fashioned way by parishioners, who mixed the more than 200,000 mud-and-straw adobe bricks and hauled them into place. The 225-ton stone reredos (altar screen) is magnificent. ⊠ *Canyon Rd. at Cristo Rey, where "lower" Canyon Rd. becomes "upper" Canyon Rd.,* ☎ *505/983–8528.* ⊙ *Daily 8–7.*

❽ Gerald Peters Gallery. While under construction, this 32,000-square-ft building was dubbed the "ninth northern pueblo," its scale rivaling that of the eight northern pueblos around Santa Fe. The suavely designed Pueblo-style gallery is Santa Fe's premier showcase for American and European art from the 19th century to the present. It feels like a museum, but all the works are for sale. Pablo Picasso, Georgia O'Keeffe, Charles M. Russell, Deborah Butterfield, George Rickey, and members of the Taos Society are among the artists represented, along with nationally renowned contemporary ones. ⊠ *1011 Paseo de Peralta,* ☎ *505/954–5700.* ⊠ *Free.* ⊙ *Mon.–Sat. 10–5.*

NEED A
BREAK?

A good place to rest your feet is the **Backroom Coffeebar** (⊠ 616 Canyon Rd., ☎ 505/988–5323), which serves pastries and light snacks. Locals congregate in the courtyard or on the front portal of **Downtown Subscription** (⊠ 376 Garcia St., ☎ 505/983–3085) a block up from Paseo de Peralta and one block east of Canyon Road. You can pick up a paper here as well as coffee, light snacks, and pastries.

Lower Old Santa Fe Trail

It was along the Old Santa Fe Trail that wagon trains from Missouri rolled into town in the 1800s, forever changing Santa Fe's destiny. This area off the Plaza is one of Santa Fe's most historic.

A Good Walk

The **Loretto Chapel** ⑩, facing the Old Santa Fe Trail, behind the La Fonda hotel (☞ Santa Fe Plaza, *above*), is a good place to start your walk. After visiting the chapel, head southeast on Old Santa Fe Trail to the **San Miguel Mission** ⑪. Across from the mission, on De Vargas Street, is the **Oldest House** ⑫. Up and down narrow De Vargas stretches the **Barrio de Analco** ⑬. There are a few galleries worth visiting on De Vargas Street east of Old Santa Fe Trail, and, back across Old Santa Fe Trail on the west side, check out the historic Santa Fe Community Theatre. In the early art colony days, literary luminaries like Mary Austin and Witter Bynner would stage shows here. Walk farther away from downtown until you come to the **New Mexico State Capitol** ⑭, which contains some interesting artwork.

TIMING

Plan on spending a half hour at each of the churches and the New Mexico State Capitol and an hour exploring the Barrio de Analco. The entire walk can easily be done in about 3½ hours.

Sights to See

⑬ **Barrio de Analco.** Along the south bank of the Santa Fe River, the barrio—its name means "district on the other side of the water"—is one of America's oldest neighborhoods, settled in the early 1600s by the Tlaxcalan Indians (who were forbidden to live with the Spanish near the Plaza) and in the 1690s by soldiers who had helped recapture New Mexico after the Pueblo Revolt. Plaques on houses on East De Vargas Street will help you locate some of the important structures. Check the performance schedule at the **Santa Fe Community Theatre** on De Vargas Street, founded by writer Mary Austin and other Santa Feans in the 1920s.

⑩ **Loretto Chapel.** A delicate Gothic church modeled after Sainte-Chapelle in Paris, Loretto was built in 1873 by the same French architects and Italian stonemasons who built St. Francis Cathedral. The chapel is known for the "Miraculous Staircase" that leads to the choir loft. Legend has it that the chapel was almost complete when it became obvious that there wasn't room to build a staircase to the choir loft. In answer to the prayers of the cathedral's nuns, an old bearded man arrived on a donkey, built a 20-ft staircase—using only a square, a saw, and a tub of water to season the wood—and then disappeared as quickly as he came. Many of the faithful believed it was St. Joseph himself. The staircase contains two complete 360-degree turns with no central support; no nails were used in its construction. The chapel closes for services and special events. Adjoining the chapel are a small museum and gift shop. ⊠ *211 Old Santa Fe Trail,* ☎ *505/984–7971.* ⊑ *$2.* ☉ *Mid-Oct.–mid-May, Mon.–Sat. 9–5, Sun. 10:30–5; mid-May–mid-Oct., Mon.–Sat. 8:30–6, Sun. 10:30–6.*

★ ⑭ **New Mexico State Capitol.** The symbol of the Zía Pueblo, which represents the Circle of Life, was the inspiration for the Capitol, also known as the Roundhouse. Doorways at opposing sides of this 1966 structure symbolize the four winds, the four directions, and the four seasons. Throughout the building are artworks from the outstanding collection of the Capitol Art Foundation, historical and cultural displays, and handcrafted furniture. The **Governor's Gallery** hosts temporary exhibits. Six acres of imaginatively landscaped gardens shelter outstanding sculptures. ⊠ *Old Santa Fe Trail at Paseo de Peralta,* ☎ *505/986–4589.* ⊑ *Free.* ☉ *Mon.–Sat. 8–5; tours at 10 AM and 2 PM.*

⑫ **The Oldest House.** More than 800 years ago, Pueblo people built this structure out of "puddled" adobe (liquid mud poured between upright wooden frames). This house, which contains a gift shop, is said to be the oldest in the United States. ⊠ *215 E. De Vargas St.*

★ ⑪ **San Miguel Mission.** The oldest church still in use in the United States, this simple earth-hued adobe structure was built in the early 17th century by the Tlaxcalan Indians of Mexico, who came to New Mexico as servants of the Spanish. Badly damaged in the 1680 Pueblo Revolt, the structure was restored and enlarged in 1710. On display in the chapel are priceless statues and paintings and the San José Bell, weighing nearly 800 pounds, which is believed to have been cast in Spain in 1356. In winter, the church sometimes closes before its official closing hour. Mass is held on Sunday at 5 PM. Next door in the back of the Territorial-style dormitories of the old St. Michael's High School, a **Visitor Information Center** distributes information on northern New Mexico. ⊠ *401 Old Santa Fe Trail,* ☎ *505/983–3974.* ⊑ *$1.* ☉ *Mission May–Oct., Mon.–Sat. 9–4:30, Sun. 3–4:30; Nov.–Apr., Mon–Sat. 10–4, Sun. 3–4:30. Information center weekdays 9–5.*

....

NEED A BREAK?   Have a slice of pizza on the patio of **Upper Crust Pizza** (⊠ 329 Old Santa Fe Trail, ☎ 505/982–0000), next to the San Miguel Mission.

Upper Old Santa Fe Trail

A Good Tour

This museum tour begins 2 mi east of the Plaza. Hearty souls could walk the 2 mi, but it's best to save energy for the museums themselves. If you don't have a car, city buses leave hourly from downtown to the outlying museums. Begin at the **Museum of Indian Arts and Culture** ⑮. To get here from the Plaza, drive uphill on Old Santa Fe Trail to Camino Lejo. From the Museum of Indian Arts and Culture, cross the parking lot to the **Museum of International Folk Art** ⑯. Nearby is the **Wheelwright Museum of the American Indian** ⑰. To reach the **Santa Fe Children's Museum** ⑱ you'll need to drive back down the hill or ask the bus driver to let you off nearby it.

TIMING

Set aside four to six hours to see all the museums on the Upper Santa Fe Trail. Kids usually have to be dragged from the Children's Museum, even after an hour or two.

Sights to See

★ ⑮ **Museum of Indian Arts and Culture.** An interactive, multimedia exhibition tells the story of Native American history in the Southwest, merging contemporary Native American experience with historical accounts and artifacts. The collection has some of New Mexico's oldest works of art: pottery vessels, fine stone and silver jewelry, intricate textiles, and other arts and crafts created by Pueblo, Navajo, and Apache artisans. You can also see art demonstrations and a video about the life and work of Pueblo potter Maria Martinez (☞ San Ildefonso Pueblo *in* Side Trips, *below*). ⊠ *710 Camino Lejo,* ☎ *505/476–1250, www.nm-culture.org.* ⊠ *$5, 4-day pass $10.* ⊙ *Tues.–Sun. 10–5.* ☒

★ ⑯ **Museum of International Folk Art.** Everywhere you look in this facility, the premier institution of its kind in the world, you'll find amazingly inventive handmade objects—a tin Madonna, a devil made from bread dough, and all kinds of rag dolls. Florence Dibell Bartlett, who founded the museum in 1953, donated its first 4,000 works. In the late 1970s Alexander and Susan Girard, major folk-art collectors, gave the museum 106,000 items. The Hispanic Heritage Wing contains art dating from the Spanish colonial period (in New Mexico, 1598–1821) to the present. The 5,000-piece exhibit includes religious works—particularly *bultos* (carved wooden statues of saints) and *retablos* (holy images painted on wood or tin). The objects in the Neutrogena Wing are exhibited by theme rather than by date or country of origin—you might, for instance, find a sheer Eskimo parka alongside a Chinese undergarment made of bamboo and cotton webbing. Lloyd's Treasure Chest, the wing's innovative basement section, provides a behind-the-scenes look at more of this collection. You can rummage about storage drawers, peer into microscopes, and, on occasion, speak with conservators and other museum personnel. ⊠ *706 Camino Lejo,* ☎ *505/476–1200, www.nmculture.org,* ⊠ *$5, 4-day pass $10 (good at all 4 state museums in Santa Fe).* ⊙ *Tues.–Sun. 10–5.* ☒

☚ ⑱ **Santa Fe Children's Museum.** Stimulating hands-on exhibits, a solar greenhouse, oversize geometric forms, and a simulated 18-ft mountain-climbing wall all contribute to the museum's popularity with kids. Puppeteers and storytellers occasionally perform. ⊠ *1050 Old Pecos Trail,* ☎ *505/989–8359.* ⊠ *$3.* ⊙ *Sept.–May, Thurs.–Sat. 10–5, Sun. noon–5; June–Aug., Wed.–Sat. 10–5, Sun. noon–5.*

⑰ **Wheelwright Museum of the American Indian.** A private institution in a building shaped like a traditional octagonal Navajo hogan, the Wheelwright opened in 1937. Founded by Boston scholar Mary Cabot

Wheelwright and Navajo medicine man Hasteen Klah, the museum originated as a place to house ceremonial materials. Those items are not on view to the public. What is displayed are 19th- and 20th-century baskets, pottery, sculpture, weavings, and paintings, including contemporary works by Native American artists. The Case Trading Post on the lower level is modeled after the trading posts that dotted the Southwestern frontier more than 100 years ago. It carries an extensive selection of books and contemporary Native American jewelry, weaving, and pottery. ✉ *704 Camino Lejo,* ☎ *505/982–4636.* ⊠ *Free.* ☉ *Mon.–Sat. 10–5, Sun. 1–5.*

Historic Guadalupe Railroad District

The historic warehouse district of Santa Fe is commonly referred to as the Railyard District. After the demise of the train route through town, the low-lying warehouses were converted to artist studios and antiques shops. Bookstores, shops, and restaurants have sprung up in the last 15 years. The restored scenic train line is once again putting the town's old depot to use. The local farmers' market turns the depot parking lot into a colorful outdoor fiesta of chiles, fresh greens, lavender, medicinal oils, baked goods, coffee, ranchero music, and socializing beginning the first weekend in May and continuing through the first weekend in November. It takes place Saturday mornings until noon, Tuesday as well from July through September.

A Good Walk

From the Plaza, head west on San Francisco Street, and then take a left on Guadalupe Street toward **Santuario de Guadalupe** ⑲, 1½ short blocks across the Santa Fe River and on your right. After you visit the Santuario, take your time browsing through the shops and eating lunch in one of the restaurants farther down Guadalupe Street. At the corner of Montezuma Street, turn right and proceed a half block to the end, where you'll find the **Sanbusco Market Place** in one of Santa Fe's largest historic warehouses. Check out the innovative shops and the photographic history on the walls near the market's main entrance. Continue south on Guadalupe, past the historic Gross Kelly Warehouse, one of the earliest Santa Fe–style buildings constructed. You'll pass two huge murals on buildings facing Guadalupe Street depicting the magical-realism that flavors so much of New Mexico culture. You will also pass Santa Fe's two train depots—one is now the sight of Tomasita's Restaurant, the other, set farther back, is the Santa Fe Depot, where the **Santa Fe Southern Railway** ⑳ departs and where the **Farmers' Market** is held. Continue south on Guadalupe until you come to Paseo de Peralta. Across the street, in a renovated bottling warehouse, is **SITE Santa Fe** ㉑ gallery and performance space.

TIMING

A visit to the Santuario de Guadalupe can take 15 minutes to an hour, depending on whether or not there's an art show in progress. If you like shopping, you might spend hours in the shops on and off Guadalupe Street.

Sights to See

⑳ **Santa Fe Southern Railway.** For a leisurely tour across the Santa Fe plateau and into the vast Galisteo Basin, where panoramic views extend for up to 120 mi, take a nostalgic ride on the antique cars of the Santa Fe Southern Railway. The train once served a spur of the Atchison, Topeka & Santa Fe Railway. In 1991, the train started taking visitors on 36-mi round-trip scenic trips to Lamy, a sleepy town without streetlights, offering picnics under the cottonwoods (bring your own or buy one from the caterer that meets the train) at the quaint Lamy train station. Aside from day trips, the railway offers special events such as a Friday-night "High Desert High Ball" cash bar with appetizers, and a "Sunset Run" on which a barbecue, a campfire, and live entertainment await you at the Lamy depot. Trains depart from the Santa Fe Depot, rebuilt in 1909 after the original was destroyed in a fire. ⊠ *410 S. Guadalupe St.,* ☎ *800/989–8600.* 🖾 *Day trips start at $25, Sunset Run starts at $45.* ☉ *Departs May–Oct., Tues.–Thurs. and Sat. 10:30* AM, *returns 2:30–3:30* PM; *Sun.–Mon. departs 1* PM, *returns 4:30* PM *(bring your own refreshments). Sunset Run departs between 6* PM *and 7:15* PM. *Call for winter schedule, Sunset Run, and High Desert High Ball times.*

⑲ **Santuario de Guadalupe.** A humble adobe structure built by Franciscan missionaries between 1776 and 1795, this is the oldest shrine in the United States to Our Lady of Guadalupe, patron saint of Mexico. The sanctuary, now a nonprofit cultural center, has adobe walls nearly 3 ft thick. Among the sanctuary's religious art and artifacts is a priceless 16th-century work by Venetian painter Leonardo de Ponte Bassano that depicts Jesus driving the money changers from the Temple. Also of note is a portrait of Our Lady of Guadalupe by the Mexican colonial painter José de Alzíbar. Other highlights are the traditional New Mexican carved and painted altar screen, an authentic 19th-century sacristy, a pictorial-history archive, a library devoted to Archbishop Jean Baptiste Lamy that is furnished with many of his belongings, and a garden with plants from the Holy Land. ⊠ *100 Guadalupe St.,* ☎ *505/988–2027.* 🖾 *Donation suggested.* ☉ *May–Oct., Mon.–Sat. 9–4; Nov.–Apr., weekdays 9–4.*

㉑ **SITE Santa Fe.** The events at this nexus of international contemporary art include lectures, concerts, author readings, performance art, and gallery shows. The facility hosts a biennial exhibition every odd-numbered year. ⊠ *1606 Paseo de Peralta,* ☎ *505/989–1199.* 🖾 *$5, free Fri.* ☉ *Wed.–Thurs. and weekends 10–5, Fri. 10–7.*

DINING

Santa Fe cuisine is a robust mixture of Pueblo, Spanish, Mexican, and Continental influences. Chefs at European-style cafés prepare superb Mexican dishes; nouvelle New Mexican cuisine is served at elegant restaurants. Hamburgers and comfort food abound at many of the contemporary grills, which manage to bring a unique Santa Fe spin to tried-and-true American cooking.

American

$$$–$$$$ ✕ **El Nido.** Since the 1920s, Santa Feans have made the 6-mi drive to the village of Tesuque to eat at this former dance hall and trading post, which has a cozy ambience and a solid menu of choice aged beef, fresh seafood, and local specialties like chunky green-chile stew. Only a five-minute drive from the Santa Fe Opera, El Nido is a favorite of opera fans. Reservations are recommended during July and August. ⊠ *U.S. 285/84, 6 mi north of Santa Fe to first Tesuque exit, then about ¼ mi farther to restaurant,* ☎ *505/988–4340. AE, DC, MC, V. Closed Mon. No lunch.*

$$$–$$$$ ✕ **Vanessie.** An à la carte menu specializing in high-quality cuts of meat,
★   fresh fish, and very simple side dishes is ideally suited for conservative tastes. The oak interior, high ceilings, and oversize windows give the restaurant a lodgelike atmosphere. Casual fare such as large burgers and onion loaf is served in the adjoining piano bar. Professional pianists perform classical to Broadway favorites nightly starting at 8 PM (no cover charge). ⊠ *434 W. San Francisco St.,* ☎ *505/982–9966. AE, DC, MC, V.*

Santa Fe Dining

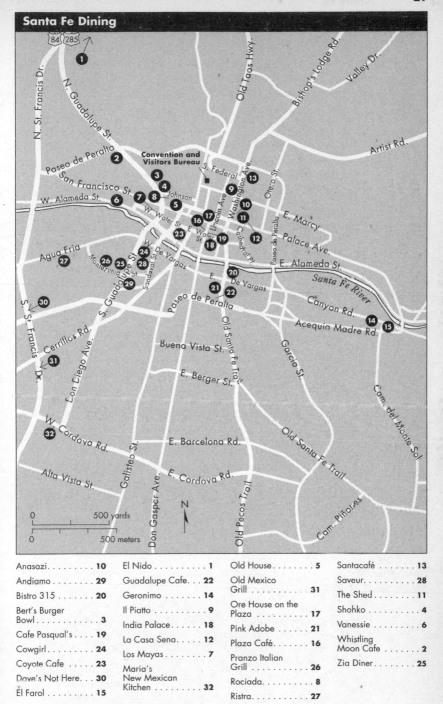

American/Casual

$$–$$$ ✕ **Zia Diner.** This slick diner with a low-key, art deco–style interior provides a menu that pleases meat-loaf lovers and vegetarians, senior citizens and families. Stop in for a full meal (try one of their weeknight blue-plate specials, like Friday night's Pescado Vera Cruz) or just a thick slice of fresh strawberry-rhubarb pie. Service is fast and friendly, and the food is fresh and more imaginative than most diner fare. Patio dining is also available. Reservations are accepted for parties of six or more. ⊠ 326 S. Guadalupe St., Railyard District, ☏ 505/988–7008. AE, MC, V.

$$ ✕ **Plaza Café.** Run with homespun care by the Razatos family since
★   1947, this café has been a fixture on the Plaza since 1918. The decor—red leather banquettes, black Formica tables, tile floors, vintage Santa Fe photos, a coffered tin ceiling, and a 1940s-style service counter—hasn't changed much in the past half century. Standard American fare is served, along with New Mexican and Greek dishes. A bowl of green chile and beans will leave your tongue burning—that's the way the locals like it. You can cool it off with an old-fashioned ice-cream treat from the soda fountain. All in all, it's a good stop for breakfast, lunch, or dinner. ⊠ 54 Lincoln Ave., ☏ 505/982–1664. Reservations not accepted. AE, D, MC, V.

$–$$ ✕ **Bert's Burger Bowl.** This tiny place has been serving up yummy charbroiled burgers since the 1950s. The No. 6 (green chile with cheese) is a staple. You can also get excellent pressure-cooked chicken, *carne adovada* (red chile–marinated pork), crispy fries, and old-fashioned shakes. There are tables outside and a few chairs indoors. ⊠ 235 N. Guadalupe St., ☏ 505/982–0215. No credit cards.

$–$$ ✕ **Dave's Not Here.** Dave may not be here, but you will find one of Santa Fe's best burgers, served with heaps of onions, mushrooms, avocado, or cheese. The cooks at Dave's prepare super made-from-scratch chiles rellenos. For dessert try the slab of deep chocolate cake. ⊠ 1115 Hickox St. (the extension of Paseo de Peralta west from St. Francis Dr.), ☏ 505/983–7060. Reservations not accepted. No credit cards. Closed Sun.

$ ✕ **Saveur.** Fresh ingredients, pleasant atmosphere, and great bread make this a good place for an inexpensive meal just a short walk from the Plaza. In the morning, make your own omelet; in the afternoon, build your own sandwich. Try a daily special, like Friday's grilled tuna with roasted red peppers. ⊠ 204 Montezuma, where Montezuma intersects with Galisteo/Sandoval, ☏ 505/989–4200. Reservations not accepted. D, MC, V. Closed weekends.

Contemporary

$$$$ ✕ **Bistro 315.** As if it were on a thoroughfare in Paris rather than on the Old Santa Fe Trail, Bistro 315 has a Continental, white-tablecloth sophistication, but the offbeat wall art gives it a contemporary feel. Chef and owner Louis Maskow prepares bistro fare using organic vegetables, locally raised beef and lamb, free-range chicken, and fresh seafood. Seasonal specialties on the ever-evolving menu might include duckling with porcini mushroom turnover. The patio opens onto the street scene. ⊠ 315 Old Santa Fe Trail, ☏ 505/986–9190. Reservations essential. AE, MC, V. No lunch Sun.

$$$$ ✕ **Coyote Café.** The Coyote gives Southwest style a dose of Hollywood with a bold decor that creates its own special effects. The inventive menu is the creation of chef-owner Mark Miller. Try "The Cowboy," a 22-ounce rib-eye steak served with barbecued black beans and onion rings dusted with red chile; the short stack of griddled corn cakes with *chipotle* (a hot, smoky chile) shrimp appetizer; or the ravioli filled with sausage made of wild boar and goat cheese. The open dining room can be loud, and it's the kind of place where people go to be seen. On the wine list are more than 500 vintages. Exotic but much less expensive dishes are served on the Rooftop Cantina April through October. The Coyote General Store, under the café, sells Southwestern foodstuffs and Miller's cookbooks. ⊠ *132 W. Water St.,* ☏ *505/983–1615. AE, D, DC, MC, V. Closed Tues.–Wed. Jan.–Feb.*

$$$$ ✕ **Geronimo.** Chef Eric DiStefano changes the menu frequently at this
★ restaurant in the Borrego House, which dates from 1756. A typical meal might start with an appetizer like cold water lobster tail on angel hair pasta. Entrées are artful, like mesquite-grilled elk tenderloin with smoked bacon and chestnut strudel, or red-corn relleno with duck and black-bean sauce. The Sunday brunch is also impressive. The intimate, white dining rooms have beamed ceilings, wood floors, fireplaces, and cushioned bancos. In summer you can dine under the front portal; in winter the bar and fireplace are inviting. ⊠ *724 Canyon Rd.,* ☏ *505/982–1500. AE, MC, V. No lunch Mon.*

$$$$ ✕ **Old House.** Chef Martin Rios changes the menu every Thursday at
★ his fashionably casual restaurant inside the equally fashionable Eldorado Hotel (☞ *Lodging, below*). Entrées have included barbecued breast of quail on a crispy corn cake and rack of lamb in a pepita-garlic crust. More than two dozen of the impressive wines are served by the glass. A separate dining room has a slightly more refined interior than the hacienda ambience of the main dining room. Reservations are essential during summer and on weekends year-round. ⊠ *Eldorado Hotel, 309 W. San Francisco St.,* ☏ *505/988–4455. AE, D, DC, MC, V. Closed Mon. No lunch.*

$$$$ ✕ **Santacafé.** Minimal elegance marks the interior of Santacafé, one
★ of Santa Fe's vanguard "food as art" restaurants, two blocks north of the Plaza in the historic Padre Gallegos House. Seasonal ingredients, like locally harvested fresh porcini mushrooms, are included in the inventive dishes. The shrimp and spinach dumplings and shiitake mushrooms and cactus spring rolls are particularly good. The patio is a joy in summer. ⊠ *231 Washington Ave.,* ☏ *505/984–1788. AE, MC, V.*

$$$–$$$$ ✕ **Ore House on the Plaza.** Popular more for its perfect location overlooking the Plaza than for its cuisine, this restaurant serves salmon, swordfish, lobster, ceviche, and steaks that are adequate if uninspired. The specialty margaritas, though, are anything but ordinary: they come in more than 80 flavors, from cool watermelon to zippy jalapeño. ⊠ *50 Lincoln Ave., upstairs on the southwest corner of the Plaza,* ☏ *505/983–8687. AE, MC, V.*

$$$–$$$$ ✕ **Ristra.** Continental dishes receive Southwestern accents here—mussels in chipotle-and-mint broth, rack of lamb with creamed garlic potatoes, and perfectly grilled salmon. The wines are well selected and the service is swift and courteous. Navajo blankets hang on stark white walls, and Pueblo pottery adorns the handful of niches. ⊠ *548 Agua Fria St., near the Railyard District,* ☏ *505/982–8608. AE, MC, V. No lunch.*

Eclectic

$$$–$$$$ ✕ **Pink Adobe.** Rosalea Murphey opened her restaurant back in 1944,
★ and the place still seems to reflect a time when fewer than 20,000 people lived in town. The intimate, rambling rooms have fireplaces and artwork and are filled with conversation made over special-occasion meals. The ambience of the restaurant, rather than the food, accounts for much of its popularity. The steak Dunnigan, smothered in green chile and mushrooms, and the savory shrimp Louisianne—fat and deep-fried crispy—are among the Continental, New Orleans Creole, and New Mexican dishes served. The apple pie drenched in rum sauce is a favorite. Particularly strong margaritas are mixed in the adjacent Dragon Room bar. Reser-

vations are essential for dinner during the summer. ⊠ *406 Old Santa Fe Trail,* ☎ *505/983–7712. AE, D, DC, MC, V. No lunch weekends.*

French

$$$–$$$$ ✕ **Rociada.** Country French has arrived in Santa Fe with this intimate bistro, which opened in 2000. Fresh ingredients are used for the Provençal specialties, including a delicious onion soup *velouté,* which combines five types of onions in a light cream and vegetable broth base. Another specialty is the chilled bisque of crawfish and corn. The list of French wines is extensive. ⊠ *304 Johnson St.,* ☎ *505/983–3800. AE, D, MC, V. Closed Mon. No lunch.*

Indian

$$ ✕ **India Palace.** East Indian cuisine was utterly foreign to most locals before the arrival of India Palace, but many Santa Feans have since become devotees of chef Bal Dev Singh's spicy dishes. The serene deep-pink interior sets the scene for tender tandoori chicken and lamb and superb curried seafood and vegetables. Meals are cooked as hot or mild as you wish, and vegetarian dishes are prepared. For lunch, try the Indian buffet to sample some of their staple dishes. ⊠ *227 Don Gaspar Ave., at the rear of the El Centro shopping center,* ☎ *505/986–5859. AE, D, MC, V.*

Italian

$$–$$$ ✕ **Andiamo.** Produce from the Farmers' Market across the street adds to the seasonal surprises of this intimate restaurant inspired by northern Italian cuisine. Fresh ingredients, natural meats, and homemade desserts are guaranteed. Try the crispy polenta with rosemary and Gorgonzola sauce for an appetizer and, if you want to go casual, a pizza or, for heartier fare, the linguine puttanesca with grilled tuna. ⊠ *322 Garfield St., near the Railyard District,* ☎ *505/995–9595. AE, DC, MC, V. Closed Tues. Oct.–May. No lunch.*

$$–$$$ ✕ **Il Piatto.** Creative pasta dishes like risotto with duck, artichoke, and truffle oil and homemade pumpkin ravioli grace the menu here. Entrées include pancetta-wrapped trout and roast chicken with Italian sausage. ⊠ *95 W. Marcy St.,* ☎ *505/984–1091. AE, MC, V. No lunch weekends.*

$$ ✕ **Pranzo Italian Grill.** Northern Italy with a touch of cream is the signature of the pastas on the menu. Try the *frito misto* (fried scallops, shrimp, and calamari with marinara sauce—plenty for two to three people). There's a large variety of individually sized, thin-crust pizzas, as well as mixed green salads. Upstairs, full meals are served on the rooftop terrace overlooking the Railyard area. You can hear the church bells ringing if you happen to be dining around 6 PM. ⊠ *540 Montezuma Ave., Railyard District,* ☎ *505/984–2645. AE, DC, MC, V. No lunch Sun.*

Japanese

$$–$$$ ✕ **Shohko.** Tasty tempura—including a Southwestern variation made with green chile—and more than 35 kinds of sushi are served at this small Japanese restaurant. At the 16-seat sushi bar you can watch the masters at work. ⊠ *321 Johnson St.,* ☎ *505/983–7288. AE, D, MC, V. No lunch weekends.*

Latin

$$$$ ✕ **Cafe Pasqual's.** A block southwest of the Plaza, this cheerful cub-
★   byhole dishes up regional and Latin American specialties for break-fast, lunch, and dinner. Don't be discouraged by lines out in front—it's

worth the wait. The culinary muse behind it all is Katharine Kagel, who for more than 20 years has been introducing specialties like Huevos Motuleños (a concoction of black beans and eggs over a blue corn tortilla, topped with tomatillo sauce and goat cheese) to diners. Dinner is a more formal affair, with Latin meals joined by Asian and French entrées. The Plato Supremo includes a taco of citrus-garlic shrimp, chicken mole puebla, rice, and exotic salad. Mexican folk art and colorful tiles and murals by Oaxacan artist Leo Vigildo Martinez create a festive atmosphere. Try the communal table if you want to be seated in a hurry. Reservations are accepted for dinner. ⊠ *121 Don Gaspar Ave.,* ☎ *505/983–9340 or 800/722–7672. AE, MC, V.*

$$–$$$ ✕ **Los Mayas.** Owners Fernando Antillas and Reyes Solano brought the spirit of Latin America with them when they opened this restaurant in 1998. They've transformed a nondescript building into a cozy setting with a patio. The menu offers a taste of the Americas. Try the enchilada banana, a baked plantain served with mole. There is music every night, including a harp player from Paraguay and a rollicking accordion player from Santa Fe. Ask Fernando to sing—he has a voice that harks back to old Mexico. ⊠ *409 W. Water St., at northwest corner of intersection with Guadalupe St.,* ☎ *505/986–9930. AE, D, MC, V. No lunch Oct.–Apr..*

Mediterranean

$$–$$$ ✕ **Whistling Moon Cafe.** Unusual spices scent the Mediterranean fare, which includes pasta calamari, Greek salad, a Middle Eastern sampler, and grilled duck. The coriander-cumin fries are irresistible, as is the homemade Greek honey cheesecake. Although the small ocher dining room with red Moroccan weavings is a touch noisy, the food and prices more than make up for it. On weekends a brunch of traditional standards like eggs Benedict and omelets is served. There's also patio dining. ⊠ *402 N. Guadalupe St.,* ☎ *505/983–3093. Reservations essential for 6 or more. MC, V.*

Mexican

$$–$$$ ✕ **Guadalupe Cafe.** Come to this informal café for hefty servings of New Mexican favorites like enchiladas and quesadillas, topped off with *sopaipillas* (fluffy fried bread). The seasonal raspberry pancakes are one of many breakfast favorites. ⊠ *422 Old Santa Fe Trail,* ☎ *505/ 982–9762. Reservations not accepted. AE, D, DC, MC, V.*

$$–$$$ ✕ **Maria's New Mexican Kitchen.** Maria's is proud to serve a walloping 80 kinds of tequila, and Jose Cuervo is the low end of the high-quality offerings. All but six of the tequilas are 100% agave. Diners enjoy their margaritas with basic dishes like rellenos, enchiladas, and *carne adovada* (red chile–marinated pork) and, on occasion, to the serenades of strolling guitarists. ⊠ *555 W. Cordova Rd.,* ☎ *505/983–7929. AE, D, DC, MC, V.*

$$–$$$ ✕ **Old Mexico Grill.** For a taste of Old Mexico in New Mexico, sam-
★ ple dishes like *arracheras* (the traditional name for fajitas) and tacos *al carbón* (shredded pork cooked in a mole sauce and folded into corn tortillas). Start the meal with a fresh ceviche appetizer and a cool lime margarita. The location in a shopping center makes parking a snap. ⊠ *2434 Cerrillos Rd., College Plaza S,* ☎ *505/473–0338. Reservations not accepted. D, MC, V. No lunch weekends.*

Southwestern

$$$$ ✕ **Anasazi.** Soft light illuminates the stone and adobe interior of this restaurant, which became a Santa Fe fixture the day it opened. Chef Randall Warder combines New Mexican and Native American flavors

to produce exotic fare like flat bread with fire-roasted sweet peppers, and cinnamon-chile filet mignon chop. The large dining room has wooden tables and *bancos* (benches built into the plastered walls) upholstered with handwoven textiles from Chimayó. Groups of up to 12 can dine in the private wine cellar, and groups of up to 40 can be served in the romantic library. If you don't want to invest in dinner, try a delicious breakfast. The Sunday brunch is excellent. ⊠ *113 Washington Ave.*, ☎ *505/988–3236. AE, D, DC, MC, V.*

$$$$ ✕ **La Casa Sena.** The Southwestern and Continental fare served at La Casa Sena is rich and beautifully presented. Weather permitting, get a table on the patio surrounded by hollyhocks, flowering shrubs, and centuries-old adobe walls. If you order the *trucha en terra-cotta* (fresh trout wrapped in corn husks and baked in clay), ask your waiter to save the clay head for you as a souvenir. Finish dinner with the wonderful citrus mascarpone tart with orange sauce and Grand Marnier–soaked berries. Weekend brunch dishes are equally elegant. For a musical meal (evenings only), sit in the restaurant's adjacent Cantina, where the talented staff belt out Broadway show tunes. Meals in the Cantina are less expensive, and less exciting. Reservations are essential in summer. ⊠ *Sena Plaza, 125 E. Palace Ave.*, ☎ *505/988–9232. AE, D, DC, MC, V.*

$–$$$ ✕ **Cowgirl.** Part restaurant, part bar, part museum, and part theater, this Western grill serves Texas-style barbecue, good New Mexican fare, hybrid Southwestern dishes such as grilled-salmon soft tacos, and butternut-squash casserole. In summer you can dine on tree-shaded patios and kids can eat in the Corral, a special area with its own menu. After dinner there's entertainment—blues and rock bands, singer-songwriters, or comedians. Brunch is served on weekends. ⊠ *319 S. Guadalupe St.*, ☎ *505/982–2565. AE, D, MC, V.*

$$–$$$ ✕ **The Shed.** The lines at lunch attest to the status of this downtown New Mexican eatery. The rambling adobe dating from 1692 is decorated with folk art, and service is downright neighborly. Even if you're a devoted green chile fan, try the locally grown red chile the place is famous for. Specialties include red-chile enchiladas, green-chile stew with potatoes and pork, *posole* (soup made with lime hominy, pork, chile, and garlic), and charbroiled Shedburgers. The homemade desserts are fabulous. Now there's a full bar too. Reservations are accepted only for parties of six or more. ⊠ *113½ E. Palace Ave.*, ☎ *505/982–9030. AE, DC, MC, V. Closed Sun. No dinner Mon.–Wed.*

Spanish

$$–$$$ ✕ **El Farol.** In this crossover cuisine town, owner David Salazar sums up his food in one word: "Spanish." Order a classic entrée like paella or make a meal from the 20 different tapas—from tiny fried squid to wild mushrooms. Dining is indoors and outdoors. Touted as the oldest restaurant and cantina in Santa Fe, El Farol (built in 1835) has a relaxed ambience, a unique blend of the Western frontier and contemporary Santa Fe. People push back the chairs and start dancing at around 9:30. The bar is smoky and noisy but unnoticeable from the back dining room thanks to the ventilating system and thick adobe walls. ⊠ *808 Canyon Rd.*, ☎ *505/983–9912. D, DC, MC, V.*

LODGING

In Santa Fe you can ensconce yourself in quintessential Santa Fe style or anonymous hotel-chain decor, depending on how much you want to spend. Cheaper motels and hotels are on Cerrillos (pronounced sah-*ree*-yos) Road—Santa Fe's strip of could-be-anywhere fast-food and lodging chains. Enchantment and prices rise the closer you get to the

Plaza. There are also many bed-and-breakfasts and campgrounds. Even if you are 5 mi from the Plaza, getting around is easy by bus or car. Rates become lower in the off-season, from November to April (excluding Thanksgiving and Christmas).

Downtown Santa Fe

$$$$ 🏨 **Campanilla Compound.** If you want to feel like a Santa Fean living on prime, downtown real estate, stay at this private, tastefully decorated compound. Each unit has its own small courtyard with barbecue grill, landscaping, wood or tile floors, high ceilings, fabulous light, and a fireplace. It's ideal for families and groups—there's a full kitchen and washer and dryer. Each one-bedroom unit sleeps up to four people, two-bedroom units up to six. This privacy and spaciousness are a pleasant five-block walk from the Plaza. There's a two-night minimum stay, and a $50 cleaning fee is added to the room charge. ⊠ *334 Otero St., 87501,* ☎ *505/988–7585 or 800/828–9700. 15 units. Outdoor hot tub. AE, MC, V.*

$$$$ 🏨 **Eldorado Hotel.** The city's largest hotel, a too-modern affair for some, is in the heart of downtown, close to the Plaza. Rooms are stylishly furnished with carved Southwestern-style desks and chairs, large upholstered club chairs, and art prints. Many rooms have terraces or kiva-style fireplaces. Baths are spacious and completely tiled. The Old House restaurant (☞ *Dining, above*) is highly rated. There's music nightly, from classical Spanish guitar to piano, in the comfortable lobby lounge. ⊠ *309 W. San Francisco St., 87501,* ☎ *505/988–4455 or 800/955–4455,* FAX *505/995–4543. 201 rooms, 18 suites, 55 casitas, 8 condos. 2 restaurants, bar, lounge, pool, hot tub, sauna, health club, shops, concierge, convention center, meeting rooms, parking (fee). AE, D, DC, MC, V.* 🐾

$$$$ 🏨 **Hilton of Santa Fe.** While this hotel claims to offer a Santa Fe experience, once you leave the lobby, which displays tasteful Santa Fe style, most of the rooms look like anywhere U.S.A. You'll get predictable, dependable Hilton service, but not much imagination or magic. ⊠ *100 Sandoval St., 87501,* ☎ *505/988–2811 or 800/221–2424,* FAX *505/986–6435. 157 rooms. Restaurant, bar, lounge, pool, hot tub, concierge, parking (fee). AE, D, DC, MC, V.* 🐾

$$$$ 🏨 **Hotel Loretto.** Formerly known as the Inn at Loretto, the Pueblo-style hotel attracts a loyal clientele year after year, many of whom swear by the friendly, outstanding service they receive. The lobby opens up to the gardens and pool, and leather couches and high-end architectural details make the hotel a pleasure to relax in. The restaurant Nellie's serves new American cuisine with plenty of meats and seafood. Next door is the Loretto Chapel. ⊠ *211 Old Santa Fe Trail, 87501,* ☎ *505/988–5531, 800/727–5531 outside NM;* FAX *505/984–7988. 140 rooms, 5 suites. Restaurant, lounge, pool, shops. AE, D, DC, MC, V.* 🐾

$$$$ 🏨 **Hotel Santa Fe.** Picurís Pueblo maintains the controlling interest in this Pueblo-style three-story hotel. Rooms and suites are done in traditional Southwestern style, with locally handmade furniture, wooden blinds, and Pueblo paintings (*Picurís* means "those who paint"), many by Gerald Nailor. The hotel gift shop, the only tribally owned store in Santa Fe, has lower prices than many nearby retail stores. The Corn Dance Cafe serves Native American cuisine with a nouvelle twist. Guests can learn about Native American history and culture from informal talks held in the lobby by Alan Osbourne, an extremely well versed scholar. Native American dances take place May through October. ⊠ *1501 Paseo de Peralta, 87505,* ☎ *505/982–1200, 800/825–9876 outside NM;* FAX *505/983–0785. 40 rooms, 91 suites. Restaurant, pool, outdoor hot tub. AE, D, DC, MC, V.* 🐾

Santa Fe Lodging

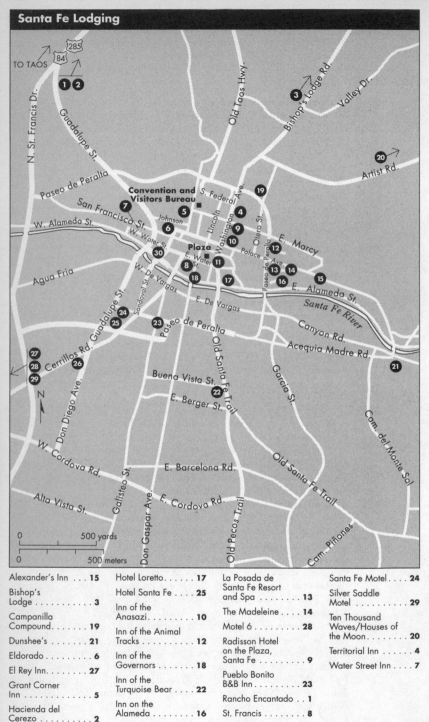

$$$$ ⊡ **Inn of the Anasazi.** In the heart of downtown, this hotel is one of
★ Santa Fe's finest, with superb craftsmanship in every architectural de-
tail. Each room has a beamed ceiling, kiva-style fireplace, and handcrafted furniture. Amenities include attentive concierge services,
twice-daily maid service, room delivery of exercise bikes upon request,
and a library with books on New Mexico and the Southwest. The
Anasazi restaurant (☞ Dining, *above*) serves contemporary cuisine with
uniquely regional accents. ⊠ *113 Washington Ave., 87501,* ☎ *505/
988–3030 or 800/688–8100,* FAX *505/988–3277. 59 rooms. Restaurant,
in-room safes, minibars, in-room VCRs. AE, D, DC, MC, V.* ❧

$$$$ ⊡ **Inn of the Governors.** The intimate lobby and gracious service at
this hotel two blocks from the Plaza will quickly make you feel at home.
The standard rooms have a Mexican theme, with bright colors, hand-
painted folk art, Southwestern fabrics, and handmade furnishings;
deluxe rooms also have balconies and fireplaces. New Mexican dishes
and lighter fare like wood-oven pizzas are served in the dining room.
⊠ *234 Don Gaspar Ave., 87501,* ☎ *505/982–4333 or 800/234–4534,*
FAX *505/989–9149. 100 rooms. Dining room, piano bar, pool, free
parking. AE, D, DC, MC, V.* ❧

$$$$ ⊡ **Inn on the Alameda.** Between the Plaza and Canyon Road is one
of the city's best small hotels. Alameda means "tree-lined lane," and
this one perfectly complements the inn's riverside location. The adobe
architecture and enclosed courtyards combine a relaxed New Mexico
country atmosphere with the luxury and amenities of a top-notch
hotel. Rooms have a Southwestern color scheme, handmade armoires
and headboards, and ceramic lamps and tiles. ⊠ *303 E. Alameda St.,
87501,* ☎ *505/984–2121 or 800/289–2122,* FAX *505/986–8325. 59
rooms, 10 suites. Bar, refrigerators, 2 hot tubs, exercise room. AE, D,
DC, MC, V. CP.* ❧

$$$$ ⊡ **La Fonda.** A rich history and charm are more prevalent in this sole
Plaza-front hotel than first-class service and amenities. The present structure, built in 1922 and enlarged many times, captures the essence of
authentic Santa Fe style—the Pueblo-inspired architecture that defines
the town today. Antiques and Native American art decorate the tiled
lobby, and each room has hand-decorated wood furniture, wrought-
iron light fixtures, and beamed ceilings. Some of the suites have fireplaces. There are 14 rooms for environmentally sensitive guests. La
Plazuela Restaurant, with its hand-painted glass tiles, is a joy to sit in,
but the food is disappointing. Folk and Latin jazz bands rotate nightly
in the bar. ⊠ *100 E. San Francisco St., 87501,* ☎ *505/982–5511, 800/
523–5002 outside NM;* FAX *505/988–2952. 143 rooms, 24 suites.
Restaurant, bar, pool, 2 hot tubs, massage, meeting rooms, parking (fee).
AE, D, DC, MC, V.* ❧

$$$$ ⊡ **La Posada de Santa Fe Resort and Spa.** In 1999 new owners un-
dertook a massive renovation, transforming the *Posada* (shelter) into
an upscale, valet-parking-only hotel. Unfortunately, gone are the gardens that once made this an oasis from the rest of downtown, but there
is a bellhop around every corner. The decor is stunning—many rooms
have fireplaces, beamed ceilings, and Native American rugs. The restaurant Fuego specializes in rotisserie dishes from around the world. The
resort and spa amenities are supported by on-site body treatment staff.
⊠ *330 E. Palace Ave., 87501,* ☎ *505/986–0000 or 800/727–5276,*
FAX *505/982–6850. 120 rooms, 38 suites. Restaurant, bar, pool, spa,
parking (fee). AE, D, DC, MC, V.* ❧

$$$$ ⊡ **Territorial Inn.** Creature comforts are a high priority at this 1890s
brick structure, set back off a busy downtown street two blocks from
the Plaza. The well-maintained rooms have Victorian decor; No. 9 has
a canopy bed and a fireplace. Afternoon treats and brandy-and-cookie
nightcaps are among the extras. ⊠ *215 Washington Ave., 87501,* ☎

505/989–7737, FAX *505/984–8682. 10 rooms, 8 with bath, 2 with shared bath. Hot tub, free parking. AE, DC, MC, V. CP.* 🐾

$$$$ 🏨 **Water Street Inn.** The large rooms in this restored adobe 2½ blocks
★   from the Plaza are decorated with reed shutters, antique pine beds, hand-stenciled artwork, and a blend of cowboy, Hispanic, and Native American art and artifacts. Most have fireplaces; all have private baths, VCRs, cable TV, and voice mail. Afternoon hors d'oeuvres are served in the living room. A patio deck is available for relaxing. ⊠ *427 W. Water St., 87501,* ☎ *505/984–1193 or 800/646–6752. 12 rooms. In-room VCRs, outdoor hot tub, free parking. AE, DC, MC, V. CP.* 🐾

$$$–$$$$ 🏨 **Grant Corner Inn.** Though this B&B is downtown, the surrounding small garden and Victorian porch shaded by a huge weeping willow make it feel private. Antique Spanish and American country furnishings share space with potted greens and knickknacks. Room accents include old-fashioned fixtures, quilts, and Native American blankets. The ample breakfast, which is open to the public, includes home-baked breads and pastries, jellies, and blue-corn waffles. A separate hacienda, located six blocks north, can accommodate groups of up to seven people. It is connected via intercom to the inn, and guests are entitled to all of the inn's amenities, including free parking at the downtown location. ⊠ *122 Grant Ave., 87501,* ☎ *505/983–6678,* FAX *505/983–1526. 8 rooms, 2 rooms in hacienda. Breakfast room, free parking. DC, MC, V. BP.* 🐾

$$–$$$$ 🏨 **Alexander's Inn.** This two-story 1903 Craftsman-style house in the
★   Eastside residential area, a few blocks from the Plaza and Canyon Road, exudes the charm of an old country inn. Rooms have American country–style wooden furnishings and flower arrangements. There are also two two-story cottages with kitchens—perfect for groups (☞ The Madeleine, *below*). ⊠ *529 E. Palace Ave., 87501,* ☎ *505/986–1431. 5 rooms, 2 with shared bath; 2 cottages. Outdoor hot tub. D, DC, MC, V. CP.* 🐾

$$–$$$$ 🏨 **Inn of the Turquoise Bear.** In the 1920s, poet Witter Bynner played host to an eccentric circle of artists and intellectuals, as well as some wild parties in this mid-19th-century adobe home. The rooms in the rambling B&B are simple—no oversize televisions or big hotel trimmings, but there's plenty of ambience and a ranchlike lobby where you can stretch out or converse with other guests. You might sleep in the room where D. H. Lawrence and Frieda slept, or perhaps Robert Oppenheimer's room. The terraced flower gardens have plenty of places to repose, away from the traffic on Old Santa Fe Trail, which borders the property. ⊠ *342 E. Buena Vista, 87504,* ☎ *505/983–0798 or 800/396–4104. 8 rooms, 2 with shared bath; 2 suites. AE, D, MC, V. CP.* 🐾

$$–$$$$ 🏨 **The Madeleine.** Carolyn Lee, who owns Alexander's Inn (☞ *above*), has named her successful establishments after her children. The Madeleine is the only Queen Anne house in the city, three blocks east of the Plaza in a quiet garden setting. The public rooms are open, sunny, and genuine Queen Anne style, with fruit bowls, original and fantastically futuristic stained-glass windows, lace curtains, and fresh-cut flowers. You'll feel as if you've made a genteel step back in time. Rooms in the main home are furnished in ornate late-19th-century fashion. ⊠ *106 Faithway St., 87501,* ☎ *505/982–3465 or 888/321–5123,* FAX *505/982–8572. 6 rooms, 2 cottages. AE, D, MC, V. BP.* 🐾

$$$ 🏨 **Dunshee's.** So romantic that its patio has been used for weddings, this B&B is in the quiet Eastside area, a mile from the Plaza, where the oldest stone irrigation ditch still runs with water in spring and summer. Acequia Madre (Mother Ditch) is one of the oldest and most enchanting roads in Santa Fe (it runs parallel to Canyon Road). The suite is the restored adobe home of artist Susan Dunshee, the proprietor; the adobe casita is good for families. The suite has a living room, a bedroom with a queen bed, kiva-style fireplaces, and viga ceilings and is decorated with antiques and works by area artists. The casita has two bedrooms, a living room, a patio, a completely equipped and stocked kitchen, and a kiva-style fireplace and is adorned with decorative linens and folk art. ✉ *986 Acequia Madre, 87501,* ☎ *505/982–0988. 1 suite, 1 small house. MC, V. BP in suite, CP in casita.* ✎

$$$ ☷ **Pueblo Bonito B&B Inn.** Rooms in this adobe compound built in 1873 have handmade and hand-painted furnishings, Navajo weavings, sand paintings and pottery, locally carved *santos,* and Western art. All have kiva fireplaces, and many have kitchens. Breakfast is served in the main dining room. Afternoon tea also offers complimentary margaritas. The Plaza is a five-minute walk away. ✉ *138 W. Manhattan Ave., 87501,* ☎ *505/984–8001 or 800/461–4599,* ℻ *505/984–3155. 11 rooms, 7 suites. Dining room, hot tub, coin laundry. AE, DC, MC, V. CP.* ✎

$$$ ☷ **Radisson Hotel & Suites on the Plaza, Santa Fe.** The rooms at the handsome, brick-trimmed, Territorial-style hotel, formerly the Plaza Real, have maintained their charm, despite incorporation into a large chain. All rooms are off an interior brick courtyard. Handcrafted Southwestern furniture decorates the large rooms, and most have patios or balconies and wood-burning fireplaces. ✉ *125 Washington Ave., 87501,* ☎ *505/988–4900 or 800/537–8483,* ℻ *505/983–9322. 13 rooms, 43 suites. Breakfast room, lounge. AE, D, DC, MC, V.* ✎

$$–$$$ ☷ **Inn of the Animal Tracks.** This restored Pueblo-style home three blocks east of the Plaza has beamed ceilings, hardwood floors, handcrafted furniture, and fireplaces. Each guest room is decorated with an animal theme, such as Soaring Eagle or Gentle Deer. On the cutsey side, the Whimsical Rabbit Room is filled with stuffed and terra-cotta rabbit statues, rabbit books, rabbit drawings. Bunny-rabbit slippers are under the bed. (This room opens directly onto the kitchen, where the cook arrives at 6 AM.) The backyard is delightful. The inn is on the curve of a busy road that loops around the historic center of town—somewhat noisy, but ideal for access to both the Plaza and Canyon Road. ✉ *707 Paseo de Peralta, 87504,* ☎ *505/988–1546,* ℻ *505/982–8098. 5 rooms. AE, MC, V. BP.*

$$–$$$ ☷ **St. Francis.** Listed in the National Register of Historic Places, this three-story building, parts of which were constructed in 1920, has walkways lined with turn-of-the-20th-century lampposts and is just one block south of the Plaza. The simple and elegant rooms with high ceilings, casement windows, brass-and-iron beds, marble and cherry antiques, and original artworks suggest a refined establishment, but the service has been known to fall short. Afternoon tea, with scones and finger sandwiches, is served daily (not complimentary) in the huge lobby, which rises 50 ft from a floor of blood-red tiles. The St. Francis Club, which has a very English feel, serves Continental fare. The hotel bar is among the few places in town where you can grab a bite to eat until midnight. ✉ *210 Don Gaspar Ave., 87501,* ☎ *505/983–5700 or 800/529–5700,* ℻ *505/989–7690. 83 rooms. Restaurant, bar, free parking. AE, D, DC, MC, V.* ✎

Cerrillos Road

$$ ☷ **El Rey Inn.** The tree-shaded, whitewashed El Rey has been a Santa Fe landmark motel for 65 years. Rooms are decorated in Southwestern, Spanish colonial, and Victorian style. Some have kitchenettes and fireplaces. The largest suite, with seven rooms, sleeps six and has antique furniture, a full kitchen, a breakfast nook, and two patios. Service is friendly. ✉ *1862 Cerrillos Rd., 87501,* ☎ *505/982–1931 or 800/ 521–1349,* ℻ *505/989–9249. 79 rooms, 8 suites. Kitchenettes, pool, 2 hot tubs, sauna, playground, coin laundry. AE, DC, MC, V. CP.*

$$ ⌂ **Santa Fe Budget Inn.** On the southern edge of the Railyard District, this inn offers affordable comfort and standard Southwestern decor within walking distance of the Plaza (six blocks). Special packages are available for three- and four-day stays during peak-season events such as Indian Market (☞ Festival and Seasonal Events *in* Chapter 1). Full breakfast is complimentary during off-season. ⊠ *725 Cerrillos Rd., 87501,* ☎ *505/982–5952,* ℻ *505/984–8879. 160 rooms. 2 restaurants, pool. AE, DC, MC, V. CP.* ✎

$$ ⌂ **Santa Fe Motel.** Walking-distance proximity to the Plaza is a prime asset of this property—an unusually successful upgrade of a standard motel. Rooms, some with kitchenettes, are decorated in contemporary Southwestern style. ⊠ *510 Cerrillos Rd., 87501,* ☎ *505/982–1039 or 800/999–1039,* ℻ *505/986–1275. 13 rooms, 8 casitas. Kitchenettes (some). AE, D, MC, V.* ✎

$ ⌂ **Motel 6.** The amenities at this well-maintained chain property several miles from the Plaza include an outdoor pool, free HBO, and free local calls. Those under 17 stay free with their parents. ⊠ *3007 Cerrillos Rd., 87505,* ☎ *505/473–1380,* ℻ *505/473–7784. 104 rooms. Pool. AE, DC, MC, V.*

$ ⌂ **Silver Saddle Motel.** If you want a taste of late 1950s Western kitsch, try this motel, built when Cerrillos Road was the main route to Albuquerque and the village of Cerrillos. Some of the rooms have kitchenettes and adjoining open carports: nothing fancy, but very nostalgic. It's next door to the Mexican-style market Jackalope (☞ Home Furnishings, *in* Shopping, *below*), which has a café. ⊠ *2810 Cerrillos Rd., 87505,* ☎ *505/471–7663,* ℻ *505/471–1066. 27 rooms with bath or shower. Kitchenettes (some). DC, MC, V.* ✎

North of Santa Fe

$$$$ ⌂ **Bishop's Lodge.** This resort established in 1918 is in a bucolic val-
★ ley at the foot of the Sangre de Cristo Mountains and yet only a five-minute drive from the Plaza. Behind the main building is an exquisite chapel that was once the private retreat of Archbishop Jean Baptiste Lamy. Outdoor activities include horseback riding, organized trail riding (with meals) into the adjacent national forest, skeet-shooting, and trapshooting. At press time, indoor exercise facilities were being expanded and rooms added. The two lodge buildings have antique Southwestern furnishings—shipping chests, tinwork from Mexico, and Native American and Western art. The restaurant serves a Continental menu with a Southwestern touch. A bountiful brunch, probably the best in Santa Fe, is served on Sunday. ⊠ *Bishop's Lodge Rd., 2½ mi north of downtown, 87501,* ☎ *505/983–6377 or 800/732–2240,* ℻ *505/989–8739. 70 rooms, 18 suites. Restaurant, bar, pool, hot tub, spa, 4 tennis courts, exercise room, hiking, horseback riding, fishing, airport shuttle. AE, D, MC, V.* ✎

$$$$ ⌂ **Hacienda del Cerezo.** Stop reading here if $600 is more than you
★ want to spend on a room. Keep in mind that the rate includes three meals for two people prepared by a master chef; dinner is a five-course candlelit affair in the great room or in the courtyard, looking out onto the vanishing-edge pool and the desert beyond. The inn sits on a splendidly isolated patch of land 25 minutes northwest of downtown. Rooms are subtly executed in prints, ornaments, carvings on the beams of the viga ceilings, and etchings in the glass shower doors. Each room has a king-size bed, a generous sitting area, a kiva fireplace, an enclosed patio, and a view of the mountains. Service is gracious and understated. ⊠ *100 Camino del Cerezo, 87501,* ☎ *505/982–8000 or 888/982–8001,* ℻ *505/983–7162. 10 rooms. Dining room, pool, outdoor hot tub, tennis court, hiking, horseback riding. FAP. AE.*

$$$$ ⊡ **Rancho Encantado.** Robert Redford, Johnny Cash, Robert Plant, and
★   the Dalai Lama are among the past guests of this resort on 168 acres.
The accommodations have Southwestern-style furniture, handmade and
hand-painted, in addition to fine Spanish and Western pieces from the
1850s and earlier. Some of the villas and rooms have fireplaces, private patios, and tiled floors; others have carpeting and refrigerators.
The dining room, with a terrific view of the Jemez Mountains, serves
good Continental fare. ⊠ *198 State Rd. 592, 8 mi north of Santa Fe
off U.S. 84/285 near Tesuque, 87501,* ☎ *505/982–3537 or 800/722–
9339,* ℻ *505/983–8269. 29 rooms, 22 villas. Dining room, pool, outdoor hot tub, 2 tennis courts, hiking. AE, D, DC, MC, V.* ☜

$$$–$$$$ ⊡ **Ten Thousand Waves/Houses of the Moon.** The Zenlike atmosphere
of this Japanese-style health spa and resort above town offers an East-
meets-West retreat for adults. Eight small hillside houses are reached
by a path through the piñons. All have brick floors, marble fireplaces,
fine woodwork, futon beds, and adobe-color walls; two come with full
kitchens. The ambience is suited toward organic rather than antiseptic
taste. The facility has private and communal indoor and outdoor hot
tubs and spa treatments. Tubs run from $19 to $26 per hour; massage
and spa treatments cost from $35 to $120. Overnight guests can use
the communal mens's and women's hot tubs free of charge. The health
bar serves sushi. ⊠ *Box 10200, 87504, 4 mi from the Plaza on road
to Santa Fe Ski Basin,* ☎ *505/982–9304,* ℻ *505/989–5077. 8 cabins.
9 outdoor hot tubs, massage, spa, gift shop, snack bar. D, MC, V.* ☜

Campgrounds

The Santa Fe National Forest is right in the city's backyard and includes
the Dome Wilderness (5,200 acres in the volcanically formed Jemez
Mountains) and the Pecos Wilderness (223,333 acres of high moun-
tains, forests, and meadows at the southern end of the Rocky Moun-
tain chain). Public campsites are open from May to October, and all
the ones listed here have hot showers.

For a report on general conditions, call the **Santa Fe National Forest
Office** (⊠ 1220 S. St. Francis Dr. [Box 1689], 87504, ☎ 505/438–7840).
For a one-stop shop for information about public lands, which includes
national and state parks, contact the **New Mexico Public Lands Infor-
mation Center** (⊠ 1474 Rodeo Rd. 87505, ☎ 505/438–7542, ℻ 505/
438–7582, ☜) on the south side of Santa Fe. It has maps, reference
materials, licenses, permits—just about everything you need to plan a
trip into the New Mexican wilderness.

⚠ **Babbitt's Los Campos RV Resort.** The only full-service RV park within
the city limits, Los Campos even has a swimming pool. There's a car
dealership on one side and open vistas on the other: poplars and Rus-
sian olive trees, a dry riverbed, and mountains rise in the background.
The fee per night is $25. ⊠ *3574 Cerrillos Rd., 87505,* ☎ *505/473–
1949. 94 RV sites. Rest rooms, showers, pool. MC, V.*

⚠ **Rancheros de Santa Fe Campground.** This camping park is on a
hill in the midst of a piñon forest. You can get LP gas service here. Tent
sites are $16.95, water and electric hookups $20.95, full hookups
$23.95–$24.95, and cabins $31.95. ⊠ *On I–25N, Old Las Vegas
Hwy. (Exit 290 on the Las Vegas Hwy., 10½ mi from the Plaza),
87505,* ☎ *505/466–3482. 95 RV sites, 37 tent sites. Rest rooms, show-
ers, grocery, pool, coin laundry. MC, V. Nov.–Feb. 28.*

⚠ **Santa Fe KOA.** In the foothills of the Sangre de Cristo Mountains,
20 minutes southeast of Santa Fe, this large campground is covered
with piñons, cedars, and junipers. Tent sites are $17.95, water and elec-

tric hookups $21.95, full hookups $23.95, and cabins $31.95. ⊠ *Old Las Vegas Hwy. (NM 3), (Box 95-A), 87505,* ☎ *505/466–1419. 44 RV sites, 26 tent sites, 10 cabins. Rest rooms, showers, LP gas, grocery, recreation room, coin laundry. D, MC, V. Closed Nov.–Feb.*

NIGHTLIFE AND THE ARTS

Santa Fe is perhaps America's most cultured small city. Gallery openings, poetry readings, plays, and dance concerts take place year-round, not to mention the famed opera and chamber-music festivals. Check the arts and entertainment listings in Santa Fe's daily newspaper, the *New Mexican,* particularly on Friday, when the arts and entertainment section, *Pasatiempo,* is included, or check the weekly *Santa Fe Reporter* for shows and events. Activities peak in the summer.

Nightlife

A handful of bars have spirited entertainment, from flamenco dancing to smokin' bands. Austin-based blues and country groups and other acts wander into town, and members of blockbuster bands have been known to perform unannounced at small clubs while vacationing in the area. But on most nights your best bet might be quiet cocktails beside the flickering embers of a piñon fire or under the stars out on the patio. Mellow entertainers perform nightly in many hotel bars. There is always one nightclub in town hosting rock-and-roll, swing, or Latin music.

Catamount Bar (⊠ 125 E. Water St., ☎ 505/988–7222) is popular with the post-college set; jazz and blues/rock groups play on weekends and some weeknights. The dance floor isn't great—too small, and with bright lights.

Club Alegría (⊠ Agua Fria Rd., just south of Siler Rd., ☎ 505/471–2324) is the venue for Friday-night salsa dance parties. Father Frank Pretto, known as the Salsa Priest (a genuine Catholic priest), and his very hot salsa band, Pretto and Parranda, pour out salsa, boleros, rhumba, and merengue in the mirrored dance hall–bar. Security is in force, and the crowd is friendly, so don't be intimidated by the location. Free dance lessons start at 8. Blues, Mexican songs, and oldies are performed other nights of the week.

Dragon Room (⊠ 406 Old Santa Fe Trail, ☎ 505/983–7712) at the Pink Adobe restaurant has been the place to see and be seen in Santa Fe for decades; flamenco and other light musical fare entertain at the packed bar.

Eldorado Hotel (⊠ 309 W. San Francisco St., ☎ 505/988–4455) has a gracious lobby lounge where classical guitarists and pianists perform nightly.

El Farol (⊠ 808 Canyon Rd., ☎ 505/983–9912) restaurant is where locals like to hang out in an old Spanish-Western atmosphere and listen to flamenco, country, folk, and blues. Dancers pack the floor on weekend nights in summer.

Evangelo's (⊠ 200 W. San Francisco St., ☎ 505/982–9014) is an old-fashioned, smoky street-side bar, with pool tables, 200 types of imported beer, and rock bands on many weekends.

Paramount (⊠ 331 Sandoval St., ☎ 505/982–8999) has a snappy theme for each night of the week. The interior is contemporary and well lit and the dance floor is large. It's a good place to meet people, especially on swing night, when all ages over 21 swing, jitterbug, and lindy. There's also a Latin dance night, trash disco, and on Fridays, live music. Cover charge varies.

Rodeo Nites (✉ 2911 Cerrillos Rd., ☎ 505/473–4138) attracts a country-western crowd. It can get a bit rough in the wee hours, so get there on the early side for line dancing and some very hot two-stepping.

The Arts

The performing arts scene in Santa Fe comes to life in the summer. Classical or jazz concerts, Shakespeare on the grounds of St. John's campus, experimental theater at Santa Fe Stages, or flamenco—"too many choices!" is the biggest complaint. The rest of the year is rather quiet, with seasonal music and dance performances. These events often double as benefits for nonprofit organizations and manage to bring top names to town. The historic Lensic Theater, Santa Fe's first and only movie palace from the 1930s, is being renovated into an 830-seat performing arts center. The Lensic Performing Arts Center is slated to open in spring of 2001.

Film

Cinematheque (✉ 1050 Old Pecos Trail, ☎ 505/982–1338) screens foreign and independent films.

Music

The acclaimed **Santa Fe Chamber Music Festival** (✉ Museum of Fine Arts, 107 E Palace Ave., ☎ 505/983–2075) presents a March Spring Music minifest and, in July and August, performances every night except Tuesday at the St. Francis Auditorium.

Santa Fe Opera (☎ 505/986–5900 or 800/280–4654, ✆) performs in a strikingly modern structure—a 2,126-seat, indoor-outdoor amphitheater with excellent acoustics and sight lines. Carved into the natural curves of a hillside 7 mi north of the city on U.S. 84/285, the opera overlooks mountains, mesas, and sky. Add some of the most acclaimed singers, directors, conductors, musicians, designers, and composers from Europe and the United States, and you begin to understand the excitement that builds every June. Richard Gaddes replaced founding director John Crosby in 2000, but no big changes are planned for the company, which presents five works in repertory each summer—a blend of seasoned classics, neglected masterpieces, and world premieres. Many evenings sell out far in advance, but inexpensive standing-room tickets are often available on the day of the performance.

The **Santa Fe Symphony** (☎ 505/983–3530 or 800/480–1319, ✆) performs eight concerts each season (from September to May) and three concerts in the summer. In 2001 performances move to the **Lensic Performing Arts Center** (✉ 1050 Old Pecos Trail).

Orchestra and chamber concerts are given by the **Santa Fe Pro Musica** (☎ 505/988–4640) from September through April. Baroque and other classical compositions are the normal fare; the annual Christmas and April's Bach Festival performances are highlights.

Santa Fe Summerscene (☎ 505/438–8834) presents free concerts (rhythm and blues, light opera, jazz, Cajun, salsa, folk, and bluegrass) and dance performances (modern, folk) in the Santa Fe Plaza every Tuesday and Thursday from mid-June to August at noon and 6 PM.

On the campus of the Santa Fe Indian School, the **Paolo Soleri Outdoor Amphitheater** (✉ 1501 Cerrillos Rd., ☎ 505/982–1889) hosts summer concert series.

Theater

The **Greer Garson Theater** (✉ College of Santa Fe, 1600 St. Michael's Dr., ☎ 505/473–6511, ✆) stages student productions of comedies, dramas, and musicals from October to May.

The **Santa Fe Community Theatre** (✉ 142 East De Vargas St., ☎ 505/988–4262) has been presenting an adventurous mix of avant-garde pieces, classical drama, and musical comedy since 1922. The Fiesta Melodrama, which started in the 1920s—a spoof of the Santa Fe scene—takes place during September's Fiestas de Santa Fe.

Santa Fe Stages (✉ 100 N. Guadalupe, ☎ 505/982–6683), an international theater festival, produces and presents professional theater, dance, and music from late June to August.

On Friday, Saturday, and Sunday during July and August, **Shakespeare in Santa Fe** (☎ 505/982–2910) presents performances of the Bard's finest in the courtyard of the John Gaw Meem Library at St. John's College (✉ 1160 Camino Cruz Blanca). A performance of Renaissance music begins at 6, followed by the play at 7:30. Seating is limited to 350, so it's best to get tickets in advance. Bring a picnic basket or buy food at the concession stand. It can get cold and the performers have been known to keep the show going in light rain. Tickets cost between $10 and $28. Grass seating is free, though a $5 donation is suggested. There are also several matinees during the season.

OUTDOOR ACTIVITIES AND SPORTS

The Sangre de Cristo Mountains (the name translates as "Blood of Christ" for the red glow they radiate at sunset) preside over northern New Mexico, constant and gentle reminders of the mystery and power of the natural world. To the south, the landscape descends into the high desert of north-central New Mexico. The dramatic shifts in elevation and topography make for a wealth of outdoor activities. Head to the mountains for fishing, camping, and skiing; to the nearby Rio Grande for kayaking and rafting; and almost anywhere in the area for bird-watching and biking.

Participant Sports

Bicycling

A map of bike trips—among them a 30-mi round-trip ride from downtown Santa Fe to Ski Santa Fe at the end of Highway 475—can be picked up at the **Santa Fe Convention and Visitors Bureau** (✉ 201 W. Marcy St., ☎ 505/984–6760) or the **New Mexico Public Lands Information Center** (☞ Campgrounds, *above*).

Bike N' Sport (✉ 1829 Cerrillos Rd., ☎ 505/820–0809) provides rentals and information about guided tours. **Sun Mountain** (✉ 107 Washington Ave., ☎ 505/820–2902) provides mountain bikes from its Plaza location. The shop will also deliver to your hotel, any day, year round.

Bird-Watching

At the end of Upper Canyon Road, at the mouth of the canyon as it wends up into the foothills, is the **Randall Davey Audubon Center,** a 135-acre nature sanctuary that harbors diverse birds and other wildlife. An educator leads free nature walks on the first Saturday of each month. The home and studio of Randall Davey, a prolific early Santa Fe artist, is here and on summer Monday afternoons, tours are given of the rambling house. ✉ *Top of Upper Canyon Rd.,* ☎ *505/983–4609.* ▦ *$1, house tour $3.* ☉ *Daily 9–5.*

Golf

Marty Sanchez Links de Santa Fe (⊠ 205 Caja del Rio, off NM 599, ☎ 505/438–5200), a relatively new, public 18-hole, par-72 golf course on the high prairie southwest of Santa Fe, has views of mountain ranges. It has driving and putting ranges, a pro shop, and a snack bar. The greens fee is $49 for nonresidents (plus $11 per rider per cart).

The 18-hole, par-72 **Pueblo de Cochiti Golf Course** (⊠ 5200 Cochiti Hwy., Cochiti Lake, ☎ 505/465–2239), set against a backdrop of steep canyons and red-rock mesas, is a 45-minute drive southwest of the city. Cochiti, one of the top public golf courses in the country, has a greens fee of $25 on weekdays and $32 on weekends and holidays; an optional cart costs $11 per person.

Santa Fe Country Club (⊠ Airport Rd., ☎ 505/471–0601), a tree-shaded semiprivate 18-hole, par-72 golf course, has driving and putting ranges and a pro shop. You can rent clubs and electric carts. The greens fee is $55 for nonresidents, and a cart costs $15 per single rider or $11 for each rider.

Hiking

Hiking around Santa Fe can take you into high-altitude alpine country or into lunaresque high desert as you head south and the elevation drops radically. For winter hiking, the gentler climates to the south are less likely to be snow-packed, while the alpine areas will likely require snowshoes or cross-country skis. In summer, wildflowers are in bloom in the high country and the temperature is generally at least 10 degrees cooler than in town. For information about specific areas, contact the **New Mexico Public Lands Information Center** (☞ Campgrounds, *above*). The **Sierra Club** (⊠ 621 Old Santa Fe Trail, ☎ 505/983–2703) organizes group hikes. You can get information from the pick-up box in front of their office.

The mountain trails accessible at the base of the Ski Santa Fe area (end of Highway 475) offer a refuge from the dry summer heat in town. Weather can change with one gust of wind, so be prepared with extra clothing, rain gear, water, and food. The sun at 10,000 ft is very powerful, even with a hat and sunscreen. **Aspen Vista** is a lovely hike along a south-facing mountainside. Take Hyde Park Road 13 mi, and the trail begins before the ski area. After walking a few miles through thick aspen groves you'll come to panoramic views of Santa Fe. The path is well marked and gently inclines toward Tesuque Peak. The trail becomes shadier with elevation—snow has been reported on the trail as late as July. In winter, after heavy snows, the trail is great for intermediate-advanced cross-country skiing. The round-trip is 12 mi, but it's just 3½ mi to the spectacular overlook. The hillside is covered with golden aspen trees in late September.

Tsankawi Trail, pronounced sank-ah-*wee,* will take you through the ancient rock trails of the Pajarito Plateau. The Pueblo people created the trails in the 1400s as they made their way from their mesa-top homes to the fields and springs in the canyon below. In the 1½-mi loop you'll see petroglyphs and south-facing cave dwellings. Wear good shoes for the rocky path and a climb on a 12-ft ladder that shoots between a crevasse in the rock and the highest point of the mesa. This is an ideal walk if you don't have time to explore Bandelier National Monument (☞ Side Trips, *below*) in depth but want to get a taste of it. It's on the way to Los Alamos, about a 35-minute drive from Santa Fe. ⊠ *25 mi northwest of Santa Fe. Take US 285/84 north to the Los Alamos exit for NM 502. Go west on 502 until the turnoff for White Rock, Hwy. 4. Continue for several mi to the sign for Tsankawi on the left. The trail is clearly marked.* ☎ *505/672–3861.*

Tent Rocks is the place to hike if you always wanted to walk on the moon. The sculpted sandstone rock formations look like stacked tents on a stark, water- and wind-eroded hillside. Located 45 minutes south of Santa Fe, near Cochiti Pueblo, Tent Rocks is excellent hiking in dry winter, spring, or fall weather. Avoid it in summer—the rocks magnify the heat. The drive to this magical landscape is equally awesome, as the road heads west toward Cochiti Dam and through the cottonwood groves around the pueblo. It's a good hike for kids. The round-trip hiking distance is only 2 mi, about 1½ hours, but it's the kind of place you'll want to hang out in for a while. Take a camera. ⌧ *I–25 south to Cochiti exit 264. Go right (west) off the exit ramp on NM 16 for 8 mi. Turn right at the T intersection onto NM 22. Continue approximately 3½ more mi (you will pass Cochiti Pueblo entrance). Turn right on NM 266 "Tent Rocks" and continue 5 mi to the "*WELCOME TO TENT ROCKS*" sign. The last stretch of road is jarring, washboarded gravel.* ☎ *505/465–2244.* 🖼 *$5 per car.*

Horseback Riding

New Mexico's rugged countryside has been the setting for many Hollywood westerns. Whether you want to ride the range that Gregory Peck and Kevin Costner rode or just head out feeling tall in the saddle, you can do so year-round. Rates average about $20 an hour.

Bishop's Lodge (⌧ Bishop's Lodge Rd., ☎ 505/983–6377) provides rides and guides from April to November. Call for reservations. Rides with **Broken Saddle Riding Co.** (⌧ High Desert Ranch, Cerrillos, ☎ 505/470–0074) take you around the old turquoise and silver mines the-Cerrillos area is noted for. On a Tennessee Walker or a Missouri Fox Trotter you can explore the Cerrillos hills and canyons, 23 mi southeast of Santa Fe. This is not the usual nose-to-tail trail ride.

Galarosa Stable (⌧ Galisteo, ☎ 505/983–6565 or 800/338–6877) provides rentals by the half day or full day south of Santa Fe in the panoramic Galisteo Basin. **Vientos Encantados** (⌧ Round Barn Stables, off U.S. 84/285, Ojo Caliente, ☎ 505/583–2233), a one-hour drive north of Santa Fe, conducts trail rides and pack trips near the Ojo Caliente mineral springs. Reserve at least one day in advance.

Jogging

Because of the city's altitude (7,000 ft), you may feel heavy-legged and light-headed if you start running shortly after you arrive. Once you've become acclimated, though, you'll find that this is a great place to run. There's a jogging path along the Santa Fe River, parallel to Alameda, and another at Fort Marcy on Washington Avenue.

Three races of note take place each year (☞ Santa Fe Convention and Visitors Bureau *in* Santa Fe A to Z, *below,* for more information). The **Santa Fe Runaround,** a 10-km race held in early June, begins and ends at the Plaza. The **Women's Five-Kilometer Run** is held in early August. Runners turn out in droves on Labor Day for the **Old Santa Fe Trail Run.**

River Rafting

If you want to watch birds and wildlife along the banks, try the laid-back Huck Finn floats along the Rio Chama or the Rio Grande's White Rock Canyon. The season is generally between April and September. Most outfitters have overnight package plans, and all offer half- and full-day trips. Be prepared to get wet, and wear secure water shoes. For a list of outfitters who guide trips on the Rio Grande and the Rio Chama, write the **Bureau of Land Management, Taos Resource Area Office** (⌧ 224 Cruz Alta Rd., Taos 87571, ☎ 505/758–8851).

Kokopelli Rafting Adventures (✉ 541 Cordova Rd., ☎ 505/983–3734 or 800/879–9035) specializes in trips through the relatively mellow White Rock Canyon as well as white water. **New Wave Rafting Company** (✉ 103 E. Water St., Suite F, ☎ 505/984–1444 or 800/984–1444) conducts full-day, half-day, and overnight river trips, with daily departures from Santa Fe. **Santa Fe Rafting Company and Outfitters** (✉ 1000 Cerrillos Rd., ☎ 505/988–4914 or 800/467–7238) customizes rafting tours. Tell them what you want—they'll do it.

Skiing

To save time during the busy holiday season you may want to rent skis or snowboards in town the night before hitting the slopes, or early in the morning so you don't have to waste your pricey lift ticket. **Alpine Sports** (✉ 121 Sandoval St., ☎ 505/983–5155) rents downhill and cross-country skis and snowboards. **Ski Tech** (✉ 905 St. Francis Dr., ☎ 505/983–5512) rents the works, including loaner ski racks and snow gear.

Ski Santa Fe (✉ end of Hwy. 475, ☎ 505/982–4429), usually open from Thanksgiving to Easter, is a fine, midsize operation that receives an average of 250 inches of snow a year and plenty of sunshine. One of America's highest ski areas—the summit is a little more than 12,000 ft above sea level—it has a variety of terrain and seems bigger than its 1,650 ft of vertical rise and 500 acres. There are some great powder stashes, tough bump runs, and many wide, gentle cruising runs. The 40-plus trails are ranked 20% beginner, 40% intermediate, and 40% advanced. Snowboarders are welcome and there's the Norquist Trail for cross-country skiers. The kids' center, Chipmunk Corner, provides day care for infants and supervised skiing for children. The ski school is excellent. Rentals, a good cafeteria, a ski shop, and Totemoff's bar are other amenities. Call for **snow-condition information** (☎ 505/983–9155, ✆).

Pajarito Mountain Ski Area, a small, low-key area near Los Alamos, has some excellent long runs and a good selection of wide-open, intermediate mogul runs. There's no artificial snowmaking, so the slopes are barely open during dry winters. But there's never a wait in lift lines. Call for **ski information** (☎ 505/662–5725) and **snow-condition information** (☎ 505/662–7669).

For other sources of ski information, call **Santa Fe Central Reservations** (☎ 505/983–8200; 800/776–7669 outside New Mexico), or **Ski New Mexico** (☎ 505/982–5300 or 800/755–7669) for general information about downhill or cross-country skiing conditions around Santa Fe.

Tennis

Santa Fe has more than two dozen public tennis courts available on a first-come, first-served basis. For information about the public facilities listed below and additional ones, call the **City Parks Division** (☎ 505/473–7236).

There are four asphalt courts at **Alto Park** (✉ 1035½ Alto St.). **Herb Martínez/La Resolana Park** (✉ Camino Carlos Rey) has four concrete courts. **Ortiz Park** (✉ Camino de las Crucitas) has three asphalt courts. There are two asphalt courts at **Fort Marcy Complex** (✉ 490 Washington Ave.).

Among the major private tennis facilities, including indoor, outdoor, and lighted courts, are **Club at El Gancho** (✉ Old Las Vegas Hwy., ☎ 505/988–5000), **Sangre De Cristo Racquet Club** (✉ 1755 Camino Corrales, ☎ 505/983–7978), **Santa Fe Country Club** (✉ Airport Rd., ☎ 505/471–3378), and **Shellaberger Tennis Center** (✉ College of Santa Fe, St. Michael's Dr., ☎ 505/473–6144).

Windsurfing

Strong summer breezes and a proximity to man-made lakes have made northern New Mexico a popular windsurfing spot, though the water can be chilly and the winds unpredictable. Early morning is the best time to go, because thunderstorms often develop in the afternoon. Devoted regulars head to **Abiquiú Lake** (⊠ U.S. 84/285, Abiquiú, ☎ 505/685–4371), 40 mi northwest of Santa Fe and backed by sculptural red-rock cliffs. **Cochiti Lake** (⊠ I–25, Santo Domingo exit, Peña Blanca, ☎ 505/242–8302) lies between Los Alamos and Santa Fe.

SHOPPING

Santa Fe has been a trading post for a long time. A thousand years ago the great pueblos of the Anasazi civilizations were strategically located between the buffalo-hunting tribes of the Great Plains and the Indians of Mexico. Native Americans in New Mexico traded turquoise, which was thought to have magical properties, and other valuables with Indians from Mexico for metals, shells, parrots, and other exotic items. After the arrival of the Spanish and the subsequent development of the West, Santa Fe became the place to exchange silver from Mexico and natural resources from New Mexico—including hides, fur, and foodstuffs—for manufactured goods, whiskey, and greenbacks from the United States. With the building of the railroad in 1880, Santa Fe had access to all kinds of manufactured goods as well as those unique to the region via the old trade routes.

The trading legacy remains, but now downtown Santa Fe caters almost exclusively to those looking for handcrafted goods. Sure, T-shirt outlets and major retail clothing shops have moved in, but shopping in Santa Fe remains a unique experience for most visitors. The enigma of Santa Fe style, as distinct as the city's architecture, continues, although in a tempered, more sophisticated version than a decade ago, when chile ristras and wooden howling coyotes took over the shops.

Santa Fe is a great place to window shop, perhaps because of the high visual standards such an artistic community commands. It is a town where color, texture, and pattern make a brave stand for diversity rather than uniformity. Canyon Road, where art galleries are within a short distance of one another, is the perfect place to find one-of-a-kind gifts and collectibles. The downtown district, around the Plaza, has unusual gift shops, clothing and shoe stores that range from theatrical to conventional, curio shops, and art galleries. The Historic Guadalupe Railroad District, popularly referred to as the Railyard District, includes Sanbusco Market Place on the southwest perimeter of downtown. It's a laid-back place to mingle with residents who don't want to fight for a parking place near the Plaza. All areas have cafés and restaurants that satisfy the need to people-watch and relax.

Art Galleries

The following are only a few of the more than 150 galleries in Santa Fe—with the best of representational, nonobjective, Native American, Latin American, cutting edge, photographic, and soulful works that defy categorization. The Santa Fe Convention and Visitors Bureau has a more extensive listing. *The Wingspread Collectors Guide to Santa Fe and Taos* (☞ Books and Videos *in* Chapter 9) is a good resource and is available in hotels. Check the *Pasatiempo* pullout in the *Santa Fe New Mexican* on Friday for a preview of gallery openings.

Andrew Smith Gallery (⊠ 203 W. San Francisco St., ☎ 505/984–1234) is a significant photo gallery dealing in works by Edward S. Curtis and

Santa Fe Shopping

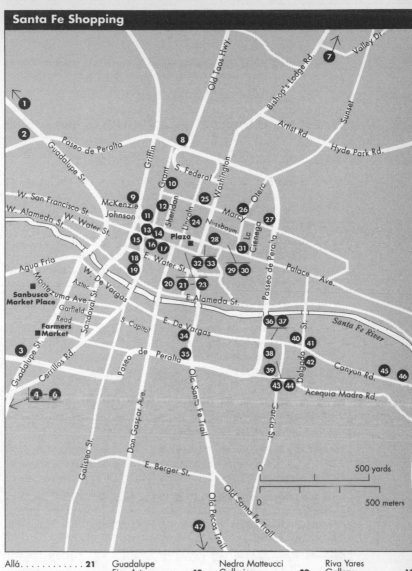

other 19th-century chroniclers of the American West. Major figures from the 20th and 21st centuries are Ansel Adams, Eliot Porter, Alfred Stieglitz, Annie Liebowitz, and regional artists like Barbara Van Cleve.

Bellas Artes (✉ 653 Canyon Rd., ☎ 505/983–2745), a sophisticated gallery and sculpture garden, has ancient ceramics and represents internationally renowned artists like Judy Pfaff, Phoebe Adams, and Olga de Amaral.

Charlotte Jackson Fine Art (✉ 123 E. Marcy St., ☎ 505/989–8688) focuses primarily on monochromatic "radical" painting. Florence Pierce, Joe Barnes, Anne Cooper, and Joseph Marionni are among the artists producing minimalist works dealing with light and space.

Dewey Galleries (✉ Catron Building, 53 Old Santa Fe Trail, ☎ 505/982–8632) shows historic Navajo textiles and jewelry, pueblo pottery, and antique Spanish colonial furniture, as well as paintings and sculpture.

Ernesto Mayans Gallery (✉ 601 Canyon Rd., ☎ 983-8068) focuses on paintings and works on paper. There's an excellent selection of contemporary photography by Mexican luminaries Graciela Iturbide and Manuel Alvarez Bravo.

Gerald Peters Gallery (✉ 1011 Paseo de Peralta, ☎ 505/954–5700) is Santa Fe's leading gallery of American and European art from the 19th century to the present. It has works by Charles M. Russell, Albert Bierstadt, the Taos Society, the New Mexico Modernists, and Georgia O'Keeffe, as well as contemporary artists.

Guadalupe Fine Art (✉ 403 Canyon Rd., across the courtyard in back, ☎ 505/982–2403) is a vibrant venue for emerging and established painters and sculptors. Owner and gallery artist Lena Bartula hosts annual, thematic group shows that are community events. The Southwest Zen-style sculpture garden is a great place to linger.

James Kelly Contemporary Gallery (✉ 1601 Paseo de Peralta, ☎ 505/989–1601) displays works by such internationally renowned artists as Susan Rothenberg and video artist Bruce Nauman in its warehouse space.

LewAllen Contemporary (✉ 129 W. Palace Ave., ☎ 505/988–8997) is a leading center for a variety of contemporary arts by Southwest artists. Arlene LewAllen has been a vital force in the Santa Fe art scene for more than 20 years.

Meredith-Kelly Gallery (✉ 135 W. Palace Ave., ☎ 505/986–8699) shows work by Latin American artists, some local, working mostly in painting. Most of the work is global in theme rather than culturally specific. Zuñega is one of the big names.

Nedra Matteucci Galleries (✉ 1075 Paseo de Peralta, ☎ 505/982–4631) exhibits works by California regionalists, members of the early Taos and Santa Fe schools, and masters of American Impressionism and Modernism. Spanish-colonial furniture, Indian antiquities, and a fantastic sculpture garden are other draws of this well-respected establishment.

Niman Fine Arts (✉ 125 Lincoln Ave., ☎ 505/988–5091) focuses on the prolific work of two contemporary Native American artists—Hopi painter Dan Namingha and the late Apache sculptor Allan Houser.

Photo-Eye Gallery (✉ 370 Garcia St., ☎ 505/988–5152) shows everything from contemporary photography that includes the beautiful and sublime to controversial works by Jock Sturges.

Plan B Evolving Arts (⊠ 1050 Old Pecos Trail, ☎ 505/982–1338) showcases young artists, with an emphasis on cutting-edge and avant-garde works.

Riva Yares Gallery (⊠ 123 Grant St, ☎ 505/984–0330) specializes in contemporary artists of Latin American descent. There are sculptures by California artist Manuel Neri, color field paintings by Esteban Vicente, and works by Santa Feans Elias Rivera, Rico Eastman, and others.

Shidoni Foundry and Galleries (⊠ Bishop's Lodge Rd., Tesuque, 5 mi north of Santa Fe, ☎ 505/988–8001) casts work for accomplished and emerging artists from all over North America. On the grounds of an old chicken ranch, Shidoni has a rambling sculpture garden and a gallery. Guided tours of the foundry take place on Saturday.

William R. Talbot Fine Art (⊠ 129 W. San Francisco St., ☎ 505/982–1559) sells antique maps and prints.

Wyeth Hurd Gallery (⊠ 229 E. Marcy St., ☎ 505/989–8380) carries the work of the multigenerational arts family that includes N. C. Wyeth; his children Andrew and Henriette Wyeth; Peter Hurd, Henriette's husband; Michael Hurd, son of Henriette and Peter; Jamie Wyeth, Andrew's son; and Peter de la Fuente, Henriette and Peter's grandson. Works include the landscape of the Delaware River valley that so inspired the Wyeth family and the New Mexico landscapes of Peter Hurd, who grew up in Roswell.

Specialty Stores

Books

More than 20 stores in Santa Fe sell used books, and a handful of high-quality shops carry the latest releases from mainstream and small presses.

Allá (⊠ 102 W. San Francisco St., upstairs, ☎ 505/988–5416) is one of Santa Fe's most delightful small bookstores. It focuses on hard-to-find Spanish-language books and records, including limited-edition handmade books from Central America. It also carries Native American books and music, as well as English translations.

Collected Works Book Store (⊠ 208B W. San Francisco St., ☎ 505/988–4226) carries art and travel books, including a generous selection of books on Southwestern art, architecture, and general history, as well as the latest in contemporary literature.

Nicholas Potter (⊠ 211 E. Palace Ave., ☎ 505/983–5434) specializes in used, rare, and out-of-print books. The quixotic shop also stocks used jazz and classical CDs.

Photo-Eye Books (⊠ 376 Garcia St., ☎ 505/988–5152) stocks new, rare, and out-of-print photography books.

Clothing

Women have been known to arrive here in Liz Claiborne and leave in a broomstick skirt and Navajo velvet shirt. Men who swore they never would, don silver *bolo* ties. Function dictates form in cowboy fashions. A wide-brimmed hat is essential in open country for protection from heat, rain, and insects. In the Southwest there's no such thing as a stingy brim. Cowboy hats made by Resistol, Stetson, Bailey, and other leading firms cost between $50 and $500, and hats made of fur and other exotic materials can fetch four figures. Small wonder that when it rains in Santa Fe or Albuquerque, some people are more concerned about protecting their hats than about getting wet.

ART IN SANTA FE

THE ARTISTIC ROOTS OF Santa Fe stretch back to the landscape and the devotion of those who roamed and settled here long before the Santa Fe Trail transplanted goods and people from the east. The intricate designs on Native American pottery and baskets, the embroidery on the ritual dancewear, the color and pattern on Rio Grande weavings, and the delicate paintings and carvings of devotional images called santos all contributed to the value and awareness of beauty that Santa Fe holds as its cultural birthright. The rugged landscape, the ineffable quality of the light, and the community itself continue to draw to Santa Fe a plethora of musicians, writers, and visual artists. The spell of beauty is so powerful here that some people call the town "Fanta Se," but for those who live in Santa Fe the arts are very real (as are economic realities; most artists hold jobs—ask your waiter). The painter and part-time Santa Fe resident Robert Henri once said, "There are moments in our lives, there are moments in a day, when we seem to see beyond the usual." Santa Fe is alive with those moments and many artists draw their inspiration from them.

With wide-eyed enchantment, visitors often buy paintings in orange, pink, and turquoise that are perfect next to the adobe architecture, blue sky, and red rocks of the New Mexican landscape. When they get home, however, the admired works sometimes end up in a closet simply because it's so hard to integrate the Southwestern look with the tone of the existing furnishings and artwork. Taking the risk is part of the experience. Rather than suffering from buyer's remorse, those who make the aesthetic leap can take the spirit of northern New Mexico home with them. Although it may shake up the home decor, the works are a reminder of a new way of seeing and of all the other values that inspire one to travel in the first place.

Most galleries will send a painting (not posters or prints) out on a trial basis for very interested clients. If looking at art is new to you, ask yourself if your interest is in bringing home a souvenir that says "I was there" or, in art that will live in the present and inspire the future, independent of the nostalgia for the "land of enchantment." Santa Fe has plenty of both to offer—use discrimination while you look so you don't burn out on the first block of Canyon Road.

SANTA FE, while holding strong in its regional art identity, emerged in the late 1990s as a more international art scene. Native American and Hispanic arts groups now include the work of contemporary artists who have pressed beyond the bounds of tradition. Bold color and the oft-depicted New Mexico landscape are still evident, but you're just as likely to see mixed-media collages by a Chinese artist currently living in San Francisco. Several Santa Fe outlets, such as the Riva Yares Gallery and the Meredith-Kelly Gallery, are dedicated to representing artists with Latin American roots. "The world is wide here," Georgia O'Keeffe once noted about northern New Mexico. And just as Santa Fe welcomed early Modernist painters who responded to the open landscape and the artistic freedom it engendered, contemporary artists working with edgier media, such as conceptual, performance, and installation art, are finding welcoming venues in Santa Fe, specifically at Plan B and SITE Santa Fe.

The pointed toes of cowboy boots slide easily in and out of stirrups, and high heels help keep feet in the stirrups. Tall tops protect ankles and legs on rides through brush and cactus country and can protect the wearer from a nasty shin bruise from a skittish horse.

Some Western fashion accessories were once purely functional. A colorful bandanna protected an Old West cowboy from sun- and windburn and served as a mask in windstorms, when riding drag behind a herd or, on occasions far rarer than Hollywood would have us believe, when robbing trains. A cowboy's sleeveless vest enhanced his ability to maneuver during roping and riding chores and provided pocket space that his skintight pants—snug to prevent wrinkles in the saddle area—didn't. Belt buckles are probably the most sought-after accessories—gold ones go for as much as $1,000.

Back at the Ranch (✉ 235 Don Gaspar, ☎ 505/989–8110 or 888/962–6687) is a musty old shop stocked with used cowboy boots, from red leather to turquoise snakeskin. Some things get better with age, especially cowboy boots.

Jane Smith (✉ 550 Canyon Rd., ☎ 505/988–4775) sells extraordinary handmade Western wear for women and men, from cowboy boots and sweaters to Plains Indians–style beaded tunics.

Mirá (✉ 101 W. Marcy St., ☎ 505/988–3585) clothing for women is slick, eclectic, and funky, combining the adventurous spirit of Mexico with global contemporary fashion. The shop has accessories and collectibles from Latin America, hemp apparel, and knock-out vintage-inspired dresses.

Montecristi Custom Hat Works (✉ 322 McKenzie St., ☎ 505/983–9598) is where the smart set goes for custom-made straw hats so snug they're all but guaranteed to stay on, even in an open convertible.

Origins (✉ 135 W. San Francisco St., ☎ 505/988–2323) borrows from many cultures, carrying pricey women's wear like antique kimonos and custom-dyed silk jackets. One-of-a-kind accessories complete the spectacular look that Santa Fe inspires.

Santa Fe Boot Company (✉ 950 W. Cordova Rd., ☎ 505/983–8415) stocks boots by all major manufacturers and more exotic styles designed by owner Marian Trujillo. Hats and Western outerwear are also sold.

Simply Santa Fe (✉ 72 E. San Francisco St., ☎ 505/988–3100) carries unusual and lovely items, such as cut velvet vests with handmade buttons, turquoise and coral watchbands, and hand-beaded evening bags. It also carries fine furnishings like leather wing chairs and forged steel beds.

Western Warehouse (✉ De Vargas Center, ☎ 505/982–3388; Villa Linda Mall, ☎ 505/471–8775) sells all the top-name hats, boots, belts, and buckles.

Home Furnishings

Artesanos (✉ 222 Galisteo St. and 1414 Maclovia St., ☎ 505/471–8020) is one of the best Mexican-import shops in the nation, with everything from leather chairs to papier-mâché *calaveras* (skeletons used in Day of the Dead celebrations), tinware, and Talavera tiles.

Doodlet's (✉ 120 Don Gaspar Ave., ☎ 505/983–3771) has an eclectic collection of stuff: pop-up books, bizarre postcards, tin art, hooked rugs, and stringed lights. Wonderment is in every display case, drawing the eye to the unusual.

Foreign Traders (✉ 202 Galisteo St., ☎ 505/983–6441), a Santa Fe institution founded as the Old Mexico Shop in 1927 and still run by the same family, stocks handicrafts, antiques, and accessories from Mexico and other parts of the world.

Jackalope (✉ 2820 Cerrillos Rd., ☎ 505/471–8539) sprawls over 7 acres, incorporating several pottery barns, a furniture store, endless aisles of knickknacks from Latin America and Asia, and a huge greenhouse. There's a lunch counter, barnyard animals, and a prairie-dog village.

Montez Gallery (✉ Sena Plaza Courtyard, 125 E. Palace Ave., ☎ 505/982–1828) sells Hispanic works of religious art and decoration, including retablos, bultos, furniture, paintings, pottery, weavings, and jewelry.

Pachamama (✉ 223 Canyon Rd., ☎ 505/983–4020) carries Latin American folk art, including small tin or silver *milagros*, the stamped metal images used as votive offerings. Milagro-inspired jewelry by Elena Solow, which combines gemstones with antique-looking images in stamped silver, is a rare find. The shop also carries weavings and Spanish-colonial antiques, including santos, devotional carvings, and painted images of saints.

Jewelry

Karen Melfi Collection (✉ 225 Canyon Rd, ☎ 505/982–3032) sells high-quality yet moderately priced handmade jewelry and other wearable art.

Ornament of Santa Fe (✉ 209 W. San Francisco, ☎ 505/983–9399) is full of cosmopolitan jewelry and unique hair accessories. Precious and semiprecious stones set in gold and silver push the envelope of tradition without being trendy.

Native American Arts and Crafts

Cristof's (✉ 420 Old Santa Fe Trail, ☎ 505/988–9881) has a large selection of pottery, sculpture, and contemporary Navajo weavings and sand paintings.

Joshua Baer & Co. (✉ 116½ E. Palace Ave., ☎ 505/988–8944) carries superb historic Navajo textiles and rare antique Pueblo weavings.

Morning Star Gallery (✉ 513 Canyon Rd., ☎ 505/982–8187) is a veritable museum of Native American art and artifacts. An adobe shaded by a huge cottonwood tree houses antique basketry, pre-1940 Navajo silver jewelry, Northwest Coast Native American carvings, Navajo weavings, and art of the Plains Indians.

Packard's on the Plaza (✉ 61 Old Santa Fe Trail, ☎ 505/983–9241), the oldest Native American arts-and-crafts store on Santa Fe Plaza, sells Zapotec Indian rugs from Mexico and original rug designs by Richard Enzer, old pottery, saddles, katsina dolls, and an excellent selection of coral and turquoise jewelry.

The **Rainbow Man** (✉ 107 E. Palace Ave., ☎ 505/982–8706), established in 1945, does business in the remains of a building that was damaged during the 1680 Pueblo Revolt. The shop carries early Navajo, Mexican, and Chimayó textiles, along with photographs by Edward S. Curtis, vintage pawn jewelry, and katsinas.

Relics of the Old West (✉ 402 Old Santa Fe Trail, ☎ 505/989–7663) stocks eclectic crafts and artifacts from cowboy-and-Indian days, as well as high-end Navajo textiles, old and new. Navajo weavers are on-site demonstrating their craft during the summer.

Trade Roots Collection (✉ 411 Paseo de Peralta, ☎ 505/982–8168) sells Native American ritual objects, such as fetish jewelry and Hopi rattles. The store is a good source of craft materials.

Flea Markets

Tesuque Pueblo Flea Market (⊠ U.S. 84/285, 7 mi north of Santa Fe), formerly known as Trader Jack's or the Santa Fe Flea Market, was once considered the best flea market in America by its loyal legion of bargain hunters. The Tesuque Pueblo now manages the market and has made a few changes. Occult services, such as palm reading, are gone and increased vendor fees have cut down on garage-sale treasures and increased the predictable goods brought in by professional flea-market dealers. You can still find everything from a half-wolf puppy or African carvings to vintage cowboy boots, fossils, or a wall clock made out of an old hubcap. On 12 acres of land belonging to the Tesuque Pueblo, the market is right next to the Santa Fe Opera and is open Friday through Sunday, May through October, and weekends in November, December, and mid-February through April.

SIDE TRIPS

One can hardly grasp the profundity of New Mexico's ancient past or its immense landscape without journeying into the hinterland. Each of the excursions below can be accomplished in a day or less. The High Road to Taos is a very full day, so start early or plan on spending the night near Taos. For a longer loop heading northeast out of town on a route that traces the historic Santa Fe Trail, *see* Chapter 4.

Jemez Country

In the Jemez region, the 1,000-year-old Anasazi ruins at Bandelier National Monument present a vivid contrast to Los Alamos National Laboratory, birthplace of the atomic bomb. You can easily take in part of Jemez Country in a day trip from Santa Fe; some of the sights beyond the end of the tour described below, among them Jemez Pueblo, are covered in Chapter 6. On the loop described you'll see terrific views of the Rio Grande Valley, the Sangre de Cristos, the Galisteo Basin, and, in the distance, the Sandias. There are places to eat and shop for essentials in Los Alamos and a few roadside diners in La Cueva, on the highway to Jemez Springs.

The 48,000-acre Cerro Grande fire of May 2000 burned much of the pine forest in the lower Jemez mountains. The once scenic drive is now scarred with charcoaled remains. Restoration of the grasslands and trees is under way. Grass will be the first vegetation to return, with aspen trees being among the first trees to reforest the area. Depending on fire hazard due to seasonal droughts, access to New Mexico wilderness may be affected. A call to the New Mexico Public Lands Information Center (☎ 505/438–7582) is advisable when planning a trip.

Los Alamos

31 mi from Santa Fe, north on U.S. 84/285 (to Pojoaque) and west on NM 502.

The town of Los Alamos, a 45-minute drive from Santa Fe, was founded in absolute secrecy in 1943 as a center of war research, and its existence only became known in 1945 with the detonation of atomic bombs in Japan. The bomb was first tested in southern New Mexico, at White Sands Missile Range (☞ Alamogordo, *in* Chapter 7), but the think tank and laboratories that unleashed atomic power were firmly planted in the forested hillside of Los Alamos (*alamos* means "trees" in Spanish). Many of those trees burned in the May 2000 Cerro Grande fire, which destroyed the surrounding hillsides and burned 260 homes in Los Alamos. Reforestation is well under way. The topography will transform slowly, first with grasses. Aspen trees will be among the first trees to root, providing the conditions necessary for pine seedlings to come back.

In time, Los Alamos (referred to by Santa Feans as the "city on the hill," or, more recently, "LA,") will be green again, with stunning fall color in its aspen groves. The fire did not damage the business district. Architecturally, it continues to look and feel like a town that is utterly out of place in northern New Mexico. It's a fascinating place to visit because of the profound role it played in shaping the modern world.

The **Bradbury Science Museum** is Los Alamos National Laboratory's public showcase. You can experiment with lasers; use advanced computers; witness research in solar, geothermal, fission, and fusion energy; and view exhibits about World War II's Project Y (the Manhattan Project, whose participants developed the atomic bomb). If you like this museum, you might also want to stop by the National Atomic Museum in Albuquerque (☞ Chapter 5). ⊠ *Los Alamos National Laboratory, 15th St. and Central Ave.,* ☎ *505/667–4444.* ⊡ *Free.* ☉ *Tues.– Fri. 9–5, Sat.–Mon. 1–5.*

The New Mexican architect John Gaw Meem designed the **Fuller Lodge,** a short drive up Central Avenue from the Bradbury Science Museum. The massive log building was erected in 1928 as a dining and recreation hall for a small private boys' school. In 1942 the federal government purchased the school and made it the base of operations for the Manhattan Project. Part of the lodge is an art center that shows the works of northern New Mexican artists. ⊠ *2132 Central Ave.,* ☎ *505/662–9331.* ⊡ *Free.* ☉ *Mon.–Sat. 10–4.*

The **Los Alamos Historical Museum,** in a log building adjoining Fuller Lodge, displays artifacts of early Native American life. Photographs and documents relate the community's history. ⊠ *2132 Central Ave.,* ☎ *505/662–4493.* ⊡ *Free.* ☉ *Oct.–Apr., Mon.–Sat. 10–4, Sun. 1–4; May–Sept., Mon.–Sat. 9:30–4:30, Sun. 11–5.*

DINING AND LODGING

$–$$ ✕ **Hill Diner.** With a friendly staff and clientele, this large diner serves some of the finest burgers in town, along with chicken-fried steaks, homemade soups, and heaps of fresh vegetables. ⊠ *1315 Trinity Dr.,* ☎ *505/ 662–9745. AE, D, DC, MC, V.*

$$ ✕⊡ **Los Alamos Inn.** Rooms in this one-story hotel have modern Southwestern decor and sweeping canyon views. Ashley's, the inn's restaurant ($$) and bar, serves American and Southwestern regional specialties; the Sunday brunch is popular. ⊠ *2201 Trinity Dr., 87544,* ☎ *505/662–7211,* ℻ *505/661–7714. 115 rooms. Restaurant, bar, pool. AE, D, DC, MC, V.*

$$ ⊡ **Hilltop House Hotel.** Minutes from the Los Alamos National Laboratory, this hotel hosts both vacationers and scientists. All the rooms are furnished in modern Southwestern style; deluxe ones have kitchenettes. ⊠ *400 Trinity Dr., at Central Ave. (Box 250), 87544,* ☎ *505/ 662–2441,* ℻ *505/662–5913. 87 rooms, 13 suites. Restaurant, lounge, indoor pool, exercise room, coin laundry. AE, D, DC, MC, V. CP.* ❧

$–$$ ⊡ **Renata's Orange Street Bed&Breakfast.** Linda Hartman is the new proprietor of this B&B. In an unremarkable 1948 wood-frame house in a quiet residential neighborhood, rooms are furnished in Southwestern and country style. The public area has cable TV and a VCR, and you can use the kitchen and the laundry. ⊠ *3496 Orange St., 87544,* ☎ ℻ *505/662–2651. 6 rooms, 2 with bath; 3 suites. AE, D, DC, MC, V. BP.* ❧

Bandelier National Monument

40 mi from Santa Fe, north on U.S. 84/285, west on NM 502, south on NM 501 (W. Jemez Rd.) to "T" intersection with NM 4; turn left (east) and drive 6 mi to the monument's entrance.

Seven centuries before the Declaration of Independence was signed, compact city-states existed in the Southwest. Remnants of one of the most impressive of them can be seen at **Frijoles Canyon** in Bandelier National Monument. At the canyon's base, beside a gurgling stream, are the remains of cave dwellings, ancient ceremonial kivas, and other stone structures that stretch out for more than a mile beneath the sheer walls of the canyon's tree-fringed rim. For hundreds of years the Anasazi people, relatives of today's Rio Grande Pueblo Indians, thrived on wild game, corn, and beans. Suddenly, for reasons still undetermined, the settlements were abandoned.

Wander through the site on a paved, self-guided trail. If you can climb primitive wooden ladders and squeeze through narrow doorways, you can explore some of the cave dwellings and cell-like rooms.

Bandelier National Monument, named after author and ethnologist Adolph Bandelier (his novel *The Delight Makers* is set in Frijoles Canyon), contains 23,000 acres of backcountry wilderness, waterfalls, and wildlife. Sixty miles of trails traverse the park. A small museum in the visitor center focuses on the area's prehistoric and contemporary Native American cultures, with displays of artifacts from 1200 to modern times. ☎ 505/672–3861. ☞ *$10 per car, good for 7 days.* ☉ *Memorial Day–Labor Day, daily 8–6; Labor Day–Memorial Day, daily 8–5.*

Valle Grande

40 mi west of Santa Fe. From Bandelier National Monument, head west on NM 4 and follow the winding road through the mountain forest.

A high-forest drive brings you to the awe-inspiring Valle Grande, one of the world's largest calderas. You can't imagine the volcanic crater's immensity until you spot what look like specks of dust on the lush meadow floor and realize they're cows. The entire 50-mi Jemez range, formed by cataclysmic upheavals, is filled with streams, hiking trails, campgrounds, and hot springs—reminders of its volcanic origin. If you're coming from Bandelier National Monument (☞ *above*), the drive should take about 45 minutes. It's particularly pretty in late September or early October when the aspens turn gold.

Galisteo

23 mi from Santa Fe. North on I–25 to Exit 290, several mi on U.S. 285, right on NM 41 for 2½ mi.

South of Santa Fe lie the immense open spaces of the sublime Galisteo Basin and the quintessential New Mexican village of Galisteo—a harmonious blend of multigenerational New Mexicans and recent migrants who protect and treasure the bucolic solitude of their home. The drive from Santa Fe takes about 25 minutes and offers a panoramic view of the surreal, sculpted landscape of the Galisteo Basin, which is an austere contrast to the alpine country of the Sangre de Cristos. It's a good place to go for a leisurely lunch or a sunset drive to dinner, maybe with horseback riding or a day of lounging and having body treatments at the local spa, Vista Clara Ranch.

Founded as a Spanish outpost in 1614 and built largely with rocks from nearby Pueblo ruins, Galisteo is a village with many artists and equestrians (trail rides and rentals are available at local stables). Cottonwood trees shade the low-lying Pueblo-style architecture, a premier example of vernacular use of adobe and stone. The small church is open only for Sunday services. The excellent gallery **Linda Durham Contemporary Art** (☎ 505/466–6600) exhibits sculpture and paintings from mainly New Mexican artists. Aside from the two restaurant-inns and the gallery, a *tiendita,* a small store that sells bare essentials, constitutes the commercial center of Galisteo.

Dining and Lodging

$$$–$$$$ ✕⊡ **The Galisteo Inn.** In the center of Galisteo is a rambling old adobe
★   hacienda that Wayne and Joanna Aarniokoski transformed into an idyllic inn more than 10 years ago. Thick adobe walls, wide-plank pine floors worn with age and rich in patina, and vistas and patios from which to enjoy them add to the privacy and romance of this refuge. The restaurant ($$$) is acclaimed for its innovative American cuisine and is open to the public (reservations are essential). Chef Julie Francis prepares a new menu each week, with specialties such as wild mushroom and leek ravioli with sweet corn and asparagus. The intimate setting of the inn and restaurant is geared toward adults. ⊠ *9 La Vega, Galisteo 87540,* ☎ *505/466–4000,* ℻ *505/466–4008. 12 rooms. Restaurant, pool. D, MC, V. BP.* ✆

$$$$ ⊡ **Vista Clara Ranch Resort and Spa.** One mile outside Galisteo, this hideaway on 80 acres combines modern spa amenities and treatments with ancient healing arts. The Southwestern-style accommodations are charming and serene. Rotating chefs from around the world prepare the healthful meals, which focus on vegetables grown in the on-site organic garden (including greenhouse). The spa and beauty treatments include herbal and aroma wraps, salt glows, massage, facials, pedicures, and even all-natural hair coloring. Daily guided hikes head to petroglyph-inscribed rock formations. You can ride horseback and visit an authentic Native American sweat lodge. Vista Clara is unpretentious and prices are surprisingly reasonable. Round-trip transportation from Santa Fe–area hotels ($30) can be arranged for day-trippers, and there are also multi-day packages. The restaurant is open to the public but requires a 24-hour advance reservation. ⊠ *HC 75 (Box 111), Galisteo 87540,* ☎ *505/466–4772 or 888/663–9772,* ℻ *505/466–1942. 10 rooms. Restaurant, pool, spa, health club. MC, V.* ✆

El Rancho de las Golondrinas

15 mi south of Santa Fe off I–25 Exit 276 in La Cienega.

The "Williamsburg of the Southwest," El Rancho de las Golondrinas (the Ranch of the Swallows) is a reconstruction of a small agricultural village. Originally a *paraje,* or stopping place, on El Camino Real, the village has buildings from the 17th to 19th century. Travelers would stop at the ranch before making the final leg of the journey north on El Camino Real, a half-day ride from Santa Fe in horse-and-wagon time. By car, the ranch is only a 25-minute drive from the Plaza and even closer if you are on the south side of town. From Interstate 25, the village is tucked away from view, frozen in time. Owned and operated by the Paloheimo family, direct descendants of those who owned the ranch when it functioned as a paraje, the restored grounds of this living museum maintain an authentic character without compromising history for commercial gain. Even the gift shop carries items that reflect life on the ranch and the cultural exchange that took place there.

Guided tours (April–October) survey Spanish-colonial lifestyles in New Mexico from 1660 to 1890: you can view a molasses mill, threshing grounds, and wheelwright and blacksmith shops, as well as a mountain village and a *morada* (meeting place) of the order of Penitentes (a religious fraternity known for its reenactment during Holy Week of the tortures suffered by Christ). Farm animals roam through the barnyards on the 200-acre complex. Wool from the sheep is spun into yarn and woven into traditional Rio Grande–style blankets, and the corn grown is dried and used to feed the animals. During the spring and harvest festivals, on the first weekends of June and October, respectively, the village comes alive with Spanish-American folk music, dancing, and food and crafts demonstrations. ⊠ *334 Los Pinos Rd.,* ☎ *505/471–2261.* ⌺ *$5.* ☉ *Wed.–Sun. 10–4.* ✎

The High Road to Taos

The main highway to Taos along the Rio Grande gorge (NM 68) provides dramatic close-ups of the river and rocky mountain faces (☞ Low Road to Santa Fe *in* Side Trips *in* Chapter 3), but if you have a couple of extra hours, the High Road to Taos provides sweeping views of woodlands and some traditional villages to explore. The High Road consists of U.S. 285 north to NM 503 (just past village of Pojoaque), to Santa Fe County Road 98 (a left at sign for Chimayó), to NM 76 northeast to NM 75 east, to NM 518 north. The drive through the rolling foothills and tiny valleys of the Sangre de Cristos, dotted with orchards, pueblos, and picturesque villages, is stunning. In mid-April the orchards are in blossom; summer turns the valleys into lush green oases; and in fall, the smell of piñon adds to the sensual overload of golden leaves and red-chile ristras hanging from the houses. In winter, the fields are covered with quilts of snow, and the lines of homes, fences, and trees stand out like bold pen-and-ink drawings against the sky. But the roads can be icy and treacherous. If your rental car isn't up to adverse weather conditions, take the "low road" to Taos. If you decide to take the High Road just one way between Santa Fe and Taos, you might want to save it for the return journey—the scenery is best enjoyed when traveling north to south.

Española

20 mi from Santa Fe, north on U.S. 285/84.

Only a 20-minute drive north of Santa Fe is the Española Valley, where rivers and state highways converge to form the epicenter of the valley—Española. This is the land of '53 turquoise Chevy pick-ups and red TransAms that practically scrape the ground, chain steering wheels, tiny tires, and shiny hubcaps. Vying for attention with these low-riders are trucks hoisted 4 ft off the ground by oversize tires. A few miles north of Española on U.S. 285/84, the highway splits, 84 heading northwest through the Rio Chama valley, and 285 cutting east and then straight north toward Ojo Caliente (☞ *below*). Highway 68 heads northeast toward Taos. All of the main arteries converge in the heart of town in a confusing maze, so watch the signs on the south side of town. Tank up here before making a road trip north. Traffic moves slowly, especially on weekend nights when cruisers bring car culture alive. Both the Low Riders Club and the Hot Rod and Drag Racing Club have chapters in Española. More of a crossroads than a destination, Española has a few outstanding restaurants that serve northern New Mexican cuisine and are worth the trip.

DINING

$$–$$$ ✕ **El Paragua Restaurant.** With a dark, intimate atmosphere of wood and stone, this place offers a more formal ambience for New Mexican and Mexican cuisine. Steaks and fish are grilled over a mesquite-wood fire. Lunch and dinner are served daily. ⊠ *603 Santa Cruz Rd. (NM 76 at Hwy. 68),* ☎ *505/753–3211 or 800/929–8226. D, MC, V.*

$–$$ ✕ **JoAnn's Ranch O Casados.** JoAnn Casados grew up on a ranch in Española, where she learned to grow chiles and squash. The ranch still provides many of the fresh ingredients used to create the great chiles rellenos, *posole* (corn with pork in a broth), and enchiladas. Half portions and a children's menu are served as well. The casual decor includes brightly striped Mexican blankets on the walls. Beer and wine are served. ✉ *418 North Riverside Dr. (on Hwy. 68),* ☎ *505/753–2837. Reservations not accepted. D, MC, V. Closed Sun.*

Chimayó
25 mi north of Santa Fe, 7 mi east of Española on NM 76

From Santa Fe, you can take the scenic NM 503, which winds past horses and orchards in the narrow Nambé Valley, then ascends into the red-rock canyons with a view of Truchas Peaks to the northeast before dropping into the bucolic village of Chimayó. New Mexico's state motto, "The Land of Enchantment," is hard to deny once you lay eyes on this village. It is not to be missed. Nestled into hillsides where gnarled piñons seem to grow from bare bedrock, Chimayó is famed for its weaving, its food, and its two chapels.

The **Santuario de Chimayó,** a small frontier adobe church, has a fantastically carved and painted wood altar and is built on the site where, believers say, a mysterious light came from the ground on Good Friday in 1810 and where a large wooden crucifix was found beneath the earth. The chapel sits above a sacred *pozito* (a small hole), the dirt from which is believed to have miraculous healing properties. Dozens of abandoned crutches and braces placed in the anteroom—along with many notes, letters, and photos—testify to this. The Santuario draws a steady stream of worshipers all year long—Chimayó is considered the Lourdes of the Southwest. During Holy Week as many as 50,000 pilgrims come here. The shrine is a National Historic Landmark, but unlike similar holy places, this one is not inundated by commercialism; a few small adobe shops nearby sell religious articles, brochures, and books. Mass is celebrated on Sundays. ✉ *Off SF County Rd. 98, look for sign and turn right,* ☎ *505/351–4889.* 🎫 *Free.* ☉ *Daily 9–5:30.*

A smaller chapel just 200 yards from El Santuario was built in 1857 and dedicated to **Santo Niño de Atocha.** As at the more famous Santuario, the dirt at Santo Niño de Atocha's chapel is said to have healing properties in the place where the *Santo Niño* was first placed. The little boy saint was brought here from Mexico by Severiano Medina, who claimed Santo Niño de Atocha had healed him of rheumatism. San Ildefonso pottery master Maria Martinez came here for healing as a child. Tales of the boy saint losing one of his shoes as he wandered through the countryside helping those in trouble endeared him to the people of northern New Mexico. It became a tradition to place shoes at the foot of the statue as an offering. 🎫 *Free.* ☉ *Daily 9–5:30.*

DINING AND LODGING

$$–$$$ ✕ **Rancho de Chimayó.** In a century-old adobe hacienda tucked into the mountains, with whitewashed walls, hand-stripped vigas, and cozy dining rooms, the Rancho de Chimayó is still owned and operated by the family that first occupied the house. There's a roaring fireplace in winter and, in summer, a terraced patio shaded by catalpa trees. You can take an after-dinner stroll on the grounds' paths. Reservations are essential in summer. ✉ *SF County Rd. 98,* ☎ *505/351–4444 or 505/ 984–2100. AE, D, DC, MC, V.*

$ ✕ **Leona's de Chimayó.** This fast-food-style burrito and chile stand at one end of the Santuario de Chimayó parking lot has only a few tables, and in summer it's crowded. The specialty is flavored tortillas—

everything from jalapeño to butterscotch. (Her business became so successful that owner Leona Tiede opened a tortilla factory in Chimayó's Manzana Center.) ⊠ *Off SF County Rd. 98, behind Santuario de Chimayó,* ☎ *505/351–4569 or 888/561–5569. AE, D, DC, MC, V.*

$$–$$$ ⊞ **Casa Escondida.** Intimate and peaceful, this adobe inn has sweeping views of the Sangre de Cristo range. The setting makes it a great base for mountain bikers. Chopin on the CD player and the scent of fresh-baked strudel waft through the rooms; owner Irenka Taurek, who speaks several languages, and manager Matthew Higgi provide an international welcome. Rooms are decorated with antiques and Native American and other regional arts and crafts. Ask for the Sun Room, in the main house, which has a private patio, viga ceilings, and a brick floor. The separate one-bedroom Casita Escondida has a kiva-style fireplace, tile floors, kitchen, and a sitting area. A large hot tub is hidden in a grove behind wild berry bushes. ⊠ *Off NM 76 at Mile Marker 0100 (Box 142), 85722,* ☎ *505/351–4805 or 800/643–7201,* FAX *505/ 351–2575. 7 rooms, 1 house. Outdoor hot tub. AE, MC, V. BP.* ⊜

$$ ⊞ **Hacienda de Chimayó.** This authentic adobe house is furnished with antiques, and each room has a private bath and fireplace. The inn doesn't offer much in the way of seclusion since it's directly on Chimayó's main road, but it is conveniently across from the lovely Rancho de Chimayó restaurant and within walking distance of the Santuario. ⊠ *Off SF County Rd. 98 (Box 11), Chimayo 87522,* ☎ *505/351–2222 or 888/270–2320. 6 rooms, 1 suite. AE, MC, V. CP.*

$$ ⊞ **La Posada de Chimayó.** New Mexico's first B&B is a peaceful place whose two suites have fireplaces, Mexican rugs, handwoven bedspreads, and comfortable regional furniture. The entire guest house can be rented by the week and the minimum stay is two nights. Views are somewhat obscured and the house is set close to the dirt road. ⊠ *279 Rio Arriba, County Rd. 0101 (Box 463), 87522,* ☎ FAX *505/351– 4605. 2 suites. BP. No credit cards.*

SHOPPING

Centinela Traditional Arts-Weaving (⊠ NM 76, approximately 1 mi east of the junction with County Rd. 98, ☎ 505/351–2180 or 877/ 351–2180) continues the Trujillo family weaving tradition, which started in northern New Mexico more than seven generations ago. Irvin Trujillo and his wife, Lisa, are both award-winning master weavers, creating Rio Grande–style tapestry blankets and rugs, many of them with natural dyes that authentically replicate early weavings. Most designs are historically based, but the Trujillos contribute their own designs as well. The shop and gallery carries these heirloom-quality textiles, with a knowledgeable staff on hand to demonstrate or answer questions about the weaving technique.

Ortega's Weaving Shop (⊠ NM 76 at County Rd. 98, look for the sign on the left if going north on SF County Rd. 98, ☎ 505/351–4215 or 877/351–4215) sells Rio Grande– and Chimayó-style textiles made by the family whose Spanish ancestors brought the craft to New Mexico in the 1600s. The Galeria Ortega, next door, sells traditional New Mexican and Hispanic and contemporary Native American arts and crafts. The shop is closed on Sunday.

Cordova

28 mi north of Santa Fe. From Chimayó, go north on NM 76 for about 4 mi, turn right onto the road at Mountain View Elementary School.

Hardly more than a mountain village with a small central plaza, a school, a post office, and a church, Cordova is the center of the regional wood-carving industry. The town supports 35 full-time and part-time carvers. Most of them are descendants of José Dolores López, who in the 1920s created the village's signature unpainted "Cordova style" of carving. Most of the *santeros* (makers of religious images) have signs outside their homes indicating that santos are for sale. The pieces are expensive, ranging from several hundred dollars for small ones to several thousand for larger figures. There are also affordable and delightful small carvings of animals and birds. The **St. Anthony of Padua Chapel,** which is filled with handcrafted retablos and other religious art, is worth a visit.

Truchas
35 mi north of Santa Fe; from Cordova, take NM 76 1½ mi north.

Truchas (Spanish for "trout") is where Robert Redford shot the movie *The Milagro Beanfield War* (based on the much-better novel written by Taos author John Nichols). This village is perched on the rim of a deep canyon beneath the towering Truchas Peaks, mountains high enough to be almost perpetually capped with snow. The tallest of the Truchas Peaks is 13,102 ft, the second-highest point in New Mexico. There are a few galleries and a small market in this town, which feels like an outpost just waking up from the colonial days.

SHOPPING

The most notable of the colorful shops and galleries in Truchas is **Cordova's Weaving Shop** (✉ Box 425, ☎ 505/689–2437).

En Route Continuing toward Taos, you'll come to the marvelous **San Tomás Church** in the village of Trampas, 7 mi north of Truchas on NM 76. It dates from at least 1760. To reach Rancho de Taos, the site of **San Francisco de Asís Church** (☞ Ranchos de Taos and Points South *in* Chapter 3), continue north on NM 76 to its intersection with NM 75 and turn right (east). After 6 mi you'll come to NM 518. Make a left and drive 14 mi; the driveway leading to the church is 500 yards south of NM 518 on NM 68. Taos Plaza is about 4 mi north of the San Francisco de Asís on NM 68.

Pueblos near Santa Fe

This trip will take you to several of the state's 19 pueblos, including San Ildefonso, one of the state's most picturesque, and Santa Clara, whose lands harbor a dramatic set of ancient cliff dwellings. Between the two reservations sits the ominous landmark called Black Mesa, which you can see from NM 30 or NM 502. The solitary butte has inspired many painters, including Georgia O'Keeffe. Plan on spending anywhere from one to three hours at each pueblo, and leave the day open if you are there for a feast day, when dances are set to an organic rather than mechanical clock. Pueblo grounds and hiking areas do not permit pets.

Pojoaque Pueblo
12 mi north of Santa Fe on U.S. 84/285.

There is not much to see in the pueblo's plaza area, which hardly has a visible core, but the state visitor center and adjoining **Poeh Cultural Center and Museum** on U.S. 84/285 are worth a visit. The latter is an impressive complex of traditional adobe buildings, including the three-story Sun Tower, which contains a museum, a cultural center, and artists' studios. There are frequent demonstrations by artists, exhibitions, and, in warm weather, traditional ceremonial dances. By the early 20th century the pueblo was virtually uninhabited, but the survivors eventually began to restore it. Pojoaque's feast day is celebrated with dancing on December 12. The visitor center is one of the friendliest and best stocked in northern New Mexico, with free maps and literature on hiking, fishing, and the area's history. Crafts in the visitor center are made by residents of Pojoaque and neighboring pueblos. ✉ *41*

Camino de Rincon (Box 71), on U.S 84/285, Santa Fe 87501, ☎ *505/ 455–3334.* ⌨ *Free.* ☉ *Daily 8–5. Sketching, cameras, and video cameras are prohibited.*

Nambé Pueblo

Head north from Santa Fe past Tesuque on U.S. 84/285; about 12 mi out of town at Pojoaque turn northeast (right) onto NM 503. Nambé Pueblo is off NM 503 about 4 mi down a side road.

Nambé Pueblo no longer has a visitor center, so the best time to visit is during a ceremonial feast-day celebration on October 4, the feast day of St. Francis. If you want to explore the landscape surrounding the pueblo, take the drive past the pueblo until you come to Nambé Falls. There's a shady picnic area and a large fishing lake that's open from March to November. The waterfalls are about a 15-minute hike in from the parking and picnic area along a rocky, clearly marked path. The water pours over a rock precipice—a loud and dramatic sight given the modest size of the river. ⌧ *Nambé Pueblo Rd. off NM 503,* ☎ *505/ 455–2036.* ⌨ *$2.*

San Ildefonso Pueblo

19 mi north of Santa Fe on U.S. 84/285. From the Pojoaque Pueblo, return to U.S. 84/285, but exit almost immediately onto NM 502 toward Los Alamos. Continue for about 7 mi until you reach the turnoff for San Ildefonso.

Maria Martinez, one of the most renowned Pueblo potters, lived here. She first created her exquisite "black on black" pottery in 1919 and in doing so sparked a major revival of all Pueblo arts and crafts. She died in 1980, and the 26,000-acre San Ildefonso Pueblo remains a major center for pottery and other arts and crafts. Many artists sell from their homes, and there are trading posts, a visitor center, and a museum where some of Martinez's work can be seen on weekdays. San Ildefonso is also one of the more visually appealing pueblos, with a well-defined plaza core and a spectacular setting beneath the Pajarito Plateau and Black Mesa. The pueblo's feast day is January 23, when unforgettable buffalo, deer, and Comanche dances are performed from dawn to dusk. Cameras are not permitted at any of the ceremonial dances but may be used at other times with a permit.

On the western edge of the reservation is **Babbitt's Cottonwood Trading Post,** where John Babbitt continues the multigenerational tradition as a trader. Babbitt provides materials for making ceremonial costumes used during feast days. Ribbons, yarn and cloth, gourds for making rattles, and dried animal skins are among the goods he sells at this contemporary trading post. He also carries an excellent selection of 19th-century and new Navajo weavings. His expertise as a trader shows in the fine selection of Native American crafts for sale. ⌧ *NM 502,* ☎ *505/455–3549.* ⌨ *$3 per car; still-camera permit $10, video recorder permit $20, sketching permit $15.* ☉ *Daily 8–5.*

Santa Clara Pueblo

27 mi northwest of Santa Fe. From San Ildefonso Pueblo, return to NM 502 and continue west across the Rio Grande to NM 30. Turn north (right) and continue 6 mi to the turnoff to the Puyé Cliff Dwellings. Proceed on this gravel road 9 mi to Santa Clara Pueblo.

Santa Clara Pueblo, southwest of Española, is the home of a historic treasure—the awesome **Puyé Cliff Dwellings,** believed to have been built in the 13th to 14th centuries. They can be seen by driving 9 mi up a gravel road through a canyon, south of the village off NM 502. The pueblo also contains four ponds, miles of stream fishing, and picnicking and camping facilities. You can tour the cliff dwellings, topped by the ruins of a 740-room pueblo, on your own or with a guide. Permits for the use of trails, camping, and picnic areas, as well as for fishing in trout ponds, are available at the sites.

Shops in the village sell burnished red pottery, engraved blackware, paintings, and other arts and crafts. All pottery is made via the coil method, not with a pottery wheel. Santa Clara is known for its carved pieces, and Avanyu, a water serpent that guards the waters, is the pueblo's symbol. Other typical works include engagement baskets, wedding vessels, and seed pots. The pueblo's feast day of St. Clare is celebrated on August 12. ⊠ *Off NM 502 on NM 30, Española,* ☎ *505/753–7326.* ⊡ *Pueblo free, cliff dwellings $5, video and still-camera permits $15.* ⊙ *Daily 8–4:30.*

Ojo Caliente

55 mi north of Santa Fe on U.S. 285.

Ojo Caliente is the only place in North America where five different types of hot springs—iron, lithia, arsenic, salt, and soda—are found side by side. The town was named by Spanish explorer Cabeza de Vaca, who visited in 1535 and believed he had stumbled upon the Fountain of Youth. He recorded his excitement in his journal:

"The greatest treasure I have found these strange people to possess are some hot springs which burst out of the foot of a mountain that gives evidence of being an active volcano. So powerful are the chemicals contained in this water that the inhabitants have a belief that the waters were given to them by their gods after weeping many tears. From the effect of the waters upon my remaining men, I am inclined to believe that the waters will do many things that our doctors are not capable of doing . . . I believe I have found the Fountain of Youth."

Modern-day visitors draw similar conclusions about the restorative powers of the springs. The spa itself, built in the 1920s (no one knows the exact date), is a no-frills establishment that includes a hotel and cottages, a restaurant, a gift shop, massage rooms, men's and women's bathhouses, a chlorine-free swimming pool, and indoor and outdoor mineral-water tubs. The hotel, one of the original bathhouses, and the springs are all on the National Register of Historic Places, as is the adjacent Round Barn, from which visitors can take horseback tours and guided hikes to ancient pueblo dwellings and petroglyph-etched rocks. Spa services include wraps, massage, facials, and acupuncture. The setting at the foot of sandstone cliffs topped by the ruins of ancient Indian pueblos is nothing short of inspiring.

$$$ ⊡ **Ojo Caliente Mineral Springs Spa and Resort.** Accommodations at this spa are decidedly spartan but clean and comfortable, with down comforters on the beds and rudimentary bathrooms without showers or tubs—you've come for the mineral springs, after all. Lodgers have complimentary access to the mineral pools and milagro (miracle) wraps, and the bathhouse is equipped with showers. The lodgings have no phones, but the morning newspaper is supplied. Some of the cottages have kitchenettes. Horseback tours of the area must be prearranged, so notify the office in advance. Poppy's Cafe serves New Mexican specialties for breakfast, lunch, and dinner. ⊠ *50 Los Banos Dr., off U.S. 285, 30 mi north of Española (Box 68), 87549,* ☎ *505/583–2233 or 800/222–9162,* ℻ *505/583–2464. 19 rooms, 19 cottages. Café. AE, D, DC, MC, V.* ✑

SANTA FE A TO Z

Arriving and Departing

By Bus

Texas, New Mexico & Oklahoma Coaches (⊠ 858 St. Michael's Dr., ☎ 800/231–2222), which is affiliated with Greyhound, serves Santa Fe. The **Greyhound bus station** (⊠ 858 St. Michael's Dr., ☎ 505/471–0008) is south of downtown.

By Car

Interstate 25 passes east–west through Santa Fe, which is 58 mi northeast of Albuquerque. U.S. 84/285 runs north–south through the city. The Turquoise Trail (☞ Side Trips *in* Chapter 5) is a scenic, two-lane approach to Santa Fe from Albuquerque.

By Plane

See Airports & Transfers *in* Smart Travel Tips A to Z.

By Train

Amtrak (☎ 800/872–7245) operates the *Southwest Chief* between Chicago and Los Angeles. The train stops in Lamy, 18 mi south of Santa Fe. You need to reserve a day ahead for the **shuttle bus** (☎ 505/982–8829) to and from Santa Fe. The cost each way is $14.

Getting Around

The majority of museums, galleries, shops, and restaurants in downtown Santa Fe are within walking distance of the Plaza. You need to take a car or a bus to get to the city's outer reaches.

By Bus

The city's bus system, **Santa Fe Trails** (☎ 505/438–1464), covers six major routes: Agua Fria, Cerrillos, West Alameda, Southside, Eastside, and Galisteo. A daily pass costs $1. Buses run about every 30 minutes on weekdays, every hour on weekends. Service begins at 6 AM and continues until 10 PM on weekdays and until 8 PM on Saturday. There is no bus service on Sunday.

By Car

For car rental companies in Santa Fe, *see* Car Rental *in* Smart Travel Tips A to Z. Parking in Santa Fe is difficult, but public and private lots can be found throughout the city. Parking meters are well monitored. There are parking garages near the Plaza on W. San Franscisco, between Sandoval and Galisteo, and on Water Street, between Don Gaspar and Shelby Street.

By Limousine

Limotion (☎ 505/820–0816) charges $65 per hour, with a two-hour minimum.

By Taxi

Capital City Cab Company (☎ 505/438–0000) controls all the cabs in Santa Fe. The taxis aren't metered; you pay a flat fee determined by the distance you're traveling. There are no cab stands; you must phone to arrange a ride. Trips within the city cost between $4 and $7. You can pick up a 40% taxi discount coupon at the Santa Fe Public Library (☞ Visitor Information, *below*).

Guided Tours

General-Interest

Aboot About (☎ 505/988–2774) has been walking groups through the history, art, and architecture of Santa Fe for 20 years. Tours ($10) leave daily at 9:30 and 1:30 from the Eldorado Hotel and at 9:45 and 1:45 from the Hotel St. Francis. Tours take about two hours. No reservations are required.

Afoot in Santa Fe Walking Tours (✉ 211 Old Santa Fe Trail, ☎ 505/983–3701) conducts a two-hour close-up look at the city. The tours ($10) leave from the Hotel Loretto from Monday to Sunday at 9:30. Several trolley tours are offered daily.

Gray Line Tours of Santa Fe (✉ 1330 Hickox St., ☎ 505/983–9491) operates guided outings to Taos, the Bandelier cliff dwellings, Los Alamos, and the Santa Clara pueblo. It also offers city tours and a minibus charter service.

Santa Fe Detours (✉ 107 Washington Ave., outdoor booth Mar.–Oct.; ✉ 54½ San Francisco St., above Häagen-Dazs, ☎ 505/983–6565 or 800/338–6877) conducts bus, river, rail, horseback, and walking tours and organizes rafting and ski packages.

Storytellers and the Southwest (☎ 505/989–4561) surveys Santa Fe through its literary history. The two-hour literary walking tour explores the history, legends, characters, and authors of the region. Tours are by appointment only and for at least two people; the cost is $15 per person.

Learning Experiences

Art Adventures in the Southwest (✉ Box 5912, 87502, ☎ 505/986–1108, FAX 505/986–3845, ✑) takes you into the New Mexico landscape for outdoor art classes with Jane Shoenfeld. All materials are supplied, as are all levels of experience.

Santa Fe Art Institute (✉ 1600 St. Michael's Dr., on the College of Santa Fe campus, ☎ 505/424–5050, ✑) is housed in the Visual Arts Center designed by Mexican architect Ricardo Legorreta (a Modernist break from Santa Fe style). The institute (not part of the College of Santa Fe) offers weeklong workshops with renowned artists such as Phoebe Adams and Nathan Olivéra. Dormitory quarters are available and studio space is provided. Workshops are offered year-round.

Santa Fe Photographic Workshops (✉ Box 9916, ☎ 505/983–1400, ✑) offers workshops in photographic processes including digital imaging, platinum, and travel photography. The workshops have an excellent reputation, and many instructors return year after year.

Santa Fe School of Cooking (✉ 116 W. San Francisco St., ☎ 505/983–4511) holds night and day classes in regional New Mexican fare.

Special-Interest

Behind Adobe Walls and Garden Tours (✉ 54½ E. San Francisco St., ☎ 505/983–6565 or 800/338–6877) generally schedules house and garden tours on the last two Tuesdays of July and the first two Tuesdays of August.

Recursos (✉ 826 Camino de Monte Rey, ☎ 505/982–9301, ✑) operates historical, cultural, and nature tours, plus a series of literary conferences and workshops.

Rojo Tours (✉ Box 15744, 87504, ☎ 505/983–8333) designs specialized trips—to view wildflowers, pueblo ruins and cliff dwellings, galleries and studios, Native American arts and crafts, and private homes—as well as adventure activity tours.

Southwestern Association for Indian Arts (⊠ 125 E. Palace Ave., ☎ 505/983–5220), which produces the annual Santa Fe Indian Market, organizes visits to Native American artists in northern New Mexico.

Contacts and Resources

Emergencies
Ambulance, Fire, and Police (☎ 911).

Lovelace Urgent Care (⊠ 901 W. Alameda, ☎ 505/995–2500; 440 St. Michael's Dr., ☎ 505/995–2400).

Medical Emergency Room, St. Vincent Hospital (⊠ 455 St. Michael's Dr., ☎ 505/820–5250).

Medical Dental Center (⊠ 465 St. Michael's Dr., Suite 205, ☎ 505/983–8089).

24-Hour Pharmacy
Walgreens (⊠ 1096 S. St. Francis Dr., ☎ 505/982–9811).

Visitor Information
Los Alamos County Chamber of Commerce (⊠ Fuller Lodge, 2132 Central Ave. [Box 460 VG], Los Alamos 87544, ☎ 505/662–8105).

New Mexico Department of Tourism (⊠ Lamy Bldg., 491 Old Santa Fe Trail, 87503, ☎ 505/827–7400 or 800/733–6396).

Española Chamber of Commerce (⊠ 417 Big Rock Center, Española 87532, ☎ 505/753–2831).

Santa Fe Chamber of Commerce (⊠ 510 N. Guadalupe St., Suite L, De Vargas Center N, 87504, ☎ 505/983–7317).

Santa Fe Convention and Visitors Bureau (⊠ 201 W. Marcy St. [Box 909], 87504, ☎ 505/984–6760 or 800/777–2489).

Santa Fe Public Library (⊠ 145 Washington Ave., ☎ 505/984–6780).

3 TAOS
WITH THE ENCHANTED CIRCLE AND TAOS SKI VALLEY

The essence of Taos lies in the easy rapport of its Native American, Hispanic, and Anglo inhabitants, a reality vividly illustrated by this small town's effusive cultural spirit and eclectic architecture. The diversity, physical beauty, and Old West feel of Taos have lured authors, painters, and other artists since the early 20th century. More recently, outdoors enthusiasts have discovered the area's world-class ski slopes and rushing rivers.

TAOS CASTS A LINGERING SPELL. The scent of piñon trees fills the air, and the fragrance of sagebrush is curiously strong here. Stately elms and cottonwoods frame sometimes narrow streets, and one- and two-story adobe buildings line the two-centuries-old Plaza. The adobes reveal the influence of Native American and Spanish settlers, and the entrepreneurial spirit here was brought by American traders. When it rains, the unpaved roads and lanes around town are not un- like the rutted streets of yesteryear.

Updated by
Jeanie Puleston
Fleming

With a population of about 6,500, Taos, on a rolling mesa at the base of the Sangre de Cristo Mountains, is actually three towns in one. The first is the low-key business district of art galleries, restaurants, and shops that recalls the Santa Fe of a few decades ago. The second area, 3 mi north of the commercial center, is Taos Pueblo, home to Tiwa-speak- ing Native Americans and also a UNESCO World Heritage site. Life at the Taos Pueblo long predates the arrival of the Spanish in America in the 1500s. Unlike many nomadic Native American tribes that were forced to relocate to government-designated reservations, the residents of Taos Pueblo have inhabited their land (at present 95,000 acres) at the base of the 12,282-ft-high Taos Mountain for centuries.

The third part of Taos, 4 mi south of town, is Ranchos de Taos, a farm- ing and ranching community settled by the Spanish. Ranchos de Taos is best known for the San Francisco de Asís Church, whose buttressed adobe walls shelter significant religious artifacts and paintings. Its massive exterior and *camposanto* (graveyard) are among the most photographed in the country.

That so many 20th-century painters, photographers, and literary fig- ures—among them Georgia O'Keeffe, Ansel Adams, and D. H. Lawrence—have been drawn to the earthy spirit of Taos has only heightened its appeal. Bert Geer Phillips and Ernest Leonard Blumen- schein, traveling from Denver on a planned painting trip into Mexico in 1898, stopped in Taos to have a broken wagon wheel repaired. En- thralled with the landscape, earth-hue adobe buildings, piercing light, and clean mountain air, they abandoned their plan to journey farther south. They returned to the Taos area often, speaking so highly of it that other East Coast artists followed them west. By 1915, the Taos Society of Artists had been established. Blumenschein and Phillips, with Joseph Henry Sharp and Eanger Irving Couse, all graduates of the Paris art school Académie Julian, formed the core of the group.

Another reason for the gathering of talented artists and other cultural lu- minaries in this community was the persuasive hospitality of transplanted socialite Mabel Dodge Luhan (☞ Close-Up: Mabel Dodge Luhan, *below*). Some of the early Taos artists spent their winters in New York or Chicago teaching painting or illustration to earn enough money to summer in New Mexico. Others became full-time New Mexicans. Living conditions were primitive then: no running water, electricity, or even indoor plumbing. But these painters happily endured such inconveniences to indulge their fascination with Native American customs, modes of dress, and ceremonies. Eventually, they co-opted the Native architecture and dress and pre- sumptuously fancied that they "knew" Indian culture. The society dis- banded in 1927, but Taos continued to attract artists. Several galleries opened and, in 1952, local painters joined together to form the Taos Artists' Association, forerunner to today's Taos Art Association. At present, sev- eral dozen galleries and shops (☞ Shopping, *below*) display art, sculp- ture, and crafts, and about 1,000 artists live in town or nearby. No mere satellite of Santa Fe, Taos is an art center in its own right.

Close-Up

HOSTESS OF TAOS

MABEL DODGE LUHAN, a progressive-minded socialite from Buffalo, New York, arrived on the scene in 1917, fell in love with Taos, and stayed. In the high-desert landscape and in the Taos Pueblo culture she found a purpose and unity that she firmly believed ought to be extended to American society at large. When she walked away from her "old, mythical life," aiding her as soul mate and spiritual mainstay was a statuesque Taos Pueblo man, Antonio Luhan, who became her fourth, and last, husband. In the house they built together next to Pueblo land, they hosted many of the era's great artists, writers, philosophers, psychologists, anthropologists, and social reformers. Mabel's friends and acquaintances included Martha Graham, Aldous Huxley, and Carl Jung. Mabel wrote to D. H. Lawrence many times and even tried to send him psychic messages until finally he, too, came to Taos and was profoundly affected by what he found. Although he stayed less than two years all together, some of his finest writing, including *The Plumed Serpent* and several novelettes, essays, and poems, grew out of his experiences in Taos and Mexico. Mabel herself penned several books; *Edge of Taos Desert: An Escape to Reality* (1937) is a part of her autobiography that vividly describes her life in Taos. She and her beloved Tony died within months of each other in 1970. Their house is now a conference center and B&B (*see* Lodging, *below*).

EXPLORING TAOS

Taos is small and resolutely rustic, and the central area is highly walkable. Sociable Taoseños make the town an even more welcoming place to explore. You'll need a car to reach the Enchanted Circle, the Rio Grande Gorge, Taos Ski Valley, and other places of interest beyond Taos proper. Traffic can be heavy in the peak summer and winter seasons; ask locals about back roads that let you avoid backed-up ones like Paseo del Pueblo.

The Museum Association of Taos includes seven properties. Among them are the Harwood Museum, the Fechin Institute, the Millicent Rogers Museum, and the Van Vechten–Lineberry Taos Art Museum, as well as those in the Kit Carson Historic Museum consortium: the Blumenschein Home and Museum, the Kit Carson Home and Museum, and La Hacienda de los Martínez. Each of the museums charges $4 or $5 for admission, but you can opt for a combination ticket—30% discount on all seven valid for one year, or buy a $10 joint ticket to the three Kit Carson museums.

Downtown Taos

More than four centuries after it was laid out, Taos Plaza remains the center of commercial life in Taos. Bent Street, where New Mexico's first American governor lived and died, is the town's upscale shopping area and gallery enclave.

Numbers in the text correspond to numbers in the margin and on the Taos map.

A Good Walk

Begin at the gazebo in the middle of **Taos Plaza** ①. After exploring the Plaza, head south from its western edge down the small unmarked alley (its name is West Plaza Drive). The first cross street is Camino de la Placita. Across it, West Plaza Drive becomes Ledoux Street. Continue south on Ledoux to the **Blumenschein Home and Museum** ② and, a few doors farther south, the **Harwood Foundation** ③. (If you're driving, the parking area for the Harwood Foundation is at Ledoux and Ranchitos Road.)

From the Harwood Foundation, walk back north on Ranchitos Road a few blocks, make a left on Camino de la Placita, and go right onto Don Fernando Road. Follow it east along the north side of the Plaza to Paseo del Pueblo Norte (NM 68), which is the main street of Taos. As you cross NM 68, Don Fernando Road changes to Kit Carson Road. On the north side of Kit Carson Road is the **Kit Carson Home and Museum** ④. After visiting the home, head back to Paseo del Pueblo Norte and walk north past the Taos Inn and **Stables Art Center** ⑤ to browse through Bent Street's shops, boutiques, and galleries.

In a tiny plaza is the **Governor Bent Museum** ⑥, the modest home of the first Anglo governor of the state. Across the street is the John Dunn House. Once the homestead of a colorful and well-respected Taos gambling and transportation entrepreneur, the Dunn House is now a small shopping plaza. At the western end of Bent Street, head north on Camino de la Placita. In about 2½ blocks you'll come to the Taos Volunteer Fire Department building, which doubles as a fire station and the **Firehouse Collection** ⑦ exhibition space.

Head east on Civic Plaza and cross Paseo del Pueblo Norte. To the north will be **Kit Carson Memorial Park** ⑧ and the **Fechin Institute** ⑨, named for the iconoclastic artist Nicolai Fechin. On 10 handsome acres north of the Fechin Institute stands the **Van Vechten–Lineberry Taos Art Museum** ⑩.

TIMING

The entire walk can be done in a half day, a whole day if you stop to lunch along the way and browse in the shops and galleries. The Fechin Institute is closed Monday and Tuesday. Hours vary by season, but visits by appointment are welcomed. Some museums are closed on the weekend, so you may want to do this walk on a Wednesday, Thursday, or Friday. You'll be able to tour each of the museums in less than an hour.

Sights to See

② **Blumenschein Home and Museum.** For an introduction to the history of the Taos art scene, start with Ernest L. Blumenschein's residence, which provides a glimpse into the cosmopolitan lives led by the members of the Taos Society of Artists, of which Blumenschein was a founding member. One of the rooms in the adobe-style structure dates from 1797. On display are the art, antiques, and other personal possessions of Blumenschein and his wife, Mary Greene Blumenschein, who also painted, as did their daughter Helen. Several of Ernest Blumenschein's vivid oil paintings hang in his former studio, and also on display are works by other early Taos artists. ⊠ *222 Ledoux St.,* ☎ *505/ 758–0505.* ✉ *$5 (or use Kit Carson Historic Museums of Taos joint ticket).* ☉ *Apr.–Oct., daily 9–5; Nov.–Mar., daily 11–4.*

★ ⑨ **Fechin Institute.** The interior of this extraordinary adobe house, built between 1927 and 1933 by Russian émigré and artist Nicolai Fechin, is marvel of carved Russian-style woodwork and furniture that glist with an almost golden sheen. Fechin constructed it to showcase his d

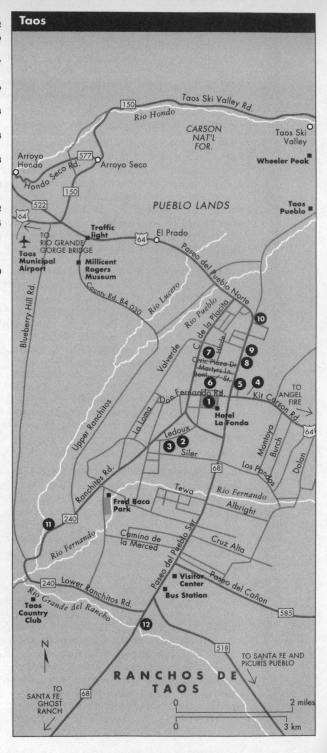

ingly colorful portraits and landscapes. Fechin's octogenarian daughter Eya oversees her father's architectural masterpiece—she loves talking about him and life "back then." Listed on the National Register of Historic Places, the Fechin Institute hosts exhibits and special workshops devoted to the artist's unique approach to learning, teaching, and creating. Open hours are often in flux, so call ahead. ⊠ *227 Paseo del Pueblo Norte,* ☎ *505/758–1710.* 🎫 *$3.* ☉ *Wed.–Sun. 10–2.*

🖐 ❼ **Firehouse Collection.** More than 100 works by well-known Taos artists like Joseph Sharp, Ernest L. Blumenschein, and Bert Phillips hang in the Taos Volunteer Fire Department building. The exhibition space adjoins the station house, where five fire engines are maintained at the ready and an antique fire engine is on display. ⊠ *323 Camino de la Placita,* ☎ *505/758–3386.* 🎫 *Free.* ☉ *Weekdays 8–4:30.*

🖐 ❻ **Governor Bent Museum.** In 1846, when New Mexico became a U.S. possession as a result of the Mexican War, Charles Bent, a trader, trapper, and mountain man, was appointed governor. Less than a year later he was killed in his house by an angry mob protesting New Mexico's annexation by the United States. Governor Bent was married to María Ignacia, the older sister of Josefa Jaramillo, the wife of mountain man Kit Carson. A collection of Native American artifacts, Western Americana, and family possessions is squeezed into five small rooms of the adobe building where Bent and his family lived. ⊠ *117A Bent St.,* ☎ *505/758–2376.* 🎫 *$1.* ☉ *Daily 10–5.*

★ ❸ **Harwood Foundation.** The Pueblo Revival former home of Burritt Elihu "Burt" Harwood, a dedicated painter who studied in France before moving to Taos with his public-spirited wife, Lucy, in 1916, is adjacent to a museum dedicated to the works of local artists. Traditional Hispanic northern New Mexican artists, early art-colony painters, post–World War II modernists, and contemporary artists such as Larry Bell, Agnes Martin, Ken Price, and Earl Stroh are represented. Mabel Dodge Luhan, a major arts patron, bequeathed many of the 19th-century and early 20th-century works in the Harwoods' collection, including *retablos* (painted wood representations of Catholic saints) and *bultos* (three-dimensional carvings of the saints). In the Hispanic Traditions Gallery upstairs are 19th-century tinwork, furniture, and sculpture. Downstairs, among early 20th-century art-colony holdings, look for E. Martin Hennings's *Chamisa in Bloom,* featuring the familiar New Mexican gray-green plant tipped with golden fall flowers and backed by a blue ridge of mountains. A tour of the ground-floor galleries shows that Taos painters of the era, notably Oscar Berninghaus, Ernest Blumenschien, Victor Higgins, Walter Ufer, Marsden Hartley, and John Marin, were fascinated by the land and the people linked to it. An octagonal gallery exhibits works by Agnes Martin. Martin's seven large canvas panels (5 ft by 5 ft) are studies in white paint, their precise lines and blocks forming textured grids. Operated by the University of New Mexico since 1936, the Harwood is the second oldest art museum in the state. ⊠ *238 Ledoux St.,* ☎ *505/758–9826.* 🎫 *$5.* ☉ *Tues.–Sat. 10–5, Sun. noon–5.*

🖐 ❹ **Kit Carson Home and Museum.** Kit Carson bought this low-slung 12-room adobe home in 1843 as a wedding gift for Josefa Jaramillo, the daughter of a powerful, politically influential Spanish family. Josefa was 14 when the dashing, twice-married mountain man and scout began courting her. Three of the museum's rooms are furnished as they were when the Carson family lived here. The rest of the museum is devoted to gun and mountain-man exhibits, such as rugged leather clothing and Kit's own Spencer carbine rifle with its beaded leather carrying case, and early Taos antiques, artifacts, and manuscripts. ⊠ *Kit Carson Rd.,*

☎ *505/758–4741.* 🎫 *$5 (or use Kit Carson Historic Museums of Taos joint ticket).* ☉ *Nov. 2–Apr., daily 9–5; May–Nov. 1, daily 8–6.*

NEED A
BREAK?

Caffe Tazza (✉ 122 Kit Carson Rd., ☎ 505/758-8706) serves great coffee, chai tea, and Italian sodas as well as pastries and vegetarian chili inside by the photo display or on the outside terrace. Or, let the coffee aroma draw you into the tiny **World Cup** (✉ 102 Paseo del Pueblo Norte, ☎ 505/737-5299).

🐾 **⑧ Kit Carson Memorial Park.** The noted pioneer is buried in the park that bears his name. His grave is marked with a *cerquita* (a spiked wrought-iron rectangular fence), traditionally used to outline and protect burial sites. Also interred here is Mabel Dodge Luhan, the pioneering patron of the early Taos art scene. The 20-acre park has swings and slides for recreational breaks. It's well marked with big stone pillars and a gate. ✉ *Paseo del Pueblo Norte at Civic Plaza Dr.,* ☎ *505/758-8234.* 🎫 *Free.* ☉ *Memorial Day–Labor Day, daily 8–8; Labor Day–Memorial Day, daily 8–5.*

⑤ Stables Art Center. It was in the stables in back of this house that the Taos Artists' Association first began showing the works of members and invited nonmember artists from across northern New Mexico. In 1952 the association purchased the handsome adobe building, which is now the visual arts gallery of the Taos Art Association. All the work on exhibit is for sale. ✉ *133 Paseo del Pueblo Norte,* ☎ *505/758-2036.* 🎫 *Free.* ☉ *Daily 10–5.*

❶ Taos Plaza. The first European explorers of the Taos Valley came here with Captain Hernando de Alvarado, a member of Francisco Vásquez de Coronado's expedition of 1540. Basque explorer Don Juan de Oñate arrived in Taos in July 1598 and established a mission and trading arrangements with residents of Taos Pueblo. The settlement actually developed into two plazas: the Plaza at the heart of the town became a thriving business district for the early colony; a walled residential plaza was constructed a few hundred yards behind; it remains active today, home to a throng of gift and coffee shops. As authorized by a special act of Congress, the American flag flies in the center of the Plaza day and night in recognition of Kit Carson's heroic stand protecting it from Confederate sympathizers during the Civil War. The covered gazebo was donated by heiress and longtime Taos resident Mabel Dodge Luhan. On the southeastern corner of Taos Plaza is the **Hotel La Fonda de Taos.** Some infamous erotic paintings by D. H. Lawrence that were naughty in his day but are quite tame by present standards can be viewed ($2 entry fee) in the former barroom beyond the lobby. As an accommodation, the hotel is in need of renovations.

NEED A
BREAK?

To fuel your walk, grab a pick-me-up at the **Bent Street Coffeehouse** (✉ 124-F Bent St., ☎ 505/751-7184).

❿ Van Vechten–Lineberry Taos Art Museum. This privately run museum shows the works of painter Duane Van Vechten, the late wife of Edwin C. Lineberry. Her former studio is the entrance to the museum, whose collection of about 130 works by more than 50 Taos artists includes works of varying quality by all of the founders of the Taos Society of Artists. The museum's signature piece is *Our Lady of Gualadupe* (1929) by Van Vechten, a painting of a solid adobe church against a deep blue sky. On a par with the exhibits are the museum grounds, a 10-acre, walled park, and the building itself, which was the home of the artist and Mr. Lineberry, who maintains the museum with his wife,

Novella. ⊠ *501 Paseo del Norte,* ☎ *505/758–2690.* ☒ *$6.* ⊙ *Wed.– Fri. 11–4, weekends 1:30–4.*

NEED A
BREAK? Join the local clientele at the north or south location of the **Bean** (⊠ 900 Paseo del Pueblo Norte, ☎ 505/758–7111; 1033 Paseo del Pueblo Sur, ☎ 505/758–5123). The south Bean offers breakfast and lunch, too.

Ranchos de Taos and Points South

The first Spanish settlers were farmers who faced raids by non–Pueblo Indians like the Comanches. Aspects of this history come alive on this meandering drive south through fields and farmland to a restored hacienda and into a former farming village with its famous, fortresslike church.

Numbers in the text correspond to numbers in the margin and on the Taos map.

A Good Drive

Head south 3 mi on NM 240 (also known as Ranchitos Road) to **La Hacienda de los Martínez** ⑪. As you pass by the adobe cottages and modest homes dotting the landscape, you'll get a sense of the area's rural atmosphere. From the hacienda continue south and east another 4 mi to NM 68 and the small farming village of **Ranchos de Taos.** Head south on NM 68 and watch for signs for **San Francisco de Asís Church** ⑫, which is on the east side of NM 68. The small plaza here contains several galleries worth checking out. Off the beaten path from Ranchos de Taos is the **Picuris Pueblo.**

TIMING

Set aside about two hours to tour the hacienda, a bit of Ranchos de Taos, and San Francisco de Asís Church. You'll need to make a day of this tour if you continue on to Picurís Pueblo.

Sights to See

⑪ **La Hacienda de los Martínez.** Spare and fortlike, this adobe structure built between 1804 and 1827 on the bank of the Rio Pueblo served as a community refuge during Comanche and Apache raids. Its thick walls, which have few windows, surround two central courtyards. Don Antonio Severino Martínez was a farmer and trader; the hacienda was the final stop along El Camino Real (the Royal Road), the trade route the Spanish established between Mexico City and New Mexico. The restored period rooms here contain textiles, foods, and crafts of the early 19th century. There's a working blacksmith's shop, and weavers create beautiful textiles on reconstructed period looms. During the last weekend in September the hacienda hosts the Old Taos Trade Fair, a reenactment of fall trading fairs of the 1820s, when Plains Indians and trappers came to Taos to trade with the Spanish and the Pueblo Indians. The two-day event includes crafts demonstrations, native foods, and entertainment. ⊠ *Ranchitos Rd. (NM 240),* ☎ *505/758–1000.* ☒ *$5 (or use Kit Carson Historic Museums of Taos joint ticket).* ⊙ *Apr.– Oct., daily 9–5; Nov.–Mar., daily 10–4.*

OFF THE
BEATEN PATH **PICURÍS PUEBLO** – The Picurís (Keresan for "those who paint") Native Americans once lived in six- and seven-story dwellings similar to those still standing at the Taos Pueblo, but these were abandoned in the wake of 18th-century Pueblo uprisings. Relatively isolated about 30 mi south of Taos, Picurís, one of the smallest pueblos in New Mexico, is surrounded by the timberland of the Carson National Forest. The 270-member Tiwa-speaking Picurís tribe is a sovereign nation and has no treaties with any country, including the United States. You can tour the village

and 700-year-old ruins of kivas (ceremonial rooms) and storage areas, which were excavated in 1961. The exhibits in the pueblo's museum include pottery and some ruins. A separate building under renovation will contain a restaurant. The uncompleted convenience store and crafts shop are occasionally open. Fishing, picnicking, and camping are allowed at nearby trout-stocked Pu-Na and Tu-Tah lakes. Fishing and camping permits can be obtained at the Picurís Market. The pueblo honors its patron saint, San Lorenzo, with a festival on August 9 and 10. An example of the Picurís people's enterprising spirit is their majority interest in the lovely Hotel Santa Fe in the state's capital city; many pueblo members commute to work there (☞ Lodging, Chapter 2). ⊠ *NM 75, Peñasco (from Ranchos de Taos head south on NM 518, east on NM 75, and turn right at signs for village; from NM 68 head east on NM 75 and make a left into village),* ☎ *505/587–2519.* ☞ *Museum free, self-guided walking or driving tours $1.75, still camera permit $5 (includes $1.75 fee for camera-holder), video camera or sketching permit $10 (includes $1.75 fee).* ☉ *Daily 9–6, but call ahead especially Labor Day–Memorial Day, when the pueblo is sometimes closed.*

Ranchos de Taos. A few minutes' drive south of the center of Taos, this village still retains some of its rural atmosphere despite the highway traffic passing through. Huddled around its famous adobe church and dusty plaza are cheerful, remodeled shops and galleries standing shoulder to shoulder with crumbling adobe shells. This ranching, farming, and budding small-business community was an early home to Taos Native Americans before being settled by Spaniards in 1716. While many of the adobe dwellings have seen better days, the shops, modest galleries, taco stands, and two fine restaurants (☞ Dining, *below*) point to an ongoing revival. The massive bulk of **San Francisco de Asís Church** (☞ *below*) is an enduring attraction. ⊠ *Paseo del Pueblo Sur (NM 68), about 4 mi south of Taos Plaza.*

⑫ **San Francisco de Asís Church.** The Spanish Mission–style church was erected in the 18th century as a spiritual and physical refuge from raiding Apaches, Utes, and Comanches. In 1979 the deteriorated church was rebuilt with traditional adobe bricks by community volunteers. Every spring a group gathers to re-mud the facade. The earthy, clean lines of the exterior walls and supporting bulwarks have inspired generations of painters and photographers. The late-afternoon light provides the best exposure of the heavily buttressed rear of the church—though today's image-takers face the challenge of framing the architecturally pure lines through rows of parked cars and a large, white sign put up by church officials; morning light is best for the front. Bells in the twin belfries call Taoseños to services on Sunday and holidays. In the parish hall nearby a 15-minute video presentation every half hour describes the history and restoration of the church and explains the mysterious painting, *Shadow of the Cross,* on which each evening the shadow of a cross appears over Christ's shoulder. Scientific studies made on the canvas and the paint pigments cannot explain the phenomenon. ⊠ *NM 68, 500 yards south of NM 518, Ranchos de Taos,* ☎ *505/758–2754.* ☞ *$2.* ☉ *Mon.–Sat. 9–4, Sun. and holy days during morning church services: Mass at 7 (in Spanish), 9, and 11:30.*

NEED A
BREAK?

The storefront **Ranchos Coffee Company** (⊠ 1807 Paseo del Pueblo Sur, ☎ 505/751–0653) has fresh coffee, tea, pastries, and sandwiches.

Taos Pueblo to Rio Grande Gorge

*Numbers in the text correspond to numbers in the margin and on the
Taos Environs and the Enchanted Circle map.*

A Good Drive

Drive 2 mi north on Paseo del Pueblo Norte (NM 68), and keep your
eyes peeled for the signs on the right, beyond the post office, directing
you to **Taos Pueblo** ⑬. To reach the **Millicent Rogers Museum** ⑭ next,
return to NM 68 to head north and make a left onto County Road
BA030. If you find yourself at the intersection with U.S. 64 and 150,
you've gone too far. Continue down the country road to the big adobe
wall; the sign for the museum is on the right. This rural road eventually connects back onto Upper Ranchitos Road. After exploring the
museum, return to the traffic light on NM 68 and make a left to follow U.S. 64 west to the **Rio Grande Gorge Bridge** ⑮, a stunning marriage of natural wonder and human engineering. Bring along sturdy
hiking shoes and plenty of water and snacks for an invigorating walk
down into the gorge. But remember that what goes down must come
up, and it's an arduous path.

TIMING

Plan on spending 1½ hours at the pueblo. Taos can get hot in summer,
but if you visit the pueblo in the morning, you'll avoid the heat and
the crowds. Winters can be cold and windy, so dress warmly. If your
visit coincides with a ceremony observance, set aside several hours, because the ceremonies, though they are worth the wait, never start on
time. Two hours should be enough time to take in the museum and
the grandeur of the Rio Grande Gorge Bridge.

Sights to See

⑭ **Millicent Rogers Museum.** More than 5,000 pieces of Native American
and Hispanic art, the core of Standard Oil heiress Millicent Rogers's private collection, are on exhibit here: baskets, blankets, rugs, jewelry,
katsina dolls, carvings, paintings, and rare religious and secular artifacts.
Of major importance are the pottery and ceramics of Maria Martinez
and other potters from San Ildefonso Pueblo. Docents conduct guided
tours by appointment, and the museum hosts lectures, films, workshops,
and demonstrations. ⊠ *1504 Museum Rd. (from Taos Plaza head north
on Paseo del Pueblo Norte and left at the sign for County Rd. BA030—
also called Millicent Rogers Rd. or Museum Rd.),* ☎ *505/758–2462.* ☜
$6. ⊙ *Apr.–Sept., daily 10–5; Nov.–Mar., Tues.–Sun. 10–5.*

Ⓒ ⑮ **Rio Grande Gorge Bridge.** It's a breathtaking experience to see the Rio
Grande flowing 650 ft underfoot. The bridge is the second-highest expansion bridge in the country. Hold on to your camera and eyeglasses
when looking down, and watch out for low-flying planes. The Taos
Municipal Airport is close by, and daredevil private pilots have been
known to challenge one another to fly under the bridge. Shortly after
daybreak, hot air balloons fly above and even inside the gorge.

★ Ⓒ ⑬ **Taos Pueblo.** For nearly 1,000 years the mud-and-straw adobe walls
of Taos Pueblo have sheltered Tiwa-speaking Native Americans. A United
Nations World Heritage Site, this is the largest multistory pueblo structure in the United States. The two main buildings, Hlauuma (north house)
and Hlaukwima (south house), separated by a creek, are believed to
be of a similar age, probably constructed between 1000 and 1450. The
dwellings have common walls but no connecting doorways—the Tiwas
gained access only from the top, via ladders that were retrieved after
entering. Small buildings and corrals are scattered about.

Taos Environs and the Enchanted Circle

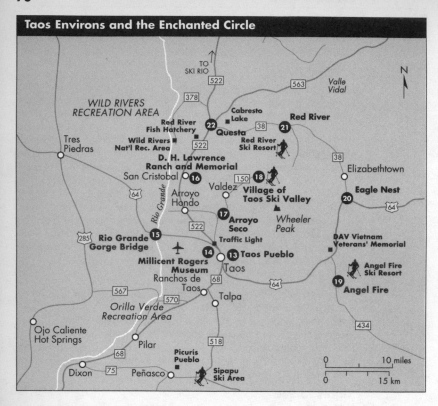

The pueblo today appears much as it did when the first Spanish explorers arrived in New Mexico in 1540. The adobe walls glistening with mica caused the conquistadors to believe they had discovered one of the fabled Seven Cities of Gold. The outside surfaces are continuously maintained by replastering with thin layers of mud, and the interior walls are frequently coated with thin washes of white clay. Some walls are several feet thick in places. The roofs of each of the five-story structures are supported by large timbers, or vigas, hauled down from the mountain forests. Pine or aspen *latillas* (smaller pieces of wood) are placed side by side between the vigas; the entire roof is then packed with dirt.

Even after 400 years of Spanish and Anglo presence in Taos, inside the pueblo the traditional Native American way of life has endured. Tribal custom allows no electricity or running water in Hlauuma and Hlaukwima, where varying numbers (usually fewer than 100) of Taos Native Americans live full-time. About 2,000 others live in conventional homes on the pueblo's 95,000 acres. The crystal-clear Rio Pueblo de Taos, originating high above in the mountains at the sacred Blue Lake, is the primary source of water for drinking and irrigating. Bread is still baked in *hornos* (outdoor domed ovens). Artisans of the Taos Pueblo produce and sell (tax-free) traditionally handcrafted wares such as mica-flecked pottery and silver jewelry. Great hunters, the Taos Native Americans are also known for their work with animal skins and their excellent moccasins, boots, and drums.

Although the population is about 90% Catholic, the people of Taos Pueblo, like most Pueblo Native Americans, also maintain their native religious traditions. At Christmas and other sacred holidays, for instance, immediately after Mass, dancers dressed in seasonal sacred garb proceed down the aisle of St. Jerome Chapel, drums beating and rattles shaking, to begin other religious rites.

The pueblo **Church of San Geronimo**, or St. Jerome, the patron saint of Taos Pueblo, was completed in 1850 to replace the one destroyed by the U.S. Army in 1847 during the Mexican War. With its smooth symmetry, stepped portal, and twin bell towers, the church is a popular subject for photographers and artists (though the taking of photographs inside is discouraged).

The public is invited to certain ceremonial dances held throughout the year: January 1, Turtle Dance; January 6, Buffalo or Deer Dance; May 3, Feast of Santa Cruz Foot Race and Corn Dance; June 13, Feast of San Antonio Corn Dance; June 24, Feast of San Juan Corn Dance; July 2 weekend, Taos Pueblo Powwow; July 25–26, Feast of Santa Ana and Santiago Corn Dance; September 29–30, Feast of San Geronimo Sunset Dance; Christmas Eve, the Procession; Christmas Day, Deer Dance or Matachines. While you're at the pueblo certain rules must be observed: respect the RESTRICTED AREA signs that protect the privacy of residents and native religious sites; do not enter private homes or open any doors not clearly labeled as curio shops; do not photograph tribal members without asking permission; do not enter the cemetery grounds; and do not wade in the Rio Pueblo de Taos, which is considered sacred and is the community's sole source of drinking water. ⊠ *Head to the right off Paseo del Pueblo Norte just past the Best Western Kachina Lodge,* ☎ *505/758–1028.* ☞ *Tourist fees $10. Guided tours by appointment. Still-camera permit $10 (note: cameras that may look commercial, such as those with telephoto lenses, might be denied a permit); video-camera permit $20; commercial photography, sketching, or painting only by prior permission from the governor's office (505/758–1028); fees vary; apply at least 10 days in advance.* ☉ *Apr.–Nov., daily 8–4; Oct.–Mar., daily 8:30–4. Closed for funerals, religious ceremonies, and for a 2-month "quiet time" in late winter or early spring, and the last part of Aug.; call ahead before visiting at these times.*

NEED A BREAK?
Look for signs that read FRY BREAD on dwellings in the pueblo: you can enter the kitchen and buy a piece of fresh bread dough that is flattened and deep-fried until puffy and golden brown and then topped with honey or powdered sugar.

DINING

For a place as remote as Taos, the dining scene is surprisingly varied and well supplied with foods from outside the area. You can find the usual coffee shops and Mexican-style eateries but also restaurants serving creatively prepared Continental, Italian, and Southwestern cuisine. Arroyo Seco, a village about 7 mi north of Taos on the way to Taos Ski Valley, has several good eateries. *See* the Glossary *in* Chapter 9 if you come across menu items you're not familiar with.

Downtown Taos

American

$$–$$$ ✕ **Ogelvie's Bar and Grill.** On the second floor of an old two-story adobe building, Ogelvie's is the perfect spot for people-watching from on high, especially from the outdoor patio in summer. You won't find any culinary surprises here, just dependable meat-and-potato dishes. The sure bets are Angus beef, grilled Rocky Mountain trout, and meat or cheese enchiladas. ⊠ *East side of Taos Plaza,* ☎ *505/758–8866. Reservations not accepted. AE, DC, MC, V.*

80

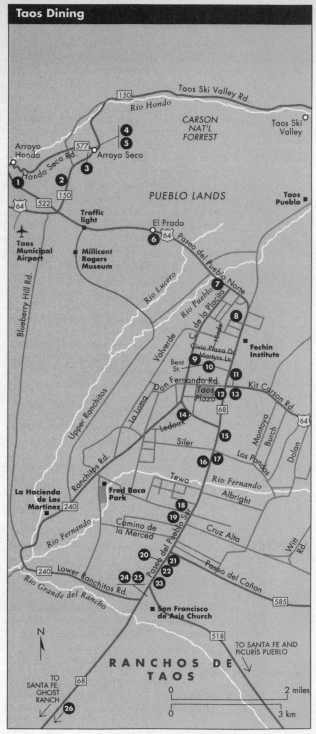

Taos Dining

$–$$ ✕ **Michael's Kitchen.** This casual, homey restaurant serves up a bit of everything—you can order a hamburger while your friend who can't get enough chile can order another enchilada. Brunch is popular with the locals, and amusing asides to the waitstaff over the intercom contribute to the energetic buzz. Breakfast, lunch, and dinner are served daily, but be sure to order dinner by 8:30 PM. ⊠ *304 Paseo del Pueblo Norte,* ☎ *505/758–4178. Reservations not accepted. AE, D, MC, V.*

$ ✕ **Eske's Brew Pub.** This casual dining and quaffing pub is favored by off-duty ski patrollers and river guides. The menu mostly covers hearty sandwiches with soup and salad. The microbrewery downstairs produces everything from nutty, dark stout to light ales. There's live music on weekends. ⊠ *106 Des Georges La.,* ☎ *505/758–1517. MC, V.*

Contemporary

$$$–$$$$ ✕ **Doc Martin's.** The restaurant of the Taos Inn takes its name from the building's original owner, a local physician who performed operations and delivered babies in rooms that are now the dining areas. Among the signature creations are the piñon-crusted salmon and the Aztec chocolate mousse with roasted-banana sauce. The wine list has won awards from *Wine Spectator* and other organizations. ⊠ *Taos Inn, 125 Paseo del Pueblo Norte,* ☎ *505/758–1977. MC, V.*

$$–$$$$ ✕ **Lambert's of Taos.** The signature dishes at this restaurant 2½ blocks south of the Plaza include crab cakes and pepper-crusted lamb. California's finest vintages receive top billing on the wine list. The desserts are tasty. ⊠ *Randall House, 309 Paseo del Pueblo Sur,* ☎ *505/758–1009. AE, DC, MC, V. No lunch weekends.*

$$–$$$ ✕ **Apple Tree.** Named for the large tree in the umbrella-shaded courtyard, this is a great lunch and early dinner spot in a historic adobe a block from the Plaza. The food is fresh—among the well-crafted dishes are grilled lamb and chicken fajitas. The restaurant has received regular awards for its wine selection, which includes many options by the glass. Sunday brunch is served from 10 to 3. Expect about a 15-minute wait if you don't have a reservation. There's an aromatherapy shop upstairs and a coffee and juice bar outside. ⊠ *123 Bent St.,* ☎ *505/758–1900. AE, D, DC, MC, V.*

$$–$$$ ✕ **Byzantium.** Off a grassy courtyard near the Blumenschein and Harwood museums, this restaurant offers an eclectic menu with touches of Asia, the Middle East, and Europe in dishes such as Wu Tang chicken, baba ghanoush, grilled polenta, and green lip mussel hot pot. ⊠ *Ledoux St. and La Placita,* ☎ *505/751–0805. AE, MC, V. Closed Tues. No lunch.*

$$ ✕ **La Luna.** In a colorful two-level space with a mural along one wall, the former New Yorkers who took charge in late 1999 have attracted a local clientele fond of the pasta such as the penne with cilantro-citrus sauce, the daily fish specials, and the pizza from the wood-fired oven in the dining room. Also for sale: bottles of the house apple-balsamic vinaigrette. ⊠ *225 Paseo del Pueblo Sur,* ☎ *505/751–0023. AE, D, MC, V. No lunch Sun.*

$–$$ ✕ **Bravo!** Short on atmosphere but by no means tacky, this restaurant and full bar inside an upscale grocery store and beer and wine shop is a great stop for gourmet picnic fixings or an on-site meal. The fare is nothing if not varied—you can feast on anything from a turkey sandwich to escargots—and there's a children's menu to boot. The beer and wine selection is formidable. ⊠ *1353A Paseo del Pueblo Sur,* ☎ *505/758–8100. Reservations not accepted. MC, V. Closed Sun.*

Deli

$$–$$$ ✕ **Bent Street Deli.** Great soups, sandwiches, salads, and desserts (cheesecake and other sweet treats) are the trademarks of the small and unassuming Bent Street Deli, which serves beer, wine, and gourmet coffees. Reubens are on the menu for East Coasters and others who can't live without a dose of pastrami. Dinners are a little fancier: fresh salmon, Sumatra primavera pasta with Indonesian peanut sauce, or shrimp in pesto sauce. Breakfast is served until 11 AM. ⊠ *120 Bent St.,* ☎ *505/758–5787. MC, V. Closed Sun.*

$ ✗ **JJ's Bagels.** In a storefront off the tourist path, this cybercafé bakes bagels on the spot and serves pastries, soups, and sandwiches along with Internet connections. Take out picnic fare or choose a table and terminal. It's open 7–5 weekdays and 7–2 weekends. ⊠ *710 Paseo del Pueblo Sur,* ☎ *505/758–0045. MC, V.*

$ ✗ **Taos Wrappers.** Owner-chefs Kim Wever and Greg Payton have a loyal clientele for take-out lunch, and a small eat-in space with tiny tables. Pesto chicken, roasted veggies, and curried tuna are among the healthful ingredients inside flavored tortilla wraps. There are soups, salads, and desserts, too. ⊠ *616 Paseo del Pueblo Sur,* ☎ *505/751–9727. No credit cards.*

Southwestern

$$–$$$ ✗ **Casa de Valdez.** A large A-frame building with wood-panel walls and beamed ceilings, Casa de Valdez has the feel of a mountain lodge. The tables and chairs are handmade, as are the colorful drapes on the windows. Owner-chef Peter Valdez specializes in hickory-smoked barbecues, charcoal-grilled steaks, and regional New Mexican cuisine. ⊠ *1401 Paseo del Pueblo Sur,* ☎ *505/758–8777. AE, D, MC, V. Closed Wed.*

$$–$$$ ✗ **Jacquelina's.** Specializing in fare of northern New Mexico, this restau-
★   rant on the south end of town has a following among longtime Taos residents. The night's menu might include a grilled salmon with tomatillo salsa or barbecued shrimp with *poblano* (a dark green, rich-tasting chile, ranging from mild to fiery) corn salsa. ⊠ *1541 Paseo del Pueblo Sur,* ☎ *505/751–0399. MC, V. Closed Mon. No lunch Sat.*

$$ ✗ **Fred's Place.** Eccentric decorations—carved crucifixes and santos and a ceiling mural of hell—set a quirky tone at this hip spot with a congenial staff. You may have to stand in line at popular Fred's, but you'll find you haven't waited in vain when you taste the subtly prepared northern New Mexican specialties like *carne adovada* (meat marinated in a spicy sauce) and blue-corn enchiladas. ⊠ *332 Paseo del Pueblo Sur,* ☎ *505/758–0514. Reservations not accepted. MC, V. Closed Sun. No lunch.*

$ ✗ **Guadalajara Grill.** Tasty Mexican cuisine is the feature here, served quickly from the open, spotless kitchens and popular enough with local patrons that there is one on each end of town. You'll hear Spanish banter across the kitchen counter while you watch your burritos or enchiladas being prepared. ⊠ *822 Paseo del Pueblo Norte,* ☎ *505/737–0816; 1384 Paseo del Pueblo Sur,* ☎ *505/751–0063. MC, V.*

$ ✗ **Orlando's.** This family-run local favorite features authentic-tasting *carne adovada* (red chile–marinated pork), blue-corn enchiladas, and an innovative shrimp burrito, among other offerings. Eat in the cozy dining room or call ahead for takeout. ⊠ *114 Don Juan Valdez La., off Paseo des Pueblo Norte,* ☎ *505/751–1450. No credit cards. Closed Sun.*

Ranchos de Taos and Points South

American

$$$–$$$$ ✗ **Stakeout Grill and Bar.** On Outlaw Hill in the foothills of the Sangre de Cristo Mountains, this old adobe homestead has 100-mi-long views and sunsets that dazzle. The sturdy fare includes New York strip steaks, filet mignon, pepper steak, shrimp scampi, swordfish steaks, duck, chicken, and daily pasta specials. The restaurant's decor will take you back to the days of the Wild West even though the owners hail from northern Italy. ⊠ *Stakeout Dr., 8½ mi south of Taos Plaza, east of NM 68 (look for the huge cowboy hat),* ☎ *505/758–2042. AE, D, DC, MC, V.*

Contemporary

$$$–$$$$ ✕ **Joseph's Table.** The funky decor and romantic lighting at Joseph's make a rustic yet dramatic stage for Italian-oriented fare like the gnocchi stuffed with white-truffle paste, seared salmon with tarragon velouté, and the pepper steak with garlic mashed red potatoes. The first-rate desserts are more ornate. ⊠ *4167 Paseo del Pueblo Sur (NM 68), Ranchos de Taos,* ☎ *505/751–4512. AE, D, DC, MC, V. Closed Mon., Tues. No lunch.*

$$$–$$$$ ✕ **Trading Post Cafe.** A postmodern Western ambience, impeccable ser-
★ vice, and an imaginative menu have made the Trading Post the most popular dining spot in Ranchos de Taos. The perfectly marinated salmon gravlax appetizer is exceptional and the paella is a bounty for two. The pasta dishes pack flavor to equal their unbelievably generous portions. The desserts—try the homemade raspberry sorbet or the flan—are delicious. Coming from the north, take the left turn onto Highway 518 (Talpa Road) just before the restaurant to reach the more ample parking lot. Be careful not to walk over the neighbor's yard; to reach the restaurant's entrance, walk back along Talpa Road. ⊠ *4179 Paseo del Pueblo Sur (NM 68), Ranchos de Taos,* ☎ *505/758–5089. D, DC, MC, V. Closed Sun.*

Arroyo Seco and Points North

Cafés

$–$$ ✕ **Taos Cow.** This growing enterprise has expanded into the former Casa Fresen Bakery building. Not only is it the world headquarters for tasty ice cream made from growth-hormone-free milk (featured in area health food stores), but the remodeled dining areas have become a fine spot for coffee, tea, chai, deli items, pastries, cookies, and fresh-baked bread (such as the tasty zucchini bread). Favorites among the three-dozen ice cream flavors are cherry ristra, piñon caramel, and the true test—vanilla. ⊠ *591 Hondo Seco Rd.,* ☎ *505/776–5640. MC, V.*

$ ✕ **Abe's Cantina y Cocina.** Have your breakfast burrito, rolled tacos, or homemade tamales at one of the small tables crowded next to the canned goods, or take it on a picnic. You never know when the place might be closed for golf outings. ⊠ *Taos Ski Valley Rd. (County Rd. 150),* ☎ *505/776–8643. No credit cards. Closed Sun.*

Contemporary

$$$$ ✕ **Momentitos de la Vida.** Opened in early 1999 in the former Casa
★ Cordova, chef Chris Maher's restaurant brings an ambitious, worldly focus to dining out in the area. There's an outdoor terrace and a playfully elegant interior (trompe-l'oeil garlands and fireplace "stonework"), but focus is on the food. An evening's entrée might be apricot-glazed game hen or or seared salmon in sun-dried tomato fish stock, but save some room for desserts, which change nightly. Live music in the piano bar several nights a week might include smoky-smooth jazz vocals by Mary Bruscini. Sunday brunch allows those on a tighter budget to enjoy the food and atmosphere. ⊠ *Taos Ski Valley Rd. (County Rd. 150),* ☎ *505/776–3333. AE, MC, V. Closed Mon. No lunch.*

Italian

$$$$ ✕ **Villa Fontana.** Entering this restaurant, which serves northern Ital-
★ ian cuisine, is like walking into a sophisticated Italian country inn: warm coral walls, candlelight, gleaming hardwood tables, starched linens, and courtly service. Notable dishes include grilled whole sole and seasonal game like venison and pheasant. Lunch is served in the garden. ⊠ *NM 522, 5 mi north of Taos Plaza, Arroyo Hondo,* ☎ *505/758–5800. AE, D, DC, MC, V. Closed Sun. No lunch Nov.–May.*

Southwestern

$$–$$$ ✕ **Tim's Chile Connection.** Young skiers flock to this place between
the turn-off for the Taos Ski Valley and Arroyo Seco for beer, country-western music, and Tim's stick-to-your-ribs Southwestern blue-corn
tortillas, homemade salsa, buffalo burgers and steaks, and fajitas. The
tab is pricey for what you get, but the margaritas are monumental and
even memorable. ☒ *Taos Ski Valley Rd. (County Rd. 150),* ☎ *505/
776–8787. AE, MC, V.*

LODGING

The hotels and motels along NM 68 (Paseo del Pueblo Sur and Norte)
suit every need and budget; rates vary little between big-name chains
and smaller establishments. Make advance reservations and expect higher
rates during the ski season (usually from late December to early April)
and in the summer. Skiers have many choices for overnighting, from
accommodations in the town of Taos to spots snuggled up right beside the slopes (☞ Taos Ski Valley *in* Side Trips, *below*).

The best deals in town are the bed-and-breakfasts. Mostly family-
owned, they provide personal service, delicious breakfasts, and many
extras that hotels charge for. The B&Bs are often in old adobes that
have been refurbished with style and flair.

❧ *following the text of a review is your signal that the property has
a Web site, where you will find details and, usually, images; for a link,
visit www.fodors.com/urls.*

Downtown Taos

$$$–$$$$ ☷ **Casa de las Chimeneas.** Regional art, tile hearths, French doors, and
★   traditional viga ceilings are among the design elements of note at the
House of Chimneys B&B, 2½ blocks from the Plaza and secluded be-
hind thick walls. Each room in the 1912 structure has a private en-
trance, a fireplace, handmade New Mexican furniture, and a tile bar
stocked with complimentary juices, sodas, and mineral waters. All rooms
overlook the gardens and fountains. The two-course breakfasts might
include cheese-filled crepes with fresh berries, and late-afternoon hors-
d'oeuvres are generous enough to be a light meal. You can also pam-
per yourself with a massage or spa treatments. ☒ *405 Cordoba Rd.
(Box 5303), 87571,* ☎ *505/758–4777 or 800/758–4777,* ℻ *505/758–
3976. 8 rooms, 2 suites. In-room VCRs, outdoor hot tub, sauna, ex-
ercise room, laundry service. No smoking. AE, MC, V. BP.* ❧

$$$–$$$$ ☷ **Fechin Inn.** This graceful Pueblo Revival structure on the grounds of
the Fechin Institute (to which guests have free admission) is adjacent to
Kit Carson Memorial Park. Painter Nicolai Fechin's daughter, Eya, par-
ticipated in the planning; Fechin reproductions adorn the rooms and hall-
ways, and the woodwork in the large, comfortable lobby is based on the
artist's designs. A generous breakfast is available every morning in the
lobby, as are cocktails in the evening. Rooms are comfortable, if non-
descript; most have private balconies or patios. Pets are welcome. ☒ *227
Paseo del Pueblo Norte, 87571,* ☎ *505/751–1000 or 800/811–2933,* ℻
*505/751–7338. 71 rooms, 14 suites. Massage, exercise room, ski stor-
age, meeting rooms, free parking. AE, D, DC, MC, V. CP.* ❧

$$$–$$$$ ☷ **Historic Taos Inn.** Mere steps from Taos Plaza, this hotel is listed on
the National Register of Historic Places. The guest rooms are pleasant
and comfortable, and in summer there's dining alfresco on the patio. The
lobby, which also serves as seating for the Adobe Bar, is built around an
old town well from which a fountain bubbles forth. Many shops and eater-
ies are within walking distance of the inn, and its own restaurant, Doc

Taos Lodging

Martin's (☞ Dining, *above*), is quite popular itself. ☒ *125 Paseo del Pueblo Norte, 87571,* ☏ *505/758–2233 or 800/826–7466,* ℻ *505/758–5776. 36 rooms. Restaurant, bar, lounge, library. AE, DC, MC, V.* ❧

$$–$$$$ ⊡ **Casa Europa.** The original adobe bricks and wood viga ceiling enhance the pastoral feeling of this classic estate on six acres with views of pastures and mountains. European antiques and Southwestern pieces decorate the rooms of the B&B. Though parts are 200 years old, the two main guest areas are light and airy with comfortable chairs to relax in while the fireplace crackles. Breakfasts are elaborate, and complimentary homemade afternoon pastries are served daily except during the ski season, when they're replaced by evening hors d'oeuvres. ☒ *840 Upper Ranchitos Rd., HC 68 (Box 3F), 87571,* ☏ *888/758–9798,* ☏ ℻ *505/758–9798. 7 rooms. 2 lounges, hot tub, sauna. AE, MC, V. BP.* ❧

$$–$$$$ ⊡ **Hacienda del Sol.** Art patron Mabel Dodge Luhan bought this house ★ in the 1920s and lived here with her husband, Tony Luhan, while building their main house, Las Palomas de Taos. It was also their private retreat and guest house for visiting notables; Frank Waters wrote *People of the Valley* here. Most of the rooms contain kiva-style fireplaces, Southwestern-style handcrafted furniture, and original artwork. The secluded outdoor hot tub has a crystalline view of Taos Mountain. The jet-black bathroom of the Los Amantes Room is a celebration in decadence with its huge black hot tub amid a jungle of potted plants below a skylight. Breakfast is a gourmet affair. Each room has two phone lines. ☒ *109 Mabel Dodge La. (Box 177), 87571,* ☏ *505/758–0287,* ℻ *505/ 758–5895. 11 rooms. Outdoor hot tub. MC, V. BP.* ❧

$$–$$$$ ⊡ **Inn on La Loma Plaza.** The walls surrounding this Pueblo Revival build-★ ing (formerly the Taos Hacienda Inn) date from the early 1800s and were designed to protect a small enclave of settlers from Indian attacks. The inn is listed on the National Register of Historic Places and behind it lies the historic, residential La Loma Plaza. The individually decorated rooms have Southwestern accents, including kiva fireplaces and bathrooms with Mexican tile work. The comfortable living room holds an interesting collection of antique cameras and a well-stocked library with books on Taos and art. Owners Jerry and Peggy Davis unobtrusively provide helpful advice about the area and serve a generous breakfast, afternoon snacks, and evening coffee daily. B&B guests also have privileges at the nearby health club (but there's an outdoor hot tub here too). ☒ *315 Ranchitos Rd. (Box 4159), 87571,* ☏ *505/758–1717 or 800/530– 3040,* ℻ *505/751–0155. 5 rooms, 2 artist studios with kitchenettes. Hot tub, library. AE, D, MC, V. BP.* ❧

$$–$$$$ ⊡ **Mabel Dodge Luhan House.** This National Historic Landmark was once the home of the heiress who drew the literati to the area. Guests from pre-B&B days included D. H. and Frieda Lawrence, Georgia O'Keeffe, and Willa Cather. The main house has nine guest rooms, and there are eight more in a separate guest house, as well as a two-bedroom cottage. The inn is frequently used for literary, artistic, cultural, and educational meetings and workshops. Don't expect glamour—this is one of the most basic B&Bs in town. The buildings have been freshened up with new paint and baths, but the stairs still creak comfortingly. Meal service is available for groups, and public tennis courts are nearby. ☒ *240 Morada La. (Box 3400), 87571,* ☏ *505/758–9456 or 800/846–2235,* ℻ *505/751–0431. 15 rooms with bath, 2 with shared bath; 1 cottage. Meeting rooms. AE, MC, V. BP.* ❧

$$–$$$$ ⊡ **Touchstone Inn.** D. H. Lawrence visited this house when Miriam De-★ Witt owned it in 1929. The inn's owner, Taos artist Bren Price, has filled the rooms, named after famous Taos literary figures, with tasteful antique and modern pieces. The grounds overlook part of the Taos Pueblo lands, and this makes for a quiet stay within a mile of Taos Plaza. Some suites have fireplaces. Early-morning coffee is poured in the living room, and breakfasts with inventive presentations are served in the glassed-in patio. ⊠ *110 Mabel Dodge La. (Box 2896), 87571,* ☎ *505/ 758–0192 or 800/758–0192,* FAX *505/758–3498. 8 rooms. In-room VCRs, hot tub. MC, V. BP.* ❧

$$$ ▣ **Ramada Inn de Taos.** More Taos than Ramada, the two-story adobe-style hotel welcomes you with a lobby fireplace, desert colors, Western art, and Native American pottery. The rooms have an inviting Southwestern flavor as does the new dining menu. ⊠ *615 Paseo del Pueblo Sur, 87571,* ☎ *505/758–2900 or 800/659–8267,* FAX *505/758– 1662. 124 rooms. Dining room, lounge, indoor pool, hot tub, meeting rooms. AE, D, DC, MC, V.*

$$–$$$ ▣ **Best Western Kachina Lodge de Taos.** Down the road from Taos Pueblo and minutes from the Taos Plaza, this hotel is in a two-story Pueblo-style adobe. From Memorial Day to Labor Day a troupe from Taos Pueblo performs nightly ritual dances outside by firelight. The katsina theme (a doll representing a masked ancestral spirit) is carried throughout, and guest rooms continue the Native American motif with handmade and hand-painted furnishings and colorful bedspreads. ⊠ *413 Paseo del Pueblo Norte (Box NN), 87571,* ☎ *505/758–2275 or 800/522–4462,* FAX *505/758–9207. 113 rooms, 5 suites. Restaurant, bar, coffee shop, pool, hot tub, shops, meeting rooms. AE, D, DC, MC, V.* ❧

$$–$$$ ▣ **Brooks Street Inn.** An elaborately carved corbel arch, the handiwork of Japanese carpenter Yaichikido, spans the entrance to a shaded, walled garden. Fluffy pillows, fresh flowers, and paintings by local artists are among the grace notes in the rooms. Blue-corn pancakes with pineapple salsa, stuffed French toast with an apricot glaze, and other home-baked delights are served at breakfast, along with coffee or espresso drinks. In warm weather, breakfast is served at umbrella-shaded tables on the patio; in winter it's served by the fireplace. ⊠ *119 Brooks St. (Box 4954), 87571,* ☎ *505/758–1489 or 800/758–1489. 6 rooms. No smoking. AE, MC, V. BP.* ❧

$$–$$$ ▣ **Comfort Suites.** Each unit at this complex contains a living room with a sofa bed, a bedroom with a king- and a queen-size bed, a television in both rooms, a microwave oven, a coffeemaker, and a refrigerator. ⊠ *1500 Paseo del Pueblo Sur (Box 1268), 87571,* ☎ *505/751– 1555 or 888/751–1555. 60 suites. In-room data ports, refrigerators, hot tub, pool. AE, D, DC, MC, V. BP.*

$$–$$$ ▣ **Holiday Inn Don Fernando de Taos.** The accommodations at this hotel with a Pueblo-style design are grouped around central courtyards and connected by walkways. Appointed with hand-carved New Mexican furnishings, the rooms have kiva-style fireplaces. There's a free shuttle to take guests to the town center. ⊠ *1005 Paseo del Pueblo Sur, 87571,* ☎ *505/ 758–4444 or 800/759–2736,* FAX *505/758–0055. 124 rooms. Restaurant, bar, lounge, pool, hot tub, tennis court. AE, D, DC, MC, V.* ❧

$$–$$$ ▣ **La Posada de Taos.** A couple of blocks from Taos Plaza, this provincial adobe has beam ceilings, a portal, and the intimacy of a private hacienda. Five of the guest rooms are in the main house; the sixth is a separate cottage with a queen-size four-poster bed, a sitting room, and a fireplace—a setting cozy and pretty enough to earn the name *La Casa de la Luna de Miel* (The Honeymoon House). The rooms have mountain views or face a flowering courtyard; all but one of the rooms have adobe, kiva-style fireplaces. Breakfasts are hearty. ⊠ *309 Juanita La. (Box 1118), 87571,* ☎ *505/758–8164 or 800/645–4803,* FAX *505/751– 4694. 5 rooms, 1 cottage. AE, MC, V. BP.*

$$–$$$ ▣ **Old Taos Guesthouse.** Once a ramshackle adobe hacienda, this homey B&B has been completely and lovingly outfitted with the owners' hand-carved doors and furniture, Western artifacts, and antiques. Some rooms have the smallest bathrooms you'll ever encounter but have private entrances and some have fireplaces. There are 80-mi views from the outdoor hot tub and it's just a five-minute drive to town. The owners welcome families. Breakfasts are healthy and hearty. ⊠ *1028 Witt Rd. (Box 6552), 87571,* ☎ *800/758–5448,* ☎ FAX *505/758–5448. 9 rooms. Hot tub. MC, V. BP.*

$$–$$$ 🏨 **Orinda.** Built in 1947, this adobe estate has spectacular views and country privacy. The one- and two-bedroom suites have separate entrances, kiva-style fireplaces, traditional viga ceilings, and Mexican-tile baths. Two rooms share a common sitting room. One suite has a Jacuzzi. The hearty breakfast is served family-style in the soaring two-story sun atrium amid a gallery of artworks, all for sale. ⊠ *461 Valverde (Box 4451), 87571,* ☎ *505/758–8581 or 800/847–1837,* FAX *505/751–4895. 5 rooms. No smoking. AE, MC, V. BP.* 🐾

$$–$$$ 🏨 **San Geronimo Lodge.** On a small street off Kit Carson Road, this lodge built in 1925 sits on 2½ acres that front majestic Taos Mountain and back up to the Carson National Forest. A balcony library, attractive grounds, many rooms with fireplaces, two rooms designed for people with disabilities, and a room for guests with a pet are among the draws. The hotel staff will arrange ski packages. ⊠ *1101 Witt Rd., 87571,* ☎ *505/751–3776 or 800/894–4119,* FAX *505/751–1493. 18 rooms. Pool, hot tub, massage. AE, D, DC, MC, V.*

$$ 🏨 **El Pueblo Lodge.** This low-to-the-ground, pueblo-style adobe a few blocks north of Taos Plaza has practical in-room amenities and guest laundry rooms. The traditional Southwestern furnishings and fireplaces lend the rooms a homey feel. ⊠ *412 Paseo del Pueblo Norte (Box 92), 87571,* ☎ *505/758–8700 or 800/433–9612,* FAX *505/758–7321. 61 rooms. Kitchenettes, refrigerators, pool, hot tub, coin laundry. AE, D, MC, V. CP.* 🐾

🏨 **Sagebrush Inn.** A tad run-down but still with a certain allure, this Pueblo Mission–style 1929 adobe 3 mi south of the Plaza contains authentic Navajo rugs, rare pottery, Southwestern and Spanish antiques, fine carved pieces, and paintings by Southwestern masters. Georgia O'Keeffe once lived and painted in one of the third-story rooms. Many of the bedrooms have kiva-style fireplaces; some have balconies looking out to the Sangre de Cristo Mountains. There's country-western music nightly. The Sagebrush Village offers condominium family lodging, too. ⊠ *1508 Paseo del Pueblo Sur (Box 557), 87571,* ☎ *505/758–2254 or 800/428–3626,* FAX *505/758–5077. 68 rooms, 32 suites. 2 restaurants, bar, lounge, pool, 2 hot tubs, meeting rooms. AE, D, DC, MC, V.* 🐾

$–$$$ 🏨 **Sun God Lodge.** Though inexpensive, this motel has old adobe charm with basic amenities—it's a good deal. Right on the main highway, the Sun God is convenient to restaurants and historic sites. ⊠ *909 Paseo del Pueblo Sur, 87571,* ☎ *505/758–3162 or 800/821–2437,* FAX *505/758–1716. 55 rooms. Hot tub. AE, D, MC, V.* 🐾

Ranchos de Taos

$$–$$$$ 🏨 **Adobe & Pines Inn.** Native American and Mexican artifacts decorate the main house of this B&B, which has expansive mountain views. Part of the main building dates from 1830. The rooms contain Mexican-tiled baths, kiva fireplaces, fluffy goose-down pillows, and comforters. A separate cottage and two equally handsome casitas also house guests. The owners serve gourmet breakfasts in a sunny glass-enclosed patio. ⊠ *NM 68 and Llano Quemado (Box 837), Ranchos de Taos 87557,* ☎ *505/751–0947 or 800/723–8267,* FAX *505/758–8423. 5 rooms, 1 cottage, 2 casitas. 5 hot tubs, sauna. No smoking. AE, MC, V. BP.* 🐾

Arroyo Seco

$$$–$$$$ 🏨 **Quail Ridge Inn Resort.** On the way to Taos Ski Valley, this large resort has one- and two-story modern adobe bungalows that are comfy

and efficient. Some suites have kitchens. The resort provides a host of recreational amenities, from organized trail rides to hot-tub soaks. Skiing, tennis, rafting, mountain-biking, and fly-fishing packages are available for groups or individuals. ✉ *Taos Ski Valley Rd. (County Rd. 150; Box 707), Taos 87571,* ☎ *505/776–2211 or 800/624–4448,* FAX *505/776–2949. 50 rooms, 60 suites. Restaurant, lounge, in-room data ports, pool, hot tub, 8 tennis courts, exercise room, racquetball, squash, volleyball, meeting rooms. AE, D, DC, MC, V.* 🏖

$$$–$$$$ 🏨 **Casa Grande Guest Ranch.** Watch the stars and the lights of Taos twinkle from the hot tub of this B&B; morning views stretch for miles. Three comfortable rooms are integrated into the family home built not far from the property's historic hacienda on the flanks of El Salto Mountain. Breakfast burritos with all the trimmings will see you through a horseback ride up to the waterfalls. Children must be 18 and over. ✉ *75 Luis O. Torres Rd., Arroyo Seco 87514,* ☎ *888/236–1303,* FAX *505/776–2177. 3 rooms. Hot tub. AE, MC, V. BP.* 🏖

$$–$$$$ 🏨 **Alma del Monte.** Mountain views abound from the rooms and the courtyard of this B&B on the high plain between Taos and the ski valley. Saltillo-tiled floors, Victorian antiques, canopies over some of the beds, generous breakfasts, and afternoon wine with hors d'oeuvres make it a hard place to leave, even for skiing. ✉ *372 Hondo Seco Rd. (Box 1434), Taos 87571,* ☎ *505/776–2721 or 800/273–7203,* FAX *505/776–8888. 5 rooms. MC, V. BP.* 🏖

Campgrounds

⚠️ **Orilla Verde Recreation Area.** You can hike, fish, and picnic at this area along the banks of the Rio Grande, 10 mi south of Ranchos de Taos, off NM 68 at NM 570. As for paying the camping fee, leave cash in an envelope provided, drop it in a tube, and the rangers will collect it. ✉ *Mailing address: Bureau of Land Management, Cruz Alta Rd., Taos 87571,* ☎ *505/758–8851. 70 tent sites. Rest rooms. No credit cards.*

⚠️ **Taos RV Park.** The sites are grassy, with a few small trees, in this park 3½ mi from Taos Plaza near the junction of NM 68 and NM 518. A recreation room has video games, TV, and a pool table. Some RV supplies are for sale. There are rest rooms and hot showers. ✉ *1799 Paseo del Pueblo Sur, next to the Taos Motel (Box 729F), Ranchos de Taos 87557,* ☎ *505/758–1667 or 800/323–6009. 29 RV and tent sites. Kitchenette, horseshoes, billiards, recreation room, playground. D, MC, V.*

NIGHTLIFE AND THE ARTS

Evening entertainment is modest in Taos. Some motels and hotels present solo musicians or small combos in their bars and lounges. Everything from down-home blues bands to Texas two-step dancing blossoms on Saturday and Sunday nights in winter. In summer things heat up during the week as well. For information about what's going on around town pick up *Taos Magazine.* The weekly *Taos News,* published on Thursday, carries arts and entertainment information in the "Tempo" section.

Nightlife

Bars and Lounges

The **Adobe Bar** (✉ Taos Inn, 125 Paseo del Pueblo Norte, ☎ 505/758–2233), a local meet-and-greet spot, books talented acts, from solo guitarists to small folk groups, and, two or three nights a week, jazz musicians. **Fernando's Hideaway** (✉ Holiday Inn, 1005 Paseo del Pueblo Sur, ☎ 505/758–4444) occasionally presents live entertainment—rock, jazz, blues, vocals, and country music. Saturday is reserved for karaoke. Lavish complimentary happy-hour buffets are laid out on weekday evenings. **Weasel Mahood's Bar and Bistro** (✉ 122 Paseo del Pueblo Sur, 2nd floor, ☎ 505/758–1778) often has dancing, karoke, or live music as well as pool, 10 beers on tap, and the house special, the Weasel Mahood martini.

Cabaret

The **Kachina Lodge Cabaret** (✉ 413 Paseo del Pueblo Norte, ☎ 505/758–2275) brings in headline acts, such as Arlo Guthrie and the Kingston Trio, on a regular basis and has dancing.

Coffeehouse

Caffe Tazza (✉ 122 Kit Carson Rd., ☎ 505/758–8706) presents free evening performances throughout the week—folk singing, jazz, blues, poetry, and fiction readings.

Country-and-Western Club

The **Sagebrush Inn** (✉ 1508 Paseo del Pueblo Sur, ☎ 505/758–2254) hosts musicians and dancing in its lobby lounge. If you hear that South by Southwest is playing, go ahead and check the three-guy band out. There's no cover charge, and if you show up on a Thursday, you can learn to two-step.

Jazz and Dance Clubs

Alley Cantina (✉ 121 Teresina La., ☎ 505/758–2121) has jazz, folk, and blues—as well as shuffleboard and board games for those not moved to dance. The piano bar at **Momentitos de la Vida** (✉ County Rd. 150 in Arroyo Seco, ☎ 505/776–3333) often presents jazz and bossa nova. At **Tim's Chile Connection** (✉ County Rd. 150, ☎ 505/776–2969) on the way to Arroyo Seco, look for lively swing and singers strumming acoustic guitar. **Thunderbird Lodge** (✉ 3 Thunderbird Rd., ☎ 505/776–2280) in the Taos Ski Valley has free jazz nights and country-and-western swing dancing.

The Arts

Summer music has become a staple in Taos, which benefits from talented performers who enjoy coming to the desert-mountain setting. But more spring and fall festivals, spurred by availability of lodgings and venues, are coming to town to enliven slow seasons, too.

The **Taos Art Association** (✉ 133 Paseo del Pueblo Norte, ☎ 505/758–2052) has information about art-related events in Taos. The **Taos Community Auditorium** (✉ 145 Paseo del Pueblo Norte, ☎ 505/758–4677) presents plays, dance, concerts, and movies.

Festivals

For information about festivals in Taos, contact the **Taos County Chamber of Commerce** (☞ Visitor Information *in* Taos A to Z, *below*).

The **Taos Spring Arts Festival,** held throughout Taos in early May, is a showcase for the visual, performing, and literary arts of the community and allows you to rub elbows with the many artists who call Taos home. The Mother's Day Arts and Crafts weekend during the festival always draws a crowd.

Held every year during the second weekend of July, the **Taos Pueblo Powwow** attracts Native Americans from across the country for traditional dances, socializing, and a market on Pueblo land.

The **Taos Fall Arts Festival,** from late September to early October, is the major arts gathering, when buyers are in town and many other events, such as a Taos Pueblo feast, take place.

On the heels of the Fall Arts Festival comes the **Wool Festival** in early October, held in Kit Carson Memorial Park, which celebrates everything from sheep to shawl, with demonstrations of shearing, spinning, and weaving; handmade woolen items for sale; and tastings of favorite lamb dishes.

Film

Taos Talking Picture Festival (☎ 505/751–0637) is a multicultural celebration of cinema artists, with a focus on Native American film and video makers. The mid-April festival presents independent films, documentaries, animation, and some classic cinema.

Music

From mid-June to early August the Taos School of Music and the International Institute of Music fill the evenings with the sounds of chamber and symphonic orchestras at the **Taos Chamber Music Festival** (☎ 505/776–2388). Nearly four decades old, this is America's oldest chamber music summer program and possibly the largest assembly of professional musicians in the Southwest. Concerts are presented every Saturday evening, and every other Friday evening from mid-June to August, at the Taos Community Auditorium (☞ *above*). Tickets cost $15. The events at Taos Ski Valley are free.

The Taos School of Music gives free weekly summer concerts and recitals from mid-June to early August at the **Hotel Saint Bernard** (☎ 505/776–2251), at the mountain base (near the lifts) of Taos Ski Valley.

Music from Angel Fire (☎ 505/758–4667 or 505/377–3233) is a series of classical and jazz concerts presented at the Taos Community Auditorium (☞ *above*) and the Angel Fire Community Auditorium in the town center from August 21 to September 2. Tickets cost about $12 per concert.

OUTDOOR ACTIVITIES AND SPORTS

Whether you plan to cycle around town, jog along Pasco del Pueblo Norte, or play a few rounds of golf, keep in mind that the altitude in Taos is over 7,000 ft. It's best to keep physical exertion to a minimum until your body becomes acclimated to the altitude—a full day to a few days depending on your constitution. With the decreased oxygen and humidity you may experience some or all of the following symptoms: headache, nausea, insomnia, shortness of breath, diarrhea, sleeplessness, and tension. If you are planning to engage in physical activity, avoid alcohol and coffee (which aggravate "high-altitude syndrome") and drink a lot of water and juice. Some locals also recommend taking aspirin in the morning and afternoon.

Participant Sports

Bicycling

Taos-area roads are steep and hilly, and none have marked bicycle lanes, so be careful while cycling. The **Enchanted Circle Wheeler Peak Bicycle Rally** (☎ 800/384–6444) takes place in mid-September. The rally loops through the entire 84-mi Enchanted Circle, through Red River, Taos, Angel Fire, Eagle Nest, and Questa, past a brilliant blaze of fall color. During the summer, you can head up the mountainside via ski lift in Red River, Angel Fire, and Sipapu. The **West Rim Trail,** a route opened in 1998, offers a fairly flat but view-studded 9-mi ride that follows the Rio Grande canyon's west rim from the Rio Grande Gorge Bridge to near the Taos Junction Bridge.

"Gearing Up" Bicycle Shop (✉ 129 Paseo del Pueblo Sur, ☎ 505/751–0365) is a full-service bike shop that also has information about tours and guides. **Native Sons Adventures** (⊠ 715 Paseo del Pueblo Sur, ☎ 505/758–9342 or 800/753–7559) offers guided tours on its mountain bikes.

Fishing

Picurís Pueblo (☞ Ranchos de Taos and Points South, *in* Exploring Taos, *above*) and Cabresto Lake in the Carson National Forest (☞ Questa *in* The Enchanted Circle, *below*) have good trout fishing. The Upper Red River valley is good for bait and fly fishing. For trout fishing far off the beaten path try Hopewell Lake, in Carson National Forest, 30 minutes by car from Tres Piedras (35 mi west of Taos). The lake is open from May to October. In Taos, **Los Rios Anglers** (⊠ 226C Paseo del Pueblo Norte, ☎ 505/758–2798 or 800/748–1707) offers free one-hour fly-casting clinics, weekly between May and August. Well-known area fishing guide **Taylor Streit** (☎ 505/751–1312) also takes individuals or small groups out for fishing and lessons. For information about fishing regulations in New Mexico, *see* Outdoor Activities and Sports *in* Smart Travel Tips A to Z.

Golf

The 18-hole, par-72 course at the **Angel Fire Country Club** (⊠ Country Club Dr. off NM 434, Angel Fire, ☎ 505/377–3055), one of the highest in the nation, is open from May to mid-October. The greens fee is $35; an optional cart costs $12.50 per person.

The greens fee at the 18-hole, PGA-rated, par-72 championship course at **Taos Country Club** (⊠ Hwy. 570, Ranchos de Taos, ☎ 505/758–7300) ranges between $25 and $42; optional carts cost $22.

Health Clubs & Fitness Centers

The **Northside Health & Fitness Center** (⊠ 1307 Paseo del Pueblo Norte, ☎ 505/751–1242) is a spotlessly clean facility with indoor and outdoor pools, a hot tub, tennis courts, and aerobics classes. Non-members pay $9 per day; passes for a week or longer are also available. The center provides paid child care with a certified Montessori teacher. About 3 mi south of the Plaza, **Taos Spa & Tennis Club** (⊠ 111 Doña Ana Dr., ☎ 888/758–1981) has tennis and racquetball courts, indoor and outdoor pools, fitness equipment, saunas, steam rooms, and hot tubs, as well as baby-sitting and massage services. Nonmembers pay $10 per day. The **Taos Youth and Family Center** (⊠ 105 Camino de Colores, ☎ 505/758–4160) has an outdoor Olympic-size ice arena, where rollerblading, volleyball, and basketball take place in summer. Other scheduled activities are open to the public.

Hiking

Strenuous trails from the Village of Taos Ski Valley lead to **Wheeler Peak,** the highest point in New Mexico, at 13,161 ft. Gentler paths head up other piney and meadow-filled mountains like **Gold Hill.** Easy nature hikes are organized by the Bavarian hotel (☞ Dining and Lodging *in* Side Trips *below*) and guided by Shar Sharghi, a botanist and horticulturist. There are also trails in the valley that pass by old mining camps. For canyon climbing, head into the wooded Italianos on the way to the Taos Ski Valley, or the rocky **Rio Grande Gorge.** The best entry point into the gorge is at the Wild Rivers Recreation Area in Cerro, 35 mi north of Taos.

Visitors from lower altitudes should take time to acclimatize, and all hikers should follow basic safety procedures. Wind, cold, and wetness can occur any time of year, and the mountain climate produces sudden storms. Dress in layers; carry water, food, sunscreen, hat, sunglasses, and a first-aid kit; and wear sturdy footwear. Maps and information about trails are available from the **U.S. Forest Service** (⊠ 208 Cruz Alta, Taos, ☎ 505/758–6200); the **Bureau of Land Management, Taos Re-**

source **Area Office** (✉ 226 Cruz Alta, Taos, ☎ 505/758–8851); and local outfitters (☞ Outdoor Equipment *in* Shopping, *below*).

Jogging

The track around the football field at **Taos High School** (✉ 134 Cervantes St., ☎ 505/758–5230) isn't officially open to the public, but no one seems to object when nonstudents jog there. The paved paths and grass of **Kit Carson Memorial Park** (☞ Downtown Taos *in* Exploring Taos, *above*) make for a pleasant run. The mountain roads north of Taos present a formidable challenge.

River Rafting

The **Taos Box**, at the bottom of the steep-walled canyon far below the Rio Grande Gorge Bridge, is the granddaddy of thrilling white water in New Mexico and is best attempted by experts only—or on a guided trip—but the river also offers more placid sections such as through the Orilla Verde Recreation Area. Spring runoff is the busy season, from mid-April through June, but rafting companies conduct tours March to November. Shorter two-hour options usually cover the fairly tame section of the river. The **Bureau of Land Management, Taos Resource Area Office** (✉ 226 Cruz Alta, ☎ 505/758–8851) has a list of registered river guides and information about running the river on your own.

Far Flung Adventures (✉ 15 State Highway 522, El Prado, ☎ 505/758–2628 or 800/359–2627) operates half-day, full-day, and overnight rafting trips along the Rio Grande and the Rio Chama.

Kokopelli Rafting Adventures (✉ 541 Cordova Rd., Santa Fe, ☎ 800/879–9035) takes you through the Taos Box or down other stretches of the river.

Los Rios River Runners (✉ Taos, ☎ 800/544–1181) will take you to your choice of spots—the Rio Chama, the Lower Gorge, or the Taos Box.

Native Sons Adventures (✉ 715 Paseo del Pueblo Sur, ☎ 505/758–9342 or 800/753–7559) offers several trip options on the Rio Grande.

Skiing

RESORTS

The five ski resorts within 90 mi of Taos have beginning, intermediate, and advanced slopes and snowmobile and cross-country skiing trails. All the resorts have fine accommodations and safe child-care programs at reasonable prices. Only Taos Ski Valley prohibits snowboarding. For more on Angel Fire, Red River, or Taos Ski Valley, *see* Side Trips, *below*.

Angel Fire Resort (✉ N. Angel Fire Rd. off NM 434, Angel Fire, ☎ 505/377–6401; 800/633–7463 outside NM) has a hotel and is open from mid-December to the first week in April.

Red River Ski Area (✉ Pioneer Rd. off NM 38, Red River, ☎ 505/754–2382) is open from Thanksgiving to Easter.

Sipapu Lodge and Ski Area (✉ NM 518, Vadito, ☎ 505/587–2240) is open from mid-December to the end of March.

Ski Rio (✉ NM 196 off NM 522, Costillo, ☎ 505/758–7707), north of Taos Ski Valley, opens for daily business from mid-December to early April. The resort has 83 runs and makes its own snow.

Village of Taos Ski Valley (✉ Taos Ski Valley Rd./County Rd. 150, Village of Taos Ski Valley 87525, ☎ 505/776–2291 for ski information and ticket office; 505/776–2233 or 800/776–1111 for lodging reservations) is open from late November until the first week in April. This world-class area is known for its alpine village atmosphere, perhaps the finest ski school in the country, and the variety of its 72 runs—51% expert (the ridge chutes, Al's Run, Inferno), 25% intermediate (Honeysuckle), 24% beginner (Bambi, Porcupine). Taos Ski Valley averages 323 inches of annual snow-fall and makes its own if needed. There's no snowboarding.

CROSS-COUNTRY

Carson National Forest (⊠ Forest Service Building, 208 Cruz Alta Rd., Taos 87571, ☎ 505/758–6200) has a good self-guided map of cross-country trails throughout the park. You can drive into the forest land via Highways 522, 150, 38, and 578.

At the **Enchanted Forest Cross-Country Ski Area** (⊠ Box 521, Red River 87558, ☎ 505/754–2374), 24 mi of groomed trails loop through meadows and pines from the warming hut; the season runs from the end of November to Easter.

Swimming

The **Don Fernando Municipal Swimming Pool** (⊠ 124 Civic Plaza Dr., ☎ 505/758–9171) is open on weekdays from 1 to 4:30 and on week-ends from 1 to 5. Admission is $2.

Tennis

Kit Carson Memorial Park (⊠ Paseo del Pueblo Norte at Civic Plaza Dr.) and **Fred Baca Park** (⊠ 301 Camino de Medio) have free public tennis courts, available on a first-come, first-served basis. The **Quail Ridge Inn and Tennis Ranch** (⊠ Taos Ski Valley Rd./County Rd. 150, ☎ 800/624–4448) has eight Laykold tennis courts (two indoor). Outdoor courts are free to guests; indoor courts cost $15 per hour, $30 per hour for visitors. **Taos Spa & Tennis Club** (⊠ 111 Doña Ana Dr., ☎ 888/758–1981) has tennis and racquetball courts; nonmembers pay $10 per day.

Spectator Sports

Spectator sports in the Taos area include the **Rodeo de Taos,** which takes place at the Taos County Rodeo Fairgrounds in mid-June, and the **Taos Mountain Balloon Rally,** held in a field south of downtown during the last week in October. Contact the Taos County Chamber of Commerce (☞ Visitor Information *in* Taos A to Z, *below*) for more information. **Paradise Balloons** (☎ 505/751–6098) and **Pueblo Balloons** (☎ 505/751–9877) conduct balloon rides over and into the Rio Grande Gorge at sunrise. The cost is $195 plus gratuities.

SHOPPING

Shopping Districts

Taos Plaza consists mostly of T-shirt emporiums and souvenir shops that are easily bypassed, though a few stores, like Blue Rain Gallery, carry quality Native American artifacts and jewelry. The more upscale galleries and boutiques are two short blocks north on Bent Street, including the John Dunn House Shops. Kit Carson Road, also known as U.S. 64, has a mix of the old and the new. There's metered municipal parking downtown, though the traffic can be daunting. Some shops worth checking out are in St. Francis Plaza in Ranchos de Taos, 4 mi south of the Plaza near the San Francisco de Asís Church.

Galleries

For at least a century, artists have been drawn to Taos by its special light, open space, and connections to nature. The result is a vigorous art community with some 80 galleries, a lively market, and an estimated 1,000 residents producing art full- or part-time. Many artists explore themes of the Western landscape, Native Americans, and adobe architecture; others create abstract forms and mixed-media works that may or may not reflect the Southwest. Some local artists grew up in Taos, but many—Anglo, Hispanic, and Native Americans—are adopted Taoseños.

Blue Rain Gallery (✉ 117 S. Plaza, ☎ 505/751–0066) carries some of the finest examples of Pueblo pottery and Hopi katsina dolls to be found anywhere, ranging in price from several hundred to several thousand dollars. The owner, Leroy Garcia, takes time to explain the materials and traditions; you'll learn a great deal during a short visit here. The gallery also sells Indian-made jewelry and art.

Clay and Fiber Gallery (✉ 210 Paseo del Pueblo Sur, ☎ 505/758–8093) has exhibited first-rate ceramics, glass, pottery, and hand-painted silks and weavings by local artists for the past quarter century.

Fenix Gallery (✉ 228-B Paseo del Pueblo Norte, ☎ 505/758–9120) is a showcase for contemporary art, exhibiting paintings, sculpture, ceramics, and lithography by established Taos artists.

La Tierra Gallery (✉ 124-G Bent St., ☎ 505/758–0101) has nature as its featured artist. Fossils and minerals that have been crafted into jewelry and graceful carvings are for sale.

Leo Weaver Jewelry Galleries represents 50 local jewelry artists at two locations (✉ 62 St. Francis Plaza, Ranchos de Taos, ☎ 505/751–1003; Historic Taos Inn, 125 Paseo del Pueblo Norte, ☎ 505/758–8171). You'll find contemporary and traditional designs in silver, gold, and precious stones, as well as beautiful silver disk concha belts.

Lumina Gallery (✉ 239 Morada La., ☎ 505/758–7282) exhibits paintings solely by artists who have worked in New Mexico for at least 20 years, as well as sculpture, photography, mixed-media pieces, and antiques. Artists represented include Joe Waldrun and Chuck Henningsen. The impressive works decorate the former adobe home of Victor Higgins, one of the original members of the Taos Society of Artists. The outdoor sculpture garden is a serene oasis conducive to lingering, which the owners happily encourage.

Michael McCormick Gallery (✉ 106C Paseo del Pueblo Norte, ☎ 505/758–1372) is home to the sensual, stylized female portraits by Miguel Martinez and the architectural paintings of Margaret Nes. An important annex is the JD Challenger studio and gallery. JD Challenger is renowned for his paintings of Native Americans.

Mission Gallery (✉ 138 E. Kit Carson Rd., ☎ 505/758–2861) carries the works of early Taos artists, early New Mexico modernists, and important contemporary artists. The gallery is in the former home of painter Joseph H. Sharp.

Navajo Gallery (✉ 210 Ledoux St., ☎ 505/758–3250) shows the works of owner and Navajo painter R. C. Gorman, well known for his ethereal interpretations of Indian imagery.

New Directions Gallery (✉ 107-B N. Plaza, ☎ 505/758–2771 or 800/658–6903) displays works by contemporary Taos artists such as Larry Bell, Ted Egri, and Maya Torres in a light-filled room.

Parks Gallery (✉ 140 Kit Carson Rd., ☎ 505/751–0343) specializes in contemporary paintings, sculptures, and prints. Mixed-media artist Melissa Zink shows here.

R. B. Ravens Gallery (✉ St. Francis Plaza, Ranchos de Taos, ☎ 505/758–7322) exhibits paintings by the founding artists of Taos, pre-1930s weavings, and ceramics.

Shriver Gallery (✉ 401 Paseo del Pueblo Norte, ☎ 505/758–499
dles drawings and etchings, traditional bronze sculptures, an
ings, including oils, watercolors, and pastels.

Six Directions (✉ 110 S. Plaza, ☎ 505/758–4376) has pain
abaster and bronze sculpture, Native American artifacts, silve
and pottery. Bill Rabbit and Robert Redbird are among the a
resented here.

Spirit Runner Gallery (✉ 303 Paseo del Pueblo Norte, ☎
1132) exhibits colorful acrylic and gold-leaf paintings by T
Ouray Meyers.

Specialty Stores

Books

Brodsky Bookshop (✉ 218 Paseo del Pueblo Norte, ☎ 505/758–9468)
has books—contemporary literature, Southwestern classics, children's
titles—sometimes piled every which way, but the amiable staff will help
you find whatever you need.

Fernandez de Taos Book Store (✉ 109 N. Plaza, ☎ 505/758–4391)
carries magazines, major out-of-town newspapers, and many books
on Southwestern culture and history.

G. Robinson Old Prints and Maps (✉ John Dunn House, 124D Bent
St., ☎ 505/758–2278) stocks rare books, Edward Curtis photographs,
and maps and prints from the 16th to 19th century.

Merlin's Garden (✉ 127 Bent St., ☎ 505/758–0985) is a funky repos-
itory of metaphysical books and literature from Ram Dass to Thomas
More. The shop also carries tapes, incense, crystals, and jewelry.

Moby Dickens (✉ No. 6, John Dunn House, 124A Bent St., ☎ 505/
758–3050), great for browsing, is a bookstore for all ages. It carries
many books on the Southwest.

Mystery Ink (✉ 121 Camino de la Placita, ☎ 505/751–1092) specializes
in high-quality used books, especially murder mysteries. The shop also
carries some foreign-language literature.

Taos Book Shop (✉ 122D Kit Carson Rd., ☎ 505/758–3733), the oldest bookshop in New Mexico, founded in 1947, specializes in out-of-
print and Southwestern books. The founders, Genevieve Janssen and
Claire Morrill, compiled the reminiscences of their Taos years in the
interesting *A Taos Mosaic* (University of New Mexico Press). Book signings and author receptions are frequently held here.

Clothing

Mariposa Boutique (✉ John Dunn House, 120F Bent St., ☎ 505/758–
9028) sells Southwestern clothing and accessories by leading Taos designers. The store also sells handcrafted jewelry.

Overland Sheepskin Company (✉ NM 522, ☎ 505/758–8822; 100-
A McCarthy Plaza, ☎ 505/758–5150) carries high-quality sheepskin
coats, hats, mittens, and slippers, many with Taos beadwork.

Taos Moccasin Co. Factory Outlet (✉ 216 Paseo del Pueblo Sur, ☎ 505/
758–4276) sells moccasins made in the building next door—everything
from booties for babies to men's high and low boots. This shop has
great discounts and interesting designs.

Home Furnishings

Casa Cristal Pottery (✉ 1306 Paseo del Pueblo Norte, ☎ 505/758–1530),
2½ mi north of the Taos Plaza, has it all: stoneware, serapes, clay pots,

When it Comes to Getting Cash at an ATM, Same Thing.

Whether you're in Yosemite or Yemen, using your Visa® card or ATM card with the PLUS symbol is the easiest and most convenient way to get cash. Even if your bank is in Minneapolis and you're in Miami, Visa/PLUS ATMs make getting cash so easy, you'll feel right at home. After all, Visa/PLUS ATMs are open 24 hours a day, 7 days a week, rain or shine. And if you need help finding one of Visa's 627,000 ATMs in 127 countries worldwide, visit **visa.com/pd/atm**. We'll make finding an ATM as easy as finding the Eiffel Tower, the Pyramids or even the Grand Canyon.

It's Everywhere You Want To Be.®

Native American ironwood carvings, straw and tin ornaments, fountains, sweaters, ponchos, clay fireplaces, Mexican blankets, clay churches, birdbaths, baskets, tiles, piñatas, and blue glassware from Guadalajara. Also in stock are wrought-iron antique reproductions.

Country Furnishings of Taos (⊠ 534 Paseo del Pueblo Norte, ☎ 505/758–4633) sells folk art from northern New Mexico; handmade furniture, metalwork lamps and beds; and many other colorful accessories.

Flying Carpet (⊠ 208 Ranchitos Rd., ☎ 505/751–4035) carries colorful rugs and kilims from Turkey, Kurdistan, Persia, and elsewhere. Owner Bill Eagleton, who wrote a book about Kurdish carpets, and his wife, Kay, have a keen eye for quality and design.

Franzetti Metalworks (⊠ 120G Bent St., ☎ 505/758–7872) displays owner Pozzi Franzetti's whimsical steelwork designs—from switch plate covers to wall hangings in animal and Western motifs.

Hacienda de San Francisco (⊠ 4 St. Francis Plaza, Ranchos de Taos, ☎ 505/758–0477) has an exceptional collection of Spanish-colonial antiques.

Lo Fino (⊠ 201 Paseo del Pueblo Sur, ☎ 505/758–0298) carries the works—hand-carved beds, tables, chairs, *trasteros* (free-standing cupboards), and benches—of the 10 top Southwestern furniture and lighting designers, as well as some Native American alabaster sculpture, basketry, and pottery.

LYNCO Design Pottery (⊠ 124-C Bent St., ☎ 505/758–3601) features the decoratively painted oven ware of Taos artist Lynn FitzGerald. The high-fired, stoneware pottery comes in serving bowls, pie plates, casserole dishes, and other forms to suit your baking needs.

Partridge Company (⊠ 241 Ledoux St., at Ranchitos Rd., ☎ 505/758–1225) sells linens, rugs, woven bedcovers, and accessories. The shop's owner fashions some eye-catching dried-flower arrangements.

Taos Blue (⊠ 101A Bent St., ☎ 505/758–3561) carries jewelry, pottery, and contemporary works by Native Americans (masks, rattles, sculpture), as well as Hispanic santos (*bultos* and *retablos*).

The **Taos Company** (⊠ 124K Bent St., ☎ 800/548–1141) sells magnificent Spanish-style furniture, chandeliers, rugs, and textiles; Mexican *equipal* (wood and leather) chairs; and other accessories.

Taos Tinworks (⊠ 1204 Paseo del Pueblo Norte, ☎ 505/758–9724) sells handcrafted tinwork such as wall sconces, mirrors, lamps, and table ornaments by Marion Moore.

Native American Arts and Crafts

Broken Arrow (⊠ 222 N. Plaza, ☎ 505/758–4304) specializes in collector-quality Native American arts and crafts, including sand paintings, rugs, prints, jewelry, pottery, artifacts, and Hopi katsina dolls.

Buffalo Dancer (⊠ 103A E. Plaza, ☎ 505/758–8718) buys, sells, and trades Native American arts and crafts, including pottery, belts, katsina dolls, hides, and silver-coin jewelry.

Don Fernando Curios and Gifts (⊠ 104 W. Plaza, ☎ 505/758–3791), which opened in 1938 (it's the oldest Native American arts shop on the Taos Plaza), sells good turquoise jewelry, katsinas, straw baskets, and colorful beads.

El Rincón (⊠ 114 E. Kit Carson Rd., ☎ 505/758–9188) is housed in a large, dark, cluttered century-old adobe. Native American items of all kinds are bought and sold here: drums, feathered headdresses, Navajo rugs, beads, bowls, baskets, shields, beaded moccasins, jewelry, arrows, and spearheads. The packed back room contains Indian, Hispanic, and Anglo Wild West artifacts.

Southwest Moccasin & Drum (✉ 803 Paseo del Pueblo Norte, ☎ 505/ 758–9332 or 800/447–3630) has 716 native moccasin styles and 72 sizes of drums, many painted by local artists.

Taos Drums (✉ Santa Fe Hwy./NM 68, ☎ 505/758–3796 or 800/424– 3786) is the factory outlet for the Taos Drum Factory. The store, 5 mi south of Taos Plaza (look for the large tepee), stocks handmade Pueblo log drums, leather lamp shades, and wrought-iron and South-western furniture.

Taos General Store (✉ 223 Paseo del Pueblo Sur, ☎ 505/758–9051) represents a good part of the world in the large showroom's selection of furniture and decorative items. You can also wander among the dis-plays of American Indian pots, rugs, and jewelry. Some items are at wholesale prices.

Outdoor Equipment

Los Rios Anglers (✉ 226C Paseo del Pueblo Norte, ☎ 505/758–2798 or 800/748–1707) is a fly-fisherman's haven for fly rods, flies, cloth-ing, books, instruction, and guide service to local streams.

Mudd 'n' Flood Mountain Shop (✉ 134 Bent St., ☎ 505/751–9100) has gear and clothing for rock climbers, backpackers, campers, and backcountry skiers.

Taos Mountain Outfitters (✉ 114 S. Plaza, ☎ 505/758–9292) supplies kayakers, skiers, and backpackers with what they need, as well as maps, books, and handy advice.

SIDE TRIPS

The Enchanted Circle

Some clever marketers conceived the moniker the Enchanted Circle to describe the territory accessed by the roads that form an 84-mi loop north from Taos and back to town (U.S. 64 to NM 522 to NM 38 back to U.S. 64), and it's likely you'll agree with their choice. A day trip around the Enchanted Circle includes a glorious panorama of alpine valleys and the towering mountains of the lush Carson National Forest. You can see all the major sights listed below on a one-day drive, or pace them out with an overnight stay.

Numbers in the text correspond to numbers in the margin and on the Taos Environs and the Enchanted Circle map.

A Good Drive

Traveling east from Taos along U.S. 64, you'll soon be winding through Taos Canyon, climbing your way toward 9,000-ft Palo Flechado Pass. On the other side of the pass, in about 25 mi you'll come to **Angel Fire** ⑲, a ski resort. Continue east on U.S. 64 about 14 mi to tiny **Eagle Nest** ⑳, an old-fashioned ski-resort village. Next take NM 38 going northwest and head over Bobcat Pass, a tad under 10,000 ft in elevation, about 16 mi from **Red River** ㉑. From Red River the Enchanted Circle heads west about 12 mi to scenic **Questa** ㉒. The **Red River Hatchery** is about 5 mi south of Questa on NM 522. Continue south on NM 522 and keep an eye out for the sign that points to the **D. H. Lawrence Ranch and Memorial** ⑯. The memorial may be visited, but the other build-ings on the ranch are closed to the public. From here, Taos is about 15 mi south via NM 522 to U.S. 64.

TIMING

Leave early in the morning and plan to spend the entire day on this trip. During ski season, which runs from late November to early April, you may want to make it an overnight trip and get in a day of skiing (☞ Skiing *in* Outdoor Activities and Sports, *above*). In spring, summer, and fall your drive should be free of snow and ice. A sunny winter day will yield some lovely scenery (but if there's snow out, don't forget your sunglasses).

Sights To See

⑲ **Angel Fire.** For hundreds of years a long, empty valley and the fall meeting grounds of the Ute Indians, the Angel Fire area is a busy ski resort these days. There are several dining options at the main resort. A prominent landmark is the **DAV Vietnam Veterans Memorial**, a 50-ft-high wing-shape monument built in 1971 by D. Victor Westphall, whose son David was killed in Vietnam. The memorial's textured surface, which captures the dazzling, colorful reflections of the New Mexican mountains, changes constantly with the sun's movement. ⊠ *U.S. 64, 25 mi east of Taos,* ☎ *505/377–6401 (24 hrs) or 800/633–7463 (8–5).*

Carson National Forest. The national forest that surrounds Taos spans almost 200 mi across northern New Mexico and encompasses mountains, lakes, streams, villages, and much of the Enchanted Circle. Hiking, skiing, horseback riding, mountain biking, backpacking, trout fishing, boating, and wildflower viewing are among the popular activities here. The forest is home to big-game animals and many species of smaller animals and songbirds; you can see some at the **Ghost Ranch Living Museum** (☞ Chapter 6). **Wheeler Peak** (☞ Taos Ski Valley, *below*) is a designated wilderness area where travel is restricted to hiking or horseback riding. Contact the Carson National Forest for maps, safety guidelines, and conditions (it's open weekdays 8–4:30). ⊠ *Forest Service Building, 208 Cruz Alta Rd., Taos 87571,* ☎ *505/758–6200.*

⑯ **D. H. Lawrence Ranch and Memorial.** The influential and controversial English writer David Herbert Lawrence and his wife, Frieda, arrived in Taos at the invitation of Mabel Dodge Luhan, who collected famous writers and artists the way some people collect butterflies. Luhan provided them a place to live, Kiowa Ranch, on 160 acres in the mountains. Rustic and remote, it's known as the D. H. Lawrence Ranch, though Lawrence never actually owned it. Lawrence lived in Taos on and off for about 22 months during a three-year period between 1922 and 1925. He wrote his novel *The Plumed Serpent* (1926), as well as some of his finest short stories and poetry, while in Taos and on excursions to Mexico. The houses here, owned by the University of New Mexico, are not open to the public; the nearby smaller cabin is where Dorothy Brett, the Lawrences' traveling companion, stayed. You can visit the D. H. Lawrence Memorial on wooded Lobo Mountain. A white shedlike structure, it's simple and unimposing. The writer fell ill while visiting France and died in a sanatorium there in 1930. Five years later Frieda had Lawrence's body disinterred and cremated and brought his ashes back to Taos. Frieda Lawrence is buried, as was her wish, in front of the memorial. Views down into the Taos area to the south and west are great. ⊠ *NM 522 (follow signed dirt road from the highway), San Cristobal,* ☎ *505/776–2245.* ☒ *Free.* ☉ *Daily dawn–dusk.*

⑳ **Eagle Nest.** Eagle Nest Lake nestles into the crook made by the intersection of NM 64 and NM 38, and the main street through town is actually NM 64. Thousands of acres of national forest surround this funky village, population 189, elevation 8,090 ft. The shops and other buildings here evoke New Mexico's mining heritage while a 1950s-style diner, Kaw-Lija's, serves up a memorable burger. ⊠ *NM 38, 14 mi north of Angel Fire.*

㉒ **Questa.** Literally "hill" in the heart of the Sangre de Cristo Mountains, Questa is a quiet village about 12 mi from the town of Red River, nestled against the Red River itself and amid some of the most striking mountain country in New Mexico. **St. Anthony's Church,** built of adobe with 5-ft-thick walls and viga ceilings, is on the main street. Questa's **Cabresto Lake,** in Carson National Forest, is about 8 mi from town. Follow NM 563 to Forest Route 134, then 2 mi of a primitive road (134A)—you'll need a four-wheel-drive vehicle. You can trout fish and boat here from about June to October.

㉑ **Red River.** A major ski resort, Red River, elevation 8,750 ft, came into being as a miners' boomtown during the 19th century, taking its name from the river whose mineral content gave it a rich, rosy color. When the gold petered out, Red River died, only to be rediscovered in the 1920s by migrants escaping the dust storms in the Great Plains. An Old West flavor remains: Main Street shoot-outs, an authentic melodrama, and square dancing and two-stepping are among the diversions here. Because of its many country dances and festivals, Red River is affectionately called "The New Mexico Home of the Texas Two-Step." The bustling little downtown area contains shops and sportswear boutiques. The **Jewelry Lady** (⊠ Main St., ☎ 505/754–2300) is a well-stocked shop. The ski area is also in the middle of town, with lifts within walking distance of restaurants and hotels. ⊠ *Off NM 38,* ☎ *505/776– 5510 for overnight reservations.*

NEED A
BREAK?

In Red River stop by the **Sundance** (⊠ High St., ☎ 505/754–2971) for Mexican food. **Texas Red's Steakhouse** (⊠ Main St., ☎ 505/754– 2964) has steaks, chops, burgers, and chicken. The **Black Crow Coffeehouse** (⊠ Main St., ☎ 505/754–3150) serves up an energizing brew.

Ⓒ **Red River Hatchery.** At this engaging facility you can feed freshwater trout and learn how they're hatched, reared, stocked, and controlled. The visitor center has displays and exhibits, a show pond, and a machine that dispenses fish food. The self-guided tour can last anywhere from 20 to 90 minutes, depending on how enraptured you become. There's a picnic area on the grounds. ⊠ *NM 522, 5 mi south of Questa,* ☎ *505/586–0222.* ☞ *Free.* ⊙ *Daily 8–5.*

Camping

The country around Taos provides a wealth of camping opportunities, from organized campgrounds to informal roadside campsites and sites that require backpacking in. If mountains, pines, and streams are your goal, stake out sites in Carson National Forest along the Rio Hondo or Red River; if you prefer high-desert country along the banks of the Rio Grande, consider Orilla Verde or Wild Rivers recreation areas.

⚘ **Carson National Forest.** Within the forest are dozens of campsites along 400 mi of cool mountain trout streams and lakes. You may also choose your own site, anywhere along a forest road. Rest rooms are provided. Contact the U.S. Forest Service for the latest camping information. ⊠ *Forest Service Building, 208 Cruz Alta Rd., Taos 87571,* ☎ *505/758–6200. 30 RV and tent sites.*

⚘ **Questa Lodge.** This campground is on the Red River off the Enchanted Circle, just off NM 522. There are rest rooms and hot showers. ⊠ *Lower Embargo Rd. (Box 155), Questa 87556,* ☎ *505/586– 0300 or 800/459–0300. 26 RV sites. Basketball, croquet, volleyball, playground, coin laundry. Closed mid-Oct.–Apr.*

⚘ **Roadrunner Campground.** The Red River runs right through this woodsy mountain campground. There are rest rooms, hot showers, and an area with video games. ✉ *NM 578 (Box 588), Red River 87558,* ☎ *505/754–2286 or 800/243–2286. 155 RV sites. Grocery, tennis court, playground, coin laundry, meeting room. Closed mid-Dec.–early spring.*

🔺 **Wild Rivers Recreation Area.** This area at the confluence of the Rio Grande and the Red River near Questa has a visitor center and rim-top campsites with parking, picnic tables, grills, drinking water, and rest-room facilities, as well as less-developed river sites that require a hike in. Inquire about special tours and campfire talks. There is a $7 per vehicle rim-top fee, $5 riverside. ✉ *Bureau of Land Management, Cruz Alta Rd., Taos 87571, about 35 mi north of Taos off NM 522 and NM 378,* ☎ *505/758–8851. 10 15-person campsites, 2 group shelters for up to 50 people. Restrooms, showers. Reservations necessary for group shelters.*

Taos Ski Valley

22 mi northeast of Taos.

⑱ Skiers from around the world return to the slopes and hospitality of the alpinelike **Village of Taos Ski Valley** every year, and the area attracts outdoor enthusiasts year-round. Aside from skiing in winter and early spring, there's also good hiking in summer and fall (☞ Outdoor Activities and Sports, *above*). There aren't many summer visitors, so you can have the trails up to Bull-of-the-Woods, Gold Hill, Williams Lake, and Wheeler Peak nearly all to yourself. The village will celebrate its sixth year of incorporation on July 4, 2001. Special events like barn dances and wine tastings occur throughout the nonskiing seasons.

⑰ To get here from Taos, take U.S. 64 north to the traffic light and turn right for NM 150 (Taos Ski Valley Road). The hamlet of **Arroyo Seco,** some 5 mi up NM 150 from the traffic light, is worth a stop for lunch or ice cream (☞ Dining, *above*) and a look at some crafts and antiques shops. Beyond Arroyo Seco the road crosses a high plain, then plunges into the Rio Hondo Canyon to follow the cascading brook upstream through the forest to the Taos Ski Valley, where NM 150 ends. (It does not continue to Red River as some misguided motorists discover.)

OFF THE **WHEELER PEAK –** Part of the Sangre de Cristo Mountains, 13,161-ft-high
BEATEN PATH Wheeler is the highest point in New Mexico. The 7-mi trail to the peak begins at the Village of Taos Ski Valley. Only experienced hikers should tackle this strenuous trail. Dress warmly even in summer, take plenty of water and food, and pay attention to *all* warnings and instructions distributed by the forest rangers.

Dining and Lodging

In winter, an espresso stand on the top level of the base lodge complex pours courage in a cup to those about to tackle the mountain.

$ ✕ **Tim's Stray Dog Cantina.** This good spot for lunch at the ski area is known for New Mexican food such as chiles rellenos. ✉ *Sutton Pl.,* ☎ *505/776–2894. MC, V.*

$$$$ ✕▣ **The Bavarian.** A luxurious secluded hideaway, this authentic re-
★ creation of a Bavarian ski lodge has the only mid-mountain accommodations in the Taos Ski Valley. The King Ludwig suite has a dining room, a kitchen, a huge marble-tiled bathroom, and two bedrooms with canopied beds. The Lola Montez has a bedroom plus a loft and is a favorite with honeymooners. Three suites have whirlpool tubs, and there's a three-bedroom, three-bath apartment. The restaurant serves Bavarian cuisine and has a comprehensive wine list. Summer activities at the Bavarian include hiking, touring with the resident botanist,

horseback riding, rafting, and fishing. Seven-night ski packages, including two meals a day and six days of lifts and lessons, range from $1,715 to $1,925 per person. There are reduced nightly rates in summer. ⊠ *Twining Rd. off County Rd. 150, Village of Taos Ski Valley 87525,* ☎ *505/776–8020,* FAX *505/776–5301. 4 suites. Restaurant, in-room VCRs, kitchenettes, hiking, horseback riding, fishing. AE, MC, V. Closed May and early Nov. BP.* ✎

$$$$ ✕⊡ **Inn at Snakedance.** This modern, spotlessly clean resort hotel epitomizes the rustic tradition of European alpine lodges. Right on the slopes, the inn has a handsome library where guests can enjoy an après-ski coffee or after-dinner drink next to a fieldstone fireplace. The dining room has a soaring ceiling with 100-year-old beams originally cut for the copper mines down the road. The rooms, some with fireplaces, have Southwestern decor. In summer the hotel offers weeklong vacation packages, including a cooking school and fitness adventure courses. ⊠ *Off Taos Ski Valley Rd. (County Rd. 150; Box 89), Village of Taos Ski Valley 87525,* ☎ *505/776–2277 or 800/322–9815,* FAX *505/776–1410. 60 rooms, 1 condo. Minibars, refrigerators, hot tub, massage, sauna, exercise room, library. AE, DC, MC, V. Closed mid-Apr.–Memorial Day.* ✎

$$$–$$$$ ⊡ **Edelweiss.** Put your skis on at the back door of this intimate lodge, and glide down to the lift. Tasty power breakfasts, lunches, and afternoon hors d'oeuvres are served in the dining room overlooking the bunny slope. The rooms upstairs are loaded with old-world touches, polished antique chests, bookshelves, and gable-framed views. An oft-requested suite has a large Jacuzzi in the bedroom nook. There is a three-night minimum. Ski-week packages include six days of lifts and lessons, seven nights' lodging, seven breakfasts, and seven dinners for $1,125–$1,890 per person. ⊠ *106 Sutton Pl., Village of Taos Ski Valley 87525,* ☎ *505/776–2301 or 800/458–8754,* FAX *505/776–2533. 8 rooms. Outdoor hot tub, ice-skating. No smoking. MC, V. Mid-Apr.–Nov. BP.*

$$$ ✕⊡ **Thunderbird Lodge and Chalets.** Only 150 yards from the main lifts, on the sunny side of Taos Ski Valley, this two-story wood-frame inn, one of the valley's first lodges, is great for families. A large conference room doubles as a games room, with board games and a library. Supervised children's activities during holiday seasons include early dinners, movies, and games. Lodge rooms are cozy and functional; the rooms in the Chalet are larger and have king-size beds. Sumptuous breakfast buffets and family-style dinners are served in the pine-paneled dining room. Reservations are recommended for dinner. Ski-week packages with two meals a day are $601–$840 per person. ⊠ *3 Thunderbird Rd., off Taos Ski Valley Rd. (County Rd. 150; Box 87), Village of Taos Ski Valley 87525,* ☎ *505/776–2280 or 800/776–2279,* FAX *505/776–2238. 32 rooms. Restaurant, bar, hot tub, massage, sauna, recreation room, library, meeting room. AE, MC, V.* ✎

$–$$$ ✕⊡ **Austing Haus.** Owner Paul Austing constructed much of this
★   handsome building 1½ mi from Taos Ski Valley himself, along with many of its furnishings. The breakfast room has large picture windows, stained-glass paneling, and an impressive fireplace. Aromas of fresh-baked goods such as Paul's apple strudel come from the kitchen. Guest rooms are pretty and quiet with harmonious, peaceful colors; some have four-poster beds and fireplaces. During the winter the inn offers week-long ski packages. A hot tub offers relaxation after skiing or hiking. ⊠ *Taos Ski Valley Rd. (County Rd. 150; Box 8), Village of Taos Ski Valley 87525,* ☎ *505/776–2649, 505/776–2629, or 800/748–2932,* FAX *505/776–8751. 22 rooms, 3 chalets. Hot tub. AE, DC, MC, V. BP.*

Shopping
Andean Softwear (⊠ 118 Sutton Pl., ☎ 505/776–2508) carries exotic clothing, textiles, and jewelry. Note the deliciously soft alpaca sweaters

from Peru. You can bring your ski boots up to the pros at the **Boot Doctor** (✉ 103 Sutton Pl., ☎ 505/776–2489)—if anyone can make 'em fit, they can; if not, they'll find a pair that does. A demo program lets you try skis out. Ski clothing and accessories fill out the store in winter, and in the summer you can stock up on hiking clothing, sandals, and clogs.

Low Road to Santa Fe

Traveling south out of town, Paseo del Pueblo Sur becomes NM 68, and wide-open views abound—from picture-perfect mountains on the east to the distant western horizon across the plain. The jagged slash cut into the land a few miles west was carved over many millennia by the Rio Grande. The highway also winds down from the high plateau into the rocky canyon of the Rio Grande. But before you reach the "Big River," watch for another river rushing in from the east about 20 mi south of Taos. This is the Embudo River, and 2 mi east across it on NM 75 lies the pretty hamlet of Dixon. New Mexico 68 continues south and begins to parallel the Rio Grande just before the Embudo Station restaurant and microbrewery, seen across a bridge on the right bank. Farther south the river canyon widens into a valley with farmers' fields and fruit orchards near Velarde, where fruit and vegetable stands tempt travelers from both sides of the road.

Dixon
20 mi south of Taos.

The small village of Dixon and its surrounding country lanes are home to a surprising number of artists. The Dixon Arts Association lists some four dozen of them, many represented in a cooperative showroom in the village center, **Casa de Piedra Gallery** (✉ State Rd. 75, No. 211, ☎ 505/ 579–4608). Artistic sensitivity, as well as generations of dedicated farmers, account for the community's well-tended fields, pretty gardens, and fruit trees—a source of produce for restaurants and farmer's markets such as the one in Santa Fe. The single main road flanked by businesses and residences simplifies finding your way around Dixon.

DINING AND LODGING

$ ✕ **Dan's Cafe.** The 100-year-old adobe building once housed a blacksmith shop but has been renovated to allow breakfast and lunch patrons to settle in for inexpensive dining. Northern New Mexican vegetarian food is the mainstay, with a few sandwiches that include turkey or ham. It's open 10 AM–2 PM and on Friday nights from 6:30–9 for homemade pizza. ✉ *State Rd. 75, No. 236,* ☎ *505/579–4532. No credit cards. Closed Sat. No dinner Sun.–Thurs.*

$$$ ✕🏠 **Embudo Station Guesthouse.** The restaurant's ($$) emphasis is on locally grown produce and the house-brewed beers. Lunch and dinner are served in the casual indoor dining room or outside on the riverside patio. Rainbow trout roasted and served on a cedar plank is one of the most-called-for entrées along with a crisp salad; also popular is a hearty sandwich of turkey cured in the smokehouse next door. Behind the restaurant is a renovated one-bedroom log cabin with a living room and kitchen unit that offers roomy digs for two to four guests. ✉ *Hwy. 68, Box 154, Embudo 87531,* ☎ *505/852–4707 or 800/852–4707,* ☏ *505/852–2479. 1 cabin. Restaurant, kitchen. AE, MC, V. Closed mid-Nov.–early Apr. and Mon.* ✆

$$ 🏠 **Rock Pool Gardens.** A two-bedroom suite with a kitchenette stocked with breakfast items is offered here. The bedrooms are connected by a bathroom, but each has its own access and patio (the suite is rented to one party only, usually a family). Decorated by the owner, who also designs opera sets, the faux-finish walls and willow twig furniture in the rooms have a country flair. Guests can use the Jacuzzi under the

trees and the heated pool set in natural rock. ⊠ *State Rd. 75, No. 249, Dixon 87527,* ☎ *505/579–4602,* ℻ *505/579–9182. 1 suite. Refrigerator, hot tub, pool. No credit cards.*

TAOS A TO Z

Arriving and Departing

By Bus

Texas, New Mexico & Oklahoma Coaches (☎ 800/231–2222), a subsidiary of Greyhound Lines, runs buses twice a day from Albuquerque to Taos. Buses stop at the **Taos Bus Station** (⊠ 1353 Paseo del Pueblo Sur, ☎ 505/758–1144).

By Car

The main route from Santa Fe to Taos is NM 68 (☞ Low Road to Santa Fe, *in* Side Trips, *above*), which winds between the Rio Grande and red-rock cliffs before rising to a spectacular view of the plain and river gorge. You can also take the wooded High Road to Taos (☞ Side Trips from Santa Fe *in* Chapter 2) from Santa Fe. From points north of Taos, take NM 522; from points east or west, take U.S. 64.

Roads can be treacherously icy in the winter months; call **New Mexico Road Conditions** (☎ 800/432–4269) before heading out. The altitude in Taos will affect your car's performance, causing it to "gasp" because it's getting too much gas and not enough air. If a smooth ride matters, you can have your car tuned up for high-altitude driving.

By Plane

Albuquerque International Sunport (⊠ 2200 Sunport Blvd. SE, off I–25, ☎ 505/842–4366) is the nearest (130 mi) major airport to Taos. **Rio Grande Air** (☎ 877/435–9742) offers several round-trips daily between Albuquerque, Los Alamos, and **Taos Municipal Airport** (⊠ U.S. 64, ☎ 505/758–4995), 12 mi west of the city.

AIRPORT TRANSFERS

Pride of Taos (☎ 505/758–8340) runs daily shuttle service to the Albuquerque International Sunport ($35 one-way, $65 round-trip) and between Taos and Santa Fe ($20 each way). Reservations are strongly recommended. **Faust's Transportation** (☎ 505/758–3410 or 505/758–7359) operates radio-dispatched taxis between Taos Municipal Airport and town ($20) and between Albuquerque's airport and Taos ($35 one-way, $65 round-trip). **Twin Hearts Express** (☎ 505/751–1201) charges $30 one-way and $55 round-trip to the Albuquerque airport and also has service to Taos Ski Valley, Red River, Questa, and Santa Fe.

Getting Around

Taos radiates around its central Plaza and is easily maneuvered on foot: many restaurants, stores, boutiques, and galleries are on or near the Plaza. The main street through town is Paseo del Pueblo.

By Bus

The town of Taos transit department's **Chile Line** (☎ 505/751–4459) bus service has two lines. The Green Line circles around town while the Red Line runs between Taos Pueblo and Ranchos de Taos post office. Tickets are 50¢, all-day passes $1.

By Car

Major hotels have ample parking. Metered parking areas are all over town; in peak seasons—summer and winter—traffic and parking can be a headache. There's a metered parking lot between Taos Plaza and Bent Street and a free lot on Kit Carson two blocks east of Paseo del Pueblo.

By Taxi

Taxi service is sparse. However, **Faust's Transportation** (☎ 505/758–3410 or 505/758–7359), based in nearby El Prado, has a fleet of radio-dispatched cabs.

Guided Tours

Orientation

Historic Taos Trolley Tours (☎ 505/751–0366) conducts two three-hour narrated tours of Taos daily, including stops at the San Francisco de Asís Church, Taos Pueblo, La Hacienda de los Martínez, and a Taos drum shop. Tours run from May to October and cost $25 each.

Special-Interest

Taos Studio Tours (☎ 505/776–9749) offers individual or small group tours to galleries and artists' studios as well as excursions in and around town. **All Aboard** (☎ 505/758–9368) guide service conducts 1½-hr walking tours in town ($10 per person). **Native Sons Adventures** (✉ 715 Paseo del Pueblo Sur, Taos, ☎ 505/758–9342 or 800/753–7559) organizes biking, backpacking, rafting, snowmobiling, and horseback and wagon expeditions. **Roadrunner Tours** (☎ 505/377–6416) is run by Nancy and Bill Burch, who rent cars, jeeps, skis, and horses and offer snowmobile tours and sleigh rides from the Elkhorn Lodge near Angel Fire. **Taos Indian Horse Ranch** (✉ 1 Miller Rd., Taos Pueblo, ☎ 800/659–3210) conducts two-hour trail rides, as well as old-fashioned horse-drawn sleigh rides through the Taos Pueblo backcountry—winter weather permitting—complete with brass bells, a Native American storyteller, toasted marshmallows, and green-chile roasts. Escorted horseback tours and hayrides are run through Native American lands during the remainder of the year. Tours are by reservation only; no alcohol is permitted. The ranch closes for 42 to 48 days each year to observe the Taos Pueblo Sweats Ceremony. Call the **Taos Pueblo Governor's Office** (☎ 505/758–9593) for exact dates.

Learning Vacations

Workshops and Educational Tours

Taos Art School (✉ Box 2588, Taos 87571, ☎ 505/758–0350) offers educational field trips and workshops from May to October in painting, sculpture, weaving, photography, creativity, Native American pottery making, Pueblo culture, and other topics. **Taos Institute of Arts** (✉ 108 Civic Plaza Dr., ☎ 505/758–2793 or 800/822–7183) holds its week-long intensive classes in ceramics, fiber arts, jewelry making, painting, photography, and writing, among others, at Mountain Village, 20 mi south of Taos, from June to October. **Fechin Art Workshops** (✉ Box 220, San Cristobal 87564, ☎ 505/776–2622) present hands-on sessions June to October—in photography, painting, drawing, and sculpture—at the Donner Ranch 18 mi north of Taos.

The **German Summer School** (✉ Dept. of Foreign Language and Literature, Ortega Hall 347A, University of NM, Albuquerque 87131, ☎ 505/277–7367) allows no English during its five-week language-learning session for teachers and students of German, held in June and July at the Thunderbird Lodge in Taos Ski Valley. **UNM's Taos Summer Writers' Conference** (✉ English Dept., University of NM, Albuquerque 87131, ☎ 505/277–6248), held in July at the Sagebrush Inn in Taos, conducts a variety of weekend and weeklong workshops from fiction to poetry to screenwriting.

Contacts and Resources

Emergencies

New Mexico state police (☎ 505/758–8878). **Taos police** (☎ 505/758–2216). **Holy Cross Hospital** (✉ 630 Paseo del Pueblo Sur, ☎ 505/758–8883).

Lodging Reservations

Taos Association of B&B Inns (TABBI; ✉ Box 5440, Taos 87571, ☎ 505/758–4246 or 800/939–2215). **Taos Central Reservations** (✉ Box 1713, Taos 87571, ☎ 505/758–9767 or 800/821–2437).

Pharmacies

Furr's Pharmacy (✉ 1100 Paseo del Pueblo Sur, ☎ 505/758–1203). **Taos Pharmacy** (✉ Piñon Plaza, 622A Paseo del Pueblo Sur, ☎ 505/758–3342). **Wal-Mart Discount Pharmacy** (✉ 926 Paseo de Pueblo Sur, ☎ 505/758–2743).

Visitor Information

Taos County Chamber of Commerce (✉ 1139 Paseo del Pueblo Sur, Drawer I, Taos 87571, ☎ 505/758–3873 or 800/732–8267, ✍).

The Village of Taos Ski Valley Visitors & Conference Bureau (✉ Box 91, Taos Ski Valley 87525, ☎ 800/992–7669, ✍).

4 NORTHEASTERN NEW MEXICO

The brilliantly clear light of northeastern New Mexico illuminates seemingly endless high-desert plains. Hawks soar overhead and antelope gallivant across the same open landscape traversed by the Native Americans and the cowboys, ranchers, miners, and railroaders who settled the West.

By Sharon
Niederman

Updated by
Andrew Collins

YOU'LL BATTLE NEITHER CROWDS NOR HYPE in northeastern New Mexico, one of the best-kept secrets in the state. You can have a wildflower-strewn trail through alpine meadows and forests of aspen and ponderosa pine all to yourself, or step back in time in small towns that treasure their past but do not exploit it. The sheer variety of terrain—mountain, grassy plain, wet, arid—and the combination of natural and social history make the region an ideal destination, whether as a short side trip or part of a journey from New Mexico toward the Plains states.

In 1908 an African-American cowboy named George McJunkin found arrowheads embedded in a bison bone. Archaeologists determined that the arrowheads had been made by ancient hominids, now known as Folsom Man, who inhabited northeastern New Mexico at least 10,000 years ago. In more recent centuries, Apaches, Utes, Comanches, and other Plains Indians hunted and camped here.

The opening of the Santa Fe Trail in the first half of the 19th century and the arrival of the railroad in the 1870s and '80s brought streams of people and goods into northeastern New Mexico, as did the coal mines. Italians, Mexicans, Greeks, Slavs, Spaniards, and Irish all headed to Raton to harvest coal in mines that first opened in 1879. German-Jewish merchants opened shops in the town of Las Vegas to serve the miners, the railroads, and the local Hispanic population.

Roughly during the railroad heyday, Civil War veterans homesteaded in the region, some working for Lucien Maxwell, onetime mountain man and fur trader who came to control the largest landholding (1,714,765 acres) in the western hemisphere. Many of New Mexico's large ranches date from the era of the Maxwell Land Grant, territory awarded to the father of Maxwell's wife and another man by the Mexican government in 1841. Modern-day land baron Ted Turner now owns an enormous chunk of open land in these parts.

History is very much alive in northeastern New Mexico, in the stories of the people who live here and their way of life, in the architecture, and in the landscape itself. Exploring this land of vast plains, rugged mesas, and wild, crystalline streams may well be the best way to immerse yourself in the American West.

Pleasures and Pastimes

Dining
This is ranching country, where hearty, straightforward meals are favored. Few locals feel any shame about sitting down to a chicken-fried steak, mashed potatoes, and biscuits slathered in gravy and accompanied by green beans boiled into the gray zone. You can find excellent New Mexican food and some pasta, but beef rules. Most restaurants stop serving dinner around 8 PM.

Fishing
Whether you prefer lake or stream fishing, gray-hackled peacocks or Powerbait, some of your greatest fishing dreams might just come true in northeastern New Mexico. Idyllic clear mountain streams and alpine lakes are regularly stocked with rainbows; in Cimarron Canyon State Park you can catch your limit on German browns. Numerous operators arrange fishing trips.

Lodging
Lodging possibilities in northeastern New Mexico fall into three categories: standard motels, memorable if quirky historic properties, and

the occasional B&B. Prices at all these establishments are reasonable. The highest concentrations of cheap chain properties lie just off I–25 in Las Vegas and Raton.

Viewing Wildlife

Early morning and late afternoon are the best times to grab your binoculars and head out to spot wildlife—elk, deer, wild turkey, bears, and bobcats—in the Raton area, or on the road to Sugarite Canyon State Park, Yankee Canyon, or York Canyon. However, it is possible to catch a glimpse of antelope any time of day, especially on the open range.

Exploring Northeastern New Mexico

Interstate 25 heading north from Santa Fe is the fastest route through the region, but try to sample as many local roads as possible to catch the area's true flavor. The destinations below are arranged in a loop from Pecos via I–25 north to Las Vegas, Springer, and Raton (with an optional side loop over Johnson Mesa to Folsom, Capulin, and Clayton). Either way the tour continues by heading west to Cimarron, and then along U.S. 64 west through Cimarron Canyon; past Eagle Nest Lake and Angel Fire (☞ Chapter 3 for details); and then south on NM 434 through stunning Guadalapita Canyon to Mora. Here you can either continue south toward Santa Fe back through Las Vegas or opt for the more dramatic mountain route, skirting over the east face of the Sangre de Cristo range.

Great Itineraries

IF YOU HAVE 2 DAYS

Stroll around the Plaza and Bridge Street in **Las Vegas** ②. After you've walked the town, drive north on I–25 to ⊞ **Raton** ⑥ and visit the **Raton Museum** and **Historic First Street.** Take a picnic up to **Lake Maloya** in **Sugarite Canyon State Park** and hike or go fishing. The next day drive west on U.S. 64 to ⊞ **Cimarron** ⑨, exploring the heart of yesteryear's Wild West. Spend the night in the allegedly haunted **St. James Hotel.** In the morning continue west on U.S. 64, stopping off to fish or walk along the Cimarron River in Cimarron Canyon, and then head south on NM 434 at Angel Fire, stopping off for a visit to Victory Ranch in **Mora** ⑩, before continuing back toward Santa Fe.

IF YOU HAVE 4 TO 5 DAYS

The main routes through northeastern New Mexico follow the path of the original Santa Fe Trail and its shortcut, the Cimarron Route (which passed near Clayton and Springer), enabling you to retrace the steps of the pioneers. Begin at **Pecos National Historic Park** ① before heading north to ⊞ **Las Vegas** ②, where you should stay at the Plaza Hotel. Detour for an hour or two to **Fort Union National Monument** ③. Back at I–25, continue north to ⊞ **Raton** ⑥. On day three head east on NM 72 over starkly captivating Johnson Mesa and visit **Capulin Volcano National Monument** ⑦. After viewing four states from the rim of the volcano, have lunch at the **Capulin Country Store,** at the junction of U.S. 64/87 and NM 325. If you have an extra day, head east to ⊞ **Clayton** ⑧ to view the dinosaur tracks at **Clayton Lake State Park.** Have dinner at the **Eklund Hotel Dining Room & Saloon** and spend the night at the Best Western. The following day drive west on U.S. 56 toward Springer, detouring first to **Dorsey Mansion. Springer** ⑤ is a good place to have lunch and browse in the antiques shops downtown. With or without the Clayton detour, continue west to ⊞ **Cimarron** ⑨ (via U.S. 64 from Capulin, or NM 58 from Springer), and from here repeat the last day of the two-day itinerary given above.

When to Tour Northeastern New Mexico

In a region where the weather is close to perfect, the only months to avoid are March and April, when "Texas blows through" and you'll find yourself dodging tumbleweeds in the highway. From late spring, when the wildflowers begin to bloom, into late summer is a wonderful time to visit—an occasional afternoon thunderstorm, often followed by a rainbow, punctuates days that are mostly sunny. Fall brings the gold of aspens, and some of the best fishing and hiking. Temperatures can remain mild through Thanksgiving, and a crisp winter with good snow is a blessing for cross-country skiers. The wide vistas on snowy days are unforgettable. Roads are well maintained throughout the year, but be alert to storm warnings.

SANTA FE TRAIL COUNTRY

Comanche, Apache, and other Native American peoples of the Great Plains and Southwest lived in northeastern New Mexico. Throughout the region you'll find reminders of them and the pioneers who traveled the Santa Fe Trail, two sections of which passed through the area. The Mountain Route entered New Mexico from southeastern Colorado, crossed through Raton Pass, and passed Cimarron and Rayado before heading on to Fort Union. Because it was so arduous, this route was less subject to Indian attack, mostly from the Comanches and Apaches, whose land was being usurped. The quicker, flatter Cimarron Route (aka Cimarron Cutoff), entering New Mexico from Oklahoma and passing across the dry grasslands, left travelers much more vulnerable. The Mountain Route, which William Becknell followed 900 mi from Franklin, Missouri, during his first successful navigation, also provided an excellent source of water—the Arkansas River. The Cimarron Route was deathly dry.

Pecos National Historic Park

❶ *25 mi east of Santa Fe on I–25.*

Pecos was the last major encampment travelers on the Santa Fe Trail reached before Santa Fe (or the first if they were headed back east). Today the little village is mostly a starting point for exploring the Pecos National Historic Park, the centerpiece of which is the **ruins of Pecos**, once a major Pueblo village with more than 1,100 rooms. Twenty-five hundred people are thought to have lived in this structure, as high as five stories in places. Pecos, in a fertile valley between the Great Plains and the Rio Grande Valley, was a trading center centuries before the Spanish conquistadors visited in about 1540. The Spanish later returned to build two missions.

The Pueblo was abandoned in 1838, and its 17 surviving occupants moved to the Jemez Pueblo (☞ Chapter 2). Anglo travelers on the Santa Fe Trail observed the mission ruins with a great sense of fascination (and relief—for they knew it meant their journey was nearly over). A couple miles from the ruins, **Andrew Kozlowski's Ranch** served as a stage depot, and a fresh spring quenched the thirsts of horses and weary passengers. The ranch now houses the park's law-enforcement corps and is not open to the public. You can view the mission ruins and the excavated pueblo on a ¼-mi self-guided tour in about two hours.

The pivotal Civil War Battle of Glorieta Pass took place on an outlying parcel of park land in late March 1862; a victory over Confederate forces firmly established the Union army's control over the New Mexico Territory. The Union troops maintained headquarters at Kozlowski's Ranch during the battle. Check out the park visitor center to go on guided park tours (in summer only) and to see exhibits on the region's checkered history. Major wildfires in spring of 2000 burned some of the wilderness within the park, but none of the ruins were touched. ⊠ *NM 63, Exit 307 off I–25, Pecos,* ☎ *505/757–6414.* ☑ *$2; $4 per car.* ☉ *Memorial Day–Labor Day, daily 8–6; Labor Day–Memorial Day, daily 8–5.*

Las Vegas

❷ *40 mi east of Pecos on I–25.*

The antithesis of the Nevada city that shares its name, Las Vegas is a town of 15,000 that time appears to have passed by. Once an oasis for stagecoach passengers en route to Santa Fe, it became, for a brief period after the railroad arrived in the late 19th century, New Mexico's major center of commerce. The seat of San Miguel County, Las Vegas, elevation 6,470 ft, lies where the Sangre de Cristo Mountains meet the high plains of New Mexico, and its name, meaning "the Meadows," reflects its scenic setting.

More than 900 structures here are listed on the National Register of Historic Places, and the town has nine historic districts, many with homes and commercial buildings of ornate Italianate design (a welcome relief if you're experiencing adobe overload). History lives in the doorways of this once rough-and-tumble stop on the Santa Fe Trail—the nearest to Santa Fe. Butch Cassidy is rumored to have tended bar here, Doc Holiday practiced dentistry, and German-Jewish merchants ran mercantile establishments. Long a popular film location, Las Vegas is where Tom Mix shot his vintage Westerns. Contemporary films with a Las Vegas background include *Wyatt Earp, The HiLo Country, All the Pretty Horses,* and episodes of *Walker, Texas Ranger* have been filmed here as well.

To gain an appreciation of the town's architecture, try some of the walking tours described in brochures available at the **Las Vegas Chamber of Commerce** (⊠ 727 Grand Ave., ☎ 505/425–8631 or 800/832–5947). Best bets include Stone Architecture of Las Vegas; the Carnegie Park Historic District; and the business district of Douglas/Sixth Street and Railroad Avenue, which includes the famous Harvey House hotel of the railroad chain, La Casteneda, where the grand lobby and dining room are still intact and you can still order a drink at the bar. Bookstores, Western-wear shops, boutiques, and coffeehouses line the streets near the downtown Plaza and Bridge Street.

Las Vegas City Museum & Rough Riders Collection houses historical photos, medals, uniforms, and memorabilia from the Spanish-American War, documents pertaining to the city's history, and Native American artifacts. Theodore Roosevelt recruited many of his Rough Riders—the men the future president led into battle in Cuba in 1898—from northeastern New Mexico, and their first reunion was held here. ⊠ *725 Grand Ave.*, ☎ *505/454–1401 ext. 283.* ☑ *Free.* ☉ *Weekdays 9–noon and 1–4, Sat. 10–3.*

A favorite fishing hole for rainbow and German brown trout is **Storrie Lake State Park.** The 1,200-acre lake also draws waterskiers, sailboarders, and windsurfers. You can camp in the area and there are 11 full hookups. ⊠ *4 mi north of Las Vegas on NM 518,* ☎ *505/425–7278.* ☑ *$4 per vehicle; tent site $8, shelter $10, hookup $14.*

Las Vegas National Wildlife Refuge has the best birding around, with 271 known species—including eagles, sandhill cranes, hawks, and prairie falcons—that travel the Central Flyway to this 8,700-acre area of marsh, wetlands, native grasslands, and timber. Here the Sangre de Cristo Mountains meet the Great Plains. A nature trail winds beside sandstone cliffs and ruins. Get oriented by dropping by the new visitor center. ⊠ *Rte. 1 (Box 399), Las Vegas 87701, 1 mi east on NM 104, then 4 mi south on NM 281,* ☎ *505/425–3581.*

Las Vegas is the home of **New Mexico Highlands University** (⊠ 901 University Ave., ☎ 505/425–7511), which puts on concerts, plays, sporting events, and lectures. Its tree-shaded campus of largely Spanish colonial and Romanesque Revival buildings anchors the eastern side of downtown.

About 5 mi northwest of town in Montezuma, students from around the world study language and culture at the **Armand Hammer United World College of the American West** (⊠ NM 65, ☎ 505/454–4200). Looming over the school property is the fantastically ornate, vaguely Queen Anne–inspired Montezuma Castle, a former resort hotel developed by the Santa Fe Railroad a century ago and designed by the famous Chicago firm of Burnham and Root. The castle will be closed through at least 2002, but you can still wander the school's majestic, rolling grounds. Check in with the guard booth at the campus entrance.

Continue another half mile north of the campus on NM 65, and you'll see the signs to the right for the **hot springs** that inspired Montezuma's tourist boom in the 1880s. You can freely bathe in the several warm springs, which overlook the castle, if you follow a few basic posted rules (no nude bathing, no alcohol, open 5 AM–midnight). The trip from the Las Vegas Plaza up to Montezuma is a favorite of mountain bikers—you'll understand the appeal once you dip into these muscle-relaxing waters.

Dining and Lodging

✑ *following the text of a review is your signal that the property has a Web site, where you will find details and, usually, images; for a link, visit www.fodors.com/urls*

$$-$$$ ✕ **El Rialto Restaurant & Lounge.** The tart, perfectly blended margaritas mixed at El Rialto will put you in the right mood for deep-fried oyster dinners, huge steaks, stuffed sopaipillas, and great tamales. American dishes, seafood, and the salad bar are other options. The attached Rye Lounge is a fun spot for drinks. ✉ *141 Bridge St.,* ☎ *505/ 454–0037. AE, D, MC, V. Closed Sun.*

$-$$ ✕ **Estella's Restaurant.** An old-fashioned storefront café with a high
★ pressed-tin ceiling, vintage photos, and a Formica counter with swivel stools, Estella's serves simple, spicy New Mexican fare—huevos rancheros, green-chile enchiladas—plus a few American favorites like burgers and chile cheese fries. It's a great spot for people-watching. ✉ *148 Bridge St.,* ☎ *505/454–0048. No credit cards. Closed Sun. No dinner.*

$-$$ ✕ **Meadows Bar & Grill.** In the downtown's eastern section, Meadows serves both new American and northern New Mexican cuisine. Locals and visitors pack the place at lunchtime, chowing down on the monstrous Reuben sandwiches served on toasted pretzel rolls. The blue-corn enchiladas are stellar, as are the artichoke-olive salad and the linguine with chicken and a sunflower seed–cilantro pesto. ✉ *500 Douglas Ave.,* ☎ *505/426–1604. AE, D, MC, V. Closed Sun.–Mon. No lunch.*

$ ✕ **Murphey's Drugs.** A Las Vegas institution, Murphey's is the place to sit at an old-fashioned soda fountain, order a lime rickey or cherry Coke, sip a milk shake, or savor a homemade dessert. ✉ *600 Douglas Ave.,* ☎ *505/425–6811. No credit cards. No dinner.*

$-$$ ✕⌂ **Plaza Hotel.** Rooms at this three-story Italianate hotel offer a bal-
★ ance of the old and new, are not fancy, but are very nice. In addition to plenty of space, rooms have painted trim and borders, high stamped-tin ceilings, a sprinkling of antiques, modernized baths, coffeemakers, TVs, and phones. Reasonably priced packages include dinner at the Landmark Grill ($$–$$$), which serves filet mignon, piñon crusted trout, and reasonably good Mexican food. ✉ *230 Old Town Plaza, 87701,* ☎ *505/425–3591 or 800/328–1882,* FAX *505/425–9659. 32 rooms, 4 suites. Restaurant, bar, room service, meeting rooms, free parking. AE, D, DC, MC, V.* ✪

$$ ⌂ **Inn on the Santa Fe Trail.** David and Lavinia Fenzi and a friendly staff run this well-kept, hacienda-style motel. The grounds are well manicured, there's a nice pool area, and the unfussy rooms have TVs with premium cable and well-chosen Southwestern furnishings created by area artisans. Guests have privileges at a nearby health club. ✉ *1133 N. Grand Ave., 87701,* ☎ *505/425–6791 or 888/448–8438,* FAX *505/ 425–0417. 28 rooms, 2 suites. Restaurant, in-room data ports, pool, hot tub, business services. AE, D, DC, MC, V. CP.*

$$ ⌂ **Pendaries Village.** While the mood here is Holiday Inn meets Kit Carson, the standard motel-room decor in no way detracts from the thrill of high-altitude golfing. The **Pendaries Golf Course** (☎ *505/425–8890*) begins at 7,500 ft with a par 73, set smack at the eastern edge of the Sangre de Cristo Mountains. Ask about special golf packages, offered seasonally. Greens fees are $32 weekdays, $40 weekends; golf cart rental is $22. The rustic lodge has a well-esteemed restaurant usually crowded with locals who come for the steaks, Southwestern food, and pastas. Pendaries is in the tiny mountain hamlet of Rociada, an exquisite place to relax. ✉ *1 Lodge Rd., on NM 105 (Box 820), Rociada 87742, 26 mi northwest of Las Vegas,* ☎ *505/425–3561 or 800/733–5267,* FAX *505/ 425–3562. 18 rooms. Restaurant, bar, 18-hole golf course. MC, V.*

$ ⌂ **Carriage House B&B.** This dramatic three-story 1893 house lies in the eastern half of the town's colorful historic district, a short drive from the downtown Plaza. Rooms are homey and inviting, abundant with frilly Victoriana, stuffed animals, delicate fabrics, and a smattering of antiques. Continental breakfast is included. ✉ *925 6th St., 87701,* ☎ *505/454–1784. 3 rooms. D, MC, V. CP.* ✪

$ ⚠ **Las Vegas New Mexico KOA.** Five miles south of Las Vegas you can camp and cook out near a piñon-juniper hillside with beautiful views. RV sites are $23–$25, tent sites are $20, and cabins are $33.50. There's a convenience store. ⊠ *HCR 31 (Box 1), Las Vegas 87701, I–25, Exit 339, at U.S. 84,* ☎ *505/454–0180 or 800/562–3423 www.koa.com. 5 cabins, 50 tent sites, 54 hookups. Showers, pool, horseshoes, volleyball, recreation room, coin laundry. D, MC, V.*

$ ⚠ **Pecos River Campground.** Just off I–25 Exit 319, 24 mi west of Las Vegas, is this appealing campground. Wagon ruts of the Santa Fe Trail run through the park, which has abundant wildflowers and nearby fishing, a national forest, and a meteor crater. A full hookup costs $10. ⊠ *HCR 73 (Box 30), San Jose 87565,* ☎ *505/421–2211. 42 hookups, 10 tent sites. Showers, grocery, coin laundry. No credit cards.*

Outdoor Activities and Sports

OUTFITTERS

Brazos River Ranch (☎ 505/425–1509) can take you on jeep tours or fishing trips. Arrange for backcountry horseback riding with **Tererro Riding Stables** (☎ 505/757–6193).

Shopping

Shops are located mainly on Bridge Street, off the Plaza. **New Moon Fashions** (⊠ 132 Bridge St., ☎ 505/454–0669) has a well-chosen selection of Western and imported women's clothing. **Rough Rider Trading Co.** (⊠ 158 Bridge St., ☎ 505/425–0246) sells Western wear, handcrafted furniture, hand weaving, and rustic wood and metal crafts. **Tome on the Range** (⊠ 116 Bridge St., ☎ 505/424–9944) is a well-appointed bookstore with good Southwestern and kids sections. **Plaza Antiques** (⊠ 1805 Old Town Plaza, ☎ 505/454–9447) contains several dealers offering a wide range of antiques from different periods; it's in a stunningly restored hip-roofed adobe 1870s Victorian. **Meadowland Antiques and Spice Co.** (⊠ 131 Bridge St., ☎ 505/425–9502) sells gourmet foods, candies, a huge selection of spices, and distinctive furnishings and has a little espresso bar in back.

OFF THE   **MADISON VINEYARDS & WINERY –** Proud producers of some very fine
BEATEN PATH   New Mexico wines, Madison has picked up quite a few awards over the years. The tasting room is open Monday–Saturday 10–5, Sunday noon–5. ⊠ *NM 3, 6 mi south from I–25, Exit 323 (which is 23 mi from Las Vegas),* ☎ *505/421–8028.*

Fort Union National Monument

❸ *26 mi from Las Vegas, north on I–25 and (past Watrous) northwest on NM 161; 94 mi northeast of Santa Fe on I–25.*

The ruins of New Mexico's largest American frontier–era fort sit on an empty windswept plain that still echoes with the isolation surely felt by the soldiers stationed here between 1851 and 1890. The fort was established to protect travelers and settlers along the Santa Fe Trail. It became a military supply depot for the Southwest, but with the "taming" of the West it was abandoned. The visitor center provides historical background about the fort and the Santa Fe Trail. Talks on the Santa Fe Trail and Fort Union are given daily, and guided tours are available by reservation. Sunset programs feature period music. Call for schedule and details. ⊠ *Off NM 161, Watrous,* ☎ *505/425–8025. ▣ $2 per person, $4 per vehicle. ☉ Labor Day–Memorial Day, daily 8–5; Memorial Day–Labor Day, daily 8–6.*

Wagon Mound

4 *40 mi north of Las Vegas on I–25.*

As you drive up I–25 from Las Vegas and Fort Union, the high prairie unfolds before you to the east, an infinite horizon of grassland that's quite breathtaking when the sun sets. Soon interrupting this view is a covered wagon–shape butte that was a famous Santa Fe Trail landmark, Wagon Mound. The butte is where travelers crossed over from the Cimarron Cutoff to journey south to Fort Union. Local lore tells of mysterious lights, ghosts, and murders committed on top of the butte. The town serves a free barbecue at noon on Labor Day to celebrate its bean-growing heritage. Other events—horseshoe tournaments, a rodeo, and a parade—take place that same weekend in this otherwise sleepy village.

Dining

$–$$ ✕ **Santa Clara Cafe.** The cattle brands of local ranchers decorate this café, which serves delectable pies—among them walnut-raisin and a knockout four-fruit cobbler. Dishes include slow-cooked roast beef, mashed potatoes, and other home-cooked vittles. The café is in a century-old building on the actual Santa Fe Trail. ⊠ *709 Railroad Ave.,* ☎ *505/666–2011. D, MC, V.*

Springer

5 *25 mi north of Wagon Mound on I–25.*

A stroll under the shady oaks of Springer's main street is a journey into the past. Add vintage cars, and you'd think Harry Truman was still president. More than a few locals here still seem a bit rankled about losing the title of county seat to Raton—in 1897. The main industry of this town of 1,262 is the Springer Boys School, an incarceration facility for minors. Long a shipping center for cattle, sheep, and mining machinery, Springer was founded in 1870 when land baron Lucien Maxwell deeded 320 acres to his lawyer, Frank Springer, for handling the sale of the Maxwell Land Grant to the Dutch East India Company.

Crammed with everything you'd expect to find at a five-and-dime, **Springer Drug** is a local hangout and site of an ongoing gabfest. The highlight is the old (not old-fashioned, this is the original article) soda fountain, where you can order a sundae, a malt, a shake, or a cone. The root-beer float comes in a glass so big you could dive into it. In winter, homemade chili is served on Wednesday. ⊠ *825 4th St.,* ☎ *505/483–2356.* ☉ *Weekdays 8:30–5:30, Sat. 8:30–1.*

When Springer was the Colfax County seat, the 1883 structure that houses the **Santa Fe Trail Museum** served as a courthouse. The museum has a curious jumble of documents, maps, memorabilia, and other artifacts. The setup is not particularly sophisticated—it takes a bit of patience to wade through the assorted bits and pieces of the past. ⊠ *606 Maxwell St.,* ☎ *505/483–2998.* ☒ *$2.* ☉ *Memorial Day–Labor Day, Mon.–Sat. 9–4, with limited hrs in early fall and late spring (call ahead).*

OFF THE BEATEN PATH   **DORSEY MANSION –** In the middle of nowhere (about 35 mi northeast of Springer) stands this curious 36-room log-and-masonry castle built in 1886 by Stephen Dorsey, a U.S. senator from Arkansas. Its grand furnishings include a cherrywood staircase from Chicago, gargoyles depicting Dorsey family members, a dining room that seats 60, and a swank billiard room. The career of the ambitious senator, who owned the mansion for 15 years, dissolved in a mail-fraud scandal. He was acquitted after two trials but went bankrupt defending himself. You must make reservations by phone to visit the mansion. ⊠ *Off U.S. 56/412; follow signs 12 mi north from hwy.,* ☎ *505/375–2222.* ⊡ *$3.* ☉ *Daily, by appointment.*

OFF THE
BEATEN PATH

MAXWELL NATIONAL WILDLIFE REFUGE – More than 300 species of migratory waterfowl, including many geese and ducks in fall and winter, stop for a spell at this low-key 2,800-acre prairie refuge 12 mi north of Springer. Sightings of great blue herons are not uncommon in mid-winter, and bald eagles are fairly plentiful at this time. Sandhill cranes usually drop by in early fall, Canada geese around December. Deer, prairie dogs, long-tailed weasels, jackrabbits, coyotes, bears, and elk live here. The fishing season (Lake 13 is a fabled spot to catch rainbows) is between March and October. You can camp (no fee, no facilities) near the fishing areas. ⊠ *Off I–25 (take Maxwell Lakes exit at Mile Marker 426; follow NM 445 north ¾ mi, then NM 505 west 2½ mi to unmarked gravel road to refuge),* ☎ *505/375–2331.* ⊡ *Free.* ☉ *Daily.*

Dining and Lodging

$–$$ ✕ **El Taco.** It seems like just about everybody in town drops by this characterful, bilevel eatery at least once a week to enjoy a good meal, to shoot pool, or to yuk it up at the carved-wood century-old bar. The kitchen churns out excellent New Mexican fare, prepared with vegetable oils and extremely fresh ingredients. The red chile that accompanies the huevos rancheros could substitute for rocket fuel, and the Mama Sofia's El Taco combination is gargantuan. The sopaipillas are light and perfect. ⊠ *704 Maxwell Ave.,* ☎ *505/483–0402. MC, V. Closed Sun.*

$ ✕⊞ **Brown Hotel & Cafe.** Granny's parlor circa 1924 is the best way to describe the Brown Hotel, where the lobby furnishings include a rocking chair by the fireplace and hooked rugs and doilies. Antiques decorate the basic rooms, some of which have chenille-covered beds. The café's claims to fame include the baked goods and made-from-scratch soups; both New Mexican and standard American dishes are on the menu. ⊠ *302 Maxwell Ave., 87747,* ☎ *505/483–2269. 11 rooms. Café. MC, V. BP.*

Shopping

Jespersen's Cache (⊠ 403 Maxwell Ave., ☎ 505/483–2349), a pack rat's paradise, is a place to get lost for a morning or afternoon. The sheer mass of stuff is astounding—boxed Barbies, railroad lanterns, Depression-era glass, carousel horses. If you've got a collector's eye, you could make your lucky find here.

Raton

⑥ *39 mi north of Springer on I–25, 100 mi northeast of Taos on U.S. 64.*

Vastly underrated as a destination, Raton occupies an appealing spot at the foot of a lush mountain pass, offering wide-open views of stepped mesas and sloping canyons from the higher points in town. Midway between Albuquerque and Denver, it's an ideal base for exploring northeastern New Mexico. Because Raton was a racetrack town from the 1940s through the early '90s, motels are plentiful. There's some talk today of bringing back horse racing.

As it has for more than a century, Raton (population 8,500), the seat of Colfax County, runs on ranching, railroading, and the industry for which it's most famous, mining. In the early 1900s there were about 35 coal camps around Raton, most of them occupied by immigrants from Italy, Greece, and Eastern Europe. It was hard living in these camps and a tough road out, but a familial, close-knit interdependence grew out of mining life—a spirit that still prevails in Raton today. People here are genuinely friendly and have a great pride in their town.

Originally a Santa Fe Trail forage station called Willow Springs, Raton was born in 1880 when the Atchison, Topeka & Santa Fe Railway established a repair shop at the bottom of Raton Pass. The town grew up around 1st Street, which paralleled the railroad tracks. Much of the Raton Downtown Historic District, which has 70-odd buildings on the National Register of Historic Places, lies along **Historic First Street,** which consists of several restored blocks of antiques shops, galleries, and everyday businesses.

The Historic 1st Street area provides a fine survey of Western architecture from the 1880s to the early 1900s. In the early 20th century the **Mission Santa Fe Depot** (⊠ 1st St. and Cook Ave.), a 1903 Spanish Mission Revival structure, serviced several dozen trains daily (Amtrak still stops here, and a ticket office was reopened recently). The **Wells Fargo Express Building** (⊠ 145 S. 1st St.), also designed in the Spanish Mission Revival style, was erected in 1910. The building houses the **Old Pass Gallery** (☎ 505/445–2052), which presents exhibits of regional art, books, and jewelry. Garlands and female figureheads adorn the 1906 **Abourezk Building** (⊠ 132 S. 1st St.), originally a drugstore, later a dry-goods and grocery store, and now the home of the Heirloom Shop (☞ Shopping, *below*).

The tiny **Raton Museum,** inside the 1906 Coors Building (the beer manufacturer used it as a warehouse), brims with artifacts of the coal camps, railroading, ranch life, and the Santa Fe Trail. The museum, which has a large and interesting photo collection, is a good first stop on a visit to the area. The docents enjoy explaining local history. ⊠ *218 S. 1st St., ☎ 505/445–8979. ⊡ Free. ☉ May–Sept., Tues.–Sat. 9–5; Oct.–Apr., Wed.–Sat. 10–4.*

Just down a couple of blocks from the train station, the **Scouting Museum** opened in 1999 and is a must-see for anyone planning a visit to Philmont Scout Ranch (☞ Cimarron, *below*). Amiable curator Dennis Downing has amassed an exhaustive collection of scouting-related books, badges, films of old jamborees, buttons, and *Boys Life* magazines. ⊠ *400 S. 1st St., ☎ 505/445–1413. ⊡ Free. ☉ June–Aug., daily 10–7, or by appointment.*

More retro 1930s and '40s than Victorian, 2nd Street—Raton's main commercial drag—also has a number of handsome old buildings. The pride and joy of the neighborhood is the **Shuler Theater** (⊠ 131 N. 2nd St., ☎ 505/445–5528), a 1915 European rococo–style structure whose lobby contains WPA murals depicting local history. The Shuler (☞ Nightlife and the Arts, *below*) is one of the few remaining stages hand-operated with hemp rope and wooden pulleys. On weekdays between 8 and 5 the staff will happily take you on a free tour.

Southern California may have its HOLLYWOOD sign; well, northeastern New Mexico has its **RATON sign**—and this neon-red beauty is completely accessible. From the north end of 3rd Street, head west on Moulton Avenue to Hill Street and follow signs along the twisting road to the parking area at Goat Hill. Here you can walk around the sign, take in 270-degree views of the countryside, or picnic while contemplating the history of Raton Pass—the original Santa Fe Trail ran up Goat Hill clear into Colorado.

★ ☙ **Sugarite Canyon State Park,** a gem of a park near the Colorado state line, has some of the best hiking, camping (☞ *below*), fishing, bird-watching ("sugarite" is a corruption of the Comanche word "chicor-

ica," meaning "an abundance of birds," and is pronounced shug-ur-
eet), and wildflower viewing in the state. The road to Sugarite twists
and turns high up into the canyon to Lake Maloya, a trout-stocked
shimmering body of water from which a spillway carries overflow down
into the canyon. From its 7,500-ft elevation, hills rise up the eastern
and western canyon walls where miners once dug for ore—you can still
see gray slag heaps and remnants of the coal camp, which thrived here
from 1910 to 1940, along portions of the park road near the visitor
center (the former coal camp post office), down near the base of the
canyon. The center contains exhibits on the mining legacy, and from
here you can hike 1½ mi to the original camp.

Hikes elsewhere in the park range from the easy ½-mi Grande Vista
Nature Trail to the pleasant 4-mi jaunt around Lake Maloya to the
challenging Opportunity Trail. "Caprock" is the name given to the park's
striking basaltic rock columns, which were formed millions of years
ago when hot lava from a nearby volcano created the 10- to 100-ft-
thick rocks. Climbing is permitted on these sheer cliffs. ⊠ *NM 526, 7
mi northeast of Raton via NM 72,* ☎ *505/445–5607.* ⌑ *$4 per vehi-
cle.* ⊙ *Daily 6 AM–9 PM.*

The vast wilderness west of Raton comprises **Vermejo Park Ranch** (⊠
Drawer E, Raton 87740, ☎ 505/445–3097), a 588,000-acre property
owned by CNN media mogul Ted Turner—the single largest private
owner of New Mexico land. Elevations within this ranch, which spans
just about every ecosystem known to the Southwest, range from 6,400
to 13,000 ft. For an enormous fee you can stay at the ranch's ultra-
private resort, where your own private guide will take you fishing among
21 stocked lakes or hunting for turkeys, mule deer, and elk. For his
part, Turner has removed miles of barbed wire, reintroduced American buffalo and other indigenous flora and fauna, and made every effort to return this land—which he purchased in 1996 from Pennzoil
Company for a plum $80 million—to its original pristine state.

OFF THE   **NRA WHITTINGTON CENTER –** About 10 mi southwest of Raton on U.S. 64,
BEATEN PATH   toward Cimarron, is the world's largest shooting range, at 52 square mi.
              You don't have to be a member of the National Rifle Association to visit the
              center, which hosts shooting competitions year-round. ⊠ *U.S. 64,* ☎ *505/
              445–3615.* ⊙ *June–Aug., weekdays 8–5, weekends 8:30–4:30; Sept.–
              May, weekdays 8–5.* ⌑ *Free to tour grounds; $10 to shoot at the range.*

Dining and Lodging

$$–$$$ ✕ **The Grapevine.** Arguably the best place to eat in Raton, this cheery
         Italian restaurant prepares tasty thin-crust pizzas (try the Rustica, a
         white pesto pie with fresh tomatoes, garlic, mozzarella, and ricotta),
         calzones, and eggplant dishes. A specialty is chicken with artichokes,
         fresh tomatoes, and basil in a marinara sauce. Amaretto cheesecake is
         a favorite dessert. ⊠ *120 N. 2nd St.,* ☎ *505/445–0969. AE, D, DC,
         MC, V. Closed Sun.*

$$–$$$ ✕ **Pappas' Sweet Shop Restaurant.** You'll feel pampered at this restau-
         rant, whose antiques and collectibles exude a sense of history and a
         pleasant nostalgia for the Greek candy maker who founded the place
         in the 1920s. It's no longer a sweets shop today but serves familiar Amer-
         ican fare, like Alaskan king crab legs, porterhouse steak, shrimp fet-
         tuccine, and a few surf-and-turf combos. ⊠ *1201 S. 2nd St.,* ☎ *505/
         445–9811. AE, D, DC, MC, V. Closed Sun. in winter.*

$–$$ ✕ **Domingo's.** It's a bit of a gimmick, but kids especially love eating
         in the cavelike restaurant with faux stalagmites and stalagtites that re-
         call Carlsbad Caverns (well, if it had a waterfall), plus a game room
         and on weekends live music. Standard Mexican and American fare is

served. Domingo's has a gift shop with salsas, sopaipilla mix, and such. ⊠ *1903 S. Cedar St., off U.S. 64/87, just east of I–25,* ☎ *505/445–2288. AE, D, DC, MC, V.*

$ ✕ **Eva's Bakery.** In a cheerful storefront across from the Shuler Theater, this inviting sit-down bakery has fabulous chocolate-cake doughnuts and oatmeal-raisin cookies and attracts old-timers who gather here to keep up with town gossip and political intrigue. Chile fries, burgers, and frito pies are big sellers. ⊠ *134 N. 2nd St.,* ☎ *505/445–3781. Reservations not accepted. No credit cards. Closed Sun. No dinner.*

$ ✕ **Hot Dog Depot.** Cute, clean, and blessedly smoke-free, this café inside a bright turquoise vintage house serves hearty breakfasts, homemade chili and soup, and salads. The fresh coffee is only 49¢ a cup. ⊠ *100 S. 3rd St.,* ☎ *505/445–9090. Reservations not accepted. No credit cards. Closed Sun.*

$$–$$$ ☷ **Holiday Inn Express.** Brand-new with clean rooms, many with fine views east to Johnson Mesa and the vast grasslands, this pleasant franchise of the reputable and affordable brand of the Holiday Inn family lies just south of downtown. An extensive Continental breakfast buffet is included. ⊠ *101 Card Ave., 87740, I–25, Exit 450,* ☎ *505/445–1500 or 800/465–4329,* ℻ *505/445–7650. 50 rooms. In-room data ports, no-smoking rooms, pool, hot tub. AE, D, DC, MC, V. CP.*

$$ ☷ **Hearts Desire Inn Bed & Breakfast.** Gregarious host Barbara Riley, who grew up on a ranch south of Springer, opened this homey B&B in the late 1990s. She has filled the rooms with mostly Victorian antiques and collectibles (many for sale), giving guests the virtual run of this 1885 former boardinghouse, which is steps from downtown dining and the historic district. The top-floor hunting-and-fishing-theme suite has a full kitchen, TV and VCR, and two twin beds—ideal for kids or a couple of friends visiting on an outdoors expedition. In addition to a full breakfast, snacks are served in the evening. ⊠ *301 S. 3rd St., 87740,* ☎ *505/445–1000. 6 rooms, 1 suite. MC, V. BP.*

$–$$ ☷ **Best Western Sands.** Some of the good-size rooms at this 1950s-style motel have refrigerators, and all have coffeemakers, queen or king beds, and TVs with premium cable. The Sands provides free transportation to and from Raton's bus depot and Amtrak station. ⊠ *300 Clayton Rd. (NM 87/U.S. 64), 87740,* ☎ *505/445–2737 or 800/518–2581,* ℻ *505/445–4053. 50 rooms. Restaurant, in-room data ports, no-smoking rooms, pool, hot tub, playground, business services. AE, D, DC, MC, V.*

$ ☷ **El Portal.** An eccentric, if a bit raggedy, hostelry that occupies a restored 1885 downtown building, the El Portal exudes personality. The antiques-filled lobby has a working fireplace and a vintage Royal typewriter. Many rooms have themes, such as the Holiday Room, with autographed photos of Hollywood stars. Expect old beds, totally unmodernized bathrooms, no room phones, and somewhat musty accommodations, but for the price of the cheapest chain motel in town you'll be treated to as authentic an Old West experience as you'll ever find. Adjoining the hotel are 39 apartments leased both short- and long term. ⊠ *101 N. 3rd St., 87740,* ☎ *505/445–3631. 15 rooms. MC, V.*

$ ⌂ **Sugarite Canyon State Park.** If you're going to camp at either of the park's two campgrounds, Lake Alice or Soda Pocket, arrive early for the best choice among the fully developed sites. Facilities include a disposal station, electric hookups, flush toilets, RV sites, showers, and tent sites. Follow park instructions regarding the resident brown bears at Soda Pocket. ⊠ *NM 526 (HCR 63, Box 386), 87740, 6 mi northeast of Raton,* ☎ *505/445–5607. 40 sites. Showers. No credit cards.*

Nightlife and the Arts

Shuler Theater (⊠ 131 N. 2nd St., ☎ 505/445–5528) presents late-summer concerts, Music at Angel Fire, and productions by the Creede

Repertory Theater. Children's theater, local college productions, and traveling dance, folk dance, and vocal evenings are scheduled throughout the year. The beautiful **El Raton Theatre** (⊠ 115 N. 2nd St, ☎ 505/445–3721) dates to the 1940s and shows first-run movies. For the better part of this century, locals have popped into the rollicking **White House Saloon** (⊠ 133 Cook Ave., ☎ 505/445–9992) for drinks after work and late into the evening.

Outdoor Activities and Sports

Raton's playground is **Sugarite Canyon State Park** (☞ *above*). Sugarite's alpine **Lake Maloya** (⊠ NM 526, 10 mi northeast of Raton, ☎ 505/445–5607) is generously stocked with rainbow trout. The profusion of wildflowers and flocks of bluebirds make the lake a joy to hike around. Boating and ice-fishing are popular as well.

Shopping

Hattie Sloan, the proprietor of the **Heirloom Shop** (⊠ 132 S. 1st St., ☎ 505/445–8876), was one of the key figures involved in the restoration of Historic 1st Street. Hattie knows her antiques and has packed her highly browsable shop with beautiful selections, from rhinestone necklaces to quilts, china, and linens.

Rubin's Family Clothiers (⊠ 113 S. 2nd St., ☎ 505/445–9492) sells Pendleton shirts, woolen skirts, and well-made shoes. Its owners, Kathryn and Leon Rubin, can tell you a thing or two about local history—their store has been in the family for almost a century.

Given the quality of some of the merchandise, the prices at **Santa Fe Trail Traders** (⊠ 100 S. 2nd St., ☎ 505/445–2888 or 800/286–6975) are surprisingly competitive. Items include earrings, sand paintings, dream catchers, Nambé hand-cast bowls, Navajo rugs old and new, beadwork, and katsinas (many by well-known artists).

You can enter **Solano's Boot & Western Wear** (⊠ 101 S. 2nd St., ☎ 505/445–2632) a city slicker and exit a cowboy or cowgirl. The enormous space, an experience as much as a store, is full of fashionable, practical Western garb. Check out the collection of cowboy hats.

En Route   To reach Capulin, skip U.S. 64 and instead take NM 72 past Sugarite Canyon State Park, a stunning road that climbs up over Johnson Mesa, from which you have amazing 100-mi views north over the mesa into the plains of eastern Colorado—it's bare and flat up here, as though you're driving across a table straddling the Colorado–New Mexico border. About halfway across the mesa (15 mi from Raton), note the **old stone church** to your right, which was built by the early farmsteaders and has since been abandoned—it's a beautiful, lonely little building with a presence that illustrates the life of solitude the mesa's settlers must have endured.

Farther along on the right a historical marker details the 1908 discovery of Folsom Man by George McJunkin, which established the existence of indigenous inhabitants in the area dating back some 10,000 years. The road trails down the eastern side of the mesa and leads into tiny **Folsom.** Here make a right turn south on NM 325 to reach Capulin Volcano, 6 mi away.

Capulin

46 mi east of Raton on NM 72 and NM 325.

Tiny Capulin has a gas station, a campground, and well—little else. If you're in luck, lunch will be on at the delightful **Capulin Country Store** (⊠ U.S. 64 and NM 325, ☎ 505/278–3900), which in addition to fine food sells crafts and gifts (like candlesticks made of elk antlers and dolls sewn from old quilts), snacks, maps, and cold drinks.

7 From the crest of **Capulin Volcano National Monument,** elevation 8,182 ft, you can see four states: Colorado, New Mexico, Texas, and Oklahoma. To the southeast is the vast section of the Santa Fe Trail that includes the Cimarron Cutoff; to the west are the snowcapped Sangre de Cristo Mountains. Unlike much of the dry surrounding territory, Capulin has fairly plentiful water supplies that support an oasis of trees, shrubs, and wildflowers. A narrow 2-mi paved road (no trailers, towed vehicles, bicycles, or pedestrians allowed) leads to the rim of the volcano, from which you can walk the final ⅛ mi into the extinct, and rather uninteresting, crater vent. (An easy-to-hike 1-mi trail circles the rim, so you can see it from different angles.) The cone of Capulin (the word is Spanish for chokecherry) rises more than 1,300 ft from its base. The visitor center has books, a brief video about the site, and interpretive exhibits. On busy summer weekends, you may have a short wait to enter the paved road. ✉ *NM 325, 3 mi north of Capulin off U.S. 64,* ☎ *505/ 278–2201.* ✇ *$4 per vehicle.* ☉ *Memorial Day–Labor Day, daily 7:30– 6:30; Labor Day–Memorial Day, daily 8–4.*

Dining

$ ✕ **Capulin Country Store.** From May to December, seven days a week, lunch is the big meal (and big deal) of the day at the Capulin Country Store, where Jenny Lee Pugh sets the tables with homemade chicken-fried steak accompanied by mounds of mashed potatoes. Everything, including the Texas chili, the volcano burger and fries, and the fantastic desserts, is fresh and made to order. Sunday dinner buffets served on holiday weekends only are not to be missed, as the ranchers who drive from miles in every direction will tell you. ✉ *U.S. 64 and NM 325,* ☎ *505/278–3900. Reservations not accepted. AE. No lunch weekdays Jan.–Apr.*

En Route Should you decide to skip Clayton and drive back west to Cimarron, take U.S. 64 west via Raton, which passes through ranch country underneath the biggest, bluest skies imaginable. Antelope herds graze alongside cattle. This is the classic West, with old windmills jutting into the sky of the rimrock country. The 29-mi stretch from Capulin passes through the **Raton-Clayton volcano field,** where the cones of quiet volcanos break the flat, green landscape.

Clayton

8 *43 mi east of Capulin on U.S. 64/87; 83 mi east of Springer on U.S. 56.*

Clayton, which lies flat on the high prairie at an elevation of 5,000 ft, seemingly grew up out of nothing. Downtown is sleepy and sunny, with the old-fashioned retro-veneer typical of little Western towns. It's nowhere near an interstate and so lacks the scads of ubiquitous chain properties found in Las Vegas and Raton; mom-and-pop-owned shops dominate. The town bills itself as the carbon-dioxide capital of the world, but the carbon dioxide here isn't hanging in the air but rather underground, embedded in sandstone southwest of town. Cattle graze on the many ranches around Clayton.

The friendly locals here may look at you cockeyed when they learn you've come to sightsee, but Clayton does have a few notable landmarks. The guest rooms of the 1892 **Eklund Hotel Dining Room & Saloon** (✉ 15 Main St., ☎ 505/374–2551) have been closed since the 1970s, but the splendid Victorian dining room, which is still open (☞ Dining and Lodging, *below*), contains crystal chandeliers, apricot tufted-velvet booths, gilt-flocked wallpaper, and marble fireplaces. The atmosphere in the saloon is quite different but no less authentic. Here you'll find a large raw-rock fireplace, wooden booths, and mounted heads of elk and buffalo, plus historic photos and clippings of Clayton's past. The town's biggest character, Black Jack Ketchum, the notorious train robber, was hanged just out front. His last words were: "I had breakfast in Clayton, but I'll have dinner in hell!" Put your boot up on the brass rail at the bar (won in a poker game) and order a cold one.

★ ⑤ More than 500 fossilized dinosaur tracks can be observed along the ½-mi wooden **Dinosaur Trackway at Clayton Lake State Park,** making this one of the few sites of its kind in the world. The tracks, estimated to be 100 million years old, were made when the area was the shore of a prehistoric sea. Eight species of dinosaurs, vegetarian and carnivorous, lived here. The sparkling lake that gives the state park its name is ideal for camping and fishing. ⊠ *NM 370, 12 mi north of Clayton,* ☎ *505/374–8808.* ☞ *$4 per vehicle.* ☉ *Daily 6 AM–9 PM.*

There are few better places in New Mexico to soak in wide-open prairie vistas, clear skies, and fresh air than in the 136,000-acre **Kiowa National Grasslands.** One section of the grasslands is near Clayton and spreads east into Oklahoma and Texas. The other is about 80 mi west of Clayton, closer to Springer (☞ *above*), south of U.S. 56. In the section near Clayton, if you look carefully, you can see the ruts made by the wagons that crossed on the Old Santa Fe Trail. The land was drought-stricken during the Dust Bowl of the 1920s and '30s, when homesteaders abandoned their farms. Following the Dust Bowl, the government purchased the land and rehabilitated it to demonstrate that it could be returned to grassland agriculture.

For an enjoyable loop drive through the grasslands, head east out of Clayton on U.S. 56; at NM 406 head north to just past Seneca to where NM 406 makes a sharp turn to the east. Take the county gravel road west 3 mi and north 1 mi, noting the interpretive sign about the Santa Fe Trail. Continue a little farther north to the green gate that leads to the trail (following the limestone markers), where you can see ancient wagon ruts. Save for the occasional house or windmill, the view from the trail is not too different from what the pioneers saw. ⊠ *Off U.S. 56, north and south of Clayton.* ⊠ *Administrative office: 714 Main St., Clayton 88415,* ☎ *505/374–9652.* ☞ *Free.*

Dining and Lodging

$$–$$$ ✕ **Eklund Hotel Dining Room & Saloon.** American standards and Mexican and New Mexican fare (good sopaipillas) are served in both the dining room and saloon. Hand-cut steaks are the house specialty, and you can order hamburgers, beef stew, chicken-fried steak, and a decent club sandwich. ⊠ *15 Main St.,* ☎ *505/374–2551. MC, V. No lunch Mon.–Sat. in dining room.*

$ ⌂ **Best Western Kokopelli Lodge.** When locals have out-of-town guests they can't put up for the night, they send them to the Southwestern-style Best Western, where the rooms are spacious and pets are allowed (by prior arrangement). ⊠ *702 S. 1st St., 88415,* ☎ *505/374–2589 or 800/ 528–1234,* FAX *505/374–2554. 44 rooms. Pool. AE, D, DC, MC, V.*

Cimarron

❾ *108 mi from Clayton via U.S. 56/412 west to Springer, I–25 north, and NM 58 west; 42 mi southwest of Raton on U.S. 64.*

As you approach Cimarron from the south or east, you can't help but notice a rock projection over the town. Known as the Tooth of Time, it indicated to Santa Fe Trail travelers that their journey was nearing an end, for Santa Fe was only seven days away by wagon. Today the Tooth of Time is the emblem of the Philmont Scout Ranch, where 25,000 Boy Scouts assemble each summer.

A holdout for gamblers and outlaws and a stopping point for soldiers, gold seekers, and mountain men, Cimarron (its name means "untamed" in Spanish), founded in the early 1840s, was the home of land baron Lucien Maxwell. These days, sleepy Cimarron is a trove of Old West artifacts and lore, as well as a base from which to head out for great fishing. Don't be surprised to find deer grazing on the edge of town or to encounter a herd of elk crossing the road.

With 27 bullet holes in the tin dining-room ceiling, resident ghosts profiled on the TV show *Unsolved Mysteries*, and a guest book signed by someone using a known alias of Jesse James, the **St. James Hotel** (⊠ NM 21 at Collinson St., ☎ 505/376–2664) is nothing if not atmospheric. Every notable outlaw of the late 19th century is said to have visited this place. Chef to presidents Lincoln and Grant, Frenchmen Henri Lambert opened the St. James first as a saloon in 1872 and then eight years later developed it into a hotel. The lobby epitomizes Western Victoriana, with overstuffed sofas; stuffed heads of bison, elk, deer, and bear on the walls; and fringe on the lamp shades. Tours of the hotel are $2.

★ The workers who toiled inside the sturdy stone building that holds the **Old Mill Museum** once processed 300 barrels of flour a day. Now the mill houses four floors of vintage photos, clothing, tools, and memorabilia depicting life in Colfax County from the 1860s into the 20th century. ⊠ 220 W. 17th St., 1 block north of St. James Hotel, ☎ no phone. ☎ $2. ☉ Memorial Day–Labor Day, Fri.–Wed. 9–5.

The largest scouting venue in the world, 137,000-acre **Philmont Scout Ranch** sees nearly 30,000 young visitors every summer—on any given day about 3,000 of them are out plying the property's miles of rugged trails. Phillips Petroleum (i.e., Phillips 66) magnate and Boy Scouts of American benefactor Waite Phillips established the mountainous ranch, hence the name. The museums of the Philmont Scout Ranch include **Villa Philmonte**, the restored 1927 Spanish-Mediterranean summer home Waite Phillips, which is furnished with European and Southwestern antiques and Native American and Southwestern art. Tours of the mansion are conducted in July and August. Scouting cofounder Ernest Thompson Seton donated most of the holdings of the **Philmont Museum & Seton Memorial Library,** among them New Mexican art and artifacts and books on natural history and the history of the Southwest. ⊠ NM 21, 4 mi south of Cimarron, ☎ 505/376–2281. ☎ Museum free, villa tours $4. ☉ Museum Sept.–May, weekdays 8–5; June–Aug., daily 8–6. Villa tours July–Aug., daily 8–11 and 12:30–4:30; by appointment rest of yr.

Also here is the **Kit Carson Museum,** where costumed reenactments of life in 19th-century New Mexico and period crafts demonstrations take place in the adobe-style buildings, which include a working horno oven, blacksmith shop, and a trading post stocked as it might have been during Santa Fe Trail days. ⊠ NM 21, 11 mi south of Cimarron, ☎ 505/ 376–2281. ☎ Free. ☉ Mid-June–Aug., daily 8–5.

OFF THE BEATEN PATH **VALLE VIDAL –** One of New Mexico's great scenic routes heads northwest from U.S. 64 toward the town of Costillo (44 mi north of Taos on NM 522), affording great opportunities for sighting elk, deer, wild turkeys, and many other birds. The roughly 80-mi road is dirt and requires several hours of driving to complete—it's okay for non–four-wheel-drive vehicles in summer and fall (assuming there hasn't been a major rainfall in a couple days, and you're comfortable driving on some pretty rough roads). The trip passes through high-mountain grasslands, ponderosa, aspen, and sandstone cliffs. The fishing (season is July–December) in Valle Vidal is mighty fine—one rare trout species is found only here—and there are two campgrounds. The western section of the road is closed May 1 to June 31 for elk-calving season, and the eastern section is closed to protect the elks from January 1 to March 31. ⊠ *Off U.S. 64, turnoff is 8 mi east of Cimarron,* ☎ *505/758–6200.*

Dining and Lodging

$ ✕ **Colfax Tavern.** Also known as Cold Beer, New Mexico, this little
★   red roadhouse continues the tradition of a bar that's been here since the Prohibition era. An ongoing card game, excellent green-chile burgers, Shiner Bock on tap, spaghetti Mondays, brisket Wednesdays, Saturday-night dances, and a winter *Jeopardy!* tournament are among the joint's trademarks. Visitors can walk into this hangout and feel right at home. Wear your cowboy boots. ⊠ *U.S. 64, Colfax, 11 mi east of Cimarron,* ☎ *505/376–2229. Reservations not accepted. MC, V.*

$–$$$ ✕▥ **St. James Hotel.** Lace curtains and Victorian-era antiques adorn the 12 rooms (there are also 10 modern but less distinctive motel rooms) at this landmark lodging. The feeling is somewhat chilly and the rooms aren't well soundproofed or especially luxurious—all you'd expect in an allegedly haunted hotel. The restaurant, Lambert's ($$–$$$), with a ceiling full of bullet holes from the old days, serves steaks and pastas, and the café, Sweetwater's ($–$$), serves American and Mexican standards. ⊠ *NM 21 at 17th St., 87714,* ☎ *505/376–2664 or 800/748–2694,* ℻ *505/376–2623. 21 rooms, 1 suite. Restaurant, café, lounge. AE, MC, V.*

$$–$$$$ ▥ **Casa del Gavilan.** On the Santa Fe Trail and directly below the Tooth
★   of Time and 10,242 Trail Peak, this early 1900s white adobe compound (the name means "house of the hawk") on 225 acres is a romantic hideaway of the first order. The original owner, industrialist J. J. Nairn, used to entertain artists and other creative types here. The furnishings—artworks of various origins and Southwestern antiques—have been carefully selected. You can enjoy breakfast in the dining room or out on the patio. ⊠ *NM 21 (Box 518), 87714, 6 mi south of Cimarron,* ☎ *505/376–2246 or 800/428–4526,* ℻ *505/376–2247. 5 rooms. No smoking. AE, D, MC, V. BP.*

$ ▥ **Kit Carson Motel.** This serviceable motel is nothing special, but it'll do the job if you're after shelter and a hot shower. The Kit Carson Restaurant serves a decent chicken quesadilla and primo fried onions. ⊠ *31039 U.S. 64, Cimarron 87714,* ☎ *505/376–2288 or 800/293–7961. 38 rooms. Restaurant, lounge. AE, D, DC, MC, V.*

Shopping

The **Cimarron Art Gallery** (⊠ 337 E. 9th St., ☎ 505/376–2614) sells Southwestern jewelry, art, and artifacts, and there's a 1930s soda fountain where you can purchase sodas, ice cream cones, and coffee drinks. **Tracy's Blue Moon Eclectics** (⊠ 333 E. 9th St., ☎ 505/376–9040) stocks handmade pottery at very reasonable prices and has other handmade gift items such as candles, jewelry, and edibles.

En Route   One of the most breathtaking stretches of highway in the state is U.S. 64 west from Cimarron through **Cimarron Canyon State Park** (☎ 505/377–6271; ▤ free day use, campsites $10 per vehicle). The road passes through a steep and lush canyon banked by crenellated granite walls. Paralleling the road is the sparkling Cimarron River, which is known for its superb trout fishing. Wildlife (including elk, deer, and bear), granite cliff formations, a natural spring, and an abandoned mine are further draws. A campground contains 100 sites with access to rest rooms but no showers.

The road continues west out of the canyon and over a high bald ridge from which you'll be awarded a magnificent view over **Eagle Nest Lake,** the Moreno Valley, and the eastern slope of the Sangre de Cristo Mountains in the distance. Continue down through Eagle Nest Lake village toward **Angel Fire** (☞ Chapter 3), making a left turn (south) onto NM 434, which passes little Black Lake, offering one final view of the valley before narrowing sharply and plummeting into dark, deep, ponderosa pine–shrouded Guadalapita Canyon. Drive slowly: the road twists and turns and crosses several one-lane bridges over Coyote Creek. The Rincon Mountains rise to 9,500 ft to your right, and on your left you can stop for a ramble at **Coyote Creek State Park** (☎ 505/387–2328), which also has exceptionally good trout fishing. Day use is free; campsites are $10 per vehicle.

You'll soon pass through a pair of tiny, insular agricultural villages, **Guadalapita** and **El Turquillo.** Here the highway widens again as it opens into a broad sunny valley—to the east you'll spy the red rock cliffs that form the face of Black Mesa, the land barrier between here and the eastern grasslands. In El Turquillo stands a pretty yellow chapel with a corrugated metal roof and red belfry. As you come around the bend toward Mora, again behold the Sangre de Cristro Range, specifically the east side of Trampas and Truchas peaks, from an angle few tourists ever see.

Just before Mora and NM 518 are an intricate network of irrigation ditches that farmers employ to keep this region so fertile.

Mora

⑩ *72 mi south from Cimarron on U.S. 64 west to Eagle Nest Lake and NM 434 south via Angel Fire; 30 mi northwest of Las Vegas on NM 518; 85 mi northeast of Santa Fe via the High Road to Taos north to Peñasco and then NM 518 south.*

Mora is a reasonably sized, mostly Hispanic farming village where you can get gas, pick up snacks, and get your bearings. Especially if you've got animal-loving kids with you, stop by **Victory Ranch,** a working 1,100-acre alpaca farm. You can pet and feed the high altitude–loving creatures as well as visit the gift shop loaded with alpaca wool sweaters, hats, and gloves. The ranch is handicapped accessible. ⊠ *NM 434, 1 mi north of NM 518,* ☎ *505/387–2254.* ☉ *Thurs.–Mon. 10–4.*

At the junction of NM 434 and NM 518 make a right and head a couple miles to **Cleveland Mill,** a fixture in Mora Valley that served as the region's main flour mill in the late 1800s. Milling demonstrations are held over Labor Day weekend, and all summer long you can visit the building's artists cooperative, where craftspersons sell their sculpture, weaving, jewelry, and other fine arts. ⊠ *NM 518,* ☎ *505/387–2645.* ☒ *Free.* ☉ *Memorial Day–late Oct., daily 10–5.*

From Cleveland Mill you can either return via NM 518 back to Las Vegas (about 30 mi), or continue north on NM 518 over the gorgeous eastern face of the Sangre de Cristo Range. You'll eventually join Peñasco on the High Road to Taos, from which you can either continue south to Santa Fe or north to Taos. A relatively untraveled route, the drive from Mora to Peñasco offers some spectacular mountain views and passes by old farmsteads.

En Route **The La Cueva Historic District.** As you head south on NM 518 toward Las Vegas, be sure to stop in this curious village. In the 1850s, pioneer Vicente Romero established his legendary ranch and stone-walled mill here to supply the soldiers of Fort Union (☞ *above*). La Cueva means "the cave," and it's said Romero slept in caves while he built the ranch. His mill generated electricity for the area until 1950. The original ranch is now known as Salmon Ranch, where you can pick raspberries early to mid-fall, or buy fresh berries, raspberry jam and vinegar, or dried flowers and herbs at the original La Cueva Ranch store. Brilliantly colored wildflower gardens, homemade tamales, and raspberry sundaes draw families out for weekend excursions. The town's San Rafael Church dating from the 1870s is also worth a look. Call ahead for the ranch's hours. ⊠ *NM 518 at 442, 10 mi south of Mora, 20 mi north of Las Vegas,* ☎ 505/387–2900.

NORTHEASTERN NEW MEXICO A TO Z

Arriving and Departing

By Bus

Texas, New Mexico & Oklahoma Coaches (☎ 505/445–9071 in Raton; 800/231–2222) makes daily runs between Albuquerque and Raton and between Taos and Raton, with stops in Las Vegas, Springer, Cimarron, and Maxwell. The company is affiliated with Greyhound Lines.

By Car

Interstate 25 is the main route into northeastern New Mexico from Santa Fe. U.S. 64 heads east into the region from Taos and west into the region from Oklahoma. U.S. 56/412 heads west from Oklahoma toward Springer, where it connects with I–25.

By Train

Amtrak (☎ 800/872–7245) operates the *Southwest Chief* between Chicago and Los Angeles; Las Vegas and Raton are the train's stops in northeastern New Mexico.

Contacts and Resources

Emergencies

Ambulance, Fire, Police (☎ 911).

Visitor Information

Cimarron Chamber of Commerce (⊠ 104 N. Lincoln Ave., 87740, ☎ 505/376–2417 or 800/700–4298). **Clayton Chamber of Commerce** (⊠ 1103 S 1st St., 88415, ☎ 505/374–9253). **Las Vegas Chamber of Commerce** (⊠ 727 Grand Ave. [Box 128], 87701, ☎ 505/425–8631 or 800/832–5947, ✎). **Raton Chamber of Commerce** (⊠ 100 Clayton Rd., 87740, ☎ 505/445–3689 or 800/638–6161, ✎). **Springer Chamber of Commerce** (⊠ 606 Maxwell St., 87747, ☎ 505/483–2998).

5 ALBUQUERQUE

WITH SIDE TRIPS ALONG THE TURQUOISE TRAIL

A modest and practical city with a long and fascinating history, Albuquerque is the center of commerce, medicine, and education in New Mexico. Founded in 1706 as an outpost of the North American Spanish Empire, the city has a central location that makes it the perfect jumping-off point for excursions to other parts of New Mexico.

A T FIRST GLANCE, Albuquerque appears to be a typical Sun Belt city, spreading out in all directions with no grand design, architectural or otherwise, holding things together. The city's growth pattern seems as free-spirited as all those hot-air balloons that take part in the Kodak Albuquerque International Balloon Fiesta every October. With a bit of exploration, however, this initial impression of an asphalt maze softens as one gets a sense of Albuquerque's distinctive neighborhoods. The charms of Albuquerque may not jump out to greet you, but the blend of Spanish, Mexican, Native American, Anglo, and Asian influences makes this a vibrant multicultural metropolis well worth exploring.

Updated by
Sharon
Niederman

An unpretentious, practical city with a population nearing 700,000, Albuquerque is the center of New Mexico's educational institutions and financial, business, manufacturing, and medical industries. Its people are friendly, and the state's three primary cultures rub elbows more comfortably here than anywhere else in New Mexico. Many Albuquerqueans have descended from one or more of three groups: Native Americans, some of whom arrived more than 10,000 years ago; 17th-century Spaniards who came on horseback to conquer and convert; or the European and American trappers, fortune seekers, traders, and merchants who made the arduous journey across the Santa Fe Trail. From its humble beginning as a settlement of Spanish families in what is now known as Old Town, Albuquerque grew into a trade and transportation center. It became an important station on the Spaniards' El Camino Real, the Royal Road, which wound from Mexico City to Santa Fe and was for centuries New Mexico's primary link to the outside world.

Albuquerque was founded in 1706 as a farming settlement near a bend in the Rio Grande. Named for Spain's duke of Albuquerque, then viceroy of Mexico, it prospered, thanks to its strategic location on a trade route and its proximity to several Native American pueblos, which were a source of commerce and provided protection from raiding nomadic tribes. The nearby mountains and river forest yielded ample wood. The settlers built a chapel and then a larger structure, San Felipe de Neri Catholic Church, named after a 16th-century Florentine saint. For protection, homes were built around a central plaza like those in other Spanish settlements. The fortresslike community could be entered from the four corners only, making it easier to defend. This four-block area, Old Town, is the city's tourist hub, filled with shops, galleries, and restaurants.

It would have made sense for the town to simply grow outward, expanding from its central hub. But the Rio Grande gradually changed its course, moving farther and farther west, and Albuquerque followed. In 1880 the railroad came to central New Mexico, its tracks missing Old Town by a good 2 mi and causing another population shift. Old Town wasn't exactly abandoned, but New Town sprouted near the depot and grew until it eventually enveloped Old Town.

Then came Route 66. Opened in 1926 and nicknamed "The Mother Road" by John Steinbeck, it sparked much of Albuquerque's modern economic development. Surging through town during the 1930s and '40s, the route's traffic had as much impact as the railroad and the river combined. The burgeoning city swelled around the asphalt—motels, gas stations, diners, and truck stops formed a sea of neon that celebrated American mobility. During World War II Albuquerque flourished with the growth of a major air base, Kirtland. It and other military-related facilities such as Sandia National Laboratory remain economic linchpins.

Albuquerque's economy continues to diversify. Intel, the world's largest computer-chip maker, has one of its biggest manufacturing centers here, across the river in Rio Rancho. Intel's presence has stimulated population and housing growth and attracted additional high-tech businesses. That the city has a substantial arts scene will be apparent the moment you step off a plane at Albuquerque International Sunport and see the works of New Mexican artists throughout the terminal. The city has significant museums and galleries and is a magnet for artists, writers, poets, filmmakers, and musicians.

Many interesting towns, parks, and Indian pueblos are just outside Albuquerque. The pueblo residents continue to preserve their customs in a changing world. Each pueblo has its own customs, history, art, and design. Visitors are generally welcome, particularly on feast days, which occur throughout the year.

EXPLORING ALBUQUERQUE

Colorful Historic Route 66 is Albuquerque's Central Avenue, unifying, as nothing else, the diverse areas of the city—Old Town cradled at the bend of the Rio Grande, the downtown business and government centers to the east, the University of New Mexico farther east, and the Nob Hill strip of restaurants and shops following the university. The railroad tracks and Central Avenue divide the city into quadrants—Southwest, Northwest, Southeast, and Northeast. Once you understand the layout, it's easy to get around. Many attractions are a considerable distance apart. A car is a necessity, but rental rates are reasonable (about $140 per week for a compact with unlimited mileage).

Albuquerque's terrain is diverse. Along the river in the north and south valleys, the elevation hovers at about 4,800 ft. East of the river, the land rises gently to the foothills of the Sandia Mountains; their 10,678-ft summit, Sandia Crest, is a grand spot from which to view the city below. West of the Rio Grande, where much of Albuquerque's growth is taking place, the terrain rises abruptly in a string of mesas topped by five volcanic cones. The changes in elevation from one part of the city to another result in corresponding changes in temperature, as much as 10°F at any time. It's not uncommon for snow or rain to fall on one part of town while another remains sunny and dry.

Numbers in the text correspond to numbers in the margin and on the Albuquerque and Albuquerque Old Town maps.

Old Town and Vicinity

A Good Tour

Soak up the air of history in **Old Town Plaza** ①, and then cross the street and visit **San Felipe de Neri Catholic Church** ②. Cutting diagonally across the Plaza, head south to the corner of San Felipe Street and Old Town Road to drop in on the **American International Rattlesnake Museum** ③. Walk south on San Felipe and west on Central Avenue to the corner of Rio Grande Boulevard, where in a strip mall you'll find the **Turquoise Museum** ④. Farther west on Central, along an historic section of Route 66 lined with shabby vintage motels, is the **Albuquerque Aquarium and Rio Grande Botanic Garden** ⑤. Leaving Old Town, take a five-minute stroll over to two of the city's cultural institutions, the **Albuquerque Museum of Art and History** ⑥ and the **New Mexico Museum of Natural History and Science** ⑦. You'll need to hop in your car (or take city Bus 66) to visit the **Indian Pueblo Cultural Center** ⑧.

130

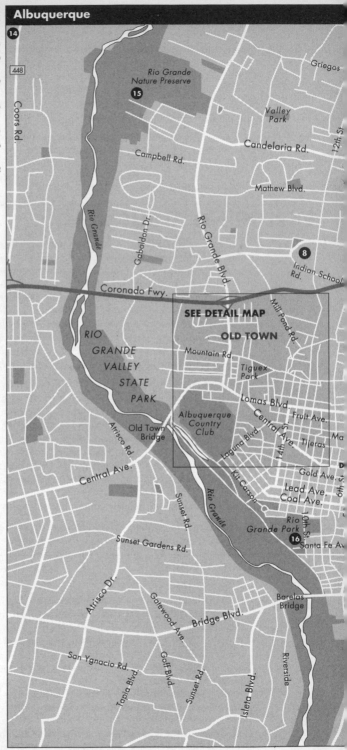

Albuquerque

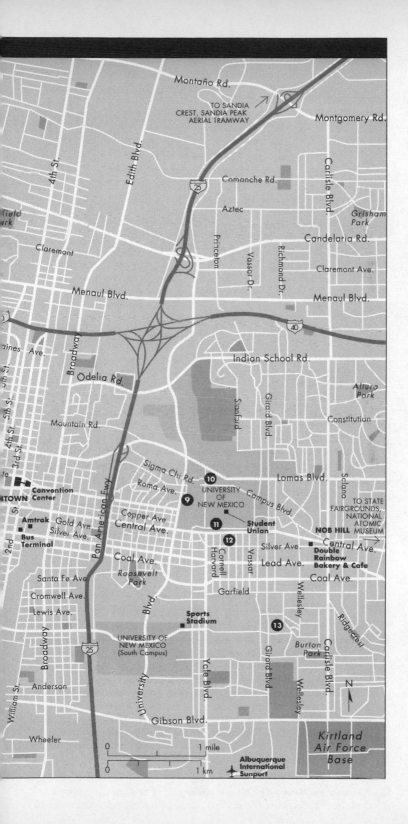

Montaño Rd.

Montgomery Rd.

TO SANDIA
CREST, SANDIA PEAK
AERIAL TRAMWAY

4th St.

Edith Blvd.

Carlisle Blvd.

Comanche Rd.

Aztec

Grisham
Park

...field
...ark

Claremont

Candelaria Rd.

Princeton

Vassar Dr.

Richmond Dr.

Claremont Ave.

Menaul Blvd.

Menaul Blvd.

...aines Ave.

Broadway

Odelia Rd.

Indian School Rd.

Stanford

Girard Blvd.

Altura
Park

Constitution

Salano

4th St.
3rd St.
5th St.

Mountain Rd.

Sigma Chi Rd.

Lomas Blvd.

Roma Ave.

10

9

UNIVERSITY
OF
NEW MEXICO

Campus Blvd.

TO STATE
FAIRGROUNDS,
NATIONAL
ATOMIC
MUSEUM

Convention
Center

DOWNTOWN

Amtrak
Bus
Terminal

Gold Ave.
Silver Ave.

Copper Ave.
Central Ave.

11

Student
Union

NOB HILL

Central Ave.

12

Cornell

Harvard

Vassar

Silver Ave.

Lead Ave.

Double
Rainbow
Bakery & Cafe

2nd St.

Coal Ave.

Roosevelt
Park

Coal Ave.

Santa Fe Ave.

Garfield

Cromwell Ave.

Lewis Ave.

Sports
Stadium

13

Wellesley

Burton
Park

Ridgecrest

Broadway

Pan American Fwy

UNIVERSITY OF
NEW MEXICO
(South Campus)

University
Blvd.

Yale Blvd.

Girard Blvd.

Carlisle Blvd.

Wellesley

Anderson

William St.

Wheeler

Gibson Blvd.

N

0   1 mile

0   1 km

Albuquerque
International
Sunport

Kirtland
Air Force
Base

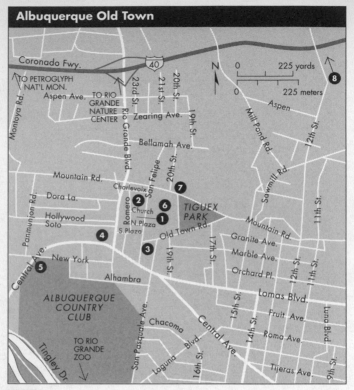

Albuquerque Old Town

TIMING

The best time to begin a visit to Old Town is in the morning, before
the stores open at 10 and the daily rush of activity begins. In the beam-
ing morning light, the echoes of the past are almost palpable (and you
might find parking). Plan to spend an hour and a half at the Old Town
sites, an hour in the Albuquerque Museum of Art and History, and two
hours in the New Mexico Museum of Natural History and Science. The
Turquoise Museum is closed on Sunday, and the Albuquerque Museum of Art and History is closed on Monday. You'll need at least an
hour and a half to take in all the exhibits at the Indian Pueblo Cultural Center.

Sights to See

✒ following the text of a review is your signal that the property has
a Web site, where you will find details and, usually, images; for a link,
visit www.fodors.com/urls.

👆 ❺ **Albuquerque Aquarium and Rio Grande Botanic Garden.** A spectacular shark tank with floor-to-ceiling viewing is among the most popular of the marine exhibits here. A video follows the path of a drop of
water as it forms in the Rocky Mountains, enters the upper Rio Grande,
and finally spills into the Gulf of Mexico. The Spanish-Moorish garden is one of three walled gardens near the entrance of the Botanic Garden. The glass conservatory has two pavilions. The smaller one exhibits
desert plants and the larger houses the Mediterranean collection.
Sharkreef Cafe (open between 7:30 and 5) serves breakfast and lunch.
✉ 2601 Central Ave., at New York Ave. NW, ☎ 505/764–6200. ✍
$4.50. ⊙ Daily 9–5.

❻ **Albuquerque Museum of Art and History.** This modern structure houses
the largest collection of Spanish-colonial artifacts in the nation, along

with relics of the city's birth and development. The centerpiece of the colonial exhibit is a pair of life-size models of Spanish conquistadors in original chain mail and armor. Perhaps the one on horseback is Francisco Vásquez de Coronado, who, in search of gold, led a small army into New Mexico in 1540—the turning point in the region's history. Among the museum's attractions are treasure chests filled with pearls and gold coins, religious artifacts, and early maps (some dating from the 15th century and showing California as an island). A multimedia presentation chronicles the development of the city since 1875. The sculpture garden contains 45 works in bronze, fiberglass, and steel by 20th-century Southwestern artists that include Glenna Goodacre, Michael Naranjo, and Luís Jiménez. ⊠ *2000 Mountain Rd. NW,* ☎ *505/243–7255 or 505/242–4600.* ▦ *Free.* ⊙ *Tues.–Sun. 9–5.*

⊞ ❸ **American International Rattlesnake Museum.** Included in this strange collection of living "rattlers" are rare and unusual specimens, such as an albino western diamondback. The museum's labels, its engaging staff, and a video will supply you with the lowdown on these venomous creatures—for instance, that they can't hear their own rattles and that the human death rate from rattlesnake bites is less than 1%. ⊠ *202 San Felipe St. NW,* ☎ *505/242–6569.* ▦ *$2.* ⊙ *Daily 10–6.*

★ ⊞ ❽ **Indian Pueblo Cultural Center.** The multilevel semicircular design at this museum was inspired by Pueblo Bonito, the prehistoric ruin in Chaco Canyon in northwestern New Mexico. Each of the state's 19 pueblos has an upper-level alcove devoted to its particular arts and crafts. Lower-level exhibits trace the history of the Pueblo people. Youngsters can touch Native American pottery, jewelry, weaving, tools, and dried corn at the Hands-on Corner and also draw petroglyph designs and design pots. Paintings, sculptures, jewelry, leather crafts, rugs, souvenir items, drums, beaded necklaces, painted bowls, and fetishes are for sale. Ceremonial dances are performed during the summer and on special holidays. ⊠ *2401 12th St. NW,* ☎ *505/843–7270 or 800/766–4405.* ▦ *$4.* ⊙ *Daily 9–5:30.* ✑

NEED A BREAK?
The **Indian Pueblo Cultural Center** (⊠ 2401 12th St. NW, ☎ 505/843–7270) has a restaurant, open for breakfast and lunch, that serves blue-corn enchiladas, *posole* (a thick soup with pork, hominy, chile, garlic, and cilantro), Native American bread pudding, and, of course, fry bread—that addictive popover-like creation that is served plain or topped with honey, beans, chile, or powdered sugar.

★ ⊞ ❼ **New Mexico Museum of Natural History and Science.** The world of wonders at Albuquerque's most popular museum includes the simulated volcano (with a river of bubbling hot lava flowing beneath the see-through glass floor), the frigid Ice Age cave, and the world-class dinosaur exhibit hall. The Evolator—short for Evolution Elevator—a six-minute high-tech ride, uses video, sound, and motion to whisk you through 35 million years of New Mexico's geological history. A film in the Dynamax Theater makes viewers feel equally involved. Arrive via the front walkway, and you'll be greeted by life-size bronze sculptures of a 21-ft-long horned pentaceratops and a 30-ft-long carnivorous albertosaur. The new LodeStar Science Center features a state-of-the-art planetarium. ⊠ *1801 Mountain Rd. NW, across from the Albuquerque Museum of Art and History,* ☎ *505/841–2800.* ▦ *Museum $5.25, combination ticket for museum and Dynamax Theater $9, LodeStar Science Center $6.* ⊙ *Daily 9–5.* ✑

★ ⊞ ❶ **Old Town Plaza.** Don Francisco Cuervo y Valdés, a provincial governor of New Mexico, laid out this small plaza in 1706. No slouch when it came to political maneuvering, he named the new town after the duke of Albuquerque, viceroy of New Spain. He hoped flattery would induce the duke to waive the requirement that a town have 30 families before a charter was issued—there were only 15 families living here in 1706. The duke acquiesced. (Albuquerque is nicknamed "The Duke City," so he's hardly been forgotten.) Today the plaza is an oasis of tranquillity filled with shade trees, wrought-iron benches, a graceful white gazebo, and strips of grass. Nearly 200 shops, restaurants, cafés, galleries, and several cultural sites in *placitas* (small plazas) and lanes surround Old Town Plaza. The scents of green chile, enchiladas, and burritos hang in the air. Mock gunfights are staged on Romero Street on Sunday afternoon, and during fiestas Old Town comes alive with mariachi bands and dancing señoritas. Event schedules and maps, which contain a list of public rest rooms, are available at the **Old Town Visitors Center** (⊠ 303 Romero St. NW, ☎ 505/243–3215), across the street from the San Felipe de Neri Catholic Church. The center is open daily from 9 to 5 in summer and from 9:30 to 4:30 the rest of the year.

NEED A BREAK?	Umbrellas shade the outdoor tables on the brick patio in front of **Zane Graze Cafe & News** (⊠ 308 San Felipe St. NW, ☎ 505/243–4377), a delightful spot where you can have a cone filled with Taos Cow ice cream, sip a latte, or sample soups, salads, sandwiches, and home-made desserts.

❷ **San Felipe de Neri Catholic Church.** More than 2½ centuries after it first welcomed worshipers, this structure erected in 1793 is still active. The building, which replaced Albuquerque's first Catholic church, has been enlarged and expanded several times, but its adobe walls and other original features remain. Small gardens front and flank the church; the inside is dark and quiet. Next to it is a small museum that displays relics—vestments, paintings, carvings—dating from the 17th century. ⊠ *2005 Plaza NW,* ☎ *505/243–4628.* ☉ *Church daily 7–7; museum weekdays 1:30–4:30, Sat. 1–4. Call ahead to confirm hrs.*

❹ **Turquoise Museum.** A novel attraction, this museum focuses on the beauty, mythology, and physical properties of turquoise, a semiprecious but widely adored gemstone that many people understandably associate with the color of New Mexico's skies. A simulated mine shaft leads to one-of-a-kind showpieces and examples from more than 60 mines on four continents. Displays show how turquoise is formed and highlight its uses by Native Americans in prehistoric times. At the education center you can learn how to distinguish the real McCoy from plastic. ⊠ *2107 Central Ave. NW,* ☎ *505/247–8650.* ▣ *$2.* ☉ *Mon.–Sat. 9:30–5:30.*

The University of New Mexico

Established in 1889, the University of New Mexico is the state's leading institution of higher education, with internationally recognized programs in anthropology, biology, Latin American studies, and medicine. Its many outstanding galleries and museums are open to the public free of charge. The university's Pueblo Revival–style architecture is noteworthy, particularly the old wing of Zimmerman Library and the Alumni Chapel, both designed by John Gaw Meem, a Santa Fe–based architect who was one of the chief 20th-century proponents of the Pueblo style.

A Good Walk

The impeccably landscaped grounds of the University of New Mexico surround a central area containing knolls, a duck pond, fountains, waterfalls, and benches. The **Maxwell Museum of Anthropology** ⑨ is in the Anthropology Building on the western edge of the campus, only a few minutes' walk from the duck pond. From the Maxwell, walk east past Alumni Chapel and turn left. At the duck pond walk north on Yale past University House. You'll come to a four-way stop at Yale and Las Lomas streets. The **Jonson Gallery** ⑩ is the second building on the northeast corner of this intersection. Walk south past the duck pond, between Zimmerman Library and Ortega Hall. Continue south under a walkway and left, past the Student Union Building, to the **University Art Museum** ⑪, in the Center for the Arts (use the Stanford Drive and Central Avenue entrance). At the corner of Central Avenue and Cornell Drive is the sales and exhibition gallery of the **Tamarind Institute** ⑫. Nine blocks south of Central along Girard Boulevard is the **Ernie Pyle Branch Library** ⑬.

TIMING

Seeing the University of New Mexico could take the better part of a day. Spend an hour strolling the grounds, maybe catching some rays by the duck pond. Allot an hour for each subsequent stop. All facilities are open year-round, but some are closed from Saturday to Monday.

Sights to See

⑬ **Ernie Pyle Branch Library.** After several visits to New Mexico, Ernie Pyle, a Pulitzer Prize–winning news reporter, built a house in 1940 that now contains the smallest branch of the Albuquerque Public Library. On display are photos, handwritten articles by Pyle, and news clippings about his career as a correspondent during World War II and his death from a sniper's bullet on April 18, 1945, on the Pacific island of Ie Shima. ⊠ *900 Girard Blvd. SE, ☎ 505/256–2065. ☜ Free. ☉ Tues.–Sat. 10–6.*

⑩ **Jonson Gallery.** The home and studio of Raymond Jonson (1891–1982) house the abstract, colorful works on paper of this Transcendentalist painter who focused on mass and form. The gallery mounts a major Jonson retrospective each summer and also exhibits works by other contemporary painters. ⊠ *1909 Las Lomas Blvd. NE, ☎ 505/277–4967. ☜ Free. ☉ Tues. 9–4 and 5–8, Wed.–Fri. 9–4.*

⑨ **Maxwell Museum of Anthropology.** Many of the more than 2½ million artifacts at the Maxwell, the first public museum in Albuquerque (established in 1932), come from the Southwest. Two permanent exhibitions chronicle 4 million years of human history and the lifeways, art, and cultures of 11,500 years of human settlement in the Southwest. The photographic archives contain more than 250,000 images, including some of the earliest photos of Pueblo and Navajo cultures. The museum shop sells traditional and contemporary Southwestern Native American jewelry, rugs, pottery, basketry, and beadwork, along with folk art from around the world. In the children's section are inexpensive books and handmade tribal artifacts. ⊠ *University of New Mexico, University Blvd., 1 block north of Grand Ave., ☎ 505/277–4405. ☜ Free. ☉ Tues.–Sat. 9–4.*

OFF THE
BEATEN PATH

NATIONAL ATOMIC MUSEUM – This fascinating and unusual museum chartered by the U.S. Congress explores atomic weaponry, the role New Mexico played in nuclear technology (check out the green trinitite sample from the Trinity test site), and pop culture perspectives on modern warfare. Exhibits include replicas of Little Boy and Fat Man, the atomic bombs dropped on Japan; a Trident missile; and a documentation of the little-remembered 1966 "Palomares Incident"—a plane crash over Spain that dropped unexploded nuclear bombs. Outdoors in the Missile Park you can examine a B-52 bomber and an F-105D fighter-bomber, touch the rocket that was used to boost Alan Shepard into space, and view historic planes. David Wolper's film, *Ten Seconds That*

Shook the World, a 53-minute documentary about the development of the atomic bomb, is shown four times daily. The gift shop has an interesting book selection as well as souvenirs. Have a picture ID and your car's registration material handy when you enter the base. You'll be directed to a parking lot and the museum's shuttle bus will fetch you. ⊠ *Kirtland Air Force Base, Wyoming Gate (from downtown take Central Ave. east and turn south on Wyoming Blvd.),* ☎ *505/284–3243.* 🖼 *$3.* ☉ *Daily 9–5.*

⑫ **Tamarind Institute.** This world-famous institution played a major role in reviving the fine art of lithographic printing, which involves working with plates of traditional stone and modern metal. Tamarind certification is to a printer what a degree from Juilliard is to a musician. A small gallery within the facility exhibits prints and lithographs. Guided tours (reservations essential) are conducted on the first Friday of each month at 1:30. ⊠ *108 Cornell Dr. SE,* ☎ *505/277–3901.* 🖼 *Free.* ☉ *Weekdays 9–5.*

⑪ **University Art Museum.** A handsome facility, the museum holds New Mexico's largest collection of fine art. Works of old masters share wall space with the likes of Picasso and O'Keeffe, and many photographs and prints are on display. Lectures and symposia, gallery talks, and guided tours are regularly scheduled. ⊠ *University of New Mexico Center for the Arts,* ☎ *505/277–4001.* 🖼 *Free.* ☉ *Tues. 9–4 and 5–8, Wed.–Fri. 9–4, Sun. 1–4.*

NEED A BREAK?   You can grab a burger or a snack or just rest your feet at the **Student Union Building** (☎ 505/277–2331), north of the university's Stanford entrance (off Central Avenue). Exhibits of art by students and others are shown in several spaces, including the Centennial (on the main level) and the ASA (south end, lower level). The coffee at **Double Rainbow Bakery & Cafe** (⊠ 3416 Central Ave. SE, 1 block west of Carlisle Blvd., ☎ 505/255–6633) is brewed from beans roasted on the premises. The bakery has delectable pastries, and the café serves scrumptious soups, quiches, sandwiches, and salads. An international selection of periodicals is available for perusing while you're munching.

Elsewhere in Albuquerque

A Good Tour

Petroglyph National Monument ⑭, **Rio Grande Nature Center State Park** ⑮, and the **Rio Grande Zoo** ⑯ are far-flung sites usually visited separately and by car.

TIMING

These three sites are open daily. Each deserves a minimum of two hours.

Sights to See

⑭ **Petroglyph National Monument.** Beneath the stumps of five extinct volcanoes, this park encompasses more than 15,000 ancient Native American rock drawings inscribed on the 17-mi-long West Mesa escarpment overlooking the Rio Grande Valley. For centuries, Native American hunting parties camped at the base, chipping and scribbling away. Archaeologists believe the petroglyphs were carved on the lava formations between the years 1100 and 1600. Walking trails provide access to them. A paved trail at **Boca Negra Canyon** (north of the visitor center on Unser Boulevard, beyond Montaño Road) leads past several dozen petroglyphs. The trail at **Rinconado Canyon** (south of the visitor center on Unser) is unpaved. To get to the visitor center from central Albuquerque take I–40 west to the NM 448/Coors Road Exit north (west of the Rio Grande) and take a left on Western Trail Road. ⊠ *Visitor center: 4735 Unser Blvd. NW,* ☎ *505/899–0205.* ⊑ *$1 weekdays, $2 weekends.* ⊙ *Daily 8–5.*

☾ ⑮ **Rio Grande Nature Center State Park.** This year-round refuge in a portion of the Bosque, the nation's largest cottonwood forest, is home to all manner of birds and migratory waterfowl. Constructed half aboveground and half below the edge of a pond, the park's Observation Room has viewing windows that provide a look at what's going on at both levels. You'll see birds, frogs, ducks, and turtles. The park has active programs for adults and children, and trails for biking, walking, and jogging. ⊠ *2901 Candelaria Rd. NW,* ☎ *505/344–7240.* ⊑ *$1.* ⊙ *Daily 10–5.*

☾ ⑯ **Rio Grande Zoo.** An oasis of waterfalls, cottonwood trees, and naturalized animal habitats, the Rio Grande Zoo is one of the best-managed and most attractive facilities of its kind in the nation. More than 200 species of wildlife from around the world live here. In keeping with its mission of wildlife care and conservation, the zoo has established captive breeding programs for more than a dozen endangered species. Concerts are performed on the grounds during the summer. There's a café on the premises. ⊠ *903 10th St. SW,* ☎ *505/764–6200.* ⊑ *$4.50.* ⊙ *Daily 9–5.*

Sandia Peak Aerial Tramway

Rising like a wave of color poised to break on Albuquerque are the majestic Sandia Mountains, which form an ever-changing panoramic backdrop to the city. Hikers, bikers, bird-watchers, climbers, painters, skiers, and sightseers all take advantage of this wild urban refuge. An ideal way to get the lay of this spectacular land northeast of downtown is to take the tram ride up to Sandia Peak and hike along the rim.

A Good Tour

Head north from downtown on I–25 and east on Tramway Road (NM 556) to reach the base station of the **Sandia Peak Aerial Tramway.** If you have more time to spend in the area, take the Sandia Crest tour described in Side Trips from Albuquerque, *below.*

TIMING

The tram excursion, best taken on warm, clear days and a superb experience at sunset, takes about 90 minutes round-trip. Allow more time if you want to explore the rim, stop for a picnic, or have a drink at the High Finance Restaurant. Autumn is an ideal time to view the changing colors of the aspens and scrub oaks. At any time of year, bring warm layers if you intend to spend more than a few minutes on the mountain.

Sights to See

☾ **Sandia Peak Aerial Tramway.** Tramway cars climb 2⁷⁄₁₀ mi up the steep western face of the Sandias, giving you a close-up view of red rocks and tall trees. From the sky-top observation deck at the summit you can see Santa Fe to the northeast and Los Alamos to the northwest. If you're lucky, you'll see birds of prey soaring above or mountain lions roaming the cliff sides. An exhibit room at the top surveys the wildlife and landscape of the mountain, as well as some trails. If you want to tie a meal into the excursion, there's the pricey High Finance Restaurant above, and the Salsa Grille & Cantina at the tram's base. ⊠ *10 Tramway Loop NE,* ☎ *505/856–7325.* ⊑ *$14 ($10 early-bird special Memorial Day–Labor Day, daily 9–11).* ⊙ *Memorial Day–Labor Day, daily 9 AM–10 PM; Labor Day–Memorial Day, Sun.–Tues. and Thurs. 9–9, Wed. 5–10 PM, Fri.–Sat. 9 AM–10 PM.*

NEON AND NOSTALGIA

MID-20TH-CENTURY American motorists came to know their country firsthand via Route 66, and as its 75th anniversary approaches, frequent flyers enviably wonder about the romance of the open road. Long before the prosperous age of the two-car family, the 2,400 mi of Route 66 opened in 1926 to link eight states, from Chicago to Los Angeles. It came to be known by the nickname John Steinbeck gave it—"The Mother Road." The nation's outlet for movement and change has become enveloped in nostalgia. Today in New Mexico, from the Texas to the Arizona border, it's still possible to experience vestiges of the old Route 66.

Built in part to aid rural communities and the transportation of agricultural goods, Route 66 evolved into a farmer's very escape from the Dust Bowl of the 1930s, and then a tryst for the love affair between Americans and their automobiles. The route's other nickname, "America's Main Street," was due to the fact that the road incorporated towns' main streets, and because of this, communities thrived. Along the highway that ran as vividly through the imagination as through the landscape, many discovered their ability to move on beyond the confines of their own home town. They found places along the road that appeared to offer a better opportunity to prosper and to reinvent their destiny.

After World War II, Route 66 saw jubilant family vacationers tumble out of cars and into roadside diners and motels. The 1940s and '50s were the heyday of the highway, as Nat King Cole crooned the lyrics to Bobby Troup's song of the road. The road's adventure was overplayed in the '60s television series Route 66, and by 1970, nearly all of the two-laner was trumped by four-lane interstate highways. Along Route 66, the possibility of connection with America's people and places lived beyond every bend in the road. By contrast, the interstate would dampen travel with franchised monotony. Most of the bypassed Route 66 communities dried up and blew away like tumbleweeds. In many of these ghost towns, only a few crumbling buildings and fading signs remain as markers to a vanished age.

By hopping on and off I–40, it's possible to find the quieter, slower two-laner that's held on to its name. The feeling of adventure still flickers in Tucumcari at twilight, when the neon signs of the Buckaroo Motel, the Westerner Drive-In, and the Blue Swallow light up the cobalt sky. In Santa Rosa, at Joseph's Cafe, the Fat Man continues to beckon. In Albuquerque, you can drive down Central Avenue, stopping at the Route 66 Diner or the Route 66 Malt Shop and heading past the El Vado. And in Gallup, dine at Earl's Restaurant or the Eagle Cafe, and book a room at the stars of yesteryear's hotel, El Rancho Hotel. Between Albuquerque and Gallup, this ribbon of road takes you through dusty towns with names like poetry: Budville, Cubero, McCartys, Thoreau. These places also once offered the traveler the filling stations, motor courts, curio shops, and cafés that gave comfort on a long drive, and every road tripper today hopes to happen upon such an undiscovered (but really just forgotten) place.

July 2001 marks the Diamond Jubilee (75th anniversary) of Historic Route 66. For information, keep posted on www.rt66nm.org. Albuquerque will hold festivities July 20–22, headquartered at the New Mexico State Fairgrounds on Route 66. For information on dining and lodging along Route 66, contact the **National Historic Route 66 Federation** (✉ Box 423, Tujunga, CA 91043, ☎ 818/352–7232, 📠). To track Route 66 through New Mexico, contact the **Route 66 Association** (☎ 505/255–4304).

DINING

Albuquerqueans love to eat out, as the city's more than 1,700 restaurants attest. Chinese, Vietnamese, Thai, Cajun, French, and Italian restaurants can all be found, along with establishments serving regional New Mexican cuisine based on the native ingredients—chile, beans, and corn—that have sustained people in this land for centuries.

The argument that Albuquerque is the Mexican food capital of the Southwest is easy to make—and tough to dispute. Fine examples of this eclectic diet, in which dishes of diverse pedigrees are doused with colorful chile sauce, can be found in paper-plate eateries and linen-tablecloth restaurants.

Downtown, Old Town, and Vicinity

Contemporary

$$$$ ✕ **Seasons Rotisserie-Grill.** Upbeat yet elegant, this Old Town eatery is an easy place to have a business lunch or a dinner date, and it's conveniently near museums and shops. The kitchen serves reliable grilled specialties, like the popular spit-roasted half-chicken with garlic mashed potatoes, as well as light northern Italian pastas. Other dishes are the double-cut pork rib chop with caramelized shallot-sage sauce and grilled Atlantic salmon with lemon beurre blanc. The rooftop patio and bar provides evening cocktails and lighter meals. Reservations are recommended. ✉ *2031 Mountain Rd. NW,* ☎ *505/766–5100. AE, D, DC, MC, V.*

$$$ ✕ **Avalon.** This white-linen, new American restaurant showcases the cuisine of chef-owner Cord McQueen. Go for the pork tenderloin in chipotle demi-glace, the sunflower seed crusted Atlantic salmon with red-pepper mashed potatoes, or the garlic-molasses-cured roast chicken with sweet potato gratin. Special desserts are chocolate souffle served with ice cream, and the apple-walnut crème brûlée. Local produce is used in season. The drink menu includes local and California wines and local microbrews. Reservations are recommended. ✉ *515 Central Ave. NW,* ☎ *505/924–1537. AE, DC, MC, V. Closed Sun.–Mon.*

$$–$$$ ✕ **Artichoke Cafe.** Locals praise the Artichoke for its service and
★ French, new American, and Italian dishes prepared, whenever possible, with organically grown ingredients. Specialties include grilled duck, pumpkin ravioli with fresh spinach and butternut squash, and grilled chicken with five onion risotto. The appetizers are so tasty you may want to make a meal out of them. The building is about a century old, but the decor is uptown modern. The two-tier dining room spills out into a small courtyard. ✉ *424 Central Ave. SE,* ☎ *505/243–0200. AE, D, DC, MC, V. Closed Sun. No lunch Sat.*

$$–$$$ ✕ **High Noon Restaurant and Saloon.** Fine dining is staged in a former woodworking shop in one of Old Town's 200-year-old adobe buildings. The setting is Territorial, with viga ceilings, brick floors, handmade Southwestern furniture, and New Mexican art. A skylight provides diffused light and glimpses of the stars. Among the menu highlights are bison rib eye, rack of lamb crusted in roasted pine nuts and flame-broiled fresh salmon. From Thursday to Sunday you'll dine to the music of a flamenco guitarist. ✉ *425 San Felipe St. NW,* ☎ *505/765–1455. AE, D, DC, MC, V.*

$ ✕ **Manhattan on the Rio Grande.** This deli serves sandwiches big enough to pass muster with a doting Jewish or Italian mother. Get a Reuben, a Siciliano, or a Stormin' Norman (nothing to do with General Schwarzkopf, it's named after a famous basketball coach at the University of New Mexico). It's open until 11 PM. ✉ *901 Rio Grande Blvd. NW,* ☎ *505/248–1514. AE, MC, V. No dinner Sun.–Tues.*

Albuquerque Dining

Continental

$$–$$$ ✕ **Maria Teresa Restaurant & 1840 Bar.** The 32-inch-thick walls of the
restored 1840s adobe have stood—like the Continental and New Mexican fare—the test of time. The rack of Colorado lamb is a good
choice. Early Spanish American chests, carvings, and tables and Southwestern paintings decorate the swank room, but in summer everyone
wants to eat in the courtyard. ⊠ *618 Rio Grande Blvd. NW,* ☎ *505/
242–3900. AE, DC, MC, V.*

French

$$ ✕ **La Crêpe Michel.** The highlights at this intimate country-French café
are its innovative chicken, beef, seafood, vegetarian, and dessert crepes.
Also prepared are classic French onion soup, escargots, and fresh-
baked French bread. You may notice that there is (Mon Dieu!) no wine
list, which has to do with the restaurant's proximity to San Felipe de
Neri Catholic Church (liquor laws prohibit alcoholic beverages from
being served near a church). ⊠ *Old Town Patio del Norte, 400 C-2
San Felipe St. NW,* ☎ *505/242–1251. MC, V. Closed Mon. No din-
ner Sun.*

Mexican and New Mexican

$$–$$$ ✕ **La Placita.** It's touristy and not particularly authentic, but this
restaurant housed in a historic hacienda on Old Town Plaza is nothing
if not convenient. Chiles rellenos, enchiladas, tacos, and sopaipillas are
all on the menu, which also includes American entrées. The building
dates from 1706—the adobe walls are 3 ft thick in places. For years
it housed Ambrosio Armijo's mercantile store, where ladies' lace gloves
sold for 10¢ a pair and gents' linen underdrawers could be purchased
for $1. The six dining rooms are also art galleries—patrons dine sur-
rounded by outstanding examples of Native American and South-
western painting, most of which may be purchased. ⊠ *208 San Felipe
St. NW,* ☎ *505/247–2204. AE, D, MC, V.*

$ ✕ **Barelas Coffee House.** Barelas may look like a set in search of a script,
but it's the real deal: diners come from all over the city to sup in this
old-fashioned chile parlor in the Hispanic Historic Route 66 neigh-
borhood south of downtown. You may notice looks of quiet content-
ment on the faces of the many dedicated chile eaters as they dive into
their bowls of Barelas's potent red. ⊠ *1502 4th St. SW,* ☎ *505/843–
7577. Reservations not accepted. D, MC, V. Closed Sun. No dinner.*

$ ✕ **Duran's Central Pharmacy.** This expanded Old Town lunch counter
with a dozen tables and a tiny patio just might serve the best tortillas
in town. A favorite of old-timers who know their way around a blue-
corn enchilada, Duran's is an informal place whose patrons give their
food the total attention it deserves. Dinner is served only until 6 PM
on weekdays and not at all on weekends. ⊠ *1815 Central Ave. NW,*
☎ *505/247–4141. No credit cards. No dinner weekends.*

$ ✕ **Garcia's Kitchen.** Authentic Mexican cooking makes the Old Town
location of this local chain a good stop for smooth red chile and daily
lunch specials like flautas or chicken enchiladas. Breakfast is served
all day at Garcia's, whose decor might best be described as early car-
nival toy. ⊠ *1736 Central Ave. SW,* ☎ *505/842–0273. Reservations
not accepted. AE, D, DC, MC, V.*

$ ✕ **M&J's Sanitary Tortilla Factory.** Ravenous travelers rub elbows with
downtown lawyers in this large, bright, nostalgic lunchroom. The hos-
pitable Bea Montoya, who knows her regulars by name, serves the best
carne adovada (red chile–marinated slow-baked pork) in town. ⊠ *403
2nd St. SW,* ☎ *505/242–4890. No credit cards. Closed Sun. No dinner.*

North of I–40

Mexican and New Mexican

$$ ✗ **Casa de Benavidez.** The fajitas at this local favorite with a romantic patio are among the best in town, and the chile is faultless. This perhaps explains why many patrons return despite prices that are higher than at similar establishments. Reservations are not accepted on weekends. ⊠ *8032 4th St. NW,* ☎ *505/898–3311. AE, D, DC, MC, V. No dinner Sun.*

$$ ✗ **El Pinto.** Expect a wait on weekends at this big indoor-outdoor restaurant in the shadow of the Sandia Mountains. The food is authentic New Mexican—some of the recipes at family-owned El Pinto have been passed down three generations—as is the ambience: mariachi bands stroll through the Spanish-style setting. Homemade tortillas accompany sopaipillas, chiles rellenos, tamales, enchiladas, and other dishes; the chiles, all of which are roasted on the premises, have a sometimes un-deserved reputation for mildness. ⊠ *10500 4th St. NW,* ☎ *505/898– 1771. AE, D, DC, MC, V.*

$$ ✗ **Garduño's of Mexico.** Tangy margaritas, elaborate Mexican decor, and generally fine cooking are the hallmarks of Garduño's, part of a successful local chain. Some diners find the food lightweight and in-consistent, but the middle-of-the-road formula appeals to many. When the place gets crowded, which is often, it has a real party feel. ⊠ *8806 4th St. NW,* ☎ *505/898–2772. AE, D, DC, MC, V.*

$ ✗ **Fajitaville.** This restaurant in a converted drive-in serves healthful, grease-less, cooked-to-order fajitas with fabulous fresh salsas. Try the chicken fajita with the roasted tomato-chipotle salsa. ⊠ *6313 4th St. NW,* ☎ *505/341–9683. Reservations not accepted. AE, D, DC, MC, V.*

University, Nob Hill, and Vicinity

Barbecue

$$ ✗ **Quarters BBQ.** All you've ever dreamed of finding in a barbecue joint awaits you when you walk into this dark den. The three-decades-old Albuquerque institution serves tender, smoky falling-off-the-bone ribs and chicken, brisket, and sausage—it's hard to know where to dive in first. You'll need a fistful of napkins, that's for sure. The sauce is more tangy than sweet, and slow smoking with a secret recipe makes for the winning combination. Top steaks and Alaskan king crab legs are also served without barbecue sauce. ⊠ *801 Yale Blvd. SE,* ☎ *505/843–7505. AE, MC, V.*

Greek

$–$$ ✗ **Yanni's Mediterranean Bar & Grill.** Something of a see-and-be-seen Nob Hill spot, Yanni's is a casual, airy place serving souvlaki and gyros dinners, marinated grilled lamb chops, grilled fresh halibut, and ro-tisserie Greek chicken seasoned with garlic and oregano. The popular vegetarian plate includes a surprisingly good meatless moussaka, tabouli, spanikopita, and stuffed grape leaves. ⊠ *3109 Central Ave. NE,* ☎ *505/268–9250. AE, D, MC, V.*

Italian

$$–$$$ ✗ **Portobello: A Taste of Tuscany.** At this spin-off of the highly respected
★ Artichoke Cafe (☞ *above*) you can dine on the best of northern Italy without leaving the country. Chef Fabrizio Ventricini prepares simple, fresh, traditional Tuscan fare, much of it with glorious mushroom-in-fused pasta sauces. The steak Portobello, a tenderloin topped with fried leeks and the namesake and scrumptious Portobello mushroom, is one of many exquisitely prepared dishes; other good choices are the veal marsala and the chicken with rosemary and olives. Fresh fish is also on the menu. The hits of the wine list are the Italian vintages pro-duced by the venerable Antinori family. ⊠ *Fashion Square, 1100 San*

Mateo Blvd., ☎ *505/232–9119. Reservations essential. AE, D, DC, MC, V. No lunch weekends.*

$$ ✕ **Scalo Northern Italian Grill.** Nob Hill trendsetters gather at this in-
★ formal eatery to experience fine Italian wines and first-rate pasta, seafood, and meat entrées. Most of the multilevel dining area looks onto the lively bar and an open kitchen, where wonders like the ravi-oli with spinach and ricotta cheese and the fried baby calamari with a spicy marinara and lemon aioli are created. The homemade desserts are mighty fine. ⊠ *Nob Hill Shopping Center, 3500 Central Ave. SE,* ☎ *505/255–8781. AE, DC, MC, V. No lunch Sun.*

$ ✕ **Il Vicino.** The gourmet pizzas at Il Vicino are baked in a European-style wood-fired oven. If a suitable combination of the 25 possible top-pings eludes you, try the Pizza Rustica, a buttery cornmeal crust topped with roasted garlic, artichokes, calamata olives, and capers. Good sal-ads, pastas, and microbrewery beers are also served here. ⊠ *3403 Central Ave. NE,* ☎ *505/266–7855. Reservations not accepted. MC, V.*

Mexican and New Mexican

$ ✕ **El Patio.** A university-area hangout, this sentimental favorite has con-sistently great food served in the funky patio. Go for the green-chile chicken enchiladas, the best in town, or any of the heart-healthy and vegetarian selections. But watch out for the fiery green chiles served at harvesttime. ⊠ *142 Harvard St. NE,* ☎ *505/268–4245. Reserva-tions not accepted. MC, V.*

$ ✕ **Los Cuates.** Frequently voted the best Mexican restaurant in local polls, Los Cuates is a classic. The soft chicken taco smothered with green chile and the chile relleno are tops. The roast beef burrito could be a contender for the best burrito in town. Fresh chips and spicy salsa are brought immediately to your table or red-vinyl booth. Portions are gar-gantuan, so you may want to order à la carte. Expect a wait on week-end nights. A second location across the street at 4901 Lomas Boulevard NE serves fine margaritas as well. ⊠ *5016B Lomas Blvd. NE,* ☎ *505/ 268–0974. Reservations not accepted. AE, D, DC, MC, V.*

LODGING

Albuquerque's hotels provide a comfortable mix of modern conveniences and Old West flavor. Homier are the many bed-and-breakfast inns, some downtown in restored Victorian-era homes, others north of town in Los Ranchos and Corrales.

Downtown, Old Town, and Vicinity

$$$$ ⊞ **Doubletree Hotel.** A two-story waterfall splashes down a marble back-drop in the lobby of this 15-story downtown hotel adjoining the Al-buquerque Convention Center. The pastel rooms contain custom-made Southwestern furniture and complementary art. The restaurant at the foot of the waterfall is called, appropriately, La Cascada (The Cascade). Breakfast, a lunch buffet, and dinner, from fresh seafood to Southwestern specialties, are served. ⊠ *201 Marquette Ave. NW, 87102,* ☎ *505/247–3344; 888/223–4113 central reservations;* ℻ *505/247–7025. 295 rooms. Restaurant, bar, room service, pool, exercise room, parking (fee). AE, D, DC, MC, V.*

$$$–$$$$ ⊞ **Hyatt Regency Albuquerque.** Adjacent to the Albuquerque Convention
★ Center, this hotel occupies one of two soaring, desert-color towers that figure prominently in the city's skyline. The gleaming Art Deco–style interior is refined and not overbearing. The contemporary rooms in mauve, burgundy, and tan combine Southwestern style with all the ex-pected Hyatt amenities. Rooms with data ports are available. The on-site McGrath's restaurant serves steaks, chops, chicken, and seafood.

✉ *330 Tijeras Ave. NW, 87102,* ☎ *505/842–1234 or 800/233–1234,* FAX *505/766–6710. 395 rooms, 14 suites. Restaurant, 2 bars, pool, health club, shops, business services. AE, D, DC, MC, V.* ✧

$$–$$$$ ☎ **Böttger-Koch Mansion.** Charles Böttger, a German immigrant, built his two-story mansion in 1912. Some of the rooms in the structure, which is on the National Register of Historic Places, have original pressed-tin ceilings and roomy four-poster beds. A grassy courtyard fronted by a patio provides a quiet escape from the Old Town crowds. Breakfast might consist of stuffed French toast or perhaps burritos smothered in green chile, which you can also enjoy in your room. ✉ *110 San Felipe St. NW, 87104,* ☎ *505/243–3639 or 800/758–3639. 8 rooms. Free parking. AE, MC, V. BP.* ✧

$$–$$$$ ☎ **Brittania & W. E. Mauger Estate B&B.** Popular with businesspeople
★ because of its downtown location, this fine B&B is in an 1897 Queen Anne Victorian, the first home in Albuquerque to have electricity. Oval windows with beveled and "feather-pattern" glass, hardwood floors, a bright redbrick exterior, and an Old West front veranda are among the noteworthy design elements. Rooms now have data ports. ✉ *701 Roma Ave. NW, 87102,* ☎ *505/242–8755 or 800/719–9189,* FAX *505/ 842–8855. 8 rooms. In-room data ports. AE, D, DC, MC, V. BP.* ✧

$$$ ☎ **Best Western Rio Grande Inn.** This member of Best Western is one of the most regionally and authentically decorated in the state. The heavy, handcrafted wood furniture, tin sconces, and artwork in the rooms come from local suppliers and artisans, whose addresses are listed in a corner of the lobby. That locals are familiar with the Albuquerque Grill is a good indicator of the restaurant's value. The hotel is conveniently just off I-40 and within an easy walk of Old Town. ✉ *1015 Rio Grande Blvd. NW, 87104,* ☎ *505/843–9500 or 800/959–4726,* FAX *505/ 843–9238. 174 rooms. Restaurant, pool, outdoor hot tub, meeting room, free parking. AE, D, DC, MC, V.* ✧

$$–$$$ ☎ **La Posada de Albuquerque.** Opened in 1939 by New Mexico na-
★ tive Conrad Hilton (who honeymooned here with bride Zsa Zsa Gabor), this 10-story hotel is listed on the National Register of Historic Places. The tiled lobby fountain, circular balcony, massive vigas, and Native American war-dance murals lend the place an easy Southwestern charm. Ranging from small to spacious, the rooms have Southwestern and Native American accents that include Hopi pottery and R. C. Gorman prints. Guests have health-club privileges at a nearby downtown health club. ✉ *125 2nd St. NW, 87102,* ☎ *505/242–9090 or 800/777–5732,* FAX *505/242–8664. 114 rooms, 4 suites. Restaurant, 2 bars, parking (fee). AE, D, DC, MC, V.*

$$–$$$ ☎ **Ramada Inn–Downtown.** An Art Deco–style hotel built in 1962 and remodeled 1998 lies in the heart of downtown, less than a mile from Old Town. The Ramada welcomes business travelers with conveniences like in-room data ports, two-line phones, and free local calls. The white-walled rooms are decorated with Art Deco–style prints and white furnishings trimmed with black. Each room has a king-size bed. ✉ *717 Central Ave. NW, 87102,* ☎ *505/924–2400 or 877/878– 4868,* FAX *505/924–2465. 125 rooms, 10 suites. Restaurant, bar, in-room data ports, exercise room, pool, free parking. AE, D, DC, MC, V.* ✧

$$–$$$ ☎ **Sheraton Old Town.** This modern 11-story hotel sits gracefully amid Old Town's ancient structures. The large rooms have desert-color appointments, hand-wrought furnishings, and big bathrooms with vanities. The Rio Grande Customs House Restaurant, with a misplaced nautical scheme, serves well-prepared prime rib, steaks, seafood, and poultry. The casual Café del Sol has a varied menu, with many Southwestern dishes. ✉ *800 Rio Grande Blvd. NW, 87104,* ☎ *505/843– 6300 or 800/237–2133,* FAX *505/842–9863. 188 rooms, 4 suites. 2 restaurants, 2 bars, pool, hot tub. AE, D, DC, MC, V.* ✧

Albuquerque Lodging

Montano Rd.

Cliff's
Amusement
Park

Montgomery Blvd.

425

Montgomery
Park

Edith Blvd.

Comanche Rd.

Ela
Park

25

Aztec

Grisham
Park

Carlisle Blvd.

Candelaria Rd.

Adams St.

Princeton Dr.

Vassar Dr.

Richmond Dr.

Claremont Ave.

Menaul Blvd.

5

6

40

Indian School Rd.

Louisiana Blvd.

Altura
Park

Constitution

University Blvd.

Stanford

Girard Blvd.

Washington

San Mateo Blvd.

San Pedro Blvd.

0

7

9

Sigma Chi Rd.

Lomas Blvd.

Campus Blvd.

Solano

Marquette

New Mexico
State
Fairgrounds

Ruina Ave.

UNIVERSITY
OF
NEW MEXICO

Grand Ave.

Central Ave.

Student
Union

Cornell

Harvard

Vassar

Silver Ave.

Central Ave.

Coal Ave.

Roosevelt
Park

Lead Ave.

Coal Ave.

Coal Ave.

Garfield

Wellesley

Ridgecrest

Zuni Rd.

Sports
Stadium

UNIVERSITY OF
NEW MEXICO
(South Campus)

Yale Blvd.

Girard

Burton
Park

Carlisle Blvd.

Trumbull Ave.

Ridgecrest Dr.

Kathryn Ave.

shine Terr. Ave.

University Blvd.

Wellesley

N

Louisiana Blvd.

13

Gibson Blvd.

10

11

12

Kirtland
Air Force
Base

Albuquerque
International
Sunport

0   1 mile

0   1 km

$–$$ 🔲 **Jazz Inn Bed & Breakfast.** This creatively restored 100-year-old home
in the historic Huning Highland District, just off Old Route 66, is convenient to both downtown and the university. Nowhere will you find
more interesting or hospitable hosts than innkeepers Sophia and Nicholas
Peron. Artists and community activists, they are up on the town's music
and art scene. Rooms are themed after jazz musicians like Bessie Smith
and Duke Ellington and are simple, elegant, and comfortable, with decor
that mixes and matches the antique with the utterly contemporary.
Music lovers can browse through the music library's 4,000 CDs, tapes,
and records. There's a grand piano for those who like to practice. The
inn is completely handicapped accessible. Smoking is not permitted indoors. ✉ *111 Walter NE, 87102,* ☎ *505/242–1530 or 888/529–9466,*
FAX *505/224–9083. 5 rooms, 2 suites. Piano. AE, D, DC, MC, V. BP.* ✺

$ 🔲 **Old Town B&B.** Part of this structure was built by local architect Leon
Watson, a pioneer in the use of adobe in Pueblo Revival–style home
design. The bright downstairs suite—with a viga and latilla ceiling, a
kiva fireplace, and Mexican leather furniture—is stylishly Southwestern without overkill. There is a bathroom with a skylight and hot tub,
shared with the owner only, and a sitting room and library. The sec-
ond-story room, with private bath, has views of the Sandias. ✉ *707
17th St. NW, 87104,* ☎ *505/764–9144 or 888/900–9144. 1 room, 1
suite with shared bath. No credit cards. BP.* ✺

East Side Near I–40

$$–$$$ 🔲 **Albuquerque Hilton.** A blend of contemporary sophistication and
Southwestern charm, the Hilton has Native American rugs, Western
and Native American art, arched doorways, and Santa Fe–style wooden
furniture. The Ranchers Club restaurant is elegant, with a roaring
fireplace. In the grill room, fish and meats are cooked over aromatic
woods like piñon or mesquite. The hotel's other restaurant, Casa
Chaco, serves coffee-shop breakfast and lunch fare but is transformed
at night, when nouvelle Southwestern cuisine is served by candlelight
on crisp linen with sparkling crystal. ✉ *1901 University Blvd. NE,
87102,* ☎ *505/884–2500 or 800/274–6835,* FAX *505/889–9118. 263
rooms, 6 suites. 2 restaurants, 2 bars, no-smoking rooms, indoor-outdoor pool, sauna, exercise room. AE, D, DC, MC, V.* ✺

$–$$$ 🔲 **Albuquerque Marriott.** This 17-story luxury property takes care of
the executive traveler with two concierge floors but doesn't forget the
vacationer. Katsina dolls, Native American pottery, and other regional
artworks decorate the elegant public areas. The rooms are traditional
American, with walk-in closets, armoires, and crystal lamps, but 1999
remodeling brought Southwestern touches. ✉ *2101 Louisiana Blvd.
NE, 87110,* ☎ *505/881–6800 or 800/334–2086,* FAX *505/888–2982.
411 rooms, 6 suites. Restaurant, bar, indoor-outdoor pool, sauna, ex-
ercise room, concierge floor, business services. AE, D, DC, MC, V.*

$$ 🔲 **Barcelona Suites Uptown.** With tile floors and wrought-iron rail-
ings, this colorful three-story hotel has the feel of Old Mexico, but its
Southwestern-tinged furnishings are contemporary. Each suite has a
galley kitchen with a wet bar and microwave. Three suites have hot
tubs. ✉ *900 Louisiana Blvd. NE, off I–40, 87110,* ☎ *505/255–5566
or 877/227–7848,* FAX *505/266–6644. 164 suites. Kitchenettes, 2 pools,
sauna. AE, D, DC, MC, V. BP.*

$ 🔲 **Midtown Econo Lodge Inn.** There's nothing special about this locally
owned chain property 5 mi east of Old Town, but it is inexpensive and
local calls are free, as is the cable TV. The clean rooms contain coffeemakers and queen- or king-size beds. ✉ *2412 Carlisle Ave. NE, at
I–40, 87110,* ☎ *505/880–0080, 800/553–2666 central reservations;*
FAX *505/880–0053. 38 rooms, 1 suite. AE, D, DC, MC, V.*

North Valley and Corrales

$–$$$ ⊞ **Inn at Paradise.** Near the first tee of the lush Paradise Hills Golf Club, this swank B&B resort atop the West Mesa is a golfer's dream: the 6,895 yards of bluegrass fairways and bent-grass greens challenge players of all levels. Works by local artists and craftspeople decorate the large rooms; the two suites have fireplaces. Golf packages are available. ⊠ *10035 Country Club La. NW, Albuquerque 87114,* ☎ *505/898–6161 or 800/938–6161,* FAX *505/890–1090. 16 rooms, 2 suites, 1 apartment. Spa. AE, D, MC, V. CP.* ✿

$$ ⊞ **Casita Chamisa.** In the pastoral cottonwood-shaded North Valley
★   village of Los Ranchos, 15 mi north of Old Town, this B&B consists of a handsome room in the main adobe-style house and a separate two-bedroom house with a fireplace, a kitchenette, and a greenhouse. The furnishings are a comfortable blend of local, Southwestern, and Mexican materials. Casita Chamisa is on an archaeological site, with a prehistoric Native American ruin still visible. Breakfast is vegetarian-friendly: juices, coffee, breads, pancakes, coffee cake, waffles, and perhaps fruit picked from the 14 fruit trees on the grounds. The sourdough bread is made with a starter that's 120 years old. ⊠ *850 Chamisal Rd. NW, 87107,* ☎ *505/897–4644. 1 room, 1 two-bedroom house. Indoor pool, hot tub. AE, MC, V. BP.* ✿

$$ ⊞ **Corrales Inn.** This solar-heated Territorial-style adobe home, 14 mi north of Albuquerque in picturesque Corrales, was built in the 1980s. Each room has a theme—Asian, Native American, Flower Garden, Cowboy, Corrales (Southwestern), and South of the Border—and each has individual temperature controls and a sitting and dressing area. Country breakfasts of quiches, soufflés, omelets, huevos rancheros, and stuffed French toast are served in the dining room. ⊠ *Box 1361, 58 Perea Rd., behind Plaza San Ysidro, Corrales 87048,* ☎ *505/897–4422 or 800/897–4410,* FAX *505/890–5244. 6 rooms. AE, MC, V. BP.* ✿

$$ ⊞ **Yours Truly.** The views are awesome from this hillside inn run by the gracious Pat and James Montgomery. Glass blocks set into the walls cast subtle light. The modern adobe rooms are not large, but they're comfortable, especially the one with a king-size bed nestled in a *banco* (adobe bench). Special touches include plush robes, afternoon wine and snacks, and fireplaces in all rooms. Pat pulls out all the stops at breakfast, which might include praline French toast or creamed gravy with sausage and green chile on biscuits. The inn is north of Albuquerque in Corrales. ⊠ *Box 2263, 160 Paseo de Corrales, Corrales 87048,* ☎ *505/898–7027 or 800/942–7890,* FAX *505/898–9022. 4 rooms. AE, MC, V. BP.* ✿

Sandia Mountain Foothills

$$ ⊞ **Elaine's, A Bed and Breakfast.** This antiques-filled three-story log
★   home is set in the evergreen folds of the Sandia Mountain foothills. Four acres of wooded grounds beckon outside the back door. The top two floors have rooms with balconies and big picture windows that bring the lush mountain views indoors. The third-floor room also has cathedral ceilings and a brass bed. Breakfast, served in a plant-filled room or outside on a patio with a fountain, often includes fresh fruit, pancakes, or waffles with sausage. ⊠ *Snowline Estate, Box 444, 72 Snowline Rd., Cedar Crest 87008,* ☎ *505/281–2467 or 800/821–3092. 5 rooms. Hot tub. AE, D, MC, V. BP.* ✿

Airport Hotels

$$$–$$$$ ⊞ **Wyndham Albuquerque Hotel.** Only 350 yards from the airport, this
★   15-story hotel provides speedy access to your flight, day or night. Rooms have Southwest accents, large work desks, data ports, and cof-

feemakers. ⊠ *2910 Yale Blvd. SE, 87106,* ☎ *505/843–7000 or 800/ 227–1117,* FAX *505/843–6307. 276 rooms, 2 suites. Restaurant, lobby lounge, in-room data ports, pool, tennis court, exercise room, airport shuttle. AE, D, DC, MC, V.* 🕸

$–$$$ 🏨 **Courtyard by Marriott.** Take advantage of corporate rates and amenities—available to everyone—at this haven for business travelers ½ mi north of the airport. Rooms, done in mauve and teal with South-west-inspired paintings, have jacks for portable fax machines and modems, large desks, and long telephone cords that actually reach the work area. ⊠ *1920 Yale Blvd. SE, 87106,* ☎ *505/843–6600 or 800/ 321–2211,* FAX *505/843–8740. 136 rooms, 14 suites. Restaurant, lobby lounge, in-room data ports, indoor pool, exercise room, business services, airport shuttle. AE, D, DC, MC, V.*

$$ 🏨 **Comfort Inn.** The rooms here have uninspired but acceptable decor and furnishings. A full-service restaurant and coffee shop is adjacent to the hotel. The airport is 1 mi away. ⊠ *2300 Yale Blvd. SE, 87106,* ☎ *505/243–2244 or 800/228–5150,* FAX *505/247–2925. 118 rooms. Pool, hot tub, airport shuttle. AE, D, DC, MC, V.* 🕸

$–$$ 🏨 **Radisson Inn Albuquerque Airport.** A mere ¼ mi from the airport, this hotel has arched balconies, tan desert colors, a year-round courtyard pool, and indoor and seasonal outdoor dining. Standard rooms are comfortable; VIP executive rooms are larger and overlook the pool. Pets are welcome in some rooms. Complimentary car service is available. ⊠ *1901 University Blvd. SE, 87106,* ☎ *505/247–0512 or 800/333–3333,* FAX *505/ 843–7148. 148 rooms. Restaurant, bar, no-smoking rooms, pool, hot tub, exercise room, airport shuttle. AE, D, DC, MC, V.* 🕸

Camping

For additional campgrounds in the Albuquerque area, *see* the listings in the town of Bernalillo *in* Chapter 6 and Isleta Pueblo, *below.*

⚠ **Albuquerque Central KOA.** At town's edge, off Historic Route 66 in the foothills of the Sandia Mountains, this well-equipped campground has expansive views and only a few trees, but there is a dog run. A tent site costs $22.95, full hookup $32.95, cabins $39.95–$49.95. Amenities include rest rooms, hot showers, LP gas, and dump facility. ⊠ *12400 Skyline Rd. NE (Exit 166 off I–40), 87123,* ☎ *505/296–2729. 169 RV sites, 24 tent sites, 16 cabins. Grocery, pool, hot tub, miniature golf, bicycles, recreation room, playground, coin laundry, meeting room. AE, D, MC, V.* 🕸

⚠ **Turquoise Trail Campground and RV Park.** Pine and cedar trees dot this 14-acre park in the Sandias, which has hiking trails with access to the Cibola National Forest. A museum on the premises—open to guests and nonguests for a $2.50 entrance fee—chronicles archaeological finds and contains artifacts dating from the Ice Age to the battle at Wounded Knee. Tent sites cost $10.50, hookups $19, cabins $25–$50. Amenities include rest rooms and hot showers. ⊠ *22 Calvary Rd., 5 mi north of I–40's Exit 175, Cedar Crest 87008,* ☎ *505/281–2005. 57 RV sites, 30 tent sites, 3 cabins. Grocery, hot tub, playground, coin laundry. AE, D, V.* 🕸

NIGHTLIFE AND THE ARTS

The entertainment options in Albuquerque include theater, dance, classical and rock concerts, and film screenings. If you like to two-step to country-and-western tunes, you've come to the right place. To find out what's going on in town, check the Friday and Sunday editions of the *Albuquerque Journal,* the Thursday edition of the *Albuquerque Tribune,*

or the *Weekly Alibi*. **Ticketmaster** has an event information line (☎ 505/
842–5387; 505/884–0999 to purchase tickets) or try **tickets.com** (☎ 505/
851–5050 or 800/905–3315). Bars and lounges close by 2 AM.

Nightlife

Bars and Lounges

Many of downtown Albuquerque's nightclubs, bars, pool halls, late-
night dining establishments, and performance spaces are within a 10-
minute walk of one another, on Central and Gold avenues between 2nd
and 7th streets.

Club Rhythm and Blues (✉ 3523 Central Ave. NE, ☎ 505/256–0849)
is open from Tuesday to Saturday for live R&B.

The **Cooperage** (✉ 7220 Lomas Blvd. NE, ☎ 505/255–1657) is where
a hip crowd goes to dance salsa, reggae, and rock and roll.

Martini Grill (✉ 4200 Central Ave. SE, ☎ 505/242–4333) provides a
sophisticated setting for a superlative piano bar.

O'Neill's Pub (✉ 3211 Central Ave. NE, ☎ 505/256–0564) serves good
Mexican and American comfort food and presents jazz, bebop, and
other musicians in a cheery neighborhood bar near the University of
New Mexico.

Outpost Performance Space (✉ 210 Yale Blvd. SE, ☎ 505/268–0044)
programs an eclectic slate, from local nuevo-folk to techno, jazz, and
traveling East Indian ethnic.

Comedy Clubs

Laff's Comedy Caffé (✉ 3100-D Juan Tabo Blvd. NE, ☎ 505/296–5653)
serves up the live laughs (and dinner) Wednesday through Sunday.

Country-and-Western Clubs

Caravan East (✉ 7605 Central Ave. SE, ☎ 505/265–7877) has been
around for five decades. Two bands play nightly, and there's a free buffet and half-price drinks during happy hour, from 5 to 7.

Midnight Rodeo (✉ 4901 McLeod Rd. NE, ☎ 505/888–0100) is a one-
stop two-step complex with a racetrack-style dance floor, several bars,
and even boutiques. The happy-hour buffet, served on Friday and
Sunday between 5 and 7, is copious.

The Arts

Music

The **New Mexico Symphony Orchestra** (☎ 505/881–8999 or 800/
251–6676) plays pops, Beethoven, and, at Christmas, Handel's *Mes-
siah*. Some performances are at 2,000-seat Popejoy Hall; others are under
the stars at the Rio Grande Zoo Bandshell.

Popejoy Hall (✉ University of New Mexico campus, ☎ 505/277–4569
or 800/905–3315) presents concerts, from rock and pop to classical.

Opera

The Albuquerque Civic Light Opera Association has changed its name
to **Musical Theater Southwest** (☎ 505/262–9301) and is still one of the
largest community-based producers of musical theater in the country.
Performances take place at Popejoy Hall (☞ *above*) and at the **Hiland
Theater** (✉ 4804 Central Ave. SE, ☎ 505/265–9119).

Theater

Albuquerque Little Theater (✉ 224 San Pasquale Ave. SW, ☎ 505/242–
4750) is a nonprofit community troupe. Its staff of professionals teams

up with local volunteer talent to produce comedies, dramas, musicals, and mysteries. The company theater, across the street from Old Town, was built in 1936 and designed by John Gaw Meem. It contains an art gallery, a large lobby, and a cocktail lounge.

KiMo Theater (⊠ 423 Central Ave. NW, ☎ 505/764–1700), a 1927 Pueblo Deco movie palace, reopened late in 2000 after extensive renovations. The decorative ceiling has been restored, the seating custommade, and the proscenium arch re-created. Jazz, dance—everything from traveling road shows to local song-and-dance acts—might turn up here. Albuquerque native Vivian Vance of *I Love Lucy* fame once performed on the stage.

La Compania de Teatro de Albuquerque (☎ 505/242–7929), a bilingual theater company based at the KiMo Theater (☞ *above*), performs classic and contemporary plays in English and Spanish during April, October, and December. The company also appears at the South Broadway Cultural Center.

Rodey Theater (⊠ University of New Mexico, UNM Arts Center, ☎ 505/277–4402) stages student and professional plays and dance performances throughout the year, including the acclaimed annual Summerfest Festival of New Plays during July and the June Flamenco Festival.

OUTDOOR ACTIVITIES AND SPORTS

Albuquerque is blessed with an exceptional setting for outdoor sports, backed by a favorable if unpredictable climate. Usually 10°F warmer than Santa Fe's, Albuquerque's winter days are often mild enough for most outdoor activities. The Sandias tempt you with challenging mountain adventures; the Rio Grande and its thick forest, the Bosque, provide settings for additional wilderness pursuits.

Participant Sports

The **Albuquerque Cultural and Recreation Services Department** (⊠ 400 Marquette Ave. NW, ☎ 505/857–8669) maintains a diversified network of cultural and recreational programs. Among the city's assets are more than 20,000 acres of open space, 4 golf courses, 200 parks, 68 paved tracks for biking and jogging, as well as swimming pools, tennis courts, ball fields, playgrounds, and a shooting range.

Ballooning

The Kodak Albuquerque International Balloon Fiesta (☞ Spectator Sports, *below*) is a town highlight, but if you'd like to give ballooning a try, contact one of the many outfitters that run trips: **Rainbow Ryders** (⊠ 11520 San Bernadino NE, ☎ 505/293–0000 or 800/725–2477) or **World Balloon Corporation** (⊠ 4800 Eubank Blvd. NE, ☎ 505/293–6800 or 800/351–9588). The ride will set you back about $150.

Bicycling

Albuquerque has miles of bike lanes and trails crisscrossing and skirting the city. Not only is Albuquerque's Parks and Recreation Department aware of bikers' needs, but bike riding is heavily promoted as a means of cutting down on traffic congestion and pollution. The elaborately detailed **Metropolitan Albuquerque Bicycle Map** can be obtained free of charge by calling 505/768–3550. For information about mountain biking in national forest land around Albuquerque call the **Sandia Ranger Station** (☎ 505/281–3304).

Bikes can be rented at several locations, including **Rio Mountainsport** (⊠ 1210 Rio Grande Blvd. NW, ☎ 505/766–9970), which is convenient to Old Town, the Rio Grande Nature Center, and the Paseo de Bosque trail.

Bird-Watching

The Rio Grande Valley, one of the continent's major flyways, attracts many migratory bird species. For details about bird-watching events and outings, contact the local chapter of the **Sierra Club** (⊠ 207 San Pedro NE, ☎ 505/265–5506 ext. 4).

Good viewing locales include the **Rio Grande Nature Center** (☞ Elsewhere in Albuquerque *in* Exploring Albuquerque, *above*) and **Elena Gallegos/Albert Simms Park** (⊠ 1700 Tramway Loop NE, ☎ 505/857–8334 or 505/873–6620), a 640-acre reserve adjoining the Sandia Mountain Wilderness Area.

Golf

The Albuquerque Cultural and Recreation Services Department (☞ *above*) operates four public golf courses. The two best ones are listed below. All the courses are open from sunup to sundown; special discount rates go into effect for sundown play. Each course has a clubhouse and pro shop, where clubs and other equipment can be rented. Weekday play is on a first-come, first-served basis, but reservations are taken for weekend use. The city's **Golf Management Office** (⊠ 6401 Osuna Rd. NE, ☎ 505/888–8115) can provide more information.

Arroyo del Oso (⊠ 7001 Osuna Rd. NE, ☎ 505/884–7505) has an 18-hole, par-72 course. The greens fee is $15; an optional cart costs $10. There's also a 9-hole, par-36 course here.

The 18-hole, par-71 **Los Altos Golf Course** (☎ 9717 Copper Ave. NE, ☎ 505/298–1897), one of the Southwest's most popular facilities, has a greens fee of $15; an optional cart costs $13. The complex includes a driving range, grass tees, and a restaurant serving mainly New Mexican food.

The University of New Mexico has two public golf courses. **UNM North** (⊠ 2201 Tucker Rd. NE, between Stanford Ave. and University Blvd., ☎ 505/277–4146) is a first-class 9-hole, par-36 course on campus; **UNM South** (⊠ Rio Bravo Blvd. east of I–25, ☎ 505/277–4546) has an 18-hole, par-72 championship course, and a beginners' 3-hole regulation course. Both are open daily and have full-service pro shops, instruction, and snack bars. Greens fees range from $20 to $42, with higher fees, in the $70 range, for out-of-staters; optional carts cost $20.

Health Clubs

A day pass ($10) at the state-of-the-art **4th Street Fitness** (⊠ 1100 4th St. NW, ☎ 505/247–1947) entitles you to a one-on-one boxing session. Should the pummeling become too intense, you can head over to the on-site masseur for an additional fee.

Gold's Gym (⊠ 5001 Montgomery Blvd. NE, Suite 147, ☎ 505/881–8500) has free weights, a cardiovascular deck, and aerobics classes. Nonmembers pay $10 per day.

Liberty Gym (⊠ 2401 Jefferson St. NE, ☎ 505/884–8012) has weight-training equipment, free weights, and a cardiovascular area. The walk-in fee is $5.

Jogging

The Albuquerque Cultural and Recreation Services Department (☞ *above*) maintains a network of Designated Recreational Trails that joggers share with bicyclists.

Skiing

Sandia Peak Ski Area (✉ NM 536, ☎ 505/242–9133) contains novice, intermediate, and expert downhill trails. Snowboarding is welcome on all trails, and there is cross-country terrain as well, whenever snow is available.

Swimming

The city of Albuquerque has pools for lap and recreational swimming; the fee is $2. Indoor pools are at **Highland** (✉ 400 Jackson St. SE, ☎ 505/256–2096), **Los Altos** (✉ 10100 Lomas Blvd. NE, ☎ 505/291–6290), **Sandia** (✉ 7801 Candelaria Rd. NE, ☎ 505/291–6279), and **Valley** (✉ 1505 Candelaria Rd. NW, ☎ 505/761–4086).

Outdoor pools are open from Memorial Day to mid-August at **Wilson** (✉ 6000 Anderson Ave. SE, ☎ 505/256–2095), and **Montgomery** (✉ 5301 Palo Duro NE, ☎ 505/888–8123).

Tennis

Albuquerque's public parks contain nearly 140 courts, some of which are lighted for night play (until 10 PM). For information call the Albuquerque Cultural and Recreation Services Department (☞ *above*). In addition, the city operates three tennis complexes.

Albuquerque Tennis Complex (✉ 1903 Ave. Cesar Chavez SE, ☎ 505/848–1381) consists of 16 Laykold tennis courts and two racquetball-handball courts, which may be reserved by phone or in person; reservations are taken two days ahead at 10 AM. It costs $2.10 per hour to play at the complex, which is open from 8 AM to dusk weekdays.

Jerry Cline Tennis Complex (✉ Louisiana Blvd. at Constitution Ave., ☎ 505/256–2032) has 12 Laykold courts; 3 are lighted. There is no charge, and no reservations are needed.

Sierra Vista Tennis Complex (✉ 5001 Montano Rd. NW, ☎ 505/897–8819) has 10 tennis courts (2 Omni courts), 2 platform tennis courts, and an outdoor pool. Court reservations are taken two days ahead at 10 AM. It costs $2.10 per hour to play at the complex, which is open from 8 to 8 on weekdays and from 8 to 5 on weekends.

Also try **Highpoint Sports & Wellness Club** (✉ 4300 Landau Dr. NE, ☎ 505/293–5820), **Tanoan Country Club** (✉ 10801 Academy Rd. NE, ☎ 505/822–0455), and the **Tennis Club of Albuquerque** (✉ 2901 Indian School Rd. NE, ☎ 505/262–1691).

Spectator Sports

Ballooning

Mention hot-air ballooning to an enthusiast, and Albuquerque automatically comes to mind. The city's high altitude, mild climate, and steady but manageable winds are ideal for ballooning. But it's the "Albuquerque Box," created by the city's location against the Sandia Mountains, that makes this a great place to fly.

Albuquerque's long history of ballooning dates from 1882, when Professor Park A. Van Tassel, a saloon keeper, ascended in a balloon at the Territorial Fair. Albuquerque has become the hot-air capital of the world, partly because of the nine-day **Kodak Albuquerque International Balloon Fiesta** (✉ 8309 Washington Pl. NE, 87113, ☎ 505/821–1000, ✆), which began in 1972. The event, held during the first two weeks of October, is the largest hot-air-balloon gathering in the world. At the Special Shapes Rodeo, hundreds of unusual balloons, including depictions of the old lady who lived in the shoe, the pink pig, and dozens of other fanciful characters from fairy tales and popular culture, soar high above the crowds, which number more than 1 million. There are night flights, obstacle races, and many other surprising balloon events. The entrance fee to the grounds is $4. Book your hotel far in advance if you plan to attend, and note that hotel rates also rise during the fiesta.

Basketball

Albuquerque now has an International Basketball League team, the New Mexico Slam. The team plays at the **Albuquerque Convention Center** (⊠ 401 2nd St. NW, ☎ 505/924–2255) with its 6,200 seating capacity.

It's hard to beat the excitement of a home basketball game at the **University of New Mexico** (⊠ University Ave. at Ave. Cesar Chavez, ☎ 505/925–5627 or 800/905–3315), when 18,000 rabid fans crowd into the school's arena, "the Pit," from November to March.

Drag Racing

Albuquerque National Speedway (⊠ 5700 Bobby Foster Rd., ☎ 505/299–9478) is the state's only sanctioned National Hot Rod Association facility. Races are held year-round, with five major events a year.

Football

The New Mexico Lobos of the **University of New Mexico** (☎ 505/925–5627 or 800/905–3315) plays at 30,000-seat University Stadium in the fall.

Hockey

The **New Mexico Scorpions** (☎ 505/881–7825) play in the Western Professional Hockey League. The home ice of the Scorps is at **Tingley Coliseum** (⊠ New Mexico State Fairgrounds, Central Ave. and Louisiana Blvd., ☎ 505/881–7825).

SHOPPING

As is the case in other large Western cities, Albuquerque's main shopping areas and malls are scattered throughout the community. Nob Hill, the trendiest district, stretches for seven blocks along Central Avenue from Girard Boulevard to Washington Street. Neon-lit boutiques, galleries, and performing-arts spaces encourage foot traffic day and night. Old Town, at the corner of Central and Rio Grande Boulevard, has the city's largest concentration of one-of-a-kind retail shops, selling clothing, home accessories, and Mexican imports. Also here are a slew of galleries, many exhibiting Native American art. Most places are open from 10 to 9 on weekdays, 10 to 6 on Saturday, and noon to 6 on Sunday.

Art Galleries

Amapola Gallery (⊠ Old Town, 2045 S. Plaza St. NW, ☎ 505/242–4311), west of the Plaza near Rio Grande Boulevard, is one of the largest co-op galleries in New Mexico. It has a brick courtyard and an indoor space, both brimming with pottery, paintings, textiles, carvings, baskets, jewelry, and other items.

Andrew Nagen (⊠ 222 Andrews La., Corrales, ☎ 505/898–5285) has been buying, selling, and appraising antique Navajo, Mexican, Rio Grande, and Pueblo textiles since 1976. His shop is open by appointment only.

Concetta D. Gallery (⊠ First Plaza Galeria, 20 1st Plaza NW, Suite 29, ☎ 505/243–5066) carries works by early Santa Fe and Taos artists, as well as contemporary regional artists such as Rod Goebel, Walter Chapman, Lincoln Fox, Don Brackett, Clifford Fragua, Ramon Kelley, Joe Horton, Carol McIlroy, Morris Ripple, and Julian Roble.

DSG (✉ 3011 Monte Vista Blvd. NE, ☎ 505/266–7751 or 800/474–7751), owned by John Cacciatore, handles works by leading regional artists, including Frank McCulloch, Carol Hoy, Leo Neufeld, John Rise, Jane Abrams, Nancy Kozikowski, and Angus MacPherson.

Mariposa Gallery (✉ Old Town, 113 Romero St. NW, ☎ 505/842–9097; Monte Vista, 3011 Monte Vista Blvd. SE, ☎ 505/265–7966; Nob Hill, 3500 Central Ave. SE, ☎ 505/268–6828) sells contemporary fine crafts, including jewelry, sculptural glass, works in mixed media and clay, and fiber arts. The changing exhibits focus on upcoming artists. The display of *Dia de los Muertos* (Day of the Dead) objects in October is always worth a look. Mariposa Gallery now has two additional locations.

516 Magnifico Art Space (✉ 516 Central Ave. SW, ☎ 505/242–8244) exhibits all styles of art, from traditional to contemporary, in all media, with a primary focus on the work of New Mexico artists.

Richard Levy Gallery (✉ 514 Central Ave. SW, ☎ 505/766–9888) carries works on paper (including photography) and small sculpture by major regional artists, including Clinton Adams, Thomas Barrow, Ed Haddaway, Frederick Hammersley, Patrick Nagatani, Ed Ruscha, and Richard Tuttle.

Weems Gallery (✉ 2801-M Eubank Blvd. NE, ☎ 505/293–6133; Old Town, 303 Romero St. NW, ☎ 505/764–0302) has paintings, pottery, sculpture, jewelry, weaving, stained glass, and original-design clothes.

Specialty Stores

Antiques

Antique Specialty Mall (✉ 4516 Central Ave. SE, ☎ 505/268–8080) is a center for collectibles and antiques. The emphasis is on memorabilia from the early 1880s to the 1950s. (When the set designers for the television miniseries *Lonesome Dove* needed props, they came here.) Items for sale include Art Deco and Art Nouveau objects, Depression-era glass, Native American goods, quilts and linens, vintage clothes, and Western memorabilia.

Cowboys & Indians (✉ 4000 Central Ave. SE, ☎ 505/255–4054) carries Native American and cowboy art and artifacts.

Books

Page One (✉ 11018 Montgomery Blvd. NE, ☎ 505/294–2026), frequently voted the best bookstore in Albuquerque, is the largest independent bookstore in the state. Besides books of general interest, it sells technical and professional titles, maps, globes, racing forms, and 150 out-of-state and foreign newspapers. Book signings, poetry readings, and children's events are frequently scheduled.

Clothing

Wear It! (✉ 107 Amherst Dr. SE, ☎ 505/266–7764) sells stylish contemporary clothing and accessories.

Western Warehouse (✉ 6210 San Mateo Blvd. NE, ☎ 505/883–7161) will outfit you in Western style with boots, hats, belts, and vests.

Gifts

Beeps (✉ Nob Hill Shopping Center, 3500 Central Ave. SE, ☎ 505/262–1900), a Nob Hill favorite, carries cards, T-shirts, and novelty items.

Home Furnishings

A (✉ 3500 Central Ave. SE, ☎ 505/266–2222) is a Nob Hill stop for housewares, soaps, candles, body-care products, and jewelry.

El Paso Import Co. (✉ 3500 Central Ave. SE, ☎ 505/265–1160) carries distressed and "peely-paint" antique-looking chests and tables loaded with character. If you love the "shabby chic" look, or want more Southwest-style in your home, head over to this Nob Hill furniture shop.

Moderno (✉ 113 Carlisle Ave. SE, ☎ 505/254–0447) stocks merchandise for contemporary living: handmade steel beds, chairs, mobiles, and modern, locally produced art, rugs, and jewelry.

Objects of Desire (✉ 3300 Central SE, ☎ 505/232–3088) is the place to find that special lamp or table from a whimsical and worldly collection of furnishings that appeal to individualized tastes.

Mexican Imports

Jackalope (✉ Hwy. 44, I–25W, Bernalillo, ☎ 505/867–9813) galloped over from its famous Santa Fe location and settled down in a second home that's acres of imported pottery, crafts, table linens, jewelry, clothing, glass, tinwork, and furniture from Mexico as well as India, Eastern Europe, and China. About 20 mi north of town, this is a good place to hunt for gifts and a great place to spend an hour (at least) browsing.

La Piñata (✉ Old Town, No. 2 Patio Market, ☎ 505/242–2400) specializes in piñatas and papier-mâché products of all kinds.

Native American Arts and Crafts

Adobe Gallery (✉ 413 Romero St. NW, ☎ 505/243–8485) specializes in historic and contemporary art by Southwestern Native Americans—Pueblo pottery, Hopi katsinas, and Navajo rugs, blankets, and paintings. The shop is in a historic *terrones* adobe (cut from the ground rather than formed from mud and dried) homestead that dates from 1878. The shop carries many books about Southwestern Native Americans.

Andrews Pueblo Pottery (✉ 303 Romero St. NW, Suite 116, ☎ 505/243–0414) carries a terrific selection of Pueblo pottery, fetishes, katsina dolls, and baskets for the beginning and seasoned collector.

Bien Mur Indian Market Center (✉ I–23 7 Tramway Rd. NE, ☎ 505/821–5400) in Sandia Pueblo showcases the best of the best in regional Indian rugs, jewelry, and crafts of all kinds. You can feel very secure about what you purchase at this trading post, and prices are fair for what you get.

Gertrude Zachary ✉ 1501 Lomas Blvd. NW, ☎ 505/247–4442) dazzles with its selection of Indian jewelry. This may be your best place to shop for a bargain in a good bracelet or ring. Locals buy here, too.

Nizhoni Moses, Ltd. (✉ 326 San Felipe St. NW, ☎ 505/842–1808) stocks Pueblo pottery, including the black earthenware pottery of San Ildefonso, as well as the work of potters from Acoma, Santa Clara, Isleta, and Zía. Rare Zuñi and Navajo jewelry is on display, as are Navajo weavings from 1900 to the present.

Skip Maisel Wholesale Indian Jewelry and Crafts (✉ 510 Central Ave. SW, ☎ 505/242–6526), in business since 1905, has been at this location since 1929. Even its exterior is a piece of art—check out the murals in the entryway alcove. Inside are quality Native American arts and crafts at wholesale prices.

Tanner Chaney Gallery (✉ 323 Romero St. NW, No. 5, ☎ 505/247–2242 or 800/444–2242) is housed in the Territorial-style new plaza in Old Town. The three showrooms contain Native American jewelry, sculpture, contemporary and historic pottery, baskets, incredible Navajo weavings, and many books on the Southwest.

Shopping Malls

Coronado Center (✉ Louisiana Blvd. NE at Menaul Blvd. NE, ☎ 505/881–4600) has Macy's, JCPenney, Mervyn's, and Sears department stores, along with 160 specialty shops and a food court.

Cottonwood Mall (✉ Coors Blvd. at Coors Bypass, ☎ 505/899–7467), Albuquerque's largest mall, contains such department stores as Dillard's, JCPenney, and Montgomery Ward. Williams-Sonoma is among the 136 specialty shops. There's a food court and a multiplex cinema.

First Plaza Galeria (✉ 20 First Plaza, ☎ 505/242–3446), near the convention center, has gift and clothing stores, a health club, restaurants, a post office, galleries, and a beauty shop.

Winrock Center (✉ Louisiana Blvd. off I–40, ☎ 505/888–3038) has Dillard's and Montgomery Ward department stores, plus Oshman's SuperSports USA, Bed Bath & Beyond, and 17 restaurants, from fast food to fancy fare.

SIDE TRIP ALONG THE TURQUOISE TRAIL

A scenic drive etched out nearly a quarter century ago and still well traveled is the Turquoise Trail, which follows an old route between Albuquerque and Santa Fe that's dotted with ghost towns now being restored by writers, artists, and other urban refugees. This 70 mi of piñon-studded mountain back road is a gentle roller coaster of panoramic views of the Ortiz, Jemez, and Sangre de Cristo mountains. It's believed that 2,000 years ago Indians mined turquoise in these hills. The Spanish took up turquoise mining in the 16th century, and the practice continued into the early 20th century, with Tiffany's removing a fair share of the semiprecious stone. In addition, gold, silver, tin, lead, and coal have been mined here. There's plenty of opportunity for picture-taking and picnicking along the way. The pace is slow, the talk is about the weather, and Albuquerque might as well be on another planet. The entire loop of this trip takes a day, the drive up the Sandia Crest a half day. Sites farther west are described *in* Chapter 6.

Tijeras

7½ mi from Albuquerque east on I–40 and south on NM 337.

Begin your tour of the Turquoise Trail and the Sandia Mountains with a quick, educational stop in the Tijeras area.

☪ At the **Sandia Ranger Station** you can pick up pamphlets and maps, and—if there are enough kids in the audience—witness a fire-prevention program with a *Smokey the Bear* movie. Tours head to the nearby **fire lookout tower** and **Tijeras Pueblo ruins.** Call ahead to reserve a tour. ✉ *11776 NM 337, south of I–40,* ☎ *505/281–3304.* ☒ *Free.* ☉ *Weekdays 8–5, weekends 8:30–noon and 12:30–5.*

☪ Carmen Sanchez, the Goat Lady, tends to the herd at **Sierra Goat Farms.** Ms. Sanchez delights in showing children how to milk the animals and care for them. The farm has plenty of outdoor grills and picnic tables, and goat cheese, cheesecake, and chocolate are for sale. You can pet the baby goats, as well as feed them. ✉ *NM 337 at Cardinal Rd., 15 mi south of I–40,* ☎ *505/281–5061.* ☒ *$1, free Sun.* ☉ *Farms Tues.–Fri. 2–4, weekends 1–4; cheese room Tues.–Sun. 10–5.*

Sandia Park

13 mi northeast of Albuquerque, 7 mi north of Tijeras. From Tijeras, take I–40 east and exit north on the Turquoise Trail (NM 14); proceed 6 mi and turn left onto NM 536.

☾ The **Tinkertown Museum** contains a world of miniature carved-wood characters. Owner Ross Ward has spent more than 35 years carving and collecting the 1,200 figures that populate this museum, including an animated miniature Western village, a Boot Hill cemetery, and a circus exhibit from the 1940s. Ragtime piano music, a 40-ft sailboat, and a life-size general store are other highlights. This is one attraction guaranteed to please all ages. The latest addition is Ward's recently completed "mystery doll house." And don't miss the "bottle wall," made of 12,000 bottles pressed into cement. ✉ *121 Sandia Crest Rd./NM 536,* ☎ *505/281–5233.* ☞ *$2.50.* ☉ *Apr.–Oct., daily 9–6.*

Sandia Crest

25 mi from Albuquerque; east on I–40, north on NM 14, and east on NM 536.

For awesome views of Albuquerque and half of New Mexico, take the side road to the Sandia Crest via the "backside" on NM 536, which ascends through the Cibola National Forest. At the 10,678-ft summit, explore the foot trails along the rim (particularly in summer) and take in the views, which include a close-up view of the "Steel Forest," the nearby cluster of radio and television towers. During the summer, a chairlift operates Thursday through Sunday, 10–4 and costs $7 round-trip. Mountain bikes may be rented at the top for $35 and a $350 deposit. Call **Sandia Ski Area** (☎ 505/242–9052) for information. Always bring an extra layer of clothing, even in summer.

If you are in need of refreshments or are searching for some inexpensive souvenirs, visit the **Sandia Crest House Gift Shop and Restaurant** (☎ 505/243–0605), on the rim of the crest.

Golden

25 mi northeast of Albuquerque. From the Sandia Crest, take NM 536 south to NM 14 north, the Turquoise Trail; in 20 mins or so you'll coast into Golden.

Golden, the site of the first gold rush (in 1825) west of the Mississippi, has a rock shop and a mercantile store. The rustic adobe church and graveyard are popular with photographers. Be aware that locals are very protective of this area and aren't known to warm up to strangers. Should you have any questions about the area, **La Casita**, a gift shop at the north end of the village, serves as the unofficial chamber of commerce.

Madrid

37 mi northeast of Albuquerque, 12 mi northeast of Golden on NM 14.

Totally abandoned when its coal mine closed in the 1950s, Madrid is slowly being rebuilt. The entire town was offered for sale for $250,000 back then, but there were no takers. Finally, in the early 1970s, a few artists fleeing big cities settled in and began the work of restoration. Weathered houses and old company stores have been repaired and turned into shops, some of which are definitely worth a visit. The big events here are Old Timers Days on July 4th weekend, and the Christmas open house, held weekends in December, when galleries and studios are open and the famous Madrid Christmas lights twinkle brightly. Sunday summer jazz concerts in the ballpark are also popular.

ⓒ Madrid's **Old Coal Mine Museum** is a remnant of a once-flourishing industry. Children can explore the old tunnel, climb aboard a 1900 steam train, and poke through antique buildings full of marvelous relics. Tickets for the museum are available at the Mine Shaft Tavern out front. On weekends between Memorial Day and Labor Day you can cheer the heroes and hiss the villains of the old-fashioned melodramas performed at the **Engine House Theater.** The theater, inside a converted roundhouse machine shop, has a full-size steam train that comes chugging onto the stage. ⊠ *Old Coal Mine Museum, 2846 NM 14,* ☎ *505/ 438–3780.* 🄼 *Museum $3, melodrama $9.* ☉ *Daily 9:30–dusk.*

Dining and Lodging

$ ✕ **Java Junction.** Here's where the locals—many of whom look like and are aging hippies—congregate for their morning brew and socializing. ⊠ *2855 Hwy. 14,* ☎ *505/438–2772. MC, V.*

$ ✕ **Mama Lisa's No Pity Cafe.** Sit at an outdoor table and watch the world go by in the company of a fresh-baked scone, fruit pie, or healthy sandwich. The café is open 11–5. ⊠ *2859 Hwy. 14,* ☎ *no phone. No credit cards. Closed Tues.*

$$ 🛏 **Heart Seed B&B.** Stay in a mountain retreat only a half-hour drive from Santa Fe. Simple but far from rustic luxury awaits, with a sensational view of the Sangre de Cristo Mountains from the hot tub deck. Among the amenities are access to 80 mi of hiking trails, hearty home-cooked breakfasts, and spa and massage treatments. About a mile north of Madrid, follow the sign to the Heart Seed, 5 mi up an unpaved road. ⊠ *Hwy. 14, 63 Corazon de Oro Rd. (Box 6019), Santa Fe 87502,* ☎ *505/471–7026. 12 rooms. Hot tub, spa. MC, V. BP.*

Shopping

The town of Madrid has only one street, so the shops are easy to find.

Maya Jones Imports (☎ 505/473–3641) stocks Guatemalan imports and one-of-a-kind creations, plus a 1934 soda fountain that pumps out phosphates, malteds, and sundaes.

Primitiva (☎ 505/471–7904) carries handmade Mexican furniture and imports from around the world.

Tapestry Gallery (☎ 505/471–0194) stocks hand-loomed knits and rugs, as well as wearable art and locally produced silver and turquoise jewelry.

Cerrillos

40 mi northeast of Albuquerque, 3 mi northeast of Madrid on NM 14.

Cerrillos was a boomtown in the 1880s—its mines brimmed with gold, silver, and turquoise, and eight newspapers, four hotels, and 21 taverns flourished. When the mines went dry the town went bust. More recently, Cerrillos has served as the backdrop for feature-film and television Westerns, among them *Young Guns* and *Lonesome Dove.* Today, it might easily be mistaken for a ghost town, which it's been well on the way to becoming for decades. Time has left its streets dry, dusty, and almost deserted.

Casa Grande (⊠ 17 Waldo, ☎ 505/438–3008), a 21-room adobe (several rooms of which are part of a shop), has a small museum ($1) with a display of early mining exhibits. There's also a petting zoo ($1) and a scenic overlook. Casa Grande is open daily from 8 AM to sunset.

Pack rats and browsers alike ought not to miss the **What-Not Shop** (⊠ 15B First St., ☎ 505/471–2744), a venerable secondhand/antiques shop of a half-century's standing packed floor to ceiling with Indian pottery, cut glass, rocks, political buttons, old postcards, clocks, and who knows what else.

Santo Domingo Pueblo

40 mi northeast of Albuquerque. From Cerrillos, take NM 14 south 9 mi and turn right (west) on NM 301 for about 12 mi to I–25; cross under I–25 onto NM 22 and proceed 4½ mi to the pueblo. To return to Albuquerque from the pueblo, take NM 14 south to I–40 west.

Santo Domingo Pueblo craftspeople sell their outstanding *heishi* (shell) jewelry and pottery, along with other traditional arts and crafts, all year long. But the Pueblo's Labor Day Arts and Crafts Fair, a three-day event, brings out artists and visitors in full force. The Corn Dance is one of the most colorful and dramatic of pueblo ceremonial events. Held in honor of St. Dominic, the pueblo's patron saint, the August 4 festivities attract more than 2,000 dancers, clowns, singers, and drummers. Painter Georgia O'Keeffe supposedly said the Corn Dance was one of the great events in her life. Santo Domingo Pueblo is not part of the Turquoise Trail. ⊠ *Off NM 22, 4½ mi west of I–25,* ☎ *505/465–2214.* ☞ *Donations encouraged. Still and video cameras, tape recorders, and sketching materials prohibited.* ☉ *Daily dawn–dusk.*

SIDE TRIPS TO PUEBLOS

When Francisco Vásquez de Coronado arrived in what is now New Mexico in 1540, he found a dozen or so villages along the Rio Grande in the ancient province of Tiguex, between what is now Bernalillo to the north of Albuquerque and Isleta to the south. Of those, only Sandia and Isleta survive today. Santo Domingo Pueblo is covered under the Turquoise Trail (☞ *above*). The Salinas Pueblo Missions ruins, about 65 mi southeast of Albuquerque, remain a striking example of the Spanish penchant for building churches on sites inhabited by native people.

Isleta Pueblo

13 mi south of Albuquerque, I–25 (to Exit 213) to NM 47 and follow signs.

Of the pueblos in New Mexico when the Spanish first arrived, Isleta Pueblo is one of two Tiwa-speaking communities left in the middle Rio Grande Valley. Isleta was one of the few pueblos that didn't participate in the Pueblo Revolt of 1680, during which Isleta was abandoned. Some of the residents fled New Mexico with the Spanish to El Paso, where their descendants live to this day on a reservation called Ysleta del Sur (☞ El Paso *in* Chapter 8). Other members went to live with the Hopi of Arizona but eventually returned and rebuilt the pueblo.

Facing the quiet plaza is Isleta's church, **St. Augustine,** built in 1629. One of the oldest churches in New Mexico, it has thick adobe walls, a viga-crossed ceiling, and simple interior decor. Legend has it that the ground beneath the floor has the odd propensity to push church and community figures buried under the floor back up out of the ground; bodies have been reburied several times, only to emerge again.

Polychrome pottery with red-and-black designs on a white background is the specialty here. The pueblo celebrates its feast days on August 28 and September 4, both in honor of St. Augustine. The tribal government maintains picnicking and camping facilities, several fishing ponds, a casino, and an 18-hole golf course. Baking in Isleta is done in the centuries-old fashion, in beehive ovens beside adobe homes bedecked with crimson chiles. ⊠ *Tribal Rd. 40,* ☎ *505/869–3111 for pueblo; 505/869–2614 for casino; 505/869–0950 for Isleta Eagle Championship Golf Course.* ☞ *Free. Camera use restricted; only church may be photographed.*

Camping

⚠ **Isleta Lakes and Recreation Area.** Near the pueblo on the Isleta Reservation, this area covered with cottonwoods contains three fishing lakes full of trout, bass, and catfish. Facilities include rest rooms, hot showers, and LP gas. Tent sites are $12, hookups $15. ✉ *NM 47 south of I–25's Exit 215, Isleta 87022,* ☎ *505/877–0370. 40 RV sites, 100 tent sites. Grocery, basketball, softball, fishing, coin laundry. MC, V.*

Salinas Pueblo Missions National Monument

58 mi (to Punta Agua/Quarai) from Albuquerque, east on I–40 (to Tijeras Exit), south on NM 337 and NM 55; 23 mi from Punta Agua to Abó, south on NM 55, west (at Mountainair) on U.S. 60, and north on NM 513; 34 mi from Punta Agua to Gran Quivira, south on NM 55.

Salinas Pueblo Missions National Monument is made up of three sites—**Quarai, Abó, and Gran Quivira**—each with the ruins of a 17th-century Spanish-colonial Franciscan missionary church and an associated pueblo. The sites represent the convergence of two Native American peoples, the Anasazi and the Mogollon, who lived here for centuries before the Spanish arrived. Quarai, the nearest to Albuquerque, was a flourishing Tiwa pueblo whose inhabitants' pottery, weaving, and basket-making techniques were quite refined. On the fringe of the Great Plains, all three of the Salinas pueblos were vulnerable to raids by nomadic Plains Indians. Quarai was abandoned about 50 years after its mission church, **San Purísima Concepción de Cuarac,** was built in 1630. The church's sandstone walls still rise 40 ft out of the earth. At Abó are the remains of the three-story church of San Gregorio and a large unexcavated pueblo. (The masonry style at Abó bore some similarity to that at Chaco Canyon, which has led some archaeologists to speculate that the pueblo was built by people who left the Chaco Canyon area.) A video about Salinas Pueblo can be viewed at Gran Quivira, which contains two churches and some excavated Native American structures. The monument headquarters is in the town of Mountainair. ✉ *201 Broadway, at U.S. 60, Mountainair,* ☎ *505/847–2585.* 🎟 *Free.* ☉ *Memorial Day–Labor Day, daily 9–7; Labor Day–Memorial Day, daily 9–5.*

ALBUQUERQUE A TO Z

Arriving and Departing

By Bus

Texas, New Mexico & Oklahoma Coaches (☎ 505/243–4435 or 800/231–2222), affiliated with Greyhound Lines, provides service to Albuquerque from cities in the Southwest and beyond.

To get from the **bus station** (✉ 300 2nd St. SW, ☎ 505/243–4435 or 800/231–2222) to the center of the city, phone for a taxi or walk south on 2nd Street two blocks to catch a municipal bus.

By Car

The main routes into Albuquerque are I–25 from points north and south and I–40 from points east and west.

By Plane

Albuquerque International Sunport (✉ 2200 Sunport Blvd. SE, off I–25, ☎ 505/842–4366), the major gateway to New Mexico, is 5 mi south of downtown. Car rentals, air taxis, and bus shuttles are readily available at the airport, which is 65 mi southwest of Santa Fe and 130 mi south of Taos. The Albuquerque Convention and Visitors Bureau maintains an information center, open daily between 9:30 and 8, on the lower level of the airport near the escalator.

AIRPORT TRANSFERS

The trip into town from the airport takes about 10 to 15 minutes by car. Taxis, available at clearly marked stands, charge about $7 (plus 50¢ for each additional rider). Sun Tran buses (☞ *below*) stop at the sunburst signs every 30 minutes; the fare is 75¢. Some hotels provide shuttle service to and from the airport. You can also rent a limousine (☞ *below*). Another option is the **Airport Express** shuttle (☎ 505/765–1234), which costs less than $10 to most downtown locations.

By Train

Amtrak (☎ 800/872–7245) operates the *Southwest Chief* daily between Chicago and Los Angeles. The train stops at **Albuquerque Station** (✉ 214 1st St. SW, ☎ 505/842–9650).

Getting Around

Albuquerque sprawls out in all directions, so with the exception of Old Town you'll need transportation to get wherever you're going.

By Bus

Sun Tran (☎ 505/843–9200) buses provide good coverage of the city for residents, but the substantial distances between some of the major sights make public transportation impractical. The fare is 75¢ (exact change is required; fare box will accept a $1 bill, but no change is returned). Bus stops are well marked with the line's sunburst signs. There is no service on some major holidays.

By Car

Getting around Albuquerque is not difficult by car, but the town's drivers are notoriously casual, rarely signaling or showing consideration if you are trying to change lanes. Use extra caution at intersections, where drivers frequently scream through yellow and even red lights. A dependable east–west route through the city is Central Avenue, but you can also rely on a few one-way streets: take Coal Avenue east toward the mountains or Lead Avenue west toward the volcanoes. To go north–south, San Mateo Boulevard and Wyoming Boulevard are good bets. Stay off the interstates (I–25 and I–40) during evening rush hour, which begins about 3 PM.

Vacant parking spaces are particularly scarce in the University of New Mexico area, where even paid parking is limited, so it's best to arrive early if attending an event. Don't exceed the posted speed limit, regardless of what you see other drivers doing: police personnel have ticket quotas. You can turn right on a red light (or left at intersecting one-way streets) after coming to a complete stop unless a sign prohibiting such a turn is posted. For information about renting a car, *see* Car Rental *in* Smart Travel Tips A to Z.

By Limousine

Rates start at $55 to $60 per hour for standard limousines and can reach $95 per hour for stretch limos. There is usually a two-hour minimum. Call for special airport shuttle rates. Companies include **Imperial Limo** (☎ 505/298–9944), **Classic Limousine** (☎ 505/247–4000), and **Dream Limousine** (☎ 505/884–6464).

By Taxi

Taxis are metered in Albuquerque, and service is around the clock. The rates run $3.80 for the first mile, $1.80 for each mile thereafter, and 50¢ for each additional passenger. Contact **Albuquerque Cab** (☎ 505/883–4888) or **Yellow Cab** (☎ 505/247–8888).

By Trolley

The **Sun Trolley** (☎ 505/843–9200) runs daily (except some holidays) past many downtown attractions between 9:30 and 8:30. The fare is 75¢ each time you board.

Guided Tours

Orientation

Gray Line of Albuquerque (✉ 800 Rio Grande Blvd. NW, Suite 22, ☎ 505/242–3880 or 800/256–8991) conducts daily tours, among them a four-hour swing through town that includes historic landmarks, downtown, Kirtland Air Force Base, and the Indian Pueblo Cultural Center.

Special-Interest

Gray Line (☞ Orientation, *above*) operates tours to Acoma Pueblo, the Anasazi cliff dwellings at Bandelier National Monument, and other Native American sites.

International Universities (✉ 1101 Tijeras Ave. NW, ☎ 505/246–2233 or 800/547–5678) conducts fascinating educational seminars and excursions (for groups only) that focus on the culture and history of New Mexico, including Indian pueblos, Santa Fe, and the Turquoise Trail.

Walking

The **Albuquerque Museum** (☎ 505/243–7255) leads hour-long historical walks through Old Town at 11 AM except Monday from mid-March to mid-December. The tour is free and available on a first-come, first-served basis, so arrive early in the museum lobby.

Contacts and Resources

Dentists

Dentist referrals (☎ 505/260–7333).

Emergencies

Presbyterian Hospital (✉ 1100 Central Ave. SE, ☎ 505/841–1111). **University Hospital** (✉ 2211 Lomas Blvd. NE, ☎ 505/272–2411).

24-Hour Pharmacies

Walgreens (✉ 6201 Central Ave. NE, ☎ 505/255–5511; 5001 Montgomery NE, ☎ 505/881–5050).

Road Conditions, Time, and Temperature

New Mexico Road Conditions (☎ 800/432–4269). **Time and temperature** (☎ 505/247–1611).

Visitor Information

The **Albuquerque Convention and Visitors Bureau** (✉ 20 1st Plaza NW, Suite 601, 87125, ☎ 505/842–9918 or 800/284–2282, ⊛) is open Monday–Friday, 8–5. To find out about current events taking place around town, you can call 800/284–2282 around the clock.

State Information Center (✉ Indian Pueblo Cultural Center, 2401 12th St. NW, 87107, ☎ 505/843–7270).

University of New Mexico Information Center (✉ 1700 Las Lomas NE, 87131, ☎ 505/277–1989).

The **Public Lands Interpretive Association** (✉ 6501 4th St. NW, Suite I, 87107, ☎ 877/851–8946 or 505/277–9498, ⊛) provides information related to public lands (both federal and state) and operates a bookstore carrying natural history books, guidebooks, maps, and educational books and toys.

6 NORTHWESTERN NEW MEXICO

Roads branch out north and west from Albuquerque like the roots of a tree, to the ruins of Anasazi civilization and to their descendants' pueblos, which have survived time and change. Journey through red-rock canyons that shelter ancient hamlets or to high, fortresslike plateaus crowned by Native American villages, and you'll encounter cultures whose art, architecture, spirituality, and knowledge of nature have ensured their existence for millennia.

By Sharon
Niederman

Updated by
Andrew Collins

W HEN A NEW MEXICAN SAYS HE OR SHE IS "on Indian time," the expression is usually meant as a joke. But when you leave Albuquerque or Santa Fe behind and wind your way through the red canyons of northwestern New Mexico's desert plateau, you do seem to enter a place impervious to the small demands of time-keeping. The enormous sweep of land and sky and its mysterious silence conjure the spirits of those who lived here long before recorded history. Standing on the edge of a sandstone cliff overlooking the San Juan River, entering the restored Great Kiva at the Aztec Ruins, or studying the pattern of a handwoven Navajo rug may give you insight into cultures past and present that honor conditions and cycles dictated by nature.

The powerful Indian spirit dominates this stark countryside as it always has. Specifics about the Anasazi people, who built great cities and roads in northwestern New Mexico and environs 1,000 and more years ago, have been revealed gradually through the discoveries of archaeologists. This region is today dominated by the Navajo people in the northwest and the Pueblo people—who have descended from the Navajo's "ancient enemies," which translates literally to "Anasazi"— closer to the Rio Grande. From the 19th century on, generations of traders, soldiers, homesteaders, and prospectors made this area their home as well. The two largest cities, Gallup and Farmington, are the legacy of these later arrivals. Gallup remains the capital of Indian art and jewelry, and Farmington, an agricultural center for more than a century, is a hub of energy exploration.

Pleasures and Pastimes

Arts and Crafts
A piece of handmade Indian pottery is among the best souvenirs of a visit to northwestern New Mexico. When you tour the Acoma Pueblo you'll find vessels of all shapes and sizes displayed outside individual artists' homes. At other pueblos potters sell their works in small studios or at outdoor stalls, usually happy to discuss the design traditions with you.

Dining
Fast-food and familiar franchise restaurants thrive in this region, but there are some reputable homegrown establishments. As elsewhere in New Mexico, the specialty is the chile—red and green—but also Western favorites like rib-eye steak and barbecue pork and chicken. Other local specialties include Navajo fry bread (not unlike a sopaipilla, served plain or topped with honey, beans, chile, or powdered sugar), tacos, and mutton stew such as you would be served at a pueblo's feast day. Delicious bread and pies, baked in beehive-shape outdoor *hornos* (ovens), are sold at roadside stands at some pueblos.

Lodging
Farmington, Grants, and Gallup are well supplied with chain motels, while Chama and Cuba have a few decent independently owned motels; there are also several appealing B&Bs in the region. You should have no problem finding a room, but book in advance if attending a special event.

Outdoor Activities and Sports
No question about it, fishing is a chief lure (pardon the pun) of the Four Corners—near Farmington. The San Juan River is fishable year-round; serious fisherfolk report some of their best experiences in winter. The large trout (up to 2 ft or more) that swim the San Juan provide exceptional catches. Bluewater Lake State Park, between Grants and Gallup, also yields good trout and catfish angling and is popular for

boating, swimming, and waterskiing. Hikers and mountain bikers share numerous trails in the region. The 3-mi hike along the San Juan River at Navajo Lake State Park is especially beautiful.

Exploring Northwestern New Mexico

This region covers an immense territory—give yourself five to seven days for a reasonably thorough exploration. Begin by heading west out of Albuquerque on I–40, planning a night or two in the Indian Country, before heading north toward Farmington for another night in the Four Corners region. From here opt for a night in Chama before heading south down through the Abiquiu area. Spend your last night near here or cut over to Cuba—either way tour Chaco Canyon your final morning, leaving the Jemez region for last. If you're daunted by squeezing so much into a short period, remember that it's easy to visit Acoma, Grants, Bernalillo, Jemez, and Abiquiu at other times as day trips from Albuquerque or Santa Fe, and Chama as a day trip from Taos. Some folks tackle Chaco as a day trip from the Rio Grande Valley—but it's far more practical to spend the night closer by, if not in Cuba than Abiquiu, Farmington, or even Grants or Gallup (the latter towns being relatively near Chaco's southern entrance).

Great Itineraries

IF YOU HAVE 2 OR 3 DAYS

The only way to tour this region adequately in two days is if you're incorporating your trip into a journey west into Arizona (via Gallup or Farmington), northwest into Utah (via Farmington), or north into Colorado (via Chama or Farmington). In just three days, however, you can make a nice loop of the region's top sites: drive west from Albuquerque on I–40, stopping in **Acoma Pueblo** ② for a couple hours before continuing west to ☷ **Gallup** ⑦. Spend the late afternoon shopping the old trading posts there, have dinner at Earl's, and stay overnight at the atmospheric El Rancho. On day two, head north on NM 371 to ☷ **Farmington** ⑧, stopping for a brief ramble through the **Bisti Wilderness Area.** If you like to fish or hike, head straight to the **San Juan River.** Otherwise, tour **Salmon Ruins** ⑨ and, in **Aztec** ⑩, the **Aztec Ruins National Monument and Museum.** Spend the final day at **Chaco Culture National Historical Park** ⑰.

IF YOU HAVE 5 TO 7 DAYS

In five to seven days you can get a real sense for the past and present of northwestern New Mexico. On day one, drive west on I–40 to **Acoma Pueblo** ② and then to the museums in ☷ **Grants** ③. The next day loop down along NM 53 for short hikes at the **Ice Cave and Bandera Volcano** ④ and **El Morro National Monument** ⑤, before stopping at ☷ **Zuñi Pueblo** ⑥ en route to ☷ **Gallup** ⑦. Next follow NM 371 to ☷ **Farmington** ⑧, visiting the **Bisti Wilderness Area** en route. After a night or two in Farmington, continue on to ☷ **Chama** ⑬, where the next morning you can make the partial trip on the Cumbres & Toltec Scenic Railroad. That afternoon drive down to visit **Ghost Ranch** ⑮ and ☷ **Abiquiu** ⑯, either spending the night there if you've got an extra day or in ☷ **Cuba** if time is tight. Either way plan to spend at least a half day exploring **Chaco Culture National Historical Park** ⑰. If you've got a full seven days, spend the final one visiting **Jemez Pueblo** ⑱, **Jemez State Monument,** and **Soda Dam.**

When to Tour Northwestern New Mexico

Weatherwise, the best months to tour the ruins of Anasazi Country are from April to early June and from late August to October, but there's no bad time. The roads to Chaco Canyon are sometimes closed because of snow or mud in winter, and cold winds can make the going rough

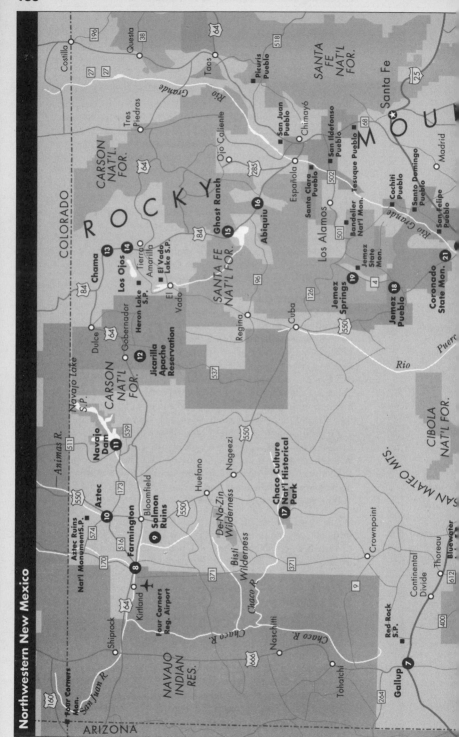

Northwestern New Mexico

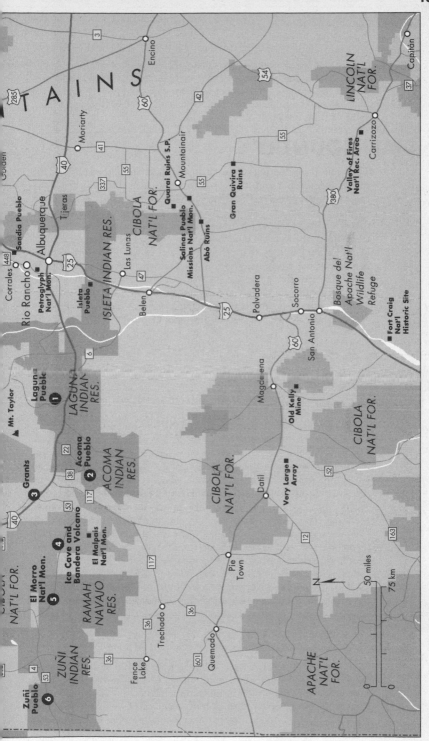

in early spring. The best seasons for attending Pueblo Indian dances are summer and fall, when harvest dances take place, and from Thanksgiving through early January. June and July are the hottest months, but by August afternoon thunderstorms begin cooling things down.

When visiting pueblos and reservations you are expected to follow a certain etiquette (☞ Pleasures and Pastimes *in* Chapter 1). Check the pueblos and monuments for dates of feast-day celebrations and fairs; some pueblos are open only on specific days.

INDIAN COUNTRY

The scent of smoldering piñon, the hypnotic chant of dancers, and the mood of reverence and joy that comes over a pueblo on a feast day leave lasting impressions on visitors to Indian Country. The spirituality that pervades a pueblo like Acoma, secluded on an imposing mesa that served as a lookout for "the people of the white rock" (as the name translates in the Keresan language), is unmistakable. Though the pueblos of Indian Country share the magnetism of so-called power spots, or vortices, the world over, they differ in a most significant way from places like Stonehenge or Machu Picchu: New Mexico's Indian pueblos are still inhabited. They are alive, their residents carrying on timeless traditions, arts, and ways of living as vibrant today as they were centuries ago. Much but not all of Indian Country lies within northern New Mexico. Among the region's important pueblos are Acoma, Laguna, Jemez, and Zuñi. Sacred grounds include portions of El Malpais and El Morro national monuments.

Laguna Pueblo

❶ *50 mi west of Albuquerque on I–40.*

Laguna Pueblo, which was established in 1697 by refugees from Zía, Cochiti, and Santo Domingo pueblos, is one of the youngest of New Mexico's pueblos. Scattered about the reservation are six villages, but most visitors are drawn to **Old Laguna**, capped by the eye-catching white facade of San José de Laguna Church, which is visible from I–40. The church, built in 1699, is a National Historic Landmark. In shops and artists' homes (the latter identified by signs) you can buy fine pottery decorated with geometric designs. The pueblo's villages celebrate many feast days and dances, including St. Joseph (March 19), Virgin Mary (September 8), and Saints Margaret and Mary (October 17). All the pueblo's residents gather at Old Laguna on September 19 to honor St. Joseph with a fair. ⊠ *Off I–40,* ☎ *505/552–6654 governor's office.* ⊡ *Free.* ☉ *Daily 8–4:30, village tours by appointment. Photography rules vary; contact the governor's office (☞ above) for information.*

Acoma Pueblo

★ ❷ *63 mi west of Albuquerque on I–40 and NM 22 south.*

Atop a 367-ft mesa that rises abruptly from the valley floor, Acoma Pueblo's terraced, multistory, multiunit Sky City is like no other pueblo structure. It's one of the oldest continually inhabited spots in North America, with portions believed to be more than 1,500 years old. Captain Hernando de Alvarado, a member of Francisco Vásquez de Coronado's Expedition of 1540, was the first European to see Acoma. He reported that he had "found a rock with a village on top, the strongest position ever seen in the world." The Spanish eventually conquered the Acomas and brutally compelled them to build **San Estéban del Rey,** the immense adobe church that stands to this day. Indians laborers cut the church's ceiling logs 30 mi away on Mt. Taylor and carried them overland. If at any time during the journey one of the enormous logs touched the ground, the men were severely beaten and sent back to the mountain for a new one—84 women and men died during construction.

About a dozen families live at the pueblo full time with most other Acomans living on Indian land nearby and returning only in summer and for celebrations, the primary one being the feast day of St. Stephen (September 2), which is open to the public. Acoma's artisans are known for their thin-walled pottery, hand-painted with intricate geometrical patterns. Visitation is by an hour-long guided tour; you're whisked by van up a steep road from the visitor center and then led about the mesa community on foot. There's no electricity or running water in the village, but you'll see cars parked outside many homes—one wonders what it must have been like to visit Acoma before the road was constructed in 1969. Open hours vary slightly, depending on the weather. ⊠ *Hwy. 22*, ☎ *505/552–6604 or 800/747–0181.* ⊡ *$9.* ☉ *Early Apr.–late Oct., daily 8–7, tours daily 8–6; late Oct.–early Apr., daily 8–4, tours daily 8–3. Closed certain periods; call first. Video cameras prohibited; still-camera permit $10.*

Grants

❸ *34 mi west of Laguna Pueblo, 29 mi northwest of Acoma via Hwy. 38 north and I–40 west.*

The largest community on old Route 66 between Albuquerque and Gallup, little Grants has a couple of intriguing museums and many chain hotels and inexpensive restaurants, making it a good base for exploring the eastern half of this region. The seat of Cibola County, Grants started out as a farming and ranching center, grew into a rail transport hub, and boomed during the 1950s when uranium was discovered in the nearby mountains. The town is gearing up for the arrival of the LodeStar-Enchanted Skies Park, which will offer an examination of the night skies through astronomy exhibits, but it will not be complete for a year or two.

In the center of Grants's sleepy downtown, the small **New Mexico Mining Museum** shares quarters with the chamber of commerce off Santa Fe Avenue. On the ground level are charts, photos, gems and minerals, and depictions of uranium-mining life in the region—this area is free. After paying admission, you can ride the elevator down into an amazingly realistic, re-created mine in the building's basement, where you can make a self-guided loop of the equipment and exhibits. ⊠ *100 N. Iron Ave.*, ☎ *505/287–4802.* ⊡ *Museum free, mine exhibit $2.* ☉ *Mon.–Sat. 9–4.*

☺ The **Dinamations Discovery Museum** opened to great acclaim in 1999. Here you'll see massive, alarmingly lifelike robotic replicas of dinosaurs that move and roar; interactive, hands-on displays; videos; and fossils and cast skeletons. Don't think this is simply a kiddie museum either—the exhibits are thoroughly engaging for all ages. ⊠ *Cibola Industrial Park, just south of I–40, Exit 85*, ☎ *505/876–6999.* ⊡ *$5.50.* ☉ *Mon.–Sat. 10–5.*

Looming high above Grants to the northeast, **Mt. Taylor** rises to 11,301 ft, the highest peak in northwestern New Mexico. You can drive fairly far up the mountain for fine views and hop out to hike on marked trails. There are also a couple campgrounds. The annual **Mt. Taylor Winter Quadrathlon** (☎ *505/287–4802 or 800/748–2142*) takes place every mid-February, when 600 unbelievably fit athletes compete in a highly challenging bicycle, foot, ski, and snowshoe race near the summit.

Dining and Lodging

🐝 *following the text of a review is your signal that the property has a Web site, where you will find details and, usually, images; for a link, visit www.fodors.com/urls*

$$ ✕ **Monte Carlo.** A fixture in town since the 1940s, this rollicking old New Mexican eatery is best known for its *chile relleno del mar* (green chile stuffed with cheese, bay shrimp, and crabmeat). The salsas here also pack quite a punch. ✉ *721 W. Santa Fe Ave.,* ☎ *505/287–9250. MC, V.*

$ ✕ **Riverwalk Cafe.** An endearingly diminutive luncheonette with green-and-white-checked valances, this place occupies an old grocery store and overlooks downtown's riverfront. Famous for chile dogs, the kitchen also prepares dependable burgers, New Mexican favorites, and sandwiches. You can make your order to-go and picnic by the river. ✉ *3rd St. and W. Stephens Ave.,* ☎ *505/287–2825. No credit cards. No dinner.*

$$ 🏨 **Zuni Mountain Lodge.** This contemporary lodge at the edge of the Zuni Mountain Range lies 1 mi from Bluewater Lake State Park, just west of Grants. Airy, white-walled rooms with simple, attractive furnishings induce tranquillity, as do their views of the lake and Cibola National Forest. Surrounded by piñon and ponderosa pines at almost 8,000 ft, this is a great spot for mountain biking or hiking. Count on a full breakfast, with a specialty of a green-chile quiche and homemade Belgian waffles, and a delicious dinner of hearty home-style favorites. The inn also offers five-day intensive workshops on Navajo weaving and pottery. ✉ *40 Perch Dr. (Box 5114), Thoreau 87323, between Grant and Gallup; from I–40, Exit 53, head south 13 mi on NM 612,* ☎ *505/ 862–7769, FAX 505/862–7616. 9 rooms. MAP. No credit cards.* 🐝

$–$$ 🏨 **Days Inn.** This is one of the newest and nicest of the numerous motels off Exit 85 of I–40, a reliable place for a restful stay. ✉ *1504 E. Santa Fe Ave., Grants 87020,* ☎ *505/287–8883 or 800/544–8313, FAX 505/287–7772. 62 rooms. AE, D, DC, MC, V. CP.*

En Route As you head toward El Morro National Monument on NM 53, you'll pass through the stark, volcanic rock–strewn **El Malpais National Monument and Conservation Area.** The conversation area contains New Mexico's largest natural arch and has miles of hiking trails. The monument is also popular for hiking, as well as spelunking. Some 40 volcanoes dot the properties' combined 114,000 acres, at least one of them active as recently as 2,000 years ago—the blink of an eye in geological terms. There are no tourist facilities here, but a visitor center has maps and knowledgeable staff. El Malpais is not much of an attraction for the pass-through visitor, but best experienced by spending a full day or two exploring the park in depth. A quick snapshot of the volcanic landscape and terrain is best gained from the Ice Cave and Bandera Volcano, ☞ *below.* ✉ *NM 53, 23 mi south of Grants,* ☎ *505/ 783–4774.* 🖼 *Free.* ☉ *Daily 8:30–4:30.*

Ice Cave and Bandera Volcano

🐾 ❹ *25 mi southwest of Grants and 1 mi west of El Malpais via NM 53.*

Despite its unabashed commercialism, this roadside curiosity, set squarely on the Continental Divide, easily merits an hour of your time—the short trail from the 1930s trading post (with gift shop and snack bar) just off NM 53 affords unusual vistas of blackened lava fields and gnarled juniper and ponderosa stands. It's about a 20-minute moderately strenuous jaunt up to the 1,200-ft-diameter crater of **Bandera Volcano,** which last unleashed a torrent of lava 10,000 years ago. An even shorter walk leads to an old wooden staircase that descends 100 ft into the bowels of a collapsed lava tube, where an eerie **Ice Cave** remains 31°F year-round and has a perpetual floor of blue-green ice. ✉ *12000 Ice Caves Rd.,* ☎ *888/423–2283.* ⊞ *$7.* ☼ *Memorial Day–Labor Day, daily 8–7; Labor Day–Memorial Day, daily 8–5.*

El Morro National Monument

★ **⑤** *43 mi southwest of Grants and 15 mi west of Ice Cave and Bandera Volcano via NM 53.*

When you see the imposing 200-ft-high sandstone bluff that served as a rest stop for explorers, soldiers, and pioneers, you'll understand how El Morro ("the Headlands") got its name. The bluff is the famous **Inscription Rock,** where wayfarers, beginning with Juan de Oñate in 1605, stopped to carve their names and leave messages. Petroglyphs mark the passage of travelers of earlier times. The **Inscription Trail** makes a quick ½-mi round-trip from the visitor center. While El Morro is justly renowned for Inscription Rock, try to allow an extra 90 minutes or so to venture along the spectacular, moderately strenuous 2-mi (round-trip) **Mesa Top Trail,** which meanders past the excavated edge of a massive field of pueblo ruins, cuts along the precarious rim of a deep box canyon, and affords panoramic views of the region. The monument's **museum** chronicles 700 years of human history in this region. ✉ *Visitor center: NM 53,* ☎ *505/783–4226.* ⊞ *$2, maximum of $4 per carload.* ☼ *Memorial Day–Labor Day, daily 9–7; Labor Day–Memorial Day, daily 9–5. Trails close 1 hr before monument.*

Zuñi Pueblo

⑥ *35 mi west of El Morro National Monument on NM 53.*

Zuñi Pueblo has been occupied continuously since at least the year 700 and its language is unrelated to that of any other pueblo. Hawikuh, a Zuñi-speaking settlement now 12 mi south of the pueblo, was the first contacted by the Spaniards, in 1539. Francisco Vásquez de Coronado came here seeking one of the Seven Cities of Gold. He'd been tipped off by his guide, Estéban, who had seen the setting sun striking the walls of the dwellings and thought the multistoried villages were made of gold.

With a population of 8,500, Zuñi Pueblo is the largest of New Mexico's 19 Indian pueblos. You may be disappointed to find the pueblo is mostly modern housing along dusty streets. But the artists and craftspeople here are famous for their fine silversmithing and carving, Zuñi needlepoint, turquoise and silver jewelry, carved animal fetishes, pottery, and katsina dolls.

The original **Our Lady of Guadalupe Mission,** built in 1629, was destroyed during the Pueblo Revolt of 1680, when the Indians ousted the Spanish. In 1699 the mission was rebuilt, and in 1966 it was excavated and reconstructed. ✉ *Old Mission Dr.,* ☎ *505/782–4403.* ⊞ *Free.* ☼ *Weekdays 9–noon (hrs sometimes vary; call).*

A:shiwi A:wan Museum and Heritage Center, which celebrates Zuñi history and culture, was built in harmony with traditional and environmental values of the Zuñi people. Food-preparation classes, storytelling, and other activities take place here in addition to exhibits. Artifacts, baskets, and pottery are also on view. ✉ *1222 NM 53,* ☎ *505/782–4403.* ⊞ *Free.* ☼ *Nov.–Apr., weekdays 9–5:30; May–Oct., Mon.–Sat. 9–5:30.*

Lodging

$$–$$$ ⊡ **Inn at Halona.** Your only opportunity to stay right in the heart of the actual Zuñi pueblo village, this bright and cheerfully decorated inn is filled with handwoven rugs, fine Zuñi arts and crafts, brightly colored linens, and locally made furniture. An annex has a few larger rooms in a more rustic design scheme. Outside you can relax in the tree-shaded, enclosed flagstone courtyard, or walk a short distance to the village plaza or an art gallery. Room-service is available from the neighboring grocery-cum-restaurant. ⊠ *23B Pia Mesa Rd. (Box 446), Zuñi 87327, off NM 53,* ☎ *505/782–4118 or 800/752–3278,* ℻ *505/782–2155. 8 rooms, 5 with bath. MC, V. BP.* 🐾

Gallup

❼ *42 mi north of Zuñi on NM 602, 138 mi west of Albuquerque on I–40.*

Heart of Indian Country. Indian Jewelry Capital of the World. With more than 100 trading posts that deal in Indian jewelry, pottery, rugs, and all manner of other arts and crafts, fine and handmade, Gallup could be the best place to acquire that concho belt or squash-blossom necklace you've always wanted. Prices are often better than those you'll find in Santa Fe, and the selection is just short of overwhelming. Many of the Navajos selling their wares are from Window Rock, Arizona, the Navajo Nation's capital, 25 mi northwest of town. As elsewhere, it's buyer beware in Gallup. Generally, if a deal seems too good to be true, it is. To assure yourself of authenticity and quality, shop at a reputable, established dealer.

Gallup originated in the 1880s as a coal-mining town and the railroad that followed encouraged a boom. Long strings of freight cars still rumble along the tracks paralleling Historic Route 66, and train whistles hoot regularly. During the late 1920s and '30s, Gallup became a fabled stop along Route 66. When you drive down its neon-illuminated main street, you enter a retro world of nostalgia that's part of the 20th-century pop culture imagination.

The 12-block downtown section bounded by **Historic Route 66,** 1st Street, Hill Avenue, and 4th Street is best explored on foot. You can browse through the trading posts and appreciate 19th-century architecture. The 1928 Pueblo Deco **El Morro Theater** (⊠ 207 W. Coal Ave., ☎ 505/722–7469) screens Hollywood features and hosts the Gallup Film Festival—which includes a generous helping of Western-theme flicks—each October. Many of Hollywood's great westerns were filmed in this area.

Clothing, furniture, tools, and typewriters are among the artifacts of the coal-mining era on display at the **Rex Museum,** operated by the Gallup Historical Society inside the former Rex Hotel. ⊠ *300 W. Historic Rte. 66,* ☎ *505/863–1363.* 🖰 *$1.* ☉ *Weekdays 8–4, Sat. 8–3 (later in summer).*

Part of the **Gallup Cultural Center,** a project of the Southwest Indian Foundation, is inside the restored 1927 Atchison, Topeka & Santa Fe Railway station, a gem of a building designed by Mary E. Coulter. Buses and trains still run in and out of the station. The cultural center includes a café (where you can lunch or sip coffee out of replicas of the china used on AT&S trains), a cinema that screens documentaries about the Southwest, and two dozen dioramas that relate the history of area native peoples, Western expansion, and the building of the railroads. ⊠ *201 E. Historic Rte. 66,* ☎ *505/722–7534 or 505/863–4131.* 🖰 *Free.* ☉ *Memorial Day–Labor Day, daily 9–9; Labor Day–Memorial Day, daily 9–6.*

During spring, summer, and early fall, wildflowers add brilliance to the landscape of **Red Rock State Park,** which has a small nature trail, and campgrounds. The park's red-rock amphitheater holds Gallup's premier event, the **Inter-Tribal Indian Ceremonial** (☎ 800/233–4528), each August. About 50,000 people come to see the dances of more than 30 tribes, watch rodeo events and parades, and stroll the market-places. The **Red Rocks Museum** contains exhibits of jewelry, pottery, rugs, architecture, and tools of the Anasazi, Zuñi, Hopi, and Navajo. ⊠ *NM 566, Exit 31 from I–40, 7 mi east of Gallup,* ☎ *505/722–3829.* 🎦 *Park free, museum $1.* ⊙ *Park Nov.–Feb., daily 8–4:30; Mar.–mid-May, daily 8–6; mid-May–mid-Sept., daily 7:30 AM–10 PM; mid-Sept.–Oct., daily 7:30–6. Museum Mon.–Sat. 8:30–4:30.*

Dining and Lodging

$$ ✕ **The Butcher Shop.** Ensconced in a questionable-looking motel, the Butcher Shop is a pleasant surprise. Almost Euro-bistro in feel, this is a wonderful place to order prime rib and a glass of fine wine. Steaks, seafood, and pastas are served with flair in a most romantic setting. ⊠ *2003 W. Historic Rte. 66,* ☎ *505/722–4711. AE, D, MC, V. Closed Sun. No lunch.*

$ ✕ **Eagle Cafe.** For a glimpse of the past, slide into a red-vinyl booth in this 80-year-old diner, where you can watch trains chug past as you munch on mutton stew, enchiladas, or a burger. Not much has changed through the years at this tasty piece of living history. ⊠ *220 W. Historic Rte. 66,* ☎ *505/722–3220. Reservations not accepted. No credit cards. Closed Sun.*

$ ✕ **Earl's Restaurant.** If you have time for only one meal in Gallup, ★ come—as do many country-and-western stars traveling through town—to Earl's, a landmark that is Gallup's de facto dining room. The home-style rib-sticking daily specials include meat loaf and fried chicken with mashed potatoes. Another plus: some of the best green chile in all New Mexico. At Earl's it's the custom for Native American jewelry vendors to go table-to-table displaying their wares. They leave very quickly if you say you are not interested. ⊠ *1400 E. Historic Rte. 66,* ☎ *505/863–4201. Reservations not accepted. AE, D, DC, MC, V.*

$ ✕🎬 **El Rancho.** Book a night in the Ronald Reagan, Katharine Hep-★ burn, or William Bendix Room—all units at this National Register his-toric property are named for vintage movie stars, many of whom stayed here back when Hollywood Westerns were shot in the region (the hotel was built in 1937 by R. E. Griffith, the brother of the legendary silent-film director D. W. Griffith). A delightful combination of nostalgic glamour, neon signage, and Old West decor, this is the premier hotel in town. The restaurant ($$), which serves decent American and Mexi-can food, is open for breakfast, lunch, and dinner. Browse through the respected on-site art gallery for pottery, katsinas, and sand paintings. ⊠ *1000 E. Historic Rte. 66, 87301,* ☎ *505/863–9311 or 800/543–6351,* 🖷 *505/722–5917. 73 rooms, 3 suites. Restaurant, bar. AE, D, MC, V.*

$ 🎬 **Sleep Inn.** Sleep here and you'll get a reasonably priced motel room with all the basics: chairs, a dresser, TV with remote, and a phone. ⊠ *3820 E. Historic Rte. 66, 87301,* ☎ *505/863–3535 or 800/753–3746,* 🖷 *505/722–3737. 61 rooms. In-room data ports, no-smoking rooms, indoor pool, hot tub. AE, D, DC, MC, V.*

$ 🏕 **Red Rock State Park.** Red rocks 500 ft high loom over the park's paved campsites, which are surrounded by red sand and shady trees. Facilities include dump stations, fire rings, full hookups, running water, and showers. The site is open year-round. ⊠ *NM 566, Exit 31 from I–40, 7 mi east of Gallup,* ☎ *505/722–3829. 160 sites. Showers. MC, V.*

Shopping

Howling Coyote Books (⊠ 112 W. Coal Ave., ☎ 505/722–6937) car-ries a good selection of books about the Southwest and Native Amer-ican culture and is a fine general-interest bookstore. **Kiva Gallery** (⊠ 202 W. Historic Rte. 66, ☎ 505/722–5577) exhibits art of the Amer-ican Indian, including many original paintings.

At **Richardson's Trading Company** (✉ 222 W. Historic Rte. 66, ☎ 505/722–4762), the great-granddaddy of trading posts, the wooden floors creak under your feet as you gawk at the knockout array of Navajo and Zuñi turquoise and silver earrings, squash blossoms, concho belts, bracelets, natural-dye handwoven rugs, beadwork, and you name it. Richardson's is also a veritable museum of old pawn (the often valuable, unclaimed items pawned by Native Americans). The fourth generation of the Tanner trading family runs **Shush Yaz Trading Co.** (✉ 1304 W. Lincoln Ave., ☎ 505/722–0130), which stocks all manner of Native American arts and crafts, including locally made Navajo squaw skirts. The store sells traditional and contemporary jewelry and is a great source of old pawn. The on-site restaurant serves native foods. **Tobe Turpen's Indian Trading Post** (✉ 1710 S. 2nd St., ☎ 505/722–3806) has been in business for more than 80 years, selling katsinas, sand paintings, jewelry, folk art, and more. Poke around—you're likely to make a real find here.

En Route   Held the third Friday of every month, the **Crownpoint Rug Auction**
★   (✉ Crownpoint Elementary School, NM 371, 26 mi north of Thoreau at I-40, Exit 53, ☎ 505/786–7386) is the foremost place to buy handwoven Navajo rugs—you're bidding with a mix of collectors and dealers, so prices on the some 300 to 400 rugs are sometimes well below what you'd pay at a store. Viewing begins at 3 PM, with the actual auction running from 7 PM till usually midnight or later.

★   Dinosaurs used to roam the adjoining **Bisti and De-Na-Zin Wilderness areas** when they were part of a shallow sea some 70 million years ago. Lending the 45,000 acres an eerie, lunarlike appearance are hoodoos, mushroom-shape rock formations in subtle shades of brown, gray, and white. De-Na-Zin (pronounced duh-*nah*-zen and named for a petroglyph found nearby) is the much larger and less visited of the two sections, and here you'll find hillier and more challenging terrain, plus numerous fossils and petrified logs. At Bisti (pronounced *Biss*-tye), you'll encounter deeply eroded hoodoos whose striations represent layers of sandstone, shale, mudstone, coal, and silt. In many spots you'll climb over mounds of crumbly clay and silt that looks a bit like the topping of a coffee cake, but gray.

Both sections are ideal for photography, and in both backcountry camping is permitted. The Bureau of Land Management, which administers the land, asks that you remove nothing from either area, preserving its magical appearance for those who follow. The most fascinating terrain is 2 to 3 mi from the parking areas, and there are no trails, so bring a compass and be alert about your surrounding and where you are in relation to the sun—it's relatively easy to get lost in the vast, lonely, and barren place. ✉ *Bisti is on NM 371, 36 mi south of Farmington; De-Na-Zin is on (unpaved) County Rd. 7500, off either NM 371 8 mi south of Bisti entrance or NM 44 at Huerfano, 34 mi south of Bloomington,* ☎ *505/599–8900.* 🄳 *Free.*

ANASAZI COUNTRY

To gain a sense of the beauty, power, and complexity of the ancient civilizations of the Americas, you can do no better than to travel to Chaco Canyon, sometimes called the "Stonehenge of the West," and the more accessible Salmon Ruins and Aztec Ruins. Discoveries of the past 20 years, notably the Sun Dagger, which appears at a particular point in Chaco Canyon on each summer solstice, have increased interest in the science of archaeoastronomy—the study of the ways in which the ancients surveyed the skies, kept track of the movement of the planets and stars, and marked their passage within the construction of elaborate stone structures. But Anasazi Country is more than ancient ruins. Spectacular hiking, golfing, and fishing can be had here, and you can poke through small towns that are the products of northwestern New Mexico's homesteading era. The best shopping is for antiques and Native American jewelry and pottery.

Farmington

8 *142 mi north of Gallup via I–40 east to NM 371 north.*

A rough-edged, gritty, unpretentious town full of giant pickup trucks, with a radio dial loaded with country-and-western stations, Farmington sits in the heart of the Four Corners region, with archaeological, recreational, and scenic wonders within easy driving distance. Its central location, reasonable prices, and friendly ways make Farmington the ideal base.

The Navajo gave the name *Totah* (Among the Waters) to the land around what is now Farmington, which lies at the confluence of three rivers— the Animas, La Plata, and San Juan. Homesteaders began planting farms and orchards in 1879 on this fertile land, and the "farming town" became Farmington.

The agricultural economy shifted to one based on oil and gas in the late 1940s, beginning a boom-and-bust cycle tied to the fluctuation of fuel prices. Diversification didn't come until the past decade or so, when Farmington began promoting its historic past with more gusto. Even more revitalizing was the creation of a regional shopping center, which swells the population by thousands on weekends, when Native Americans and other country people make their weekly or monthly trip to town to stock up on supplies.

You can get an inkling of what the Four Corners area was like during the trading-post days at the **Farmington Gateway Museum and Visitors Center,** in a spectacular modern sandstone building whose stonework closely resembles the Aztec and Chaco ruins. Landscaped grounds behind the building, where the Farmington Convention and Visitors Bureau is, extend down to the Animus River—an ideal spot for a picnic. The museum contains a permanent trading post exhibit and also presents art, science, Native American, and regional history exhibits throughout the year. ✉ *3041 E. Main St.,* ☎ *505/599–1174.* ✆ *Free (except for certain exhibits).* ۞ *Mon.–Sat. 9–5, Sun. noon–5.*

The **River Corridor,** a 5-mi walkway between Scott Avenue and U.S. 64 along the Animas River, winds alongside Berg Park. The corridor contains trails for walkers, runners, cyclists, and wildlife- and bird-watchers, and a new man-made, 300-yard-long, white-river course.

OFF THE
BEATEN PATH

SHIPROCK PINNACLE – West of Farmington, at U.S. 666 and U.S. 64, the 1,700-ft **Shiprock Pinnacle** rises from the desert floor like a massive schooner. It's sacred to the Navajo, who call it "rock with wings." No climbing or hiking is permitted. The pinnacle is composed of igneous rock flanked by upright walls of solidified lava.

FOUR CORNERS MONUMENT – About 30 mi west of Shiprock you'll reach the only place in the United States where you can stand in four states at the same time—at the intersection of New Mexico, Arizona, Colorado, and Utah. There's an Indian marketplace at this popular—if somewhat cheesy—attraction, which has no view to speak of. ✉ *U.S. 160, north from U.S. 64,* ☎ *520/871–6647.* ✆ *$2.50.* ۞ *May–Aug., daily 7 AM–8 PM; Sept.–Apr., daily 8–5.*

Dining and Lodging

$$$$ ✕ **K. B. Dillon's.** Fresh fish, beef, steamed vegetables, and pasta dishes are on the menu at this clubby steak house with a Western-Victorian feel. There's live music some nights. ⊠ *101 W. Broadway,* ☎ *505/325–0222. AE, MC, V.*

$$ ✕ **Three Rivers Eatery & Brewhouse.** In a historic downtown structure
★   with a gorgeous pressed-tin ceiling, exposed air ducts, and walls lined with historic photos, this microbrewery whips up more than 10 kinds of beer (also available to go) with names like Power Plant Porter and Chaco Nut Brown Ale. The brews go well with the enormous portions of tasty soups, salads, burgers, ribs, and other pub grub served here. It's open late most nights. ⊠ *101 E. Main St.,* ☎ *505/324–2187. Reservations not accepted. AE, D, MC, V.*

$ ✕ **Bagel Conspiracy.** This urbane little bagelry and delicatessen with a bright sunny interior serves commendable fresh-baked bagels with daily changing cream cheeses (like cranberry-orange-nut), coffees, and Italian sodas. A full range of creative sandwiches is also served. ⊠ *3030 E. Main St.,* ☎ *505/564–8888. Reservations not accepted. No credit cards. No dinner.*

$ ✕ **El Charro Cafe.** Don't be put off by El Charro's out-of-the-way location or shabby carpet. Locals who demand authentic Mexican fare head here for lunch. The pulse of life beats within the red chile. The combination plate—a tamale, an enchilada, a burrito, and guacamole, rice, and beans—won't leave you hungry. ⊠ *737 W. Main St.,* ☎ *505/327–2464. Reservations not accepted. AE, D, DC, MC, V.*

$ ✕ **The Spare Rib.** The decor here is nothing fancy, just plastic table-cloths over picnic tables, but the whole family can fill up on generous portions of delicious smoked barbecue. ⊠ *1700 E. Main St.,* ☎ *505/325–4800. Reservations not accepted. AE, D, MC, V. Closed Sun.*

$$ ▥ **Kokopelli's Cave.** Few accommodations in the world can claim a
★   more fascinating history and unusual setting than this fully furnished cave carved into cliffside 250 ft above the La Plata River and an adjoining wildlife refuge. The exposed sandstone walls of this spacious one-bedroom unit trace 70 million years of erosion history. Geologist Bruce Black had the 1,650-square-ft cave blasted out in 1980, to serve as his office. It now contains a bedroom, fireplace, full kitchen (with Continental breakfast supplies included), gas barbecue, washer-dryer, TV and VCR, phone, and a romantic stone shower with a waterfall that trickles into a hot tub—there's even wall-to-wall carpeting. From the two terraces you may see the occasional ring-tail cat or gray fox— a trail leads up the cliff face, some 70 vertical ft, to the parking area. The cave has two futons in the living area and accommodates up to six persons. ⊠ *206 W. 38th St., 87401,* ☎ *505/325–7855,* ☏ *505/325–9671. 1 unit. Kitchenette. AE, MC, V. CP.* ⊛

$$–$$$ ▥ **Casa Blanca Bed & Breakfast Inn.** Luxury without pretension is the trademark of the innkeepers of the Mission-style Casa Blanca, which stands atop a bluff overlooking Farmington. You can relax in the Southwestern-style den, watch city lights twinkle from the solarium, or zone out near the patio's fountain. One room has a double hot tub; another has a fireplace; all have cable TV and VCRs and receive turn-down service. Breakfast is a gourmet affair, and fresh-baked goodies are served in the afternoon. Business travelers seeking a homey atmosphere make it a point to stay here. ⊠ *505 E. La Plata St., 87401,* ☎ *505/327–6503 or 800/ 550–6503,* ☏ *505/326–5680. 4 rooms, 1 suite. AE, D, MC, V. BP.*

$$–$$$ ▥ **Silver River Adobe Inn.** This red-roof adobe sits on a sandstone cliff 30 ft above where the San Juan River meets the La Plata, at the west end of town. Rough-hewn timbers, fluffy quilts, and complete privacy make this rustic getaway ideal for romance or rumination. ⊠ *3151 W. Main St. (Box 3411), 87499,* ☎ *505/325–8219 or 800/382–9251. 2 rooms, 1 suite. AE, MC, V. BP.*

$–$$ ⊡ **Comfort Inn.** This well-run motel with warmly decorated, up-to-date rooms and a hospitable staff provides comfort indeed after a long day of sightseeing. ⊠ *555 Scott Ave., 87401,* ☎ *505/325–2626 or 800/ 341–1495,* 📠 *505/325–7675. 42 rooms, 18 suites. Pool. AE, D, DC, MC, V. CP.*

Nightlife and the Arts
Several of the restaurants in Farmington and Aztec are popular for cocktails, notably **K. B. Dillon's** and **Three Rivers Eatery & Brewhouse** (☞ *above*). From Wednesday to Saturday, regional-history and other plays are performed at the **Outdoor Summer Theater** (⊠ Lion's Wilderness Park, College Blvd. and Piñon Hills Blvd., ☎ 505/327–9336 or 800/ 448–1240) between mid-June and mid-August at 8 PM in a sandstone amphitheater. An optional Southwestern-style dinner is served prior to each performance. **San Juan College Theater** (⊠ 4601 College Blvd., ☎ 505/326–3311 ext. 364) presents concerts, student recitals, lectures, and theatrical performances.

Outdoor Activities and Sports

FISHING
San Juan Troutfitters (☎ 505/324–8149) conducts fly-fishing classes and operates guided fishing trips.

GOLF
Piñon Hills Golf Course (⊠ 2101 Sunrise Pkwy., ☎ 505/326–6066), an 18-hole, par-72 course, is one of New Mexico's best links. The greens fee ranges from $20 to $25; an optional cart costs $16.

WATER SPORTS
Farmington Aquatic Center (⊠ 1151 N. Sullivan St., ☎ 505/599– 1167), a public water-wonderland, has a 150-ft-long water slide and three pools.

Shopping
Stores at the gargantuan **Animas Valley Mall** (⊠ 4601 E. Main St., ☎ 505/326–5465) include Dillard's, Sears, JCPenney, and the very fine Western Warehouse, plus specialty shops like Home Sweet Home. The ubiquitous Gap clothing chain debuted in 2000, a sign of the region's steadily growing prosperity. The historic trading-post district along Main Street downtown, a good place to look for antiques, provides a nostalgic alternative to the mall.

It's easy to while away an afternoon at the **Dusty Attic** (⊠ 111 W. Main St., ☎ 505/327–7696), a 17,000-square-ft downtown mall where you'll find antiques, arts, crafts, and gifts. **Fifth Generation Trading Co.** (⊠ 232 W. Broadway, ☎ 505/326–3211), an old trading post run by the Tanner family since 1875, has a wealth of Indian wares and is known for sand paintings. Creaky wooden floors add to the charm of **Foutz Indian Room** (⊠ 301 W. Main St., ☎ 505/325–9413), which sells superb Navajo folk art and old pawn. **Sentimental Journey Antiques** (⊠ 218 W. Main St., ☎ 505/326–6533), a multidealer operation, is crammed with interesting treasures and collectibles. About a half-hour drive west of town is the **Hogback Trading Co.** (⊠ 3221 U.S. 64, ☎ 505/598–5154), a trading post known for fine, handwoven Navajo rugs.

Salmon Ruins

⑨ *10 mi east of Farmington on U.S. 64.*

Salmon Ruins (pronounced *sol*-mon), which dates from the 11th century, is a large Chacoan Anasazi apartment complex on the northern edge of the San Juan River. A stunning example of pre-Columbian Pueblo architecture and stonework, the site is named for a homesteader whose family protected the ruins for nearly a century. **Heritage Park** contains the restored Salmon Homestead and other traditional habitations of the people of this region. ⊠ *6131 U.S. 64,* ☎ *505/632-2013.* ☞ *$3.* ☉ *Apr.–Oct., daily 8–5, Nov.–Mar., Mon.–Sat. 8–5, Sun. noon–5.*

Aztec

⑩ *14 mi northeast of Farmington on U.S. 550, 10 mi north of Bloomfield on NM 544.*

The many Victorian brick buildings and quaint outlying residential blocks give charming Aztec, the seat of San Juan County, the feeling of a picture-book hometown. Adding to the allure are the views had in the very distance of the snowcapped mountains north of Durango, Colorado, toward Telluride. The village part of the **Aztec Museum, Pioneer Village and Oil Field Exhibit** contains more than a dozen late-19th-century buildings—a blacksmith shop, a schoolhouse, a wooden oil derrick, and a log cabin, among others—that convey a sense of life as it used to be. ⊠ *125 N. Main St.,* ☎ *505/334-9829.* ☞ *Free.* ☉ *Memorial Day–Labor Day, Mon.–Sat. 9–5; Labor Day–Memorial Day, Mon.–Sat. 10–4.*

★ With the largest reconstructed Great Kiva in North America and a pueblo dwelling that once contained more than 500 rooms, **Aztec Ruins National Monument and Museum,** a World Heritage Site, dates from the early 1100s. Early homesteaders thought the dwelling was a Mexican Aztec ruin, but it actually is a section of what is known as the Chaco Phenomenon, the extensive social and economic system that reached far beyond Chaco Canyon. This pueblo was abandoned by the mid-1200s. You only need an hour or so to tour the ruin, which is less spectacular but considerably more accessible than those at Chaco. ⊠ *Near U.S. 550 and Ruins Rd.,* ☎ *505/334-6174.* ☞ *$4.* ☉ *Memorial Day–Labor Day, daily 8–6; Labor Day–Memorial Day, daily 8–5.*

Dining and Lodging

$–$$ ✕ **Hiway Grill.** Don't be put off by its location adjoining a package store: this is a lively restaurant with vintage car photos, a super-friendly staff, art deco tables, and red vinyl booths—it all has the feel of a '50s malt shop. Many of the American and New Mexican dishes—like the Mustang Melt (a burger with grilled onions and melted Swiss on rye with Thousand Island dressing) are named for classic cars. The sign outside has an actual '50s automobile stuck through it. ⊠ *401 N.E. Aztec Blvd.,* ☎ *505/334-6533. AE, D, DC, MC, V. Closed Sun.*

$$ ✕🏠 **Miss Gail's Inn.** On Main Street just steps from the town's best antiquing (and the Aztec Museum), this rambling redbrick Victorian offers characterful accommodations—some rooms have kitchenettes, and all are enlivened with quilts, antiques, and collectibles. You can grab lunch on weekdays and dinner on Friday and Saturday nights only (and only by advance reservation) at Giovanni's Restaurant ($$), a cheerful dining room in back with very good Italian food. ⊠ *300 S. Main St. 87410,* ☎ *505/334-3452 or 888/534-3452,* FAX *505/334-9664. 8 rooms. Kitchenettes (some). AE, D, MC, V. CP.*

$$ 🏠 **Step Back Inn.** Though technically a modern motor hotel, this Victorian-style clapboard structure on the north edge of downtown offers a considerably more memorable experience than you'll have at any of the countless chain properties in nearby Farmington, and at similar prices. The public areas are inviting, and individually decorated rooms have a mix of newer pieces and reproduction antiques, floral wallpapers, and chenille bedspreads. ⊠ *U.S. 550 at NM 544, 87410,* ☎ *505/334–1200 or 800/334–1255,* 𝔽𝔸𝕏 *505/334–9858. 40 rooms. AE, MC, V. CP.*

Navajo Dam

⓫ *26 mi east of Aztec on NM 173.*

Navajo Dam is the name of a tiny town a few miles below Navajo Lake State Park and the name of the dam itself. At the base of the dam lie the legendary trout waters of the San Juan River. One of the country's top five trophy-trout streams, the San Juan has year-round fishing for rainbow, brown, and cutthroat trout. Many areas are catch and release only. The San Juan carves a scenic gorge of stepped cliffs alongside cottonwood-lined banks that attract elk, Barbary sheep, golden and bald eagles, blue herons, and not a few fly-fisherfolk in waders.

As you drive up over the dam you'll be rewarded with panoramic views down into the valley. **Navajo Lake State Park** is a popular boating and fishing spot; you can rent boats at two marinas. Short trails lead to the lakeshore, and the 3-mi-long cottonwood-shaded San Juan River Trail parallels the river down below the dam. The park has three campgrounds and 200 sites; some sites sit among piñon and juniper trees and overlook the lake. Running water and hot showers are available at Sims Mesa and Pine campgrounds Cottonwood Campground has modern rest rooms but no showers. A disposal station, fire rings, and flush toilets are other facilities. Driving the narrow road across the top of the dam, with no guardrails, is a slightly hair-raising, memorable experience. ⊠ *1448 NM 511, off NM 173,* ☎ *505/632–2278.* ⊡ *Park $4 per vehicle; campsites $10, $14 with electricity, $18 with full hookup.*

Outdoor Activities and Sports

Stop by **Abe's Motel & Fly Shop/Born-n-Raised on the San Juan** (⊠ 1791 NM 173, ☎ 505/632–2194) to find out what flies you need to snare the wily San Juan rainbows. "If Abe's don't have it, you don't need it." You can also pick up a cold drink and snacks at Abe's or book a wade or float trip. At the revered **Rizuto's Fly Shop** (⊠ 1796 NM 173, ☎ 505/632–3893 or 800/525–1437), you can pick up some tips or book a guide.

Jicarilla Apache Reservation

⓬ *55 mi east of Navajo Dam on U.S. 64.*

The Spanish named the Jicarilla tribe, a group of Native Americans related to the Navajo and Apache, for the baskets they made. For centuries before the arrival of the Spanish, they were a nomadic people who roamed across northeastern New Mexico, southeastern Colorado, and the Oklahoma and Texas panhandles. Their tribe of 10,000 was decimated to 330 by 1897. The federal government relocated the tribe to this isolated area of almost a million acres a century ago. The tribe has made something of a comeback with the sale of timber, oil and gas development, casino gambling, and savvy investing.

Dulce ("sweet") on U.S. 64 is the capital of the reservation. The **Arts & Crafts Museum** remains the best place to see the fine historic Jicarilla baskets, beadwork, and pottery. ⊠ *¼ mi west of downtown, U.S. 64,* ☎ *505/759–3242 ext. 274.* ⊡ *Free.* ☉ *Daily 8–5.*

The **Cultural Center** (☎ 505/759–1343) is a small gift shop that sells mostly beadwork. It's at the corner of Basket Lane and U.S. 64.

This country is known for fishing, particularly at Stone Lake, and for hunting; contact the **Game & Fish Department** (☎ 505/759–3442). Visitors may also hike and camp. In recent years, the casino has become a big draw as well. Some Jicarilla celebrations are open to the public. The Little Beaver Roundup, the third weekend in July, entails a rodeo, powwow, and carnival and draws participants from Indian tribes and pueblos throughout the United States.

Lodging

The tribe also operates the Lodge at Chama, a hunting and fishing resort (☞ Chama, *below*).

$$ ☲ **Best Western Jicarilla Inn.** This is the only place to stay in Dulce. The accommodations preserve the flavor of the cultural and natural setting, with dark woods, Native American art, and stone fireplaces. The restaurant, the Hill Crest, is a favorite gathering spot for celebration dinners. Train packages are available (☞ Chama, *below*). ☒ *U.S. 64, 12 mi west of Jct. 84 (Box 233), Dulce 87528, ☎ 505/759–3663 or 800/528–1234, FAX 505/759–3170. 42 rooms. Restaurant, bar. AE, D, DC, MC, V.*

CHAMA AND GEORGIA O'KEEFFE COUNTRY

A railroad town nestled at the base of 10,000-ft Cumbre Pass, lush and densely wooded Chama offers outdoors activities year-round, as well as a scenic railroad. From there, U.S. 84 hugs the Rio Chama and leads southward through monumental red rocks and golden sandstone spires that inspired Georgia O'Keeffe's vivid paintings of creased mountains, stark crosses, bleached animal skulls, and adobe architecture. The artist abandoned her position in the center of the New York art world to spend her life painting this landscape. To see what O'Keeffe saw is to understand her work.

Chama

⑬ *30 mi east of Jicarilla Apache Reservation and 95 mi west of Taos on U.S. 64, 59 mi north of Abiquiu on U.S. 84.*

The booms and busts of Chama have largely coincided with the popularity of train transportation. The town's very earliest boom, which precipitated its founding, occurred in the 1880s when workers piled into town to construct the Denver & Rio Grande Railroad. In those days, narrow-gauge trains chugged over the high mountain tracks carrying gold and silver out from the mines of the San Juan Mountains, which straddle the nearby Colorado–New Mexico border. Gambling halls, moonshine stills, speakeasies, and brothels were a fixture along the main drag, Terrace Avenue. The lumber industry also thrived during the early years, and the town still has quite a few houses and buildings fashioned out of spare hand-hewn railroad ties.

Chama offers an assortment of outdoor recreation opportunities that's hard to beat. Vast meadows of wildflowers and aspen and ponderosa pines blanket the entire region. Hunters are drawn here by the abundant wildlife. There's cross-country skiing and snowmobiling in winter; camping, rafting, hiking, and fishing in summer, all in a pristine, green, high-mountain setting that feels like the top of the world.

All directions are given in terms of "the Y," the town's only major intersection (of U.S. 64/84 and NM 17). The big attraction is the historic **Cumbres & Toltec Scenic Railroad,** the narrow-gauge coal-driven steam engine that runs through the San Juan Mountains and over the Cumbres Pass. You'll chug over ancient trestles, around breathtaking bends, and high above the Los Pinos River—if the terrain looks at all familiar, you may have seen this railroad's "performance" in *Indiana Jones and the Last Crusade*. Midway through the trip you break for lunch and can switch to an awaiting Colorado-based train to complete the 64 mi to Antonito, Colorado (from which you'll be shuttled back by bus), or return from this point on the same train. Train trip packages including stays at area lodgings are available. ⊠ *15 Terrace Ave., Chama,* ☎ *505/756–2151 or 888/286–2737.* ⊠ *$38–$58.* ⊘ *Late May–mid.-Oct., daily departures at 8 AM and 10:30 AM.*

Dining and Lodging

$$ ✕ **Whistle Stop Cafe.** "We serve real food here," says the proprietor, meaning fresh seafood and fresh roasted turkey. The $10 dinners and $5 lunch are the big draw. Recommended are the twice-baked duck, with honey-almond sauce; the blackened salmon; and halibut in lemon-dill sauce. The café is also open for breakfast. ⊠ *425 Main St., across from train station,* ☎ *505/756–1833. MC, V. Closed Nov.–Apr.*

$$$$ ⊡ **The Lodge at Chama.** An outdoor-oriented vacation can also be luxurious. The lodge and working ranch, owned by the Jicarilla Apache tribe, is on 32,000 idyllic acres on the Colorado border, at an elevation between 9,000 and 11,000 ft, with 10 lakes. Horseback riding, trophy fishing, touring the ranch, and sitting by the huge stone fireplace ought to relax the most stressed-out executive. Meals and the bar tab are included. ⊠ *16263 U.S. 84 (Box 127), 87520,* ☎ *505/756–2133,* FAX *505/756–2519. 9 rooms, 2 suites. Restaurant, bar, hot tub, sauna. FAP. D, MC, V.*

$$ ⊡ **Cardin's Crossing B&B.** Fancy a cup of tea on a Victorian front porch filled with white wicker furniture? Or a stroll through a lovingly tended flower garden? At Cardin's Crossing, there's an all-out breakfast with fresh fruit and homemade cinnamon rolls. Apple pie is served every night as a snack. The Narrow Gauge Room has a model train running overhead, and the Victorian dollhouse room has a dollhouse and canopy bed. ⊠ *551 Maple Ave. (Box 180), 87520,* ☎ *505/756–2542 or 800/852–6400. 2 rooms. MC, V. BP.*

$$ ⊡ **The Lightheart Inn.** This cozy house emphasizes the nourishment of body and soul with a massage therapist on the premises and health-conscious breakfasts. ⊠ *63 Terrace Ave. (Box 223), 87520,* ☎ *505/ 756–2908. 2 rooms. Hot tub. MC, V. BP.*

$ ⊡ **River Bend Lodge.** This comfortable but not fancy lodge has one of the few hot tubs in town. It's right on the Chama River, so you can walk out your door and cast a fly. But be careful—you might surprise a black bear and her cub. Management here is especially sensitive and accommodating, particularly for groups or family reunions. It also offers train packages. ⊠ *U.S. 84 (Box 593), 87520,* ☎ *505/756–2264 or 800/ 288–1371,* FAX *505/756–2664. 19 rooms. Hot tub. AE, D, DC, MC, V.*

$ ⊡ **Spruce Lodge.** So you like roughing it, but not too rough? These 12 little cabins with kitchenettes beside the Rio Chama are the perfect balance: rustic but comfortable. You know you're away from it all when you can hear the river and the wind sifting through the pines. Pets are welcome. ⊠ *U.S. 84 (Box 365), 87520,* ☎ *505/756–2593. 12 cabins. Kitchenettes. D, MC, V.*

Nightlife and the Arts

To hear local bands on Saturday night, head for **Ben's Lounge** (⊠ NM 17, ☎ 505/756–2922). The **Chama Valley Music Festival** (☎ 505/ 756–2836) takes place every Friday and Saturday in July.

Outdoor Activities and Sports

Plenty of outfitters are here to help out with equipment and tours. **Adventures** (☎ 888/660–9878) provides snowmobiles. **Chama Ski Service** (☎ 505/756–2493) rents cross-country ski equipment. For river rafting, there's **Far Flung Adventures** (☎ 800/359–2627), **Los Rios** (☎ 505/776–8854 or 800/544–1181), and **Canyon REO** (☎ 520/774–3377 or 800/637–4604). **Lone Pine Hunting and Outfitting Co.** (☎ 505/756–2992 or 800/704–4087) offers horseback riding.

Shopping

Local Color Gallery (✉ 567 Terrace Ave., ☎ 505/756–2604) carries photography and jewelry of local artisans. The sales of many goods at **Trackside Emporium** (✉ 611 Terrace Ave., ☎ 505/756–1848) support the preservation of the railroad; here you'll find books, signs, and other memorabilia pertaining to the trains. **Chama Valley Supermarket** (✉ 2451 U.S. 84, ☎ 505/756–2545) at the Y intersection sells groceries and fishing supplies.

Los Ojos

⑭ *13 mi south of Chama on U.S. 64/84.*

Los Ojos, midway between Tierra Amarilla and Chama (☞ *above*), could well serve as a model for rural economic development worldwide. The little town has experienced an economic revival of sorts by returning to its ancient roots—the raising of churro sheep (the original breed brought over by the Spanish, prized for its wool) and weaving. Ganados del Valle, the community-based, nonprofit economic development corporation headquartered here, has created many new jobs and increased prosperity by returning to the old ways, with improved marketing. You'll also find a smattering of artists studios, most of them in rustic buildings with corrugated metal roofs.

The cooperative **Tierra Wools** produces some of the finest original weavings in the Southwest. Designs are based on the old Rio Grande styles, and weavers make rugs and capes of superb craftsmanship entirely by hand, using old-style looms. Weaving classes are available. ✉ *91 Main St., Los Ojos,* ☎ *505/588–7231.* ⊙ *June–Aug., Mon.–Sat. 9–6, Sun. 10–4; Sept.–May, Mon.–Sat. 10–5.*

Heron Lake State Park (✉ NM 95 and U.S. 64, ☎ 505/588–7470) and **El Vado Lake State Park** (✉ NM 112 [Box 1147], Santa Fe 87504, ☎ 505/588–7247) are within 15 mi of Los Ojos and less than an hour's drive south of Chama. They offer boating, fishing, wildlife viewing, and bird-watching, and Heron Lake has several campgrounds. From Heron Lake State Park, the 5½-mi Rio Chama Trail crosses the Rio Chama, winds along the south slope of the canyon, goes up to a mesa top, and descends to the shore of El Vado Lake, a wintering ground for bald eagles and many other birds.

Dining and Lodging

$ ✕ **Pastore's Feed and General Store.** Inside a century-old general store,
★   this funky café serves up homemade cinnamon rolls, muffins, and burritos for breakfast and gourmet sandwiches, homemade soup, and salad for lunch and early dinner. It's a fun hangout with better food than just about anything else in Chama, and everyone seems to know one another. ✉ *100 Market St.,* ☎ *505/588–7821. No credit cards. Closed Sun.*

$$ ▥ **El Vado Ranch.** This old-time hunting camp with gas-heated cabins on the river is a launch site for rafters and a favorite haunt of fishermen. They're still bragging over here about the state-record brown trout they caught in 1946. ✉ *3150 NM 112 (Box 129), Tierra Amarilla 87575,* ☎ *505/588–7354. 9 cabins. AE, MC, V. Closed Jan.–Feb.*

$ ⚠ **El Vado RV Resort.** Tent and RV travelers can plant themselves 2 mi from El Vado Lake and 5 mi from El Vado Lake State Park at this campsite among trees and sagebrush. Senior citizens are the majority here. Hookups cost $19. ⊠ *NM 112 W (Box 89), Tierra Amarilla 87575,* ☎ *505/588–7225. 110 sites with 5 RV rental units. Showers, grocery, pool, recreation room. Closed Oct. 15–Apr. 15.*

Ghost Ranch

⑮ *36 mi south of Los Ojos and 10 mi northwest of Abiquiu on U.S. 84.*

For art historians, the name Ghost Ranch brings to mind Georgia O'-Keeffe, who lived on but a small parcel of this 20,000-acre dude and cattle ranch. The ranch's owner in the 1930s—conservationist and publisher of *Nature Magazine* Arthur Pack—first invited O'Keeffe here to visit in 1934; Pack soon sold the artist the 7-acre plot on which she lived summer through fall for most of the rest of her life.

In 1955, Pack donated the rest of the ranch to the Presbyterian Church, which continues to use Pack's original structures and about 55 acres of land as the Ghost Ranch Conference Center, which is open year-round. Summer is the busiest season, when dozens of workshops take place, on subjects ranging from poetry and literary arts, to photography, horseback riding, and every conceivable traditional craft of northern New Mexico. Guests camp or stay in semi-rustic cottages or casitas. After registering at the main office, you may come in and hike high among the wind-hewn rocks so beloved by O'Keeffe (but her original house is closed to the public). ⊠ *Ghost Ranch Conference Center, U.S. 81,* ☎ *505/685–4333.*

The **Ghost Ranch Living Museum** is on the edge of Ghost Ranch. A trail passes by native trees and wildlife enclosures (containing rolly-polly beavers, jittery prairie dogs, brilliant red-and-blue-headed wild turkeys, and formidable elk). Newer exhibits trace how mankind has lived on and utilized the land around Ghost Ranch for more than 1,000 years. ⊠ *Off U.S. 84, just north of Ghost Ranch Conference Center,* ☎ *505/ 685-4312.* ▣ *$3.* ☉ *Tues.–Sat. 9–4.*

The **Florence Hawley Ellis Museum of Anthropology** contains Indian tools, pottery, and other artifacts excavated from the Ghost Ranch Gallina digs. Pioneer anthropologist Florence Hawley Ellis conducted excavations at Chaco Canyon and at other sites in New Mexico. Adjacent to the Ellis Museum, the **Ruth Hall Museum of Paleontology** exhibits the New Mexico state fossil, the coelophysis, also known as "the littlest dinosaur," originally excavated near Ghost Ranch. ⊠ *Ghost Ranch,* ☎ *505/685–4333.* ▣ *Donation $2.* ☉ *Memorial Day–Labor Day, Tues.– Sat. 9–5, Sun. 1–5; Labor Day–Memorial Day, Tues.–Sat. 9–12, 1–5.*

The **Dar al Islam** (⊠ Hwy. 155 at sign 42A, ☎ 505/685–4378) adobe mosque was built by Egyptian architect Hassan Fathy, and visitors are welcome. The annual North American Muslim Pow-wow is held here each June. To reach the mosque from Bode's (☞ *below*), drive ¼ mi north, turn right onto unpaved County Road 155, and proceed 3 mi, making a left at the main entrance sign.

OFF THE BEATEN PATH   **MONASTERY OF CHRIST IN THE DESERT –** Designed by a Japanese monk, this remote rock-and-adobe church can be visited for the 9:15 AM Sunday Mass, on holidays, and for silent retreats (if requested in advance by mail or e-mail). ⊠ *Guestmaster, Christ in the Desert (Box 270), Abiquiu 87510 (pass Ghost Ranch Visitor's Center and turn left on Forest Service Rd. 151. Follow dirt road 13 mi to monastery; road is impassable during rainy weather).* ☎ *No phone.* ✎

En Route Down U.S. 84 toward Abiquiu, subjects of O'Keeffe's work unfold before you, from the precipitous vermilion and ocher cliffs surrounding deep-blue Abiquiu Reservoir, which you'll pass on the right shortly after leaving Ghost Ranch, to old adobe homes and churches. If you stop at the roadside picnic area overlooking the reservoir (at the junction with NM 96), you'll glean a perfect view of Cerro Pedernal, a mountain, sacred to many Native Americans, which figured prominently in many of O'Keeffe's works. High over Ghost Ranch is Chimney Rock, another notable feature favored by the artist.

Abiquiu

16 *15 mi southeast of Ghost Ranch and 50 mi northwest of Santa Fe on U.S. 84.*

This tiny, very traditional Hispanic village was home to *genizaros,* people of mixed tribal backgrounds with Spanish surnames. The surnames came from Spanish families who used Indians as servants. Many descendants of original families still live in the area, although in the past 20 years, Abiquiu has become a nesting ground for those fleeing big-city lifestyles. A feeling of insider versus outsider, and old-timer versus newcomer, still prevails. Newcomers or visitors may find themselves resented; it's best to observe one very important local custom: no photography is allowed in and around the village.

You can visit **Georgia O'Keeffe's home** through advance reservation (four months recommended) with the **Georgia O'Keeffe Foundation** (☎ 505/685–4359), which conducts tours Tuesday, Thursday, and Friday, April–November, for $20. In 1945 Georgia O'Keeffe bought a large, dilapidated late-18th-century Spanish colonial adobe compound just off the Plaza. Upon the 1946 death of her husband, photographer Alfred Stieglitz, she left New York City and began dividing her time permanently between this home, which figured prominently in many of her works, and the one in Ghost Ranch. She wrote about the house, "When I first saw the Abiquiú house it was a ruin. . . . As I climbed and walked about in the ruin I found a patio with a very pretty well house and a bucket to draw up water. It was a good-sized patio with a long wall with a door on one side. That wall with a door in it was something I had to have. It took me 10 years to get it—three more years to fix the house up so I could live in it—and after that the wall with the door was painted many times." The patio is featured in *Black Patio Door* (1955) and *Patio with Cloud* (1956). O'Keeffe died in 1986 at the age of 98 and left provisions in her will to ensure that the property's houses would never be public monuments.

Bode's (✉ U.S. 84, ☎ 505/685–4422), across from the Abiquiu post office, is much more than a gas station. It's a popular stop for newspapers, cold drinks, supplies, and excellent green chile stew and sandwiches. The station serves as an exchange post for news and gossip.

OFF THE   **EL RITO –** This center of crafts, particularly Rio Grande weaving, has a
BEATEN PATH general store and **El Farolito** (✉ Main St., ☎ 505/581–9509), a minuscule dinner restaurant on the town's tree-shaded Main Street that serves State Fair blue-ribbon chili at its eight tables. The ride here offers a stunning view of the Sangre de Cristos. ✉ *East of Abiquiu on U.S. 84, take a left and head north 12 mi on NM 554.*

Dining and Lodging

$$$$ ✕🏨 **Rancho de San Juan.** Technically in Española, this secluded 225-
★   acre Relais & Châteaux compound lies within close proximity of Abiquiu, hugging the base of Black Mesa. Many of the rooms at this

understatedly and very romantic inn are self-contained suites, some set around a central courtyard and others farther out amid the wilderness. All rooms have museum-quality Southwestern furnishings, CD-stereos, and local artworks; some rooms have fireplaces, Jacuzzi tubs, and full kitchens. A full health spa is planned for the near future, and a four-course prix-fixe dinner of some of New Mexico's finest contemporary cooking is available (by reservation only) in the intimate restaurant ($$$), Wednesday through Sunday. Guests can also hike up to a serene hand-carved sandstone shrine on a bluff high above the property. ⊠ *U.S. 285, 3½ mi north of U.S. 84 (Box 4140), Española, 87533,* ☎ *505/ 753–6818 or 800/726–7121,* ℻ *505/753–6818. 9 rooms, 8 suites. Restaurant, kitchens (some), hiking. AE, D, DC, MC, V.* ⊛

$$–$$$ ✕⊡ **Abiquiu Inn and Cafe Abiquiu.** Deep in the Chama Valley, the inn has a secluded, exotic feel, almost like an oasis, with lavishly decorated rooms, including several four-person casitas, with wood stoves or fire-places and tiled baths. Middle Eastern and Mediterranean cuisine are on the menu at the café ($–$$). The inn is owned and operated by the Dar al-Islam mosque (☞ Ghost Ranch, *above*) and is the departure point for tours of the O'Keeffe home; it also has an exceptional art gallery, crafts shop, and gardens. ⊠ *U.S. 84 (Box 120), Abiquiu, 87510,* ☎ *505/685–4378 or 800/447–5621,* ℻ *800/447–5621 ext. *2. 19 rooms, 5 casitas. Restaurant, shops. AE, D, DC, MC, V.* ⊛

CHACO CANYON AND THE JEMEZ MOUNTAINS

The rough access roads to Chaco—and that there are no gas service, food concessions, or hotels—keeps this archaeological treasure free from the overcrowding that can mar other national park visits: only about 85,000 people visit annually, compared with at least 10 times that number to Canyon de Chelly, which is just 80 mi away as the crow flies. In terms of fascinating history and the amazing degree to which it has been preserved, Chaco is without peer in North America. Make every possible attempt to see it. Farther south, the Jemez Mountains abound with mountain springs and are home to the thriving Jemez Pueblo, whose people are believed to have descended from the original Chacoans.

Chaco Culture National Historical Park

★ ⑰ *144 mi west of Abiqui via NM 96 to NM 44/U.S. 550 to (unpaved) NM 57 south; 90 mi south of Farmington via NM 44/U.S. 550 to (un-paved) NM 57 south; 78 mi north of Grants via I–40 west to (unpaved) NM 57 north.*

The roads accessing **Chaco Canyon** are rutted and generally awful, even impassable during inclement weather, but persevere and you'll even-tually reach the entrance (and paved loop road) of the largest exca-vated ruins in North America. The more than 2,000 sites were constructed between 900 and 1,150 years ago. You'll learn volumes about the sophistication, scientific knowledge, craftsmanship, and sheer ingenuity of the Anasazi, the ancestors of today's Pueblo Indi-ans. The Anasazi built a system of 400 mi of roads radiating out in straight lines from Chaco Canyon, as well as irrigation ditches to water their cultivated fields. The complexity of the masonry and ve-neered walls of these dwellings, such as Pueblo Bonito, which once stood five stories tall and held 800 rooms, is astounding. Did 5,000 people once live here? Or was Chaco maintained as a ceremonial and trade center? The more that is learned about such phenomena as the Sun Dag-ger—a spear of light that appears in the same specific location at each summer solstice—the more questions arise about the creators of this truly marvelous place.

At the visitor center you can meander through a small museum on Chaco culture, peruse the bookstore, and buy bottled water (but no food). From here drive along the paved loop road to the various trailheads for the ruins; at each you'll find a small box containing a detailed self-guided tour brochure (a 50¢ donation per map is requested). Many of the 13 ruins at Chaco require a significant hike, but a few of the most impressive are just a couple hundred yards off the road.

Pueblo Bonito is perhaps the most brilliant of the ruins, a massive semi-circular "great house" that once stood four stories in places and encompasses many kivas and interconnected cells. The park trail runs alongside the outer mortar-and-sandstone walls, up a hill that allows a great view over the entire canyon, and then right through the ruin and several rooms. It is the most substantial of the structures—the ritualistic and cultural center of a Chacoan culture that may once have comprised some 150 settlements. Pueblo Bonito was used from AD 850 to about AD 1150, longer than any other area ruin.

Not far from the visitor center is a park service–operated campground, with tables, fireplaces, and toilets. Camping is limited to seven days and costs $10 per site per night. The campsite's primitiveness is its greatest asset: the nights come alive with bursts of stars, and the only noise is that of nature. The primary advantage of staying here is being here early in the morning and having a full day to explore the ruins and perhaps hike some of the backcountry trails. ⊠ *NM 57,* ☏ *505/786–7014.* ▣ *$8 per car.* ☉ *Memorial Day–Labor Day, daily 8–6; Labor Day–Memorial Day, daily 8–5.*

En Route   As you head back toward Albuquerque on NM 44/U.S. 550, it's a 52-mi drive from Nageezi to Cuba, but it can feel longer because there isn't much happening along the roadside. **Cuba** is a good place to stop for gas and, depending on your inclination and the season, hot coffee or cold pop. There are gas stations, a convenience store, and **El Bruno's** (⊠ NM 44/U.S. 550 at NM 126, ☏ 505/289–9429), a very good Mexican restaurant that's right on the highway, plus a handful of inexpensive motels—your best bet in this regard is the **Cuban Lodge** (⊠ 6332 NM 44/U.S. 550, ☏ 505/289–3475).

Jemez Pueblo

⑱   *46 mi south of Cuba via NM 44/U.S. 550 to NM 4 northeast; 47 mi north of Albuquerque via I–25 north to NM 44/U.S. 550 north to NM 4 northeast; 50 mi southwest of Los Alamos via NM 4.*

Jemez Pueblo is set along the Jemez River, where fields of chile and corn stand bright green beneath soaring cliffs of red rock. After Pecos Pueblo (☞ Chapter 4) was abandoned in the 1838, Jemez was the state's only pueblo with residents who spoke Towa (different from Tiwa and Tewa). In addition to the pueblo, the Jemez Reservation encompasses 88,000 acres, with two lakes, Holy Ghost Springs and Dragonfly Lake, off NM 4. The lakes are open from April to October on weekends and holidays; to fish you must purchase a permit. The only part of the pueblo open to the public is the **Walatowa Visitor Center,** which includes a gift shop, a photo display, and a short wheelchair-accessible nature walk. On weekends, from 10 to 6 when weather permits, arts and crafts and traditional foods are sold at **Jemez Red Rocks,** an area of stalls and shops about 2½ mi north of the visitor center on NM 4. The pueblo is noted for its polychrome pottery. Red Rocks hosts arts-and-crafts fairs on Memorial Day weekend, the second weekend in October, and on the first weekend in December. The Walatowa Convenience Store, on NM 4 across from Jemez Red Rocks, has a gas station (one of the few in this area). Interesting group educational tours and demonstrations can be arranged in advance; call for information. ⊠ *Trading Post Rd. off NM 4,* ☎ *505/834–7235.* ⚑ *Free.* ☉ *Weekdays 10–4, weekends 10–4. Photographing, sketching, and video recording are prohibited.*

Jemez Springs

⑲ *13 mi north of Jemez Pueblo on NM 4.*

The small town of Jemez Springs is a year-round vacation destination, with hiking, cross-country skiing, and camping in the nearby U.S. Forest Service areas. The town's biggest tourist draws are Jemez State Monument and Soda Dam, but many people come here for relaxation at the town's bathhouse.

The original structure at the **Jemez Spring Bath House** was erected in the 1870s near a mineral hot spring. Many other buildings were added over the years, and the complex was completely renovated into an intimate Victorian-style hideaway in the mid-1990s. You can soak in a mineral bath for $8. Massages cost between $30 (for 30 minutes) and $65 (for 90 minutes). An acupuncturist is available with advance notice. Beauty treatments include facials, manicures, and pedicures. One bathhouse package ($72) includes a half-hour bath, an herbal blanket wrap, and a one-hour massage. It's best to make reservations for services. ⊠ *NM 4,* ☎ *505/829–3303.* ☉ *Memorial Day–Labor Day, daily 9–9; Labor Day–Memorial Day, daily 10–7:30.*

Jemez State Monument contains impressive Spanish and Native American ruins. About 600 years ago ancestors of the people of Jemez Pueblo built several villages in and around the narrow mountain valley. One of the villages was Guisewa, or "Place of the Boiling Waters." The Spanish colonists built a mission church beside it, San José de los Jemez, which was abandoned in 1630. ⊠ *NM 4, Jemez Springs,* ☎ *505/829–3530.* ⚑ *Apr.–Oct. $3, Nov.–Mar. $2.* ☉ *Daily 8:30–5.*

The geological wonder known as **Soda Dam** was created over thousands of years by travertine deposits—minerals that precipitate out of geothermal springs. With its strange mushroom-shape exterior and caves split by a roaring waterfall, it's no wonder the spot was considered sacred by Native Americans. In summer, it's popular for swimming. ⊠ *NM 4, 1 mi north of Jemez State Monument.*

Dining and Lodging

$ ✕ **Los Ojos.** Burgers, beer, and billiards are the trademarks of this jolly restaurant and bar. Take a log stool at the bar or dine in a booth. A huge stone fireplace is topped by an elk rack and the walls are covered with local doodads. ⊠ *17596 NM 4,* ☎ *505/829–3547. D, MC, V.*

$$$ 🏠 **Riverdancer Inn.** On 5½ acres along the Jemez River beneath towering mesas, this inn has rooms with cove ceilings, tile floors, and Native American arts and crafts. All open onto a plaza with a natural spring. Wellness packages include massage, acupuncture, and aromatherapy. ⊠ *16445 NM 4, 87025,* ☎ *505/829–3262 or 800/809–3262,* 🖷 *505/ 829–3262. 6 rooms. D, MC, V. BP.*

Bernalillo

⑳ *42 mi south of Jemez Springs via NM 4 to NM 44/U.S. 550, 17 mi north of Albuquerque via I–25.*

Once a rather tranquil Hispanic village, Bernalillo is today one of New Mexico's fastest-growing towns—it's increasingly absorbing the suburban growth northward from Albuquerque, just 17 mi south. The town holds a Wine Festival each Labor Day weekend. But the most memorable annual event is the Fiesta of San Lorenzo, which has honored the town's patron saint for nearly 400 years. On August 10, San Lorenzo Day, the entire town takes to the streets to participate in the traditional masked *matachine* dance. Matachines, of Moorish origin, were brought to this hemisphere by the Spanish. In New Mexico various versions are danced to haunting fiddle music, in both Indian pueblos and old Spanish villages at different holidays. Though interpretations of the matachines are inexact, one general theme is that of conquest. One dancer, wearing a devil's mask and wielding a whip, presides over the others. A young girl, dressed in white, is also present.

㉑ **Coronado State Monument** is named in honor of Francisco Vásquez de Coronado, the leader of the first organized Spanish expedition into the Southwest, from 1540 to 1542. The prehistoric **Kuaua Pueblo**, on a bluff overlooking the Rio Grande, is believed to have been the headquarters of Coronado and his army, who were caught unprepared by severe winter weather during their search for the legendary Seven Cities of Gold. A worthy stop, the monument has a museum in a restored kiva, with copies of magnificent frescoes done in black, yellow, red, blue, green, and white. The frescoes depict fertility rites, rain dances, and hunting rituals. The original artworks are preserved in the small visitor center. Adjacent to the monument is **Coronado State Park**, which has campsites and picnic grounds, both open year-round. In autumn the views at the monument and park are especially breathtaking, with the trees turning russet and gold. ⊠ *NM 44/U.S. 550*, ☎ *505/867–5351.* ☞ *May–Sept. $3, Sept.–May $2.* ⊙ *Daily 8:30–5.*

Dining and Lodging

$$$ ✕ **Prairie Star.** Residents of Albuquerque often make the 20-minute drive to this 1940s Pueblo Revival hacienda. It's renowned for the sunset views from its patio. The menu combines new American, Southwestern, and classical cuisine, including trout with piñon nuts, tender Greek-style rack of lamb, nightly seafood specials, and blue-corn crabcake appetizers. The breads and desserts are made on the premises. The culinary quality doesn't always live up to the fabulous setting, but this is still a safe bet for a memorable meal. ⊠ *255 Prairie Star Rd.,* ☎ *505/867–3327. AE, D, DC, MC, V.*

$–$$ ✕ **Range Cafe & Bakery.** Huevos rancheros, giant cinnamon rolls, grilled Portobello-mushroom burgers, roast-turkey sandwiches, homemade meat loaf with garlic mashed potatoes, and the signature dessert, "Death by Lemon," are among the highlights at this favorite New Mexican restaurant. All the above, plus a full complement of rich, decadent Taos Cow ice cream (cinnamon is the house special flavor, available only here), is served in a refurbished mercantile building with a dead-center view of the Sandia Mountains. ⊠ *925 Camino del Pueblo,* ☎ *505/867–1700. Reservations not accepted. AE, D, MC, V.*

$ 🏕 **Albuquerque North Bernalillo KOA.** Cottonwoods, pines, evergreens, and willows shade this park, where morning brings a free pancake breakfast and in summer free outdoor movies are screened. ⊠ *555 S. Hill Rd., 87004,* ☎ *505/867–5227 or 800/562–3616. 57 RV sites, 36 tent sites, 6 cabins. Rest rooms, showers, LP gas, café, heated pool, badminton, basketball, croquet, horseshoes, video games, coin laundry, meeting room. D, MC, V.*

En Route Serene **Corrales,** 10 mi south of Bernalillo via NM 528 to NM 448, is an ancient agricultural community now inhabited by artists, craftspeople, and the affluent—plus a few descendants of the old families. Small galleries, shops, and places to eat dot the town, and in the fall, roadside fruit and vegetable stands open. Bordered by Albuquerque and Rio Rancho, Corrales makes a pleasant escape to winding dirt roads, fields of corn, and apple orchards. On summer weekends, visit the Corrales Farmers' Market; in October, the village holds a Harvest Festival.

NORTHWESTERN NEW MEXICO A TO Z

Arriving and Departing

By Bus

Texas, New Mexico & Oklahoma Coaches (☎ 505/325–1009 or 800/231–2222), affiliated with Greyhound Lines, provides service to Grants, Gallup, Farmington, and other towns.

By Car

A car is your best bet getting to and around the region. Interstate 40 heads due west from Albuquerque toward Arizona. U.S. 64 leads west from Taos into northwestern New Mexico and east from Arizona. NM 44/U.S. 550 travels to the northwest from I–25 (15 mi north of Albuquerque), intersecting with U.S. 64 at Bloomfield, 14 mi east of Farmington. Road conditions vary with the seasons. Winter can create snowy, icy roads; summer can bring ferocious thunderstorms, hailstorms, and flash flood warnings.

By Train

Amtrak (☎ 800/872–7245) has service to Gallup from Albuquerque on the *Southwest Chief*, which departs Albuquerque daily at 4:23 PM and arrives in Gallup at 6:45 PM.

Contacts and Resources

Emergencies

Ambulance, Fire, Police (☎ 911). **Rehoboth McKinley Christian Health Care Services** (✉ 1901 Red Rock Dr., Gallup, ☎ 505/863–7141).

Late-Night Pharmacies

Walgreens (✉ Main and 30th Sts., Farmington, ☎ 505/325–1749; 1626 Historic Rte. 66, Gallup, ☎ 505/722–9499).

Visitor Information

Chama Valley Chamber of Commerce (✉ 499 S. Terrace Ave., 87520, ☎ 505/756–2306 or 800/477–0149). **Farmington Convention and Visitors Bureau** (✉ 3041 E. Main St., 87402, ☎ 505/326–7602 or 800/448–1240, 🖎). **Gallup Convention and Visitors Bureau** (✉ 701 Montoya St., 87301, ☎ 505/863–3841 or 800/242–4282, 🖎). **Grants/Cibola County Chamber of Commerce** (✉ 100 N. Iron Ave., 87020, ☎ 800/748–2142, 🖎). **Tourism Department, Jicarilla Apache Tribe**(✉ Box 507, Dulce 87528, ☎ 505/759–3242, FAX 505/759–3005). **Navajo Nation Tourism Office** (✉ Box 633, Window Rock, AZ 86515, ☎ 520/871–6436 or 520/871–7371, FAX 520/871–7942 or 520/871–7381).

7 SOUTHEASTERN NEW MEXICO

INCLUDING WHITE SANDS NATIONAL MONUMENT AND TEXAS'S GUADALUPE MOUNTAINS

There is beauty in simplicity—in the graceful curve of a stark white sand dune or the smooth dome of a stalagmite millions of years in the making. Even the desert's seemingly barren hills are rich in shadow, light, and color during sunset. In higher elevations, fragrant pines and cold mountain streams are oblivious to the summer heat below. Southeastern New Mexico was one of the country's last frontiers, and uncivilized charm lingers in its patches of unspoiled wilderness.

Updated by
Marilyn
Haddrill

BURSTING WITH GEOLOGICAL CONTRAST, southeastern New Mexico transforms before your eyes as you drive from one ecological zone to the next. Parched red earth that musters up little more than scrub oak leads to the blindingly white gypsum dunes of White Sands National Monument. From nearby Alamogordo, you can double your altitude in a 19-mi climb through Lincoln National Forest to the cool air of Cloudcroft (8,600 ft). Mule deer, with their large, curious ears, can be spotted in either the Lincoln National Forest's juniper and pines or among sand dunes along the Pecos River farther east. The Chihuahuan desert, a seemingly monotonous landscape left behind by a long-vanished ocean, holds the underground wonderland of Carlsbad Caverns, the hulking El Capitán peak, and, in Guadalupe Mountains National Park, pure, bubbling streams and prickly cactus.

For all its beauty, the area can seem harsh to strangers. Spanish settlers quickly bypassed the region in favor of the more friendly environs of the Rio Grande area in the western and northern portions of New Mexico. Yet, it was in this very region—at Black Water Draw near what is now Portales and Clovis—that evidence of some of the earliest inhabitants of North America was unearthed. Primitive hunters and gatherers lived here as long as 11,000 years ago. Artifacts prove their coexistence with such fantastic creatures as the monstrous wooly mammoth.

Native Americans lived here for hundreds of years before the eventual Spanish encroachment. Though some Hispanic settlers had established scattered communities, the area was seen primarily as the homeland of Mescalero Apaches and other tribes. In the mid-1800s, Fort Sumner and Fort Stanton became symbols of a determined U.S. takeover, offering protection for miners and Anglo settlers during intensified skirmishes with tribes. Near Ruidoso, in what is left of their traditional homeland in the Sacramento Mountains, the Mescalero Apaches now own a luxury resort and ski area that attracts tens of thousands of visitors annually.

The grasslands in southeastern New Mexico came to be ruled by cattle kings such as John Chisum, who moved from Texas in 1872 to ranch near what is now Roswell. During the first half of 1878, baby-face outlaw Billy the Kid (Henry McCarty) became a living legend during the infamous Lincoln County War, waged by rival entrepreneurs. Even the toughest of Texans referred to this neighboring corner of New Mexico as the "badlands" for its hostile terrain and notoriety as a hideout for outlaws (you'll find many "Billy the Kid was here" references in the area). In the vanished town of Seven Rivers, between Carlsbad and Artesia, shoot-outs were said to be so common that "you could read your newspaper by the light of the gunfire." Many thought the accounts were exaggerated, until the old Seven Rivers Cemetery was moved in the early 1980s to make way for Brantley Dam and reservoir. Bullets, knife blades, and crushed bones were found with the young cowboys buried there.

The discovery of valuable minerals in the early 1900s—including oil, gas, and potash—attracted roughnecks and miners who tackled the formidable task of forcing the land to surrender its wealth. As reminders of this effort, grasshopper-like pumping jacks slurp oil from below dunes and plains. Potash mine refineries are scattered near Carlsbad, though many are closing as the ore—used primarily as a fertilizer ingredient—is depleted. The Pecos River merely trickles in places as precious water has been diverted to cultivate crops such as alfalfa and cotton. But local springs still feed the river in downtown Carlsbad, where a watery oasis provides a haven for waterfowl and those who swim, boat, or fish.

More than any other corner of the state, southeastern New Mexico retains a delicious feeling of wildness. The nearest interstate is generally as far as 200 mi away. Stargazing is no idle pastime here—no lights from strip malls or urban sprawl pollute the heavens. The Milky Way splashes across a sky so dark that if you had the time to count them, you'd swear you could see billions of stars. Scientists built one of the largest solar observatories in the world in Cloudcroft, owing to the clean view. The town of Alamogordo below it has special lights to reduce any glare. Despite the clear skies, this corner is the home of Roswell and the unending debate over an unidentified flying object (UFO) that passed through the night sky in July 1947.

Pleasures and Pastimes

Dining

Leave the fancy duds at home, because you're unlikely to find a formal dining room to strut into. Much of southeastern New Mexico is cowboy country: thick steaks and barbecue make the meal. The dress code is casual at all the restaurants reviewed below, with the possible exception of evening meals at the elegant Dan-Li-Ka Restaurant near Ruidoso. While you wouldn't be out of place in dressy clothes here, informal attire also is welcome.

Lodging

Southeastern New Mexico has the usual chain motels and your best choice for a luxury resort, quaint cabin, or B&B would be in the Sacramento Mountains (Ruidoso and Lincoln), which is primarily a resort area. Otherwise, you'll find most communities offer the type of practical, comfortable lodging meant for business travelers.

Outdoor Activities and Sports

Fishing, hiking, and boating on the Pecos River and in Brantley Lake State Park are among the popular activities in southeastern New Mexico. Except on certain lakes operated by the Mescalero Apaches, who charge separate fees and set their own catch limits, you'll need a fishing license. Clerks at most sporting-goods shops can inform you of fishing regulations, which can vary. If you're hiking, be aware that trails in arid and even mountainous regions seldom have water available. Always carry water with you if you plan an excursion of more than a mile. Before you pack simply a purifier, call the administrators of the area in which you'll be hiking and find out about water sources. You might have to pack in all the water you need.

Exploring Southeastern New Mexico

The wildly rugged Guadalupe and Sacramento mountain ranges cut through the south-central portion of the state, dividing the Pecos River valley to the east from the Mesilla River valley to the west. Make the Carlsbad Caverns National Park and White Sands National Monument on opposite sides of these mountains a top priority: they are truly among the world's greatest natural wonders.

Great Itineraries

You can explore a cross section of the southeast's attractions in three days by moving quickly. If you start your trip from El Paso, Texas, swing through Guadalupe Mountains and Carlsbad Caverns national parks first. If you're dropping down from Albuquerque, reverse the itinerary and make cities such as Ruidoso and Roswell your first stops before traveling on to the national parks.

IF YOU HAVE 3 DAYS

It's best to start from the gateway of El Paso, Texas, and make **Guadalupe Mountains National Park** ① your first rest stop. Just north of the mountains, over the Texas state line is **Carlsbad Caverns National Park** ②. Take the Big Room Tour in the late morning or early afternoon, and in warmer months, be sure to catch the spectacular evening bat exodus out of the cave's mouth. Afterward, you can drop by Granny's Opera House in **White's City** for a live melodrama performance and overnight in ⊞ **Carlsbad** ③. On the morning of day two, stop by **Living Desert Zoo and Gardens State Park** before heading north to **Roswell** ④ to learn about alleged alien visitors at the **International UFO Museum and Research Center** and view the impressive collections of the **Roswell Museum and Art Center,** including the Goddard rocketry display and paintings by Southwestern artists. Push on to overnight in ⊞ **Lincoln** ⑦. You'll awaken in a town of 70, where the ghosts of past gunslingers loom large. Make time for some outdoor activities in the mountains surrounding **Ruidoso** ⑧. A ski resort is open in the winter, while horse racing takes place at **Ruidoso Downs** in summer. Arrange your schedule so that you'll have at least an hour for **White Sands National Monument** ⑪, which is open during the summer until 9 PM.

IF YOU HAVE 5 DAYS

Spend most of your first day at **Guadalupe Mountains National Park** ① in Texas. At **McKittrick Canyon** are three trails of varying lengths. On your first evening, view the bat flight at **Carlsbad Caverns National Park** ② and spend the night in ⊞ **White's City.**

On the morning of day two, return to Carlsbad Caverns to take the Natural Entrance Route into the depths of the cavern, after which you can loop through the interior, and then take the Big Room Tour. That afternoon, visit **Living Desert Zoo and Gardens State Park** in ⊞ **Carlsbad** ③. In the evening, consider strolling some of the scenic walkways along the Pecos River at the **Lake Carlsbad Recreation Area.**

On day three, drive north on U.S. 285 to **Roswell** ④, where you can stop at the **Roswell Museum and Art Center** and **International UFO Museum and Research Center.** Continue to ⊞ **Lincoln** ⑦ on U.S. 70/380 west and take in a bit of the Wild West before settling down for the night. Spend day four perusing the museums and galleries of ⊞ **Ruidoso** ⑧ and **Ruidoso Downs.** In the morning take your post-breakfast hike in **Cloudcroft** ⑫ before examining the space ware at the **Space Center** in **Alamogordo** ⑩. Close your day and finish up the last roll of film at **White Sands National Monument** ⑪.

When to Tour Southeastern New Mexico

Winters tend to be gentle in the desert regions, but between May and early September blistering heat is not uncommon. Even the mountainous areas can be uncomfortably warm during a hot spell. Plan summer outdoor excursions for early morning or late evening. Spring is cooler, but it's often accompanied by nasty, dust-laden winds. One of the best times to visit is between late September and early November, when skies are clear blue and the weather is usually balmy. In winter months, keep in mind that the higher elevations of Ruidoso can accumulate some hefty snows.

THE SOUTHEAST CORNER

Some folks refer to the southeast as "Little Texas," and geographically and in other ways it is indeed an extension of its neighbor to the east. The biggest attraction—Carlsbad Caverns National Park—is just above the state line. Cattle and sheep roam miles of arid pastures, reminiscent of days when livestock growers challenged a harsh, defiant land

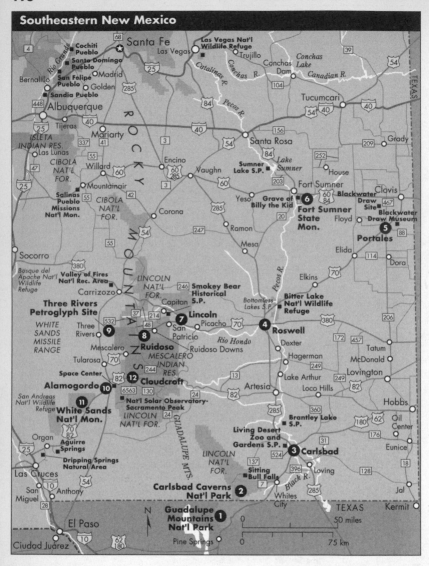

Southeastern New Mexico

that didn't yield easily to civilization. During the past two decades a steady migration of newer residents—many of them retirees leaving crowded metropolitan areas for wide-open spaces and clean air—has introduced a more rounded mix of cultures and viewpoints.

Guadalupe Mountains National Park

❶ *U.S. 62/180, 110 mi northeast of El Paso, Texas; 40 mi southwest of Carlsbad Caverns National Park.*

The vast Guadalupe Mountains jut out of the desert, and El Capitán peak, a lordly symbol of the mountains themselves, is visible for miles in all directions. The mountains provide sanctuary for diverse populations of vegetation and wildlife, including hundreds of mule deer and the occasional mountain lion. Fossils left over from an ancient sea are part of a geological terrain popular with students and researchers.

This national park is relatively new, created by Congress in 1966 and formally established in 1972. The heart of the acreage is from a gift of 5,632 acres given to the federal government by the Wallace Pratt family. Pratt had worked as a geologist for Humble Oil, later known as Exxon, when he first viewed and later acquired the wildly beautiful McKittrick Canyon area of the park in 1921. Most of the remaining acreage was added in a purchase of 70,000 acres from the J. C. Hunter Ranch.

These untamed foothills and canyons have never been tapped for development because of a general lack of water. If you don't have time for a hike, you can pull into the **visitor center** to view exhibits and a slide show that can give you a quick introduction to what this 86,416-acre park is all about. You'll see panoramic vistas and glimpses of wildflowers. But photos just can't do justice to the real thing. There are 80 mi of hiking trails, from short excursions to grueling adventures. Take your pick. But try not to leave without giving one of the trails a try.

About 1 mi northeast of the visitor center, turn west off U.S. 62/180 to see the **Pinery Butterfield Station Ruins**. This was one of the stops along the old Butterfield Overland Mail Coach route in the mid-1800s, where passengers en route from St. Louis or San Francisco could pause for rest and refreshment. There is a paved ⅔-mi round-trip trail. At the **Frijole Ranch History Museum** you can view cultural exhibits representing the Guadalupe Mountains area. Turn west off U.S. 62/180, about 2 mi northeast of the visitor center.

★ The **McKittrick Canyon** gate opens from 8 until 4:30 daily in winter months and from 8 through 6 when Daylight Saving Time is in effect. In this day-use area you can hike almost 1 mi on a nature loop or take a 4½-mi round-trip excursion to the Pratt Lodge (now vacant). Another option is a 6¾-mi round-trip to the Grotto picnic area. Turn west off U.S. 62/180 6 mi northeast of the visitor center and travel 4 mi to McKittrick Canyon Visitor Center, where the trails begin. ✉ *Guadalupe Mountains National Park (HC60, Box 400), Salt Flat, TX 79847, off U.S. 62/180 55 mi southwest of Carlsbad, and 110 mi northeast of El Paso,* ☎ *915/828–3251.* ☞ *Free.*

Camping

🏕 **Cornudas High Desert RV Park & Motel.** This pit stop in the middle of nowhere is on your way to the Guadalupe Mountains, 63 mi east of El Paso. It offers eight full-utility hookups for $16.50 nightly. A six-room hotel decorated with a Western storefront was scheduled to reopen by 2001. Owner May Carson makes a great green-chile burger (☞ Dining, *below*). ✉ *Off U.S. 62/180,* ☎ *915/964–2409.*

🏕 **Dog Canyon Campground.** This campground is a little tricky to find—as well as remote—but well worth the effort. On the north side of Guadalupe National Park, it can be accessed by turning west on County Road 408 off U.S. 62/180, about 9 mi south of Carlsbad. Drive 23 mi on this county road; then turn south on NM 137. Travel 43 mi through Lincoln National Forest until the road dead-ends just at the park boundary, at the New Mexico–Texas state line. Here, you'll find a very well-maintained camping area in a coniferous forest, where hiking trails are available. Standard fees for sites are $8 nightly. ✉ *Guadalupe Mountains National Park,* ☎ *505/981–2418. 4 RV spaces, 9 tent sites.*

🏕 **Pine Springs Campground.** This site behind the visitor center has no dump stations or hookups for recreational vehicles although 18 sites are available. Another 20 sites are available for tent campers. ✉ *Guadalupe Mountains National Park, off U.S. 62/180,* ☎ *915/828–3251. 18 RV sites, 20 tent sites.*

Dining

$ ★ ✕ **Cornudas Café.** Your first thought when you see the colorful flags flapping outside this remote roadside café will be: "How did this get here?" Food has been served at this site for almost a century, dating from the construction of the first roadway through the area. Try the café's famous green chile hamburgers, and enjoy the quirky, ornery ambience. Levi-clad cowboy legs with boots hold up the tables. Visitors leave everything from caps to license plates to business cards to add to the clutter. Owner May Carson never throws any of it away. Mexican imports are for sale in the gift shop. The annual Cornudas Chile Cook-off takes place in September. ✉ *Box 32, HC 60, off U.S. 62/180, 63 mi east of El Paso, Texas, and 103 mi southwest of Carlsbad,* ☎ *915/964–2409. AE, D, DC, MC, V.*

Carlsbad Caverns National Park

★ ❷ *167 mi east of El Paso, Texas, on U.S. 62/180; 320 mi from Albuquerque.*

✎ *following the text of a review is your signal that the property has a Web site, where you will find details and, usually, images; for a link, visit www.fodors.com/urls.*

Hundreds of thousands of people come each year to Carlsbad Caverns National Park to view its subterranean chambers, fantastic rock formations, and delicate mineral sculptures, which have evocative names like Hall of the White Giant, the Kings Palace, the Devils Den, the Caveman, and Iceberg Rock. In this setting you can feel insignificant and yet connected to eternity itself. Near the Rock of Ages stalagmite, a now abandoned tradition called for visitors to sit in the utter darkness during the singing of the hymn *Rock of Ages.*

The park is in the Chihuahuan Desert, which extends north from Mexico into southwestern Texas and southeastern New Mexico. Pictographs near the main cave entrance indicate that pre-Columbian Native Americans took shelter here more than 1,000 years ago, though archaeologists doubt that they ventured far inside. It wasn't until the 19th century that nearby settlers rediscovered the caverns, their attention captured by the smokelike swirling columns of bats leaving the caverns each night to feed on insects. Area caves were mined for bat dung, which was used as fertilizer for many years. No one was interested in the caves for any other reason until the early 1920s, after cowboy Jim White had explored them for two decades. White finally secured a photographer, Ray Davis, to bear witness to his extravagant claims about this amazing underground environment. Davis's photos sparked interest in the caverns. White turned tour operator, taking people down 170 ft in a bucket left over from the days of mining bat guano. The federal government got wind of this natural wonder, and in 1923 President Calvin Coolidge designated the caverns a national monument; in 1930 the area was upgraded to the status of a national park.

The origins of Carlsbad Caverns go back 250 million years, when the 300-mi-long Capitán Reef formed around the edge of the warm, shallow sea that once covered this region. The sea evaporated and the reef was buried until a few million years ago, when a combination of erosion and earthquakes brought parts of it back above ground. Rainwater seeping down through the reef's cracks gradually enlarged them into cavities, which eventually collapsed, forming huge rooms. For eons the evaporated limestone deposited on the cave ceilings grew into great hanging stalactites, which in turn dripped onto the floor. In time massive stalagmites grew up to meet them, and other more fragile formations such as cave pearls, draperies, popcorn, and lily pads were formed.

Don't give in to the temptation to touch the cave's walls and jutting rock formations. Oil from the human hand forms a type of waterproofing that inhibits the natural water seepage. You also shouldn't leave the guided pathways; if you do, you not only risk serious injury but can damage the cave.

The temperature inside Carlsbad Cavern remains at a constant 56°F. It's damp, so bring a sweater and comfortable shoes with rubber soles—because of the moisture, the paved walkways can get slippery. The cavern is well lighted and park rangers provide assistance and information. Electronic signals along the way trigger the CD-ROM audio guide—recorded commentary by park rangers, geologists, and cavers—for the Natural Entrance and Big Room trails. Exhibits at the visitor center describe park history and geology and the lives of bats. You can eat aboveground at the visitor center, or at an underground lunchroom. ⊠ *Carlsbad Caverns National Park, 3225 National Parks Hwy., Carlsbad 88220,* ☎ *505/785–2232 for recorded information and direct contact; 800/967–2283 for reservations (the central National Park Service number).* ☑ *General entrance fee $6; see individual cave descriptions below for additional fees and hrs of operation.* ✆

There are two self-guided routes into Carlsbad Cavern: the **Natural Entrance Route** and the **Big Room Route.** If you take the Natural Entrance Route, you'll proceed on foot along a paved walkway that winds into the caverns' depths for about a mile, passing through underground rooms and descending slowly to a depth of about 750 ft. It takes about one hour to complete; the trail can be slick and the grades are fairly steep, so be prepared for a strenuous hike. The Big Room Route is less difficult. A high-speed elevator from the visitor center carries you down 750 ft to an underground lunchroom where you can begin your exploration. This mile-long route also takes about an hour to walk. A portion of the main cavern is accessible to visitors using wheelchairs. In both cases you'll visit the Big Room, large enough to hold 14 football fields; the highest part of the ceiling reaches 255 ft. ☑ *Combined ticket to Natural Entrance Route and Big Room Route $6.* ☉ *Natural Entrance Route June–mid-Aug., daily 8:30–3:30 (last entry to the caverns); mid-Aug.–May, daily 8:30–2 (last entry to the caverns). Big Room Route June–mid-Aug., daily 8:30–5 (last elevator down); mid-Aug.–May, daily 8:30–3:30 (last elevator down).*

A third option for exploring the caverns is the ranger-led **Kings Palace Tour** through the Kings Palace, the Queens Chamber, the Papoose Room, and the Green Lake Room. The tour covers about a mile, including an uphill 80-ft climb on a switchback trail, and takes about 1½ hours to complete. ☑ *$8 (in addition to $6 general entrance fee to caverns).* ☉ *June–mid-Aug., daily 9–3 on the hr; mid-Aug.–May, daily at 9, 11, 1, and 3.*

A few other **off-trail tours** are available within Carlsbad Caverns. Lefthand Tunnel is in an undeveloped part of the caverns and contains clear pools and ancient reef fossils. Lower Cave, billed as a "moderately strenuous" tour, involves climbs on 50 ft of vertical ladders. Children younger than six are not allowed on this tour. Hall of the White Giant is a strenuous tour that requires squirming long distances on your hands and knees through tight passageways into a remote chamber with glistening white formations. The tour of "wild" Spider Cave takes you through the park's backcountry and involves tight crawlways; avoid this one if you're squeamish. Reservations are essential for the special tours. The minimum age for visitors to the Hall of the White Giant and the Spider Cave is 12. ☎ *505/785–2232; 800/967–2283 for reservations.* ☑ *In addition to general entrance fee to cavern: Lefthand Tunnel $7, Lower Cave $20, Hall of the White Giant $20, Spider Cave $20.* ☉ *Lefthand Tunnel, daily at*

9 AM; Lower Cave, daily at 1; Hall of the White Giant, Sat. at 1; Spider Cave (separate from main cavern), Sun. at 1.

Slaughter Canyon Cave, 25 mi from the main cavern, is much less accessible. Millions of years old, the cave was discovered by Tom Tucker, a local goatherd, in 1937. The cave consists primarily of a 1,140-ft-long corridor with numerous side passages. The total extent of the surveyed passage is 1¾ mi, and the lowest point is 250 ft below the surface. Outstanding formations are the Christmas Tree, the Monarch, the Tear Drop, and the China Wall.

Rangers lead groups of 25 on a two-hour lantern tour of the cave. Children under age six are not permitted. The cave temperature is a constant 62°F, and the humidity is a clammy 90%. You'll need to bring along your own flashlight, hiking boots or good walking shoes (sneakers aren't recommended), and drinking water. Photographs are permitted, but no tripod setups are allowed because the group moves along at a relatively brisk pace. Unless you're in great physical shape and have a long attention span, Slaughter Canyon Cave may be more cave viewing than you bargained for. But it's a great adventure if you want to experience what cave exploration is really like, minus paved pathways and electric lighting.

Make reservations at least a day ahead of your visit; in summer it's recommended you reserve a place at least two weeks ahead. The last few miles of the road to the cave are gravel. The mouth is at the end of a ½-mi path up a 500-ft rise. Allot sufficient time to complete the drive and climb or you might arrive late for the tour. ☎ *505/785–2232; 800/967–2283 for reservations.* ✉ *$15.* ☉ *Tour June–mid-Aug., daily at 10 and 1; mid-Aug.–May, weekends at 10 and 1.*

The newest discovery in Carlsbad Caverns National Park is **Lechuguilla Cave,** the deepest limestone cave in the United States. Scientists began mapping the cave network in 1986, and though they've located more than 106 mi of caverns extending to a depth of 1,567 ft, much more of this area along the park's northern border remains to be investigated. Lechuguilla is not open to the public, but an exhibit describing it can be viewed at the visitor center.

★ Every evening between late May and mid-October at about sunset, Mexican freetail bats swirl by the tens of thousands out of the cavern's entrance to scout for flying insects. Watching the **nightly bat flights** has been one of the greatest attractions at Carlsbad Caverns since 1929. (No scientist has yet figured out how a bat hanging upside down in a dark cave knows when the sun has set outside.) The population of bats in the late 1990s was estimated at about 500,000. Collectively, the bats consume more than 3 tons of bugs per night. Prior to the exodus, which begins at dusk, a park ranger gives an informative talk about these much-maligned creatures. The time of the bat flights varies, so ranger lectures are flexible as well; the time is posted at the visitor center. The bats leave for the warmer climates of Mexico in winter. ✉ *Bat Flight Amphitheater (near visitor center).* ✉ *Free.*

The scenic 9½-mi **Walnut Canyon Desert Drive** begins ½ mi from the visitor center and travels along the top of the ridge to the edge of Rattlesnake Canyon and back down through upper Walnut Canyon to the main entrance road. The backcountry scenery on this one-way gravel loop is stunning; go late in the afternoon or early in the morning to enjoy the full spectrum of changing light and dancing colors. You might also spot some of the many inquisitive mule deer that inhabit the park. The self-guided, partially wheelchair-accessible Desert Nature Walk, about ½ mi long, begins near the cavern's entrance.

Trees shade the picnic and recreation area at **Rattlesnake Springs**, near the Black River—don't let the name scare you; you wouldn't find any more rattlesnakes here than at any other similar site in the Southwest. A favorite of bird-watchers, the springs were a source of water for Native Americans hundreds of years ago. Today it's the main source of water for the park. Overnight camping and parking are not allowed.

Camping

Backcountry camping is by permit only in Carlsbad Caverns National Park; free permits can be obtained at the visitor center, where you can also pick up a map of areas closed to camping. You'll need to hike to campsites. There are no vehicle or RV camping areas in the park.

Nearby Brantley Lake State Park (☞ Carlsbad, *below*) and Dog Canyon Campground (☞ Guadalupe Mountains National Park, *above*) in Lincoln National Forest have camping facilities. Commercial sites can be found in White's City and Carlsbad (☞ *below*).

Outdoor Activities and Sports

BIRD-WATCHING

From turkey vultures to golden eagles, more than 200 species of birds have been identified in Carlsbad Caverns National Park. The best place to bird-watch in the park, if not the entire state, is **Rattlesnake Springs** (☞ *above*). Ask for a checklist at the visitor center and then start looking for red-tailed hawks, red-winged blackbirds, white-throated swifts, northern flickers, pygmy nuthatches, yellow-billed cuckoos, roadrunners, mallards, American coots, and green and blue-winged teal.

HIKING

Hiking in Carlsbad Caverns National Park can be exhilarating—the desert terrain is stark and awe-inspiring—but few trails are marked. A topographical map, available at the visitor center, is helpful for finding some of the old ranch trails. Permits aren't required except for overnight backpacking, but all hikers are requested to register at the information desk at the visitor center. Bring water; there's none available. No pets or guns are permitted.

White's City

7 mi east of Carlsbad Caverns National Park on NM 7, at junction with U.S. 62/180.

At the turnoff from the highway to Carlsbad Caverns, the one-road town of White's City contains motels, restaurants, a saloon, a campground, a grocery store, a post office, a gas station, souvenir shops, a museum, a water park for registered guests, and even a place to take in staged melodramas—all along a simple, Western-style boardwalk. The town is one of the few privately owned towns in the country. The owners, the White family, live in a cluster of homes above the hotel properties.

Early American memorabilia and artifacts—antique dolls and dollhouses, guns and rifles, music boxes, old cars, and a 6,000-year-old mummified Native American (or so the label says)—fill the homespun **Million Dollar Museum.** The collection has undergone some rearranging and renovation including the addition of four new rooms, granting more space to move between exhibits. Thirty-two mostly German dollhouses made between the late-19th and mid-20th centuries are also on display. ⊠ *21 Carlsbad Caverns Hwy off the White's City boardwalk,* ☎ *505/785–2291.* ⊡ *$3.* ⊙ *Mid-May–mid-Sept., daily 7 AM–10 PM; mid-Sept.–mid-May, daily 7–6.*

★ **Granny's Opera House** is the place to go if you're ready to shed your inhibitions and whoop it up. During the hour-long old-fashioned melodramas, you can boo at the villain, throw popcorn, cheer on the heroes, tune up your vocal cords for a sing-along, and be pulled on stage. ⊠ *13 Carlsbad Caverns Hwy.,* ☎ *505/785–2291.* 🎫 *$7 (includes popcorn).* ☉ *June–Sept., Fri.–Mon. at about 7:30 PM, depending on when bats fly at Carlsbad Caverns National Park (☞ above)* .

Dining and Lodging

$–$$ ✕ **Velvet Garter Restaurant and Saloon.** This eatery dishes up steaks, chicken, shrimp, and Mexican food in an Old West atmosphere. Food prices are old-style, too. A 10-ounce rib-eye steak costs $14.95, and all the entrées come with soup and salad. ⊠ *26 Carlsbad Caverns Hwy.,* ☎ *505/785–2291. AE, D, MC, V.*

$ ✕ **Jack's.** A good spot to have a hearty breakfast before heading off to the caverns, this fast-food favorite shares an adobe-style building with the Velvet Garter Restaurant (☞ *above*). Grab a booth and order eggs, a burger, or Mexican food. ⊠ *26 Carlsbad Caverns Hwy.,* ☎ *505/ 785–2291. No credit cards.*

$$ 🏨 **Best Western Cavern Inn.** This Territorial-style, two-story motor inn just outside the entrance leading to Carlsbad Caverns has rooms with Southwestern decor. Under the same ownership next door is the hacienda-style Best Western Guadalupe Inn, with the same rates and Southwestern furnishings. The Guadalupe Inn has 42 rooms. Many tour groups and families stay at both hotels, which share facilities. All guests are free to use the new water park. The high-desert landscaping includes piñon pines, ocotillo cacti, and yucca plants. Mule deer often amble down from their protected haven at Carlsbad Caverns National Park. ⊠ *17 Carlsbad Caverns Hwy. (look for large registration sign on the south side of the road), 88268,* ☎ *505/785–2291 or 800/228–3767,* 🖷 *505/785–2283. 63 rooms. 2 pools, spa, playground. AE, D, DC, MC, V.* ✹

Lincoln National Forest

Access via NM 137 (turn southwest off U.S. 285 12 mi northwest of Carlsbad), U.S. 82 west from Artesia, U.S. 70 west from Roswell, U.S. 82 east from Alamogordo, U.S. 70 east from Tularosa, and U.S. 380 east from Carrizozo. Numerous other gravel or dirt roads lead into the forest.

Covering 1.1 million acres of Eddy, Otero, Chaves, and Lincoln counties, this magnificent forest is distinguished by a diversity of plant and animal life. It encompasses two distinct regions, ranging from arid, lower elevations near Carlsbad to the towering pines and mountain peaks of the Ruidoso area. The forest's southernmost portion of piñon and juniper stretches through the Guadalupe Mountains to connect with the Carlsbad Caverns and Guadalupe Mountains national parks. The forest land has many caves, some of which can be accessed free by permit. Call the **Guadalupe Ranger District** (☎ 505/885–4181) for permit information. These caves are not developed, so be prepared for primitive conditions. The only private development you'll find other than scattered ranches is at **Queen** (49 mi southwest of Carlsbad, on NM 137). This site consists of a small mobile-home community, a restaurant, store, gas station, and church camp. This forested area is hugely popular with hunters lured by ample populations of mule deer.

Water sources in the southernmost forest are virtually nonexistent, except for livestock catchments maintained by ranchers. Coming upon ★ **Sitting Bull Falls**, you'll think you've wandered onto a Hollywood movie set of an oasis. Water cascades off a 150-ft-high cliff face to create clear, sparkling pools below. A 1-mi hike from the parking lot over a paved trail takes you to a desert riparian area with ferns, watercress, and cottonwoods. At the parking lot, the forest service provides rock ramadas for picnic areas. Viewing decks are also available, along with rest rooms. Swimming is permitted, and 16 mi of hiking trails lace the area. The park is open for day use only. If you want to camp overnight, drive southwest on NM 137 until you reach the New Mexico–Texas state line and Dog Canyon Campground (☞ Camping *in* Guadalupe Mountains National Park, *above*). ⊠ *From Carlsbad take U.S. 285 north about 12 mi, then turn west on NM 137 for 27 mi,* ☎ *no phone.* ☜ *$5 per vehicle.* ⊙ *Daily dawn–dusk.*

The northernmost portion of the Lincoln forest, surrounding the resort community of **Ruidoso** (☞ *below*), has some of the more traditional evergreen attributes of snowy mountain peaks, lakes, and gurgling mountain streams. Development has capitalized on this beauty, so the forest becomes part of the ambience of cabins, resorts, church camps, condos, and ski runs. Still, there are many miles of pristine areas. Hiking trails often thread wilderness that is free from civilization's encroachment.

More than 25 camping sites are scattered throughout Lincoln National Forest. While fishing lakes and streams are available on private, municipal, or tribal lands, there is very little opportunity for the sport on public forest land. To obtain more information about hiking, camping, hunting, and other recreation, contact the forest service's main headquarters in Alamogordo (☎ 505/437–6030).

Carlsbad

➌ *27 mi northeast of Carlsbad Caverns National Park, east on NM 7 and north on U.S. 60/180; 20 mi north of White's City on U.S. 62/180.*

On the Pecos River, with 2½ mi of beaches and many picturesque riverside pathways, Carlsbad, population 25,000, seems suspended between the past and the present. The Territorial town square, a block from the river, encircles a Pueblo-style country courthouse designed by New Mexican architect John Gaw Meem, who also designed many of the buildings on the University of New Mexico campus in Albuquerque. Some of the city's fanciest houses occupy quiet residential areas along the riverbanks.

A boat parade and evening fireworks attract thousands of visitors to the Lake Carlsbad Recreation Area for Fourth of July festivities. During the annual **Christmas on the Pecos** (☎ 505/887–6516), dazzling Christmas displays decorate backyards and lots along a 2½-mi stretch on the Pecos River. Boat tours ($7) are operated from Thanksgiving night through December 31. Tickets for the event usually sell out early, so it's best to buy them in advance; they are available beginning August 1. The night breeze blowing across the water can be chilly, so dress warmly. Boats leave from the **Pecos River Village** (⊠ 710 N. Muscatel Ave.), once an amusement park and now a convention center.

The **Carlsbad Museum and Arts Center** houses Pueblo pottery, Native American artifacts, and early cowboy and ranch memorabilia along with exhibitions of contemporary art. The real treasure, though, is the McAdoo Collection, with works by painters of the Taos Society of Artists. ⊠ *418 W. Fox St.,* ☎ *505/887–0276.* ☜ *Free.* ⊙ *Mon.–Sat. 10–5.*

★ ☾ Atop Ocotillo Hills on the northwest edge of Carlsbad, **Living Desert Zoo and Gardens State Park** contains impressive plants and animals native to the Chihuahuan Desert. The Desert Arboretum has hundreds of exotic cacti and succulents, and the Living Desert Zoo—more a reserve than a traditional zoo—is home to mountain lions, deer, elk, wolves, buffalo, rattlesnakes, and other indigenous species. Nocturnal exhibits and dioramas let you in on the area's nighttime wildlife. Though there are shaded rest areas, rest rooms, and water fountains, in hot weather try to visit during the early morning or early evening, when it's cooler. In spring the Living Desert hosts the four-day Annual Mescal Roast and Mountain Spirit Dances demonstrated by members of the Mescalero Apache Indian tribe. Tribal members once harvested the revered desert plant, mescal, for food. ⊠ *1504 Miehls Dr., off U.S. 285,* ☎ *505/887–5516.* ⊴ *$4.* ⦿ *Memorial Day–Labor Day, daily 8–8; Labor Day–Memorial Day, daily 9–5. Last admission 1½ hrs before closing.*

Ⓒ **White's Animal Kingdom Zoo** opened in 1999. More than 45 species of unusual animals are on display here, including a pair of extremely rare Rothschild giraffes, distinguished by a middle horn. Paths wind through 7 acres of irrigated greenery. A snack bar and gift shop are on the premises. Plans were being made in 2000 to add Safari jeeps for children. ⊠ *512 E. Fiesta Dr.,* ☎ *505/887–3398.* ⊴ *$5.* ⦿ *Daily 9–5.*

Dining and Lodging

This rural community is ultracasual, so don't expect to find nouvelle cuisine restaurants or sophisticated nightspots here.

$–$$ ✕ **Bamboo Garden Restaurant.** Possibly the best Chinese food in south-
★   ern New Mexico can be found right here in cowboy country. Kung Pao chicken, a dish with vegetables and peanuts stir-fried in chile pepper sauce, is among menu items that include standard favorites such as sweet-and-sour pork and cashew shrimp. Surroundings are pleasant but not elegant, with Asian decor. The food is fresh, crisp, and skillfully prepared. ⊠ *1511 N. Canal St.,* ☎ *505/887–5145. AE, D, MC, V. Closed Mon.*

$ ✕ **Furr's Cafeteria.** For a chain establishment, the food at roomy Furr's is exceptionally good. The fare includes fried chicken, roast beef, and lasagna. ⊠ *901 S. Canal St.,* ☎ *505/885–0430. AE, D, MC, V.*

$ ✕ **Lucy's Mexicali Restaurant & Entertainment Club.** "The best margaritas and hottest chile in the world" is the motto of this family-owned oasis of great Mexican food. All the New Mexican standards are prepared here, along with some not-so-standard items such as chicken fajita burritos, Tucson-style chimichangas, and brisket *carnitas* (meat sautéed with chiles and seasonings). Low-fat and fat-free Mexican dishes and 12 microbrewery beers are served. Live entertainment is offered on weekends. ⊠ *701 S. Canal St.,* ☎ *505/887–7714. AE, D, DC, MC, V.*

$ ✕ **Red Chimney.** If you hanker for sweet and tangy barbecue, try this restaurant, which has log-cabin decor and an Early American atmosphere. Sauce from an old family recipe is slathered on chicken, pork, beef, turkey, and ham. Fried catfish and other home-style dishes are also served. ⊠ *817 N. Canal St.,* ☎ *505/885–8744. MC, V. Closed weekends.*

$$ ✕⌂ **Holiday Inn Carlsbad Downtown.** The rugs, paintings, and room
★   decor of this two-story lodge harmonize with the building's Territorial theme. Children under 19 stay free if they're in a room with their parents. The hotel's Phenix Bar & Grill is a pub that earned its name and quirky spelling from a rip-roaring Old West town that once flourished a few miles away. Ventanas serves fine Continental cuisine. ⊠ *601 S. Canal St. 88220,* ☎ *505/885–8500 or 800/742–9586,* ℻ *505/887–5999. 100 rooms. 2 restaurants, bar, pool, hot tub, exercise room, playground, laundry service. AE, D, DC, MC, V. BP.*

$–$$ ⌂ **Days Inn.** Rooms at this motel on the south side of town have Southwestern decor, king-size beds, and sofa beds. ⊠ *3910 National Parks Hwy., 88220,* ☎ *505/887–7800; 800/329–7466 central reservations;* ℻ *505/885–9433. 42 rooms, 8 suites. Indoor pool, airport shuttle. AE, D, DC, MC, V. CP.*

$–$$ ⌂ **Stagecoach Inn.** A family-style motor inn, the Stagecoach has basic rooms at affordable rates (that go up during holiday periods). On the premises is a tree-shaded park with a playground and a picnic area. ⊠ *1819 S. Canal St., 88220,* ☎ ℻ *505/887–1148. 55 rooms. Restau-*

rant, kitchenettes, refrigerators, pool, wading pool, hot tub, playground, laundry service. AE, D, DC, MC, V.

$ ⊞ **Best Western Stevens Inn.** Scenes of cavern formations and Carlsbad's
★ historic courthouse are etched in mirrored glass and carved into wooden doors at this motel, which provides a touch of elegance at bargain prices. Prints of Western landscapes decorate the spacious rooms, which have voice mail. Prime rib and steaks are served in the evening at the motel's Flume Room, and Mexican food and sandwiches are served throughout the day at the Green Tree Room. ⊠ *1829 S. Canal St. (Box 580), 88220,* ☎ *505/887–2851 or 800/730–2851,* FAX *505/887–6338. 202 rooms. 2 restaurants, bar, kitchenettes (some), in-room data ports, pool, wading pool, hot tub, playground, coin laundry. AE, D, DC, MC, V.* ☜

$ ⊞ **Carlsbad Super 8.** This three-story motel 2 mi from the regional airport and one block from Carlsbad's convention center has rooms in Southwestern tones with generic furnishings and coffeemakers. Outdoor grills are available, and nearby is a fast-food restaurant that's open 24 hours. The outdoor pool is heated. ⊠ *3817 National Parks Hwy., 88220,* ☎ *505/887–8888, 800/800–8000 central reservations;* FAX *505/ 885–0126. 60 rooms. Pool, hot tub. AE, D, DC, MC, V. CP.*

$ ⊞ **Continental Inn.** This inn is south of Carlsbad, about 30 minutes from Carlsbad Caverns. The simple rooms have typical matching curtains and bedspreads in Southwestern patterns. The small grounds are well kept. ⊠ *3820 National Parks Hwy., 88220,* ☎ *505/887–0341 or 877/887–0341,* FAX *505/885–1186. 57 rooms, 3 suites. Pool, airport shuttle. AE, D, DC, MC, V.*

$ ⊞ **Quality Inn.** One mile from the municipal airport, this two-story stoneface inn surrounds a landscaped patio with a pool and a sundeck about as large as an aircraft hangar. Rooms are comfortable, with nondescript modern furnishings. The Cafe in the Park serves free Continental breakfasts to guests, from 5:30 AM to 10 AM. The Chaparral Grill Room is open for dinner. ⊠ *3706 National Parks Hwy., 88220,* ☎ *505/887–2861 or 800/321–2861,* FAX *505/887–2861. 120 rooms. 2 restaurants, bar, pool, hot tub, shop, laundry service, airport shuttle. AE, D, DC, MC, V. CP.*

$ ⚲ **Brantley Lake State Park.** Twelve miles north of Carlsbad, the campground in this state park is filled with Afghan pines, Mexican elders, and desert plants. Some camping and picnic sites (with grills) have views of the 3,000-acre lake and dam—an inviting haven in this upper Chihuahuan desert region. ⊠ *U.S. 285 (Box 2288), 88221,* ☎ *505/ 457–2384,* FAX *505/457–2385. 51 RV sites (water and electric hookups $14); primitive-area camping with no facilities ($8). Rest rooms, showers, boating, fishing, playground, dump station. Reservations not accepted. No credit cards.*

$ ⚲ **Carlsbad RV Park & Campgrounds.** This tree-filled, full-service campground inside the city limits has level gravel sites and an indoor swimming pool. Camping cabins with heating and air-conditioning also are available. Other facilities include grills, public phones, and phone hookup. Reservations are recommended in summer. A professional RV service is next door. ⊠ *4301 National Parks Hwy., 88220,* ☎ *505/885– 6333,* FAX *505/885–0784. 96 RV sites (full hookups $19.75), 41 tent sites ($14.50). Rest rooms, showers, grocery, indoor pool, sewage disposal, playground, coin laundry, meeting room. D, MC, V.* ☜

Nightlife and the Arts

Like many other small towns, Carlsbad tends to fold up at night—you're pretty much limited to special events and the lounge circuit. **Lucy's Mexicali Restaurant & Entertainment Club** (☞ Dining and Lodging, *above*) has bands on the weekend. On Saturday, popular country-and-western bands play at the **Silver Spur Lounge** (⊠ Best Western Motel Stevens, 1829

S. Canal St., ☎ 505/887–2851), a favored local hangout where dancing takes place all week long.

Artesia

36 mi north of Carlsbad on U.S. 285, 40 mi south of Roswell on U.S. 285, 110 mi west of Alamogordo on U.S. 82.

Artesia got its name from the artesian wells that were dug in the late 1800s to tap the plentiful supply of water just below the ground's surface. The underground bounty includes more than clear liquid, however. Oil and gas were discovered in the 1920s; today there are more than 20,000 oil and 4,000 natural-gas wells in the area. Pumping jacks cover the dunes and fields to the east. The Navajo Oil Refinery, alongside U.S. 285, is a major employer for this city of about 12,000.

A Federal Law Enforcement Training Center took over the abandoned campus of a private liberal arts college in 1989. Thousands of law-enforcement employees from agencies such as the U.S. Bureau of Land Management and U.S. Customs Service train at its driving and shooting ranges. Other than grabbing a meal, there isn't much to do here. On football-season Fridays you can't miss the array of orange banners and bulldog emblems touting the local high-school team, the Bulldogs, in this highly sports-conscious town.

Dining

$–$$ ✕ **La Fonda.** While en route to or from Carlsbad Caverns, consider
★ stopping at this popular restaurant known for its milder style of Mexican cuisine. Try the house special, the Guadalajara, for a palate-pleasing blend of seasoned beef, cheese, and guacamole served on a corn tortilla. Plants and bright Southwestern scenes decorate the dining room. ⊠ *210 W. Main St.,* ☎ *505/746–9377. AE, D, MC, V.*

En Route   If you would like a closer look at some of the irrigated farmland and dairies of the Pecos Valley, veer northeast off the main highway (U.S. 285) just north of Artesia and take Alt. U.S. 285. This 40-mi route meanders through quaint farming villages of Lake Arthur, Dexter, and Hagerman and will rejoin the main highway at Roswell. If you want to view one of the valley's little-known but fascinating attractions, turn east onto Hatchery Road in Dexter. One mile's journey will take you to the **Dexter National Fish Hatchery & Technology Center,** a facility with the noble mission of studying, propagating, and possibly salvaging endangered species of warm-water fish such as the Colorado squawfish (once common to the Colorado River). You can view live exhibits and read all about the center's activities at a small visitor center on site. ⊠ *7116 Hatchery Rd., Dexter,* ☎ *505/734–5910.* ▣ *Free.* ☉ *Daily 7–4.*

Roswell

❹ *40 mi north of Artesia on U.S. 285; 205 mi southeast of Albuquerque, south on I–25 and east on U.S. 380; 78 mi southwest of Fort Sumner, via NM 20 and U.S. 285.*

It's not surprising that the true town of Roswell has been lost in the waves of Unidentified Flying Object (UFO) debates (☞ Close-Up: UFO over Roswell). Rather than being exclusively the hotbed of UFO activity, Roswell is in reality a conservative city with an economy based on manufacturing, agriculture, oil, and gas. The population of around 50,000 grew out of a farming community founded in the fertile Pecos Valley about a century ago; artesian wells still provide the water used to irrigate crops like alfalfa, hay, and cotton. That most visitors come only in search of UFOs elicits a few heavy sighs from res-

UFO OVER ROSWELL

OF ALL THE SIGHTINGS of Unidentified Flying Objects in the world, it's the one that took place more than 50 years ago outside Roswell, New Mexico, that remains most credible in people's minds. Rumors of alien bodies and silenced witnesses are the real-life happenings that inspired fantastical entertainment like the TV series *The X-Files* and *Roswell*. The most likely reason so many people refuse to dismiss the Roswell Incident is the undisputed fact that in July 1947 *something* fell from out of the sky. To the exasperation of the U.S. military—which itself helped spark the original rumors of a spacecraft—its explanations of what made up the glittering silver debris at a ranch northwest of Roswell have never totally convinced the public. Roswell's International UFO Museum and Research Center keeps visitors informed of the latest research on the Roswell Incident, and the annual UFO Encounter festival in July provides a forum for enthusiasts.

On July 8, 1947, officers at Roswell Army Airfield announced to the *Roswell Daily Record* that the military had retrieved wreckage of a UFO nearby. The next day, Army Air Force officials retracted the story, saying it was in fact a weather balloon that had crashed. Over the years, theories of a cover-up and suspicions that the military had also recovered alien bodies linked the town of Roswell with aliens as strongly as Loch Ness is with its monster. Backing up the alien bodies theory is the testimony of people like mortician Glen Dennis, who today works with Roswell's International UFO Museum and Research Center. He maintains that a nurse at the military hospital passed him sketches of aliens and that the military called him in 1947 to ask odd questions about embalming bodies.

In the 1990s a flood of information, including books like *UFO Crash at Roswell* and accounts from eyewitnesses who claim they were silenced, rekindled the conspiracy theories. The Air Force responded in 1994 with a report revealing that fragments mistaken for a flying saucer came not from a weather balloon but from an Air Force balloon used in the top-secret Project Mogul. The true nature of the balloon had to be concealed in 1947, because its purpose was to monitor evidence of Soviet nuclear tests.

AS THIS NEW explanation didn't address the alien bodies issue, the Air Force issued a 231-page report, "The Roswell Report, Case Closed," in 1997. This document explains that from 1954 to 1959, life-size dummies were used in parachute drop experiments. That this time frame postdates the 1947 Roswell Incident is immaterial to the Air Force, which claims people have simply confused dates in their memories.

The holes in every story, whether from the military or eyewitnesses, have allowed the Roswell UFO legend to mushroom extravagantly. It now incorporates tales of captured aliens (alive and dead) that further feed our imaginations, thanks in part to the capitalizing media. You'll see depictions of slender, doe-eyed aliens, known as the "Grays," all over storefronts and souvenir shops in Roswell. These spooky, diminutive creatures might even be called the New Mexico version of leprechauns, with only the rare treasure seeker truly hoping to encounter one.

idents. The town's notoriety may chagrin the locals a little, but they've learned to have fun with it—and also cash in on the tourist trade.

★ ⓒ Depending on your point of view, the **International UFO Museum and Research Center** will be a folly of only-in-America kitsch or an opportunity to examine UFO documentation and other phenomena involving extraterrestrials. This homespun, nonprofit facility is surprisingly low-tech—some of the displays look like they've seen previous duty on B-movie sets (the museum is, coincidentally, inside an old movie house). The blowups of newspaper stories about the Roswell crash, its fallout, and 1950s UFO mania make interesting reading, and you can view the videotaped recollections of residents who say they saw the Roswell crash. Dummies used in movies about the Roswell incident are also on exhibit. The gift shop sells all manner of souvenirs depicting wide-eyed extraterrestrials, along with books and videos. Though some of the exhibits are whimsical, the portion of the museum devoted to research accumulates serious written collections and investigations of reported UFOs. A 2,000-square-ft library addition opened in July 1999. ⊠ *114 N. Main St.,* ☎ *505/625–9495.* 🎫 *Free.* ☉ *Oct.–Apr., daily 10–5; May–Sept., daily 9–5.*

Roswell's **Encounter Festival** (☎ 505/624–6860) takes place during the first week in July, with lectures about UFOs, science-fiction writers workshops, and events such as alien-costume competitions.

The impressive **Roswell Museum and Art Center** often gets overlooked next to the alien hoopla. It holds a good survey of Southwestern artists, highlighted with works by Georgia O'Keeffe, Henriette Wyeth, Peter Hurd, and Luis Jimenez. The extensive Rogers Aston Collection has displays of Plains Indian cultures, Spanish armor, and the gear of those who settled the land. Robert H. Goddard's collection exhibits the inventions and journals of the rocketry genius, who conducted some of his early experiments near Roswell. The **Robert H. Goddard Planetarium** presents star talks and multimedia programs. ⊠ *100 W. 11th St.,* ☎ *505/624–6744.* 🎫 *Free.* ☉ *Mon.–Sat. 9–5, Sun. 1–5. Planetarium shows 1 wk each month, Aug.–May, and daily June–July; call for schedule.*

A note of warning: don't be caught out on the highway in winter during a heavy snowstorm. Blinding, blizzardlike conditions can prevail, creating heaps of snow.

Portales

❺ *From Roswell, take U.S. 285 north 5 mi and U.S. 70 east 92 mi. Or, if you want a nice drive through sand dunes and rural farmland, from Artesia, take U.S. 82 east 65 mi to Lovington and S.R. 206 north to Portales 109 mi.*

Along with neighboring Clovis, this farming and ranching community bills itself as the world's top producer of Valencia peanuts, a specialty crop ideally suited to red, sandy soil. In October, Portales hosts a peanut festival where nuts are sold in raw form or cooked up in candies and other delicacies.

ⓒ The nation's largest **windmill collection** is found on Portales's Kilgore Street (you can't miss it). Resident Bill Dalley has collected the 80 windmills in his own backyard. Since he's the president of the International Windmillers' Trade Fair Association, meetings of the group are conducted here annually. Portales also is home to Eastern New Mexico University, a four-year college.

In the early 1930s, archaeologists in eastern New Mexico unearthed remnants of prehistoric animals like mammoths, camels, and saber-tooth tigers. More importantly, this was the first site in the contiguous United States that provided conclusive evidence that humans lived here at least 11,300 years ago. The culture and artifacts associated with these earliest inhabitants take their name from the nearby city of Clovis. The **Black Water Draw Museum** contains photographs of early excavations, along with artifacts from Clovis, Folsom, and later Native American civilizations. The museum looks a little lonely on the side of U.S. 70, 8 mi northeast of Portales, but its interior certainly shows considerable tender loving care. The exhibits are very informative and well presented. The museum also contains a "touch and feel" table for children.

★ The **Black Water Draw Archaeological Site** remains active and is open at regular hours to visitors during the summer and on weekends in spring and fall. Self-guided tours on developed trails are well worth the effort for the privilege of viewing work in progress at a major archaeological site. Stay strictly on the trails. An exhibit building offers a fascinating look at ongoing excavations of prehistoric animal bones. A proposed master plan calls for building a major interpretive and research complex at the Black Water Draw site itself. ⊠ *West side of NM 467, 5 mi north of Portales (turn at Mile Marker 5),* ☎ *505/356–5235.* ⊒ *Site and museum $2.* ⊙ *Museum and site Memorial Day–Labor Day, Mon.–Sat. 10–5, Sun. noon–5. Museum Labor Day–Memorial Day, Tues.–Sat. 10–5, Sun. noon–5. Site Labor Day–early Nov., Sat. 10–5, Sun. noon–5; late-Mar.–Memorial Day, Sat. 10–5, Sun. noon–5.*

Dining and Lodging

$–$$$ ✕ **Cattle Baron.** This Portales steak house in the heart of cattle coun-
★ try was the founding establishment for the popular chain that now extends into Roswell, Ruidoso, and Las Cruces. Prime rib is the specialty, and the trademark salad bar never disappoints with its fresh greens, crisp veggies, and homemade soups. The interior is decorated with plenty of wooden accents and skylights. ⊠ *1600 S. Ave. D,* ☎ *505/356–5587. AE, D, DC, MC, V.*

$–$$ ✕ **Mark's Eastern Grill.** Tasty breakfast omelets, steaks, and sandwiches attract the hungry college crowd from nearby Eastern New Mexico University. Try the house specialty, a chicken fried steak dinner. This diner-style hangout has a fun atmosphere. The tables are inlaid with tile, the chairs are covered with brightly colored vinyl, and there are a few exotic parrot decorations. All food is prepared fresh. ⊠ *1126 W. 1st St., across from airplane display next to Eastern New Mexico University,* ☎ *505/359–0857. D, MC, V.*

$ ⌂ **Morning Star Bed & Breakfast & Gifts.** Antiques and brass highlights accent the fresh, bright decor of this adobe-style bed-and-breakfast in downtown Portales. The rooms have color themes—violet, blue, and peach. The bridal suite is a two-bedroom apartment with its own bath and kitchen. The other three rooms share a common area, which has a refrigerator. Guests are greeted with soft drinks and fruit upon arrival. ⊠ *620 W. 2nd St., 88130,* ☎ *305/356–2994. 3 rooms, 1 suite. Refrigerators, pool. AE, MC, V. CP.*

$ ⌂ **Super 8.** Decorated with contemporary furnishings and pastel colors, this motel has large rooms and bathrooms. It's one of the newer (built in 1993) establishments in Portales and is close to Eastern New Mexico University. ⊠ *1805 W. 2nd St., 88130,* ☎ *505/356–8518,* FAX *505/359–0431. 45 rooms. Hot tub. AE, D, DC, MC, V.*

$ ⚠ **Oasis State Park.** Six miles north of Portales via U.S. 70 and NM 467, you can hike, bird-watch, and fish at a 3-acre lake stocked with rainbow trout and catfish. Horseback riding also is allowed on the premises. The park has 23 picnic and camping sites, 13 of which offer electrical hookups for recreational vehicles. ⊠ *Off N.M. 467, 6 mi north of Portales,* ☎ *505/356–5331.* ⊒ *$4 per vehicle. 23 sites. Rest rooms,* *showers.* ⊘ *Daily 7 AM–sunset; overnight camping allowed ($11, plus additional $4 for electrical hookup).*

Fort Sumner

70 mi northwest of Black Water Draw Museum, north on U.S. 70 and west on U.S. 60/84; 85 mi northeast of Roswell, north on U.S. 285 and northeast on NM 20; 159 mi southeast of Albuquerque, east on I–40 and south on U.S. 84.

Besides its historic significance as one of the area's earliest military outposts and the place where on-the-run Billy the Kid was killed, the town of Fort Sumner has other solid credentials like farming and ranching. The National Aeronautics and Space Administration uses the Fort Sumner Air Park for launching balloons used in scientific research. Nearby Sumner Lake provides both irrigation water and boating and fishing opportunities. In June, the De Baca County Chamber of Commerce hosts the annual Old Fort Days here with living-history demonstrations and mock shoot-outs.

❻ Artifacts and photographs at **Fort Sumner State Monument** illustrate the history of the fort, which was established in 1862 on the east bank of the Pecos River. From 1863 to 1868 it was the headquarters for a disastrous attempt to force the Navajo people and some Apache bands—after their defeat on various battlefields in the Southwest—to farm the inhospitable land. Natural disasters destroyed crops, wood was scarce, and even the water from the Pecos proved unhealthy. Those who survived the harsh treatment and wretched conditions (3,000 didn't) were allowed to return to reservations elsewhere in 1868. The post was then sold and converted into a large ranch. This is the same ranch where, in 1881, Sheriff Pat Garrett gunned down Billy the Kid, who's buried in a nearby cemetery. His headstone was secured in a barred cage after it was stolen and recovered. ⊠ *Billy the Kid Rd. (from town of Fort Sumner, head east on U.S. 60/84 and south on Billy the Kid Rd., parts of which are signed NM 212),* ☏ *505/355–2573.* 🎟 *$1.* ⊘ *Daily 8:30–5.*

The small **Old Fort Museum,** next to Fort Sumner, has displays about Billy the Kid and ranch life. ⊠ *Billy the Kid Rd.,* ☏ *505/355–2942.* 🎟 *$3.* ⊘ *Call for hrs, which vary.*

The **Billy the Kid Museum** houses 17,000 square ft of exhibits about the young scofflaw, as well as antique wagon trains, guns, household goods, and other artifacts of the frontier era. ⊠ *1601 Sumner Ave. (U.S. 60/84),* ☏ *505/355–2380.* 🎟 *$4.* ⊘ *mid-May–Sept., daily 8:30–5; Oct.– Dec. and mid-Jan.–mid-May, Mon.–Sat. 8:30–5, Sun. 11–5.*

At **Sumner Lake State Park** you can boat, fish, camp, picnic, hike, sightsee, swim and water-ski. Fishing opportunities vary, since the lake is periodically drained for irrigation. ⊠ *10 mi north of Fort Sumner on U.S. 84, then west on NM 203 for 6 mi,* ☏ *505/355–2541.* 🎟 *$4 per vehicle, $8 overnight camping; extra fees for hookups. 40 developed camping sites, including 18 with utility hookups, 50 primitive camping sites, boat ramp, dock, picnic sites, dump station, rest rooms with showers.*

En Route To continue touring southeastern New Mexico, the easiest route (132 mi) is to backtrack to Roswell via NM 20 to U.S. 285 and head west on U.S. 70/380 toward Lincoln County. Look for the many pronghorn grazing alongside roadways in the flat eastern plains, which are the ideal habitat for these delicate creatures. If you count the number of pronghorn spotted, the total can sometimes surpass 100 along even short stretches of road, when rains have made grassland abundant.

A more adventurous route (178 mi) to Lincoln County would be to loop west from Fort Sumner on U.S. 60. At the town of Vaughn head south on U.S. 54 and travel through the southernmost region of Cibola National Forest to the fringes of the Lincoln National Forest. These areas are mountainous but semiarid, as evidenced by sparse hillsides dotted with brush and junipers. On this route you'll pass through **Corona,** near where the Roswell UFO is said to have crashed. No signs designate the site. At **Carrizozo** (☞ *below*) head east on U.S. 380. You'll pass the towns of **Capitan** and **Lincoln** (☞ *below*) before you reach U.S. 70. Cut back west on U.S. 70 to get to San Patricio (☞ *below*).

HEADING TO HIGH COUNTRY

From the hub city of Roswell (☞ *above*), U.S. 70 shoots out of the flatlands west toward mountain peaks. The route's slow climb in elevation is apparent beginning near San Patricio. Here, in an area known as the Hondo Valley, the shrubs and scattered forest dotting the otherwise naked hillsides provided inspiration for many of the late artist Peter Hurd's stunning landscapes.

Onward and upward, the pines thicken and grow taller. The Rio Ruidoso (Spanish for "river of noisy water") dances alongside the highway as the air grows cooler and fragrant. Imagine this majestic land as it was when outlaws, Indians, merchants, ranchers, and lawmen battled each other for control of the frontier. Consider a solitary horseback ride or hike on a wilderness trail, or try lake fishing on reservation land controlled by the Mescalero Apaches. Near the town of Ruidoso, more modern diversions are skiing, shopping, horse racing, and casino gambling.

Lincoln

★ ❼ *12 mi east of Capitan on U.S. 380; 47 mi west of Roswell on U.S. 70/ 380 to Hondo, then 10 mi northwest on U.S. 380 to Lincoln.*

It may not be as well known as Tombstone, Arizona, or Deadwood, South Dakota, but Lincoln ranks right up there with the toughest of the tough old towns of the Old West. Mellowing with age, the notorious one-street town has become a National Historic Landmark and a state monument. Its well-preserved museums and historic houses are managed by the state and Ruidoso's Hubbard Museum of the American West, and a single ticket ($6) grants entry to all attractions.

The violent, gang-style Lincoln County War flared up more than a century ago, as two factions, the Tunstall-McSween and the Murphy-Dolan groups, clashed over lucrative government contracts to provide food for the U.S. Army at Fort Stanton and area Indian reservations. The local conflict made national news and President Hayes ordered Lew Wallace, Governor of New Mexico, to settle the conflict. One of the more infamous figures to emerge from the bloodshed was a short, slight, sallow young man with buck teeth, startling blue eyes, and curly reddish-brown hair. His name was Billy the Kid.

He is said to have killed 21 men (probably an exaggeration), including Lincoln County's sheriff William Brady—for whose murder Billy the Kid was convicted in 1881 and sentenced to hang. Billy managed to elude the gallows, however. On April 28, 1881, though manacled and shackled, he made a daring escape from the old Lincoln County Courthouse, gunning down two men and receiving cheers from townspeople who supported his group, the Tunstall-McSweens. Three months later a posse led by Sheriff Pat Garrett tracked down Billy at a home in Fort Sumner, surprised him in the dark, and finished him off with two clean shots. One of the West's most notorious gunmen, and ultimately one of its best-known folk legends, was dead at age 21.

🕭 The **Historic Lincoln Center,** on the eastern end of town, serves as an information center and has a 12-minute video about Lincoln and exhibits devoted to Billy the Kid, the Lincoln County War, cowboys, Apaches, and Buffalo Soldiers. The center's guides and attendants dress in period costumes and lead a walking tour through town on the hour, vividly describing each building's role as a setting in the Lincoln County War. ⊠ *Main St. (U.S. 380),* ☎ *505/653–4025.* ⊠ *$6 pass grants access to all historic buildings.* ⊙ *Daily 8:30–5.*

Lincoln was first settled by Spanish settlers in the 1840s. The short, round **Torreon** fortress served as protection from Apache raids. The building would come in handy during the Lincoln County War, too. José Montaño ran a saloon and boardinghouse within his **Montaño Store** for more than 30 years after the Civil War. Governor Lew Wallace stayed here when trying to arrange a meeting with Billy the Kid. On view today are written displays about adobe making and Lincoln's Hispanic community. **Dr. Woods House** was once occupied by a country doctor specializing in tuberculoses treatments. ⊠ *Main St. (U.S. 380),* ☎ *no phone.* ⊠ *$6 pass grants access to all historic buildings.* ⊙ *Daily 9–5.*

🕭 Nothing has changed much at the **Tunstall Store Museum,** the rival store to L. G. Murphy & Co. (which now houses the Lincoln County Courthouse Museum; ☞ *below*). John Chisum and Alexander McSween had law offices here as well. When the state of New Mexico purchased the store in 1957, boxes of unused stock dating from the late-19th and early 20th centuries were discovered. The clothes, hardware, butter churns, kerosene lamps, and other items are displayed in the store's original cases. ⊠ *Main St. (U.S. 380),* ☎ *505/653–4049.* ⊠ *$6 pass grants access to all historic buildings.* ⊙ *Daily 9–5.*

🕭 The **Lincoln County Courthouse Museum** is the building from which Billy the Kid made his famous escape. You can walk in the room where Billy was imprisoned and view a hole in the wall that just might have been caused by the gun he fired during his escape. Display cases contain historical documents. You can read one of Billy's handwritten, eloquent letters to Governor Lew Wallace, defending his reputation. The Lincoln State Monument office is here. ⊠ *Main St. (U.S. 380),* ☎ *505/653–4372.* ⊠ *$6 pass grants access to all historic buildings.* ⊙ *Daily 8:30–5.*

Dining and Lodging

$$–$$$$ ✕▥ **Ellis Store & Co. Bed-and-Breakfast.** This B&B has a rich history
★   dating from 1850, when it was a modest two-room adobe in a territory where settlers and Mescaleros clashed. During the Lincoln County War, Billy the Kid was known to frequent the place. Rooms in the main house are decorated with antiques. Behind the main house is the Mill House, which has four guest rooms, a large common room, and is ideal for families. Casa Nueva has two suites with reproduction antiques and a country-French feeling. Owner Jinny Vigil, who's won *New Mexico* magazine's chef-of-the-month award more than once, cooks six-course gourmet meals in the evening (by reservation only), served in a wood-panel dining room. Vigil's well-manicured garden is becoming increasingly popular for June weddings. ⊠ *U.S. 380, Mile Marker 98 (Box 15), 88338,* ☎ *505/653–4609 or 800/653–6460,* ☒ *505/653–4610. 10 rooms (4 share 2 baths), 2 suites. Restaurant. No smoking indoors. AE, D, DC, MC, V. BP.*

$ ✕▥ **Wortley Pat Garrett Hotel.** This ranch-style inn relives the past by shedding the modern distractions of phones, faxes, and televisions. Rooms are named after characters in the Lincoln County War, and antiques and old newspaper accounts are displayed throughout the inn. Historical field trips and classes are part of the experience. For leisurely chats, rocking chairs are set up on the front porch. Rebuilt after a fire in 1935, the inn is on the site of the real thing, where Deputy U.S. Marshal Bob Olinger ate his last meal at noontime on April 28, 1881. As the lawman consumed roast beef and mashed potatoes, he heard gunfire from the courthouse down the street. He ran outside, becoming a casualty after meeting up with one of Billy the Kid's bullets during the outlaw's famous escape. In the **Wortley Dining Room** (☎ 505/653–4438), open daily 8–3, the town's Irish-American heritage is honored with a menu featuring old-time favorites such as corned beef and cabbage. The lodge and restaurant are closed during winter months. ⊠ *U.S. 380, 88338,* ☎ *505/653–4300 or 877/967–8539,* FAX *505/653–4686. 7 rooms. Restaurant (no credit cards). AE, MC, V. Nov.–Apr.* ❧

$$–$$$ ★ ⛺ **Casa de Patrón Bed-and-Breakfast.** This B&B is in the former adobe home of Juan Patrón, an early settler and father of three who was gunned down at age 29 in the violence that swept Lincoln County. Billy the Kid really did sleep here, as a guest of Juan Patrón, and while being held by the sheriff under protective custody. The main house has high viga ceilings and Mexican-tile baths; the adjacent Old Trail House has two large rooms—one decorated in Hispanic-cowboy style and the other in a garden motif—with fireplaces. With vigas and portals, the two small adobe casitas have a traditional New Mexican flavor (Casa Bonita has cathedral ceilings). All rooms are furnished with antiques and collectibles and one is wheelchair accessible. Full country breakfasts are served to guests staying in the main house, Continental breakfasts to those in the casitas. No smoking is permitted indoors. ⊠ *U.S. 380 (Box 27), 88338,* ☎ *505/653–4676 or 800/524–5202,* FAX *505/653–4671. 5 double rooms, 2 casitas (1 with a 2-bedroom suite). Meeting rooms. MC, V. BP, CP.* ❧

San Patricio

14 mi south of Lincoln, 45 mi west of Roswell on U.S. 70/380

Ranchers, farmers, artists, and others who appreciate the pastoral pleasures of the Hondo Valley live in San Patricio and the nearby villages of Tinnie and Hondo. The Rio Ruidoso flows into the Rio Hondo here, a boon to farmers and wildlife alike. During the harvest, fresh cider and produce are sold at roadside stands.

★ The late artist Peter Hurd lived in the Hondo Valley on the Sentinel Ranch, which is still owned by his son, Michael Hurd. The **Hurd-La Rinconada Gallery** displays Peter Hurd's landscapes and portraits. The artist is famous for Western scenes but gained some notice when a portrait he painted of Lyndon B. Johnson displeased the president, who refused to hang it in the White House. Also on display are the works of Hurd's late wife, Henriette Wyeth Hurd (Andrew Wyeth's sister), and Michael Hurd, who runs the ranch. Michael is an amiable host who has established an international reputation with a series of paintings he calls "The Road West," his vision of the lonely desert scenery surrounding his home. Michael's sister Carole Hurd Rogers and her husband, Peter Rogers, also an artist, live near the ranch as well. Paintings by Andrew Wyeth and his father, N. C. Wyeth, round out the impressive presentation at the gallery. Signed reproductions and some original paintings are for sale. ⊠ *U.S. 70, Mile Marker 281,* ☎ *505/653–4331.* ☉ *Mon.–Sat. 9–5, Sun. 10–4. Closed Sun. Labor Day–May.*

Lodging

$$$–$$$$ ★ ⛺ **Hurd Ranch Guest Homes.** Modern and Western furnishings and paintings, sculpture, and Native American artifacts decorate the adobe casitas

on the Sentinel Ranch. Peter Hurd made them available to friends and to customers who needed accommodations while he painted their portraits. The rooms have washing machines and dryers, fully equipped kitchens, and fireplaces. The newest one is named after actress Helen Hayes, who was a family friend and frequent visitor. A wing of the Hurd–La Rinconada Gallery has a spacious apartment with an enclosed patio for rent. Facilities also are available for weddings and conferences. ⊠ *U.S. 70 (Box 100), 88348,* ☏ *505/653–4331 or 800/658–6912,* �℻ *505/653–4218. 4 casitas, 1 apartment. Kitchenettes. AE, D, MC, V.* ⊛

Ruidoso

❽ *20 mi west of San Patrico on U.S. 70*

A sophisticated year-round resort town on the eastern slopes of the pine-covered Sacramento Mountains, Ruidoso retains a certain rustic charm. Shops, antiques stores, bars, and restaurants line its main street, and in winter, skiers flock to nearby Ski Apache. **Ruidoso Downs** is so close to Ruidoso you won't realize it's a separate township, but its Ruidoso Downs Racetrack and museums are the area's huge draws. The summer horse-racing season keeps the 9,800 or so permanent residents entertained after the snow and ski bunnies disappear.

Ruidoso Downs Racetrack & Casino, the self-proclaimed Home of the World's Richest Quarter Horse Race, has a fabulous mountain vista as the setting for cheering the ponies. On Labor Day the track is the site of the All-American Quarter Horse Futurity, with a total purse of as much as $2.5 million. The 1999 season opened in May with the addition of the **Billy the Kid Casino,** a considerable boost to the racing sport. Twenty percent of casino revenues are allocated to increase purses, attracting quality horses and competition. Decades ago, purses brought future contenders in prestigious events such as the Kentucky Derby. The casino, which has 300 slot machines, is decorated with murals suggesting nearby historic Lincoln (☞ *above*), where Billy the Kid once hung out. The facility also offers year-round, full card simulcasting from the nation's largest tracks. ⊠ *U.S. 70, Ruidoso Downs,* ☏ *505/ 378–4431.* ▦ *Racetrack open seating free, reserved seating $3 and up; Turf Club $9 (higher on special weekends).* ⊙ *Racing late May–Labor Day, Fri.–Sun. (post time 1 PM, earlier on Labor Day); Casino Mon.– Thurs. 11–11, Fri. 1 PM–midnight, Sat. noon–1 AM, Sun. 11–10.*

★ ⓒ About ½ mi east of the racetrack you can pay further respects to horses at the **Hubbard Museum of the American West.** The museum houses the **Anne C. Stradling Collection** of more than 10,000 artworks and objects related to the horse—paintings, drawings, and bronzes by master artists; saddles from Mexico, China, and the Pony Express; carriages and wagons; a horse-drawn grain thresher; and clothing worn by Native Americans and cowboys. The **Racehorse Hall of Fame** celebrates accomplished horses and jockeys and screens rare and contemporary video footage. Activities at the children's interactive center include pony rides, horse demonstrations, and puzzles. Youngsters can don Old West attire and have their photos taken in a jockey outfit. In front of the museum is a bronze sculpture of eight galloping horses—*Free Spirits at Noisy Water.* Not only beautiful, the monument represents a minor feat of engineering, since of the eight horses only nine hooves actually touch the ground. In early 1999, the museum took over operation of many of the exhibits in the nearby historic town of Lincoln (☞ *above*). ⊠ *U.S. 70 E, Ruidoso Downs,* ☏ *505/378–4142 or 800/263–5929.* ▦ *$6.* ⊙ *Daily 10–5.*

The **Mescalero Apache Indian Reservation,** bordering Ruidoso to the west, is inhabited by more than 2,500 Mescalero Apaches, most of whom work in tourism-related enterprises. The Inn of the Mountain Gods (☞ Dining and Lodging, *below*), one of the state's most elegant resorts, is Apache owned and operated. Also on the reservation are a general store, a trading post, and a museum that has clothing and crafts displays and screens a 12-minute video about life on the reservation. Regular talks survey the history and culture of the Mescalero Apaches. There are also campsites (with hookups at Silver and Eagle lakes only) and picnic areas. Ritual dances are occasionally performed for the public, the most colorful of which is on the Fourth of July. ⊠ *Tribal Office, U.S. 70, Mescalero,* ☎ *505/671–4494.* ☎ *Free.* ⊙ *Reservation and tribal museum weekdays (weekends on major holidays) 8–4:30.*

Dining and Lodging

$$–$$$$ ✕ **La Lorraine.** The colonial French decor with flower arrangements and chandeliers sets the perfect mood for traditional French cuisine—chateaubriand, veal chop, duck breast, and the like. Select your favorite wine from a comprehensive list. La Lorraine was opened by French owners in 1984. Kathy Garber took over the establishment in 1996 and has remained true to the original concept. ⊠ *2523 Sudderth Dr.,* ☎ *505/257–2954. AE, MC, V. Closed Sun. No lunch Mon.*

$–$$$ ✕ **Cattle Baron.** This southern New Mexico franchise serves up steaks, scampi, and more exotic dishes such as mustard grilled pork chops, while offering the chance to graze a generous salad bar. Succulent prime rib is the house specialty. Ample greenery and tile floors add a pleasant country ambience. ⊠ *657 Sudderth Dr.,* ☎ *505/257–9355. AE, D, DC, MC, V.*

$–$$ ✕ **Pub 48.** This happening place for hip families was opened by the Sierra Blanca Brewing Co. (☞ Carrizozo, *below*) in early 1999. An adobe brick fireplace, wooden ceilings, and a play station for kids help create a cozy, mountain cabin atmosphere. Try some of the excellent microbeers, such as the nut brown ale served from a copper bar, while sampling pizzas or barbecued brisket. ⊠ *441 Mechem Dr. (NM 48),* ☎ *505/257–9559. AE, D, MC, V.*

$ ✕ **Lincoln County Grill.** The locals come here for quick service and good, inexpensive food. Step up to the counter to order hearty Texas chili, old-fashioned hamburgers, or chicken-fried steak. At breakfast you can grab eggs served with fluffy, homemade "Lincoln County" biscuits. Vinyl-covered tables are decorated with old coffee, tea, and tobacco tin images. This is a great stop for families in a hurry and on a budget. ⊠ *2717 Sudderth Dr.,* ☎ *505/257–7669. AE, D, MC, V.*

$$$ ✕🏨 **Inn of the Mountain Gods.** The Mescalero Apaches own and oper-
★ ate this sprawling resort on the shore of Lake Mescalero, about 3 mi southwest of Ruidoso. Among the myriad recreational choices are a casino offering poker, lotto machines, and table action; horseback riding; big-game hunts; boating; and a video arcade. The inn rightfully retains its luxury status and reputation as New Mexico's top resort, but aging hall carpeting and worn fixtures in rooms detract from the luster. The rooms, each with a balcony, are large and have handsome Western and Native American flourishes. Lodging rates are substantially lower during the off-season—in fall and from late winter to early spring. The inn's best restaurant, Dan-Li-Ka ("good food" in Apache), serves Continental cuisine and overlooks Lake Mescalero and the Sacramento Mountains. The casual Apache Tee restaurant overlooks the well-designed championship golf course, which in turn has amazing views. A dinner and lunch buffet is offered on the casino's second floor. ⊠ *Carrizo Canyon Rd. (Box 269), 88340,* ☎ *505/257–5141 or 800/545–9011,* 𝔽𝔸𝕏 *505/257–6173. 230 rooms, 23 suites. 4 restaurants, 2 lounges, bar, pool, hot tub, 18-hole golf course, tennis court, basketball, horseback riding, volleyball, boating, fishing, casino. AE, D, MC, V.*

$$–$$$ ✕▥ **Best Western Swiss Chalet.** With a sweeping view of the forest, this property is 16 mi from the Ski Apache slopes. The Swiss owner adds character to the restaurant and common spaces with Swiss and German touches like cowbells, an alpenhorn, and cuckoo clocks, but otherwise, guest-room decor is basic, but with some painted headboards and furnishings. The restaurant serves no-nonsense German and American cuisine—try the Wiener schnitzel or the three-sausage platter. The cozy bar, which has a small fireplace, is a convivial place to decompress after a day of skiing. On the walkways and decks facing the forest, you can relax near the fragrant pines. ✉ *1451 Mechem Dr., 88345,* ☎ *505/258–3333 or 800/ 477–9477,* 🆛 *505/258–5325. 82 rooms. Restaurant, bar, indoor pool, hot tub, sauna, hiking, meeting room. AE, D, DC, MC, V. BP.*

$$ ▥ **Park Place Bed & Breakfast.** Guests at this cozy lodge (opened in
★ 1999) are blessed with both hospitality and privacy. Three rooms are available, accessible through a private entrance leading into a slant-roof hallway. Each room has a VCR and access to a video library. You can choose seclusion in your own luxurious space or stroll into an inviting lobby where you might meet up with other guests for conversation or games in front of a toasty fireplace. Friendly owners Eddie and Donna Parker discreetly entertain by stepping in from their portion of the house, connected through the kitchen and dining area. Eddie will cook you up a breakfast like pecan waffles, raspberry cream-cheese French toast, or green chile breakfast burritos. Outside, you can enjoy the hot tub, play volleyball, or watch the deer feed in the evenings. The more expensive Parker's Room has its own private Jacuzzi. ✉ *137 Reese Dr., 88345 (turn off U.S. 70 north onto Sudderth Dr., left on Thomas St., then right on Reese Dr. to cross the river),* ☎ *505/257–4638 or 800/ 687–9050,* 🆛 *505/630–0127. 3 rooms. Outdoor hot tub, tennis court, croquet, horseshoes, volleyball, fishing. MC, V.*

$–$$$$ ▥ **Days Inn Ruidoso Downs.** This standard, contemporary lodge is next to the Sierra Blanca Mountain foothills and only ½ mi from the Ruidoso Downs Racetrack. Some rooms have balconies. Rates for standard rooms can vary drastically if you happen to roll into town during peak demand, so check first. The next-door restaurant, Café Wanda, is open for breakfast and lunch. ✉ *2088 Hwy. 70 W, 88346 Ruidoso Downs,* ☎ 🆛 *505/378–4299. 50 rooms. Indoor pool, coin laundry. AE, D, DC, MC, V. CP.*

$$–$$$ ▥ **Ruidoso Lodge Cabins.** In the heart of Ruidoso's gorgeous, tree-filled
★ Upper Canyon, owners Judy and Kurt Wilkie oversee a placid retreat of 1920s, knotty-pine abodes. The immaculate one- and two-bedroom cabins are decorated in Western and Southwestern decor. Some have hot tubs, and all have fireplaces and decks with gas grills offering serene views. The cabins are fully equipped with kitchen utensils and dishes—but no phones. Prices vary widely depending on the season. You can trout fish here, right along the Rio Ruidoso, but arrange for your own gear. Hiking trails lead off from the property. ✉ *300 Main St., 88345 (take Sudderth Dr. north from U.S. 70 through downtown Ruidoso, and continue west through Upper Canyon where Sudderth turns into Main St.),* ☎ *505/257–2510 or 800/950–2510. 10 cabins. Kitchenettes, refrigerators. D, MC, V.*☜

$–$$$ ▥ **Sierra Blanca Cabins.** Log cabin–style abodes tucked between the pines alongside the Rio Ruidoso offer a gorgeous outdoor setting while providing convenient access to downtown shopping and other attractions. This is an affordable option for families. Discounts are offered for area food outlets and ski rentals. Each cabin has a fireplace, outdoor grill, picnic area, and cable TV. ✉ *215–217 Country Club Rd. (west on Sudderth Dr. to Country Club Rd.), 88345,* ☎ *505/258–4061 or 505/257– 2103. 9 cabins. Kitchenettes, playground. AE, D, MC, V.*☜

$$ ▥ **Shadow Mountain Lodge.** Designed for couples, this lodge is located on the west side of town in the unique Upper Canyon. Room amenities include hair dryers and irons. Each suite has a fireplace with pressed wood that is either complimentary or offered for purchase, depending on the season. You can enjoy views of tall pines and the landscaped gardens from the front veranda. Outside in the gazebo you can take a relaxing soak in the hot tub. ✉ *107 Main Rd., 88345,* ☎ *505/257–4886 or 800/441–4331,* ℻ *505/257–2000. 19 suites. Air-conditioning, kitchenettes, hot tub, coin laundry. AE, D, DC, MC, V.* ✍

Nightlife and the Arts

A 512-seat venue hosting top-tier performances from jazz musicians to international ballet dancers can be found in the **Spencer Theater for the Performing Arts** (✉ NM 220 [off NM 48, take NM 220 north], ☎ 505/336–0010; 888/818–7872; 800/905–3315 for ticket orders). The white, templelike building looms majestically amid mountain vistas just north of Ruidoso and is one of the state's cultural icons. Tickets run $20–$40, and free tours are given Tuesday and Thursday, 10–2. Professionals often train local children to act in special free summer performances. Children's theater and outdoor summer concerts also are offered at the site.

Outdoor Activities and Sports

Run by the Mescalero Apaches on 12,003-ft Sierra Blanca, **Ski Apache** (✉ Ski Run Rd./NM 532, ☎ 505/336–4356; 505/257–9001 for snow report) has powder skiing for all skill levels on 55 trails and 750 acres. One of Ski Apache's distinctions is its high mountain elevation surrounded by desert. This unique climate can produce mounds of snowfall (averaging about 15 ft each winter) followed by days of pleasant, sunny weather. With the largest lift capacity in New Mexico, this huge resort can transport more than 16,500 people hourly. Ski Apache also has the state's only gondola. The season typically runs from Thanksgiving through Easter, and the snow-making system is able to cover a third of the trails. Open daily from 8:45 AM to 4 PM, the ski area charges adults $40 for a full day with lift tickets and $28 for a half day. Multiday discounts are offered. Snowboarding is allowed on all trails. Families should check out the Kiddie Korral Program for children ages 4–6. While there are no overnight accommodations at the resort, day lodges have two cafeterias, three snack bars, and two outdoor hamburger stands. From Ruidoso take NM 48 6 mi, and turn west on NM 532 for 12 mi.

Capitan

22 mi north of Ruidoso on NM 48, 12 mi west of Lincoln on U.S. 380.

Capitan is famous as the birthplace and final home of Smokey Bear, the nation's symbol of wildfire prevention. The original bear concept was created in 1944, and the poster bear is still seen in public service announcements issued by the Ad Council. After a devastating 1950 forest fire in the Capitan Mountains, a bear cub was found badly burned and clinging to a tree. Named Smokey after the poster bear, he lived in the National Zoo in Washington until his death in 1976, when he was returned home for burial.

☺ Displays at the **Smokey Bear Historical Park** visitor center explain forest-fire prevention and fire ecology. A theater and computer games are among the family-oriented entertainment. The 3-acre park also contains a playground and picnic area, and Capitan's original train depot, adjacent to the museum and gift shop. The site hosts special events for youngsters, such as an Easter egg hunt, Halloween night, and Smokey's Christmas at the Park. ✉ *118 Smokey Bear Blvd., off NM 380,* ☎ *505/354–2748.* ▦ *$1.* ☉ *Daily 9–5.*

Carrizozo

37 mi northwest of Capitan on U.S. 380, 58 mi north of Alamogordo on U.S. 54.

Back when railroad crews began using this site as a supply center, the community that rose up was named after *carrizo*, the reedlike grass growing in the area. The extra "-zo" appeared when the carrizo grew so thick a ranch foreman added it to the town's name for emphasis. The ranching community incorporated in 1907 and in 1912 became the county seat of Lincoln County. About 1,000 residents live in this charming, isolated town at the junction of U.S. 54 and U.S. 380.

The **Sierra Blanca Brewing Co.,** modestly hidden on a back street of Carrizozo, is the largest brewery in New Mexico, with a maximum capacity of 3,800 beer barrels annually. The high-tech brewing process is reflected in the smooth taste of creations such as pale ale, which you can sample free on the premises. Free tours also are offered. ✉ *503 12th St.,* ☎ *505/648–6606.* ⊙ *Free tours daily 9–4.*

Near Carrizozo is the **Valley of Fires Recreation Area.** According to Indian legend, a volcanic eruption about 1,000 years ago created a valley of fire here. When the lava cooled, a dark, jagged landscape remained. A ¾-mi trail penetrates the lava-flow area, which looks like a *Star Trek* backdrop and covers 44 mi (it's 5 mi wide in some places). Crevices and bowls trapping precious water nurture branchy ocotillo and blooming cactus, creating natural landscaping along the well-maintained trail. The visitor center has a gift shop with souvenirs and books. Caving is allowed with the proper permits. A tent camping area, which includes a large group shelter, was added to the park in 1999. ✉ *U.S. 380, 4 mi west of Carrizozo,* ☎ *505/648–2241.* ✑ *$3 per individual; $5 per carload; primitive camping $5; developed camping $7; sites with hookups $11.* ⊙ *Information center daily 8–4.*

Dining and Lodging

$ ✕ **Outpost Bar & Grill.** Rural restaurants in southern New Mexico have a longstanding rivalry over who makes the best green-chile hamburgers in the region. Many fans will tell you that the winner is right here. Besides cooking awesome burgers, this bar and grill has a wacky hunting lodge decor full of animal heads, snakeskins, and painted cow skulls. The massive antique wooden bar is the centerpiece of the establishment. ✉ *U.S. 54 south,* ☎ *505/648–9994. No credit cards.*

$ ▥ **Rainbow Inn.** New furnishings and modern amenities such as remote-control TVs are generally unusual in small rural motels such as this one. You can find most of the comforts of a major establishment here, including refrigerators and microwaves in rooms. ✉ *Intersection of U.S. 308 and U.S. 54 (Box 873), Carrizozo 88301,* ☎ *505/648–4006,* FAX *505/648–2989. 11 rooms. AE, D, DC, MC, V.*

$ ▥ **Sands RV Park & Motel.** Both the Rainbow Inn and this establishment are under the same ownership, so you'll find similar amenities in refurbished and nicely maintained rooms. An RV park with full hookups, cable, and showers is also on the premises. ✉ *South U.S. 54 (Box 873), Carrizozo 88301,* ☎ FAX *505/648–2989. 9 rooms, 23 RV spaces ($16 daily). Showers, coin laundry. AE, D, DC, MC, V.*

En Route Twenty-eight miles south of Carrizozo, take Country Road B-30 east
★ ❾ off U.S. 54 and in 5 mi you'll come to **Three Rivers Petroglyph Site,** one of the Southwest's most comprehensive and fascinating examples of prehistoric rock art. The 21,000 sunbursts, lizards, birds, hand prints, plants, masks, and other symbols are thought to represent the nature-worshiping religion of the Jornada Mogollon people, who lived

in this region between AD 900 and 1400. Between 1987 and 1992, two members of the Archaeological Society of New Mexico's Rock Art Recording Field School located, identified, and recorded the symbols. Fragrant desert creosote and mesquite can be found here, along with cacti that blossom brilliant colors in early summer. A rugged trail snakes for 1 mi, and from its top you can see the Tularosa Basin to the west and the Sacramento Mountains to the east. A short trail leads to a partially excavated prehistoric village. You can camp at the site, and there are six covered shelters with picnic tables, barbecue grills, rest rooms, and water. ⊠ *County Rd. B-30 east off U.S. 54,* ☎ *505/525– 4300. 27 RV hookups.* 🎫 *$2 per car; camping $10 daily.*

Alamogordo

⑩ *58 mi south of Carrizozo on U.S. 54, 46 mi southwest of Ruidoso; 68 mi northeast of Las Cruces on U.S. 70.*

Defense-related activities are vital to the town of Alamogordo and to Otero County, which covers much of the Tularosa Basin desert. Look up and you might see the dark, bat-shape outline of a Stealth fighter swooping overhead—Holloman Air Force Base is home to these high-tech fighter planes, which played a crucial role in the Gulf War in 1991. Many residents work at White Sands Missile Range, where the nation's first atomic bomb exploded at Trinity Site on July 12, 1945. If you find U.S. 70 closed temporarily, it's due to test launches (locals have grown accustomed to this). South of Alamogordo, huge military exercises involving both U.S. and foreign troops are conducted at the Fort Bliss Military Reservation along Route 54. It's not all that surprising that flying objects can be mistaken for Unidentified Flying Objects in this state.

ⓒ The multistory structure that houses the **Space Center** and museum gleams metallic gold when the sun hits it at certain angles. Its centerpiece is the **International Space Hall of Fame,** into which astronauts and other space-exploration celebrities are routinely inducted. A simulated red Mars landscape is among the indoor exhibits. Outside, the **Stapp Air and Space Park** displays a rocket sled from the 1950s and other space-related artifacts. The scenic **Astronaut Memorial Garden** has a view of White Sands National Monument. The **Clyde W. Tombaugh IMAX Dome Theater and Planetarium** screens films and presents planetarium and laser light shows. Weeklong annual space-shuttle camps for children take place from the first week in June through the first week in August. ⊠ *At the top of NM 2001 (from U.S. 70 take Indian Wells Rd. to Scenic Dr.; from U.S. 54 take Florida Ave. to Scenic Dr.),* ☎ *505/437–2840 or 800/545–4021.* 🎫 *Museum $2.50, IMAX show (1 film) $5.50, IMAX show (2 films) $9, evening IMAX film $6 (film and show fees sometimes vary).* ☉ *International Space Hall of Fame daily 9–5. Tombaugh IMAX Dome Theater and Planetarium Memorial Day–Labor Day, shows daily at 10, 11, noon, 1, 2, 3, 4, and 7; Labor Day–Memorial Day, shows weekdays at 10, noon, 2, and 4; weekends at 10, 11, noon, 2, 3, and 4; Fri.– Sun. evening shows at 7.*

ⓒ A narrow-gauge train at the **Toy Train Depot** rumbles along a 2½-mi track through Alamogordo's Alameda Park. The depot, built in 1898, also displays toy trains in five rooms, with elaborate layouts including one that depicts the Alamogordo area's train era for the past century. Displays include live steam engines and active model train layouts. Whistles and rumbles from nearby heavy freight trains (these are real) help set the scene, since the attraction is only 50 yards from the Union Pacific main line. If you make advance reservations, you can take a guided tour of the abandoned Alamogordo and Sacramento Railway roadbed and trestles. ⊠ *1991 N. White Sands Blvd (Alameda Park),* ☎ *505/ 437–2855.* ☞ *Train fare $2, displays $2.* ☉ *Wed.–Sun. 12:30–4:30.*

Tasty nuts are the crop at **Eagle Ranch Pistachio Groves,** where you can buy nutmeats in varieties of forms from chocolate candies to cranberry biscotti or linger in the coffee shop or art gallery. George and Marianne Schweers own the family farm that in 1972 diversified into pistachios, an unusual crop for New Mexico. The ranch now has 12,000 pistachio trees, the largest such grove in the state. Ask for permission at the store to camp at the picnic area—there's no charge for self-contained vehicles. ⊠ *7288 Hwy. 54/70, 4 mi north of White Sands Mall, Alamogordo,* ☎ *800/432–0999.* ☞ *Free farm tours Sept.–May, weekdays at 1:30 PM; June– Aug., Mon.–Fri. at 10 AM and 1:30 PM.* ☉ *Daily 9–6.*

★ ⓒ ⑪ **White Sands National Monument,** with shifting sand dunes 60 ft high, encompasses 145,344 acres and the largest deposit of gypsum sand in the world. The monument, one of the few landforms recognizable from space, has displays in its **visitor center** that describe how the dunes were formed. A 17-minute introductory video that's very helpful if you intend to hike among the dunes is screened at the visitor center, where there's a gift shop, snack bar, and bookstore.

A 16-mi round-trip car ride takes you into this eerie wonderland of gleaming white sand. You can climb to the top of the dunes for a photograph, then tumble or surf down on a sled sold at the visitor center. As you wade barefoot in the gypsum crystals you'll notice the sand is not hot, and there's even moisture to be felt a few inches below the surface. Gypsum is one of the most common minerals on earth, and unlike the silica sand on beaches, gypsum is finer and used for making Sheetrock and plaster of paris. A walk on the 1-mi **Big Dune Trail** will give you a good overview of the site; other options are the 4½-mi **Alkali Flat Trail** and the 600-yard **Boardwalk.** The **Nature Center in the Dunes** museum has exhibits and other information. The picnic area has shaded tables and grills. Backpackers' campsites are available by permit, obtainable at the visitor center, but there aren't any facilities. Once a month from May to September, White Sands celebrates the full moon by remaining open until 11 PM, allowing you to experience the dunes by lunar light. Call for information and reservations for monthly auto caravans to **Lake Lucero,** the source of the gypsum sand deposit. In summer rangers lead tours daily at sunset. ⊠ *Off U.S. 70, 15 mi southwest of Alamogordo, Holloman AFB,* ☎ *505/679–2599.* ☞ *$3 (day use or camping).* ☉ *Memorial Day– Labor Day, 7 AM–9 PM; visitor center 8–7. Labor Day–Memorial Day, 7 AM–dusk; visitor center 8–5.*

OFF THE **WHITE SANDS MISSILE RANGE MUSEUM & MISSILE PARK –** Here you BEATEN PATH can see outdoor displays of more than 50 rockets and missiles along with indoor exhibits honoring historic contributions of scientists including rocketry genius and inventor Werner Von Braun. The museum also contains accounts of early Native American inhabitants who occupied the surrounding Tularosa Basin. ⊠ *White Sands Missile Range (turn east off U.S. 70 40 mi south of Alamogordo or 25 mi north of Las Cruces; take access road 4 mi to gate and stop there to obtain a visitor's pass [you must have current driver's license and insurance to enter]),* ☎ *505/678–8824.* ☞ *Free.* ☉ *Museum weekdays 8–4:30, Missile Park daily dawn–dusk.*

Dining and Lodging

$–$$ ✕ **Compass Rose Brewpub.** Patterned after a Bavarian-style tavern, this unusual establishment has wooden bench seating and cozy surroundings along with selections of cheese, meat, bread, and salads. Hot sandwiches and stews also are served, and you can eat on an outdoor patio during balmy weather. The tasty food is a change of pace from Southwestern fare and might be a reflection of the presence of German air force troops training at nearby Holloman Air Force Base. ⊠ *2203 E. 1st St.,* ☎ *505/434–9633. AE, D, MC, V.*

$–$$ ✕ **Margo's.** *Chalupas* (beans, meat, and cheese served on crisp tortillas) is the specialty Mexican dish at family-owned Margo's. In winter, *menudo,* made of hominy and tripe, is served hot and steaming. The Southwestern decor includes colorful blankets. ⊠ *504 1st St.,* ☎ *505/ 434–0689. AE, D, MC, V.*

$ 🖭 **Days Inn.** Contemporary rooms with standard furnishings assure one a pleasant stay, with extra touches such as hair dryers and microwaves in every room. ⊠ *907 S. White Sands Blvd., 88310,* ☎ *505/ 437–5090,* 𝖥𝖠𝖷 *505/434–5667. 40 rooms. Refrigerators, pool, exercise room. AE, D, DC, MC, V. CP.*

$ ⚠ **Alamogordo KOA Kampground.** Motel-style amenities such as a pool and lounge are available at this facility, where patches of green lawn and trees, along with grills and picnic tables, make the outdoors inviting. ⊠ *412 24th St., 1 block east of U.S. 70/54,* ☎ *505/437–3003. 67 sites ($24 for RV hookups, $18 for tents), 2 camping cabins ($31.50). Showers, grocery, lounge, pool, recreation room, playground, coin laundry.*

Cloudcroft

⑫ *19 mi east of Alamogordo on U.S. 82.*

Cloudcroft is a quiet mountain resort town with cabins and church camps tucked into secluded woods. Longtime weekenders don't mind telling you that they hope their haven remains a secret. A low-key version of Ruidoso, Cloudcroft has a small stretch of specialty shops and some log cabin–style restaurants and lodgings. The headquarters of the **Lincoln National Forest Sacramento Ranger District** (⊠ 61 Curlew St., off U.S. 82, ☎ 505/682–2551) has maps showing area hiking trails.

The **National Solar Observatory–Sacramento Peak,** 12 mi south of Cloudcroft on the Sunspot Highway at elevation 9,200 ft, is designated for observations of the sun. The observatory, established in 1947, has four telescopes, including a 329-ft Vacuum Tower that resembles a pyramid. One observation point has a majestic view of White Sands and the Tularosa Basin. During the day you can inspect the telescopes on a self-guided tour and watch live filtered television views of the sun. This is a working community of scientists—not a tourist attraction— so you're pretty much on your own. About half of the 50 people who work at the site also live here amid ponderosa pines. In the summer of 1998, a new $1.5 million visitor center was constructed at the site. ⊠ *National Solar Observatory–Sacramento Peak, Sunspot,* ☎ *505/434– 7000.* 🎫 *Free.* ☉ *Visitor center May–Oct., daily 10–6; Nov.–Apr., call for hrs. Self-guided tours daily dawn–dusk.*

Dining and Lodging

For cabin rental information, call the Cloudcroft Chamber of Commerce, or try **Cabins at Cloudcroft** (☎ 505/682–2396; 800/248–7967 within New Mexico, ✍). Rates are $75–$170 for one- to four-bedroom cabins.

$$–$$$$ ✕🖭 **The Lodge.** The Mexican revolutionary Pancho Villa and Holly-
★ wood celebrities Judy Garland and Clark Gable are among the past guests at this Victorian lodge, originally a retreat owned by the Alamogordo and Sacramento Mountain Railway. The Lodge was originally built in 1899, burned down in 1909, and was rebuilt in about 1911. The Bavarian-style interior seems right out of a gothic novel. Rooms have comforters, period antiques, and ceiling fans. Rebecca's restaurant is named after a flirtatious redheaded ghost who is said to haunt

the hallways in search of a new lover, but more important, executive chef Timothy Wilkins has won five gold medals in New Mexico culinary competitions for his Southwestern and classical cuisine. While steam heaters in the rooms add a classical, charming look, it can be difficult to control settings. Affiliated with the lodge is the off-premises **Lodge Pavilion**, a rustic 10-room B&B. On the premises is a private, historic "minilodge," the **Retreat**, which has three one-bedroom suites and one two-bedroom suite. A huge common area includes a large table and kitchen facilities. ⊠ *1 Corona Pl. (Box 497), 88317,* ☎ *505/682–2566 or 800/395–6343,* ℻ *505/682–2715. 61 rooms. Restaurant, lounge, refrigerators, pool, outdoor hot tub, sauna, 9-hole golf course, croquet, exercise room, horseshoes, volleyball, cross-country skiing, snowmobiling. AE, D, DC, MC, V.* ✍

SOUTHEASTERN NEW MEXICO A TO Z

Arriving and Departing

By Bus

Texas, New Mexico & Oklahoma Coaches (☎ 505/887–1108 in Carlsbad; 800/231–2222 for all other destinations), which is affiliated with Greyhound Lines, provides bus service to Carlsbad, White's City, and other destinations in southern New Mexico.

By Car

To get to Roswell and other points in southeastern New Mexico, drive east from Albuquerque on I–40 for about 60 mi, exit on U.S. 285 heading south, and continue for 140 mi to Roswell. From Roswell take U.S. 285 to Carlsbad, about 75 mi away (320 mi from Albuquerque). From El Paso, Texas, take U.S. 62/180 east and north 154 mi to Carlsbad Caverns (187 mi to Carlsbad).

By Plane

Albuquerque International Sunport (☞ Arriving and Departing by Plane *in* Chapter 5) is 380 mi north of Carlsbad and 295 mi north of Roswell.

El Paso International Airport (⊠ 6701 Convair Dr. [take I–10's Exit 25–Airway or U.S. 54's Fred Wilson Rd. Exit to Airway], ☎ 915/772–4271) is the main gateway to southern New Mexico. The major airlines with scheduled service to the airport are America West, American, Continental, Delta, Frontier, and Southwest. *See* Air Travel *in* Smart Travel Tips A to Z.

Municipal airports in Carlsbad and Roswell have daily shuttle-flight service offered by **Mesa Airlines** (☎ 800/637–2247). Roswell is southeastern New Mexico's major flight hub, offering the most daily flights and scheduling options. Charter flights can be arranged at municipal airports including Ruidoso's **Sierra Blanca Regional Airport** (☎ 505/336–8111), **Carlsbad Aviation** (☎ 505/887–1500), and **Roswell Great Southwest Aviation** (☎ 505/347–2054).

Getting Around

By Bus and Van

Silver Stage (☎ 800/522–0162) operates van service to Carlsbad Caverns National Park from any point on the Carlsbad–El Paso route.

By Car

The major highway south through southeastern New Mexico is U.S. 285, accessible from I–40 at the Clines Corner exit, 59 mi east of Albuquerque. If you're destined for Roswell or Carlsbad from southwestern New Mexico, the best route is U.S. 70 east from Las Cruces or U.S. 62/180 east from El Paso, Texas.

The quality of the roadways in southeastern New Mexico varies widely, particularly in remote rural areas. Drive with caution on the region's narrow highways, which particularly in mountainous areas have no shoulders. On minor roadways, even if paved, be alert for curves, dips, and steep drop-offs.

Contacts and Resources

Car Rental

Cars can be rented at El Paso International Airport and Albuquerque International Sunsport (☞ Car Rentals *in* Smart Travel Tips A to Z). Auto dealerships in some southeastern New Mexico cities rent cars. Your best bet for finding car rentals in smaller communities, such as Ruidoso, Roswell, and Carlsbad, is at municipal airports. Both Avis and Hertz rent cars at the Roswell airport.

Guided Tours

Around and About Tours (✉ 6716 Mesa Grande Ave., El Paso 79912, ☎ 915/833-2650) has excursions of several days to a week into New Mexico. The rates vary.

Gray Line of Albuquerque (✉ 8401-A Jefferson Ave., Albuquerque, NM 87113, ☎ 800/256-8991 or 505/242-3880, FAX 505/243-0692) provides sightseeing tours to Carlsbad Caverns National Park by special request from groups.

Tour Company Guide Service (✉ 116 La Nell St., Canutillo, TX 79835, ☎ 915/877-3002) conducts cultural, architectural, historical, and other tours of southern New Mexico sites. In some cases, you drive your own car.

Late-Night Pharmacies

Some Walgreens pharmacies in Roswell, Carlsbad, and other southeastern communities have late-night or 24-hour pharmacies. Wal-Mart and large grocery chain stores including Albertson's also have pharmacies.

Visitor Information

For cities or areas not listed below, contact the **New Mexico Department of Tourism** (✉ 491 Old Santa Fe Trail, Santa Fe 87503, ☎ 505/827-7400 or 800/545-2070).

Alamogordo Chamber of Commerce (✉ 1301 North White Sands Blvd., 88310, ☎ 505/437-6120 or 888/826-0294). **Capitan Chamber of Commerce** (✉ Box 441, 88316, ☎ 505/354-2273). **Carlsbad Chamber of Commerce** (✉ 302 S. Canal St., 88220, ☎ 505/887-6516). **Carrizozo Chamber of Commerce** (✉ Box 567, 88301, ☎ 505/648-2732). **Cloudcroft Chamber of Commerce** (✉ Box 1290, 88317, ☎ 505/682-2733, ✍). **Lincoln State Monument** (✉ U.S. 380, Box 36, 88338, ☎ 505/653-4372). **Portales Chamber of Commerce** (✉ 200 E. 7th St., 88130, ☎ 800/635-8036). **Roswell Chamber of Commerce** (✉ 121 W. 2nd St., ☎ 505/623-5695). **Ruidoso Valley Chamber of Commerce** (✉ 720 Sudderth Dr., 88345 ☎ 505/257-7395).

8 SOUTHWESTERN NEW MEXICO

INCLUDING EL PASO, TEXAS, AND CIUDAD JUÁREZ, MEXICO

Lakes along the Rio Grande reflect serene clouds, dust devils dance across the plains, a distant horseback rider searches for a calf lost from a cattle herd. In the far southwestern corner's wilderness of pines and sheer canyons, wild creatures find refuge from encroaching civilization. Of the Old West, adobe sanctuaries and cobbled plazas are surviving remnants.

Updated by
Marilyn
Haddrill

W IDELY DIVERSE CULTURES mingle in southwestern New
Mexico, and their respective art, architecture, and ethnic
foods beckon the traveler in search of adventure. The pre-
cursor to this rich variety, however, was frequent and ongoing power
struggles. Apache Indians and the Spanish threatened each other for
three centuries; the Apache leader Geronimo would close out his life
battling Anglo encroachment. Once the United States secured the lands
for its own in the mid-1800s, ranchers and the infighting of lawmen
and outlaws would create a unique American West mythology.

Where caravans of horses and wagons from Mexico's interior once
snaked cautiously, urban development booms in the borderland of New
Mexico, west Texas, and Mexico. More than 400 years ago, the vast
desert area in south-central New Mexico was known as the "Pass of
the North," a vital pathway for Spanish explorers in North America.
Cabeza de Vaca led the first Spanish expedition into the area in 1593.
Five years later Juan de Oñate brought 500 colonists from Mexico across
the Rio Grande into what is now New Mexico. Trade between the eventual northern colonial outposts and old Mexico followed El Camino
Real (The Royal Road), a route that for the most part traveled parallel to the Rio Grande. The portion of the trek north of Las Cruces and
east of the Rio Grande became known as Jornada del Muerto (Journey of Death) because of the physical hardship and Indian attacks travelers often endured. Conquistadors left behind armor, helmets, and other
relics leading to many stories of lost treasure.

El Paso, Texas, named after the Spanish explorers' route, is the area's
largest city and most convenient gateway. But the nerve center of
southern New Mexico is Las Cruces (The Crosses), with a population
of about 75,000. The Organ Mountains overlooking the city dominate
the landscape and the works of area painters and photographers. Sunset can color the jagged peaks a brilliant magenta, called "Las Cruces
purple." Nearby Old Mesilla once served as the Confederate territorial capital of New Mexico and Arizona.

Parched Spanish sojourners of the 16th century would be shocked to
witness the agrarian lifestyle in the fertile Mesilla Valley, just north of
El Paso. Miles of lush fields and pecan orchards track the path of the
Rio Grande. The huge Elephant Butte reservoir is the source of much
of the water that irrigates some of the country's most prolific pecan
and chile farms. As New Mexico's largest body of water, Elephant Butte
Lake is a mecca for water sports and fishing. At nearby Truth or Consequences you can soak at bargain prices in natural hot springs.

Outdoor enthusiasts also head to the Gila National Forest and Gila
Wilderness areas, where quaint old mining towns are the relics of
fevered quests for silver, copper, and other minerals once found abundantly in the ore-rich hills. Area museums contain comprehensive displays of locally found minerals, along with colorful pottery created by
early Native American inhabitants. The mountainous area where both
Geronimo and Billy the Kid lived provides breathtaking vistas.

North of Gila National Forest, Highway 60 runs east–west through
ranching communities whose lifestyles and isolation evoke a simpler
past. In this lonely landscape you'll find the gleaming white, dish-shape
radio telescope antennas of the Very Large Array, focusing its attention a billion light-years away.

Pleasures and Pastimes

Dining
The cost of a meal in this area is extremely reasonable. The Mexican restaurants in the Mesilla Valley and Las Cruces rival those in Santa Fe except in price. Almost any Mexican-style eatery in the valley is sure to please, especially if you're a fan of the locally grown green chiles. Barbecue joints and steak houses are just as popular as Mexican restaurants.

Lodging
The Las Cruces area has two very fine bed-and-breakfasts—Meson de Mesilla in Old Mesilla and Lundeen Inn of the Arts—both of which would stand out in any major metropolitan area. Another inn, the Cottages in Silver City, is highly recommended. You can also check out guest ranches and the usual selection of standard chain motels.

Outdoor Activities and Sports
Outdoor opportunities abound in this corner of New Mexico. Elephant Butte Lake near Truth or Consequences offers world-class competition fishing for monstrous striped bass, though other varieties such as catfish are also abundant. All sorts of water sports take advantage of the lake's miles of surface. Elephant Butte is on a flat, open plain and can get pretty toasty during summer months. The Gila National Forest and mountains near Silver City provide a cooler environment for trout fishing or hiking, but don't expect large streams or lakes here: this forest land is dryer than what you would find in higher elevations. The mountains are still immense and fun to explore, either on foot or via scenic drives. Camping is another popular activity in this area. Birdwatchers will be busy just about anywhere they go along the Rio Grande, Gila National Forest, Elephant Butte Lake, or Bosque del Apache Wildlife Refuge.

Exploring Southwestern New Mexico

The Rio Grande carves through the fertile Mesilla Valley, known for its plump green chiles and acres of thick, shaded pecan groves. Try leaving I–10 and follow the green agriculture fields along NM 28, which begins just north of El Paso and ends at Old Mesilla. You must stop in the shops and restaurants in Old Mesilla's historic plaza; its adobe structures appear much as they did a century ago. From Las Cruces, take NM 185 north through the farm valley on a route that leads to Hatch. During the fall harvest the valley is scented with the aroma of roasting chiles.

Surrounding the old mining town of Silver City is the vast and scenic Gila National Forest, which includes the Black Range mountains. New Mexico's largest lake, Elephant Butte, begins at Truth or Consequences and tracks north for miles alongside I–25. The Bosque del Apache Wildlife Refuge near Socorro provides a haven for many species of waterfowl. Another opportunity to leave the beaten path awaits at Socorro, where you can turn west on U.S. 60 to explore tiny rural villages such as Magdalena and Datil. On the Plains of San Augustin, look for the awesome array of giant, gleaming white radio antennas that are part of the National Radio Astronomy Observatory.

Great Itineraries
In this highly diverse region, you can balance a mix of historical, cultural, and outdoor experiences. Adjust your schedule to your own tastes, but be open to a little adventure. This is an ideal opportunity to leave behind urban pleasures for those of a quiet rural inn or remote forest trail. The Old West city of El Paso, Texas, serves as the gateway to southern New Mexico, which is why it is included here.

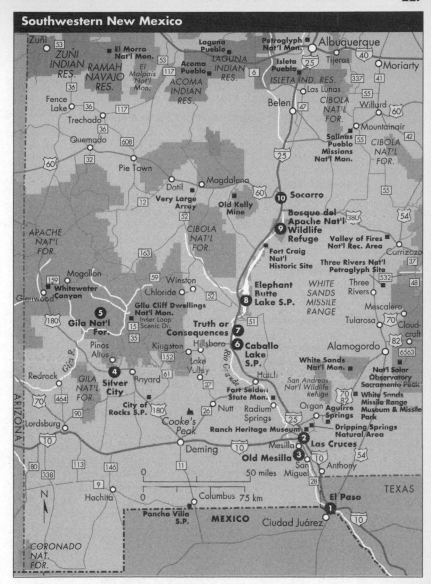

Southwestern New Mexico

IF YOU HAVE 3 DAYS

Spend your first day exploring the history and Spanish missions of ⌂ **El Paso** ①. On day two, travel north on NM 28 through shady pecan orchards to **Old Mesilla** ③ and visit the galleries, shops, and restaurants. In the afternoon, take U.S. 70 northeast to **White Sands National Monument** (☞ Chapter 7). Return to ⌂ **Las Cruces** ② to spend the night, and if you're in Las Cruces on a Wednesday or Saturday morning, stop by the open-air downtown farmers' market. Next take I–10 west 61 mi to **Deming,** and turn northwest onto U.S. 180 to drive 51 mi to ⌂ **Silver City** ④. If there's still time, you can hike, fish, or visit ghost towns in the **Gila National Forest** ⑤.

IF YOU HAVE 7 DAYS

Follow the three-day itinerary above and spend your fourth day on a scenic drive east on NM 152 through **Hillsboro** to ⌂ **Truth or Consequences** ⑦ and **Elephant Butte Lake State Park** ⑧. Spend part of your fifth day in the area before continuing north on I–25 to **Bosque del Apache National Wildlife Refuge** ⑨ and overnighting in 🏨 **Socorro** ⑩. On day six, take U.S. 60 west to investigate the **Very Large Array,** and **Datil,** among other small towns, and overnight at one of the small places along U.S. 60. Spend your seventh day making your way back south along I–25 to El Paso, stopping at one of the forts, or Hatch for some chiles to bring home.

When to Tour Southwestern New Mexico

Winters tend to be gentle in the desert regions of southern New Mexico, but between May and early September the days can be blisteringly hot. Even the mountainous areas can be uncomfortably warm during a hot spell. Plan summer outdoor excursions for early morning or late evening. Wear sunscreen, sunglasses, and hats in the midday sun, and carry plenty of water. Spring is cooler, but it's often accompanied by nasty, dust-laden winds. One of the best times to visit is between late September and early November, when skies are clear blue and the weather is usually balmy.

BORDERLAND

Lines drawn on a map do little to divide the inhabitants of two countries and three states who share an ancestry dating back to the arrival of Spanish colonists. In the small border cities of Columbus, New Mexico, and Las Palomas, Mexico, families live and do business on both sides of the international boundary line. Housing and commercial developments along I–10 are quickly joining Las Cruces, New Mexico, to El Paso, Texas. The city of Anthony marks a midway point, straddling the two states. This "Borderland" of New Mexico, Texas, and the Mexican state of Chihuahua also draws transplants from the eastern and western United States, who come to take advantage of the mild weather and placid way of life.

You might be surprised to find U.S. Border Patrol checkpoints on all major highways leading away from the El Paso area to destinations such as Carlsbad, Deming, Truth or Consequences, and Alamogordo. Uniformed officers will simply ask your citizenship, though trained dogs sometimes circle vehicles in searches for illegal drugs. The stops are routine, and law-abiding citizens should encounter no difficulty.

El Paso

❶ *267 mi south of Albuquerque, I–25 to I–10.*

&*following the text of a review is your signal that the property has a Web site, where you will find details and, usually, images; for a link, visit www.fodors.com/urls.*

Yes, El Paso *is* in Texas—but just barely. At one time, the city along the now streamlike Rio Grande was part of the New Mexico Territory. One glance at a map will explain why this area has become the transportation hub for southern New Mexico.

In April 1598, Spanish explorer Don Juan de Oñate dubbed the entire Rio Grande Valley "Paso del Rio del Norte" (the pass through the river of the north)—from which El Paso derives its name. Oñate was so grateful that the expedition of about 500 ragged colonists had reached the Rio Grande that he ordered his people to don their best clothes for a feast of thanksgiving—a celebration that preceded the arrival of the pilgrims in Massachusetts by nearly a quarter century. On that feast day, April 30, Oñate issued a formal proclamation of *La Toma*, claiming the land for the King of Spain.

Today El Paso is most strongly associated with Anglo-America's Old West tales of cattle drives and gunfighters. Between the southern end of the Rockies and the northern terminus of Mexico's Sierra Madre, the city was a major stopping point on the way west during the California gold rush. The downtown area in about 1850 was sparsely settled, with a dirt trail leading to the Rio Grande. Adobes began to appear along an established roadway about eight years later. San Jacinto Plaza soon became the official town square. The arrival of the railroad, the real life giver to towns, came in 1888.

Many of El Paso's downtown buildings date from the early 20th century, when architect Henry C. Trost produced his finest work, from the pillars and stained glass of the grandiose Camino Real Paso del Norte to the sturdy, reinforced concrete of the Mills Building. Trost, whose influences were many—from adobe to Frank Lloyd Wright—received much acclaim for his buildings at the University of Texas at El Paso. Based on Bhutanese structures, the campus buildings have an almost monastic design. Unfortunately, many downtown gems, like the historically protected Plaza Hotel (one of Conrad Hilton's first hotels), stand empty. During the 1950s hotels could be filled, sometimes with Hollywood stars and the wealthy heading for a cheap and easy divorce in Ciudad Juárez across the border. Adding to the town's bravado were live alligators in the plaza pond (a sculpture of writhing alligators has replaced the real reptiles, which ended their residency in the 1960s).

The **El Paso Museum of Art** has an American collection that includes Southwest artists Tom Lea, Frederic Remington, Henrietta Wyeth, and native son Luis Jimenez. In the Spanish Viceroyal and Mexican folk *retablos* room is striking religious art. Drawings and prints by masters like Picasso, Goya, and Rivera, and works by contemporary artists are other museum highlights. ⊠ *One Arts Festival Plaza,* ☎ *915/532–1707.* ☜ *$1, free Sun.* ◷ *Tues.–Sat. 9–6, Sun. noon–5.*

Magoffin Home State Historical Park, a Territorial-style adobe homestead near downtown El Paso, was erected in 1875 by an early El Paso pioneer, Joseph Magoffin. The home's traditional design includes thick adobe walls and an enclosed patio. Paintings and furniture belonging to the original owners lie within, including an imposing 13-ft-tall half-canopy bed with rose-color silk upholstery. The bed is part of a five-piece bedroom set purchased at the 1884 World's Fair in New Orleans. ⊠ *1120 Magoffin St. (follow signs off I-10; westbound traffic takes Cotton St. exit, eastbound traffic takes Downtown exit to Kansas St.),* ☎ *915/533–5147.* ☜ *$2.* ◷ *Daily 9–4.*

In the lower valley outside El Paso are some of the Southwest's earliest Spanish missions and other historic structures. The **Mission Trail Association** (☎ 915/534–0630, ✍) has information about them. Also, the **El Paso–Juárez Trolley Co.** (☎ 915/544–0061 or 800/259–6284) in association with **Tour Company-Guide Service** (☎ 915/877–3002), owned by Jo Ann Shaw, conducts regularly scheduled mission tours. To start your own mission trail tour, take the Zaragoza exit off I-10 just east of El Paso southwest for 4 mi, and then turn south onto Socorro Road and follow the mission trail signs.

★ Spanish refugees from Santa Fe's Pueblo Revolt of 1680 established the **Mission Ysleta** (*ysleta* means "small island") circa 1681. The clergy converted members of the Tigua tribe who had accompanied the refugees on their southern flight. The thick-walled adobe structure has a small door, which the settlers hoped would leave them less vulnerable to attacks by hostile Native Americans. Like the other old missions in the area, this structure remains an active church. A guide from the

Mission Trail Association is available to conduct free tours through noon, Friday through Sunday, depending on church schedules. ⊠ *Old Pueblo Rd. at Zaragosa and Alameda (take Zaragosa exit off I–10, east of El Paso),* ☎ *915/859–9848.* ☜ *Free.* ☉ *Daily 8–4 (varies with church service schedules).*

Adjacent to Mission Ysleta is the **Tigua Indian Reservation** (⊠ 119 S. Old Pueblo Rd., ☎ 915/859–7913), home of the oldest ethnic group in Texas. Tigua pottery, jewelry, art, and replicas of ancient Native American homes are sold here. The **Speaking Rock Casino & Entertainment Center** (⊠ Tigua Indian Reservation, 122 Old Pueblo Rd., ☎ 915/860–7777), which never closes, includes a restaurant, slots, bingo, poker, and blackjack in a mildly upscale setting.

Socorro Mission, to the south of the Tigua Indian Reservation, is famed for its fine vigas—the carved ceiling beams that support adobe architecture. Because it is so small, the building is used only for special occasions such as weddings and funerals. The church structure, weakened by rains, has been undergoing renovations that should be complete within a few years. The Mission Trail Association has a free tour guide here through noon, Friday through Sunday, unless it conflicts with services. ⊠ *328 S. Nevares Rd.,* ☎ *915/859–7718.* ☜ *Free.* ☉ *Daily 8–4 (call ahead).*

Presidio Chapel San Elceario in San Elizario (yes, the two spellings conflict) is 6 mi south of the Socorro Mission. The 1789 Spanish fortress provided settlers protection from raiding Comanches and Apaches. After fire damaged the chapel in 1936, a bell tower and stained glass were added. It was near this site that the expedition of Spanish explorer Don Juan de Oñate stopped to conduct a thanksgiving celebration in 1598. ⊠ *1556 San Elizario Rd.,* ☎ *915/851–2333.* ☜ *Free.* ☉ *Daily 8–4 (generally).*

The **San Elizario County Jail** is thought to have been built as a private residence in the early 1800s, but at some point the adobe structure transitioned into El Paso County's first courthouse and jail. Outlaw Billy the Kid is said to have helped break a friend out of one of the iron cages here, though the story cannot be verified. The account is included in a book written by former Lincoln County Sheriff Pat Garrett, who ultimately tracked down and shot Billy the Kid. In the same vicinity, you'll find other historic structures including Los Portales, originally built in the 1850s as a private residence. ⊠ *San Elizario Plaza,* ☎ *915/851–1682 (San Elizario Genealogy and Historical Society).* ☜ *Free guided tours of jail and plaza beginning at the Los Portales building.* ☉ *Tues.–Sun. 10–2.*

A new casino with 300 slot machines has boosted profits and purses for the **Sunland Park Racetrack** (⊠ 101 Futurity Dr., Sunland Park, ☎ 505/589–1131), which now has race days Friday–Sunday and Tuesday from November through early April. Post time is 1:30. It's an attractive facility, enhanced by an artificial lake in the middle of the track. A restaurant, lounge, snack bar, and live entertainment on weekends are offered, including mariachi music on Sunday afternoons. The casino stays open year-round, from noon to midnight. From El Paso, take Sunland Park exit off I–25 near the northern city limits.

Dining and Lodging

$–$$$ ✕ **Cattleman's Steakhouse.** What the owners describe as "Dakota-style
  ★   badland bluffs" signal your arrival at this restaurant and attraction, and a cowboy on horseback greets you in the parking lot. Cattleman's is pretty much in the middle of nowhere—20 mi east of El Paso—but it's worth the trip, as much for the fun ambience as for the terrific steaks. The succulent slabs are so tender they almost melt in your mouth. A zoo, donkey rides, deer display, playground, party facilities, a lake walk,

and a Western town are among the nonculinary diversions. Free hayrides are given on Sunday. Cattleman's is part of Indian Cliffs Ranch, which provided the backdrop for scenes in the movie *Courage Under Fire*. Open hours are weekdays 4:30–10, Saturday 4–10, and Sunday noon–9. ✉ *Off I–10, Exit 49 (follow signs), Fabens*, ☎ *915/ 544–3200. Reservations not accepted. AE, D, MC, V.*

$–$$ ✕ **La Norteña y Cafe Deluxe.** The after-work and singles crowd pack into this casual, hip meeting point for Mexican cuisine and pool shooting. Behind the long bar, cooks dish up staple dishes and surprises like a shark and potato taco, and quail. Breakfast here is a good bet, too. Booths and tables fill the cavernous space, which served as a jail and Chinese laundry in its past lives. Beer and alcohol logos are painted on the brick walls. The eatery is close to the Greyhound terminal and in walking distance from the civic center and Camino Real Hotel (☞ *below*). ✉ *212 W. Overland*, ☎ *915/533–0533. AE, MC, V. Closed Sun.*

$–$$ ✕ **The State Line.** The best barbecued ribs and smoked chicken in the
★ region can be found in northwestern El Paso (near Sunland Park Race-Track). Bring an appetite because the trimmings include generous helpings of potato salad, coleslaw, and beans. For dessert try the ultrarich brownie. Drinks are served in an outdoor courtyard, where you can wait for your table. ✉ *1222 Sunland Park Dr. (Sunland Park exit off I–10)*, ☎ *915/581–3371. Reservations not accepted. AE, D, MC, V.*

$ ✕ **Leo's.** You'll not be disappointed at any of this El Paso establishment's five locations. The Mexican food is repeatedly voted an ethnic favorite by locals in annual newspaper polls. Enchiladas, tacos, combination plates, and fluffy sopaipillas are served in helpings that will leave you stuffed—that is, if you can elbow your way through the crowds and get a table. ✉ *2285 Trawood St.,* ☎ *915/591–2511; 5103 Montana St.,* ☎ *915/566–4972; 5315 Hondo Pass,* ☎ *915/751 9025; 315 Mills Ave.,* ☎ *915/544–1001; 8001 N. Mesa St.,* ☎ *915/833 1189. AE, D, MC, V.*

$$$ ✕🏨 **Camino Real Hotel, El Paso.** This towering, redbrick downtown hotel is listed on the National Register of Historic Places and has a great location across from the art museum and civic center. The guest rooms are quite large, if a bit ordinary. The jewel of the hotel is the high-ceiling Dome Bar, surrounded by marble and beneath a 1912 Tiffany stained-glass dome of rich blues. In the days when the hotel was the Hotel Paseo del Norte, cattlemen filled the bar with smoke as they cut their deals. Today, locals sink into deep chairs while enjoying the evening musical entertainment. The Dome Restaurant offers fine dining, and brunch is popular at the more casual Azulejo. ✉ *101 S. El Paso St., 79901,* ☎ *915/534–3000 or 800/769–4300,* 𝖥𝖠𝖷 *915/534–3024. 359 rooms. 2 restaurants, coffee shop, pool, sauna, exercise room, babysitting, airport shuttle, parking (fee). AE, D, DC, MC, V.* ⊛

$$$ 🏨 **Hilton El Paso Airport.** Just 200 yards from the El Paso International Airport, this modern hotel has luxurious rooms and underwent a complete renovation in 2000. More than half the rooms can be converted into two-room suites. The two restaurants on the premises provide a choice of standard or northern Italian dishes. The pool here has a 200-ft water slide. ✉ *2027 Airway Blvd., 79925,* ☎ *915/778–4241,* 𝖥𝖠𝖷 *915/ 772–6871. 272 rooms. 2 restaurants, lounge, pool, hot tub, spa. AE, D, DC, MC, V.*

$–$$ 🏨 **Holiday Inn Sunland Park.** Outdoor courtyards contribute to the atmosphere of this Holiday Inn, on a hill with 6½ acres near Sunland Park RaceTrack. The Southwestern-style rooms have ironing boards, hair dryers, and coffeemakers; suites also have refrigerators and microwaves. Breakfast buffets are served in the Sierra Grille Restaurant, and a Sunday brunch is available from 11 to 3. ✉ *900 Sunland Park*

*Dr., 79922, ☏ 915/833–2900 or 800/658–2744, FAX 915/833–6338.
178 rooms. Restaurant, pool, lounge, hot tub. AE, D, DC, MC, V.
www.holidaysunland.com.*

Nightlife and the Arts

Locals drink to free musical entertainment on weekends at the **Camino Real Hotel** (⊠ 101 S. El Paso St., ☏ 915/534–3000) Dome Bar. The year's highlight for the city is the annual **Viva El Paso!** (☏ 915/565–6900 or 800/915–8482), a musical celebrating the El Paso region's history and legendary characters with music, dance, and drama. It takes place at the outdoor McKelligon Canyon Amphitheater in the Franklin Mountains, June through August, Thursday through Saturday. You can opt to take in the barbecue dinner served prior to the show, but make reservations for that, too. The **El Paso–Juárez Trolley Co.** (☏ 915/544–0062) provides a shuttle service to Viva El Paso! from downtown and airport hotels. By car, take I–10 east to Route 54 north. Take the Fred Wilson Road exit, turn left on Fred Wilson Road and left on Alabama Street, and you'll shortly arrive at the canyon's entrance on McKelligon Canyon Road.

Shopping

El Paso has some delightful specialty outlets reflecting the tastes of economy-minded residents. Colorful blankets, leather goods, ceramics, tile for home building, and household decorative items are among the most popular Mexican imports. At the **Butterfield Trading Post** (⊠ I–10 and Airway Boulevard, ☏ 915/771–7723) you'll find an open-air market and bargains such as $4 Mexican blankets. Handcrafted wooden furniture with Southwestern flourishes is sold at **Casa Rustica** (⊠ 6600 Montana Ave., ☏ 915/771–9096), along with exotic imports such as African masks. If you really want to immerse yourself in cowboy trappings, visit **El Paso Saddleblanket Co.** (⊠ 601 N. Oregon St., downtown Exit 19 off I–10, ☏ 915/544–1000). You'll find saddles, cowhides, skulls, horns, Indian pottery, and cowboy antiques such as branding irons in this 36,000-square-ft wholesale warehouse.

El Paso is *big* on cowboy boots and has several factory outlet stores. Even though the boots stocked are discontinued styles or irregular, the **Tony Lama Factory Stores** (⊠ 5040 N. Desert Blvd., ☏ 915/581–8192; 12151 Gateway West, ☏ 915/858–0124; 7156 Gateway East, ☏ 915/772–4327) carry a most prestigious name, and the boots are handcrafted in El Paso. If your boots were made for riding, not walking, check out **Barnett Harley-Davidson** (⊠ 8272 I–10, between Lomaland and Lee Trevino, ☏ 915/592–5804 or 800/736–8173), the world's largest dealership for the famed motorcycles. New, used, and rare bikes are showcased and parts and accessories are also for sale.

Ciudad Juárez

Across the Rio Grande border from El Paso.

Just across the shallow Rio Grande lies the Mexican city that at one time made up a single Spanish settlement with El Paso. Juárez is a city of tremendous contrast, from residential districts of handsome, hacienda-style mansions to outlying colonias with tiny makeshift residences and dirt streets. In recent years, the establishment of numerous *maquiladora* factories—"twin" plants operated by U.S. companies—has boosted the city's population to more than 1,700,000. Workers in maquiladoras assemble electronic and automobile components that are then shipped to the United States for further assembly.

In addition to other safety concerns, driving here is not recommended (☞ Safety *in* Smart Travel Tips A to Z). You can park in El Paso near the Santa Fe Street Bridge and walk to Juárez, or catch a ride with the **El Paso–Juárez Trolley Co.** Border Jumper (⊠ One Civic Center Plaza, El Paso, ☎ 915/544–0062 or 800/259–6284), which leaves hourly from 10 to 5. Eleven dollars will buy you a day's worth of transportation along the route that weaves through Juárez shopping areas and restaurants. Trolleys make hourly stops at the designated points and drivers provide narration and border-incident stories along the way. The trolley company also provides free shuttle transportation to and from participating El Paso hotels. Juárez is a sprawling city, and although there are sidewalks, there are dull stretches past graffiti-covered storefronts, parking lots, and strip malls. Distances between points of interest can be great, so it's best to catch the next trolley coming through.

Juárez became an official settlement with the building of its first church, **Nuestra Señora de Guadalupe Misión** (Our Lady of Guadalupe Mission), which was completed in 1668. The church and the **Juárez Cathedral** (⊠ Corner of Av. 16 de Septiembre and Mariscal, ☎ 52/155–505) next door still have an active congregation. The downtown **Mercado** (Old City Market; ⊠ Av. 16 de Septiembre) is where most day-trippers spend their time shopping. For a better view of local life, walk down Francisco I. Madero Street from the mercado, and you'll reach a park centered by a statue of Benito Juárez.

Dining

$ ✕ **Chihuahua Charlie's.** One local resident calls this establishment "hyper" Mexico, but it's a lot of fun. Sombrero-clad entertainers strum guitars and serenade guests in garishly decorated surroundings. A separate half of the restaurant is a calm and bright setting for breakfasts and lunches, and you'll see more Mexican families here. An extensive menu includes Mexican specialties along with standard fare such as steak or seafood. Order a 16-ounce margarita and you'll get another free. Prices are given in pesos, but you can pay with U.S. dollars. The trolley from El Paso stops here every hour. ⊠ *Paseo Triunfo de la Republica 2525, Zona Pronaf,* ☎ *52/139–940. AE, D, DC, MC, V.*

Shopping

In a city of nearly 2 million, shops are numerous, but you're best off sticking to tourist-oriented locales such as the **Mercado** (⊠ Av. 16 de Septiembre). Merchants hawk wares in a labyrinth of booths carrying piñatas (papier-mâché animals stuffed with candy), wooden figurines, belts, and jewelry. You're expected to barter. Don't hesitate to quibble or you'll be snickered at behind your back for paying the first asking price. You'll also be approached by insistent vendors on the street. Watch out for these street entrepreneurs, or you might end up purchasing a cassette tape that turns out to be a fuzzy recording of a radio broadcast. For a change of pace, try the three-story **Decor** (⊠ Av. Ignacio Mejia and Av. Lincoln, ☎ 52/131–415), where you can browse through fine, handcrafted furniture along with ceramics and jewelry. On the third floor are glassblowing demonstrations. **Avenida de Juárez** has many small individual shops where you can purchase items such as handwoven shawls and serapes. Be extra alert to your safety west of Avenida de Juárez. Many stores in Juárez are closed on Sunday.

Las Cruces

2 *45 mi north of El Paso on I–10.*

A mixture of old and new, Las Cruces is a city of diverse neighborhoods. The ones with adobe structures near the downtown area date back more than a century. The city, which celebrated its 150th anniversary in 1999, has for many years struggled to find ways to showcase its historic downtown. Improvements include the elimination of a dark, covered shopping mall that had proven to be more foreboding than attractive. In 2000, the transformation of this now open-air, pedestrian district was apparent. Outdated shops were being replaced with museums, a performing arts center, and a renovated old movie house. Take note of beautifully crafted, life-size bronze statues that represent different generations of travelers along the ancient Camino Real trade route.

The city and surrounding area represent one of the fastest-growing metropolitan areas in the United States, with an economy closely linked to the border factories of El Paso, Texas, and Ciudad Juárez, Mexico; defense and commercial activities at White Sands Missile Range; and a major land-grant college, New Mexico State University.

Increasing commitment to the fine arts is represented in various city-owned downtown sites known as the the **Cultural Complex,** which operates from headquarters at the Branigan Cultural Center. The center itself is the hub of educational activities, arts conferences, and traveling exhibits honoring different crafts such as quilting. The **Museum of Fine Arts And Culture,** open Tuesday–Friday 10–2, Saturday 9:30–2:30, features works of regional artists with an eclectic mix of styles, including emphasis on the Southwest and desert earth tones. The **Log Cabin Museum** is an original structure transferred from southern New Mexico's Black Range Mountains. Hands-on displays include a cider press and butter churn. Free admission can be obtained by inquiring at the cultural center headquarters. In 2001, the city plans to open the **New Mexico Railroad and Transportation Museum,** by converting an abandoned Santa Fe Railroad Depot several blocks west of the downtown strip. ⊠ *500 N. Water St.,* ☎ *505/541–3155,* ▧ *Free.* ☉ *Weekdays 9–5, Sat. 9–3.*

The handsomely designed **New Mexico Farm and Ranch Heritage Museum** contains 70,000 square ft of exhibition space, and though it opened in 1998 it's still a work in progress. The mission of the gallery and farm exhibits is to document 3,000 years of agriculture in New Mexico and the Southwest. One exhibit re-creates a Mogollon pit house—an early farmhouse—from 1,200 years ago. (The Mogollon were the first people in what is now New Mexico to cease being nomadic.) Longhorn cattle, churro sheep, and some of the dairy cows are among the heritage breeds—descendants of animals the Spanish brought from Mexico—raised here. Newly added animals include burros called "Jerusalem donkeys" for the crosslike markings on their backs. At calf-feeding time (11 AM and 3 PM), you can learn about the history of dairy production in New Mexico and pet a calf. ⊠ *4100 Dripping Springs Rd. (from Las Cruces head east on University Ave., which becomes Dripping Springs Rd.; the ranch is 1½ mi east of I–25),* ☎ *505/522–4100.* ▧ *$4.* ☉ *Tues.–Sat. 9–5, Sun. noon–5.*

Dining and Lodging

$–$$$ ✕ **Cattle Baron.** Part of a regional chain, this restaurant serves prime
★   rib, steaks, seafood, and pastas and has a well-stocked salad bar. The plant-filled, skylit dining room is done in brass and wood. The outdoor patio has city views. ⊠ *790 S. Telshor Blvd.,* ☎ *505/522–7533. AE, D, MC, V.*

$–$$ ✕ **Lemongrass.** One of the newer and more elegant eateries in Las Cruces
★   is this Thai establishment. The decor includes pastel colors and lush green carpeting, and gentle Asian music plays in the background. Dishes are authentic, such as Gang Dang Gai, featuring a scrumptious combination of green chile curry simmered in coconut milk with

SACRED GROUND

SYMBOLS OF CATHOLICISM seem to be a hallmark of New Mexico, and visitors seek out adobe churches to photograph and colorful religious icons and minishrines to buy as souvenirs. More intimate and poignant expressions of New Mexicans' deep religiosity are found in homemade shrines and centuries-old churches of healing.

Alongside the state's roadways are small memorials of flowers and crosses known in Spanish as *descansos*, or resting places, for those who have died in automobile accidents. The monuments are erected by family or friends to honor the memory of the dead and on narrow, curving roads and steep embankments serve as chilling reminders to the living not to take safe passage for granted.

Some historians say the custom of highway shrines was introduced to the Western hemisphere four centuries ago by the first Spanish explorers, who experienced so many losses of life that their trails were strewn with crosses marking the fallen. Las Cruces, New Mexico, is thought to have obtained its name, "The Crosses," after one such site where Spanish explorers were slaughtered in an Indian ambush. Tragedy along the famous trade route Camino Real in south-central New Mexico was so common for early Spanish explorers, merchants, and missionaries that one segment was known as Jornada del Muerto, or Journey of Death.

In modern times, those of Hispanic descent and others practicing the Southwest's shrine tradition have seen their custom thwarted elsewhere in the country. State highway departments in more densely populated regions order the roadside shrines to be removed because of the problems they present for road maintenance crews.

But in New Mexico, road department officials go out of their way to honor the shrines held so sacred by the loved ones who maintain them. If the shrines need to be temporarily moved for mowing or other maintenance, crews work with families to make sure the monuments are returned to their original spots.

CROSSES in general are a revered symbol in this state, where they often can be seen high atop a barren hill where religious treks are made. The crosses are placed either by a community or, as in Lincoln (☞ Chapter 7), by a single, devout individual. New Mexico also is known for a variety of spontaneous shrines, created by those who report experiencing miracles or religious visions. One woman in Lake Arthur, near Artesia in southeastern New Mexico, saw the image of Christ in a tortilla she was cooking. She built her own shrine surrounding the tortilla, complete with flickering candles, and the faithful and curious can make pilgrimages to it.

In an awesome display of religious faith during Holy Week, thousands of people journey miles by foot to reach Chimayó in northern New Mexico. They seek the blessing and healing of the holy soil found in the town's Santuario (sanctuary) church. The ground's sacredness dates from 1810, when a man discovered a crucifix glowing in the dirt. Though several attempts were made to relocate the cross, legend says the crucifix always reappeared where it was first found. Today the cross hangs above the altar, and the holy dirt can be taken from a sacred *pozito* (a small hole) in the floorboards of an adjoining room. Those seeking healing or giving thanks leave small photographs or tokens of their faith within an anteroom.

chicken and vegetables. ⊠ *2540 El Paseo Rd. (Hadley Center)*, ☎ *505/ 523–8778. AE, D, DC, MC, V.*

$–$$ ✕ **Lorenzo's.** Convenient to New Mexico State University, this is the largest of the three Lorenzo's locations in the Las Cruces area. Grilled fish and chicken are served along with Sicilian sandwiches, pizzas, pastas, and salads. The smaller outlet on North Alameda Street is open in the evening on Thursday and Friday only. ⊠ *University Plaza, 1753 E. University Ave.,* ☎ *505/521–3505; 741 N. Alameda St.,* ☎ *505/ 524–2850. AE, D, MC, V.*

$–$$ ✕ **My Brother's Place.** *Tostadas compuestos* (a concoction of red or
★   green chile, meat, pinto beans, and cheese in a crispy tortilla cup) and other Southwestern dishes are served with flair at this exceptional Mexican restaurant, where you can order pitchers of beer or margaritas to wash down the fire. Try an *empanada* (Mexican pastry) or crème caramel flan for dessert. The upstairs lounge is a pleasant watering hole decorated with brightly colored chairs and piñatas. Several varieties of Mexican beer are served here. (Try Negra Modelo or Tecate.) ⊠ *334 S. Main St.,* ☎ *505/523–7681. AE, D, DC, MC, V.*

$–$$ ✕ **Si Señor Restaurant.** Popular with businesspeople, this immaculate restaurant has spacious rooms with Southwestern decor and paintings. Mexican entrées emphasize three distinct chile sauce types—Las Cruces green (mild and flavorful), Deming red, and a variety described as "smoke," known as Hatch green. Friendly service and a pleasant atmosphere make for a relaxing meal. ⊠ *1551 E. Amador,* ☎ *505/527–0817. AE, D, MC, V.*

$ ✕ **The Durango Bagel.** The Durango caters to a college crowd. Conversation usually flows with the gourmet coffee and specialty bagels like apple-walnut and cranberry-orange. Muffins, cookies, and sandwiches are also served. ⊠ *2460 S. Locust St.,* ☎ *505/522–3397. No credit cards.*

$ ✕ **Mesilla Valley Kitchen.** Sidle up to the counter and order a gourmet sandwich, breakfast special, or beef burger accompanied by spud chips. Homemade baked goods in this Southwestern-style eatery include cinnamon rolls, cookies, and muffins. ⊠ *Arroyo Plaza, 2001 E. Lohman Ave.,* ☎ *505/523–9311. AE, D, DC, MC, V.*

$ ✕ **Nellie's.** It's tough to find seating in the tiny, Mexican diner, but that's because the food is incredible. You wouldn't give this place a second look if you judged it only by its plain appearance, but locals eat here in droves. The restaurant has gained national recognition for its mouthwatering dishes, such as chiles rellenos and combinations of enchiladas and tacos. ⊠ *1226 Hadley Ave.,* ☎ *505/524–9982. No credit cards.*

$ ✕ **Red Mountain Café.** This café serves a booming business district on the northeast side of Las Cruces. The variety of food here runs from standard deli sandwiches to imported fare and vegetarian pita pockets stuffed with smoked cheeses or hummus. The quaint setting has a European air. ⊠ *1120 Commerce Dr., Suite A (Commerce Plaza), off Telshor Blvd.,* ☎ *505/522–7584. AE, D, MC, V. Closed Sun.*

$ ✕ **Scoopy's.** Within a former hamburger stand, Scoopy's offers all manner of delectable sundaes and sodas using homemade, custard-style ice cream. The low-fat treats can be supplemented with specialty hot dogs, mesquite-smoked turkey sandwiches, or prime rib on a sourdough bun. Order from the window, and eat in your car or on the outside benches. ⊠ *590 S. Valley Dr.,* ☎ *505/647–5066. No credit cards.*

$$–$$$ ⊞ **Lundeen Inn of the Arts.** You'll think you've accidentally detoured
★   to Santa Fe at this art-filled B&B, but you'll luckily be paying Las Cruces prices. Architect Gerald Lundeen seamlessly joined two 1895 adobe houses, one Mexican colonial and the other Territorial. Linda, his wife, runs the impressionist gallery on the premises. Guest rooms pay homage to Western artists like Georgia O'Keeffe and Frederic Rem-

ington. Five rooms have balconies, and all the accommodations are furnished with a whimsical mix of antiques and newer handcrafted pieces. One suite has spectacular views of the Organ Mountains. Gourmet breakfasts might include french toast with apple-and-raisin frosting, sweet-potato pancakes, or pumpkin waffles. You can work it off at a local health club, where membership is extended free to guests. The Lundeens also offer crafts and art classes, which guests can attend. ⊠ *618 S. Alameda Blvd., 88005,* ☎ *505/526–3326,* ℻ *505/647–1334. 18 rooms, 2 suites, 2 casitas. No-smoking rooms. AE, D, MC, V. BP.* ✎

$$ ☷ **Days Inn Las Cruces.** Tidy and relatively inexpensive—rooms start at $49 for a single—this two-story motel is near I–10 and convenient to New Mexico State University and Old Mesilla. ⊠ *2600 S. Valley Dr. (Exit 142 off I–10), 88005,* ☎ *505/526–4441 or 800/829–7466,* ℻ *505/526–1980. 131 rooms. Restaurant, bar, room service, indoor pool, sauna, coin laundry. AE, D, DC, MC, V.*

Nightlife and the Arts

New Mexico State University (⊠ Corbett Center, University Park, ☎ 505/646–4411 for information center; 505/646–1420 for special events office) presents lectures, concerts, and other special events. **Popcorn's** (⊠ 2205 S. Main St., ☎ 505/525–9050), formerly known as Rita's, is a popular dance club. Good ol' country-and-western music and dancing are found at **Rodeo USA** (⊠ 170 W. Picacho, ☎ 505/524–5872). The locally based **Tierra del Encanto Ballet Folklorico** performs folk dances of Mexico at the annual weekend **International Mariachi Festival** (☎ 505/534–0360) in November.

Outdoor Activities

Aguirre Springs is beneath the towering spires of the Organ Mountains in a juniper-oak woodland zone. Trails lead into the upper regions of the ponderosa pines, including **Pine Tree Trail** (4-mi loop) and **Baylor Pass National Recreation Trail** (6 mi one-way), two developed paths. There are 60 campsites here. ⊠ *Off U.S. 70 (from Las Cruces take U.S. 70 northeast for 12 mi, then head south at the road marked "Aguirre Springs" for an additional 5 mi),* ☎ *505/525–4300.* ☷ *$3 per vehicle per day (includes camping).* ☉ *Apr.–Oct., daily 8–8; Nov.– Mar., daily 8–6.*

At the **Dripping Springs Natural Area** is an abandoned mountain resort built in the 1870s and converted decades later into a sanatorium for tuberculosis patients. Also here is **Hermit's Peak,** a hill where a local legend—Agostini Justiniani, an Italian nobleman—lived in solitude during the 19th century. Agostini was rumored to have miraculous healing powers and treated sick people with his abundance of herbs. He was found murdered at the site in 1869. Trails lead from the area to the Organ Mountains. This site is for day use only. ⊠ *Dripping Springs Rd. (from Las Cruces head east on University Ave. for 10 mi),* ☎ *505/ 522–1219.* ☷ *$3 per vehicle.* ☉ *Daily 8 AM–dusk.*

Shopping

At the **outdoor market** on North Main Street, approximately 200 vendors sell produce, handcrafted items, and baked goods on Wednesday and Saturday between 8:30 AM and 12:30 PM. The recently opened **Adobe Patio Gallery** (⊠ 2600 El Paseo Rd., ☎ 505/524–7091) has exhibits that include Native American figurines by Arizona artist Susi Nagoda-Bergquist. The upscale **Glenn Cutter Gallery** (⊠ 2640 El Paseo Rd., ☎ 505/524–4300) has regional and historic scenes from artists such as Fred Chilton, and fine jewelry as well. The small gallery (closed on Monday) run by **Mesilla Valley Fine Arts, Inc.** (⊠ Mesilla Valley Mall, 700 N. Telshor Blvd., ☎ 505/522–2933) exhibits the works of regional artists and photographers and carries note cards, bookmarks, and limited-edition prints.

Old Mesilla

★ ❸ *2 mi south of Las Cruces on NM 28.*

Historians disagree about the origins of Mesilla (today, Old Mesilla), which in Spanish means "little table." Some say the town occupies the exact spot that Don Juan de Oñate declared "the first pueblo of this kingdom." Other historians say Oñate instead meant the entire Mesilla Valley. Still, the reference to a "little table" does imply a small area. Village residents might be correct when they refer to their town as the first place in New Mexico officially proclaimed Spanish territory by Oñate. Old Mesilla is often referred to simply as Mesilla, and another town named Mesilla Park exists nearby.

Shops, galleries, and restaurants line the cobbled streets of Old Mesilla. With a Mexican-style plaza and gazebo where many weddings and fiestas take place, the village retains the charm of bygone days. The **San Albino Church** (⊠ Old Mesilla Plaza) was established in 1851. The present building of adobe and stained glass was erected in 1906 on the foundation of an earlier church.

Foreign films are shown and amateur theater productions take place in one of Mesilla's historic buildings, the **Fountain Theater** (⊠ 2468 Calle de Guadalupe, ½ block off the plaza, ☎ 505/524–8287), named for one of Mesilla's early pioneering families.

Native Americans very likely lived here before the Spanish and other Europeans, though over the years signs of earlier habitation were erased by bulky adobe structures that date back as much as 150 years. As elsewhere in New Mexico, the thick walls served as sturdy residences or businesses but also as fortification against frequent Apache Indian attacks.

By some accounts, residents determined to escape U.S. rule built Mesilla in the early 1850s in Mexican territory on the Rio Grande's west side. Mesilla and Las Cruces coexisted on opposite sides of the international boundary line until the river changed its course in 1865—leaving both villages east of the Rio Grande. By this time Mesilla had already been officially annexed by the United States—the area was among 30,000 square mi purchased from Mexico in 1854. For a brief time in 1861, Mesilla was the Confederate territorial capital of an area that included Arizona and western New Mexico.

A notorious event took place on August 27, 1871, when an argument between opposing political factions erupted into a bloodbath. The riot began after Republicans and Democrats staged political rallies in Mesilla's plaza on the same day—a terrible idea as it turned out. A Republican candidate for probate judge was clubbed over the head and died. Gunfire broke out, and eight people were killed before troops finally stormed the village to restore order.

Another milestone was the trial of Billy the Kid, at which a Mesilla jury convicted the outlaw for the murder of Matthew Brady, the sheriff of Lincoln County. The Kid was transferred to the Lincoln County Courthouse (☞ Lincoln *in* Chapter 7) to be hanged for the crime but briefly staved off the inevitable by escaping.

Mesilla was the largest station between El Paso and Los Angeles along the east–west Butterfield Stage Line in the mid-1800s. In 1881 the Santa Fe Railroad extended its line into Las Cruces, bypassing Mesilla and establishing Las Cruces as the area's major hub of commerce and transportation.

OFF THE
BEATEN PATH

STAHMANN FARMS – Pecan trees cover about 4,000 acres at one of the largest pecan orchards in the world. You can take a shaded drive through the trees and drop by the farm's store to sample pecan products. ✉ *NM 28, 8 mi south of Old Mesilla, San Miguel,* ☎ *505/526–8974 or 800/654–6887.* ⊙ *Store Mon.–Sat. 9–5:30, Sun. 11–5.*

Dining and Lodging

$$–$$$ ✕ **Double Eagle.** Chandeliers, century-old wall tapestries, and gold-leaf ceilings are among the noteworthy design elements of this restaurant inside an 1848 mansion on Old Mesilla's plaza. Some say that ghosts, including one of a young man who incurred his mother's wrath by falling in love with a servant girl, haunt the structure. Continental cuisine, steaks, and flambé dishes are served in the main restaurant. The fare at Pepper's, the adjoining Southwestern-style café-bar, includes borderland chile dishes, shark fajitas, and green-chile cheese wontons. The Double Eagle Sunday champagne brunch is worth a stop. ✉ *308 Calle de Guadalupe,* ☎ *505/523–6700. AE, D, DC, MC, V.*

$–$$ ✕ **La Posta.** Once a way station for the Butterfield Overland Mail
★ and Wells Fargo stages, the adobe restaurant that has hosted celebrities including comedian Bob Hope and Mexican revolutionary Pancho Villa noted its 60th anniversary in 2000. Some of the Mexican entrées follow recipes dating back more than a century; other fare includes Southwestern favorites like chiles rellenos and red or green enchiladas. Exotic birds and tropical fish inhabit the lushly planted atrium. ✉ *2410 Calle de San Albino,* ☎ *505/524–3524. AE, D, DC, MC, V. Closed Mon.*

$–$$ ✕ **Lorenzo's.** A hand-painted mural of the Mesilla Valley decorates this intimate restaurant, where red tablecloths and bottles of imported oil set an appropriately Italian mood. The pizzas, pasta, sandwiches, and salads served at Lorenzo's are based on old Sicilian recipes. ✉ *Oñate Plaza, 2000 Hwy. 292,* ☎ *505/525–3170. AE, D, MC, V.*

$–$$ ✕ **Old Mesilla Pastry Cafe.** Melt-in-your-mouth baked goods and spe-
★ cialty items like grilled buffalo and ostrich meat make this café a good stop for breakfast or lunch. The savory pizzas include one made with green chiles and chicken. ✉ *2790 Av. de Mesilla,* ☎ *505/525–2636. AE, MC, V. Closed Mon.–Tues. No dinner.*

$ ✕ **Chope's Bar & Cafe.** About 15 mi south of Old Mesilla, this earthen-color adobe establishment in La Mesa looks unremarkable from the outside. But the fiery Southwestern-style food served inside is highly popular with the locals. The bar serves as a favorite watering hole. ✉ *NM 28, La Mesa,* ☎ *505/233–9976. No credit cards.*

$–$$$ ✕▥ **Meson de Mesilla.** Folks drive to Mesilla from all over southern
★ New Mexico and west Texas to enjoy this inn's Continental cuisine ($$–$$$; reservations recommended). Dishes like the seared sturgeon in pesto, chateaubriand for two, and filet mignon are standard house specials. For inn guests only, a gourmet breakfast is served in a glass-enclosed atrium. The views of the jagged Organ Mountains and lower mesas from the back patio and second-floor balcony are additional lures. Rooms are done in Southwest tones and furnished with light-wood furniture and some antiques. They also have TVs, clock radios, and ceiling fans. The lower-priced single rooms are a good option for businesspeople on a budget. ✉ *1803 Av. de Mesilla, 88046, Exit 140 off I–10, and 3/4 mi west into Mesilla,* ☎ *505/525–9212 or 800/732–6025,* ⟰ *505/527–4196. 15 rooms. Restaurant, pool. AE, D, DC, MC, V. BP.*

Shopping

High-quality Native American jewelry and crafts are surprisingly economical, making shopping even more pleasing in the authentic adobe ambience of the **Old Mesilla Plaza.** Art and jewelry outlets include **El**

Platero (⊠ 2350 Calle de Principal, ☎ 505/523–5561) and **Rio de Oro** (⊠ 2000 Calle de Parian, ☎ 505/525–1934).

An interior-design firm and art gallery, **Charles Inc.** (⊠ 1885 W. Boutz St., corner of Av. de Mesilla, ☎ 505/523–1888) has an extensive collection of fine works, such as bronze and marble pieces by master stone carver Jesús Mata. Custom designs with a Southwestern flair can be found in handcrafted furniture, doors, and cabinets at **Mesilla Woodworks** (⊠ 1802 Av. de Mesilla, ☎ 505/523–1362).

Fort Selden State Monument

13 mi north of Las Cruces, off I–25's Radium Springs Exit.

Fort Selden was established in 1865 to protect Mesilla Valley settlers and travelers. The flat-roof adobe brick buildings at Fort Selden State Monument are arranged around a drill field. Several units of Buffalo Soldiers, the acclaimed African-American cavalry troops, were stationed here. Indians thought the soldiers' hair resembled that of a buffalo and gave the regiments their name. Knowing the respect the Apaches held for the animal, the soldiers interpreted the comparison as a show of admiration by their enemy and did not take offense. Buffalo Soldiers were also stationed at Fort Bayard, near Silver City, and Fort Stanton, in Lincoln County, to shield miners and travelers from Apache Indian attacks.

In the early 1880s, Capt. Arthur MacArthur was appointed post commander of Fort Selden. His young son spent several years on the post and grew up to become World War II hero General Douglas MacArthur. A permanent exhibit called "Fort Selden: An Adobe Post on the Rio Grande" depicts the roles of officers, enlisted men, and women on the American frontier during the Indian Wars. Camping facilities can be found at the adjacent Leasburg State Park. ⊠ *Off I–25's Radium Springs exit, Radium Springs,* ☎ *505/526–8911.* 🎟 *$2.* ☉ *Daily 8:30–5.*

Deming

60 mi west of Las Cruces on I–10.

In the 1800s Deming was considered so out of control that Arizona outlaws were sent here (with one-way stage tickets) as punishment. A stop on the Butterfield Stage Trail, Deming received an economic boost when the Atchison, Topeka & Santa Fe Railway met up with the Southern Pacific line here in 1881. Farming and small industry are now the main sources of income for the town's roughly 15,000 residents.

OFF THE   **PANCHO VILLA STATE PARK –** Early on the morning of March 9, 1916,
BEATEN PATH   Francisco "Pancho" Villa, a revolutionary from Mexico, crossed into
New Mexico to attack the town of Columbus and nearby Camp Furlong, a U.S. military outpost. This was the first time since the War of 1812 that the United States had experienced an armed invasion. A general who later would be commander of Allied forces in World War I—General John Joseph "Black Jack" Pershing—led 10,000 troops into Mexico for a grueling but futile search for Villa that lasted almost a year. This park on the site of Camp Furlong has exhibits depicting the raid, along with a 20-minute documentary film. You can camp, picnic, or hike, and there's a playground. ⊠ *35 mi south of Deming on NM 11,* ☎ *505/ 531–2711. Campground with 61 RV sites and 5 primitive sites, dump station.* 🎟 *$4 per car, $8 tent sites, $10 RV sites plus $4 extra for electrical hookup.* ☉ *Visitor center daily 8–5.*

Dining and Lodging

$–$$ ✕ **Si Señor Restaurant.** Tasty, spicy Mexican food in various combinations is served at Si Señor. Also on the menu are steaks and other standard American fare. This family-owned restaurant isn't fancy, but the food's good and the prices are reasonable. ⊠ *200 E. Pine St.,* ☎ *505/546–3938. AE, D, MC, V.*

$ 🛏 **Holiday Inn Deming.** The spacious rooms at this member of the national chain have Southwestern and contemporary accents. Room amenities include irons and ironing boards. ⊠ *Off I–10 (Exit 85 east), 88031,* ☎ *505/546–2661. 117 rooms. Restaurant, bar, refrigerators, pool. AE, D, DC, MC, V.*

GILA NATIONAL FOREST

Cliff dwellings, ghost towns, and sprawling ranches interspersed among miles of unspoiled forests are the legacy of the hearty individualists who have inhabited this remote area over the centuries. The desert and alpine terrain is gouged with deeply carved canyons, and the jagged scenery ranges from tall timber to sparser juniper forests. The early cliff dwellers mysteriously disappeared sometime after the year 1000, leaving behind the ruins and relics of a culture replaced half a millennium later by Spanish explorers, roving bands of Apaches, and occasional trappers. In the 1800s Apache leaders including Cochise, Geronimo, and Victorio waged war against the encroaching Mexican and American settlers. For a time, the sheer ruggedness of the mountains provided refuge for the Apaches. The area changed forever, though, when in the late 1800s the mineral-laden mountains lured crazed but hardy prospectors determined to make their fortunes in gold, silver, and copper. Scenic drives lead to several ghost towns, including the old gold-mining settlement of Mogollon.

Silver City

④ *53 mi northwest of Deming; 115 mi northwest of Las Cruces, west on I–10 and northwest on U.S. 180.*

Silver City sprouted as a tough and lawless mining camp in 1870, struggling to become a more respectable—and permanent—settlement. Henry McCarty spent part of his boyhood here, perhaps learning some of the ruthlessness that led to his later infamy under his nickname—Billy the Kid. Other mining towns in the area sparked briefly and then died, but Silver City flourished and became the area's most populated city (now with 12,000 residents). Even today the Silver City area remains aloof and beautiful, which is part of its charm. Its privacy is buffered by the Gila National Forest and vast Gila Wilderness.

Thanks to efforts of preservationists, Silver City's origins are evident in the many distinctive houses and storefronts that have been salvaged. A stroll through the historic downtown district, a haven for artists, will take you by many of the town's three dozen or so art galleries. With the area's copper ore fast being depleted, the town's traditional ties to mining are being upstaged with newcomers. New agers drive around in retro Volkswagen vans alongside sports utility vehicles owned by the newly retired or outdoor enthusiasts.

In the historic district, the **Murray Ryan Visitor's Center** (⊠ 201 N. Hudson St., ☎ 800/548–9378; 800/290–8330 Old West information line) also houses the Silver City Grant County Chamber of Commerce. If you're traveling north on NM 90, the highway turns into Hudson

Street. If you're traveling on U.S. 180, it turns into Silver Heights Boulevard within the city limits and intersects Hudson Street.

The Ailman House, built in 1881, serves as headquarters for the **Silver City Museum,** whose backlit painting of the mining and ranching community circa 1882 provides a good overview of the area's colorful history. Displays include pottery and other relics from the area's Mimbres and Mogollon Native American cultures. From the museum's upper level you can catch a glimpse of Silver City's three historic districts. Self-guided walking tours with maps are sold in the museum's store, which carries Southwestern gifts and books. Free guided walking tours of the neighboring historic district are offered on Memorial Day and Labor Day. The museum also features a local-history research library. ⊠ *312 W. Broadway,* ☎ *505/538–5921.* ⊠ *Free.* ⊙ *Tues.– Fri. 9–4:30, weekends 10–4.*

The **Western New Mexico University Museum** contains the world's largest collection of Mimbres pottery, basketry, and other artifacts. Delicate artistry on pottery includes finely drawn black-and-white geometric designs along with animal symbols representing an ancient Native American civilization that once dominated the area. Mimbres designs have influenced modern artisans throughout the world. Exhibits also include the famous, intricately decorated Casas Grandes pottery from northern Mexico. The museum's fourth floor displays photos and other memorabilia of the university, which is more than a century old. From this lofty height, you also can see a 360-degree view of Silver City. Quite unusual are the antique urinals in the men's rest room. ⊠ *1000 W. College Ave. (on campus, west end of 10th St.),* ☎ *505/538– 6386.* ⊠ *Free.* ⊙ *Weekdays 9–4:30, weekends 10–4.*

OFF THE
BEATEN PATH

CITY OF ROCKS STATE PARK – About 30 mi southeast of Silver City is this aptly named park with wondrous temples and towers of stone, spewed forth from an ancient volcano. To appreciate these natural marvels you'll need to don a pair of good walking shoes and penetrate the interior. You can't help but imagine yourself in a bizarre city as you peer down "streets" and "alleyways" lined with all shapes and sizes of solid-rock structures. The 680-acre park has 50 campsites, 10 with electrical hookups. Fire rings and picnic tables sit in the shade of the stone monoliths. The visitor center contains rest rooms and showers. ⊠ *Off U.S. 180, Faywood,* ☎ *505/536–2800. 50 campsites, 10 with electrical hookups.* ⊠ *$4 per vehicle day use, $10 per vehicle camping with no hookups, $14 per vehicle overnight camping with electrical hookups.*

Dining and Lodging

$–$$ ✕ **Adobe Springs Cafe.** This adobe-style establishment is a popular place for breakfasts, business lunches, and leisurely dinners. Greenery and paintings add a touch of class. Pastas, steaks, and Southwestern entrées such as blue-corn enchiladas are among the specialties. New owner Steve May continues popular traditions such as exhibits by local artists. ⊠ *1617 Silver Heights, Piñon Plaza,* ☎ *505/538–3665. AE, MC, V.*

$–$$ ✕ **Diane's Restaurant.** This quaint eatery was named business of the
★   year in 1999 by Silver City's MainStreet Project. Chef-owner Diane Barrett was honored for her continued expansion and quality, including meals such as blackened pork loin with apple Bourbon demi-glace and potatoes. Imported beer and specialty wines also are served in casual surroundings. Diane still offers fabulous sandwiches on bread she bakes. All her baked goods are light and exceptionally tasty, but her cinnamon rolls are knockouts. ⊠ *510 N. Bullard St.,* ☎ *505/538–8722. AE, D, MC, V. Closed Mon.*

$–$$ ✕ **Vicki's Downtown Deli.** A hint of Germany can be detected in this deli and café, which sells sausages, imported cheeses, soups, and sandwiches. Dinner menus vary but can feature pork tenderloin cordon bleu, seafood ravioli marinara, as well as regularly included vegetarian and German dishes. The outdoor patio is open in summer. Plans were in the works to move the deli portion of the business across the street. ⊠ *107 W. Yankie St.,* ☎ *505/388–5430. AE, MC, V.*

$ ✕ **A.I.R. Espresso, Art, Ice Cream.** A.I.R. stands for Artist-In-Residence, which is exactly what owner Jacqueline Shaw is. While painting her own masterpieces, she operates this ice-cream and coffee shop, where her peers often gather for long chats. Relax on a plump sofa or enjoy the mountain breeze while lounging on the rear patio. Shaw specializes in mochas and cappuccinos, along with hot chocolate, truffles, and toffee. Waffle cones, gourmet ice cream, and frozen yogurt are also served. ⊠ *112 W. Yankie St.,* ☎ *505/388–5952. No credit cards. Closed Sun.*

$ ✕ **Gregorio's Kountry Kitchen.** Though small and informal, this diner serves huge helpings of Southwestern food. If you're just plain hungry and not choosy about atmosphere, drop in. The restaurant is attached to the Maxwell House building, which houses a clothing and jewelry store. ⊠ *1500 N. Hudson St.,* ☎ *505/388–4512. AE, D, DC, MC, V. Closed Sun.*

$ ✕ **Higher Grounds Coffeehouse & Café.** Overlooking Silver City's historic district, this business can be accessed by taking a flight of stairs to a comfy loft with hardwood floors and old-fashioned vinyl kitchen chairs and tables. Specialty coffees and teas are served, along with desserts, pizza, and sandwiches such as lamb and onion or artichoke melt. Live entertainment is featured on Saturday nights. ⊠ *501 N. Bullard St.,* ☎ *505/534–0966. No credit cards.*

$ ✕ **Jalisco's.** George and Cecilia Mesa, along with son Michael Mesa,
★ own this family restaurant noted for such Mexican dishes as enchiladas and chiles rellenos based on old family recipes. Imports from nearby Palomas, Mexico, help brighten the restaurant, which exhibits colorful paintings of Mexican marketplaces by local artist Mark Wilson. ⊠ *103 S. Bullard St.,* ☎ *505/388–2060. MC, V. Closed Sun.*

$$ ▦ **Carter House Bed & Breakfast Inn.** This regal mansion built in 1906 is next door to the original site of the "Legal Tender" Silver Mine, which started a frenzy of prospecting in the area in 1870 and led to Silver City's name. Rooms are decorated with both antiques and contemporary furnishings, which are sturdy and designed for comfort; the common area features some Mission-style furniture and ornate oak trim. A hostel is operated—quietly—in the downstairs portion of the building. A laundry and fully equipped kitchen are provided in the hostel. ⊠ *101 N. Cooper St., 88061,* ☎ *505/388–5485. 4 rooms, 1 suite. AE, MC, V. BP.*

$$–$$$ ▦ **The Cottages.** Virgin forests, a friendly wild fox, and a lost silver
★ mine add to the romantic allure of this modern inn with detached country French–style cottages and B&B-style rooms. Water from hot mineral springs is piped directly into the private baths. Owners Robert "Mike" and Colleen Michael operate this 80-acre estate, which has access to miles of pristine trails (you're invited to wander them in search of the silver mine). The detached cottages are stylishly furnished and supplied with cooking utensils and staples like eggs, milk, and fresh fruit, along with snacks and frozen items for lunch or dinner. ⊠ *2037 Cottage San Rd. (Box 2562), 88062,* ☎ *505/388–3000 or 800/938–3001. 2 rooms, 3 cottages. Kitchenettes, hiking. AE, D, MC, V.* ✆

$$ ▦ **Holiday Inn Express.** Bright, contemporary decor provides a cheery atmosphere in one of Silver City's newest motels, opened in the summer of 1999. ⊠ *1103 Superior St., 88061,* ☎ *505/538–2525. 60 rooms. Exercise room, hot tub. AE, D, DC, MC, V. CP.*

$–$$ 🛏 **Comfort Inn.** This modern motel contains Southwestern-style rooms with good views of Silver City. The suite has a Jacuzzi. ✉ *1060 E. Hwy. 180, 88061,* 📞 *505/534–1883; 800/228–5150 central reservations;* 📠 *505/534–0778. 52 rooms, 1 suite. Indoor pool, hot tub, coin laundry. AE, D, DC, MC, V. CP.*

$ 🛏 **Econo Lodge Silver City.** This lodge on a mesa overlooking Silver City has economy accommodations and contemporary decor. Room amenities include hair dryers, microwaves, and data ports. ✉ *1120 Hwy. 180 E., 88061,* 📞 *505/534–1111; 800/553–2666 central reservations;* 📠 *505/534–2222. 62 rooms. In-room data ports, refrigerators, pool, hot tub, exercise room, laundry. AE, D, DC, MC, V. CP.* ❧

$ 🛏 **Palace Hotel.** Owners Nancy and Cal Thompson have replicated the intimacy of a small European hotel at the Palace, a grand structure that was a first-class lodging when it opened in 1900. It saw less fabulous times as an apartment building before the Thompsons carefully renovated it in the late 1980s and early 1990s. Some rooms have Western furnishings, others a distinctly Victorian decor. The upstairs garden room provides solitude for playing games or reading. ✉ *106 W. Broadway, 88061,* 📞 *505/388–1811. 11 rooms, 7 suites. AE, D, DC, MC, V. CP.* ❧

$ 🛏 **Super 8.** A forest of piñon and juniper trees surrounds this two-story motel. Most of the rooms have double beds; the five business minisuites have recliners, refrigerators, data ports, and coffeemakers. ✉ *1040 E. U.S. 180, 88061,* 📞 *505/388–1983; 800/800–8000 central reservations;* 📠 *505/388–1983. 64 rooms. In-room data ports (some), no-smoking rooms, refrigerators (some). AE, D, DC, MC, V.*

Shopping

Southern New Mexico's only complete birding outlet, **Birdsong** (✉ 414 N. Bullard St., 📞 505/534–2154 or 888/468–8585), opened in late 1999 with elaborately decorated feeders, adobe bird houses, and scientifically constructed bat lodging. Recordings of chirrupy birds set the upbeat mood in this unusual shop. **Hester House Candy & Gifts** (✉ 316 N. Bullard St., 📞 505/388–1360) sells highly edible homemade fudge, chocolates, and truffles, along with porcelain dolls, Tiffany-style lamps, wind chimes, jewelry, bath products, and garden art. The shop is open daily except Sunday. A family-owned clothing and jewelry store, the **Maxwell House** (✉ 1500 N. Hudson St., 📞 505/388–1573) offers a unique selection of hand-picked designs at economical prices.

Cool off with an ice cream cone and visions of Santa as you inspect Christmas ornaments or sample other treats at **Pretty Sweet Emporium** (✉ 312 N. Bullard St., 📞 505/388–8600). Vendors at the **Silver City Trading Co.'s Antique Mall** (✉ 205 W. Broadway, 📞 505/388–8989) stock antiques, collectibles, and Navajo katsina dolls; works of area artists also are displayed. It's also the only place in the area where you can buy the Sunday *New York Times*. A local artists' cooperative runs **Yankie Creek Gallery** (✉ 217 N. Bullard St., 📞 505/538–5232 or 505/388–4775), where gourd art and blown-glass items can be found in addition to paintings.

Gila National Forest

❺ *8 mi northeast of Silver City via NM 15 to Pinos Altos Range and Gila Cliff Dwellings portion of Gila National Forest; 60 mi northwest of Silver City via U.S. 180 to western portions of the forest. From I–25 the eastern edge of the forest can be accessed via NM 152: 62 mi north of Las Cruces take NM 152 west toward Hillsboro; 91 mi north of Las Cruces take NM 52 west through Winston and Chloride.*

The Gila National Forest covers 3.3 million acres—about 65 mi by 100 mi—and includes the nation's first land designated (in 1924) as wilderness by the U.S. Forest Service. About 1,500 mi of hiking trails lace the forest. Open camping is permitted, and there are 18 developed campgrounds (7 have toilets and potable water). The forest roads are ideal for mountain biking, but the trails are often too rough for bicycles. White-water rafting usually begins in April, and you can fish (there are trout aplenty) in streams, rivers, and three lakes. About a quarter of the forest is designated wilderness and closed to vehicular traffic, but much of the rest remains open for touring.

The gorgeous **Inner Loop Scenic Drive** circles 75 mi around part of the forest. Though the roads are paved, some turns are sharp, narrow, and steep—it's best not to take large RVs on this route. Starting from Silver City, take NM 15 north to Gila Cliff Dwellings National Monument (☞ *below*). From the monument backtrack on NM 15 to NM 35 heading southeast to NM 152, which leads west back to Silver City.

About 700 years ago the Mogollon Indians built the 42 rooms of stone and mud that compose the **Gila Cliff Dwellings National Monument.** The visitor center has a small museum and books and other materials about the wilderness and the Mogollon Indians. A 1-mi loop trail that's steep in parts (wear sturdy footwear) leads to the dwellings; along the wheelchair-accessible Trail to the Past you can view pictographs. ⊠ *Off NM 15, 44 mi north of Silver City,* ☎ *505/536–9461 or 505/536–9344.* ⊠ *$3.* ☉ *Monument Memorial Day–Labor Day, daily 8–6; Labor Day–Memorial Day, daily 9–4. Visitor center Memorial Day–Labor Day, daily 8–5; Labor Day–Memorial Day, daily 8–4:30.*

U.S. 180 leads west about 50 mi from Silver City to Glenwood and the **Whitewater Canyon.** The **Catwalk** (⊠ Catwalk Rd. off U.S. 180), a 250-ft-long metal walkway attached to the sides of boulders, was built in 1935 as an access route to the canyon and a breathtaking view of water cascading over rocks. Several miles north of the Catwalk on U.S. 180 is the **Glenwood State Trout Hatchery** (⊠ U.S. 180, ☎ 505/539–2461), where there are picnic tables and a fishing pond. Rocky Mountain bighorn sheep graze nearby. East of the Glenwood State Trout Hatchery on NM 159 is **Mogollon.** The gold-mining town, established in the 1880s, was a ghost town but it's been revived by a dozen or so residents who open art galleries and conduct tours during the summer.

As you drop down into **Pinos Altos** 7 mi north of Silver City on NM 15, check out the **Log Cabin Museum** (⊠ NM 15, ☎ 505/388–1882), where you'll find a structure originally built in 1865 by George Shafer. The property still remains in the family. Dusty artifacts tell the story of more than a century of occupation. You'll find two diverse galleries sharing the same phone number along this tiny town's Main Street, **Silver Winds Gallery** (⊠ 29 Main St., ☎ 505/388–5202), featuring Native American and Southwestern art, and **Gallery at the Fort** (⊠ 25 Main St., ☎ 505/388–5202), which has more contemporary Southwestern art and sculptures.

On the eastern edge of the Gila National Forest, NM 52 leads west from I–25 to **Winston** and **Chloride,** two fascinating mining towns about 35 mi northwest of Truth or Consequences. Prospectors searching for silver in the nearby ore-rich mountains founded the towns in the late 1800s; abandoned saloons and pioneer relics remain from the mining days. Though the communities are designated ghost towns, the 50 or so residents of each place dispute the moniker. ⊠ *Gila National Forest Headquarters, 3005 E. Camino del Bosque, Silver City,* ☎ *505/388–8201.*

Dining and Lodging

$$–$$$ ✕ **Buckhorn Saloon and Opera House.** Mosey up to the wooden bar
★ at this genuine 1800s saloon and slug down a taste of the Old West.
Dance-hall girl "Debbie deCamp"—a life-size doll—strikes a sultry pose
on a balcony overlooking the saloon. After visiting the bar (which opens
at 3 PM), order up a steak or other entrée in the adjoining dining room
and from Wednesday to Saturday listen to folk singers croon their mellow tunes. Food served here is all homemade, fresh and without preser-
vatives. The kitchen excels at homemade salad dressings and desserts.
Reservations are recommended. This complex also includes the Opera
House, where melodramas are performed (on Friday and Saturday at
8), and Pinos Altos Mercantile, a business founded in the 1860s that's
now an ice cream parlor and soda shop. ⊠ *32 Main St., Pinos Altos,
7 mi north of Silver City on NM 15,* ☎ *505/538–9911, 505/388–3848
for opera house. MC, V. Closed Sun. No lunch.*

$$–$$$$ ⌂ **Bear Creek Motel & Cabins.** Gold panning, hiking, and fishing are
among the activities that take place at this mountain getaway, one of
the better accommodations in the Silver City area. A ponderosa pine
forest surrounds the well-kept A-frame cabins, half of which have
kitchens, cookware, and fireplaces. ⊠ *NM 15, 6 mi north of Silver City
(Box 53082), Pinos Altos 88053,* ☎ *505/388–4501,* ℻ *505/538–5583.
1 3 cabins. Kitchenettes, refrigerators, hiking. AE, D, DC, MC, V.* ☙

$$$ ⌂ **Casitas de Gila.** Truly a place to get away from it all, these tidy adobe
guest houses near the village of Gila are a perfect place to see the bril-
liance of the night stars. Owners Becky and Michael O'Connor provide star charts and a spotting scope for optimal viewing, along with
an outdoor hot tub for long, tranquil soaks. Plan for an extended stay
(you must book for at least two nights), bring your favorite books, and
prepare for quiet the way nature intended it. Kitchens are stocked with
supplies, and there's wood for the kiva fireplaces. The nearby Double
E Guest Ranch offers horseback riding. The O'Connors will give you
exact driving directions to this rural location when you book your stay.
⊠ *310 Hooker Loop (Box 325), Gila 88038,* ☎ *505/535–4455,* ℻
505/535–4456. 5 casitas. AE, D, DC, MC, V. ☙

$$ ⌂ **Los Olmos Guest Ranch.** Tall trees shade this San Francisco Valley ranch,
whose stone cabins sleep from two to six people. The cabins are furnished
with contemporary pieces, and though there are minimal amenities (no
phones or TVs), you can count on maximum seclusion. Guests sign up
from Wednesday to Sunday for optional gourmet dinners—chicken,
lamb, pastas, trout, steaks, and vegetarian entrées. The ranch is near the
Glenwood State Trout Hatchery, and within hiking distance of White-
water Canyon and the Catwalk. Pets are welcome. ⊠ *U.S. 180 and Cat-
walk Rd., Glenwood 88039,* ☎ *505/539–2311,* ℻ *505/539–2312. 14
cabins. Dining room, pool, hot tub, hiking, horseback riding, horseshoes,
volleyball, billiards, playground. AE, D, MC, V. BP.* ☙

Lake Valley National Back Country Byway

★ *From Silver City: head east on U.S. 180/NM 152 to junction with NM
27. From Hatch: head west on NM 26 and north on NM 27.*

The 48-mi Lake Valley National Back Country Byway provides an ex-
citing link to the Wild West. This remote drive (there are no gas sta-
tions)—NM 27 between Nutt and Hillsboro (31 mi) and NM 152 east
from Hillsboro to Truth or Consequences (17 mi)—follows part of the
route taken by the Kingston Lake Valley Stage Line, which operated
in a region terrorized by Apache leaders like Geronimo and outlaw bands
led by Butch Cassidy and other notorious figures. A Lake Valley–area
landmark, west of NM 27, is Cooke's Peak, where the first wagon road
through the Southwest to California was opened in 1846.

Not much is going on these days in the old silver mining town of **Lake Valley**—the last residents departed in the mid-1990s—but it once was home to 4,000 people. Its mine produced 2.5 million ounces of pure silver and gave up one nugget weighing several hundred pounds. You can visit the schoolhouse (which later served as a saloon) and walk around the chapel, the railroad depot, and some old homes. At the junction of NM 152 and NM 27 is another mining-era boomtown, **Hillsboro,** where gold was discovered as well as silver (about $6 million worth of the two ores was extracted). The town has a small museum and some shops, restaurants, and galleries.

6 **Caballo Lake State Park** provides a nesting ground for golden and bald eagles, often sighted as they glide aloft searching for prey. Activities at the lake include fishing and various water sports. Hiking trails lead through desert areas. Late March or early April, when prickly pears and other succulents bloom, is a good time to visit. ✉ *Take state park exit off I–25, about 58 mi north of Las Cruces and 16 mi south of Truth or Consequences,* ☎ *505/743–3942,* FAX *505/743–0031.* ✉ *$4 per vehicle day use, $8–$18 campsites.* ☉ *Visitor center 7:30–4:30 (open later in summer).*

Lodging

$–$$ 🛏 **Black Range Lodge Bed & Breakfast.** Built from the ruins of an old casino and saloon that date from the 1880s, this getaway has sturdy log beam ceilings and rock walls. Breakfast is included in the room rate, and you can use the kitchen to prepare other meals. Don't expect the ruffles and flourishes of your typical B&B. The payoff is an informal, rustic atmosphere, indoors and out. Pets and children are welcome. An outdoor hot tub was slated to be added in late 2000. A one-bedroom guest house has a kitchen, deck, satellite TV, indoor Jacuzzi, and spectacular views. ✉ *NM 152, 119 Main St. (Star Rte. 2, Box 119), Kingston 88042,* ☎ *505/895–5652,* FAX *505/895–3326. 7 rooms, 3 suites, 1 guest house. Hiking, billiards, recreation room. D, MC, V. BP.* 🐾

$ ⛺ **Caballo Lake State Park.** Three camping areas offer views of the lake, which is within walking distance of each site. Cottonwoods and other trees shade two sites; the other has desert landscaping. The tent sites ($8) are lakeside. You can stock up on goods at a grocery store, bait shop, and gasoline station 3 mi from the park. Developed sites for RVs cost $10–$14 (some have sewer). ✉ *Take state park exit off I–25, about 58 mi north of Las Cruces and 16 mi south of Truth or Consequences,* ☎ *505/743–3942,* FAX *505/743–0031. 136 sites. Rest rooms, showers. No credit cards.*

ALONG THE CAMINO REAL

Four centuries ago, caravans of Spanish colonists and traders made the desolate 1,200-mi journey from Mexico City to Santa Fe via El Camino Real. As they came up from what is now El Paso and were nearing the Las Cruces area, they veered away from the Rio Grande to avoid its treacherous passages. The hostile, arid terrain they traversed is visible east off I–25, which traces this part of El Camino Real. Hazards such as frequent attacks from hostile Native Americans led to a chilling nickname for this stretch of road—Jornada del Muerto—or Journey of Death. Portions of the well-worn path still can be spotted from the air and ground, but there is no formal designation or access to the route from the highway. Interstate 10 heads west at Las Cruces, at which point I–25 continues north more or less parallel to El Camino Real. East of I–25, Elephant Butte Lake now covers part of the Jornada del Muerto route, and visible tracks are inaccessible on private land. Funding has been made available to establish a state museum along the route, which ends southwest of Socorro, where Camino Real travelers rejoined the river to complete the journey north.

Truth or Consequences

❼ *72 mi north of Las Cruces on I–25, 140 mi south of Albuquerque on I–25.*

Truth or Consequences really did get its name from the game show of the same name. The show's producer, Ralph Edwards, suggested that a town adopt the name to honor the production's 10th anniversary, in 1950. The community that had been known as Hot Springs accepted the challenge, earning national publicity for the stunt. A portion of the community rebelled, though, withdrawing from T or C (as the town is sometimes called) and incorporating as Williamsburg. T or C's name remains a sore spot in some circles.

The area's earliest Native American inhabitants believed the natural hot springs found here had magical healing properties long before modern settlements were built or names were changed. **Bathhouses** tapping into the soothing mineral waters were established near the downtown district in the 1930s. About a half dozen of those still operate at bargain prices (as low as $4 an hour). The facilities are clean but modest. Healers at the springs practice natural methods such as massage, reflexology, and Ayurvedic science.

Hay-Yo-Kay Hot Springs has five naturally flowing pools and is the largest complex in the hot-springs district. The standard price for the hot baths is $4 per person for a half-hour soak. Massage therapists are on call for fees of $60 for a 90-minute massage, and $45 for a 60-minute massage. You can pay $30 for a 30-minute massage or reflexology session. In 2000, owner Steve Kortemeier was in the process of rebuilding the old Yucca Bathhouse adjacent to his property, which will mean the addition of two new pools. ⊠ *300 Austin Ave.,* ☎ *505/894–2228. No credit cards.*

At the well-maintained **Geronimo Springs Museum** you can visit an authentic miner's log cabin that was transported from the nearby Gila National Forest or view the giant skull of a mammoth. Pottery on display includes examples of Mimbres, Tularosa, Alma, and Hohokam. The farm and ranch section has tools used by early settlers. ⊠ *211 Main St.,* ☎ *505/894–6600.* 🖼 *$2.* ☉ *Mon.–Sat. 9–5.*

★ **❽** More than a million people each year visit **Elephant Butte Lake State Park,** whose 36,500-acre lake is New Mexico's largest. At night, campfires flicker along the beaches of the many sandy coves, which have primitive and partially developed campgrounds. Showers and modern rest rooms are available throughout the park, as are picnic tables and grills. Bass, catfish, pike, and crappie fishing takes place year-round; trout are stocked in the Rio Grande River below the dam in colder months. Elephant Butte is a world-class competition lake for bass fishing. Boaters come here in droves, and when the wind picks up so do the windsurfers. Special events include an April balloon festival and July drag boat racing. The lake, which is also known as Elephant Butte Reservoir, was created by **Elephant Butte Dam,** a concrete structure 306 ft high and 1,674 ft long that was completed in 1916. The dam holds back water from the Rio Grande for irrigation purposes. The lake and Rio Grande below the dam attract many species of waterfowl, along with raptors and songbirds.

The state park straddles Elephant Butte Lake and the Rio Grande east of I–25 for about 50 mi (from south of Fort Craig to just north of Truth or Consequences). To take a **scenic drive** from Truth or Consequences, head east on NM 51, turn north at NM 179 for about 2 mi, head southeast on NM 195, and take a loop drive of about 5 mi to Elephant Butte Dam. At the end of the dam turn north for overlooks of the lake water and a view of the rocky elephant-shape island formation that inspired the name of the reservoir (look for a head, with ears and a long trunk). To visit the **Dam Site Recreation Area** turn west on NM 177, where you'll find a terraced picnic area with striking views and tall trees providing shade. A private concessionaire operates a restaurant, lounge, marina, and cabins (☞ Dining and Lodging, *below*). ⊠ *Off several I–25 exits (5 mi east of Truth or Consequences)*, ☎ *505/744–5421.* ☜ *$4 per vehicle day use, $8–$14 campsites. 108 developed sites with electrical hookups, many primitive or partially developed campsites.*

Dining and Lodging

$$–$$$ ✕ **Los Arcos Restaurant and Bar.** Steaks and seafood are the draws at this slump block adobe-style establishment with a Southwestern decor, complete with cactus garden. Homemade soups, desserts, and freshly baked bread add to the aromas and the ambience. ⊠ *1400 N. Date St.,* ☎ *505/894–6200. AE, D, MC, V. No lunch.*

$–$$ ✕ **Hodges Corner Restaurant.** Owners Ray and Linda Hodges believe in hearty food and lots of it—heapin' helpin's of thick barbecued pork ribs, cube steaks, and deep-fried fish. The atmosphere is ultracasual at this great stop for anglers who want to relax and chow down after a day boating and fishing at Elephant Butte Lake. ⊠ *915 NM 195, Elephant Butte,* ☎ *505/744–5626. D, MC, V.*

$–$$ ✕ **Town Talk Cafe.** Locals really do drop into this diner-style eatery in the heart of Truth or Consequences to catch up on the latest gossip. The breakfasts and other fare are standard but generous. ⊠ *426 Broadway,* ☎ *505/894–3119. No credit cards.*

$$ ✕⊞ **Quality Inn.** Formerly known as the Inn at the Butte, this establishment sits atop a mesa offering serene views of Elephant Butte Lake. Rooms have either two queen-size beds or one king-size bed, and all have irons, hair dryers, and coffeemakers. Executive suites have a desk and speaker phone. The restaurant serves steaks, seafood, and Southwestern cuisine. ⊠ *NM 195 (Box E), Elephant Butte 87935,* ☎ *505/744–5431,* FAX *505/744–5044. 44 rooms, 4 suites. Restaurant, lounge, pool, 2 tennis courts, hiking, meeting rooms. AE, D, DC, MC, V. CP.*

$$ ⊞ **Dam Site Recreation Area.** Located in an official historic district, the Elephant Butte Dam site offers standard cabins with one to four bedrooms and no phones or televisions. All of the cabins have lake views, and some have kitchenettes (but no utensils). The combination bar-restaurant serves steaks, seafood, and sandwiches. On weekends between about Easter and Labor Day, dance bands play blues or rock on the outdoor patio. A new bed-and-breakfast was scheduled to open in the summer of 2000 in a historic building, which once was administrative headquarters during the construction of the original dam. The building overlooks the restaurant and marina. ⊠ *77B Engle Star Rte., 87901, 5 mi east of the 3rd St. light in Truth or Consequences,* ☎ *505/894–2073,* FAX *505/894–0776. 16 cabins. Restaurant, lounge, kitchenettes (some), boating, playground. AE, D, DC, MC, V.*

$ ⊞ **Best Western Hot Springs Inn.** Large rooms with pastel colors and modern furnishings make this lodge a restful haven. The oversize pool comes in handy on hot summer days. A steak house is next door. ⊠ *2270 N. Date St., 87901, off I–25's Exit 79,* ☎ *505/894–6665. 40 rooms. Refrigerators, pool. AE, D, DC, MC, V.*

$ ⊞ **Charles Motel & Bath House.** This laid-back facility attracts healers and artists who explore spiritual and physical health through sometimes unorthodox methods. The therapies practiced here include massage, reflexology, and Ayurvedic science. Costs depend on the treatment and its length, but $5 should buy you a good long soak in the hot tub. The single-story motel and its rooms are well maintained if dated looking. The downtown Truth or Consequences location is convenient to small restaurants and shops. ⊠ *601 Broadway, 87901,* ☎ *505/894–7154. 20 rooms. Kitchenettes, refrigerators, outdoor hot tub, spa. AE, D, MC, V.*

$ ▦ **Riverbend Hot Springs.** This facility offers something for everyone, including standard motel rooms, dormitory-style accommodations in a hostel, camping areas, and RV parking. It's also the only place in the area where you can soak in open-air hot mineral baths while viewing the gently flowing Rio Grande and shifting shadows on Turtleback Mountain. The three communal hot baths are free to guests at designated hours. Private, concrete hot tubs were being built in 2000 for use alongside the river. Murals, hand-painted by appreciative guests, decorate the outside walls. The accommodation is basic, but clean and welcoming, and the atmosphere extremely casual. If you want to camp, ask for one of the three tepees that are available. ⊠ *100 Austin Ave., 87901,* ☎ *505/ 894–6183. 2 cabins, 2 motel suites, 2 double rooms in dormitory-style hostel ($15 nightly), 10 RV spaces with full hookups ($25 nightly), 3 tepees (prices vary). Kitchenettes (some), no-smoking rooms, mineral baths, hiking, camping, lockers, coin laundry. AE, D, MC, V.*

Outdoor Activities and Sports

The **Dam Site Recreation Area Marina** (⊠ 77B Engle Star Rte., 5 mi east of the 3rd St. traffic light in Truth or Consequences, ☎ 505/894– 2041) rents runabouts, ski boats, and pontoon boats. The vessels cost between $20 and $45 hourly ($110 and $220 daily).

Shopping

Paintings, sculptures, baskets, and postcards can be found at the **Main Street Gallery** (⊠ 306 Main St., ☎ 505/894–0615), an artists' cooperative open Wednesday–Saturday 1–5.

En Route As you head north on I–25 toward Socorro you can take a break at two attractions. At **Fort Craig National Historic Site,** signs describe the various buildings and life at the outpost, where only a couple of masonry walls and foundations remain. After the New Mexico Territory became part of the United States, the adobe Fort Craig was established to prevent raids by the Apache and Navajo peoples and to secure the trade routes within the region. The growth of Socorro and what is now Truth or Consequences can be traced to the protection the fort provided between 1854 and the mid-1880s, when it was decommissioned. Battles west of the Mississippi River during the American Civil War were relatively rare, but in 1862 the Confederate army crossed the Rio Grande and headed to Valverde, which is north of Fort Craig, with the goal of cutting off the fort from the Union military headquarters in Santa Fe. The Confederate forces first were sent into retreat but later won a few battles and made the Union forces withdraw. The Rebels later occupied Santa Fe for a few months. The roads to Fort Craig, which is about 40 mi south and east of Socorro, can become hard to pass during rainy weather. ⊠ *Off I–25 San Marcial exit (follow signs from exit for about 10 mi),* ☎ *505/835–0412.* ▣ *Free.* ☉ *Daily dawn–dusk.*

Snow geese, cranes, and eagles can be spotted from viewing platforms ❾ at the popular **Bosque del Apache National Wildlife Refuge.** Besides serving as a rest stop for migrating birds, the Bosque del Apache also shelters mule deer, turkeys, quail, and other wildlife. Photo opportunities abound on the 15-mi auto loop tour; you can also hike through arid shrub land or bike through the refuge or take a van tour. ⊠ *1001 NM 1, off I–25 Exit 124 (San Marcial) for northbound traffic and Exit 139 for southbound traffic, San Antonio,* ☎ *505/835–1828.* ▣ *$3 per vehicle.* ☉ *Daily dawn–dusk.*

Socorro

⑩ *72 mi north of Truth or Consequences; 77 mi southwest of Albuquerque, south on I–25 and west on U.S. 60.*

The town of Socorro, population about 7,000, traces its roots back to the earliest Spanish expeditions into New Mexico, when explorer Juan de Oñate established (in 1598) a permanent settlement along the Rio Grande. Native Americans provided corn to the expedition, inspiring Oñate to give the community a name that means succor, or help. The first Spanish settlement was virtually erased during the Pueblo Revolt of 1680 and did not reestablish itself until 1816.

The business of Socorro is conducted in historic buildings that surround its square, which has a park with a gazebo and a plaque commemorating the arrival of Juan de Oñate. The town's claim to fame is the highly regarded New Mexico Institute of Mining and Technology (New Mexico Tech), founded in 1893. The institution's original specialties were chemistry and metallurgy, but along with scientific research now there are programs in medicine, engineering, and business.

More than 1,200 minerals and fossils are on display at the **New Mexico Bureau of Mines and Mineral Resources Mineral Museum,** among them samples from the area's ore-rich mining districts of Magdalena, Hansonburg, Santa Rita, and Tyrone. Many rocks here, from glittering pyrite to the deep-blue azurite, have exotic colors like those of tropical fish. Special tours can be arranged. ⊠ *New Mexico Institute of Mining and Technology, 801 Leroy Pl. (from I–25 Exit 150, follow signs to institute),* ☎ *505/835–5140.* ⛛ *Free.* ☉ *Weekdays 8–5, weekends 10–3. Closed weekends during academic holidays.*

Only a monument remains at **Trinity Site,** where the world's first atomic bomb exploded on July 16, 1945. The resulting crater has been filled in, but the test site and monument are open for public viewing two days of the year. The McDonald ranch house, where the first plutonium core for the bomb was assembled, can be toured on those days. ⊠ *5 mi south of U.S. 380. Turn east at the San Antonio exit off I–25, 10 mi south of Socorro. Visitors will be met at the gate off U.S. 380 and allowed to drive 17 mi east to the site,* ☎ *505/678–1134.* ⛛ *Free.* ☉ *First Sat. of Apr. and Oct., 8–2.*

Dining and Lodging

$–$$$$ ✕ **Val Verde Steak House.** The curiosities inside this restaurant in the Val Verde Hotel, which opened in 1919, include an old oak-and-brass cooler and a series of mural landscapes, painted in 1923 by a patron who was working off his bar tab. The fare includes seafood such as shrimp and lobster, steak, and Southwestern dishes. ⊠ *203 Manzanares St.,* ☎ *505/835–3380. AE, D, DC, MC, V.*

$ ✕ **Martha's Black Dog Coffeehouse.** Martha has an extensive offering of vegetarian items, but she does have dishes and deli sandwiches for carnivores, too. Meals are served three times daily, but closing hours vary. Call in ahead of time if it's past 6 PM. Locals make themselves at home here over coffee and homemade desserts. Art exhibits decorate the walls. ⊠ *110 Manzanares,* ☎ *505/838–0311. AE, D, MC, V.*

$ ▥ **Super 8.** Pastel Southwestern colors and prints of adobe architecture and pottery decorate this establishment's rooms, most of which have microwaves and refrigerators. K-Bob's, a franchise restaurant specializing in steaks, is next door. ⊠ *1121 Frontage Rd. (I–25 Exit 150), 87801,* ☎ *505/835–4626, 800/800–8000 central reservations;* FAX *505/835–3988. 88 rooms. Pool, hot tub. AE, D, MC, V. CP.*

HEADING WEST ON U.S. 60

By Sharon
Niederman

Maybe you're a traveler who prefers to stay off the beaten path, to venture to places you've never even heard of. If you're in the mood to take the slow road and encounter an authentic Western America decades removed from today's franchise operations, head west on old Highway 60 out of Socorro and keep going—as far as the Arizona border if you'd like. The speed limit is 55, there's not a fast-food restaurant within 200 mi, and the scenery hasn't changed for 50 years.

This long, lonely highway opened in 1917 as the first numbered auto route to cross the United States. Called the "Ocean to Ocean Highway," U.S. 60 ran from Norfolk, Virginia, to Los Angeles. Earlier in the 20th century it was a "hoof highway," the route of cattle drives from Springerville, Arizona, to Magdalena, New Mexico. Walk into any café along this dusty roadside and you're still likely to be greeted by a blue-eyed cowboy in spurs on his way to brand a herd.

People really ranch here, much the way they have for more than 100 years. (Prior to the era of homesteaders and ranchers, the Apaches ruled.) Livestock production and timber are still the leading industries. Highway 60 takes you through the heart of Catron County, New Mexico's largest county by area. Notoriously politically incorrect and proud of it, this is a place where Confederate flags fly and animal trophies are proudly displayed.

After you've headed as far west as Quemado you can make an interesting loop by continuing north on NM 36 to NM 117, which skirts the east side of El Malpais National Monument (☞ Chapter 6), eventually hooking up with I–40 east of Grant. To get to Albuquerque take I–40 east.

Magdalena

27 mi west of Socorro on U.S. 60.

Magdalena, population 300, enjoyed its heyday about a hundred years ago as a raucous town of miners and cowboys. It was once the biggest livestock shipping point west of Chicago. The Atchison, Topeka & Santa Fe Railway built a spur line from Socorro in 1885 to transport timber, wool, cattle, and ore. Lead, zinc, silver, copper, and gold all were mined in the area, but now there are more ghosts than miners.

The town took its name from Mary Magdalene, protector of miners, whose face is supposedly visible on the east slope of Magdalena Peak, a spot held sacred by the Indians of the area. To get a feel for the place, walk down to the **Atchison, Topeka & Santa Fe Railway depot,** now the town hall and library. Across the street is the Charles Ilfeld Warehouse, where the company's motto, "wholesalers of everything," is a reminder of that great trade empire of the late 19th century.

The biggest event of the year in Magdalena is the **Magdalena Old-Timers Reunion** (☎ 505/854–2139), held in early July. The festival, which draws about 5,000 and has the biggest parade in New Mexico after the State Fair's, began quietly 30 years ago. With the end of cattle drives and the shutdown of the rail spur in the early 1970s, cowboys began returning at the same time each year to greet each other and reminisce. Over the past three decades, the reunion has grown into an event-packed weekend including both kids' and adult rodeos, Western swing dances on Friday and Saturday nights, a fiddling contest, a barbecue dinner, and an authentic chuck-wagon cook-off. The parade takes place Saturday morning, and the crowned reunion queen must be at least 60 years old. Most events are held at the Magdalena Fairgrounds, and admission is free. The deserted **Old Kelly Mine** (✉ Kelly Rd. off U.S. 60, ☎ no phone), 4 mi south of town, is reputed to be haunted, and during the Old Timers Reunion a 7K race finishes here (it begins in the village).

Dining and Lodging

$–$$　✕ **Magdalena Cafe.** Burgers, hot sandwiches, and homemade pie and Mexican pineapple cake are served on red-and-white checkered tablecloths here. Thursday's dinner is quite the event around these parts, with a big $12.95 steak dinner and a $5.95 all-you-can-eat salad bar. ✉ *U.S. Hwy. 60, across from Trail's End Supermarket,* ☎ *505/854–2696. No credit cards. No dinner except Thurs.*

$　⊡ **Western Bed & Breakfast Motel & RV Park.** To inspire dreams of riding the range, rooms of beveled pine are set off with Western paintings and Indian artifacts, and some are Victorian-like with flowered upholstery and matching art. Quilts handmade in Magdelena decorate the walls. ✉ *U.S. Hwy. 60, town center, 87835,* ☎ *505/854–2417,* FAX *505/854–3217. 6 rooms. AE, D, DC, MC, V. BP.*

Shopping

Lebanese immigrant George Salome built **Salome Store** (✉ U.S. Hwy. 60, at Oak St., ☎ 505/854–2341) in 1910, and his family still runs it. This general store with creaky wooden floors and a pressed-tin ceiling supplies locals with everything from boots and hats to groceries and feed. You'll also find saddles, dishes, giant jars of pickles on the counter, and sunbonnets hanging from elk antlers.

En Route　With its 27 glistening white 80-ft radio-telescope antennas arranged in patterns, **Very Large Array** is a startling sight when spotted along the Plains of San Augustin. The complex's dish-shape ears, each weighing 230 tons, are tuned in to the cosmos. The array is part of a series of facilities that compose the National Radio Astronomy Observatory. The antennas, which provided an impressive backdrop for the movie *Contact,* based on the Carl Sagan book, form the largest, most advanced radio telescope in the world. The telescope chronicles the birth and death of stars and galaxies from 10 to 12 billion light-years away. Hundreds of scientists from around the world travel to this windy, remote spot to research black holes, colliding galaxies, and exploding stars, as well as to chart the movements of planets. Visitors are permitted to stroll right up to the array on a self-guided walking tour that begins at the unstaffed visitor center. The staff emphasize that their work does *not* involve a search for life on other planets. ✉ *Off U.S. 60, 23 mi west of Magdalena,* ☎ *505/835–0424 Socorro County Chamber of Commerce.* ⊡ *Free.* ☉ *Daily 8:30–dusk.*

Datil

36 mi west of Magdalena on U.S. 60.

More a crossroads than a town (blink at the wrong time and you might miss it), Datil is named for the datelike fruit that once grew wild here. Datil Well, in the **Datil Well Campground,** was once an important stop on cattle drives. The scenic and popular picnic and camping area has 22 campsites ($5 camping fee). Along the ridges west of the campground there's a 3-mi trail through piñon-juniper and ponderosa pine woodlands, with overlooks of the San Augustin Plains and surrounding mountains. Drinking water, firewood, and toilets are provided at the camp. ✉ *At the intersection of U.S. Hwy. 60 and NM 12, go left on Hwy. 12 (south) 5 mi,* ☎ *505/835–0412.*

Dining and Lodging

$ ✕▦ **Eagle Guest Ranch.** At the Datil intersection sits the one reason to stop, and it's a pretty good one. Since the Eagle opened in the 1920s, it has had various incarnations: roadside store, café, lounge, and dance hall. The dark-wood walls of the restaurant are saturated with tall tales, recollections of hard winters and dry summers, and the talk and laughter of big families and old friends who continue to share generous platters of food (mainly beef dishes, though there's a salad bar). The recipes for the pies served here are more than a half century old. On Friday only, Mexican food is served. The salsa could substitute for rocket fuel, and you'd better have an asbestos tongue if you order the red chile. Beer in a frosty Kerr canning jar will come to your mouth's aid. The guest rooms are low-end affairs, but if you're in need of accommodations in a place this remote, you have to think like an Old West traveler: "When you're at the Last Chance Hotel, you don't look for luxury." ✉ *U.S. 60 at NM 12 (Box 68), 87821,* ☎ *505/772–5612. 8 rooms. AE, D, DC, MC, V. Restaurant closed Sun.*

Pie Town

21 mi west of Datil on U.S. 60.

Do they still serve pie in Pie Town? The quest to find the answer is worth heading out on U.S. 60. During the 1930s and '40s, it was said, the best pie in New Mexico was served at a little café in Pie Town, a homesteading community west of the Continental Divide. Cowboys on cattle drives and tourists heading to California spread stories of the legendary pies. Thanks to the Pie-O-Neer Cafe, the tradition of great pie in this part of the world is alive and well.

Pie Town's reputation can be traced to 1922, when World War I veteran Clyde Norman came from Texas and filed a mining claim on the Hound Pup Lode. Gold mining didn't go as well as he'd hoped, but he began selling kerosene and gasoline, as well as doughnuts he'd brought from Magdalena in his Model T. Eventually, he learned to bake pies with dried apples, which were an immediate success. Spanish American War veteran Harmon L. Craig, who made a great sourdough, arrived in 1923 or '24, and the two went into partnership. The post office granted the place the name Pie Town in 1927.

Craig bought Norman out in 1932. He ran the mercantile end while his wife, Theodora Baugh, and her two daughters took over the pie baking. Nowadays, aficionados can dig in at the annual Pie Festival, held on the second weekend in September, with pie-eating and pie-baking contests, horny-toad races, and hot-air balloon flights.

Dining

$ ✕ **Pie-O-Neer Cafe.** "Life goes on and days go by. That's why you should stop for pie." Such is the motto of one of New Mexico's most legendary roadside stops. Kathy Knapp serves three squares during the summer, but pie is her stock in trade. She always keeps these varieties on hand: apple, cherry, peach, coconut cream, lemon meringue, and banana cream. Her best sellers are the apple and the oatmeal-pecan. The butterscotch–chocolate chip and peanut butter pies are also big favorites, as is the apple-raisin-walnut. Everything here, from the cinnamon rolls to the chile-cheese fries, with your choice of green chile stew or Texas chili, is made from scratch. On some Sunday afternoons, local talent drops by for guitar strumming. The café closes at 7 PM in summer, and fall and winter hours are limited to 10–4. ✉ *U.S. 60,* ☎ *505/772–2900. No credit cards. Closed Mon.*

Quemado

22 mi west of Pie Town on U.S. 60.

Quemado (pronounced kay-*ma*-dough) means "burnt" in Spanish, and the town is supposedly named for a legendary Apache chief who burned his hand in a campfire. The bustling village, which contains several motels and cafés, is busiest in fall, when it is a favorite base for hunters. **Quemado Lake,** about 20 mi south of town on NM 32 and 103, is a man-made fishing and hiking area where it's not unusual to spot herds of elk. Quemado Lake has three **campgrounds** (☎ 505/773–4678), including RV sites. Rates are $6 a day for a campsite, $10 a day for an RV site.

OFF THE
BEATEN PATH

LIGHTNING FIELD – The sculptor Walter De Maria created *Lightning Field,* a work of land art composed of 400 stainless-steel poles of varying heights (the average is 20 ft) arranged in a rectangular grid over 1 mi by ½ mi of flat, isolated terrain. Groups of up to six people are permitted to stay overnight between May 1 and October 31—the only way you can experience the artwork—at a rustic on-site 1930s cabin (the fee ranges from $85 to $110 per person). Dia Center for the Arts administers *Lightning Field,* shuttling visitors from Quemado to the sculpture, which is on private land to the northeast. High thunderstorm season is usually from July to mid-September; book way ahead for visits during this time. If you're lucky, you'll see flashes you'll never forget (though lightning isn't required to appreciate the artwork). ⊠ *Box 2993, Corrales, 87048,* ☎ *505/898–3335 for Corrales office and reservations, 505/773–4560 for Quemado shuttle;* FAX *505/898–3336. Reservations essential. Closed Nov.–Apr.*

Dining and Lodging

$ ✕ **Snuffy's Steak House.** On the road to Quemado Lake, this true Western bar serves steaks, burgers, and Mexican food. The enchiladas aren't bad, but this is a place to soak up local color. There's an antique bar, and the walls are plastered with pictures of homesteaders and folks with their fish and wild-game trophies. Snuffy's is open for breakfast on Saturday and Sunday and for early dinner (until 8) on Friday and Saturday. ⊠ *NM 103,* ☎ *505/773–4672. MC, V. No dinner Sun.–Thurs.*

$ ✕🏠 **Largo Motel.** With plain, comfortable rooms, the Largo is as good a motel as you're going to find to wash off the trail dust and find a night's rest. The Largo has the best café in town, a busy little spot known for homemade corn tortillas and biscuits, gravy and chicken-fried steak, as well as red and green chile. The Navajo tacos are famous. They serve "a real full plate," too. Above the spacious booths are mounted trophies (the owner is a hunting guide). ⊠ *U.S. Hwy. 60 on west side of town, 87829,* ☎ *505/773–4686. 6 rooms. MC, V.*

SOUTHWESTERN NEW MEXICO A TO Z

Arriving and Departing

By Bus

Texas, New Mexico & Oklahoma Coaches (☎ 505/524–8518 in Las Cruces; 800/231–2222 for all other destinations), which is affiliated with Greyhound Lines, provides bus service throughout southwestern New Mexico (though not Silver City). For transportation between Silver City and the El Paso Airport, contact **Silver Stage** (☎ 800/522–0162).

By Car

Two major interstates travel through southwestern New Mexico, I–10 from west to east, and I–25 from north to south. U.S. 70 connects Las

Cruces to Alamogordo and the southeast. From Albuquerque, the drive
is about two hours to Truth or Consequences, three hours to Las Cruces.

By Plane

Albuquerque International Sunport (☞ Arriving and Departing by
Plane *in* Chapter 5) is 210 mi north of Las Cruces. **Mesa Airlines** (☎
800/637–2247) provides air-shuttle service from Albuquerque to Silver City, Alamogordo, and Las Cruces.

El Paso International Airport (✉ 6701 Convair Dr. [take I–10's Exit
25–Airway or U.S. 54's Fred Wilson Rd. exit to Airway], ☎ 915/772–
4271) is the main gateway to southern New Mexico. The major airlines with scheduled service to the airport are America West, American, Continental, Delta, Frontier, and Southwest.

Almost all New Mexico rural communities have a municipal airport,
even those with populations of only a few thousand. Larger municipal airports have charter services such as **Grimes Aviation** (☎ 505/538–
2142) in Silver City and **Adventure Aviation** (☎ 505/525–0500) in Las
Cruces.

By Train

Amtrak (✉ Union Station, 700 San Francisco St., El Paso, TX, ☎ 800/
872–7245) serves El Paso and Deming, New Mexico, with the *Sunset
Limited* train, which operates between Los Angeles, New Orleans, and
Florida.

Getting Around

By Bus and Van

Las Cruces Shuttle Service (☎ 505/525–1784) makes regular runs daily
between Las Cruces and the El Paso International Airport and will drop
you off at your chosen destination. **Silver Stage** (☎ 800/522–0162)
provides shuttle services to Las Cruces from El Paso International Airport, as well as regular runs to Silver City. **Roadrunner City Bus** (☎
505/525–2500) operates public buses in Las Cruces.

By Car

Silver City can be accessed from minor highways leading off I–10 and
I–25. From Las Cruces, I–10 leads south to El Paso. The quality of the
region's roadways varies widely, particularly in remote rural areas. Drive
with caution on the narrow highways, which particularly in mountainous
areas have no shoulders. On minor roadways, even if paved, be alert
for curves, dips, and steep drop-offs.

Contacts and Resources

Car Rental

Cars can be rented at either Albuquerque International Airport or El
Paso International Airport (☞ Car Rentals *in* Smart Travel Tips A to
Z). Auto dealerships in some communities, including Las Cruces, rent
cars. In Las Cruces try **Hertz** (✉ Las Cruces Hilton, 705 Telshor Blvd.,
☎ 505/521–4807).

Entry Requirements to Mexico

On a day trip into Mexico, citizens of the United States and Canada
need only carry a government-issue photo ID as documentation, but
it's always a good idea also to have a valid passport or certified copy
of a birth certificate. All other citizens must have a valid passport to
enter. Mexico has one of the strictest policies about children entering
the country. Though it's not always checked for, all children, including infants, must have proof of citizenship for travel to Mexico. All
children up to age 18 traveling with a single parent must also have a

notarized letter from the other parent stating that the child has his or her permission to leave the home country. If the other parent is deceased or the child has only one legal parent, a notarized statement saying so must be obtained as proof. If you're visiting for less than 72 hours and are not traveling past a border town like Ciudad Juárez and into the country's interior, you don't have to pay Mexico's $15 visitor fee (tourist card).

You do not have to buy Mexican auto insurance if you're only traveling to Mexico for the day. Be sure the insurance you do have covers you if you drive your vehicle across the border. If you're caught transporting a gun into Mexico, you can be jailed indefinitely.

Guided Tours

El Paso–Juárez Trolley Co. (✉ 1 Civic Center Plaza, El Paso, TX, ☎ 915/544–0062 or 800/259–6284) in association with **Tour Company-Guide Service** (✉ ☎ 915/877–3002 or 915/490–7294) has regular guided tours, some that are a combination of riding and (optional) walking, into areas such as Old Mesilla, near Las Cruces and the old Spanish missions of El Paso, Texas, and Ciudad Juárez, Mexico. Eleven dollars buys a trolley tour of Juárez, while $30 (prepaid) or $33 (no advance reservation) pays for an excursion through shaded pecan groves to Old Mesilla, including lunch and a guided walking tour. Call for schedules and rates for other specialized tours.

Around and About Tours (✉ 6716 Mesa Grande Ave., El Paso, TX, ☎ 915/833–2650) specializes in El Paso, Texas; Ciudad Juárez, Mexico; and tours of several days or a week into southern New Mexico.

El Paso Mission Trail Association (✉ 1 Civic Center Plaza, El Paso, TX, ☎ 800/351–6024) provides volunteers to lead groups of at least 10 people on visits to the old Spanish missions of the El Paso area. A donation of at least $2.50 per person is requested.

Late-Night Pharmacies

Some Walgreens pharmacies in El Paso, Texas, and in Las Cruces stay open late or are open 24 hours. Wal-Mart and large grocery chain stores including Albertson's found throughout southwestern New Mexico also have pharmacies.

Visitor Information

For cities or areas not listed below, contact the **New Mexico Department of Tourism** (✉ 491 Old Santa Fe Trail, Santa Fe 87503, ☎ 505/827–7400 or 800/545–2070, ✉). **El Paso Convention & Tourism Department** (✉ 1 Civic Center Plaza, 79901, ☎ 915/534–0696 or 800/351–6024, ✉). **Las Cruces Convention & Visitors Bureau** (✉ 211 Water St., 88001, ☎ 505/541–2444 or 800/343–7827, ✉). **Old Mesilla Association** (✉ c/o Mesilla Book Center, Box 1005, Mesilla Plaza, 88046, ☎ 505/526–6220 or 800/343–7827). **Silver City Murray Ryan Visitor's Center** (✉ 201 N. Hudson St., 88061, ☎ 800/548–9378 or 800/290–8330, ✉). **Truth or Consequences/Sierra County Chamber of Commerce** (✉ 103 Francisco de Avondo, 87901, ☎ 505/894–3536, ✉).

9 BACKGROUND

Books and Videos

Chile Time

Glossary

BOOKS AND VIDEOS

General Interest

Classic books on New Mexico include *Death Comes for the Archbishop,* by Willa Cather, a novel based on the life of Archbishop Jean Baptiste Lamy, who built, among other churches, the St. Francis Cathedral in Santa Fe. Other significant works about the state include *Great River,* by Paul Horgan; *The Wind Leaves No Shadow,* by Ruth Laughlin; *Miracle Hill,* by Barney Mitchell; *Navajos Have Five Fingers,* by T. D. Allen; *Santa Fe,* by Oliver La Farge; *New Mexico,* by Jack Schaefer; and *Moon over Adobe,* by Dorothy Pillsbury.

Norman Zollinger's *Riders to Cibola* chronicles the conquistadors' search for the legendary Seven Cities of Gold. In 1974 Albuquerque author Tony Hillerman received an Edgar Allan Poe Award from the Mystery Writers of America for his book *Dance Hall of the Dead.* He has since written a series of mystery novels revolving around the character of a Navajo police officer. Hillerman also edited *The Spell of New Mexico,* an anthology of New Mexican writers. *A Sense of Place, a Sense of Time,* by pioneering landscape architect and environmentalist John Brinckerhoff Jackson, explores New Mexico's landscape, past and present. Several strands of New Mexico's history merge in Peggy Pond Church's *The House at Otowi Bridge,* the story of Edith Warner, an Anglo woman who lived near San Ildefonso Pueblo in the period before, during, and after the atomic bomb was developed in the neighboring town of Los Alamos.

Las Cruces author Linda G. Harris and photographer Pamela Porter offer an unusual look at New Mexico's past in *Houses in Time.* Harris's explanations of architectural styles intermingle with historical perspective. *The Wood Carvers of Cordova, New Mexico,* by Charles L. Briggs, is a prizewinning study of the making and selling of religious images in a northern New Mexico village. *Eliot Porter's Southwest* is the famed photographer's poetic view of the region, much of it focused around his Tesuque home. In *An Illustrated History of New Mexico,* Thomas E. Chavez, director of the Palace of the Governors in Santa Fe, uses quotes to provide context for his visual chronicle of New Mexican history.

Native American Lore and Pueblo Life

The Man Who Killed the Deer, by Frank Waters, is a classic of Pueblo life. *Masked Gods,* by the same author, has a following that reaches cult proportions. J. J. Brody's illustrated book *Anasazi and Pueblo Painting* is an indispensable volume for art historians and students of Southwestern culture. *Mornings in Mexico,* by D. H. Lawrence, contains a number of essays pertaining to Taos and the Pueblo ritual dances. *Pueblo Style and Regional Architecture,* edited by Nicholas C. Markovich, Wolfgang F. E. Preiser, and Fred G. Strum, covers the evolution of architecture in the Southwest, with particular emphasis on New Mexico.

New Mexican Personalities

Billy the Kid: A Short and Violent Life, by historian Robert M. Utley, is considered the definitive work on the notorious outlaw. Utley also penned *High Noon in Lincoln,* another account involving the Kid. In *Edge of Taos Desert: An Escape to Reality,* New York socialite turned Taos art patron Mabel Dodge Luhan eloquently describes the transformative power Taos and the Pueblo Indians had on her life, beginning with her Taos arrival in 1917. *The Life of D. H. Lawrence,* by Keith Sagar is a good biography of the world-renowned author so strongly associated with (and buried in) New Mexico. Taos is also Georgia O'Keeffe country, and there is a wealth of books about the artist. Among the best is *Georgia O'Keeffe: Arts and Letters,* published by the New York Graphic Society in conjunction with a retrospective of her work at the National Gallery of Art, in Washington, D.C. Also worthy of note is the reissue of the coffee-table book *Georgia O'Keeffe,* with text by the artist herself. *Portrait of an Artist: A Biography of Georgia O'Keeffe,* by Laurie Lisle, spans the artist's life and career. *Georgia O'Keeffe: Some Memories of Drawings,* edited by Doris Bry, is a collection of the artist's major 1915–63 drawings, with comments on each.

Albuquerque, Santa Fe, and Taos

Albuquerque—A Narrative History, by Marc Simmons, is a fascinating look at the city's birth and development. *Lautrec,* by Norman Zollinger, is an entertaining mystery set in Albuquerque. *The Wingspread Collectors Guide to Santa Fe and Taos* and *The Wingspread Collectors Guide to Albuquerque and Corrales* (☞ Shopping *in* Smart Travel Tips A to Z) provide high-quality reproductions and useful information about art galleries, art, and crafts of the region; they also include listings of museums, hotels, restaurants, and historic sites. *A Short History of Santa Fe,* by Susan Hazen-Hammond, chronicles Santa Fe's history with text and photos. *Taos: A Pictorial History,* by John Sherman, contains numerous black-and-white historical photographs of the major characters, events, and structures that formed the backbone of Taos.

Southern New Mexico

Roswell author Carole Larson gives a fascinating and comprehensive account of the sometimes violent settling of southeastern New Mexico in *Forgotten Frontier.* El Paso, Texas, author Leon Metz, a nationally recognized historian, has written many accounts of southern New Mexico including mentions in the novel *Riders Along the Rio Grande: A Collection of Outlaws, Prostitutes and Vigilantes.* Historic photographs and colorful narratives are found in *Las Cruces: An Illustrated History,* by Linda G. Harris. Ferenc Morton Szasz tells a compelling story of the explosion of the world's first atomic bomb at the remote Trinity Site in *The Day the Sun Rose Twice.* *Tularosa,* by C.L. Sonnichsen, is a dramatic account of the Alamogordo area's old frontier.

Videos

Northern New Mexico has provided memorable scenic backdrops for several feature films, particularly Westerns. *Silverado* (1985) and *Wyatt Earp* (1994) were photographed in the Santa Fe vicinity. For television, two miniseries based on popular Larry McMurtry novels with Old West settings, *Lonesome Dove* (1989) and *Buffalo Girls* (1995), were shot near Santa Fe. *Lonesome Dove* was actually shot at Galisteo's movie ranch, Cook Ranch; most of the set there was blown up by accident during the filming of *The Wild Wild West* (1999). *The Milagro Beanfield War* (1988), directed by Robert Redford and based on the novel by Taos author John Nichols, was filmed in Truchas, on the High Road to Taos. Most agree the novel is far better than the film.

The Albuquerque area appears in director Oliver Stone's *Natural Born Killers* (1994). Southern New Mexico provides settings for *Young Guns* (1988), *Gas, Food, Lodging* (1992), *White Sands* (1992), and *Mad Love* (1995). Other movies photographed around New Mexico include *The Cowboys* (1972), starring John Wayne; *Outrageous Fortune* (1987), with Bette Midler and Shelley Long; *Powwow Highway* (1985); and *City Slickers* (1991), starring Billy Crystal.

The National Radio Astronomy Very Large Array of antennae in western New Mexico provided dramatic backdrops in the science fiction movies *Armageddon* (1998), starring Bruce Willis, and *Contact* (1997), starring Jodie Foster. The alien-sighting history of New Mexico made the state a good setting for "star man" David Bowie in *The Man Who Fell to Earth* (1976), in which an Artesia church service and White Sands National Monument are featured. You won't see White Sands in *Star Wars,* but recordings of missiles launched at White Sands Missile Range were used by the sound effects team. Carlsbad Caverns was the underground wonderland seen in the movies *King Solomon's Mines* (1950) and *Journey to the Center of the Earth* (1959).

CHILE TIME

Chile, an ancient, locally grown mainstay, is the defining ingredient of New Mexican cuisine. Combined with corn tortillas, beans, tomatoes, and potatoes, chile binds together the New Mexico that for centuries sustained indigenous people, the Spanish, and subsequent arrivals. A dedicated chile lover will travel any distance down any highway in pursuit of a great chile sauce. From Chope's south of Las Cruces to M&J's Sanitary Tortilla Factory in Albuquerque and JoAnn's Ranch-o-Casados in Española (to name a few classic hot spots), the pursuit of the most flavorful—or the hottest—chile remains a personal quest akin to proving one's honor.

When Christopher Columbus set out across the ocean in 1492, he was looking for a sea route to the lucrative spice trade of Asia. Instead, he stumbled onto the New World, where he tasted chile. He took some back to Spain, and from there chile spread around the world on trade routes, transforming the cuisines of Spain, Portugal, Italy, Hungary, North Africa, India, Nepal, Tibet, and China. In addition to its distinction as one of the world's favorite spices, chile is one of the oldest: it's believed to have originated 10,000 years ago in the Amazon region of South America in the area of Brazil land Bolivia.

How chile first arrived in New Mexico is the subject of debate. Some believe the Spanish introduced it to the Pueblo Indians on their travels north from Mexico. Others hold that chile was grown in New Mexico centuries prior to the arrival of the Spanish, having been introduced through trade with the peoples of Mexico and South America. It is interesting to note that chile is not used in the traditional ceremonies among the Pueblo Indians as is corn, but red and green chile dishes are served at all feasts and ceremonies.

The source of the chile's heat is the chemical capsaicin, found in the pepper's heart and membrane. The seeds themselves are not hot, but they absorb capsaicin from their contact with the heart and membrane. (Though "chile" is a Spanish spelling of chilli, the Aztec, or Nahuatl, word for pepper, "capsicum," comes from the Latin *capsicon,* meaning chest or box.) In addition to providing a culinary delight to chile lovers, capsaicin has a long tradition as a healing substance and pain reliever. Medicinal uses of chile extend from prehistory into modern medicine. Chile may protect against blood clots and prevent heart attacks, and it is known to hinder cholesterol absorption. Chile is low in fat and high in vitamins A and C and beta-carotene. It also speeds up metabolism and helps digestion by intensifying stomach-acid production and sometimes working as a laxative. New Mexican old-timers chop up chile and place it on arthritic limbs; more recently topical creams made from capsaicin have become available. Chile-based products

also bring relief from chronic pain caused by cluster headaches, shingles, and herpes—even amputation and other surgery.

Chile derives much of its reputation as a painkiller and bringer of well-being from the chemical effect the burning capsaicin has on the brain. When you eat or touch chile, the skin sends a pain signal to the brain, releasing endorphins, the hormones of pleasure. So, the same chemical reaction that produces "chile addiction" also blunts pain.

The green variety of chile, generically called "Hatch" (for the New Mexico town that produces the bulk of the state's crop), is the commercially developed type known as New Mexico 6-10 and the Big Jim. When it comes to red chile, the best is said to be grown from the old stock cultivated in Chimayó and other high mountain villages of the north—Española, Dixon, Velarde, and Peñasco.

By far the state's most important vegetable crop, New Mexico chile is grown on 30,000 acres, mostly in Luna and Doña Ana counties. Sixty percent of the nation's chile crop comes from the Land of Enchantment. Since 1980 chile consumption has doubled in the United States, much of it going into salsa, which in the 1990s surpassed ketchup to become the country's most popular condiment.

From mid-August through the fall, the New Mexican air is scented with the warm, enticing fragrance of chiles roasting out-of-doors in large, wire, propane-fired cages. Around State Fair time in September, people head for their favorite roadside stand to buy a sack of fresh-roasted green chiles. Once stored in the freezer, the chile is used all winter long, in stews, enchiladas, salsas, and burritos.

As the season progresses into October, it's time to buy a red chile ristra, a string of chiles, to hang full, heavy and sweet, near the front door, a sign of warmth and welcome. It's said the ristra brings good luck—and it certainly is convenient to have the makings of soul-warming red-chile salsa right at hand.

— Sharon Niederman

GLOSSARY

Perhaps more than any other region in the United States, New Mexico has its own distinctive cuisine and architectural style, both heavily influenced by Native American, Spanish-colonial, Mexican, and American frontier traditions. The brief glossary that follows explains terms frequently used in this book.

As befits a land occupied—in several senses of the word in some cases—by so many diverse peoples, the use of accents on place and other names is a tricky matter. For some people, among them many Hispanic residents, accents are a matter of identification and pride—Río Grande, for instance, represents more clearly the linguistic origins of the current name of the river that runs so grandly through the state. On the other hand, though including the accent for Picurís Pueblo or Jémez Pueblo might be linguistically accurate, it's also a reminder of the Spanish conquest of Pueblo Native Americans. ("I couldn't care less whether you use accents or not—I don't," said a woman at the governor's office of Jemez Pueblo when asked whether having an accent above the first "e" in the pueblo's name would be more accurate.)

In general in this book we've applied accents when they're part of an official place or other name. Signs for and official documents of Española, for instance, tend to have a tilde above the "n" in the city's name. On the other hand, though the names of Capulin Volcano and the city of Raton are sometimes written Capulín Volcano and Ratón, we have not employed the accents because New Mexican residents rarely do. A generally workable solution, this strategy does lead to some apparent inconsistencies (Picurís Pueblo; Jemez Pueblo), an illustration of the conflicting cultural sentiments still at play within New Mexico.

Art and Architecture

Adobe: A brick of sun-dried earth and clay, usually stabilized with straw; a structure made of adobe.

Banco: A small bench, or banquette, often upholstered with handwoven textiles, that gracefully emerges from adobe walls.

Bulto: Folk-art figures of a santo (saint), usually carved from wood.

Camposanto: A graveyard.

Capilla: A chapel.

Casita: Literally "small house," this term is generally used to describe a separate guest house.

Cerquita: A spiked, wrought-iron, rectangular fence, often marking grave sites.

Equipal: Pigskin-and-cedar furniture from Jalisco, Mexico, these chairs have rounded backs and bases rather than legs.

Farolito: Small votive candles set in paper-bag lanterns, farolitas are popular at Christmastime. The term is used in northern New Mexico only. People in Albuquerque and points south call the lanterns *luminarias,* which in the north is the term for the bonfires of Christmas Eve.

Heishi: Shell jewelry.

Hornos: Outdoor domed ovens.

Kiva: A ceremonial room, rounded and built at least partially underground, used by Native Americans of the Southwest. Entrance is gained from the roof.

Kiva fireplace: A corner fireplace whose round form resembles that of a kiva.

Latilla: Small pole, often made of aspen, used as a lath in a ceiling.

Placita: A small plaza.

Portal: A porch or large covered area adjacent to a house.

Pueblo style: Most homes in this style, modeled after the traditional dwellings of the Southwest Pueblo Indians, are cube shaped. Other characteristics are flat roofs, small windows, rounded corners, and viga beams.

Retablo: Holy image painted on wood or tin.

Santero: Maker of religious images.

Territorial style: This modified Pueblo style evolved in the late-19th century when New Mexico was still a U.S. territory. The Territorial home incorporates a broad central hallway and entryway and adds wooden elements, such as window frames, in neoclassical style; some structures have pitched rather than flat roofs, and brick copings.

Terrones adobes: Adobe cut from the ground rather than formed from mud.

Viga: Horizontal roof beam made of logs, usually protruding from the side of the house.

Flora and Fauna

Cholla: A term for various species of spiny cactus, which grow irregular branches with clustered berries.

Collared peccary: Known also as javelina hogs, these piglike animals are aggressive and highly protective of their young. They're commonly found in the mountains of southwestern New Mexico.

Creosote: Rare desert rain enhances the strong, medicine-like fragrance of this somewhat scraggly plant common to arid regions. Nicknamed greasewood for its oily resins, creosote produces evergreen leaves and small yellow or green flowers.

Desert horned lizard: Called horned or horny toads by locals, this species has a flattened body and rows of tiny spikes that resemble formidable armor.

Desert tarantula: It's a rare but startling sight to see thousands of large, dark tarantulas skittering across New Mexico highways after a heavy rain. With a leg span of up to 4 inches, this cousin of tropical spiders can look terrifying. It rarely bites, and its venom usually produces only a mild swelling on human skin.

El lobo: The Spanish term for the Mexican gray wolf once common in New Mexico, but no longer found in the wild. Efforts are being made to reintroduce this genetically unique species to its original home range.

Jackrabbit: Tall, rangy, and graceful, this long-eared rabbit can sprint and hop at astonishing speeds.

Juniper: A shrub or tree, common to arid regions, with a waxy covering that retains moisture.

Kangaroo rat: This nocturnal rodent is a master of water conservation, as well as leaping, which help it evade predators. Its kidneys expel very little water, and its body can convert a meal of dry seeds to moisture.

Lechuguilla: This fleshy desert plant has daggerlike leaves and tall stalks of yellow flowers.

Mesquite: Thorny branches and bean pods distinguish this common range plant, technically a small tree, which grows in thickets.

Mexican freetail bat: These bats are harmless to humans, except for the rare rabid individual. The half million bats living in Carlsbad Caverns during summer months can consume 3 tons of insects in one night.

Mountain lion: Solitary and stealthy, the mountain lion long has been a legend of the Old West. Habitats are disappearing, making remaining wildernesses of New Mexico a refuge for the creature.

Mule deer: The long ears of this timid deer explain the name. The animal thrives in virtually every corner of New Mexico, from forests to sand dunes.

Ocotillo: This common desert plant grows in clusters of thorny branches capped by red, tubular blossoms.

Piñon pine: These robust pines found in mountains and foothills throughout the Southwest survive drought through taproots that plunge as deep as 40 ft into the soil. The resinous wood produces fragrant scents from Santa Fe fireplaces, while tasty piñon nuts garnish foods.

Prickly pear cactus: The fleshy, rounded pads of this common cactus inspired its nickname "elephant ears."

Pronghorn: Look alongside roadways for a flash of white from the rear of this delicate creature, incorrectly called an antelope. Pronghorns roam in bands and prefer open rangeland.

Quail: Highly tolerant of dry weather, this sociable bird generally is found in a covey, which tries to sneak out of danger by running through the cover of brush. The birds take wing in short bursts of flight.

Raptor: A bird-of-prey, such as a hawk or owl.

Roadrunner: The crested head and speckled feathers of this desert dweller can be seen making mad dashes across or alongside New Mexico highways. The fearless fowl eats lizards and snakes. Its curiosity is well known to state residents, who sometimes find themselves face-to-face with a roadrunner peering through a window.

Soaptree yucca: White flowers adorn the broomsticklike protrusions of this plant, New Mexico's state flower.

Tamarisk: Imported from overseas, the tamarisk (or salt cedar) is a small evergreen found choking waterways throughout the Southwest. The nonnative plant is a major nuisance, sucking up precious moisture and providing very little benefit as animal habitat.

Texas madrone: The reddish, smooth bark of this unusual evergreen gives it the nickname "lady's legs." The tree dresses up with urn-shape white-and-pink flowers and red fruit. A relic of the last ice age, this variety is found only in isolated regions of west Texas and southeastern New Mexico. Look for it at Guadalupe Mountains National Park.

Vinegaroon: You'll know it when you see it. This dark, whip-tail scorpion appears fearsome at up to 3 inches long. It waves wicked-looking pincers and sprays an acid that reeks of vinegar. Yet, it's harmless to humans—unlike some of its more venomous cousins.

Western diamondback: This rattlesnake is usually found coiled under shady bushes or lounging in cool cave entrances. Watch your step.

Menu Guide

Aguacate: Spanish for avocado, the key ingredient of guacamole.

Albóndigas: Meatballs, usually cooked with rice in a meat broth.

Bolsa del pobre: A seafood and vegetable dish; a specialty from Colima.

Burrito: A warm flour tortilla wrapped around meat, beans, and vegetables, and smothered in chile and cheese.

Carne adovada: Red chile–marinated pork.

Chalupa: A corn tortilla deep-fried in the shape of a bowl, filled with pinto beans (sometimes meat), and topped with cheese, guacamole, sour cream, lettuce, tomatoes, and salsa.

Chile relleno: A large green chile pepper peeled, stuffed with cheese or a special mixture of spicy ingredients, dipped in batter, and fried.

Chiles: New Mexico's infamous hot peppers, which come in an endless variety of sizes and in various degrees of hotness, from the thumb-size jalapeño to the smaller and often hotter serrano. They can be canned or fresh, dried or cut up into salsa.

Chili: A stewlike Tex-Mex dish typically containing beans, meat, and red chile.

Chimichanga: The same as a burrito (☞ *above*) only deep-fried and topped with a dab of sour cream or salsa.

Chipotle: A dried smoked jalapeño with a smoky, almost sweet, chocolaty flavor.

Chorizo: Well-spiced Spanish sausage, made with pork and red chiles.

Enchilada: A rolled or flat corn tortilla filled with meat, chicken, seafood, or cheese, an enchilada is covered with chile and baked. The ultimate enchilada is made with blue Indian corn tortillas. New Mexicans order them flat, sometimes topped with a fried egg.

Fajitas: Grilled beef, chicken, or fish with peppers and onions, served with tortillas; traditionally known as arracheras.

Flauta: A tortilla filled with cheese or meat and rolled into a flutelike shape ("flauta" means flute) and lightly fried.

Frijoles refritos: Refried beans, often seasoned with lard or cheese.

Guacamole: Mashed avocado, mixed with tomatoes, garlic, onions, lemon juice, and chiles, used as a dip, a side dish, a topping, or an additional ingredient.

Hatch: A small southern New Mexico town in the Mesilla Valley, known for its outstanding production and quality of both green and red chile. The "Hatch" name often is found on canned chile food products.

Huevos rancheros: New Mexico's answer to eggs Benedict—eggs doused with chile and sometimes melted cheese, served on top of a corn tortilla (they're good accompanied by chorizo).

Pan de cazón: Grilled shark with black beans and red onions on a tortilla; a specialty from Campeche.

Posole: Resembling popcorn soup, this is a sublime marriage of lime, hominy, pork, chile, garlic, and spices.

Quesadilla: A folded flour tortilla filled with cheese and meat or vegetables, and warmed or lightly fried so the cheese melts.

Queso: Cheese; an ingredient in many Mexican and Southwestern recipes.

Ristra: String of dried red chile peppers, often used as decoration.

Salsa: Finely chopped concoction of green and red chile peppers, mixed with onion, garlic, and other spices.

Sopaipilla: Puffy deep-fried bread, served with honey.

Taco: A corn or flour tortilla baked or fried and made into a shell that's then stuffed with vegetables or spicy meat and garnished with shredded lettuce, chopped tomatoes, onions, and grated cheese.

Tacos al carbón: Shredded pork cooked in a mole sauce and folded into corn tortillas.

Tamale: Ground corn made into a dough and filled with finely ground pork and red chiles, then steamed in a corn husk.

Tortilla: A thin pancake made of corn or wheat flour, a tortilla is used as bread, as an edible "spoon," and as a container for other foods. Locals place butter in the center of a hot tortilla, roll it up, and eat it as a scroll.

Trucha en terra-cotta: Fresh trout wrapped in corn husks and baked in clay.

Verde: Spanish for "green," as in chile verde (a green chile sauce).

INDEX